THE ROUTLEDGE HANDBOOK OF WINE AND CULTURE

The link between culture and wine reaches back into the earliest history of humanity. *The Routledge Handbook of Wine and Culture* brings together a newly comprehensive, interdisciplinary overview of contemporary research and thinking on how wine fits into the cultural frameworks of production, intermediation and consumption.

Bringing together many leading researchers engaged in studying these phenomena, it explores the different ways in which wine is constructed as a social artefact and how its representation and use acquire symbolic meaning. Wine can be analysed in different ways by varying disciplines involved in exploring wine and culture (anthropology, economics and business, geography, history and sociology, and as text). The *Handbook* uses these as lenses to consider how producers, intermediaries and consumers use and create cultural significance. Specifically, the work addresses the following: how wine relates to place, belief systems and accompanying rituals; how it may be used as a marker of the identity and mechanisms of civilising processes (often in conjunction with food and the arts); how its framing intersects with science and nature; the ideologies and power relations which arise around all these activities; and the relation of this to wine markets and public institutions.

This is essential reading for researchers and students in education for the wine industry and in the humanities and social sciences engaged in understanding patterns of human ingenuity and interaction, such as sociology, anthropology, health, geography, business, tourism, cultural studies, food studies and history.

Steve Charters is Professor of Wine Marketing and a researcher at Burgundy School of Business in Dijon, and is responsible for developing teaching and research programmes focusing on all aspects of the business, culture and history of wine. He is also adjunct professor in the Adelaide Business School at the University of Adelaide, Australia.

Marion Demossier is Professor of Social Anthropology in the Department of Modern Languages and Linguistics at the University of Southampton. She has recently completed a monograph on the anthropology of wine and terroir: *Burgundy, a Global Anthropology of Place and Taste*.

Jacqueline Dutton is Professor in French Studies at the University of Melbourne, where she also lectures in wine courses.

Graham Harding is a wine historian attached to the history faculty of the University of Oxford. His *Champagne in Britain, 1800–1914: How the English Transformed a French Luxury* was published in 2021.

Jennifer Smith Maguire is Professor of Cultural Production and Consumption at the Sheffield Business School, Sheffield Hallam University. Her expertise lies in the socio-cultural study of consumer culture and cultural intermediaries, with a special focus on the construction of markets, tastes and value.

Denton Marks is Professor Emeritus of Economics at the University of Wisconsin–Whitewater and fellow of the American Association of Wine Economists. His research involves a range of aspects of wine as a cultural good, and his *Wine and Economics: Transacting the Elixir of Life* is used internationally in various oenological programs.

Tim Unwin is Emeritus Professor of Geography at Royal Holloway, University of London. He co-founded the *Journal of Wine Research* in 1990 and was external examiner and academic advisor to the Institute of Masters of Wine from 2004 to 2011.

'Food and eating as a component of culture has been a prosperous field of study for the last few decades. For myself, I always felt a bit daunted at taking on the often esoteric-seeming culture of wine. But in this book, the international, interdisciplinary and learned team of editors have produced a wonderful introduction to the field that allays all anxieties. It is an impressive collection, and written in a lively fashion.'

Stephen Mennell, author of *All Manners of Food*,
Professor Emeritus of Sociology, University College Dublin

THE ROUTLEDGE HANDBOOK OF WINE AND CULTURE

*Edited by Steve Charters, Marion Demossier,
Jacqueline Dutton, Graham Harding,
Jennifer Smith Maguire, Denton Marks
and Tim Unwin*

LONDON AND NEW YORK

Cover image credit: © Getty Images
First published 2022
by Routledge
4 Park Square, Milton Park, Abingdon, Oxon OX14 4RN

and by Routledge
605 Third Avenue, New York, NY 10158

Routledge is an imprint of the Taylor & Francis Group, an informa business

© 2022 selection and editorial matter, Steve Charters, Marion Demossier, Jacqueline Dutton, Graham Harding, Jennifer Smith Maguire, Denton Marks and Tim Unwin; individual chapters, the contributors

The right of Steve Charters, Marion Demossier, Jacqueline Dutton, Graham Harding, Jennifer Smith Maguire, Denton Marks and Tim Unwin to be identified as the authors of the editorial material, and of the authors for their individual chapters, has been asserted in accordance with sections 77 and 78 of the Copyright, Designs and Patents Act 1988.

All rights reserved. No part of this book may be reprinted or reproduced or utilised in any form or by any electronic, mechanical, or other means, now known or hereafter invented, including photocopying and recording, or in any information storage or retrieval system, without permission in writing from the publishers.

Trademark notice: Product or corporate names may be trademarks or registered trademarks, and are used only for identification and explanation without intent to infringe.

British Library Cataloguing-in-Publication Data
A catalogue record for this book is available from the British Library

Library of Congress Cataloging-in-Publication Data
A catalog record for this book has been requested

ISBN: 978-0-367-47290-0 (hbk)
ISBN: 978-1-032-19807-1 (pbk)
ISBN: 978-1-003-03471-1 (ebk)

DOI: 10.4324/9781003034711

Typeset in Bembo
by Apex CoVantage, LLC

Printed in the United Kingdom
by Henry Ling Limited

CONTENTS

List of figures	*x*
List of tables	*xii*
List of contributors	*xiii*
Preface	*xx*

Culture and wine: an introduction   1
Tim Unwin

PART I
Context: disciplinary perspectives on wine and culture   **13**

1 Anthropology, wine and culture   15
  Marion Demossier and Clelia Viecelli

2 Business, wine and culture   20
  Steve Charters

3 Economics, wine and culture   27
  Denton Marks

4 Geography, wine and culture   35
  Tim Unwin

5 History, wine and culture   41
  Graham Harding

6 Sociology, wine and culture   46
  Jennifer Smith Maguire

7 Text, wine and culture *Jacqueline Dutton*	51

PART II
Production and place — 59

8 Cultures of terroir *Tim Unwin*	61
9 Sites and sights of production: spaces and performances of winemaking *John Overton*	72
10 Wine islands: colonial cultures of the vine *Jacqueline Dutton*	82
11 Expressing sense of place and terroir through wine tourism encounters: antipodal reflections from France and New Zealand *Rory Hill and Joanna Fountain*	90
12 Wine, culture and environment: a study of the Sierra (Nevada) Foothills American Viticultural Area *Michele M. Tobias and Colleen C. Myles*	99
13 Making wine, making home *William Skinner*	110
14 *Climats* and the crafting of heritage value in Burgundy terroir *Marion Demossier*	117
15 Wine, deep in the heart of Texas *Colleen C. Myles, Kourtney Collins and Christi G. Townsend*	125

PART III
Intermediation and consumption — 133

16 Characters of wine: the cultural meanings of typefaces and fonts in wine labels *Franck Celhay*	135
17 'Making the right impression': Irish wine culture, c. 1700–present *Charles C. Ludington and Graham Harding*	145
18 Wine as part of Polish identity in early modern times: constructing wine culture in non-wine countries *Dorota Dias-Lewandowska*	155

19 The shape of luxury: three centuries of the champagne glass in British material culture   165
    Graham Harding

20 'For us as experimentalists': an Australian case study of scientific values in nineteenth-century New World winegrowing   176
    Julie McIntyre

21 Tasting as expertise: scientific agronomists and sommeliers in France in the first half of the twentieth century   187
    Sénia Fedoul

22 Wine writing as lifestyle writing: communicating taste and constructing lifestyle in *The Saturday Times* wine column   196
    Ana Tominc and Nikki Welch

23 Some practical economics of selling wine as a cultural good   204
    Ben Christiansen and Denton Marks

24 Champagne – a global symbol of contemporary consumer culture   217
    Joonas Rokka

PART IV
Belief and representation   231

25 Wine and religion: Part 1, antiquity to 1700   233
    Mack P. Holt

26 Wine and religion: Part 2, 1700 to the present   241
    Rod Phillips

27 Wine as metaphor   250
    Azélina Jaboulet-Vercherre

28 New World wine and the evolution of universal, vernacular, metro-rural and indigenous idylls   259
    Peter J. Howland

29 Narratives of science and culture in winemaking   269
    Ian Malcolm Taplin

30 Applying fashion theory to wine: a production of culture example   277
    Richard Mitchell

31 Spending, taste and knowledge: logics of connoisseurship and good taste in the age of cultural democratisation 288
Sarah Cappeliez

PART V
Power and contestation 297

32 Competing and complementary utopias: towards an understanding of entangled wine ideals 299
Jacqueline Dutton and Peter J. Howland

33 Threats of pleasure and chaos: wine and gendered social order 311
Anna-Mari Almila and David Inglis

34 Women in wine . . . occasionally: gendered roles in the wine industry 320
Florine Livat and Clara Jaffré

35 Sustainable wine: the discursive production of sustainability in the wine field 331
Gianmarco Navarini and Lorenzo Domaneschi

36 The triumph of the holy trinity: terroir, typicity and quality anchoring the AOC model in the second half of the twentieth century 342
Olivier Jacquet

37 What can winemakers' business models tell us about the cultural traits of wine regions? A comparative analysis 353
Jean-Guillaume Ditter, Paul Muller and Corinne Tanguy

38 Repudiation not withstanding: critics and the case for hybrid grape wines 363
Connor Fitzmaurice

39 If it's famous, it must be good: the social construction of brand value in the US wine market 372
Gregory S. Carpenter and Ashlee Humphreys

PART VI
Change and the future 383

40 Internationalisation of winegrape varieties and its implications for terroir-based cultural assets 385
Kym Anderson and Signe Nelgen

41 Cultural heritage and migration in the wine world 396
Chantal Crenn

42 The China wine market: how wine is gaining cultural value
    in Chinese culture   405
    *Justin Cohen, Larry Lockshin, Armando Corsi, Johan Bruwer, Carl Driesener
    and Richard Lee*

43 Beyond white: on wine and ethnicity   415
    David Inglis and Hang Kei Ho

44 Climate or technical change in wine? Confronting climatologists' and
    winegrowers' analyses   424
    Geneviève Teil

45 Winegrowing, climate change and a case for biodynamic viticulture   434
    Robert Swinburn

    Conclusion   442
    Graham Harding and Steve Charters

Index   *455*

FIGURES

0.1	Disciplinary approaches to an understanding of wine and culture	6
4.1	Towards a simplified multidisciplinary framework for an understanding of wine and culture	36
8.1	The winegrowing village of St. Romain in the Hautes Côtes de Beaune, looking out across the Côte de Beaune and the Saône Valley	63
8.2	Late twentieth-century advertisement for wines from the Graves, emphasising the importance of the precious earth	65
8.3	Geovino: Terroir tourism above Riquewihr, Alsace	66
9.1	The entrance to Montes Winery, Colchagua, Chile	73
9.2	A wine-processing facility, Fresno, California	73
9.3	The Barrel Room, Mission Hill Family Winery, Okanagan Valley, Canada	77
9.4	Winemaking equipment and yard, Summerhill Pyramid Winery, Okanagan Valley, Canada	78
12.1	(A) Average annual rainfall (cm), (B) average annual temperature (°C), (C) elevation (m)	102
12.2	Winery permit locations in August 2020 within the Sierra Foothills AVA boundary	104
13.1	The backyard crush	111
15.1	Map of Texas wineries with the High Plains and Hill Country American Viticultural Areas	126
15.2	Mourvèdre vines at Hoover Valley Vineyards in Marble Falls, nestled in the Central Texas Hill Country	128
16.1	Typefaces variation (horizontally) versus fonts variation (vertically)	136
16.2	Example of a blackletter typeface: Amador	138
16.3	Example of a formal cursive typeface: Bickham script pro	138
16.4	Example of a casual manual typeface: Professor	139
16.5	Examples of serif typefaces	139
16.6	Example of a sans serif typeface: Acumin Pro	140
16.7	Example of a tuscan typeface: Zebrawood	140
16.8	Example of a stencil typeface: Stencil	141
16.9	Lowercase versus uppercase fonts	142

16.10	Thin versus extrablack fonts	142
16.11	Roman versus italic fonts	142
17.1	'The Comforts of Life' by Henry Heath, c. 1826	150
19.1	'Mr Punch' holding a flute glass	166
19.2	'Mr Punch' with a saucer glass	167
19.3	Masked cellarmen	169
19.4	Saucer glass	171
19.5	Riedel Veritas glass	173
19.6	Champagne glass effect	174
23.1	Waterford Wine and Spirits sales of Old World wines as a share of total wine sales	208
24.1	Champagne brands expressed on official Instagram accounts	222
24.2	Expressions of heritage, class and magic in official accounts	222
24.3	Brand selfies and aestheticised bodies of various kinds	224
24.4	Brand selfies and consumer celebrities	224
24.5	Assemblages of connected brands	227
24.6	Microcelebrity looks and visual play	228
30.1	Visualisation of Nixon and Blakley's (2012) fashion thinking approach	284
37.1	Business Model Canvas (Osterwalder et al. 2010)	354
40.1	Cumulative varietal shares of global winegrape area, 2000 and 2016 (%)	389
40.2	Share of nation's top 10 varieties in national winegrape area, 2000 and 2016 (%)	389
40.3	Index of similarity between national and global varietal mixes, 2000 and 2016	390
40.4	Share of national bearing area that is planted to own-country prime varieties, by country of planting, 2000 and 2016 (%)	391
40.5	Share of global bearing area of prime varieties that is outside the country of origin, by country of origin, 2000 and 2016 (%)	391
40.6	Index of internationalisation of prime varieties, by country of origin, 2000 and 2016	392
40.7	Shares of global winegrape-bearing area by varietal country of origin, 1990 to 2016 (%)	392
40.8	Shares of premium varieties in the world's total winegrape-bearing area, 1990 and 2016 (%)	393
42.1	Self-reported (n = 1093) monthly penetration of category entry points for imported and domestic wine buying in China (May 2019)	410

TABLES

12.1	Annual precipitation in millimeters by AVA	102
12.2	Mean temperature (°C) by AVA	103
12.3	Elevation (metres above sea level) by AVA	103
12.4	Area of grape growing by AVA within the Sierra Foothills AVA	105
21.1	Synthesis of faults and diseases of wine, oenotechnical manuals (1822 to 1903)	189
23.1	Waterford (WWS) and two major competitors	207
23.2	Tasting Note History as of August 2020	212
24.1	Instagram data used in visual analysis (2014, 2018)	221
24.2	Comparison of champagne selfie coding frequencies, 2014 vs. 2018	225
30.1	Fashion diffusion models	282
34.1	Women's roles in the wine industry: Regions and methodologies	321
34.2	Gender Inequality Index (GII) rank and women's total entrepreneurial activity (TEA) of the main wine-producing countries	327
35.1	Certification data by region and date established	336
39.1	Artisanal logic and commercial logic in the US wine market	379
42.1	Self-reported (n = 2440) six-month penetration (percentage of people buying) of alcohol subcategory buying in China (July 2019)	407
42.2	Self-reported (n = 2440) six-month channel penetration of wine buying in China (July 2019)	407
42.3	Average number of stock-keeping units in brick-and-mortar retail	409
42.4	Consumer ethnocentrism (CET) and product involvement: purchased imported vs. local (May 2019)	413
44.1	Interviewees	426

CONTRIBUTORS

Anna-Mari Almila is a research fellow in the sociology of fashion, London College of Fashion, UAL. She writes in the fields of cultural, global and historical sociology. Topics include the materiality of dressed bodies and their environments, fashion globalisation and the history of fashion studies, the historical/political construction of urban spaces and wine and gender. She is co-editor of (*inter alia*) *The Globalization of Wine* and *The Sage Handbook of Cultural Sociology*.

Kym Anderson is George Gollin Professor Emeritus at the University of Adelaide and founding executive director of its Wine Economics Research Centre. He is also an honorary professor at the Australian National University and vice president of the American Association of Wine Economists and co-editor of its *Journal of Wine Economics*.

Johan Bruwer is a research professor of marketing at the UniSA Business School, University of South Australia. He specialises in marketing and consumer behaviour psychology research and has published 170 research journal articles, book chapters, etc.

Sarah Cappeliez holds a PhD from the University of Toronto, where she researched and taught in the sociologies of food, culture and consumption. Her diverse background includes work for Slow Food in Italy and France and as a restaurant critic and food writer, all of which inform her research in the cultural production of taste in a globalised cultural context.

Gregory S. Carpenter is Harold T. Martin Professor of Marketing, Kellogg School of Management, Northwestern University. He focuses on understanding how firms succeed with consumers. His recent book *Resurgence: The Four Stages of Market-Focused Reinvention* (Palgrave Macmillan, 2014) examines how firms that face serious challenges create a more customer-focused culture and renewed success.

Franck Celhay is associate professor at Montpellier Business School. He graduated in marketing and graphic design. Major topics of research are communication design and wine marketing. His research has been published in journals such as *Journal of Product Innovation Management*, *International Journal of Design* and *International Journal of Research in Marketing*.

Steve Charters is professor of wine marketing and a researcher at Burgundy School of Business in Dijon and is responsible for developing teaching and research programmes focusing on all aspects of the culture, history and business of wine. He is also adjunct professor in the Adelaide Business School at the University of Adelaide, Australia, and a member of the Institute of Masters of Wine. His research concentrates on consumer behaviour and wine and place (including terroir, wine tourism, and territorial wine management). He is the author of *Wine and Society: The Social and Cultural Context of a Drink* (Butterworth Heinemann, 2006) and has a blog on wine and culture at https://wineandculture.net/.

Ben Christiansen is chief officer of Waterford Wine and Spirits (est. 2005). Waterford is a multi-site retail wine shop (some with wine bars) and restaurant partnership. A graduate of Whitman College, the Cooking and Hospitality Institute of Chicago (CHIC) and the University of Wisconsin–Madison, he resides with his family in Shorewood, Wisconsin, USA.

Justin Cohen is a senior marketing scientist at the Ehrenberg-Bass Institute for Marketing Science, UniSA Business School, University of South Australia. His key areas of research are wine, China, brand growth, media and retailing.

Kourtney Collins is an assistant winemaker at Hawk's Shadow Winery in Dripping Springs, Texas. She has a master's in sustainability studies from Texas State University.

Armando Corsi is an associate professor in wine business at the University of Adelaide. His key area of research is the analysis of consumer behaviour, particularly towards wine and other premium foods and beverages.

Chantal Crenn is a professor of anthropology at the University of Montpellier Paul Valéry and a researcher at the UMR SENS. She is a fellow at the Institut Convergences Migrations (Paris). She is PI France of the project Food2gather: exploring foodscape as public spaces for integration.

Marion Demossier is professor of social anthropology in the Department of Modern Languages and Linguistics at the University of Southampton. She has published more than 20 scholarly articles in leading academic journals in Britain, France and the United States, including the *Journal of the Royal Anthropological Institute*, *Cultural Analysis*, the *Anthropological Journal of European Cultures* and *Modern and Contemporary France*.

Dorota Dias-Lewandowska is an anthropologist and historian working at the Institute of Archaeology and Ethnology, Polish Academy of Science in the Department for the History of Material Culture of the Middle Ages and Modern Times. She is also co-convenor of the 'Women and Alcohol' cluster of the Drinking Studies Network. Her research interests include alcohol and intoxicants; drinking culture; discourse on drunkenness, sobriety and excesses and women and alcohol, and she has published widely on Polish wine and food history.

Jean-Guillaume Ditter is an associate professor at Burgundy School of Business. He teaches industrial and international economics, strategy and international business. His research interests include the analysis of local factors affecting the global competitiveness of traditional and locally embedded industries such as wine.

Lorenzo Domaneschi is assistant professor of cultural sociology at the University of Milano-Bicocca. His main research interests include food and wine culture, consumption studies, ethnography and theories of social practice. His last book about cooking practices and the issue of quality in Italy is *Fare cucina: La cultura della qualità alimentare tra arte e artigianato* [*The Practice of Cooking: The Culture of Food Quality between Art and Craftmanship*], 2018.

Carl Driesener is a senior marketing scientist at the Ehrenberg-Bass Institute for Marketing Science, UniSA Business School, University of South Australia. His key areas of research are consumer behaviour, loyalty, brand growth and advertising.

Jacqueline Dutton is professor in French studies at the University of Melbourne, where she also lectures in wine courses. Her recent work includes an in-depth analysis of French geographers' role in shaping twentieth-century discourses for narrating wine culture (*Global Food History* 5: 2019). She is co-editor (with Peter J. Howland) of *Wine, Terroir and Utopia: Making New Worlds* (Routledge 2019) and is currently writing a cultural history of wine in Bordeaux, Burgundy and Champagne.

Sénia Fedoul is a PhD student in history at the University of Lyon. Her work discusses the concept of 'quality' applied to the taste of wine in the twentieth century with the internationalisation of the wine market. She has focused on the scientists and experts of wine and how they gained the status of experts in wine quality, with a major role in the worldwide influence of French wines. Since 2015, she has been an associate researcher at the UNESCO Chair 'Culture and Tradition of Wine' of the University of Dijon.

Connor Fitzmaurice is a sociologist studying food at the intersection of markets and culture. He writes on the everyday economic realities of organic farming, food bartering economies and the reappraisal of delicious, 'disreputable' wines. He is a lecturer in the Boston University gastronomy program.

Joanna Fountain is a senior lecturer in tourism management at Lincoln University, New Zealand. She has diverse research interests, many of which are related to agro-food and wine value chains, including tourism, and analysis of change and resilience in rural regions.

Graham Harding is a wine historian attached to the history faculty of the University of Oxford. His 2018 DPhil thesis, *The Establishment of Champagne in France and Britain, 1800–1914*, focused on the links between England and France in the long nineteenth century and how French producers and English merchants and agents created the oenological and marketing template for champagne as we know it today. He has written several books, and recent publications on wine include articles on the nineteenth-century distributors and on the branding and advertising of champagne as well as the gifting of wine, the development of Champagne as a 'cultural terroir' and wine connoisseurship.

Rory Hill is lecturer in wine business and innovation at the Eastern Institute of Technology in New Zealand. He has research interests in wine, terroir, sense of place, gastronomy and rural economy.

Mack P. Holt is professor emeritus of history at George Mason University and received his PhD in history from Emory University in 1982. He specialises in early modern Europe, especially France, the Reformation, the history of wine and the history of the book.

Peter J. Howland is a lecturer in sociology at Massey University, New Zealand. He is the founding editor of *Critical Beverage Studies* (Routledge) and the editor of a number of books about wine. He has researched – from anthropological and sociological perspectives – wine production, tourism and consumption in New Zealand and the United Kingdom as a means to critically examine the values, beliefs and practices of the middle classes.

Ashlee Humphreys is associate professor of integrated marketing communications, Medill School of Journalism, and associate professor of marketing, Kellogg School of Management, Northwestern University. Professor Humphreys studies the role of institutions in markets and the influence of language on both consumer judgements of legitimacy and the broader process of legitimation. She is the author of *Social Media: Enduring Principles*, 2016.

Hang Kei Ho is a post-doctoral scholar in the sociology discipline within the faculty of social sciences at the University of Helsinki, Finland. He held academic positions in the Netherlands, Sweden and the UK, operating across the fields of business management, development studies, economic geography, public health and urban sociology.

David Inglis is professor in the sociology discipline within the faculty of social sciences at the University of Helsinki, Finland. He writes in the areas of social theory, cultural sociology and historical sociology, with special reference to globalisation, food and wine.

Azélina Jaboulet-Vercherre received her PhD degree in history (Yale University, 2011) and since then has created wine history and culture courses tailored to various higher education institutions, particularly Ferrandi Paris (where she currently is an associate professor). In 2019, the OIV Scientific and Technical Committee appointed Azélina to the position of president of the International OIV Award jury.

Olivier Jacquet works on the history of wine in the eighteenth to the twentieth centuries as a researcher with the UNESCO Chair 'Culture and Tradition of Wine' of the University of Burgundy and is a researcher at the UMR CNRS/uB 7366 Georges Chevrier Centre. His work focuses on the construction of wine production and marketing in France, ranging from viticultural syndicalism and the establishment of the AOC system in Burgundy to the international history of prescriptions and descriptions in wine tasting during the long twentieth century.

Clara Jaffré holds an MSc degree in international business (Kedge Business School) with interests in psychology and neuroscience. Her master's thesis analyses the role of women in the wine industry. She is currently a professional coach specialising in change management.

Richard Lee is a member of the marketing faculty of the UniSA School of Business. His research focuses on international and ethnic marketing in Asian markets. He sits on the board of China Business Network.

Florine Livat is an associate professor of economics at Kedge Business School (Bordeaux). Her field is agricultural economics, with research specialising in empirical wine economics.

Larry Lockshin is adjunct professor of wine marketing at the University of South Australia. He has published over 120 academic articles, over 250 trade articles and a book on wine marketing, *This Little Pinot Went to Market*.

Charles C. Ludington is a professor at North Carolina State University, where he teaches early modern British and European history. After undergraduate history at Yale University, he completed his master's and doctoral degrees at Columbia University. He has published on British and Irish political thought in the late Stuart era and the history of wine consumption in Britain from the mid-seventeenth century to the mid-nineteenth century (*The Politics of Wine in Britain: A New Cultural History*, 2013).

Jennifer Smith Maguire is professor of cultural production and consumption at the Sheffield Business School, Sheffield Hallam University. Her expertise lies in the socio-cultural study of consumer culture and cultural intermediaries, with a special focus on the construction of markets, tastes and value. Jennifer has published widely on the cultural production of emerging wine markets, wine and cultures of consumption (e.g. China, France) and the construction of forms of value and legitimacy for and through wine (e.g. provenance, authenticity, heritage).

Denton Marks is professor emeritus of economics at the University of Wisconsin–Whitewater and fellow of the American Association of Wine Economists (AAWE). His book *Wine and Economics: Transacting the Elixir of Life* (2015), an introduction to the economics of wine for students and the public, is used internationally in various oenological and business programs.

Julie McIntyre is a senior lecturer in history and director of the Wine Studies Research Network at the University of Newcastle, Australia. Honours for her book *Hunter Wine: A History* (with John Germov) include an OIV Jury Prize, 'Special Mention for History'. She has held a Fulbright Scholarship at the University of California, Davis, and co-instructs in the UC Davis course Wine and Society for viticulture and oenology students.

Richard Mitchell is a professor at Otago Polytechnic, College of Work-Based Learning, Dunedin, New Zealand. His work has four broad areas of food and beverage research: consumer behaviour, business networks and clusters, experience design and teaching and learning. He has presented in more than a dozen countries and has held positions in national and international industry and research bodies in the food and beverage sector.

Paul Muller is associate professor in economics at the University of Lorraine and researcher at BETA. His research investigates the territorial governance of (business model and social) innovations and creative processes, with a focus on the wine and music industries.

Colleen C. Myles is an associate professor in the department of geography at Texas State University in San Marcos, Texas. She has a PhD in geography and an MS in community development from the University of California, Davis.

Gianmarco Navarini is full professor of cultural sociology at the University of Milano-Bicocca. His main research interests include wine culture, taste and tasting; social rituals; ethnography and discourse analysis and the sociology of language. He is the author of several articles and books on wine, including *Mondi del vino: Enografia dentro e fuori il bicchiere* [*Wine Worlds: Oenography Inside and Outside the Glass*], 2015.

Signe Nelgen is a research associate at Geisenheim University's Institute for Wine and Beverage Business Research. She is also an affiliate of the Wine Economics Research Centre of the University of Adelaide, the university where she completed her PhD and then worked as a post-doctoral fellow before joining the UN Food and Agriculture Organisation.

John Overton is professor of development studies at Victoria University of Wellington, New Zealand. He is a geographer who has studied the wine industry for the past 25 years and has a particular interest in the way places are used in the production, marketing and consumption of wine.

Rod Phillips is a professor of history at Carleton University, Ottawa, Canada. He is a specialist in the history of wine, and his books include *A Short History of Wine* (2000), updated as *9000 Years of Wine* (2017); *Alcohol: A History* (2014); *French Wine: A History* (2016); *The Wines of Canada* (2017) and *Wine: A Social and Cultural History of the Drink That Changed Our Lives* (2018). He also judges wine competitions and writes for the wine media, including *The World of Fine Wine* in the UK.

Joonas Rokka is professor of marketing and director of the Lifestyle Research Center at EMLYON Business School, France. He received his PhD in marketing from Aalto University School of Business, Finland. His research examines champagne, brands, consumer experience, busy lifestyles and digital technology.

William Skinner is based at the University of Adelaide and holds a PhD in anthropology. His research focuses on wine, agricultural production and regional identity and place in South Australia. He is also an amateur winemaker.

Robert Swinburn is a winegrape grower, winemaker and consultant in the Geelong wine region. He completed his PhD in anthropology at the University of Melbourne. His publications include chapters in *Wine and Culture: Vineyard to Glass*, Rachel Black and Robert Ulin (eds), and *Wine, Terroir and Utopia: Making New Worlds*, Jacqueline Dutton and Peter J. Howland (eds).

Corinne Tanguy is a professor in industrial economics at AgroSup Dijon and a researcher at Centre d'économie et de sociologie appliquées à l'agriculture et aux espaces ruraux (CESAER). She specialises in the economics of innovation and studies innovation processes in the agro-food sector and the territorial dimension of these processes.

Ian Malcolm Taplin is professor of sociology, management and international Studies at Wake Forest University, North Carolina, USA, and has also taught at Kedge Business School, Bordeaux. He has published extensively on the wine industry in North Carolina (*The Modern American Wine Industry*, 2011), Napa (*Napa Valley Wine: Organizing Excellence*, 2021) and Bordeaux. He has also written a book on the luxury goods industry (*The Evolution of Luxury*, Routledge, 2020).

Geneviève Teil is a sociologist at INRAE Paris. She is working on the interactions between humans and non-humans: namely, perception, appreciation, qualification and the variety of the existence mode of objects. Wine, its market, its critics, its appreciation and its various quality certifications, as well as wine critics' judgement activity, constitute her main research fields.

Michele M. Tobias has a PhD from the University of California, Davis (UC Davis) in geography. She works as a geospatial data scientist at the UC Davis DataLab.

Ana Tominc is an assistant professor in Food, Communication and Media Studies at Queen Margaret University Edinburgh, United Kingdom. She has published on contemporary food discourses related to lifestyle and class; veganism and far-right cooking shows on social media; cookbooks and food television in socialist Yugoslavia. She is the author of *The Discursive Construction of Class and Lifestyle: Celebrity Chef Cookbooks in Post-Socialist Slovenia* and the editor of *Food and Cooking on Early Television* (Routledge 2021).

Christi G. Townsend is a senior lecturer in the department of geography at Texas State University in San Marcos, Texas. She has a PhD and master's in environmental geography from Texas State University.

Tim Unwin is professor emeritus of geography at Royal Holloway, University of London. His seminal book *Wine and the Vine: An Historical Geography of Viticulture and the Wine Trade* was published by Routledge in 1991, and he has written extensively about wine-related subjects as diverse as terroir, wine labels and Locke's interests in wine. He co-founded the *Journal of Wine Research* in 1991 and was external examiner and academic advisor to the Institute of Masters of Wine from 2004 to 2011.

Clelia Viecelli is a PhD candidate based in the faculty of humanities at the University of Southampton (UK). She holds a MSc in social anthropology from the London School of Economics (LSE). Her PhD thesis is an anthropological account of female winegrowers producing natural wines in Italy.

Nikki Welch studied economics and languages at the University of Surrey and has an MSc in gastronomy from Queen Margaret University. She has spent the last 20 years working in the commercial wine industry and now runs her own business demystifying wine, whiskey and beer for hospitality staff with her through her award-winning training app, Quenchable, and for consumers through events, staff training and the use of her WineTubeMap, WhiskyTubeMap and BeerTubeMap.

PREFACE

When I was contacted by Emma Travis at Routledge and asked to edit a volume on wine and culture for their *Handbook* series, I immediately declined. I'd just come out of editing two other books (always a fraught process), and – more significantly – I knew instantly that such a project would have so wide a disciplinary context that it would be beyond my experience and knowledge.

Twenty-four hours later, I rang back and said I had changed my mind; the project was certainly fascinating, but I said that I was only agreeing on the condition that I could assemble a team of editors from different backgrounds and experience who would complement what I had to offer and enable us to create a truly interdisciplinary text. This has allowed me to work with a number of colleagues with whom I had already researched and who I was confident would strive to create a wide-ranging and genuinely useful book. The process has been difficult at times (how do engaged researchers from seven different fields even agree on a definition of culture?), but it has been collegial and creative, as well as intellectually challenging and enriching. Throughout, I have seen myself only as the *primus inter pares* and not the director of the project. The editors have all worked together to construct the volume, and we have passed ideas and literature on to each other, recommended reviewers and critiqued each other's contributions. We have, I believe, sincerely attempted to support each other, with good humour tempering our scepticism about the others' disciplines.

Why wine and culture? Each of us editors is fascinated by this relationship, and each of us has a different story to tell about what piqued our interest in it. Before I became an academic, I spent a few years selling wines in liquor stores in Sydney. The wine was interesting – but equally so were the people. There was the lady who, every few days, would come in for the 'cheapest red wine that you have'; when after some months of this, I asked her why it was always the cheapest, she answered that she didn't like the taste – but had been told that it was good for her health to have a glass each evening. The businessman, a self-confessed connoisseur, who insisted on 'a man's drink – full-bodied red' and refused the suggestion of pinot noir as you only have to look at it to see it is weak and a wine for women. The elderly couple I encountered outside a professional tasting of French wines who were interested in what was happening, but then, when I explained it to them, retorted, 'Why do that? We have perfectly good wines here in Australia and don't need any of that French stuff'. The wine store owners who insisted that they weren't running a business but were 'living a lifestyle'. The office worker who didn't drink wine often but, when she did, enjoyed it because it took her back to her youth in Croatia when she would be sent by her father to the corner shop with a plastic bottle to fill with wine from their barrel; 'it would last us about two days'. The winemaker who claimed that idea of terroir was just a French excuse for badly made wine. All these stories and myriad others were as intriguing as the wines themselves, and an interest in what sparked such various views of the drink led me a decade later to write a book about its cultural and social context.

There is not space for all of us to tell our stories, but, in lieu of this, we have compiled an idiosyncratic selection of cultural artefacts that have sustained, inspired and accompanied our own journeys with wine (see Appendix). These are offered not as an exhaustive compendium, but as a tasting menu that may be of use to others in search of complementary resources for teaching or research or simply something to watch, read or listen to while enjoying a glass of wine.

This book has been produced in the shadow of COVID-19, which has made life difficult in different ways for each of us. Some had family responsibilities; most found academic demands and new ways of working intruded substantially on working life; all suffered at times from the various constraints and confinements imposed by the pandemic. I want to take this opportunity to thank my six colleagues for the effort they have given in trying circumstances and the support they have offered me. It is invidious to single out any one person; nevertheless, I must particularly express my gratitude to Graham Harding, who took over the coordination of the book at a late stage when I became sick and thereafter continued to do an immense amount of work on finishing the manuscript, especially the proofing.

One of my aims in asking my colleagues to work with me on this *Handbook* was to ensure it would have a high academic quality. All chapters have been blind peer reviewed to maintain academic rigour. Thanks are therefore also due to all our reviewers, who gave time to this process. Many of these were contributors, but additionally, the following have been helpful, often more than once: Angela McShane, Boris Petric, Claude Chapuis, David R. Green, David Throsby, Diarmaid McCulloch, Donna Senese; George R. McEachern, Gergely Szolnoki, Heidi Armbruster, Iza Kaninska, James Crick, James Shackelford, Jessica Yuan, Joan Kiese, Joe Bohling, Kevin Goldberg, Mark Anthony Arceno, Natalia Velikova, Nathalie Spielmann, Nathaniel Chapman, Nelson Graburn, Paul Freedman, Percy Dougherty, Rachel Black, Roberta Capitello, Susan Boyle, Xiangchun Zheng, Eammon Maher and Agnieszka Whelan.

In addition, the work would not have been possible without the initial proposal from Emma Travis, who guided us through the submission and review stage, and support and assistance later from Lydia Kessell at Routledge.

We note in the conclusion to this volume that one of the negative aspects of wine is the vast amount of water consumed in its production. We, the editors, enjoy wine immensely. In partial reparation for the environmental problems caused by our passion, we have decided to donate the royalties from this book to the charity WaterAid (www.wateraid.org/uk/).

Steve Charters, Coordinating Editor

CULTURE AND WINE

An introduction

Tim Unwin

This introductory chapter has three main objectives: to explain how the *Handbook* was crafted, to provide an overview of its conceptual framing and to offer a guide to how it might be read. The *Handbook*'s origins lay in a conversation between Steve Charters and the editorial staff at Routledge in mid-2019, and its design and content owe much to Steve's persistence and determination in bringing together a very diverse group of editors and authors to work collaboratively with him and help bring it to fruition. He claims to be merely one among many, but without his vision and direction, the book would not have taken shape in the way that it has done.

Crafting the *Handbook*

At the *Handbook*'s heart is a vision that it should be a diverse, multidisciplinary collection of essays that shed light on the complexity and varied fascinations surrounding the interface between culture and wine. The co-editors all come from very different intellectual traditions, each bringing their own varied perspectives and personal histories to the *Handbook*. Many of us have also crossed several intellectual, linguistic and professional boundaries; indeed, it might be suggested that this is a central requirement for anyone interested in truly beginning to understand culture and wine. Steve himself has an original background in history, then worked in the wine industry in Australia, subsequently found his home in business schools (gaining the Master of Wine qualification on the way) and is now based in France; Marion Demossier combines backgrounds in linguistics and anthropology and is based in the UK; Jackie Dutton is another linguist, specialising in French culture but hailing from Australia; Graham Harding is a UK-based historian, having previously worked as a brand consultant and market researcher; Jennifer Smith Maguire, a Canadian based in the UK, is a sociologist specialising in the study of consumer culture; Denton Marks is an economist, based in the USA and Tim Unwin is, by origin, a geographer.

As co-editors, we each took responsibility for identifying relevant authors in our respective fields and for writing a short introductory overview to the ways in which previous authors in our disciplines (anthropology, business, economics, geography, history, sociology and text) have approached the interface between wine and culture. These essays provide fascinating reading and emphasise very clearly how the ways that colleagues in our different disciplines address culture and undertake research on its linkages with wine vary significantly. These understandings have also changed through time as our disciplines have been shaped to serve the interests of academics building their careers within them. Having solicited abstracts and identified potential authors, including those from disciplines other than our own, all the co-editors reviewed the submitted offerings and reached a provisional shortlist of chapters. Gaps were also identified and additional authors invited to submit contributions during 2020. Authors were requested to submit chapters of 5,000 words, and these were reviewed by two co-editors as well as external reviewers (see Preface for details). The resultant chapters are of two broad kinds: a small number address overviews of particular fields, such as those on religion or terroir, whereas the majority address much more specific aspects of the intersections between wine and culture in particular places and periods.

We also, though, wanted to craft a *Handbook* that reflected interdisciplinary collaboration and the diversity of approaches that could be taken to address specific topics, rather than producing a book simply containing sections that only included chapters by authors from the same discipline. To this end, we explored the notion of encouraging authors from different disciplines to work collaboratively on specific themes but ultimately largely rejected this, mainly because of logistical constraints and the time that such an approach would require. Consequently, we had considerable discussion around the broad themes within which the chapters could be clustered, combining our own thoughts about structure with the subject matters of the chapters that had been accepted. Ultimately, the chapters have been grouped into five thematic sections:

- Production and place
- Intermediation and consumption
- Belief and representation
- Power and contestation
- Change and the future

In part, this reflects the strong opinions each of us held about what should be included within the notion of culture. Not all of us agree with all the headings, but we each respect that some among us do, indeed, consider that there are cultural dimensions to most, if not all, of the themes. This mutual respect for other opinions and understandings is a key feature of the *Handbook*, and all of us consciously support the fundamental principle of diversity. This diversity of understandings and meanings is itself an important dimension of the *Handbook*. We reject attempts to construct a single dominant 'truth' and suspect that readers will also come to the collection with their own understandings of culture that may well differ from our own. We welcome and encourage such intellectual and practical exploration and challenge; it is these complex interactions that the *Handbook* seeks to promote and encourage.

We are also conscious of the gaps that have not been addressed in this collection of essays. In part, this reflects the lack of current scholarship on certain themes; in part, it reflects emerging fields in which exciting new research will undoubtedly emerge. We hope that the conclusions from the book can, indeed, be used by others to forge new understandings about wine and culture. The *Handbook*, with its 45 chapters, is already quite lengthy, but we recognise that five areas in particular are but briefly addressed here and could usefully be explored in more detail: the material cultures of paintings, sculpture, advertisements and music; the darker side of wine use and its connections with health, not least issues around addiction and the use of substances to escape the harsh realities of physical life, as well as the balance between the health benefits and costs of wine consumption; the dominant cultural practices of viticulture and winemaking in response to environmental change; emergent and residual forms of wine culture (such as natural wine or orange wine) that reflect new taste regimes and our understandings of human and non-human relations and, above all, contrasting understandings of culture in different linguistic traditions (Kuper 2000). We are very conscious that this book is also written in various forms of English, although many editors and authors do, indeed, speak multiple languages, and the *Handbook* as a whole does seek to draw on these varying cultural traditions. It would, however, have been very different if written by Chinese, Hindi or Arabic scholars and crafted within their own cultural contexts.

Understanding wine and culture

This *Handbook* is fundamentally about two things: the ways in which reflections about wine can enhance understandings of culture, and how wine itself can be better understood through a focus on culture. This section shares some thoughts about the variety of ways in which we, as editors, have considered the terms 'wine' and 'culture'; the disciplinary chapters delve into these complexities in much greater detail.

On wine

We have adopted the internationally accepted definition of wine as 'the beverage resulting exclusively from the partial or complete alcoholic fermentation of fresh grapes, whether crushed or not, or of grape must. Its actual alcohol content shall not be less than 8.5% vol.' (OIV 2015). In certain environmental circumstances, legislation permits the alcohol level to be reduced to 7%, but this book focuses exclusively on wine from grapes and excludes the many other different 'fruit wines' made from plums, cherries, currants and other plants. We also exclude alcoholic spirits made from grapes, such as brandies, as well as those from other plants, such as tequila made from agave. It is explicitly a handbook about wine and culture and not of alcohol and culture.

This choice reflects our view that there are very specific features about the intersections between wine and culture that are worthy of analysis and understanding. In particular, there is strong evidence that wine was first discovered or made in a particular place, variously called southwest Asia and the Caucasus region, and that there was a close relationship between its use as a religious and social symbol throughout the expansion of grape growing and winemaking subsequently into the Mediterranean region. Wine, specifically from grapes, has deep resonance in all European societies and cultures, and with the colonial expansion, first by the Spanish and Portuguese in the sixteenth century and then by the Dutch and English from the seventeenth century onwards, this element of culture was taken with Europeans as part of their wider cultural baggage and grafted into new environments.

We recognise that other cultures have long contained aspects that involved the ingestion (eating, smoking or drinking) of different elements of nature for religious purposes and to escape from or relieve tension and pain: the Aztecs maintained strict cultural traditions and restrictions around the drinking of *pulque* made from the maguey/agave plant; opium, originating from southwest Asia around 4,000 years ago, was widely used to relieve pain and bring joy (Norn *et al.* 2005); the indigenous hunting-gathering peoples of northwestern North America traditionally smoked tobacco long before the introduction of 'trade tobacco' by Europeans (Tushingham *et al.* 2018); and cannabis has been widely consumed in India for some 4,000 years. All these substances, along with many others, have played important cultural roles in different societies for millennia; our focus is on wine alone and the ways through which it is now not only a global commodity but also a global symbol. There nevertheless remains much comparative research to be done on the wider cultural roles of different elements of nature in human life and the way that these have intertwined and competed over more than five millennia.

On culture

We chose to let the authors who have contributed to this *Handbook* define culture in the ways that they chose to and deliberately did not seek to impose any single definition of culture on them. Not only would this have been an impossible task, but we also wanted to reveal the richness of meanings associated with the varied notions of culture adopted by the authors. In a sense, this can therefore be seen as reflecting a very loose and fluid notion of 'culture' rather than a formal or 'tight' definition, not least acknowledging its transitional and global dimensions. Indeed, we recognise that many people, including some academics, consider culture to be something that is everyday, obvious and boring and not worthy of deeper exploration. We fiercely challenge this notion of 'banal culture'.

However, we are also very conscious that in editing an academic collection, we have crafted a book that could itself be seen as a product of the 'high culture' or 'elite culture' of the intelligentsia and upper classes. Yet we are very committed to understanding more popular cultures, sometimes referred to by the derogatory term 'low culture' (Gans 1999). Furthermore, we also recognise the male dominance of both academia and the wine sector and acknowledge the important contributions that women have made to both, especially in recent years.

Definitions of culture are contested and vary hugely (Baldwin *et al.* 2006; Jahoda 2012), but in order to understand the special place within which wine is held in European culture, as well as those cultures that it has increasingly come to dominate, it is important here to explore some of the meanings of culture that are addressed in the *Handbook*. In its most basic form, culture is often seen as comprising both material forms (the physical expression of cultures such as art, architecture, clothes, or indeed technologies) and immaterial forms associated with the principles through which societies are organised.

In origin, 'culture' is fundamentally tied to the idea of cultivation and thus deeply resonant in the context of the cultivation of grapes and wine. The word in English is ultimately derived from the Latin *colere*, meaning to cultivate or tend the land, which is also the root of the English words 'colony' (from Latin *colonia*) and 'cult', in a religious sense. All these meanings and senses of agricultural cultivation, religion and colonialism feature prominently in this book. The link between the cultivation of the physical land and our more conceptual understanding of culture today is often seen as being derived from the Roman orator Cicero's use of the term *cultura animi* as a metaphor for the cultivation of a philosophical soul; it was what made Roman citizens different from the 'barbarians'. Over time, it has become increasingly abstracted and adapted so that as well as being found in the word 'agriculture', 'culture' itself gradually came to be used to refer to the improvement of many aspects of the human condition through education, especially of the mind.

From the Enlightenment of the seventeenth century onwards, this association of the word 'culture' with a sense of betterment of the human condition grew in prominence, not least through the writings of Germans such as Samuel von Pufendorf (1632–1694), Johann Gottfried Herder (1744–1803) and Johann Wolfgang von Goethe (1749–1832). The von Humboldt brothers Willhelm (1767–1835) and Alexander (1769–1859) – the former a politician, linguist and philosopher, the latter a geographer, naturalist and explorer – both played important roles in the subsequent evolution of notions of culture. Willhelm contributed to the development of linguistic philosophy, especially through his notion of a linguistic worldview, and Alexander sought to unite many branches of science and culture in his voluminous *Kosmos*, published between 1845 and 1862 (Von Humboldt 2014). In a sense, the two brothers represented the tension between culture and nature that the Genevan Jean-Jacques Rousseau (1712–1778) had put forward a century earlier, in which he suggested that humans had developed from a primitive condition to people of culture. Elsewhere in Europe, English humanists such as Matthew Arnold (1822–1888) also promoted the idea of culture as an ultimate ideal, which, in turn, fostered the notion of an elite or high culture. However, there was also a counter-current in the nineteenth century that saw the emergence of this elite culture as being corrupting and promoted the importance of traditional folk culture as being somehow nearer people's fundamental nature. This tradition of enquiry into the relative balance between nature and culture was fundamental to the emergence of geography and anthropology as formal academic disciplines in the nineteenth century. One of the founders of British anthropology, Edward Tyler, thus defined culture as the 'complex whole that includes knowledge, belief, art, morals, law, custom and any other capabilities and habits acquired by man as a member of society' (Tyler 1871: 1). This definition is often still cited, although modern scholarship has evolved substantially and rightly prefers the gender-neutral 'people as members of society'.

European people have since antiquity often constructed their understandings of the communities in which they live in terms of their economic, political, social and cultural or ideological contexts or structures. This owes much to Greek thought, particularly as expressed in Plato's *Republic*. In his lecture on culture and society in Plato's work, Burnyeat (1997) thus provides a fascinating account of these inter-relationships and the important role that wine played in such exchanges. Economic, political and social activities and phenomena provided a clear basis for the emergence of the formal disciplines named after them. Meanwhile, Immanuel Kant (1724–1804) had explored the philosophical distinction between space and time (Janiak 2020) that has often been used to justify a disciplinary distinction between geography and history, the former examining the ways through which phenomena vary across space and the latter through time (Unwin 1992). However, this left spheres of life and human endeavour such as art, religion and ideology – everything encapsulated within the broad term 'culture' – without an equivalent single disciplinary home, although religion fell clearly within the realms of theology, and anthropologists sought to assert their authority over all aspects of humanity.

Karl Marx (1818–1883), in his influential dialectical materialism, developed a clear vision of how these different spheres of life were related, in which the material economic base or infrastructure in effect determined the characteristics of the social, ideological and political superstructure. His arguments were vastly more nuanced and complex than such a brief summary suggests, but for the purposes of this *Handbook*, it is important to appreciate the lasting impact that these ideas had during the twentieth century, particularly through the primacy they gave to economics and economists. From a very different direction, economists such as Adam Smith, John Maynard Keynes and Milton Friedman have also sought to reinforce this dominance of economics for the foundation of modern capitalist societies. There therefore remains a deep undercurrent of thought among people from very different backgrounds that implicitly sees all other dimensions and disciplines, especially including culture, as being subservient to, or determined by, the theory and practice of economics.

Such views were, though, vehemently challenged in a range of directions from the late 1950s onwards. Althusser's (Althusser and Balibar 1970) work within a Marxist tradition, for example, postulated a relational distinction between dominant and determinant instances. For him, all social phenomena exist in relation to each other, and any one can dominate in particular circumstances, but ultimately Althusser retained the notion of the primacy of the economic structure, which, in the last instance, determines the autonomy and dependence of the non-economic (Resch 1992). Similarly, Raymond Williams (1973) reflected on the complex relationships between base and superstructure and, in so doing, emphasised his objection to crude economic reductionism.

Put simply, during the 1970s, culture became separated from the shackles of economics, regardless of their political hue, giving rise to a widespread 'cultural turn' within the social sciences and humanities (Jacobs and Spillman 2005). This was also, in part, a result of the rejection of logical positivism in favour of more hermeneutic approaches focused on understanding rather than explanation by a new generation of academics across the social sciences who turned to cultural concepts such as meanings, symbols, affect and cognition in both their theoretical and their methodological practices. This cultural turn, though, was not just in academic disciplines and was paralleled by a substantive shift in society, at least within the world's richer economies. It also led to a dramatic expansion in what was considered to be 'culture'. Indeed, there are multiple understandings of culture; Williams (1976) identified 110 different words associated with definitions of culture, and the number has expanded further since then. This has led some to suggest that in the pursuit of meaning, any notion of culture has thus itself become meaningless; if everything is culture, what indeed is culture? By the early years of the twenty-first century, cultural studies were again reinventing themselves, and new 'new cultural' studies were being forged, as expressed in volumes such as Hall and Birchall's

(2006) edited collection of *New Cultural Studies*. One thing is certain, and that is that the cultural understandings of wine will continue to evolve, and possible directions in which these may flow are examined further in this volume's conclusion.

Against this liberating background, academics from many disciplines began to explore potent expressions of culture; few expressions of human interaction with the non-human world were riper for exploration than wine. Figure 0.1 draws on these previous conceptions of human communities in order to provide a heuristic device through which some of this complexity can be understood and serves as a map through which the chapters in this handbook can be interpreted. As it seeks to portray, there is immense overlap between the aspects of culture that social scientists from different disciplines have considered, and each has tended to do so primarily from their own contrasting disciplinary backgrounds. This disciplinary diversity of approaches to culture has often meant that academics in one discipline have not read similar works by scholars from other disciplines. One of the purposes of this *Handbook*, therefore, is to bring these understandings of wine together in a single volume where they can be shared in a collaborative spirit through which both the authors and readers may indeed become enriched.

From this account of the emergence of different interpretations and understandings of culture, it will be readily apparent not only that different disciplines maintain their own languages of culture but also that even within disciplines, different researchers will have their own individual approaches to culture and wine. In very general terms, the editors of this volume consider culture to be the way in which a group of people organise themselves, including beliefs and values, formalised structures of behaviour and informal norms, all of which are mediated in its ideology, ritual, customs and language. It has a material dimension that links to technology, art and scientific development, and it sees wine as a product of the intersection between the physical environment (often seen as nature) and the cultural. It explores how and why humans have, through time and space, made a 'natural' product into a potent societally specific cultural symbol that varies in different places.

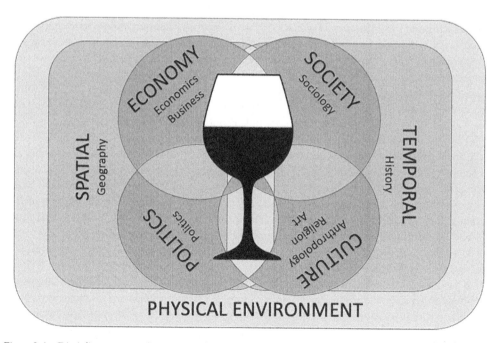

Figure 0.1 Disciplinary approaches to an understanding of wine and culture

Each editor has had the unenviable task of making sense out of this complexity by providing an overview of the emergence and current research practices of research on wine and culture in their own disciplines. These chapters, which follow on immediately from the Introduction, could clearly have been much longer, but they provide both a synthesis of past research and an individually distinctive reflection on the meanings attributed to the culture of wine in their own disciplines. One striking conclusion from reading them is how different and yet how similar they are. They approach the same basic subject – the interactions between humans and the physical environment that make and enable the appreciation of wine – but do so from very different perspectives and using rather different language and styles. Instead of repeating what each editor has written in their chapter, this section of the Introduction seeks to provide a broad overview of their key arguments (in alphabetical order of the disciplines), and the *Handbook*'s conclusion then draws together and synthesises the substantive evidence of the new contributions made by its many authors.

Anthropology

For anthropologists, 'culture' is the prism through which particular understandings, beliefs and practices are articulated in a comparative and reflexive fashion between specific groups (such as winemakers or consumers), professions (such as wine educators or lawyers) and institutions (such as the OIV or the Institute of Masters of Wine). As discussed in the previous section of this Introduction, the concept of culture has evolved considerably within anthropology, as indeed it has in other disciplines, and it is still subject to considerable internal debate and theoretical positioning.

Traditionally, anthropology has been defined through the arbitrary location of the fieldsite(s), be they local, regional, national or transnational. It has also been characterised by the ethnographic gaze and practice of the anthropologist that often seek to privilege holism (making sense of a 'total social fact', which means trying to integrate all that is known to human beings) as well as structural complexities. In methodological terms, ethnography has long been the key mode of critical research enquiry into the modern world of anthropologists who have tended to focus on the micro, the ordinary, the mundane and everyday life.

As with other social science disciplines, the cultural turn of the 1970s led to many claims about the creation of a new anthropology (Ardener 1971; Clifford and Marcus 1986) and new ethnographies (Goodall 2000). These problematise in particular the relationships between the researcher and the researched, as well as bringing to the fore the socio-cultural position and identity of the researcher. Indeed, some of the most exciting such research has been concerned with uncovering how the researcher comes to an understanding of what they claim and the extent to which this is consonant with the everyday experiences of those about whom academic publications are written.

Business

A strong tradition of academic research and teaching in business globally only really took off in the 1960s, although business and management courses had, indeed, been taught in some institutions from the second half of the nineteenth century; the first business school was the Aula do Comércio in Lisbon, which opened in 1759. Some see the discipline largely as an offshoot of economics, and there are, indeed, often institutional tensions between the two disciplines. In broad terms, though, research in business studies tends to focus mainly on aspects of finance, accounting, organisations, management, marketing and human resources. All of these have cultural dimensions to them, but as with economics, they have often taken a very instrumental view of culture. In essence, this has meant that culture has not been understood for its own value, but rather for how it can be used by managers so that they can perform their roles more effectively, or those involved in marketing so that their companies can be made more profitable. Indeed, many business academics would not be happy engaging with the complexities of culture since it is not easily measurable.

Nevertheless, in recent years, there has been a growing research focus on culture as an area of specific intrinsic interest. Businesses clearly all have their own institutional culture, and culture itself has become a vibrant business opportunity. In particular, research on wine tourism has grown significantly, focusing on issues such as the interactions between tourists and local cultures, the marketing of wine landscapes and the business of wine festivals and events (Carlsen and Charters 2006). Some of this research has also focused on the negative impacts of such tourism as well as the positives (Hill and Fountain in this book). A second broad area of increasing cultural research from a business perspective has been the application of consumer culture theory (Rokka 2021 and in this book). This examines both how consumers are culturally situated and also how they also shape culture.

Economics

Economists have long been interested in culture, but because of the need to consider it within traditional disciplinary conceptualisations, constraints and boundaries, there has been rather little research until recently by economists specifically on culture and wine. An important turning point in the ways through which economists have studied wine over the last 30 years has been the concept of cultural goods (often abbreviated to CG) and services. Throsby (2001, see also 2003) has defined these as something that is produced and valued that embodies creativity in production, intellectual property and symbolic value and whose customers have developed a taste for it from prolonged experience and assign to it cultural and perhaps economic (monetary) value. Traditional economic value alone is neither necessary nor sufficient for something to be considered a cultural good. Four important implications arise from this for the study of wine and culture. First, the discipline itself can be enhanced through convincingly defining a new type of good, such as wine, that has unique market characteristics. Second, as Beckert (2019) has suggested, the value of CG emerges from markets of meaning rather than traditionally measurable attributes. These derive from discursive practices and mutual observation of participants to arrive at intersubjective conclusions. Quality is thus endogenous to the market process as previously conceived. The role of wine experts is particularly important here, especially in shaping the perceptions of wine quality and thus its value as a cultural good. Third, it is extremely complex and difficult – and thus especially interesting – to measure and observe such value, and fourth, CGs are inspiring in the sense that production inspires further production without there necessarily being any commercial or purely financial motivation. The concept of cultural good and services, therefore, offers an exciting opportunity to be explored by future research by economists, especially when this is combined with interdisciplinary understandings of neuroscience and psychology.

Geography

Geographers have long engaged with wine, not least in terms of its spatial distribution, its contribution to the identity of places and its expression of the intimate relationships between humans and the physical environment. Much recent research by geographers on wine, though, does not overtly claim to be related to culture, and the traditionally privileged position of economics discussed earlier also had its impact on geography through the many studies of the wine trade by economic geographers. Claims *ex post facto* that economics lies completely within the domain of culture are problematic, and so such studies have not been included within the remit of this volume. Historical geographers, though, especially in France and among those who have followed their intellectual tradition elsewhere, have, indeed, focused especially on the culture of wine and viticulture as an integral part of their research, typified by the many studies of French regional *pays* and research undertaken with in the Berkeley School on cultural landscapes.

Research in historical geography waned from the 1980s onwards, and as the next generation of scholars entered the discipline, they established a 'new cultural geography' that some claim to have become hegemonic by the end of the first decade of the twenty-first century (Creswell 2010). This was inspired not only by the wider 'cultural turn' occurring within the social sciences but also, in part, by the tradition of radical geography (Peet 1977) that had risen to the fore in the previous decade. Somewhat paradoxically, rather little research on wine has been undertaken by cultural geographers within this new tradition. Much could, indeed, be gained from a wider engagement by geographers at this intersection of culture and geography. Chapters by geographers in this *Handbook* nevertheless reflect the diversity of approaches they have taken towards this intersection, ranging from studies of the emergence of demarcated vineyard areas to spaces of wine production and a long tradition of work on terroir.

History

Historians in winemaking societies have long written about wine. They have a deep embeddedness with culture through a focus on understanding how societies and cultures change over time, not least so that we can learn lessons from the past in shaping the future. Indeed Auslander *et al.* (2009: 1364) have suggested that 'cultural singularities and changes [are] the stuff that history is made of'. As a result, there have been numerous studies of the history of wine, or histories that address wine culture, ever since Herodotus wrote on the subject in the fifth century BCE. Nevertheless, as with many other disciplines in the social sciences, the cultural turn in the 1970s and 1980s had a significant impact on the ways in which historians addressed history, very much bringing culture to the fore at the heart of the discipline's theoretical and methodological concerns.

In recent years, historians have thus explored a very wide range of aspects of wine cultures, and it is important here to emphasise the plural; there is no wine culture, but many cultures of wine. Detailed historical research has examined the cultural dimensions of wine's production and consumption, its role as an expressive marker of social and economic status and, indeed, as a symbol of political allegiance. Cultural historians, with their focus on understanding change, have also interestingly explored the balance between the individual and the collective in changing culture and, indeed, the role of culture in shaping individuals and communities. Historical studies of the varying cultures of wine in economic, social and political contexts provide a powerful lens for understanding how societies and cultures change more widely.

Sociology

A sociological imagination simultaneously places wine within its cultural and structural contexts, seeking critically to decentre wine, winemakers and wine consumers in understanding how wine is 'done'. It explores the otherness beyond these usual characters in other studies of wine. Wine has served sociologists as a productive lens through which conceptualisations of legitimacy, taste, status and value and the cultural dynamics of markets and production can be examined.

Culture, in both material and immaterial forms, makes some social actions more or less likely, thus enabling and constraining different ways of 'doing' wine. These can include ways of thinking, talking, making and judging wine. For example, the taste *of* wine is shaped by shared conventions, such as tasting techniques, expectations about typicity, social esteem accrued by particular regions and the views of producers; the taste *for* wine is implicated in performances of identity, making and maintaining boundaries between groups and processes of social reproduction and stratification.

Culture for sociologists is also bound up with discourses of legitimacy and processes of legitimation – and thus also with power, stratification, differentiation and evaluation. A recurrent focus in sociological research on wine concerns how notions of legitimate taste are made, circulated and deployed, as well as by whom. Such studies, for example, explore evidence of shared conventions across a global cultural regime of fine winemaking in terms of place specificity (if not terroir *per se*), heritage, authenticity and artisanality.

Reading the *Handbook*

There are many ways in which readers can engage with this *Handbook*. As should be clear from this Introduction, we see the *Handbook* itself as a piece of material culture crafted through the editors' and authors' own diverse experiences of the two-way engagement between wine and culture. We had many reasons for labouring to produce it: we needed better to understand the complexity of the culture of wine, and the wine of culture, ourselves; we wished to develop new ideas and suggest pathways for future research as summarised in the conclusion; and we have the intention that any royalties will be used to support WaterAid. However, as we hope is clear from our enthusiasm and passion for 'wine culture' and 'culture wine', above all, we wished to share these ideas with a wider readership to encourage new ways of thinking and acting about wine and culture. The book is not just intended for an academic audience but is hopefully for all with an interest in either wine or culture; we hope it will encourage readers to explore this fascinating and important area of enquiry and that, by so doing, they will be enriched.

An orthodox way of approaching the *Handbook* would be to read it from cover to cover, theme by theme, noting the varied colours and textures referred to within it, scenting the aromas associated with different aspects of the production of wine, reflecting on the qualities and characteristics of its flavours and, hopefully, closing it at the end with lengthy memories of its complexity and finesse. Such a reading would be challenging, with adjacent chapters in each theme often focusing on rather different topics, but this would not be dissimilar to enjoying a light *vinho verde* from Portugal followed by a rich Shiraz from the Barossa Valley in Australia.

An alternative reading would be to adopt a disciplinary approach, not necessarily in the sections and order in which the chapters have been published. Those from a sociological background, for example, might begin with the introductory thematic chapter on sociology and then turn immediately to the various chapters distributed through the different thematic sections of the book that have been written by sociologists. This would be akin to tasting a flight of Chardonnays from all different parts of the world. The frequent use of cross-references to other chapters in the *Handbook*, as well as a comprehensive index, would then enable the reader to follow specific threads across its rich and diverse tapestry.

A third way of reading the *Handbook* would be to take a particular theme that is not directly apparent in its formal structure – perhaps reflecting an interest in the historical evolution of wine or its status as an elite symbol – and seek out the ways in which different authors have sought to share their understandings thereof. Again, the title of each chapter and the index should help such navigation. To use the wine analogy once again, this might be rather like identifying the varying amounts of Petit Verdot in blended Cabernet (Sauvignon and Franc) and Merlot wines from Bordeaux, California, South Africa, Chile, Australia and New Zealand.

However you approach this book as the reader, we, as the editors, hope that you will enjoy it, learn from it and be challenged by it. As noted at the beginning of this Introduction, we are fully aware that it is but a stage in an incomplete journey and that there are many topics that we would like to have included that are absent. Nevertheless, we have sought to bring together a diverse set of contributions covering a wide range of topics associated with the interface between wine and culture, and we trust that it will provide a framework that will not only inform but also inspire other researchers from our disciplines to build on the ideas contained within its material and virtual covers.

Acknowledgements

With the advice and support of all the co-editors Unwin, Charters, Demossier, Marks, Dutton, Harding, and Smith Maguire.

References

Althusser, L. and Balibar, E. (1970) *Reading Capital*, London: New Left Books.
Ardener, E. (1971) "The New Anthropology and Its Critics," *Man, New Series* 6(3), 449–467.
Auslander, L., Bentley, A., Halevi, L., Sibum, H.O. and Witmore, C. (2009) "Conversation: Historians and the Study of Material Culture," *American Historical Review*, 114(5), 1355–1404.
Baldwin, J.R., Faulkner, S.L., Hecht, M.L. and Lindsley, A.L. (2006) *Redefining Culture: Perspectives Across the Disciplines*, Mahwah, NJ, and London: Lawrence Erlbaum Associates.
Beckert, J. (2019) "Markets from Meaning: Quality Uncertainty and the Intersubjective Construction of Value," *Cambridge Journal of Economics*. DOI:10.1093/cje/bez035.
Burnyeat, M.F. (1997) "Culture and society in Plato's *Republic*," in *The Tanner Lecture on Human Values*, Cambridge: Harvard University Press, December 10–12.
Carlsen, J. and Charters, S. (eds) (2006) *Global Wine Tourism*, Wallingford: CABI.
Clifford, J. and Marcus, G. (eds) (1986) *Writing and Culture: The Poetics and Politics of Ethnography*, Berkeley: University of California Press.
Creswell, T. (2010) "New Cultural Geography – An Unfinished Project," *Cultural Geographies* 17(2), 169–174.
Gans, H. (1999) *Popular Culture and High Culture: An Analysis and Evaluation of Taste*, 2nd edition, New York: Basic Books.
Goodall, H. (2000) *Writing the New Ethnography: 7 (Ethnographic Alternatives)*, Lanham, MD: AltaMira.
Hall, G. and Birchall, C. (eds) (2006) *New Cultural Studies: Adventures in Theory*, Edinburgh: Edinburgh University Press.
Jacobs, M. and Spillman, L. (2005) "Cultural Sociology at the Crossroads of the Discipline," *Poetics* 3(1), 1–14.
Jahoda, G. (2012) "Critical Reflections on Some Recent Definitions of 'Culture'," *Culture & Psychology* 18(3), 289–303.
Janiak, A. (2020) "Kant's Views on Space and Time," in E.N. Zalta (ed), *The Stanford Encyclopedia of Philosophy*, Spring 2020 edition, Stanford, CA: Stanford University, https://plato.stanford.edu/archives/spr2020/entries/kant-spacetime/.
Kuper, A. (2000) *Culture: The Anthropologists' Account*, Cambridge, MA: Harvard University Press.
Norn, S., Kruse, P.R. and Kruse, E. (2005) "Opiumsvalmuen og morfin gennem tiderne," *Dansk Medicinhistorisk Arborg* 33, 171–184.
OIV. (2015) *International Code of Oenological Practices*, OIV Code Sheet – Issue 2015/01 1.1.3–1, www.oiv.int/public/medias/3921/e-code-i-31.pdf.
Peet, R. (1977) *Radical Geography*, London: Methuen.
Resch, R.P. (1992) *Althusser and the Renewal of Marxist Social Theory*, Berkeley: University of California Press.
Rokka, J. (2021) "Consumer Culture Theory's Future in Marketing," *Journal of Marketing Theory and Practice* 29(1), 114–124.
Throsby, D. (2001) *Economics and Culture*, Cambridge: Cambridge University Press.
Throsby, D. (2003) "Determining the Value of Cultural Goods: How Much (or How Little) Does Contingent Valuation Tell Us?" *Journal of Cultural Economics* 27(3), 275–285.
Tushingham, S., Snyder, C.M., Brownstein, K.J., Damition, W.J. and Gang, D.R. (2018) "Biomolecular Archaeology Reveals Ancient Origins of Indigenous Tobacco Smoking in North American Plateau," *PNAS* 115(46), 11742–11747.
Tyler, E. (1871) *Primitive Culture: Researches into the Development of Mythology, Philosophy, Religion, Language, Art, and Custom*, London: John Murray.
Unwin, T. (1992) *The Place of Geography*, Harlow: Longman.
Von Humboldt, A. (2014) *Kosmos: Entwurf einer physischen Weltbeschreibung, editiert und mit einem Nachwort versehen von Ottmar Ette und Oliver Lubrich*, Berlin: Die Andere Bibliothek (5 volumes first published 1845–1862).
Williams, R. (1973) "Base and Superstructure in Marxist Cultural Theory," *New Left Review* 82(1), 3–16.
Williams, R. (1976) *Keywords: A Vocabulary of Culture and Society*, London: Croom Helm.

PART I

Context: disciplinary perspectives on wine and culture

1
ANTHROPOLOGY, WINE AND CULTURE

Marion Demossier and Clelia Viecelli

Introduction

Anthropology has traditionally been associated with the concept of culture, producing detailed, empirical ethnographies of the places and people studied, often over long periods of time. Most analyses have privileged the study of human diversity through people's key values, social practices and understandings of their place in the world. Comparison and cultural relativism are fundamental to the discipline (Candea 2019). Ethnography, described as a 'potentially revolutionary praxis' (Shah 2017: 45), still characterises the uniqueness of the anthropological approach compared to other disciplines through its long-term participant observation, reflexivity, critical positionality and immersion by being in location. The history of the concept of culture includes the idealised norms and values that we hold in our minds and the symbolic nature of culture, which is understood and interpreted by individuals and groups. Political and economic forces, social institutions, and biological processes take their place in any complete explanation of why people think and behave as they do, against an explanation based on cultural determinism (Kuper 2000). The study of wine culture has benefited from this broader intellectual endeavour, bringing people back and engaging critically with what they say and what they do.

Core disciplinary concepts and scholars relevant to the anthropological study of wine and culture

Anthropology, like other human and social sciences, has long demonstrated an interest in the study of drinking and alcohol (Wilson 2005), but wine was often studied alongside other beverages such as tea, coffee, rum and brandy and was never given top billing. If, in the English-speaking world, it is easy to trace back the genealogy of the anthropological contribution to wine culture, it requires multilingual skills to navigate the field when exploring European anthropologies.[1] If the work by the British structuralist anthropologist Mary Douglas, *Constructive Drinking* (first edition 1987), opened the door to an anthropology of alcohol and *de facto* wine, it, nevertheless, treated wine like other types of fermented substances without making it a particular commodity. However, Douglas's contribution set out a new agenda whereby drinking was defined as an essential social act performed in a recognised social context, with the potential to construct the world both as it is and as an idealised commodity through rituals (Fabre-Vassas 1989). This dichotomy between ideal and real indeed remains key to most of the anthropological literature on wine (Howland and Dutton 2019).

Nearly a decade later, two landmark publications established more firmly the anthropological study of wine, despite 'the disease prevention stance and the shadow of intoxication' (Black and Ulin 2013: 6) accompanying it. Both had France as their main object of study, illustrating the disciplinary shifts which saw the closure of traditional areas of fieldwork following decolonisation and the rising opportunities offered by new European funding. In this context, American anthropologists started to turn their attention to rural communities, and France offered an original site for the study of rural Europe (Rogers 1987, 2002). The publication in 1996 of *Vintages and Traditions: An Ethnography of Southwest French Wine Cooperatives* by the American anthropologist Robert C. Ulin (1996) provided the first original contribution to the ethnographic study of wine and culture. The novelty of the book is to question the French idea of terroir as a naturalised and mythicised construct under capitalism. The cooperatives provide *de facto* a striking example of the ambiguities attached to labour in capitalist societies and offer a unique example of collective resistance in neo-liberal times. In her work on the Languedoc, Winnie Lem (1999) examined wine production and capitalism through the gender lens and discussed their impact on traditional rural communities. Focusing on gender relations and the reproduction of the family farms, Lem aptly questioned how local cultures are produced and changed while paying attention to cultural discourses about collective identity and agency.

Yet it was only in 2013[2] that wine acquired its own legitimate status in anthropology with the publication of *Wine and Culture: Vineyard to Glass*, edited by Rachel E. Black and Robert C. Ulin. For both anthropologists, the study of wine breaks new ground, but it is also linked to critical issues at the forefront of the social sciences and humanities, especially debates on neo-liberalism and capitalism (Crenn 2015). The object of their scrutiny has followed the intricacies of capitalism and provides a productive window for the study of social change. Their volume can be seen as the first deliberate attempt to give wine a legitimate academic status, separate from the boom witnessed in the last two decades in food studies (Black and Ulin: Introduction). It also provides a new direction to the field by shifting the geographic focus outside France to include Bulgaria, Galicia, Lebanon, Italy and Slovakia, as well as moving the focus away from Old European wine-producing regions. These ethnographies contribute to a critical perspective over locality, communities and globalisation and argue for complexities (Ong and Collier 2003).

Key themes and questions relating to wine within the discipline

The main contribution of anthropology to the study of wine has been to engage critically with the mythologisation attached to the commodity and to its corollary expression, terroir. Anthropologists have increasingly focused on terroir as a social construct, 'how terroir has been used and represented historically, socially, culturally and politically to support the reputedly unique characteristics of particular wines in particular places' (Black and Ulin 2013: 12). In these ethnographies, stories deployed as narratives, maps or discourses historically produced by wine producers, wine organisations or wine intermediaries have played a major role in wine culture, often legitimising the politics of value (meaning here how wines are ranked and valued) and the complex systems of wine classifications but obscuring the social processes at stake. The processes of engagement with terroir underline how individual and collective agencies are central to a sense of identification and the production of sociality and social representations (Demossier 2011).

Several anthropologists, in the footsteps of Ulin, have examined how these imaginaries contribute to the construction of place or quality or how they have become, with time, contested or transformed by social and economic change. Interestingly, it is against rapid and differentiated globalisation that wine has become the centre of new anthropological research concerns (Black and Ulin 2013; Demossier 2018). If France has remained a point of reference in the terroir discussion, an increasing number of anthropologists have shifted their attention to other geographic areas following the deployment of the concept of terroir in other locations, which has become customised, interpreted, translated and appropriated according to local conditions of reception (Appadurai 1995: 16). The New World, for example, has been explored by William Skinner (2015, 2018, 2019) in his study of McLaren Vale in South Australia. Bringing a more philosophical gaze, Robert Swinburn (2018) has concentrated his attention on how terroir, as an idea taken up by winegrowers in Geelong (Australia), could be better conceptualised as a sensibility – the poetry, rather than science or economics. More recently, China has become the place of original ethnographic research (Galipeau 2017; Zheng 2019). The anthropologist and filmmaker Boris Petric has even visually documented the relationship between the Chinese and the French when it comes to wine and, more generally, the challenge of conveying a relationship to nature and to time beyond cultural differences in his film *Château Pékin* (2018).

Another fundamental contribution lies with the politics of scale around wine production and consumption (micro and macro), in which anthropologists have shifted the terms of the debate, especially when moving the debate to new horizons beyond France. Wine culture as an object of study in European anthropology was traditionally confined to the nation and formed part of a wider European cultural imperialistic project (Black and Ulin 2013: 2). The growing importance of wine as a cultural product is beyond doubt, and its study, as an object sensitive to the socio-political structures in which it is made and consumed, deepens our understanding of the contemporary world. Territorialisation was thus a key ingredient of this long historical process, and wine communities featured prominently as part of both national and regional narratives about wine producing regions. Thus, the question of territory, its mapping and legitimacy is key to a sense of collective identification and the positioning of place within the world hierarchy (Jung 2014). The work of Monterescu (2017, with Handel in 2019) focuses on exploring food politics through wine production in Israel and Palestine, territorial mapping, and investigating borders and frontiers in reassessing the New and Old Worlds paradigms. McGonigle (2019), on the other hand, has recently explored in depth how claims of authentic indigeneity are mobilised to naturalise the Jewish presence in this contested territory through a reconnection to biblical sites. Moreover, it repositions Israel with a wine identity on the basis of the creation of so-called indigenous plants.

A growing number of exciting works have also emerged in the former socialist countries following their integration into the European community under the aegis of quality foodstuff regulations. Bulgaria has also been the object of several ethnographic publications by Yuson Jung (2014, 2019) illustrating how a new wine region engages with the politics of taste. Buzalka (2013) and Kopzynska (2013) have also engaged with the anthropology of wine in post-socialist states. Inspired by the work of the Marxist anthropologist Chris Hann (1985), a new generation of scholars have turned their attention to wine production as an area in which capitalism meets more traditional forms of cooperation and economic collectivism. Moldova has been the focus of attention by Cash (2013) and Ana (2019). Ana concentrates on the Moldovan wine industry (Purcari Winery) and its recent transition to what she describes as 'flexible capitalism' following both the collapse of the Soviet Union and, more recently, the successive bans on the export of wines to the Russian Federation. Her analysis focuses on the workers' livelihoods within the context of their employment in the local winery and the shift into the market economy, which results in ambiguities and paradoxes around the emergence of quality wine.

Locality has become a fetish which disguises the globally dispersed forces that actually drive the production process (Appadurai 1990: 307). The anthropology of wine, with its primary focus on terroir, has been extremely thought-provoking to analyses of processes of heritagisation and debates about food quality connected to locality and systems of denomination. Moreover, it has offered a perfect window into the study of these processes, especially when increasingly connecting wine to global dynamics, illustrating the need to include wine in issues of contemporaneity and the Anthropocene. A convincing example of such a shift is illustrated by the new environmental agenda

(Demossier 2015, 2018). Responding to climate change and the growing ecological preoccupation of consumers, several anthropologists have been attracted by the study of biodynamic, natural or organic wines (Black 2013; Pineau 2019; Viecelli forthcoming), representing an emerging trend in wine anthropological research. Environmental health and ecologies of production are new avenues to explore.

The study of political and institutional developments has, however, been a neglected area in the anthropology of wine (Crenn 2015). In the context of global health policy, the issue of wine as alcohol versus cultural product is also relevant. The study of wine lobbying or wine and alcohol policies are still worth investigating. The field of politics and the world of wine are in some cases close, and their joint analysis would bring some interesting materials to the table. It is worth pointing out that this emerging field of research still has lots to offer, from the ethnographies of industrial wine production and wine labs to the new virtual platforms dedicated to wine education as well as the ethnographic study of the famous Masters of Wine or the cellars of Trinity College in Cambridge. If the number of PhDs submitted recently in the field of the anthropology of wine and the recent special issue of the journal *Ethnologie Française* (Crenn *et al.* 2021) are good indicators of this new trend, then it promises a great future...

Notes

1 Indeed, in wine-producing countries, fine ethnographies were produced either in relation to the field of folklore or ethnology/anthropology at home forming part of a broader European and national project (Thiesse 1999). For an overview of works on the anthropology of wine in France, see Philippe Chaudat, 2012, 'Vin et monde viticole' in *Dictionnaire des cultures alimentaires*, Paris, PUF. Charles Parrain, Claude Royer and Jacques Bonniel are amongst the anthropologists often cited.
2 Despite these two original contributions to the field of anthropology of wine, the volume *Drinking Cultures, Alcohol and Identity* published in 2005 by the anthropologist Thomas Wilson illustrates the growing importance of alcohol consumption in anthropological studies and also the marginalised position of wine, with only two chapters out of twelve. The specificity of the anthropological perspective here lies with the examination of the consumption of alcohol as a way of life, one element of a given culture.

References

Ana, D. (2019) Produced and Bottled in Moldova: Winemaking in Flexible Capitalism (PhD Max Planck Institute).
Appadurai, A. (1990) "Disjuncture and Difference in the Global Cultural Economy," in M. Featherstone, S. Lash and R. Robertson (eds), *Global Modernities*, London: Sage, 109–133.
Appadurai, A. (1995) "The Production of Locality," in *Modernity at Large: Cultural Dimensions of Globalization*, London: Routledge, 178–200.
Black, R. E. (2013) "Vino Naturale: Tensions Between Nature and Technology in the Glass," in R. E. Black and R. C. Ulin (eds), *Wine and Culture: Vineyard to Glass*, London and New York: Bloomsbury Academic, 279–294.
Black, R. E. and Ulin, R. C. (2013) *Wine and Culture: Vineyard to Glass*, London and New York: Bloomsbury Academic.
Buzalka, J. (2013) "Tasting Wine in Slovakia: Post-Socialist Elite Consumption of Cultural Particularities," in R. E. Black and R. C. Ulin (eds), *Wine and Culture: Vineyard to Glass*, London and New York: Bloomsbury Academic, 89–108.
Candea, M. (2019) *Comparison in Anthropology. The Impossible Method*, Cambridge: Cambridge University Press.
Cash, J. (2013) "Economy as Ritual: The Problems of Paying in Wine," in A. Gudeman and C. Hann (eds), *Economy & Ritual. Studies of Postsocialist Transformations. Max Planck Studies in Anthropology and Economy*, New York and Oxford: Berghahn, 31–51.
Crenn, C. (2015) "Le vin comme objet de recherche anthropologique," *Anthropology of Food* [Online], été 2015, comptes-rendus de lecture, Online Since 04 August 2015, Connection on 30 March 2016, http://aof.revues.org/7831, accessed 31 March 2016.
Crenn, C., Demossier, M. and Petric, B. (eds) (2021) *"Mondialités du Vin"*. Special Issue of Ethnologie Française 51(3).

Demossier, M. (2011) "Beyond *Terroir*: Territorial Construction, Hegemonic Discourses and French Wine Culture," *Journal of the Royal Anthropological Institute* 17(4), 685–705.

Demossier, M. (2015) "The Politics of Heritage in the Land of Food and Wine," in N. Logan, M. Nic Craith and U. Kockel (eds), *A Companion to Heritage Studies*, Chichester, GB: Wiley-Blackwell, 87–100.

Demossier, M. (2018) *Burgundy: A Global Anthropology of Place and Taste*, New York and London: Berghahn.

Douglas, M. (1987) *Constructive Drinking. Perspectives on Drink from Anthropology*, London: Routledge.

Fabre-Vassas, C. (1989) "La boisson des ethnologues," *Terrain* (13), 5–14.

Galipeau, B.A. (2017) "Tibetan Wine Production, Taste of Place, and Regional Niche Identity in Shangri-La, China," in D.S. Yü and J. Michaud (eds), *Trans-Himalayan Borderlands. Livelihoods, Territorialities*, Amsterdam: Amsterdam University Press, 209–228.

Handel, A. and Monterescu, D. (2019) "Liquid Indigeneity: Wine, Science and Colonial Politics in Israel/Palestine," *American Ethnologist* 46(3), 313–327.

Hann, C. (1985) *A Village Without Solidarity: Polish Peasants in Years of Crisis*, New Haven, CT: Yale University Press.

Howland, P.J. and Dutton, J. (2019) *Wine, Terroir and Utopia: Making New Worlds*, London: Routledge.

Jung, Y. (2014) "Tasting and Judging the Unknown Terroir of the Bulgarian Wine: The Political Economy of Sensory Experience," *Food and Foodways* 22(1), 24–47.

Jung, Y. (2019) *Balkan Blues: Consumer Politics after State Socialism*, Bloomington: Indiana University Press.

Kopzynska, E. (2013) "Wine Histories, Wine Memories and Local Identities in Western Poland," in R. E. Black and R. C. Ulin (eds), *Wine and Culture: Vineyard to Glass*, London and New York: Bloomsbury Academic, 109–124.

Kuper, A. (2000) *Culture. The Anthropologist's Account*, Cambridge and London: Harvard University Press.

Lem, W. (1999) *Cultivating Dissent, Work, Identity and Praxis in Rural Languedoc*, Albany: State University of New York Press.

McGonigle, I. (2019) "In Vino Veritas? Indigenous Wine and Indigenization in Israeli Settlements," *Anthropology Today* 35(4), August, 7–12.

Monterescu, D. (2017) "Border Wines: Terroir Across Contested Territory," *Gastronomica: The Journal for Food Studies* 17(4), Winter, 127–140.

Monterescu, D. and Handel, A. (2019) "Liquid Indigeneity: Wine, Science and Colonial Politics in Israel/Palestine," *American Ethnologist* 46(3), 313–327.

Ong, A. and Collier, S-J. (2003) *Global Assemblages: Technology, Politics, and Ethics as Anthropological Problems*, Malden, MA and Oxford: Blackwell Publishing.

Pétric, B. (2018) *Château Pékin*. Documentary Film, Marseille: La Fabrique des Ecritures.

Pineau, C. (2019) *La corne de vache et le microscope, le vin "nature", être sciences, croyances et radicalités*, Paris: Editions La Découverte.

Rogers, S-C. (1987) "Good to Think: The 'Peasant' in Contemporary France," *Anthropological Quarterly* 60, 56–63.

Rogers, S-C. (2002) "Which Heritage? Nature, Culture and Identity in French Rural Tourism," *French Historical Studies* 25, 475–503.

Shah, A. (2017) "Ethnography? Participant Observation, a Potentially Revolutionary Praxis," *HAU: Journal of Ethnography* 7(1), 45–59.

Skinner, W. (2015) *Fermenting Place: Wine Production and Terroir in McLaren Vale, South Australia* (PhD Thesis, University of Adelaide).

Skinner, W. (2018) "Presence Through Absence: Phylloxera and the Viticultural Imagination in McLaren Vale, South Australia," *The Asia Pacific Journal of Anthropology* 19(3), 245–263.

Skinner, W. (2019) "A Gift from God: Autochtonous Grapes and Wine Heritage on the Island of Hvar, Croatia," *Journal of Wine Research* 30(4), 294–311.

Swinburn, R. (2018) *The Winegrowers of Geelong and Their Search for the Things That Count* (PhD Thesis, University of Melbourne).

Thiesse, A-M. (1999) *La création des identités nationales. Europe XVIIIe-XXe siècles*, Paris: Seuil, coll L'Univers historique.

Ulin, R. C. (1996) *Vintages and Traditions: An Ethnohistory of Southwest French Wine Cooperatives*, Washington, DC: Smithsonian Institution Press.

Viecelli, C. (forthcoming) *Crafting Alternatives Through Wine: An Ethnography of Female Natural Winegrowers in Italy* (PhD Thesis, University of Southampton).

Wilson, T. (2005) *Drinking Cultures. Alcohol and Identity*, New York and London: Berg.

Zheng, X. (2019) "Narrating Terroir: The Place-Making of Wine in China's Southwest," *Food, Culture & Society* 22(3), 280–298.

2
BUSINESS, WINE AND CULTURE

Steve Charters

Introduction

Academic 'business' disciplines such as marketing and management and related sectoral specialities (e.g. human resources, tourism or hospitality) have, until recently, largely neglected the notion of culture *per se* and, even more so, the intersection of wine with culture.[1] Their focus on culture from the 1970s onwards was not aimed at understanding the dimensions of a culture ('intrinsic culture'), but rather at helping organisations function better in different cultures (e.g. staff management, marketing products, financial control); this we can term instrumental culture.

This chapter examines the lack of attention to intrinsic culture, the evolution of interest in 'culture' in the business disciplines and the emergence of a nascent, more wine-relevant intrinsic view of culture within tourism and consumer behaviour.

The origins and evolution of the idea of culture in the business disciplines

Among several antecedents to the business academe, economics is the most prominent. Thus, like economics in the twentieth century, these disciplines were positivist. Researchers attempted to establish them as 'sciences' and focused on quantitative analysis to model, measure and predict efficiency, sales or profitability. Because it is difficult to model and quantify, culture had a minor place in this evolution, which concentrated on predictive rules for the management of enterprises. The study of consumer choice exemplified this neglect. The dominant model was 'information processing'. Consumers are seen as rational beings who evaluate available information about competing products and, within the context of price, make a rational choice of the most satisfying product for their requirements. Cultural context, social norms, myths and taboos were perceived to have little or no relevance to the decisions consumers would make.

The business disciplines subsequently drew from other disciplines. Psychology became significant. (Experimental psychology was also positivist.) Only later, from the 1970s onwards, did the influence of anthropology, sociology and even geography and history begin to challenge the dominant, positivist paradigm (and later, integrate with it). Until then, to the extent that culture was considered, it was merely a background factor which produced a level of uncertainty in the data used.

There were two key results of the positivist origins of the business disciplines in the context of their understanding and use of culture. First, culture became the focus of a type of good in product-focused fields (e.g. marketing, tourism). Its definition concentrated on civilisation, refinement or good taste rather than the broader notion of the nature of a particular society or group as used in this *Handbook*; thus, culture management or cultural tourism (originally) would be about high art or a material environment. Only later, especially in tourism (see later in this chapter) did understanding widen to include engagement with the cultural environment of particular groups of individuals. Fine wine could, conceivably, be included in the first category of refined goods (along with fine dining); wine as the product of a specific social milieu was considered irrelevant.

The second development from the positivist approach was the influence of Edward Hall's notion of high-context and low-context cultures (Hall 1976) and then the work of Geert Hofstede (Hofstede 1980, 1991; Hofstede et al. 2010). Hofstede used a large international database of IBM employees to establish national (cultural) differences in approach to organisations and management. There were originally four dimensions (Hofstede 1980) – power distance, individualism or collectivism, masculine versus feminine attitudes and uncertainty avoidance – subsequently joined by a fifth (long-term versus short-term orientation) (Hofstede 1991) and then a sixth (indulgence versus restraint) (Hofstede et al. 2010). The analyses of national differences challenged the prevailing view of a single global model of organisations and revolutionised our understanding of management and marketing. However, they also reinforced the positivist approach to 'culture' as instrumental rather than intrinsic (and thus a subject worth studying in itself); given the focus of the business disciplines, this was both inevitable and necessary. However, the instrumental approach tended to reduce cultures to ciphers (often by applying Hofstede's analysis) which need to be managed for desired outcomes (Hofstede 1991). First designed for organisational science, this approach has also been widely used in marketing as the dominant paradigm. Thus, for instance, Seidemann et al. (2017), in an exploration of wine as a gift, use both Hall and Hofstede to explain that role for wine in China. Nevertheless, some streams of contemporary marketing thought view Hofstede's approach as both essentialist (and thus universal) and static, rather than historically and interculturally dynamic.

The evolution and use of culture in marketing

One would expect marketing to have a major focus on culture, given its concentration on consumers and (sometimes) producers. However, a typical marketing textbook devotes perhaps a few pages to culture. Over the last 30 years, marketing thought has evolved away from the product (thus the producer) and sales and towards consumers and their experience (Gilmore and Pine 1999). A result of this is that the significance of intermediaries is often minimised, although their role (and thus their cultural context) are significant for products like wine (see later in this chapter).

Consumer behaviour and consumer culture theory

It is within the field of consumer behaviour that culture (albeit often unacknowledged) is most relevant to marketing. Important here – amongst other influences – is the work first of Levy (1959) and subsequently of Appadurai (1986). Following on from them, researchers have explored not merely what products do for people but also what they mean and the meanings which people ascribe to them (seminal works include – amongst many others – Belk 1988; Belk et al. 1991; Holbrook and Hirschman 1980; McCracken 1986; Solomon 1983). Although this 'interpretivist' stream of research did not always explicitly focus on culture, its exploration of symbolic meaning is rooted in an approach, often phenomenological, which seeks to understand the society which fosters those consumers and shapes their worldview.

The cultural analysis of wine has tended to be more limited, usually to denote ethnic variation, such as an early study of Australian wine consumers (Hall et al. 1997), concluding that ethnic origin significantly affected the occasions of wine consumption. A later study on UK consumers did include identity, ritual and wine as a form of material culture but finally focused primarily on buying behaviour (Ritchie 2007). More recent research on Generation Y analyses their consumption values (Mueller Loose and Remaud 2011), their relationship to images of wine (Velikova et al. 2016) and the appeal of pink wine (Velikova et al. 2015). Meanwhile, the burgeoning Chinese wine market has stimulated interest in that country's cultural approach to wine, though the focus is still more instrumental than intrinsic (Capitello et al. 2017; Jenster and Cheng 2008; Liu and Murphy 2007; for an 'intrinsic' exception, see Smith Maguire and Lim 2015). Another Chinese study, which uses a semiotic approach to examine wine culture, is by Celhay et al. (2020). Celhay has also previously researched young Basque drinkers (2008), who developed the *kalimoxto* – a mix of Coca Cola and red wine – ostensibly as an exploration of generational identity, though its focus on a specific ethnic sub-group is noteworthy. Yet without defining it, all these studies use 'culture' as a variable assumed to explain difference rather than exploring wine's place in a wider cultural framework.

More recently, a sub-domain of consumer behaviour – 'consumer culture theory' (CCT) – has concentrated explicitly on consumption's more intrinsic cultural dimension. CCT is an extension of the interpretivist approach noted earlier (Arnould and Thompson 2005) and focuses explicitly on individuals' emic ('lived') experiences with products within a specific culture, group or 'tribe'; it concentrates on the relationship of identity to markets and how, structurally, consumption operates in different cultural contexts; it also has a clear historical perspective, noting that markets change with time in response to changing culture (Rokka 2021). So far, CCT has had a limited focus on the study of wine, with Beverland (2004, 2005, 2006), Rokka (2017; Rokka and Canniford 2016; also chapter 24 in this book) and Humphreys and Carpenter (2018 and chapter 39 in this book) as the exceptions who have begun work within this paradigm.

How marketing shapes culture

Rokka's research examining how consumers use social media to influence champagne brand meaning highlights one area in which marketing has a recognised and direct interaction with culture: how, especially in the contemporary world, marketing shapes culture. The dramatic global expansion of consumer marketing in the late twentieth century (stimulated partly by the impact of modern marketing) means that now (as noted earlier), products lend meaning to consumers' lives. It also means that they, in turn, impute meaning to products (e.g. Holt 2002; Schroeder and Salzer-Morling 2006; Solomon 1983). As a result, the culture of consumers (and a culture of consumption) help 'shape' brand meaning; in turn, brands affect a culture's structure and evolution. However, with the exceptions of Rokka and Smith Maguire (2010), these approaches, emphasising the co-creation of meaning, have not been used widely to explain cultures of wine consumption and have mainly been used – again instrumentally – as a means of understanding value.

Tourism, wine and culture

Tourism (and hospitality, which overlaps with tourism), unlike other business disciplines, has focused more broadly on intrinsic rather than just instrumental culture, perhaps because much of the early research was sociological rather than commercial or economic – which is still the case. Researchers examine both cultural tourism (i.e. culture as an attraction) and the culture of tourist destinations (as the context for the tourism offer). The result is that wine tourism has provided substantial research examining the cultural context of both suppliers and consumers.

The first explicit examination of the intersection of culture with wine tourism was offered by Ravenscroft and van Westering (2001). They addressed the theoretical issues behind the significance of wine consumption as a social practice and, within this, the significance of tourism in wine consumption and especially the creation of social boundaries based on levels of wine knowledge and the relationship between tourism and the personal journey. In the process, they identified the methods that Western connoisseurs used to assert their prestige. From a different perspective, Frochot (2001) examined the world of French winemakers and how they established brotherhoods which emerged in local wine regional cultures and have, over time, acted as convivial, cohesive institutions in rural regions and also powerful bodies in representing the regional wines; they fulfil both historical and cultural needs and economic requirements. At the same time, Williams and Kelly (2001) also reinforced the intimate relationship of culture to (rural) wine for some tourists.

More recent studies have examined the comparative spatial structuring and social relationships of wine regions and wine tourism in France and Australia in the context of Bonnemaison's cultural systems approach[2] (Mitchell *et al.* 2012) and the combining of wine with culture (specifically, the cultural values of a place) to create a transformative tourism experience (Sigala 2019). Fountain *et al.* (2020) have studied the cultural perspective of wine tourism providers in Burgundy, framing their research with cultural notions of place, particularly the tensions arising from globalisation and rural change. Even in wine tourism, however, the instrumental approach to culture remains at least as important as the intrinsic.

Directions for future research

A number of themes for future study emerge from this review of research on the interaction of wine business and culture.

Place branding and the management of terroir

Place branding has been widely researched at the intersection of marketing, tourism and non-business disciplines. The wine-related research has focused on terroir (see Chapters 8 and 11 in this volume), very much in conjunction with the idea of value (Charters *et al.* 2017) or branding (Fort and Fort 2006; Spielmann and Gelinas-Chebat 2012). Only occasionally have studies within the discipline of business gone behind the instrumental to examine the cultural construction of terroir as an idea (e.g. Charters 2019; Smith Maguire 2010). Nevertheless, place as a general concept (including terroir but also place attachment and the nature of place image) is ripe for further research. Specifically the interaction between ecosystem (on a large and a small scale), identity, geography, social history and structure and rural economy would be a fruitful area for exploration in the context of culture.

Authenticity

Terroir can be seen as one component of a larger theme currently significant in consumer research – authenticity, including consumers' interpretation of and need for it, and producers' portrayal of it. It is one lens for viewing culture. Beverland (2005, 2006) has done some fundamental work in the area and noted the importance of culture as a referent without specifically investigating how culture shapes authenticity. One study examined Russian 'champagne' in a historic-cultural context (Kniazeva and Charters 2014), and another looks at family heritage as a marketing frame for Australian producers (Strickland *et al.* 2013). Nevertheless, the wine, culture and authenticity nexus remains largely unexamined, with a specific need for taking the authenticity element of the triad out of a Western context (see, for instance, Seidemann *et al.*, 2017).

Luxury

Luxury products as a category have been widely explored by business academics, including their cultural dimensions. Wine spans a range of product categories, including beverage, commodity, premium and luxury. Luxury wine markets work well as a means of examining luxury as an expression of culture. Beverland's studies, already noted (2004, 2005) are specifically focused on luxury wines and offer a useful starting point. Other business researchers have alluded to the cultural dimension of luxury (Ritchie 2007; Thach *et al.* 2018), and it is particularly important in the growing Chinese market (Seidemann *et al.* 2017; Cohen *et al.* in this volume). The management of wine as a luxury product is ripe for further cultural investigation.

Intermediaries

The business disciplines' focus on consumers has neglected intermediaries, but they are necessarily important in wine business (Dodd 1997; Seidemann *et al.* 2017; Smith Maguire 2010; Spielmann *et al.* 2014; Thode *et al.* 2002), especially given the fragmented market and consumers' difficulty in evaluating wine. Smith Maguire (2010, 2013; Smith Maguire and Zhang 2016) has focused on this and provided a strong cultural context for wine intermediaries, but the role warrants more attention, particularly the cultural factors influencing the consumer's response to critics and writers and those intermediaries' own cultural influences.

Taste

There has been substantial sociological investigation of the taste and taste construction (e.g. Grunow 1997), including in the area of wine (Smith Maguire 2018). Less has been done within the domain of business, but CCT is beginning to stimulate a research stream here (Arsel and Bean 2013; Maciel and Wallendorf 2017; Pomies *et al.* 2021), with a focus on the cultural construction of consumer taste. Wine, which one 'tastes' and which implies the use of 'good taste' as a means of discrimination (and, consequently, of consumption choice) is ideally placed for increasing our understanding of the intersection of culture and taste construction. This is especially relevant given the (sometimes contradictory) impact of physiological taste preferences as well as cultural drinking expectations and rituals (note here Cowan and Spielmann, 2017, on rituals in luxury consumption). Taste is one of the key drivers of culture and is strongly influenced by changes in markets; it also offers a framework for exploring differences in practices across various communities, and thus directly feeding back into cultural change.

Acknowledgements

I would like sincerely to thank Joanna Fountain, Joonas Rokka, Nathalie Spielmann and an anonymous reviewer for very useful comments which have all improved the clarity and precision of this chapter.

Notes

1 One exception to the lack of material at the intersection of wine, business and culture is my own work, *Wine and Society: The Social and Cultural Context of a Drink* (Elsevier, 2006), which considers *inter alia* some cultural factors on both production and consumption, many of which are addressed in this chapter. However, it was introductory rather than the product of detailed research and is now rather dated.
2 An ethno-geographical approach which posits that knowledge, techniques, beliefs and space are the four key 'pillars' which sustain a cultural system (Bonnemaison 2005).

References

Appadurai, A. (ed) (1986) *The Social Life of Things: Commodities in Cultural Perspective*, Cambridge: Cambridge University Press.

Arnould, E.J. and Thompson, C.J. (2005) "Consumer Culture Theory (CCT): Twenty Years of Research," *Journal of Consumer Research* 31(4), 868–882.

Arsel, Z. and Bean, J. (2013) "Taste Regimes and Market-Mediated Practice," *Journal of Consumer Research* 39(5), 899–917.

Belk, R.W. (1988) "Possessions and the Extended Self," *Journal of Consumer Research* 15, September, 139–168.

Belk, R.W., Wallendorf, M. and Sherry, J.F. (1991)" The Sacred and the Profane in Consumer Behaviour: Theodicy on the Odyssey," in R.W. Belk (ed), *Highways and Buyways: Naturalistic Research from the Consumer Behaviour Odyssey*, Provo, UT: Association for Consumer Research, 59–101.

Beverland, M. (2004) "Uncovering 'Theories-in-Use': Building Luxury Wine Brands," *European Journal of Marketing* 38(3/4), 446–466.

Beverland, M. (2005) "Crafting Brand Authenticity: The Case of Luxury Wines," *Journal of Management Studies* 42(5), 1003–1029.

Beverland, M. (2006) "The 'Real Thing': Branding Authenticity in the Luxury Wine Trade," *Journal of Business Research* 59, 251–258.

Bonnemaison, J. (2005) *Culture and Space: Conceiving a New Cultural Geography*, trans J. Penot-Demetry, London: I.B. Tauris.

Capitello, R., Charters, S., Menival, D. and Yuan, J. (eds) (2017) *The Wine Value Chain in China: Consumers, Marketing and the Wider World*, Kidlington: Elsevier.

Celhay, F. (2008) "Le kalimotxo: Cocktail hérétique ou nouvelle opportunité pour la filière vin?" *Decisions Marketing* 52, October, 67–71.

Celhay, F., Cheng, P., Masson, J. and Li, W. (2020) "Package Graphic Design and Communication Across Cultures: An Investigation of Chinese Consumers' Interpretation of Imported Wine Labels," *International Journal of Research in Marketing* 37(1), 108–128.

Charters, S. (2006) *Wine and Society: The Social and Cultural Context of a Drink*, Oxford: Butterworth-Heinemann.

Charters, S. (2019) "Terroir Wines in Champagne: Between Ideology and Utopia," in J. Dutton and P.J. Howland (eds), *Wine, Terroir, Utopia: Making New Worlds*, Abingdon: Routledge, 111–125.

Charters, S., Spielmann, N. and Babin, B. (2017) "The Nature and Value of Terroir Products," *European Journal of Marketing* 51(4), 748–771.

Cowan, K. and Spielmann, N. (2017) "The Influence of Rituals on Luxury Product Consumption: Implications for Brands," *Journal of Brand Management* 24(5), 381–404.

Dodd, T.H. (1997) "Factors That Influence the Adoption and Diffusion of New Wine Products," *Hospitality Research Journal* 20(3), 123–136.

Fort, F. and Fort, F. (2006) "Alternatives marketing pour les produits de terroir," *Revue Française de Gestion* 32, March, 146–159.

Fountain, J., Charters, S. and Cogan-Marie, L. (2020) "The Real Burgundy: Negotiating French Wine Tourism in a Global Countryside," *Tourism Geographies*, 1–21.

Frochot, I. (2001) "French Wine Brotherhoods and Wine Tourism: A Complex Relationship," *Tourism Recreation Research* 26(2), 53–62.

Gilmore, J.H. and Pine, B.J. (1999) *The Experience Economy: Work Is Theatre and Every Business as Stage*, Boston: Harvard Business School Press.

Grunow, J. (1997) *The Sociology of Taste*, London: Routledge.

Hall, E.T. (1976) *Beyond Culture*, New York: Doubleday.

Hall, J., Shaw, M. and Doole, I. (1997) "Cross-Cultural Analysis of Wine Consumption Motivations," *International Journal of Wine Marketing* 9(2/3), 83–91.

Hofstede, G. (1980) *Culture's Consequences: International Differences in Work-Related Values*, Beverly Hills, CA: Sage.

Hofstede, G. (1991) *Cultures and Organisations: Software of the Mind*, 1st edition, London: HarperCollins.

Hofstede, G., Hofstede, G.J. and Minkov, M. (2010) *Cultures and Organisations: Software of the Mind*, 3rd edition, New York: McGraw Hill.

Holbrook, M.B. and Hirschman, E.C. (1980) "Symbolic Consumer Behaviour: An Introduction," Paper presented at the Consumer Esthetics and Symbolic Consumption Conference, New York.

Holt, D.B. (2002) "Why Do Brands Cause Trouble? A Dialectical Theory of Consumer Culture and Branding," *Journal of Consumer Research* 29, June, 70–90.

Humphreys, A. and Carpenter, G.S. (2018) "Status Games: Market Driving Through Social Influence in the US Wine Industry," *Journal of Marketing* 82(5), 141–159.

Jenster, P. and Cheng, Y. (2008) "Dragon Wine: Developments in the Chinese Wine Industry," *International Journal of Wine Business Research* 20(3), 244–259.

Kniazeva, M. and Charters, S. (2014) "Authenticity in the Mirror of Consumer Memories, or Drinking Champagne in Russia," in C. Wang and X. He (eds), *Brand Management in Emerging Markets*, Hershey: IGI Global, 121–136.

Levy, S.J. (1959) "Symbols for Sale," *Harvard Business Review*, July–August, 117–124.
Liu, F. and Murphy, J. (2007) "A Qualitative Study of Chinese Wine Consumption and Purchasing," *International Journal of Wine Business Research* 19(2), 98–113.
Maciel, A. and Wallendorf, M. (2017) "Taste Engineering: An Extended Consumer Model of Cultural Competence Constitution," *Journal of Consumer Research* 43(5), 726–746.
McCracken, G. (1986) "Culture and Consumption: A Theoretical Account of the Structure and Movement of the Cultural Meaning of Consumer Goods," *Journal of Consumer Research* 13, June, 71–84.
Mitchell, R., Charters, S. and Albrecht, J. (2012) "Cultural Systems and the Wine Tourism Product," *Annals of Tourism Research* 39(1), 311–335.
Mueller Loose, S. and Remaud, H. (2011) "How Strong and Generalisable Is the Generation Y Effect? A Cross-Cultural Study for Wine," *International Journal of Wine Business Research* 23(2), 125–155.
Pomies, A., Arsel, Z. and Bean, J. (2021) "Taste," *Consumption Markets & Culture* 24(1), 1–5. (special issue).
Ravenscroft, N. and van Westering, J. (2001) "Wine Tourism, Culture and the Everyday: A Theoretical Note," *Tourism and Hospitality Research* 3(2), 149–162.
Ritchie, C. (2007) "Beyond Drinking: The Role of Wine in the Life of the UK Consumer," *International Journal of Consumer Studies* 31, 534–540.
Rokka, J. (2017) "Champagne: Marketplace Icon," *Consumption, Markets & Culture* 20(3), 275–283.
Rokka, J. (2021) "Consumer Culture Theory's Future in Marketing," *Journal of Marketing Theory and Practice*, 1–11.
Rokka, J. and Canniford, R. (2016) "Heterotopian Selfies: How Social Media Destabilizes Brand Assemblages," *European Journal of Marketing* 50(9/10), 1789–1813.
Schroeder, J. and Salzer-Morling, M. (2006) "Introduction: The Cultural Codes of Branding," in J.E. Schroeder and M. Salzer-Morling (eds), *Brand Culture*, Abingdon: Routledge, 1–12.
Seidemann, V., Atwal, G. and Heine, K. (2017) "Gift Culture in China: Consequences for the Fine Wine Sector," in R. Capitello, S. Charters, D. Menival and J. Yuan (eds), *The Wine Value Chain in China: Consumers, Marketing and the Wider World*, Kidlington: Elsevier, 47–61.
Sigala, M. (2019) "The Synergy of Wine and Culture: The Case of Ariousios Wine, Greece," in M. Sigala and R. Robinson (eds), *Management and Marketing of Wine Tourism Business*, Cham: Palgrave MacMillan, 295–312.
Smith Maguire, J. (2010) "Provenance and the Liminality of Production and Consumption: The Case of Wine Promoters," *Marketing Theory* 10(3), 269–282.
Smith Maguire, J. (2013) "Provenance as a Filtering and Framing Device in the Qualification of Wine," *Consumption, Markets & Culture* 16(4), 368–391.
Smith Maguire, J. (2018) "Taste as Market Practice: The Example of 'Natural' Wine," in *Consumer Culture Theory*, Bingley, UK: Emerald Publishing Limited.
Smith Maguire, J. and Lim, M. (2015) "Lafite in China," *Journal of Macromarketing* 35(2), 229–242.
Smith Maguire, J. and Zhang, D. (2016) "Shifting the Focus from Consumers to Cultural Intermediaries: An Example from the Chinese Fine Wine Market," in *Consumer Culture Theory*, Bingley, UK: Emerald Group Publishing.
Solomon, M.R. (1983) "The Role of Products as Social Stimuli: A Symbolic Interactionism Perspective," *Journal of Consumer Research* 10, December, 319–329.
Spielmann, N. and Gelinas-Chebat, C. (2012) "Terroir? That's Not How I Would Describe It," *International Journal of Wine Business Research* 24(4), 254–270.
Spielmann, N., Jolly, S. and Parisot, F. (2014) "Terroir in the Media: The Poetry of People, Place and Palate," *International Journal of Wine Business Research* 26(3), 224–240.
Strickland, P., Smith Maguire, J. and Frost, W. (2013) "Using Family Heritage to Market Wines: A Case Study of Three 'New World' Wineries in Victoria, Australia," *International Journal of Wine Business Research* 25(2), 125–137.
Thach, L., Charters, S. and Cogan-Marie, L. (2018) "Core Tensions in Luxury Wine Marketing: The Case of Burgundian Wineries," *International Journal of Wine Business Research* 30(3), 343–365.
Thode, S.F., Taylor, L.W. and Maskulka, J.M. (2002) "Information Asymmetries in the Pricing of Fine Wines," *International Journal of Wine Marketing* 14(1), 5–16.
Velikova, N., Charters, S., Bouzdine-Chameeva, T., Fountain, J., Ritchie, C. and Dodd, T. (2015) "Seriously Pink: A Cross-Cultural Comparison of Consumer Preferences, Perceptions and Attitudes Towards Rosé Wine," *International Journal of Wine Business Research* 27(4), 281–298.
Velikova, N., Charters, S., Fountain, J., Ritchie, C., Fish, N. and Dodd, T. (2016) "Status or Fun? A Cross-Cultural Examination of Younger Consumers' Responses to Images of Champagne and Sparkling Wine," *British Food Journal* 110(8), 1898–1913.
Williams, P. and Kelly, J. (2001) "Cultural Wine Tourists: Product Development Considerations for British Columbia's Resident Wine Tourism Market," *International Journal of Wine Marketing* 13(3), 59–76.

3
ECONOMICS, WINE AND CULTURE

Denton Marks

Introduction

Economists' interest in cultural industries is at least as old as their interest in Adam Smith's pin factory. In a recent presentation, one of the foremost scholars of cultural economics cited not only Smith but also other pioneers of economics such as Jevons, Marshall, Robbins and Keynes as precursors of the field – while acknowledging that the field is 'not well defined' (Ginsburgh 2016b). In their contributions, pioneers in the field have generally not sown the seeds of modern theory or econometrics with studies of museum admissions, production costs or art auction results (though auction theory more generally has been a fertile field). Indeed, in its statement of aims and scope, the well-established *Journal of Cultural Economics* (JCE), first published in 1977, does not delineate rigorously the cultural sector it covers. For example, is wine culture included? Throsby observed some years ago (2001: 61) that the content of another prominent journal, *Economic Development and Cultural Change* (est. 1952) – among the top journals in economic development – has little to do with culture, and that pattern has continued.

Digging deeper, we realise that economic analysis of culture's content – for example, symbols, norms and institutions – is limited, perhaps because of its perceived marginal significance to economic forces or resistance to formal modelling and quantification. We expect that culture has formative effects on the preferences of buyers, sellers and the state, which, in turn, have formative effects on economic outcomes and performance. Then we take preferences as given. Nevertheless, it may be that emerging shared interests among economists, neuroscientists and psychologists (e.g. Kahneman 2011) and other social scientists represent early signs of the study of formation of those preferences and even changes of consciousness – and the economics and psychology of changing consciousness.

While economists' interest in culture has been longstanding but latent, collections of their formal research on wine have appeared more recently and formally, with the appearance of the *Journal of Wine Economics* (est. 2006) and *Wine Economics and Policy* (est. 2012), as well as other economics and business scholarly journals. Most of the published research has had a significant empirical orientation and has come from established fields in economics, such as consumer theory, agricultural economics and industrial organisation.

This chapter discusses the connection between economists' interest in culture and the emerging field of wine economics, with an eye towards drawing connections among wine, culture and economics. Attention goes first to the concept of cultural goods as a valuable bridge between cultural studies and traditional economics. While many cultural products fit easily into the definition, we then discuss wine as a cultural good and a view of the unique nature of cultural goods markets with their special role for experts. We close with suggestions for future directions for this research. Throughout the chapter, we note connections between this discussion and several chapters in this volume.

Cultural goods

A turning point and touchstone in the emergence of cultural economics was the Baumol/Bowen study (1966) of the performing arts that highlighted the 'economic dilemma' of the performing arts 'cost disease': by their nature as live performances, they could not experience the technology-driven productivity gains and corresponding cost reductions available in other sectors (most obviously, manufacturing). The concern was that relative wages would continue to fall, or intervention such as state subsidies would be required to keep them viable.

More important for economics scholarship was the application of the Baumol/Bowen logic to all service industries, though the service/nonservice dichotomy became better understood as a spectrum of industries as economists detected the subtle impacts of technological change on other industries' productivity and different degrees of capital-labour substitution. Also, the dire prediction of higher cost, unaffordable services (including cultural) has been mitigated by incomes rising due to greater overall productivity (e.g. Blaug 2001: 131).

The Baumol/Bowen study provided an intellectual challenge to accompany many economists' (and their spouses') avocational interest in cultural industries and thereby helped legitimise such research. However, the field has lacked a dominant paradigm beyond the 'cost disease' (ibid.: 124) so that most of it is conventionally applied economics, primarily microeconomics.

In that spirit, an important innovation has been the concept of cultural goods (CG) (e.g. Throsby 1994, 2001; Aylward 2008) which has contributed to wider recognition of a unique paradigm. The development of the concept follows a reliable route towards recognition within the discipline – the characterisation of a different category of goods with the corresponding suggestion of a different type of market.

Reflecting one of the foremost modern barometers of economists' research interest in cultural processes, the JCE's website lists six core topics: microeconomics, economic policy and regional and cultural studies (traditional disciplinary lines), along with arts, music and 'cultural economics' (left undefined). The JCE has published research on a wide array of cultural industries and on numerous topics that would apply to a cultural industry – for example, consumer demand, contingent valuation, performance quality, effects of critics, production costs and government subsidies and policy more generally. However, while its attention to gastronomy seems a step in that direction, the JCE has never published a paper on wine.

Wine as a cultural good

There may, however, be good reasons to consider wine a CG. Distinct from other types of goods, CG must have characteristics that distinguish them on both the demand and supply side and may even elude conventional transactions:

> When we think about culture in a functional sense – that is, as cultural activities producing goods and services – [we ask] what distinguishes cultural goods and services from 'ordinary' commodities. . . . A definition [includes] . . . creativity in their production . . . some form of intellectual property and . . . symbolic meaning. . . . [A] designation from the demand side might point to the accumulation of taste and the dependence of present on previous consumption. Finally . . . cultural goods embody or give rise to both cultural and economic value, 'ordinary' economic goods yield economic value only.
>
> (Throsby 2001: 160)

> [For producers] the creation of economic value is not their only *raison d'etre*. Processes of production and consumption in the arts and culture, and the broader role of culture in articulating essential values by which human beings express their identity and work out ways of living together, have a crucial content of cultural value, defined against different yardsticks from those we use to measure economic success. Any consideration of the cultural industries . . . cannot afford to overlook or downplay this critical dimension.
>
> *(ibid.: 134)*

It is in this context that a strong connection between cultural economics and wine emerges. For example, all visual, nonverbal representations fall somewhere along a spectrum from snapshots and children's scribbles to iconic art. Harmonic sounds can range from humming a tune to the musical classics. At its most basic level, wine is a commodity beverage, but, in some forms, it embodies creativity, intellectual property and symbolic meaning.

With their varieties of grapes, treatment of grapes (e.g. planting, tending, harvesting, crushing) and options for blending and storing and releasing for sale, it is self-evident that winemakers have a palette from which to create (e.g. Smith 2013). This yields intellectual property – a delineated, created object of value either legally (geographic indications, labels) as with music and writing or perhaps only conceptually (the juice itself). Religious examples may be the most familiar of wine as symbol – a role shared with water that extends to ancient times (e.g. Crowther 1979). Over time, wine has had many meanings, with one of the richest being its association with place that is a central theme of this *Handbook*.

For those sympathetic to granting it CG status, a taste for wine reflects previous consumption, and, at their best, its producers and cultural intermediaries aspire to something beyond maximising profit to cultivating public appreciation for something that captures and expresses a place and a culture, a point developed and documented in this volume (e.g. Christiansen and Marks 2022).

Wine's potential as art has attracted considerable interest for some time (e.g. Joy *et al.* 2021 and sources cited; Charters 2005; Fretter 1971), and Throsby (2011) has acknowledged that, in some forms, it satisfies his definition of CG. Another senior scholar has acknowledged that 'wine is close, but not identical to, art' (Ginsburgh 2016a: 262) and thus might grant it CG status. While unusual, a recent application to Central and Eastern European wines (Marks 2011) has been cited often.

One difficulty with the designation is that, as with almost all types of goods in the economic taxonomy, CG status is not easily testable because its characteristics are not easily quantifiable or even observable. We can sometimes test whether a good is normal or complementary (i.e. how demand for it changes with consumer income or changes in other goods' prices), but we cannot observe whether it is cultural or 'Veblen' (luxury goods for which demand increases as price increases) or 'experience' (see later in this chapter) – other types of goods in the taxonomy – though for some categories we can try experimentally (e.g. Clingingsmith and Sheremeta 2018).

Despite these difficulties, having an operational definition of cultural goods can be critical. For example, trade negotiations typically allow the exclusion of cultural goods from negotiations as 'cultural exceptions'. UNESCO has used the Throsby approach in its 2005 Convention on the Protection and Promotion of the Diversity of Cultural Expressions (https://en.unesco.org/creativity/convention) and required in its definition that such goods have 'more than just commercial value'. Wine may not have fallen under this designation yet, but there is no *a priori* reason why it could not, and, of course, assigning that designation could have significant implications for the international wine trade.

The lack of a testable definition of CG means that, as with the identification of cultural economics, its definition can evolve. Evidence of this includes the continuing discussion of the distinction between 'willingness to pay' economic value at the core of contemporary economics and multi-dimensional and more ephemeral cultural value with considerations such as group identity value and value to other generations. The key element here is 'symbolic value', which arguably cannot be measured in monetary terms (e.g. Angelini and Castellani 2019). Wine, with its strong symbolic function, is clearly in this category.

CG are also a subset of public goods that tend to have a special impact on those who consume – or appreciate – them: their production may motivate further production. They can be inspiring. A change of consciousness may precede that when group members come to recognise a shared CG – for example, the shared cultural significance of a place or the realisation of a shared group identity.

Given the usual group-delineated definition of culture – its examples are associated with well-defined groups (e.g. nationalities, ethnicities, genders, generations, professions) – CG must have significant public goods characteristics: costly exclusion from enjoying the CG and non-rival enjoyment or appreciation of it (i.e. one's enjoyment does not interfere with another's). This is, indeed, a defining characteristic of CG: the group must freely draw some significant element of valued identity from the CG. While a bottle of wine is not literally a public good, the existence of the wine, its producer and related producers and the community and history and traditions around them can be critical components to its CG content.

Group identification with wine will depend on the group and the wine. For example, regardless of drinking practices, family and community traditions in southwest France will likely identify with wine with finer distinctions of place associating with narrower designations of wine (e.g. the St. Estephe appellation within the Medoc appellation within the Bordeaux appellation). Such identification will vary directly with the age and economic impact of the industry. Much French identification may be deeper and wider – more intensely felt at the place and still felt farther from the place – than in the Finger Lakes or Mendoza. Of course, in some regions, community place identification with wine may be weak, despite aspirational and skillful local wine production (e.g. Dane and Door Counties in Wisconsin).

Less obvious may be the cultural value of winemaking techniques, ritual and celebrations – and an appreciation of wine more generally – that began in one place but may spread with the movement of people and their winemaking skills, traditions, and varieties to new areas (e.g. Anderson and Nelgen 2022).

We know that many physical CG are not pure public goods. Even the larger ones (e.g. the Eiffel Tower, the Great Wall) are subject to congestion costs – that is, we can imagine consumption becoming rival. Pure publicness here derives from the enjoyment provided from the knowledge that the good exists. A nation's flag or anthem can provide value to its citizens even when it is out of sight or hearing. These examples suggest the sometimes subtle cultural value of CG, often taken for granted until we pause to consider what loss we might feel without them.

The inspiration to produce often lacks a dominant commercial motive. National flags and anthems inspire the production of more nations' flags and anthems. Iconic music and art inspire more, and the same can occur with wine: some may undertake production, inspired by their wine experience, with limited or little determination to make a profit (Morton and Podolny 2002). If producing wine is not a realistic option, then evidence of inspiration may appear in other parts of the market (Christiansen and Marks 2022).

The nature of cultural markets: value derived from 'meaning'

The elementary economic model of consumer behaviour assumes that the perfectly informed consumer makes the best purchasing choices, expressing economic value constrained only by purchasing power (personal income) and prices. Typically in economics, the complications arise once we introduce the details of specific markets which violate our assumptions. For the wine consumer, one assumption violated is 'perfect information' and learning what will yield economic value, cultural value and how much. We consider three types of learning challenges: goods known only or primarily by the producer (asymmetric information), goods that can only be known by using them (experience goods – EG – a way to solve the asymmetric information problem) and goods known only or primarily by 'discursive practices' in the market, such as the behaviour and opinions of experts and 'influencers'. The first two challenges apply to learning the instrumental characteristics of the product – how its technical performance can yield consumer enjoyment (e.g. a used car, a home appliance) – and focus on economic value. The third type of challenge is different, especially allowing for both cultural and economic value.

Economists often characterise wine as an 'experience good' (Nelson 1970) – a product that is most reliably known by experiencing it (e.g. Ashton 2014 and sources cited). A Google Scholar search of 'wine' with 'experience good' yields over 2,400 listings, yet this is also a designation for wine that, while testable, remains untested. Nelson argues that, allowing for some questions about the degree of competition, markets for EG are like other markets. The distinction is simply how consumers get to know these goods (his examples: canned tuna fish, home appliances).

The case for wine as an EG is not strong: it is difficult to know a wine well enough either to recognise it subsequently simply by experiencing it or to guarantee future enjoyment. Trained wine tasters can sometimes recognise wines they have tasted, but this is spotty as extensive evidence from wine competitions has demonstrated (e.g. Hodgson and Cao 2014). If, in fact, ignorance is common on the consumer side of wine markets – especially fine wine markets – then the wine market may instead resemble Akerlof's 'market for lemons' (Akerlof 1970), in which the problem of adverse selection (uninformed buyers tending to undervalue a product of unknown benefit such as a used car, which might be a 'lemon') elicits no apparent solution to the information asymmetry and threatens to shrink or even eliminate the market. Producers likely know the product better than consumers but, even if they would tell them, are unlikely to know exactly what consumers want to know.

A recent analysis (Beckert 2019) highlights the important distinction between markets *for* goods, in which value derives from potentially observable and measurable 'instrumental' product attributes ('intrinsic characteristics') such as Akerlof's market for lemons, and 'markets *from* meaning':

> *where quality cannot be based on intrinsic characteristics of the good exchanged. In such markets, quality uncertainty is not an information problem as described by Akerlof in the market for lemons model. Instead, defining quality is a problem of contingent assessments that are arrived at intersubjectively through discursive practices and mutual observation of market participants. Quality is endogenous to the market process.* . . . Prices [reflecting economic and perhaps cultural value] emerge in such markets from a combination of intersubjectively established quality assessments, institutions and existing structural [market] characteristics.
>
> (ibid.: 1; emphasis added)

'Quality' here is better understood as enjoyment, which is the assumed ultimate goal of the consumer's purchase: what will produce consumer enjoyment is endogenous to the market process. The argument is that enjoyment of wine *qua* cultural good comes not simply from using ('experiencing' or drinking) it or from learning its characteristics (e.g. appellation, producer, age) as with a used car but from the market discursive practices surrounding it and the intersubjectivity involved in establishing this.

Beckert chooses the market for fine art as his prime example to illustrate this and applies it to financial as well as wine and fashion markets. Unlike the measurable attributes of a used automobile, the measurable attributes of a painting (e.g. size, materials, age) are not what determine all or even most of its value. One might say that the artist is a measurable attribute, but that leaves the question of why some artists are valued more than others. While one might question their validity as a basis for value determination, 'discursive practices' such as publicity and reviews can affect valuation, as does deference to the 'intersubjectively established quality assessments' of experts and 'influential' owners. Such is less the case in markets where value flows from objectively measurable, functional characteristics. This analysis from an economic sociologist is consistent with Ginsburgh's (2016b) observation that cultural economics is relatively interdisciplinary economics (just as econometrics arises from statistics and economics) because it draws on other disciplines such as philosophy, history, sociology and law.

If some wine's market – one we would consider cultural – is closer to fine art's 'market from meaning' than it is to the used car market, then the consumer's problem is more daunting than lemons and experience goods and encourages a level of consumer cultural involvement greater than Nelson's model anticipates.

Expertise and its role

Beckert's market from meaning relies heavily on the influence of experts who contribute to the perception of quality endogenous to the market-from-meaning process. Perhaps without recognising experts' role in contributing to meaning, economists have paid considerable attention to the role of experts in establishing economic value – in particular, the relationship between wine prices and expert wine ratings as a proxy variable measuring wine enjoyment distinct from other indicators such as vintage, winemaker and producer. Theoretically, more enjoyable wine should command a higher transaction price, *cet. par.* The requirement here is that buyers are willing to pay more for more enjoyment, but, perhaps lacking first-hand hedonic experience with the wine, they adopt expert evaluation as a proxy signal of enjoyment, yielding the prediction that higher ratings yield higher paid prices. Well over 100 econometric studies of wine price determinants have been published over the last 25 years (Outreville and Le Fur 2020), reflecting both subtlety in analysis and challenges such as use of appropriate data (e.g. transaction prices instead of suggested/asking prices), the potential two-way causality between prices and ratings (if prices affect experts' ratings) and other difficulties (Marks 2015, 2020).

Beckert's interpretation may be different. He claims that the buyer's economic and cultural valuation emerges, at least in part, from the market from meaning: 'arrived at intersubjectively through discursive practices and mutual observation of market participants. . . . Quality is endogenous to the market process', not exogenously determined by either the buyer's personal experience with the wine, should that be available, or vicariously by accepting expert opinion as a good predictor of own enjoyment. Becker's view is consistent with evidence (Ashenfelter and Jones 2013) of a demand for expert opinion, not simply the wine itself.

Economists' widespread interest in the impact and value of wine experts raises the question of the determination and evaluation of expertise, one of two core questions in wine economics (Ashenfelter 2016). Where is the market for expertise, and how efficient is it?

Topics in the cultural economics of wine: prospects

Considering the culture as the social context in which economic activity occurs suggests the breadth of topics one might include in the cultural economics of wine, hoping to expand economists' research interest in such topics. Especially if one thinks broadly beyond its alcoholic effects, Hugh Johnson's simple but profound description of the importance of wine – 'The Power to Banish Care' (1989: 10) – signifies its economic importance.

Viewing wine as a cultural good suggests various research directions. One is differences in wine's integration into the community. How has wine's role in the economy changed over time? What social indicators track the evolution of the wine industry – for example, the divergence in evolution between Austria and northern Italy and the Central and Eastern European countries next door? How might climate change affect wine's cultural vitality as optimal growing conditions shift, and wines – or a region's variety of viable wines – change? Does the internationalisation of winegrape varieties (Anderson and Nelgen 2022) show indications of cultural importing and exporting?

The identification of traditional wine regions with wine production invariably involves agriculture. Loss of the wine identity would be structurally disruptive, but few if any wine regions have invested in diversifying their economies accordingly. Economic development has instead tended to capitalise by developing related industries such as gastronomy, tourism and hospitality. The analysis of terroir has attracted some interest among economists (e.g. Ashenfelter *et al.* 2013; Cross *et al.* 2011a, 2011b; Gergaud and Ginsburgh 2008), but the scope has been limited. The role of wine production in regional economics, heritage economics and tourism economics seems relatively unexplored and a topic for fruitful research collaboration between economics and more culture-oriented disciplines.

Cultural impact on non-agricultural regions can also be significant. The global wine trade can have a cultural impact virtually anywhere, especially through gastronomy and hospitality. Wine lists can affect the success and even the identity of restaurants and their role in local economies. This volume's chapter on wine retailing (Christiansen and Marks 2022) discusses the cultivation of wine culture and nurturing wine appreciation in a region far from any significant viticulture. A question implicit there is access to wine as a cultural good. Is the cultural appreciation of wine only for those who can afford 'ultra-premium' wines? Many cultural goods are available in some form to everyone who appreciates them or is open to that – public concerts, low- or no-fee museums, recordings and public libraries. Relatively few who inhabit the world's wine cultures drink ultra-premium wines regularly – or ever. Should that be the price of admission for everyone else?

Recent examples of evolving wine culture appear in some large Asian cities. Popularised initially as a luxury good amidst rising affluence, how might its growing popularity spread into the middle class and even working class and affect tastes and even cuisines? How does that affect attitudes and practices around the location and content of meals inside or outside the home?

Throsby's requirements – creativity, intellectual property, symbolic meaning, cultivation of taste – suggest further enquiry. How have winemaking and even winery ownership traditions evolved across different cultures – experimentation along with adherence to tradition, for example? How do different traditions of gender status affect how gender roles in the industry are changing (Livat and Jaffré 2022)? How does state protection of wine-related property – and intellectual property – vary by culture? How are cultural differences in the symbolism of wine (e.g. liturgical staple, national treasure, narcotic) reflected in regulations and wine's larger role in the culture?

As suggested earlier, once we realise the impact of culture on what propels the economy, we appreciate the importance of studying that. One hopes that the economic analysis in this volume represents a helpful contribution to – or at least effective encouragement to pursue – that effort.

Acknowledgements

I have benefited greatly from careful readings by and comments from an external reviewer, Steve Charters, Graham Harding and Anita Purkis. Of course, responsibility for the final content is mine.

References

Akerlof, G.A. (1970) "The Market for 'Lemons': Asymmetrical Information and Market Behavior," *Quarterly Journal of Economics* 83(3), 488–500.
Anderson, K. and Nelgen, S. (2022) "Internationalization of Winegrape Varieties and Its Implications for Terroir-based Cultural Assets," this volume.
Angelini, F. and Castellani, M. (2019) "Cultural and Economic Value: A Critical Review," *Journal of Cultural Economics* 43, 173–188, https://doi.org/10.1007/s10824-018-9334-4.
Ashenfelter, O. (2016) "Remarks, Plenary Session, American Association of Wine Economists (AAWE)," 10th Annual Conference, Bordeaux FR, June 21–25.

Ashenfelter, O., Gergaud, O., Ginsburgh, V. and Storchmann, K. (2013) "Wine Tasting: Is 'Terroir' a Joke and/or Are Wine Experts Incompetent?" https://voxeu.org/article/wine-tasting-terroir-joke-andor-are-wine-experts-incompetent, accessed 6 June 2020.

Ashenfelter, O. and Jones, G. (2013) "The Demand for Expert Opinion: Bordeaux Wine," *Journal of Wine Economics* 8(3), 285–293.

Ashton, R. (2014) "Wine as An Experience Good: Price Versus Enjoyment in Blind Tastings of Expensive and Inexpensive Wines," *Journal of Wine Economics* 9(2), 171–182.

Aylward, D. (2008) "Towards a Cultural Economy Paradigm for the Australian Wine Industry," *Prometheus* 26(4), 373–385.

Baumol, W. and Bowen, W. (1966) *Performing Arts: The Economic Dilemma*, New York: The Twentieth Century Fund.

Beckert, J. (2019) "Markets from Meaning: Quality Uncertainty and the Intersubjective Construction of Value," *Cambridge Journal of Economics*. DOI:10.1093/cje/bez035.

Blaug, M. (2001) "Where Are We Now on Cultural Economics?" *Journal of Economic Surveys* 15(2), 123–143.

Charters, S. and Pettigrew, S. (2005) "Is Wine Consumption an Aesthetic Experience?" *Journal of Wine Research* 16(2), 121–136.

Christiansen, B. and Marks, D. (2022) "Some Practical Economics of Selling Wine as a Cultural Good," this volume.

Clingingsmith, D. and Sheremeta, R.M. (2018) "Status and the Demand for Visible Goods: Experimental Evidence on Conspicuous Consumption," *Experimental Economics* 21(4), 877–904.

Cross, R., Plantinga, A.J. and Stavins, R.N. (2011a) "The Value of Terroir: Hedonic Estimation of Vineyard Sale Prices," *Journal of Wine Economics* 6(1), 1–14.

Cross, R., Plantinga, A.J. and Stavins, R.N. (2011b) What Is the Value of Terroir?" *American Economic Review* 101(3), 152–156.

Crowther, N.B. (1979) "Water and Wine as Symbols of Inspiration," *Mnemosyne* 32(1–2), 1–11.

Fretter, W.B. (1971) "Is Wine an Art Object?" *Journal of Aesthetics and Art Criticism* 30(1), 97–100.

Gergaud, O. and Ginsburgh, V. (2008) "Natural Endowments, Production Technologies and the Quality of Wines in Bordeaux: Does Terroir Matter?" *The Economic Journal* 118(529), F142–F157.

Ginsburgh, V. (2016a) "On Judging Art and Wine," in I. Rizzo and R. Towse (eds), *The Artful Economist: A New Look at Cultural Economics*, Switzerland: Springer, 245–265.

Ginsburgh, V. (2016b) "Economics of the Arts: A Subjective and Personal View," Presentation at Doshisha University, Kyoto.

Hodgson, R. and Cao, J. (2014) "Criteria for Accrediting Expert Wine Judges," *Journal of Wine Economics* 9(1), 62–74.

Johnson, H. (1989) *Vintage*, New York: Simon and Schuster.

Joy, A., LaTour, K.A., Charters, S.J., Grohmann, B. and Peña-Moreno, C. (2021) "The Artification of Wine: Lessons from the Fine Wines of Bordeaux and Burgundy," *Arts and the Market* 11(1), 24–39.

Kahneman, D. (2011) *Thinking, Fast and Slow*, New York: Farrar, Strauss, & Giroux.

Livat, F. and Jaffré, C. (2022) "Women in Wine . . . Occasionally: Gendered Roles in the Wine Industry," this volume.

Marks, D. (2011) "Competitiveness and the Market for Central and Eastern European Wines: A Cultural Good in the Global Wine Market," *Journal of Wine Research* 22(3), 245–263.

Marks, D. (2015) "Seeking the Veritas About the Vino: Fine Wine Ratings as Wine Knowledge," *Journal of Wine Research* 26(4), 319–335.

Marks, D. (2020) "Erring Experts? A Critique of Wine Ratings as Hedonic Scaling," *Journal of Wine Economics* 15(4), 386–393.

Morton, F. and Podolny, S. (2002) "Love or Money: The Effects of Owner Motivation in the California Wine Industry," *Journal of Industrial Economics* 50(4), 431–456.

Nelson, P. (1970) "Information and Consumer Behavior," *Journal of Political Economy* 78(2), 311–329.

Outreville, J.F. and Le Fur, E. (2020) "Hedonic Price Functions and Wine Price Determinants: A Review of Empirical Research," *Journal of Agricultural & Food Industrial Organization* 18(2), 1–27.

Smith, C. (2013) *Postmodern Winemaking*, Berkeley: University of California Press.

Throsby, D. (1994) "The Production and Consumption of the Arts: A View of Cultural Economics," *Journal of Economic Literature* 32(1), 1–29.

Throsby, D. (2001) *Economics and Culture*, Cambridge: Cambridge University Press.

Throsby, D., Personal Correspondence (email), 14 May 2011.

Websites: https://en.unesco.org/creativity/convention.

4
GEOGRAPHY, WINE AND CULTURE

Tim Unwin

Wine is geography

Geographers have written about wine since classical antiquity. Much of this writing has focused on cultural issues, from the early spread of grape growing across the Mediterranean, wine's deep symbolic and ritual significance and the nineteenth-century impact of *Daktulosphaera vitifoliae* (formerly *Phylloxera vastatrix*) to much more recent work on the role of culture in the contemporary wine trade. However, as this book has emphasised throughout, the word 'culture' is very contested. Thus, cultural geography, as a distinct field, has ebbed and flowed in importance within the discipline, and most geographical writing on wine has not overtly focused on culture. Indeed, those at the forefront of the so-called 'new cultural geography' that emerged in the 1980s (Clarke 2017) sadly had rather little to say about viticulture and winemaking. This introduction, therefore, provides some context within which the diverse chapters by geographers specifically chosen for this book may be appreciated and interpreted as contributions to a geographical understanding of wine's cultural resonances.

Until the latter part of the twentieth century, two main themes ran through most geographical thinking and writing: the interactions of humans within the physical environment, often characterised as 'people and nature', and the ways in which human activities have different spatial expressions, giving rise to the character of distinct 'places' (Unwin 1992). From the 1960s onwards, though, the increasing fragmentation of the discipline into ever smaller specialities has meant that geographers often have rather little to say about substantive issues to do with the place of humans on the earth. Nevertheless, the distinctive interactions that humans have had with the vine in different parts of the world over many thousands of years and the ways that people have turned grapes into wines with a myriad of flavours, tastes and colours mean that wine growing can itself be seen as a powerful metaphor for these two traditional conceptualisations of the discipline of geography.

The interaction between humans and nature that lies at the heart of geography is particularly well expressed in Blachon's wonderful cartoon depicted in Figure 4.1 (Humoristes Associés 1980) and used previously as one of the defining images in my *Wine and the Vine* (Unwin 1991). This perfectly captures the connections between people and the physical environment that shape the character and culture of wine. The bottle, the wine, has its roots in the soil, going down through the different horizons into the bedrock itself. In the background, across the rolling fields, is the village, the home of the wine growers. The church spire, reaching heavenwards, parallels the verticality of the bottle and emphasises the cultural and religious significance of the wine. The red-tiled roofs of the houses match the red seal on the bottle. This could be nowhere other than France, but just so that we make

Figure 4.1 Towards a simplified multidisciplinary framework for an understanding of wine and culture

no mistakes, Blachon shows part of the label 'CHAT . . . MONJ. . .'. 'Culture', of course, is derived from the Latin *colere*, meaning to cultivate, till and worship, capturing the essence of mutual responsibility between the land and the farmer.

This interaction between people and the environment that makes geography, as well as wine, is wonderfully captured in a little-known but beautiful book by four French geographers – Alain Huetz de Lemps, Jean-Robert Pitte, Xavier de Planhol and Philippe Roudié (1990) – entitled *Les Vins de L'impossible*. This lavishly illustrated work shows how vines have been grown and wines made in what many would see as being impossible physical environments in Peru, Japan, Trabzon (Turkey), Shiraz (Iran), the Tropics and 'Third World', Afghanistan and even the British Isles. It emphasises the intricate and complex interactions throughout history that have shaped the distinct landscapes of the vine and culture of wine.

The next section of this introduction provides an historical overview of writings by geographers on the culture of wine, emphasising wine's expression as a particular interaction between people and the physical environment in which they live, and this is followed by a brief thematic summary of the main recent topics and issues addressed by geographers on the culture of wine.

Historical context

Geographers in classical antiquity and the medieval world

The word 'geography' combines the two Greek words – γεω and γραφία – literally meaning 'earth-writing'. Early such works were essentially descriptions of the earth, primarily intended for rulers and merchants interested in knowing more about other places. The first surviving writings with some claim to being formal 'geography' are the *Geography* of Strabo (c. 60 BCE–post-21 CE), and Pliny's (23–79 CE) *Natural History*, which has four books specifically devoted to geography (Unwin 1992). Both of these classical works provide detailed descriptions of grape growing and winemaking in different parts of the Mediterranean world. In particular, they provide considerable information about many themes that have subsequently resonated in discussions by geographers about the culture of wine: the suitability of particular vines to certain types of environment (see Chapter 8 on terroir), the quality and reputation of certain wines and, particularly in Pliny's works, the spread of grape-growing and winemaking culture into what is now southern France and Spain.

The collapse of the Roman Empire during the latter part of the fifth century meant the loss of a European tradition of geographical writing until the later medieval period. However new cartographic traditions emerged in China in the fourth century CE, and by the twelfth century, Arab geographers, most famously al-Idrisi (1100–1165), were once again describing the cultivation of vines, notably in Spain and Portugal (Unwin 1991). The rich tradition of Persian poetry from the eleventh to the fourteenth centuries has also provided a source for more recent work by geographers and historians on the culture of wine in the Islamic world during this period (Unwin and Saeidi 2004). Geography re-emerged in Europe in the later medieval period, mainly allied with cartography as geographers sought to serve the political and commercial interests of Spain and Portugal overseas.

It was not, though, until the eighteenth century that geography became in any sense a formal academic discipline. Geography, especially following Immanuel Kant's lectures in Königsberg on *Physische Geographie* between 1756 and 1796, had by then become primarily an empirical science providing the basis for our understanding of space; there was little room for the culture of wine in the Germanic traditions of geography that ensued. However, it was in Germany later in the nineteenth century that a different and distinctive new tradition emerged that was to play a major role in subsequent geographical accounts of wine. This was the concept of *Kulturlandschaft* (cultural landscape), apparently first used in 1832 by Carl Ritter (1779–1859) (Potthoff 2012).

Geographical writing on the culture of wine in the twentieth century

Three important traditions can be identified in the work by geographers at the interface between wine, culture and geography in the second half of the twentieth century (see Unwin 2017 for an indicative bibliography): French historical geography, especially the work of Roger Dion (1959); research on cultural geography in the USA emanating from the ideas of Carl Sauer at Berkeley; and research by English-speaking geographers across the Commonwealth.

France was, and in many ways still is, a country of *pays*, those particular areas that share common cultural, social and economic characteristics, made visible in their distinctive landscapes. By the middle of the twentieth century, French geographers and, to a lesser extent, historians, had made these *pays* their specific focus of study. One of the most distinguished of these was Roger Dion (1896–1981), who held the Chaire de Géographie Historique de la France at the Collège de France from 1948 to1968 (Baker 2003). As well as a classic study of the Loire, he is best known for his magnificent *Histoire de la vigne et du vin en France: Des origines au XIXe siècle*, first published in 1959, which revealed how important landscapes of the vine were to the identity of many French *pays*. This set the scene for much subsequent writing by French geographers, as well as historians from the Annales School (Burguière 2011), on the culture of wine (Dutton 2019).

A very different tradition of geographical work on the culture of wine emerged on the West Coast of the USA at Berkeley, where Carl Sauer (1889–1975) had been appointed founding chair of the geography department in 1923. Drawing in part on German traditions, although highly critical of Ritter, he emphasised the importance of studying cultural landscapes and exploring the various human forms that were superimposed on the base provided by the physical environment. His own focus was primarily on Latin America, but one of his graduate students, Dan Stanislawski (1903–97) (Pedersen 1998), applied these notions of cultural landscapes to vineyards and wine, first in Portugal (Stanislawski 1970) and then more widely across the Mediterranean (Stanislawski 1975).

This US interest in the geography of wine culminated in Harm de Blij's (1935–2014) (1983) *Wine: A Geographic Appreciation*, which included a specific chapter on the cultural landscapes of viticulture. A great populariser of geography in the public sphere, he subsequently edited an important collection of papers on wine presented at the annual meeting of the Association of American Geographers in Miami in 1991 (de Blij 1992). It was not, though, until 2004 that the association's board formally agreed that a Wine Specialty Group should be created, and this continues to the present, albeit with a broadened agenda and name (Geography of Wine, Beer and Spirits).

Britain has long played an important role in the international wine trade, and the place of geography has also been particularly prominent in its education system (Unwin 1992). It is scarcely surprising therefore that British geographers in the second half of the twentieth century also turned their attention to research on wine. Historical geographers in particular focused on diverse aspects of culture, from agricultural syndicates in Loir-et-Cher (Baker 1986) and the spread of phylloxera in the Hérault (Stevenson 1980) to studies on viticulture and winemaking in Latin America (Dickenson and Unwin 1992; see also Crowley 1989) and the evidence provided in *Domesday Book* for the study of eleventh century vineyards in England (Unwin 1990). My own *Wine and the Vine: An Historical Geography of Viticulture and the Wine Trade* (Unwin 1991) sought to build on much of this material to provide an overview of cultural changes in viticulture, vinification and the wine trade very much within the *longue durée* tradition of the Annales School. Similarly, elsewhere in the English-speaking Commonwealth, especially in countries where winemaking was growing in importance at this time, other geographers developed their own distinctive research traditions on the culture of wine, notable among whom was Warren Moran, who wrote his master's thesis in 1958 on viticulture and winemaking in New Zealand and has recently published a major new book on the same subject (Moran 2017). He is notable also for having encouraged a raft of younger geographers to explore aspects of the wine trade in the region and beyond over the last half century.

Themes in contemporary geographical writing on the culture of wine

Among the most important recent reviews and collections of geographical research on wine-related issues are those by Dickenson and Salt (1982), de Blij (1983, 1992), Dickenson (1990) and Dougherty (2012). These show overwhelmingly that, whereas in the past there was much explicit writing by geographers on culture and wine, few geographers in the last 25 years have overtly discussed this theme. This is also reflected in the papers presented to annual meetings of the AAG's Wine Specialty Group, one of the most active communities of geographers working on wine in the English language. Nevertheless, much geographical writing is, indeed, of relevance for understanding the broader culture of wine.

In the early 1990s, Dickenson and Salt (1982) explored a wide range of works beyond those written specifically by geographers that purported to address aspects of what they saw as the geography of wine and classified these into five main groups: general backgrounds on wine, growing and processing (divided into sections on the vine, the physical environment, the farm structure of wine-producing areas and wine laws), distribution, consumption and the landscapes and culture of wine. These highlight once again views of geography primarily as interactions between the physical and human worlds and as the spatial distribution of economic activities.

Percy Dougherty's (2012: vii) much more recent edited volume acknowledges the importance of the AAG's Wine Specialty Group's activities in 'awakening a new interest in the geographical analysis of wine and viticulture', and the book's organisation, focusing on overviews, regional, physical, cultural/economic and techniques sections, largely reflects the broad areas of interest in which geographers are currently undertaking research. Interestingly, the combination of cultural/economic is heavily dominated by the latter, reflecting a rich vein of research over many years by economic geographers into the structure and organisation of the wine industry, especially in the USA (see, for example, Holly 1994).

My own bibliographical review of work over the last 50 or so years by geographers (Unwin 2017) likewise noted seven main themes: overviews (subdivided by languages), geography and the physical environment (with sections on terroir and climate), geography and wine in antiquity, geography in the history of wine, geography of wine appellations and demarcations (also see, for example, Gade 2004), the economic geography of wine (including a section on wine tourism) and the spatial distribution of wine and geographic accounts of wine regions. Interestingly, the lack of a section specifically on culture indicated not only that few geographers have recently explicitly focused on culture but also that, implicitly, it remains an underlying theme in much other geographical work on viticulture and winemaking. For example, the notion that vineyards and winemaking are essential elements of the cultural landscapes of different countries is central to the use of the term 'geography' in most popular guides to wine regions across the world. In such guides, 'geography' is merely a term to describe what is to be found where and how the character of wines is often influenced by the physical environment. Hence, any discussion of terroir becomes central to popular notions of wine's geography (see Chapter 8).

In selecting work by geographers for this volume, we have sought to encourage them to draw out from their previous research and make more explicit their understandings of the culture of wine. Myles, Collins and Townsend (Chapter 15) thus explore the evolution of the wine industry in Texas, paying particular attention to the two AVAs (American Viticultural Areas) in the state. Likewise, Tobias and Myles (Chapter 12) also explore the contested character and value of AVAs in the very different context of the Sierra Nevada mountains of California. Overton, a geographer with a chair in development studies, explores the distinction between the sites and sights of production and the contrasting ways in which the contemporary performance of winemaking takes place in different spaces (Chapter 9). Two chapters written by people from other disciplines have also been edited in a geographical context because of their interdisciplinary approaches to topics often previously addressed by geographers. Holt's chapter (25), written by a historian, is thus one of two chapters in the *Handbook* (the other is by Phillips, Chapter 26) that address the historical and geographical connections between wine and religion. Dutton's chapter (10), although written by a linguist, is included broadly within this geographical tradition, not least because of her previous explorations of the writings by French geographers about wine (see Dutton 2019). However, her chapter in this book also explores the fascinating connections between islands and wine from antiquity to the twentieth century through the lens of 'colonial cultures'.

In conclusion

Culture is an elusive notion. In Western societies, academics have frequently sought to group people into specific social, political, economic and cultural systems or structures; historians have tended to explore how these vary over time, and geographers have frequently examined their spatial representations and distribution. However, in reality, these are fluid concepts that themselves change over both space and time. Hence, much of the most exciting work on understanding the place (and culture) of wine in society has been undertaken by scholars crossing traditional boundaries at the interface between history and geography (as, for example, in Chapters 26 and 25 by Phillips and Holt in this *Handbook*). Traditionally, geographers with a sound understanding of both the physical and human processes shaping viticulture and winemaking have thus been able to provide valuable insights into the culture of wine by exploring both how culture has shaped wine growing and how wine itself has become an important cultural symbol and representation of the societies in which we live. The chapters that follow provide insights into both and highlight three main themes: the significance of cultural landscapes of the vine in many aspects of human life for millennia, the ways in which constructs such as appellation systems are themselves cultural artefacts and the deep symbolic significance that wines and vines have retained from antiquity to the present.

References

Baker, A.R.H. (1986) "The Infancy of France's First Agricultural Syndicate: The Syndicat des Agriculteurs de Loir-et-Cher 1881–1914," *The Agricultural History Review* 34(1), 45–59.
Baker, A.R.H. (2003) *Geography and History: Bridging the Divide*, Cambridge: Cambridge University Press.
Burguière, A. (2011) *The Annales School: An Intellectual History*, Ithaca, NY: Cornell University Press.
Clarke, D.B. (2017) "New Cultural Geography," in *International Encyclopedia of Geography: People, the Earth, Environment and Technology*, Chichester and New York: Wiley, https://doi.org/10.1002/9781118786352.wbieg0002.
Crowley, W. (1989) "The Growth of the Mexican Wine Industry," *Yearbook of the Association of Pacific Coast Geographers* 51, 25–47.
De Blij, H. (1983) *Wine: A Geographic Appreciation*, Totowa, NJ: Rowman and Allanheld.
De Blij, H. (ed) (1992) *Viticulture in Geographic Perspective: Proceedings of the 1991 Miami AAG Symposium*, Miami, FL: Miami Geographical Society.
Dickenson, J. (1990) "Viticultural Geography: An Introduction to the Literature in English," *Journal of Wine Research* 1(1), 5–24.
Dickenson, J. and Salt, J. (1982) "In Vino Veritas: An Introduction to the Geography of Wine," *Progress in Human Geography* 6(2), 159–189.
Dickenson, J. and Unwin, T. (1992) *Viticulture in Colonial Latin America: Essays on Alcohol, the Vine and Wine in Spanish America and Brazil*, Liverpool: University of Liverpool.
Dion, R. (1959) *Histoire de la vigne et du vin en France: Des origines au XIXe siècle*, Paris: Clavreuil.
Dougherty, P. (ed) (2012) *The Geography of Wine: Regions, Terroir and Techniques*, New York: Springer.
Dutton, J. (2019) "Geographical Turns and Historical Returns in Narrating French Wine Culture," *Global Food History* 5(1–2), 113–131, https://doi.org/10.1080/20549547.2019.1570781.
Gade, D.W. (2004) "Tradition, Territory, and Terroir in French Viniculture: Cassis, France and Appellation Contrôlée," *Annals of the Association of American Geographers* 94(4), 848–867.
Holly, B.P. (1994) "Organisational Structure of Wine Production in the US," *Journal of Wine Research* 5(2), 91–101.
Huetz de Lemps, A., Pitte, J-R., de Planhol, X. and Roudié, P. (1990) *Les Vins de l'Impossible*, Grenoble: Glénat.
Humoristes Associés. (1980) *Le Vin*, France: Ha! Humoristes Associés.
Moran, W. (2017) *New Zealand Wine: The Land, the Vines, the People*, London: Hardie Grant Books.
Pedersen, L.R. (1998) "Dan Stanislawski, 1903–1997," *Annals of the Association of American Geographers* 88(4), 699–705.
Potthoff, K. (2012) "The Use of 'Cultural Landscape' in 19th Century German Geographical Literature," *Norsk Geografisj Tidsskrift* 67, 49–54.
Stanislawski, D. (1970) *Landscapes of Bacchus: The Vine in Portugal*, Austin: University of Texas Press.
Stanislawski, D. (1975) "Dionysus Westward: Early Religion and the Economic Geography of Wine," *Geographical Review* 65(4), 427–444.
Stevenson, I. (1980) "The Diffusion of Disaster: The Phylloxera Outbreak in the Département of the Hérault, 1862–80," *Journal of Historical Geography* 6(1), 47–63.
Unwin, T. (1990) "Saxon and Early Norman Viticulture in England," *Journal of Wine Research* 1(1), 61–76.
Unwin, T. (1991) *Wine and the Vine: An Historical Geography of Viticulture and the Wine Trade*, London: Routledge.
Unwin, T. (1992) *The Place of Geography*, Harlow: Longman.
Unwin, T. (2017) *Geography of Wine*, Oxford Bibliographies. DOI:10.1093/obo/9780199874002-0166.
Unwin, T. and Saeidi, A. (2004) "Persian Wine Tradition and Symbolism: Evidence from the Medieval Poetry of Hafiz," *Journal of Wine Research* 15(2), 97–114.

5
HISTORY, WINE AND CULTURE

Graham Harding

Introduction

Wine has played a central role in human societies for many millennia. Whilst we do not yet know and may never know the precise role it had among the first peoples to make wine, we can be certain of its centrality to the earliest documented societies. Texts such as the *Epic of Gilgamesh* (c. 2100–1800 BCE) and items of material culture such as those deposited some half a millennium later in the tomb of Tutankhamun (Varriano 2010: 13–16) attest to wine's social and religious role. Wine has been central not only to rich ritual practices but also to the daily nourishment, health and pleasure of untold millions for millennia. Leora Auslander has argued cogently that changes in taste, usage and style can enlighten us not just about the people 'who had imagined, crafted, sold, bought, and used these objects' but also about the institutions of their societies. In other words, concrete objects can be linked to abstract societal transformations such as monarchical to republican systems of governance or patriarchal to (more) egalitarian familial structures, commercialism to capitalism and form a bridge between past and present (Auslander *et al.* 2009: 1371).

Understanding change

A – perhaps the – primary task of the historian is to understand change. How were the societies of the past different from those of today and why? In what Peter Stearns has called the 'unavoidable quest to figure out why our complex species behaves as it does in societal settings', history provides the evidence. Only through history, he continues, 'can we grasp how things change' (Stearns 1998). Furthermore, the analysis of how we reached our present can also inform how we think about the future and how we might 'avoid repeating the errors of our predecessors' (Gorman 2004: 109). Seventy years ago, E. H. Carr wrote of the importance of the 'unending dialogue' between past and present (Carr and Davies 1987: 56). To maintain that dialogue, we need both to be aware of the language(s) and culture(s) that each of us as individuals has inherited and to use that awareness to develop the mental frameworks needed to understand self and society (Corfield 2008). Hence, as the historian of Islam, Leor Halevi, has insisted, 'cultural singularities and changes [are] the stuff that history is made of' (Auslander *et al.* 2009: 1364).

As noted in the Introduction, however, 'culture' is a problematic word. Writing as an historian in 1997, Peter Burke identified a 'cloud' of over 200 different definitions (Burke 1997: 1). According to Andrew Grant Wood, these fall into two basic groups: first, culture as a system of beliefs and behaviours that underpins everyday life, and second, culture as the product of creative processes (Wood 2011).

Nineteenth- and early twentieth-century historians such as Jacob Burckhardt and Johann Huizinga focused on the second element of Wood's typology: Burckhardt in *The Civilisation of the Renaissance in Italy* and Huizinga in *The Waning of the Middle Ages* (Burckhardt and Middlemore 1878; Huizinga and Hopman 1924). That strand of cultural history still persists, but the focus has moved to beliefs and values and how they have affected social and individual behaviour with numberless titles on subjects as various as depression, angels, twin beds, food – and wine.

The cultural turn

Such titles represent the outworking of a 'cultural turn' in historical studies that dates back into the 1970s. This turn derived from a new-found determination within academia to place culture at the heart of the discipline's methodological and theoretical focus. It owed much to anthropology, particularly the work of Clifford Geertz (Geertz 1973), though it also drew on Foucault, Bourdieu and the work of those historians who, in Miri Rubin's summary, 'showed that peasants and artisans could be studied historically, and that historians could try to understand their ideas and aspirations, the words that comforted or excited them, the symbols they cherished or rejected'. For Rubin, the essence of cultural history is that it is 'best characterized as an approach which considers the domain of representation and the struggle over meaning as the most fruitful areas for the pursuit of historical understanding' (Rubin c2008).

With the proliferation of approaches and studies came further theoretical challenges and counter-challenges. For Ian McKay, the term was too 'malleable' to lead to anything but 'incomprehensibility', and this inability to 'stand up to scrutiny' meant that it could have no explanatory value. McKay further argued that 'cultures of. . .' were 'artificial' – nothing more than an 'intellectual pastime' (McKay 1981: 213, 224, 226). Peter Mandler's article 'The Problem with Cultural History', arguing for a 'reinfusion of discipline' to historical studies, provoked heated rebuttals and the raising or reiteration of further 'problems' (Mandler 2004; Jones 2004). The key problems – as well as the power – of this approach were summarised by Anna Green in her survey of cultural history (Green 2007) and in the remainder of this chapter, I will consider some of the key issues through the lens of wine and wine studies.

Wine, history and culture

In this context, I will argue that 'cultures of. . .' provide a valuable tool for historians looking to understand societal change and its effects. No country has a single, unitary wine culture. Regional, class and economic differences permeate both low- and high-consumption societies. Whilst the French (for instance) may mostly share a strong reverence for wine as a symbol of France, this does not mean that there is a single wine culture. As Pierre Bourdieu's influential studies showed, differing tastes in and attitudes to wine and food marked the consumption of different groups in French society (Bourdieu 1984: 177, 184–185). Hence, 'culture' can be a valuable 'exploratory methodology' in areas as diverse as international diplomacy (Jackson 2008: 155–157) and facial expression (Jones 2014). As Burke wrote in 2012, 'almost everything seems to be having its cultural history written these days' (Burke 2012: 1).

Wine, as a widely traded consumable product, offers particular benefits to the historian in consequence of its economic importance, its power as a social marker, its deep links to cultural production and its value as a national and social symbol.

First, the economic value of wine. As an item of production and/or consumption, it has carried significant economic weight for many centuries in many countries. The work of Susan Rose and others on the medieval European wine trade shows how early it became widely traded across the continent and how important it was to national revenues (Rose 2011). Wine rapidly became and remained an item of daily or occasional consumption for very many people; as Withington has written, there have always been intoxicants to suit 'most tastes and budgets' (Withington 2014: 22). Trading across regional or national borders demanded the intervention of both economic and cultural intermediaries: the former to facilitate trade, the latter to communicate the habit, value and variety of wine. Such intermediaries, it has been cogently argued, are essential components of cultural change. Cultures of all forms are never static. There is always movement at the edges where those of different backgrounds may meet as trading or intellectual intermediaries (Ben-Zaken 2013: 4; see also Burke 2012: 10).

Secondly, wine has been for many centuries an expressive marker of social and economic status both in countries where there was local production and those – like England – where the emphasis was primarily on consumption. The 'battle' between Burgundy and Bordeaux in medieval and early modern France had social and economic as well as gustatory and medicinal dimensions (Pitte 2012). In seventeenth-century England, to consume the wine of the Champagne region was a mark of closeness to the court, where the fashion for these wines had been introduced and exploited by the Marquis de St. Evremond, in exile from the French court (Simon 1905: 5–9). In the Victorian period, to affirm or affect a taste for dry champagne was to proclaim social status. The Victorian narrative insisted that to tolerate, let alone like, dry champagne demanded that the consumer start young and drink often. Merchants, who made their money in later life, were thus categorised as unlikely to demand dry champagne. The Pommery agent, Adolphe Hubinet, was explicit in his instructions to his principals in Reims that in British territories where merchants dominated society, the firm should supply sweeter champagne; colonies dominated by 'high' civil servants or army officers would require drier wine (Harding 2018: 155). David Mandelbaum has stressed that 'drinking . . . is part of a larger cultural configuration' which divides social groups (Mandelbaum 1965: 281–282), a point reiterated by Thomas Wilson, who insists that '[d]rinking is the veritable stuff of any and perhaps every level and type of culture, and is implicated in the behaviours, values, ideologies and histories of these cultures. Drinking is itself cultural' (Wilson 2004), and wine is deeply imbricated in cultural production. For centuries, it has been central to not only to ritual and sacramental practice but also to the symbolism and inspiration of artists (Withington 2014: 25).

Lastly, wine has been a powerful symbol of political – even national – allegiance. In the seventeenth and eighteenth centuries, as Charles C. Ludington has shown, to choose claret rather than port was to display allegiance to the monarchy (Ludington 2013: 28–29). In 1860, the British characterised wine as the means of the next French 'invasion' (*Punch, or, The London Charivari*, 11 February 1860: 59). In 1860, the *Glasgow Herald* quoted the French paper *Le Siècle* as saying that 'our [French] wines carry everywhere with them the genius of our people – its generous aspirations and liberal ideas. Whenever people drink our [wines] they must perforce become French'. The *Herald* added somewhat dourly that these wines in question must 'be very strong indeed' (*Glasgow Herald*, 17 April 1860: 2). As the *Herald* demonstrated and as Marion Demossier has insisted in her work on the French and wine, drinking is a political act: a means of demonstrating regional, class and national identity (Demossier 2005).

A marker of change?

Yet, like food, wine does not fundamentally change the collective culture. Most scholars would accept Stephen Mennell's view that tastes in food and are 'culturally shaped and socially controlled' (Mennell et al. 1992: 8). Though consumption patterns may be affected by external forces such as the switch from grape wine to raisin wine or industrial alcohols in the decades following France's phylloxera crisis after 1870, such changes typically follow rather than lead societal changes (see Simpson 2005: 533–535; Phillips 2016: 177–180).

Hence, wine, like food, can be used as a marker of change. Tastes in general are deeply embedded. Though some attempts to force change on society are successful, others fail. The British taste for port in the eighteenth century was created by politics – notably, the provision in the Methuen Treaty of 1703 that guaranteed that the duty on Portuguese wines would be one-third less than that on French wines (Ludington 2013: 2–3). Yet William Gladstone, who removed this restriction in an attempt wean consumers from the 'black, sweet, and strong' fortified wines that he believed were destructive of national health and well-being, failed to create the light wine-drinking culture he desired (Harding 2018). As Britain's premier trade journal wrote in 1908 of Gladstone's duty changes, 'neither then nor since has light Claret become the beverage of those who earn their bread by manual labour' (*Ridley's Wine and Spirit Circular*, 9 January 1908: 52). As these examples suggest, economic essentialism has an impact but cannot be given the dominant role in changing society.

Yet both societies and cultures change. Can the case of wine provide indications on how change occurs? As noted earlier, wine is a highly traded commodity. Cross-cultural encounters between producers, merchants and consumers are central to the wine trade. The interactions and power struggles across the total value chain between these groups produce change in taste, production and distribution. In the nineteenth century, the British switch from sweet to very dry champagne was driven by a consumer dynamic in which an aristocratic elite sought to distance itself from the middle-class adopters of the champagne habit by adopting steadily drier wine (Harding 2020). In twentieth-century Burgundy, the desire of the producers to emancipate themselves from the power of the merchants led to the creation of Burgundian folk festivals such as 'La Paulée' that changed the style of Burgundian wine and contributed to the formalisation of the 'Appellation Contrôlée' system that has largely governed French winemaking and branding practice since the 1930s (Laferté 2011). Although Mary Norton, in her work on the adoption of chocolate in Spain in the seventeenth century, has argued that 'taste . . . is an autonomous force', her account suggests that it was contact between returners and mainlanders that built up the 'critical mass of aficionados' (Norton 2006: 675–677, 691).

Change is consequent on contact with the other. Peter Burke has argued that

> [h]istorians and anthropologists alike once treated cultures as if they were homogenous. In contrast (he argued) it may be illuminating to approach the history of all cultures as the product of a series of encounters: not only encounters with other places, but also encounters between social classes, between regions, between the sexes, between town and country, and so on.
>
> (Burke 2012: 10)

This argument raises the issue of the balance between the individual and the collective in changing culture. Anna Green, in her survey of cultural history, suggests that scholars are coalescing around a rejection of 'fixed cultural scripts' and 'moving towards a perspective that acknowledges the interplay between cultural systems and cultural practices'. She accepted, however, that for historians of culture, an important question articulated by Gabrielle Spiegel remained: can history be 'culturally ordered without being culturally prescribed'? (Green 2007: 121; Spiegel 2005: 21). The contributions to this *Handbook* suggest that the study of the culture of wine – so economically important, so socially distinctive, so dependent on cross-cultural contacts of all kinds – can be a powerful lens in illustrating the central concern of historians: how do societies and cultures change?

References

Auslander, L., Bentley, A., Halevi, L., Sibum, H.O. and Witmore, C. (2009) "Conversation: Historians and the Study of Material Culture," *American Historical Review* 114(5), 1355–1404.
Ben-Zaken, A. (2013) "Cultural History: Difficulties and Possibilities," *Cultural History* 2(1), 1–15.
Bourdieu, P. (1984) *Distinction: A Social Critique of the Judgement of Taste*, London: Routledge.
Burckhardt, J. and Middlemore, S.G.C. (1878) *The Civilisation of the Period of the Renaissance in Italy*, London: C. K. Paul & Co.
Burke, P. (1997) *Varieties of Cultural History*, Cambridge: Polity Press.
Burke, P. (2012) "Strengths and Weaknesses of Cultural History," *Cultural History* 1(1), 1–13.
Carr, E.H. and Davies, R.W. (1987) *What Is History? The George Macaulay Trevelyan Lectures Delivered in the University of Cambridge January-March 1961*, Harmondsworth: Penguin.
Corfield, P.J. (2008) *Making History*, Institute of Historical Research, https://archives.history.ac.uk/makinghistory/resources/articles/why_history_matters.html, accessed 3 February 2020.
Demossier, M. (2005) "Consuming Wine in France," in T. Wilson (ed), *Drinking Cultures in France*, Oxford: Berg.
Geertz, C. (1973) *The Interpretation of Cultures: Selected Essays*, New York: Basic Books.
Gorman, J. (2004) "Historians and Their Duties," *History and Theory* 43(4), 103–117.
Green, A. (2007) *Cultural History*, Basingstoke: Palgrave Macmillan.
Harding, G. (2018) *The Establishment of Champagne in Britain, 1860–1914* (D Phil, University of Oxford).
Harding, G. (2020) "The Making of Modern Champagne: How and Why the Taste for and the Taste of Champagne Changed in 19th Century Britain," *Consumption, Markets and Culture* 24(1), 6–29.
Huizinga, J. and Hopman, F.J. (1924) *The Waning of the Middle Ages: A Study of the Forms of Life, Thought and Art in France and the Netherlands in the XIVth and XVth Centuries*, London: E. Arnold.
Jackson, P. (2008) "Pierre Bourdieu, the 'Cultural Turn' and the Practice of International History," *Review of International Studies* 34(1), 155–181.
Jones, C. (2004) "Peter Mandler's 'Problem with Cultural History', or, Is Playtime Over?" *Cultural and Social History* 1(2), 209–215.
Jones, C. (2014) *The Smile Revolution in Eighteenth Century Paris*, Oxford: Oxford University Press.
Laferté, G. (2011) "The Folklorization of French Farming: Marketing Luxury Wine in the Interwar Years," *French Historical Studies* 34(4), 679–712.
Ludington, C. (2013) *The Politics of Wine in Britain: A New Cultural History*, Basingstoke: Palgrave Macmillan.
Mandelbaum, D.G. (1965) "Alcohol and Culture," *Current Anthropology* 6(3), 281–293.
Mandler, P. (2004) "The Problem with Cultural History," *Cultural and Social History* 1(1), 94–117.
Mckay, I. (1981) "Historians, Anthropology, and the Concept of Culture," *Labour/Le Travail* 8/9, 185–241.
Mennell, S., Murcott, A. and Van Otterloo, A.H. (1992) *The Sociology of Food: Eating, Diet and Culture*, London: Sage.
Norton, M. (2006) "Tasting Empire: Chocolate and the European Internalization of Mesoamerican Aesthetics," *The American Historical Review* 111(3), 660–691.
Phillips, R. (2016) *French Wine: A History*, Berkeley: University of California Press.
Pitte, J-R. (2012) *Bordeaux/Burgundy: A Vintage Rivalry*, Berkeley and London: University of California Press.
Punch, or, The London Charivari (1860, February 11), London: Bradbury & Evans, p. 59.
Rose, S. (2011) *The Wine Trade in Medieval Europe 1000–1500*, London: Continuum.
Rubin, M. (c2008) *Cultural History I: What's in a Name?* Institute of Historical Research, https://archives,history.ac.uk/makinghistory/resources/articles/cultural_history.html, accessed 9 January 2020.
Simon, A.L. (1905) *History of the Champagne Trade in England*, London: Wyman.
Simpson, J. (2005) "Cooperation and Conflicts: Institutional Innovation in France's Wine Markets, 1870–1911," *Business History Review* 79(3), 527–555.
Spiegel, G.M. (2005) *Practicing History: New Directions in Historical Writing After the Linguistic Turn*, New York and London: Routledge.
Stearns, P.N. (1998) *Why Study History?* American Historical Association, www.historians.org/about-aha-and-membership/aha-history-and-archives/historical-archives/why-study-history-(1998), accessed 7 February 2020.
Varriano, J. (2010) *Wine: A Cultural History*, London: Reaktion Books.
Wilson, T. (2004) "Globalization, Differentiation and Drinking Cultures, an Anthropological Perspective," *Anthropology of Food*, https://doi.org.10.4000.aof.261, accessed 20 February 2020.
Withington, P. (2014) "Introduction: Cultures of Intoxication," *Past & Present Supplements* 9, 9–33.
Wood, A.G. (2011) "Cultural History," in *Latin American Studies*, Oxford: Oxford University Press.

6
SOCIOLOGY, WINE AND CULTURE

Jennifer Smith Maguire

Introduction

Wine is located within a complex array of intersecting socio-cultural formations and processes. It is connected to both formal rituals and mundane practices, elites and everyday folk, tradition and technology, ranking and regulations, pleasures and conviviality. Wine's production, consumption and distribution have been shaped by agriculture, commercial culture and elite culture; it is marked by both worldwide diffusion and local differentiation. In short: wine is a fertile focus for sociology.

Sociological perspectives on wine and culture reflect the wider sociological project. Broadly, sociology involves the study of social systems and social actions. Social systems, ranging in scale and complexity, comprise interdependent elements that operate together as figurations, more than the sum of their parts. Social actions, ranging in scale and complexity, are constituted through interaction: relations with and to others. These ideas underpin a 'sociological imagination': an attempt to 'grasp history and biography and the relations between the two within society' (Mills 2000: 6). A sociological perspective is thus often oriented to decentring the individual in understanding social life: the 'individual' and 'society' are not ontologically separate entities but two sides of the same coin (Elias 1978).[1]

Core sociological problems include social structures and institutions (e.g. the state, market, family, politics, religion), identities and roles (e.g. associated with class, gender, race/ethnicity), patterns of differentiation and stratification (including questions of authority, power and inequality) and processes of social reproduction and change. Culture is central to understanding these problems. Cultural forms, both material (objects, artefacts and physical structures involved in social life) and non-material (symbols, norms, values, beliefs, discourses), permeate and animate social life.

The development of cultural sociology and cultural studies, and the social science 'cultural turn' more generally, have underlined the intertwined, co-constitutive roles of culture and economy in the lived practices and social reproduction of various fields, institutions and practices (Santoro 2011; Warde 2014). Sociological questions of culture are less about what culture *is* and more about how and what culture *does* (and by and for whom). How does culture shape the development, character and functioning of social systems? How do artefacts, symbols, values and norms shape the course and consequences of social actions? And who and what 'speak' and are 'muted' in the process?

Key research concerns and themes

There is no sociology of wine *per se*. Sociological research on wine and culture spans the sociology of culture, economic sociology, sociology of science, organisation studies, tourism studies and sub-fields focused on place, food, taste and consumption.[2] Overall, such research is concerned with understanding how various material products, symbolic means and discourses, norms and beliefs have enabled and constrained specific ways of 'doing wine'. In turn, this entails an interest in how specific ways of thinking, feeling, talking, making, using, judging, sensing, sharing, pricing, marketing and regulating wine are implicated in the reproduction of larger social systems and sociological processes. In foregrounding the significance of context, sociological research on wine and culture tends to be methodologically diverse, spanning – and often combining – both interviews and field observations (and occasionally sustained ethnographic fieldwork) to examine the lived experiences of the social actors, and archival, media and material analyses to examine the representations, devices, sites and artefacts that constitute socio-cultural wine figurations at particular points in time and/or as they develop over time.

Cultural dynamics shape the social systems of wine in various ways. National cultural contexts underpin the development of different systems of classification (Zhao 2008) and distribution (Ouvrard and Taplin 2018). Conventions and myths (e.g. what counts as 'quality' winemaking) shape production practices, price formation, market barriers and product differentiation (Beckert *et al.* 2017; Garcia-Parpet 2008; Hills *et al.* 2013). At the same time, wine has a powerful capacity to signify place, prestige and heritage, serving as repository and marker of social, cultural and symbolic capital (Bourdieu 1984). As a result, wine norms, values and material objects feature in the ongoing accomplishment of everyday social structures such as class and national identities (Brierley-Jones *et al.* 2014; Howland 2019; Spielmann *et al.* 2020) and large-scale processes such as globalisation and democratisation (Inglis and Almila 2020; Howland 2013).

Three interrelated themes characterise recent research in this area. First: wine and the 'doing' of wine are understood as contingent results of highly distributed social actions. Multiple actors and organisations shape wine's social relations of use. Consumers, cultural producers and cultural intermediaries – winemakers, winery staff, marketing representatives, journalists, critics, sommeliers, restaurateurs, educators and wine scholars – play roles in the cultural construction of the meaning and value of wine. A wine's properties are not objective, static attributes but outcomes of socio-cultural processes of qualification (Dans *et al.* 2019; Smith Maguire 2013), consecration (Allen and Germov 2011), classification (Karpik 2010; Zhao 2005) and quantification (Phillips 2016). The work of 'making wine' encompasses not only the vineyard, winery and winemaking paraphernalia (e.g. Mitchell *et al.* 2012) but also settings and devices such as wine fairs (Vannini *et al.* 2010), blind tasting practices (Teil 2001), critical reviews and buying guides (Karpik 2010).

Second: discourses of legitimacy and processes of legitimation shape the cultural production and consumption of wine. Ideas about what is (and is not) 'good' coalesce and become concretised over time as relatively coherent, stable systems. For example, accumulated symbolic capital (e.g. celebrity winemakers, critical acclaim) enables high-status wine brands to influence the marketplace (Humphreys and Carpenter 2018). Associations with luxury and elite lifestyles are central to the long-term market dominance of champagne (Rokka 2015), the rise of 'cult' wines (Taplin 2016) and the rehabilitation of rosé (Fitzmaurice 2017). A discourse of fine winemaking is especially crucial in shaping how wine is made, priced, bought, consumed and evaluated. Despite local variations and tensions (e.g. around the fidelity due to tradition; Negro *et al.* 2011), the global cultural regime of fine winemaking is characterised by shared conventions, including an emphasis on terroir and place, heritage, artisanal craft, uniqueness, a disavowal of commercial motives and authenticity (Beverland 2005; Diaz-Bone 2013; Krzywoszynska 2015; González and Dans 2018; Rössel *et al.* 2018; Smith Maguire 2018b).

These two themes intersect in conceptualising terroir as a contingent outcome of various actors and organisations attempting to make terroir 'real' and to articulate, defend and monopolise terroir-based quality claims (Carter 2019; Fourcade 2012; Teil 2012). While the 'Old World' (especially France) is the typical referent for terroir discourses, research highlights the locally specific cultural constructions of 'New World' terroir in Canada (Cappeliez 2017; Voronov et al. 2013), China (Zheng 2019) and Israel/Palestine (Monterescu and Handel 2020). Even in regions with long-institutionalised terroir conventions, new ideas about what constitutes terroir, and how best to express it, continue to emerge, leading to contestation among producers, critics and industry organisations (Smith Maguire and Charters 2021).

Third: wine is fundamentally bound up with questions of taste. Taste is a significant hinge linking individuals and society: it is shaped (not determined) by culture in the form of pre-existing know-how, vocabularies and aesthetic hierarchies (Bourdieu 1984). This has several implications for wine. The taste *of* wine is impacted by culturally legitimate preferences and practices into which tasters are socialised. This is not only a matter of learning to taste wine according to established conventions (e.g. detecting acidity and tannin) but also a matter of 'completing' the wine itself. That is, the embodied sensation of wine tasting can be understood as a situated activity that manifests a wine's properties (e.g. varietal typicity, terroir influences) through what the taster selectively attaches their attention to (Hennion 2007; Schwarz 2013). Additionally, taste is a device impacting how wine is made. A producer's sense of taste will inform judgements throughout production from grape to glass, steering towards more or less emphasis on quality, terroir and commercial success (Scott Morton and Podolny 2002; Smith Maguire 2018a). Considered a sign of 'good taste', the taste *for* wine also plays a part in the reproduction of social stratification (who is/is not considered a proper wine consumer or producer) and contestations over boundaries around legitimate culture (what is/is not considered a worthy wine or manner of drinking). These dynamics become especially apparent through disruptions to established wine cultures, as with the emergence of new groups of wine consumers in China (Smith Maguire and Lim 2015; Smith Maguire and Zhang 2017), and invite further research on the wine world's social structural conditions of inclusion and exclusion.

A sociological imagination simultaneously places wine within its cultural and structural contexts, seeking to critically decentre wine, winemakers and wine consumers in understanding how wine is 'done'. Wine has served as a productive lens through which to sharpen sociological conceptualisations of legitimacy, taste, status and value and the cultural dynamics of markets and production. However, much work remains to be done, particularly around core disciplinary concerns with power, stratification and the reproduction of inequality – for example, in relation to the absence of (often migrant) vineyard labourers and lack of ethnic diversity in normative discourses of fine wine. As climate destabilisation, globalisation and technology (among other factors) disrupt established features of wine's cultural production and consumption, wine remains a fertile focus through which to explore the ongoing, contingent and contested accomplishment of social worlds.

Notes

1 A comprehensive account of sociology is clearly beyond the scope of the chapter. Useful introductions can be found in Elias (1978), Mills ([1959]2000), Johnson (1995) and Thompson et al. (2019). It should be noted that sociology, like any social science discipline, encompasses a range of ontological and epistemological positions and may overlap with (for example) the macroscopic orientation of economics, the microscopic orientation of anthropology or the developmental orientation of history in making sense of how the present is structured, how it is experienced and how it emerges out of the past.
2 This is neither an exhaustive list nor a suggestion that sociological research on wine is necessarily undertaken either by self-declared sociologists or under the disciplinary umbrella of sociology.

References

Allen, M.P. and Germov, J. (2011) "Judging Taste and Creating Value: The Cultural Consecration of Australian Wines," *Journal of Sociology* 47(1), 35–51.

Beckert, J., Rössel, J. and Schenk, P. (2017) "Wine as a Cultural Product: Symbolic Capital and Price Formation in the Wine Field," *Sociological Perspectives* 60(1), 206–222.

Beverland, M.B. (2005) "Crafting Brand Authenticity: The Case of Luxury Wines," *Journal of Management Studies* 42(5), 1003–1029.

Bourdieu, P. (1984) *Distinction: A Social Critique of the Judgement of Taste*, Cambridge, MA: Harvard University Press.

Brierley-Jones, L., Ling, J., McCabe, K.E., Wilson, G.B., Crosland, A., Kaner, E.F.S. and Haighton, C.A. (2014) "Habitus of Home and Traditional Drinking: A Qualitative Analysis of Reported Middle-Class Alcohol Use," *Sociology of Health and Illness* 36(7), 1054–1076.

Cappeliez, S. (2017) "How Well Does Terroir Travel? Illuminating Cultural Translation Using a Comparative Wine Case Study," *Poetics* 65, 24–36.

Carter, E. (2019) "From Myths to Markets: Power, Institutions, and the Reification of Imagined Histories," *European Journal of Sociology* 60(2), 211–236.

Dans, E.P., González, P.A. and Vázquez, A.M. (2019) "Taste and Knowledge: The Social Construction of Quality in the Organic Wine Market," *Human Ecology* 47, 135–143.

Diaz-Bone, R. (2013) "Discourse Conventions in the Construction of Wine Qualities in the Wine Market," *Economic Sociology: The European Electronic Newsletter, Max Planck Institute for the Study of Societies (MPIfG), Cologne* 14(2), 46–53.

Elias, N. [1970] (1978) *What Is Sociology?* trans. S. Mennell, London: Hutchinson & Co.

Fitzmaurice, C. (2017) "How Rosé Became High Class: Categorical Divestment and Evaluation," *Poetics* 61, 1–13.

Fourcade, M. (2012) "The Vile and the Noble: On the Relation Between Natural and Social Classifications in the French Wine World," *The Sociological Quarterly* 53, 524–545.

Garcia-Parpet, M.-F. (2008) "Markets, Prices and Symbolic Value: Grands Crus and the Challenges of Global Markets," *International Review of Sociology* 18(2), 237–252.

González, P.A. and Dans, E.P. (2018) "The 'Terroirist' Social Movement: The Reawakening of Wine Culture in Spain," *Journal of Rural Studies* 61, 184–196.

Hennion, A. (2007) "Those Things That Hold Us Together: Taste and Sociology," *Cultural Sociology* 1(1), 97–114.

Hills, S., Voronov, M. and Hinings, C.R. (2013) "Putting New Wine in Old Bottles: Utilizing Rhetorical History to Overcome Stigma Associated with a Previously Dominant Logic," in M. Lounsbury and E. Boxenbaum (eds), *Institutional Logics in Action, Part B (Research in the Sociology of Organizations*, 39(B), 99–137), Bingley: Emerald Publishing.

Howland, P.J. (2013) "Distinction by Proxy: The Democratization of Fine Wine," *Journal of Sociology* 49(2–3), 325–340.

Howland, P.J. (2019) "Drinking the Divine: Fine Wine, Religion and the Socio-Political in Aotearoa New Zealand," *Journal of Wine Research* 30(4), 275–293.

Humphreys, A. and Carpenter, G.S. (2018) "Status Games: Market Driving Through Social Influence in the U.S. Wine Industry," *Journal of Marketing* 82, 141–159.

Inglis, D. and Almila, A-M. (eds) (2020) *The Globalization of Wine*, London: Bloomsbury Academic.

Johnson, A.G. (1995) *The Blackwell Dictionary of Sociology: A User's Guide to Sociological Language*, Oxford: Blackwell Publishers.

Karpik, Lucien. (2010) *Valuing the Unique: The Economics of Singularities*, Princeton, NJ: Princeton University Press.

Krzywoszynska, A. (2015) "Wine Is Not Coca-Cola: Marketization and Taste in Alternative Food Networks," *Agriculture and Human Values* 32, 491–503.

Mills, C. Wright. [1959] (2000) *The Sociological Imagination*, Oxford: Oxford University Press.

Mitchell, R., Charters, S. and Albrecht, J. (2012) "Cultural Systems and the Wine Tourism Product," *Annals of Tourism Research* 39(1), 311–335.

Monterescu, D. and Handel, A. (2020) "Terroir and Territory on the Colonial Frontier: Making New-Old World Wine in the Holy Land," *Comparative Studies in Society and History* 62(2), 222–261.

Negro, G., Hannan, M.T. and Rao, H. (2011) "Category Reinterpretation and Defection: Modernism and Tradition in Italian Winemaking," *Organization Science* 22(6), 1449–1463.

Ouvrard, S. and Taplin, I.M. (2018) "Trading in Fine Wine: Institutionalized Efficiency in the Place de Bordeaux System," *Global Business and Organizational Excellence* 37(5), 14–20.

Phillips, C.J. (2016) "The Taste Machine: Sense, Subjectivity, and Statistics in the California Wine World," *Social Studies of Science* 46(3), 461–481.

Rokka, J. (2015) "Champagne: Marketplace Icon," *Consumption, Markets & Culture* 20(3), 275–283.

Rössel, J., Schenk, P. and Eppler, D. (2018) "The Emergence of Authentic Products: The Transformation of Wine Journalism in Germany, 1947–2008," *Journal of Consumer Culture* 18(3), 453–473.

Santoro, M. (2011) "From Bourdieu to Cultural Sociology," *Cultural Sociology* 5(1), 3–23.

Schwarz, Ori. (2013) "Bending Forward, One Step Backward: On the Sociology of Tasting Techniques," *Cultural Sociology* 7(4), 415–430.

Scott Morton, F.M. and Podolny, J.M. (2002) "Love or Money? The Effects of Owner Motivation in the California Wine Industry," *Journal of Industrial Economics*, L(4), 431–456.

Smith Maguire, J. (2013) "Provenance as a Filtering and Framing Device in the Qualification of Wine," *Consumption, Markets and Culture* 16(4), 368–391.

Smith Maguire, J. (2018a) "Taste as Market Practice: The Example of 'Natural' Wine," in A. Venkatesh, S. Cross, C. Ruvalcaba and R. Belk (eds), *Consumer Culture Theory Research in Consumer Behavior*, 19, 71–92, Bingley: Emerald Publishing.

Smith Maguire, J. (2018b) "The Taste for the Particular: A Logic of Discernment in an Age of Omnivorousness," *Journal of Consumer Culture* 18(1), 3–20.

Smith Maguire, J. and Charters, S. (2021) "Aesthetic Logics, *Terroir* and the Lamination of Grower Champagne," *Consumption, Markets and Culture* 24(1), 75–96, https://doi.org/10.1080/10253866.2020.1730823.

Smith Maguire, J. and Lim, M. (2015) "Lafite in China: Media Representations of 'Wine Culture' in New Markets," *Journal of Macromarketing* 35(2), 229–242.

Smith Maguire, J. and Zhang, D. (2017) "Shifting the Focus from Consumers to Cultural Intermediaries: An Example from the Emerging Chinese Fine Wine Market," in D. Rinallo, N. Özçaglar-Toulouse and R. Belk (eds), *Consumer Culture Theory Research in Consumer Behavior*, 18, 3–27, Bingley: Emerald Publishing.

Spielmann, N., Smith Maguire, J. and Charters, S. (2020) "Product Patriotism: How Consumption Practices Make and Maintain National Identity," *Journal of Business Research*, 1–11, https://doi.org/10.1016/j.jbusres.2018.05.024.

Taplin, Ian M. (2016) "Crafting an Iconic Wine: The Rise of 'Cult' Napa," *International Journal of Wine Business Research* 28(2), 105–119.

Teil, G. (2001) "La production du jugement esthétique sur les vins par la critique vinicole," *Sociologie du travail* 43, 67–89.

Teil, G. (2012) "No Such Thing as Terroir? Objectivities and the Regimes of Existence of Objects," *Science, Technology, and Human Values* 37(5), 478–505.

Thompson, W.E., Hickey, J.V. and Thompson, M.L. (2019) *Society in Focus: An Introduction to Sociology*, 9th edition, Lanham, MD: Rowman and Littlefield Publishers.

Vannini, P., Ahluwalia-Lopez, G., Waskul, D. and Gottschalk, S. (2010) "Performing Taste at Wine Festivals: A Somatic Layered Account of Material Culture," *Qualitative Inquiry* 16(5), 378–396.

Voronov, M., De Clercq, D. and Hinings, C.R. (2013) "Institutional Complexity and Logic Engagement: An Investigation of Ontario Fine Wine," *Human Relations* 66(12), 1563–1596.

Warde, A. (2014) "After Taste: Culture, Consumption and Theories of Practice," *Journal of Consumer Culture* 14(3), 279–303.

Zhao, W. (2005) "Understanding Classifications: Empirical Evidence from the American and French Wine Industries," *Poetics* 33, 179–200.

Zhao, W. (2008) "Social Categories, Classification Systems, and Determinants of Wine Price in the California and French Wine Industries," *Sociological Perspectives* 51(1), 163–199.

Zheng, X. (2019) "Narrating Terroir: The Place-Making of Wine in China's Southwest," *Food, Culture & Society* 22(3), 280–298.

7
TEXT, WINE AND CULTURE

Jacqueline Dutton

Introduction

Wine cultures have been shaped by text since the first representations of making and drinking wine emerged in the images and sculptures of ancient peoples in the Fertile Crescent and the Mediterranean. As writing became a more nuanced means of communicating facts as well as ideas, more complex narratives around wine developed in the form of manuals on how to make wine (Hesiod and Strabo) and philosophers' treatises on how to drink it (Plato and Pliny). Religious rituals related to wine were recorded in pictorial and scriptural texts which differentiated wine cultures throughout the region. Over the following millennia, wine cultures were practised and performed, repeated and revised through the written word as information and appreciation were communicated in this textual form for posterity. When the mechanics of the wine press inspired Gutenberg's first inklings for the printing press in the 1430s, wine and text were effectively elided as intertwined cultural products. The printing press offered possibilities to disseminate viticultural advice, wine rankings and prices and, therefore, comparative (dis)advantages more widely across the industry. Much later, the advent of journalism, photography, film, advertising, criticism and the multiple digital modes of media and storytelling that exist today have expanded the ways of recounting wine cultures through text. In parallel, these texts influence the evolution of the wine cultures they represent through increased interaction and exposure.

'Text' as the focus of this disciplinary (or positioning) chapter requires some definition and explanation. Clearly, 'text' is not a discipline in the same way that anthropology, business, economics, geography, history and sociology are recognised as discrete fields of academic study. Nor is 'text' a particularly stable term, given its broad usage in both mainstream and academic discourses, across practically every discipline, though with differing weight and meaning, because it refers generally to the content rather than the genre of a given work. In cultural studies, following the post-structuralist semiotic approach proposed by Roland Barthes in 'De l'œuvre au texte' [From Work to Text] (1971), 'text' can refer to any cultural object – not just printed matter – that has representational or symbolic value, offering multi-dimensional layers of understanding and encouraging reader engagement. Texts are therefore semiotic systems, combinations of signs or signifiers, signifieds and mechanisms – like metaphors or metonyms – that can be read with reference to certain cultural contexts in order to decode their meanings.

According to this interpretation, all the ways of representing wine mentioned in the introductory paragraph – from ancient cave paintings to digital media – are considered wine texts. A wide variety of wine texts are used across all the chapters in this *Handbook*, ranging from wine bottles and labels to historical archives, from anthropological and sociological data sets to geographical and geological analyses, from interviews to intertextual referencing. Text is arguably the most interdisciplinary thread in this multifaceted series of studies, interwoven into every element of wine and culture and serving as a support for more dominant disciplinary attachments. As a result, it facilitates our understanding of both material and immaterial cultures of wine.

Three textual fields in wine culture

The transversal and ubiquitous presence of the text in research on wine and culture renders attempts to outline core concepts, key thinkers and prominent themes problematic. In lieu of an introduction to a discipline as a cultural field, this chapter offers three textual fields that draw inspiration from and contribute to wine culture: literature, art and film. These fields are constituted through production of texts rather than historical events, demographic categories or marketing practices. They are not included, nor could they be readily classified in the other disciplinary areas of study of this *Handbook*. Yet they are highly relevant to understanding the ways in which wine is represented across the range of cultural products we are referring to as texts.

Literature, wine and culture

Wine is often interpreted as a muse in literature and the arts. Wine inspires and liberates true creative genius, as Pliny the Elder's famous quote neatly encapsulates: *In vino veritas* [In wine is truth]. The relationship between intoxication and inspiration has been the subject of many studies in cognitive theory and creativity, which indicate that the disinhibiting effects of alcohol improve divergent thinking, originality and creative cognition, though higher levels of consumption can impair creative productivity (Benedek *et al.* 2017; Norlander 1999; Norlander and Gustafson 1998). But wine is not just alcohol – it is inspirational in its own creative form and also unleashes creativity by consumption. Some of the world's best-known writers, artists and composers have articulated their praise for wine through metaphors relating their creative choices, practices and outputs to wine itself. In her novel *Jacob's Room*, Virginia Woolf's Erasmus Cowan recites luscious lines from the classical Roman poets Virgil and Catullus 'as if language were wine upon his lips' (Woolf 2005: 34). Surrealist artist Salvador Dali renders wine a mystery in *The Wines of Gala*: 'A real connoisseur does not drink wine but tastes of its secrets' (Dali 2017). And the memorable metaphor by composer Robert Fripp equates wine with music to fill the void: 'Music is the wine that fills the cup of silence' (Fripp 1980: 34–35).

The rich polysemy of wine – its capacity to contain so many allusions, including language, mystery and music – makes it an evocative word for any writer to use. As a metaphor, it flows from the ancient Greek writer Homer's 'wine-dark sea' frequently employed in *The Iliad* and *The Odyssey* to contemporary French author Michel Houellebecq's Meursault as a symbol of purity – 'the perfect synthesis of all wine' – in his 2015 novel *Submission* (Dutton 2020). 'Wine as metaphor' is the subject of another chapter in this *Handbook*, but here the aim is to present some studies of wine and literature and demonstrate the scope that exists for further work on the literary analysis of wine.

In *Wine Reads: A Literary Anthology of Wine Writing*, published in 2018, Jay McInerney brings together a selection of 27 texts about wine from a range of fictional and nonfictional sources. Announced as 'the first of its kind' and edited by a respected wine writer in his own right, *Wine Reads* does fill a gap in English-language publications. Its contents range from Roald Dahl's sinister story 'Taste', about a dinner guest who bets high stakes on his ability to guess the wine served by his host, to an extract from Stephanie Danler's *Sweetbitter*, the runaway success debut novel of a sommelier's experience in high-end New York restaurants. There are also texts by well-known wine writers Jancis Robinson, Matt Kramer, Kermit Lynch and Eric Asimov, many of whom incorporate literary references and allusions into their work. Several wine writers have academic backgrounds in literary studies, like Lisa Perrotti-Brown MW, current editor in chief of *Wine Advocate*, who was a playwright in London before entering the wine world and Hugh Johnson OBE, who read English literature at Cambridge.

Despite this wealth of literary knowledge to draw on, as well as a wide variety of novels, poetry and plays written in English that do feature wine as a dominant theme, most references to and reviews of wine literature are found in the columns of wine magazines such as *Decanter, World of Fine Wine*, and *Wine Advocate* or on an established wine blog rather than published in a book or scholarly article dedicated to the subject. *Wine Reads* does not extend the anthology genre to offer any critical insights into wine and literature. There are few academic articles on wine in literature either: Anne Lill's 'Wine and a Trial of Character in Horace's Poems' appeared in the *Journal of Wine Research* in 2000, and my own work on 'Wine in Houellebecq', published in *French Cultural Studies* in 2020, are among the rare examples of such criticism in English. The lack of appropriate venues for publishing on the intersections of wine and literature may be at the root of this lacuna, with specialised academic wine journals catering to more widely accepted areas of interest – viticulture, business, history, geography – and literary journals less open to accepting such trope-focused papers. Studies of wine in ancient Persian poetry and in biblical texts are more readily located, but there is a serious dearth of mainstream and specialist texts on wine in literature in English.

In European winemaking cultures, there is longer-standing and more evident interest in the intersections of wine and literature – and the arts. Interdisciplinary research groups, such as the Centre d'Etudes et de Recherche sur la Vigne et le Vin (CERVIN), created in the humanities section of the University of Bordeaux (Université Michel de Montaigne-Bordeaux 3) in 1970 by a professor of geography, Alain Huetz de Lemps, included literature scholars alongside geographers, historians, sociologists, anthropologists and many others. Although geography was the founding and dominant disciplinary attachment of many of CERVIN's members, conferences and publications also included research on wine and literature (https://cervinbordeaux.monsite-orange.fr/). Today, it is part of the Institut Universitaire de la Vigne et du Vin (Bordeaux), which also embraces interdisciplinary research (www.isvv.u-bordeaux.fr/fr/cervin.html). In 2016, professor emerita of comparative literature Ana Maria Binet and professor of oenology Gilles de Revel launched 'Les Vendanges du savoir' [Vintages of Knowledge] in collaboration with the Fondation pour la culture et les civilisations du vin at the Cité du Vin in Bordeaux (www.isvv.u-bordeaux.fr/fr/isvv/les-vendanges-du-savoir.html). Many of the speakers on the monthly programme are academics from literature programmes, as well as best-selling authors such as Amélie Nothomb.

Such interdisciplinary hubs for wine research exist elsewhere in France – including the dynamic UNESCO Chair 'Culture and Tradition of Wine' at the University of Burgundy, held by Professor Jocelyne Pérard. The conferences and publications hosted by this organisation since 2007 are internationally renowned and highly prestigious, including literature and the arts as well as philosophy among its privileged disciplines (https://chaireunesco-vinetculture.u-bourgogne.fr/). Burgundy is also home to the only dedicated wine book fair in the world, 'Livres en vignes' at Clos Vougeot, dating from 2007, and one of the most well-resourced specialist wine bookshops, the Athenaeum in Beaune (www.athenaeum.com/).

The proximity of major universities and cultural centres to winegrowing regions is key to the cross-pollination of literary text, wine and culture. All these intellectual and commercial supports for publishing a wider range of scholarly and mainstream writing on wine have had an impact on studies in the field of wine and French literature. Anthologies abound, ranging from Sophie Guermès's *Le Vin et l'encre* [Wine and Ink] (1997), the three-volume *Le Vin des Ecrivains* [Writers' Wines] series edited by Jean-Noël Mouret for Mercure de France (1999) and Pierre Cordier's *Lectures du vin* [Reading Wine] (2000) to slightly more critical approaches in recent years, with *Les Ecrivains du vin* [Writers on Wine] by Marc Lagrange and Philippe Lorin (2017). In this illustrated volume,

Lagrange and Lorin associate authors with their preferred wines: Colette and Jurançon, Houellebecq and Gewurztraminer, Rabelais and Chinon etc., and the follow-up volume *Les Ecrivains du champagne* (2021) performs similar pairings with '*les grandes marques*': Voltaire and Aÿ, Amélie Nothomb and Laurent Perrier, as well as classics like de Gaulle and Drappier and Churchill and Pol Roger. However, there is still very little analysis, except in the specialised interdisciplinary collections such as *Vin et altérité: le vin à l'épreuve des sciences humaines* [Wine and Alterity: Wine in the Social Sciences] (2020), which includes four articles on wine in literature, notably in the poetry of Henriette de Coligny, Countess of La Suze and Baudelaire, and in *La Nouvelle Héloïse* by Rousseau.

As might be expected, Italy, Spain, Portugal, Greece and Germany have their own wine literatures, which have not been much studied by academics either. Italian wine writers Giusi Mainardi and Pierstefano Berta's *Il vino nella storia e nella letteratura: feste, magie, storie e leggende di un simbolo universale: il fascino del vino raccontato attraverso la letteratura* [Wine in History and Literature: Feasts, Magic, Stories and Legends of a Universal Symbol: The Charm of Wine Told through Literature] (1991) is an excellent study of wine in literature, as is Pietro Gibellini's chapter on wine in the works of Alessandro Manzoni and Giovanni Verga (2003). Regional studies like *La vite e il vino nell'arte nella letteratura del Friuli* [Vine and Wine in the Art and Literature of Friuli] by G. Bergamini and M. Michelutti (2007) are more descriptive anthologies, like Spanish wine specialist Serafin Quero's *El vino: historia, arte, literature* [Wine: History, Art, Literature] (2008). Portuguese pharmacist Luis Falcao da Fonseca's *Aspectos Socio-Culturais do Vinho – arqueologica, literatura, arte* [Socio-Cultural Aspects of Wine – Archaeology, Literature, Art] (2008) is one of many examples revealing wine and literature as the domain of the amateur rather than the academic, while Fernando Pessoa's much-cited appreciation of wine should surely provide scope for research: '*Boa é a vida, mas melhor é o vinho*' [Life is good, but wine is better].

One of the more unusual literary wine texts is the Japanese *manga* – comic book series – entitled *Kami no shizuku* [Drops of God] by Tadashi Agi and Shu Okimoto (2004–2014), which has been translated into many languages and has had phenomenal success around the world. The series traces the protagonist's quest to identify and evaluate 12 famous wines – the '12 apostles' – and finally the 13th, known as the 'Drops of God'. This challenge was created by his famous wine-writer father to ensure that his son would understand the value and power of wine before inheriting his wine collection. *Kami no shizuku* features in much mainstream and academic criticism in several different languages, including two recent articles in English by Nadine Normand-Marconnet and Jason Jones on anthropomorphic wine metaphors and cross-cultural translation (2016, 2020). Mo Yan's brilliant satirical novel 酒國 (Jiǔguó) [The Republic of Wine](2000 [1992]) is a political statement on representations of wine in Chinese culture as a sign of decadence (Yang 1998), but there is little criticism in English on this novel, despite Yan's Nobel Prize–winning status.

The range and scope of literary texts on wine are much broader and more diverse than the examples mentioned, whether they emerge from winegrowing regions or from areas that do not produce their own wines. However, the relative lack of academic criticism on literary texts, wine and culture presents a field for future scholarly exploration, following in the footsteps of a few lone researchers and some interdisciplinary teams, notably in France. The value of such enquiry is considerable, contributing to understanding metaphors; (cross)-cultural representations; discourse analysis; and regional, national and transnational identities formed through wine growing, production and consumption.

Art, wine and culture

Works of art, including realist works, are narratives to be read like texts, redolent with pictorial semiotics and charged with symbolic messages (Bal and Bryson 1991). One of the most frequently used art wine images is Caravaggio's 'Bacchus' (1596), depicting a young man, who may well be Caravaggio himself, dressed in Greco-Roman attire with an almost overflowing chalice of wine, surrounded by decaying fruit and vine leaves. Caravaggio's painting has prompted addiction specialists Carolina L. Haass-Koffler and George A. Kenna (2013) to diagnose the figure with alcohol use disorder – drawing also on Caravaggio's earlier portrait 'Sick Bacchus' (1593–94). This is one of the more unusual examples of scholarship related to wine art, whereas art historian John Varriano's *Wine: A Cultural History* (2010) is much more traditional in its approach to reading wine artworks. The wine god figure recurs frequently – in the form of Bacchus or Dionysius – as in Michelangelo's sculpture of 'Bacchus' (1496–97) and Diego Velasquez's '*El Triunfo di Baco o Los Borrachos*' [The Triumph of Bacchus] (1628–29); scholars like Philippe Morel have studied these figures in art in *Renaissance dionysiaque: inspiration bachique, imaginaire du vin et de la vigne dans l'art européen (1430–1680)* [Dionysian Renaissance: Bacchic Inspiration, the imaginary of wine and vine in European Art (1430–1680)] (2014). However, as art historians like Varriano demonstrate, ancient Egyptian, Phoenician, Greek and Etruscan frescos and medieval tableaux by Dutch, Flemish and Italian masters showed people planting and tending vines, picking grapes and making wine and drinking the fruits of their labours. While Renaissance and Classical artworks tend to focus on mythical representations of wine, Romantic, Impressionist, and Post-Impressionist paintings depict both production and consumption of wine in al fresco scenes by Claude Monet and August Renoir, Joan Miro's '*La Bottiglia di vino*' [The Bottle of Wine] (1924) and Jean Dupas's Art Deco symbolist work '*La Vigne et le vin*' (1925).

Hellenic amphorae and drinking vessels were often decorated with artworks, beginning the trend of beautifying the receptable for the wine while identifying (and adding prestige branding to) its source. Château Mouton-Rothschild is undoubtedly the best-known contemporary proponent of this trend, commissioning every year since 1945 the world's finest artists – ranging from Dali, Picasso and Chagall to Warhol, Kandinsky and Xu Bing – to paint a picture for their labels (Ray 1974; Rothschild and Beaumarchais 1983; Herman and Pascal 2003). While there are beautiful books displaying the labels and a few more insightful books and articles (Caldeway and House 2003; Dickenson 2001; Croidieu *et al.* 2017), there is no significant semiotic or art-oriented research published on this extraordinary corpus. Critical studies of the Leeuwin Art Series labels (Negrin 2015) and decoding cross-cultural images on wine labels (Dutton and Normand-Marconnet 2019) contribute to the emerging scholarship on art wine labels, but there is more research oriented towards reading wine labels as text for marketing and brand positioning (Celhay and Remaud 2018). Art in wine advertising is another important area to be further explored (Unwin 1992; Venturini 1988), with champagne posters being the most closely analysed to date (Guy 2003; Rabaudy Montoussin 1998; Bonal 1990).

Philanthropy is another bridge often observed between art and wine. Many wineries around the world fund emerging and established artists, including residencies and sponsored exhibitions. However interesting these links may be for promotion of art through wine and vice versa, this relationship rarely results in the production of wine texts as wine is not normally a criterion for selection of artists or artworks.

Film, wine and culture

Hundreds of films feature wine in a starring role, as a meaningful symbol or in many other guises. *Sideways* (2004) is the most cited, studied and appreciated wine film in the world to date. Its real impact on the sales of merlot, which was derided by the tragic protagonist Miles, versus pinot noir, which he revered, was more anecdotal than evidence based, as Cuellar *et al.* (2009) have shown. Yet it inaugurated a new trend of wine-focused Hollywood-style films that portray vineyards, winemakers and the wine industry as culturally significant markers in a cinematic dichotomy that attributes value to authentic wine experiences and condemns those that fall short. *A Good Year* (2006) followed in this vein soon after, then *Bottleshock* (2008), which presents a fictionalised dramatisation of the 1976 'Judgement of Paris'. These filmic texts and many others are analysed by Raphaël Schirmer in

'Holly[wine] ou le vin dans le cinéma américain' [Holly(wine) or Wine in the American Cinema] (2014), which in turn draws on Bernardo Sanchez Salas's *El Cine del Vino* [The Cinema of Wine] (2007) to establish its corpus of 100 American fictional films referencing wine – in a central or marginal way – dating from 1932 to 2012. Schirmer identifies several stages in the journey towards representing American wine appreciation, from the early 'apprenticeship' films through democratisation, to develop a new discourse on wine that foregrounds greater connoisseurship, including knowledge of specific varieties, styles and refined practices of production and degustation. He concludes that American cinema's soft power has initiated and empowered American and global audiences to integrate wine as a positive, glamourous yet accessible product for consumption by all.

The French cinematic tradition contains many fictional films with wine references, but recent examples such as *Tu seras mon fils* [You Will Be My Son] (2011), *Premiers crus* [First Growths] (2015), and *Ce qui nous lie* [Back to Burgundy] (2017) extend the genre in new directions to explore current issues, including identity and heritage, family dynamics and economic pressures, in an increasingly globalised industry. Other European cinemas also include references to their winemaking regions and products, but it is interesting that outside America, there are very few feature-length fictionalised narratives about New World winemaking that focus on vineyards, winemakers and the wine industry.

Documentaries about winemaking and wine drinking are a different category of text altogether. In the same year that *Sideways* launched a new global discourse via the American wine film, the French-American production by Jonathan Nossiter *Mondovino* (2004) presented a new challenge to the rapidly globalising wine industry, exposing flaws in a system that seemed to be encouraging homogenisation rather than terroir-based differentiation in winemaking. Nominated for a prestigious competition slot in the official selection of the 2004 Cannes Film Festival, *Mondovino* quickly became a global phenomenon, even though Nossiter did not win the Palme d'Or, which went to fellow documentary disruptor Michael Moore with *Fahrenheit 9/11* (2004). Even more widely analysed than *Sideways*, *Mondovino* has attracted Bourdieusian critiques (Halley 2018) as well as psychoanalytical perspectives (Beuvelet 2011) and socio-economic international market studies (Roese 2008). The spinoff ten-part series of the same name released in 2006 was not as successful, but the cinematic storytelling of the wine world had started, and the documentary proved its best medium.

By 2010, wine documentary films were arriving in cinemas, on television screens and on streaming platforms, and instead of just Europe and America, they covered the world. The Northern Arizona wine industry is unpacked in *Blood into Wine* (2010) and Australia in *Chateau Chunder: A Wine Revolution* (2012). The classic Old World regions of Bordeaux, Burgundy and Champagne were depicted in *Red Obsession* (2013), *A Year in Burgundy* (2013) and *A Year in Champagne* (2014), and Italy's Barolo featured in *Barolo Boys* (2014). The duo of Argentinian films *El Camino del vino* [The Ways of Wine] (2010) followed by *El duelo del vino* [The Duel of Wine] (2015) by Nicolás Carreras are about a famous sommelier, Charlie Arturaola, losing his palate and searching for it again, in a strange mélange of staged and documentary scenes. The American series of three *Somm* movies (2012, 2015, 2018) was more clearly aspirational, presenting candidates competing in the notoriously difficult master sommelier exam. The exposé-style documentary continued with *Sour Grapes* (2016) about convicted wine fraud Rudy Kurniawan and the international network of wine people around him, whereas *Bitter Grapes* (2016), by contrast, denounced exploitation in the South African wine industry. The Napa Valley is celebrated in *Decanted* (2016) and the New Zealand wine industry in *A Seat at the Table* (2019).

These cinematic texts have found a home in various wine film festivals, the most famous being the mobile feast of Oenovideo, held in a different French wine region each year since 1993 (www.oenovideo.com/). The MOST festival in its tenth edition in 2021 is held in the Vinseum of Catalunya in Barcelona (www.mostfestival.cat/el-festival/), and the online International Wine Film Festival, which began in 2015 in Santa Barbara, showcases short and feature films about wine (http://

winefilmfestival.com/). There is clearly so much to be written about the burgeoning corpus of fictional and documentary films on wine and the events dedicated to promoting them. And there are also many opportunities to make more films about the rich and complex world(s) of wine.

Conclusion

Text, wine and culture are inextricably linked throughout history and into the present, but there is relatively little scholarly research that focuses on the textual interplay of wine and literature, wine and art or wine and film. To return to where this chapter began, with Roland Barthes and his *Mythologies*, featuring one of the most famous studies of the symbolic significance of wine in French culture, 'Le Vin et le lait' [Wine and Milk], in which he wrote: '*Le vin est senti par la nation française comme un bien qui lui est propre, au même titre que ses trois cent soixante espèces de fromages et sa culture. C'est une boisson-totem*' [Wine is felt by the French nation to be a possession which is its very own, just like its three hundred and sixty types of cheese and its culture. It is a totem-drink] (Barthes 1957: 69). Wine is here equated to culture itself – both attributes that the French possess – but Barthes also underscores the links of wine culture with text when referring to the cultural practices and meanings associated with wine: '*Tout cela est connu, dit mille fois dans le folklore, les proverbes, les conversations et la Littérature*' [All this is well known and has been said a thousand times in folklore, proverbs, conversations and Literature] (Barthes 1957: 70). Mythologies represent cultures, and in scriptural societies, they are carried across the centuries by texts of different kinds – including literary, artistic and filmic manifestations. To understand wine cultures in their depth and breadth, we need to pay more scholarly attention to these evocative and informative literary, artistic and filmic texts from around the world.

References

Agi, T. and Okimoto, S. (2004–2014) *[2011] Drops of God*, New York: Vertical Inc.
Bal, M. and Bryson, N. (1991) "Semiotics and Art History," *The Art Bulletin* 73(2), 174–208.
Barthes, R. (1957) *Mythologies*, Paris: Seuil.
Barthes, R. (1971) "De l'œuvre au texte," *Revue d'esthétique* 3, 225–232.
Benedek, M., Panzierer, L., Jauk, E. and Neubauer, A.C. (2017) "Creativity on Tap? Effects of Alcohol Intoxication on Creative Cognition," *Consciousness and Cognition* 56, 128–134.
Bergamini, G. and Michelutti, M. (2007) *La vite e il vino nell'arte nella letteratura del Friuli*, Udine: Aviani & Aviani.
Beuvelet. (2011) "Le Goût du sujet dans Mondovino: Une éthique du cadrage," *Psychoanalytische Perspectieven* 29(3–4), 1–24.
Bonal, F. (1990) *Anthologie du champagne: Le champagne dans la littérature universelle*, Chaumont: Editions Dominique Guéniot.
Caldeway, J. and House, C. (2003) *Icon: Art of the Wine Label*, San Francisco: The Wine Appreciation Guild, Board and Bench Publishing.
Celhay, F. and Remaud, H. (2018) "What Does Your Wine Label Mean to Consumers? A Semiotic Investigation of Bordeaux Wine Visual Codes," *Food Quality and Preference* 65, 129–145.
Cordier, P. (2000) *Lectures du vin*, Paris: Hachette Pratique.
Croidieu, G., Soppe, B. and Powell, W.W. (2017) "Cru, Glue and Status: How Wine Labels Helped Ennoble Bordeaux," *Multimodality, Meaning, and Institutions: Research in the Sociology of Organizations, Volume 54B*, Emerald Publishing, 37–69, https://doi.org/10.1108/S0733-558X2017000054B002.
Cuellar, S.S., Karnowsky, D. and Acosta, F. (2009) "The Sideways Effect: A Test for Changes in the Demand for Merlot and Pinot Noir Wines," *Journal of Wine Economics* 4(2), 219–232.
Dali, S. (2017) *Dali: The Wines of Gala*, Köln: Taschen.
Dickenson, J. (2001) "Wine and Art: Artistic Images and the Selling of Wine," *DOURO: Estudos & Documentos* 6(11), 85–93.
Dutton, J. (2020) "Wine in Houellebecq: Cultural Transgression or Literary Device?" *French Cultural Studies* 31(1), 73–90.

Dutton, J. and Normand-Marconnet, N. (2019) "Visual Codes on French Wine Labels for Cross-Cultural Marketing in China and Australia," in N. Terblanche and C.D. Pentz (eds), *Proceedings of the 11th Conference of the Association of Wine Business Research*, 53–67.

Fonseca, L.F. da. (2008) *Aspectos Socio-Culturais do Vinho – arqueologica, literatura, arte*, Chamusca: Zaina Editores.

Fripp, R. (1980) "The Vinyl Solution," *Musician, Player and Listener* 24, 34–35.

Gibellini, P. (2003) "Il vino nella letteratura italiana moderna: il caso di Manzoni e di Verga," in *La civiltà del vino. Fonti, temi e produzioni vitivinicole dal Medioevo al Novecento. Atti del convegno (Monticelli Brusati, Antica Fratta, 5–6 ottobre 2001)*, Brescia: Centro culturale artistico di Franciacorta e del Sebino, 751–775.

Guermès, S. (1997) *Le Vin et l'encre: la littérature française et le vin du XIIIe au XXe siècle*, Bordeaux: Mollat.

Guy, K. (2003) *When Champagne Became French: Wine and the Making of a National Identity*, Baltimore, MD: Johns Hopkins University Press.

Haass-Koffler, C.L. and Kenna, G.A. (2013) "Bacchus by Caravaggio as the Visual Diagnosis of Alcohol Use Disorder from the Fifth Edition of the Diagnostic and Statistical Manual of Mental Disorders (DSM-5)," *Frontiers in Psychiatry* 4(86), DOI:10.3389/fpsyt.2013.00086.

Halley, J. (2018) "Mondo Vino: Rationalization, Resistance, and Taste in the Wine World," in *Bourdieu in Question: Recent Developments in the French Sociology of Art*, Boston: Brill, 403–425.

Herman, S. and Pascal, J. (2003) *Mouton Rothschild: The Museum of Wine in Art*, Arles: Actes Sud.

Lagrange, M. and Lorin, P. (2017) *Les Ecrivains du vin*, Paris: L'Archipel.

Lagrange, M. and Lorin, P. (2021) *Les Ecrivains du champagne*, Paris: Max Chaleil.

Lill, A. (2000) "Wine and a Trial of Character in Horace's Poems," *Journal of Wine Research* 11(1), 35–47.

Mainardi, G. and Berta, P. (1991) *Il vino nella storia e nella letteratura: feste, magie, storie e leggende di un simbolo universale: il fascino del vino raccontato attraverso la letteratura*, Bologna: Edagricole.

McInerney, J. (2018) *Wine Reads: A Literary Anthology of Wine Writing*, New York: Grove Press.

Morel, P. (2014) *Renaissance dionysiaque: Inspiration bachique, imaginaire du vin et de la vigne dans l'art européen (1430–1630)*, Paris: Editions du Félin.

Mouret, J-N. (1999) *Le Vin des Ecrivains*, Paris: Mercure de France.

Negrin, L. (2015) "Art and Fine Wine: A Case Study in the Aestheticization of Consumption," *Continuum* 29(3), 419–433.

Norlander, T. (1999) "Inebriation and Inspiration? A Review of the Research on Alcohol and Creativity," *Journal of Creative Behavior* 33(1), 22–44.

Norlander, T. and Gustafson, R. (1998) "Effects of Alcohol on a Divergent Figural Fluency Test During the Illumination Phase of the Creative Process," *Creativity Research Journal* 11, 265–274.

Normand-Marconnet, N. and Jones, J. (2020) "Anthropomorphic Metaphors in Wine Discourse, with Special Reference to Japanese Wine Manga," *International Journal of Language and Culture* 7(2), 274–301.

Normand-Marconnet, N. and Jones, J. (2016) "From West to East to West: A Case Study on Japanese Wine Manga Translated in French," *Transcultural: A Journal of Translation and Cultural Studies* 8(2), 155–173.

Quero, S. (2008) *El vino: historia, arte, literatura*, Torremolinos: Revista Litoral.

Rabaudy Montoussin, D. de. (1998) *Les affiches du Champagne d'hier et d'aujourd'hui*, Paris: Citédis.

Ray, C. (1974) *Mouton Rothschild: The Wine, the Family, the Museum*, London: Christie's Wine Department.

Roese, M. (2008) "O mondovino de cabeça para baixo: as transformações no mercado internacional do vinho e o novo empresariado vinícola," *Revista Sociologica e Politica* 16(31), 71–83.

Rothschild, P. de and Beaumarchais, J.-P. de. (1983) *Mouton Rothschild: Paintings for the Labels 1945–1981*, Boston: Little Brown.

Salas, B.S. (2007) *El Cine del Vino*, Logroño: Fundación Dinastía Vivanco.

Schirmer, R. (2014) "Holly[wine] ou le vin dans le cinéma américain," *Annales de géographie* 697(3), 867–889.

Unwin, T. (1992) "Images of Alcohol: Perceptions and the Influence of Advertising," *Journal of Wine Research* 3(3), 205–233.

Varriano, J.L. (2010) *Wine: A Cultural History*, London: Reaktion Books.

Venturini, N. (1988) *World Drink Advertising Posters*, Padova: Franco Muzzio Editore.

Voegele, A., Goldblum, S., Nicklas, T., Toudoire-Surlapierre, F. and Faure, M. (2020) *Vin et altérité: le vin à l'épreuve des sciences humaines*, Reims: Presses Universitaires de Reims.

Woolf, V. (2005) *Selected Works*, Hertfordshire: Wordsworth Editions.

Yan, M. (2000 [1992]) *The Republic of Wine*, translated by Howard Goldblatt, London: Hamish Hamilton.

Yang, X. (1998) "*The Republic of Wine*: An Extravaganza of Decline," *Positions* 6(1), 7–31.

PART II

Production and place

8
CULTURES OF TERROIR

Tim Unwin

Imaginations

There is not a single 'idea' or 'thing' that is terroir. It is instead a word that has been used by people from many different 'cultures' and backgrounds, frequently to represent and enhance their own interests. Whilst some may seek to maintain single, pure definitions of words such as 'terroir', the reality is that most words mutate and change in the context of specific cultures and milieux (Cappelliez 2017). Ideas about terroir continually evolve, but it is also essential to recognise that the idea of terroir has itself played a significant role in shaping the wider culture of wine (Demossier 2011).

The term 'terroir' is used to refer to many other products than wine alone (Paxson 2010; Whited 2018; Angles et al. 2013), but it is in wine that it reaches its apogee (see Lesh and Lally 2020). At its simplest, it conveys the notions that products made in different places can be considered unique to those specific locations and thus that they reflect a particular environment, both 'natural' and 'human', that shaped their creation. In essence, 'terroir' conjures up that elusive sense of being that lies in place; physically drinking wine is also a way in which that sense can be translated through both time and space. 'Terroir' is singular and non-replicable and is fundamentally different from the notion of typicity (French *typicité*), which implies that a wine is typical in its general flavours of those produced from its constituent grape varieties. Terroir seeks to capture what makes places – and their wines – special to people.

This linkage between product and place is also of profound economic, social and political importance, not least because, as Karl Marx (1981) so clearly elucidated in the late nineteenth century, affirmation of such a connection can be used to create a monopoly price from which surplus profit may then be generated (Unwin 1991; Ulin 2013). This reality lies at the heart of many controlled appellation systems, which seek both to guarantee the genuineness of a product and to enable additional profit to be generated from it.

Terroir: in the ground and in the glass

The environment, grapes and wine

Winegrowers and writers about wine have observed for millennia how the nature of the physical environment contributes significantly to the character and flavours of wine. From the earliest beginnings of grape cultivation and winemaking (McGovern 2003), winegrowers gradually discovered that particular cultivars grew better and produced finer wines in certain environments. By the first century CE, it is evident that the Romans were very well aware of the relationships between different types of vine and the environments in which they grew (Columella 1941, 1954, 1955; see also Cato c. 160 BCE, 1933, Varro c.37 BCE, 1912, Pliny, CE 77–79, 1945–50). The Romans also attributed different qualities and reputations to the wines produced in different places (Strabo 1949–54; Unwin 1991). The essential ingredients of what much later was to be termed 'terroir' and its association with wine quality were therefore well known two millennia ago.

The gradual process of selection of the optimal grape varieties and methods of cultivation by winegrowers throughout the medieval and early modern periods subsequently led to the specific assemblages of vines that emerged in different parts of Europe. However, it was not until the twentieth century that scientific analysis really began to unravel the complexities of the relationship between viticulture (the cultivation of vines), grape characteristics (Gladstones 1992, 2011; Coombe and Dry 2005, 2006) and eventually wine. Despite recent claims, though, that 'Groundbreaking research proves existence of terroir' (Perrett 2021; see also Urvieta et al. 2021), there remains much uncertainty about how exactly different elements of the physical environment combine to influence the characteristics and flavours of the wines produced from them in different wine regions. This uncertainty and lack of precision are among the things that have given rise to so much debate over the meanings and value of terroir.

The environments in which vines are grown do, indeed, influence the characteristics of the fruit emanating from them. Every parcel of land has its own unique combination of environmental parameters: geology, soil, temperature, sunlight, rainfall, humidity, wind, altitude, slope and aspect/exposure (Pomerol 1989; see also Maltman 2018). Because these interact in different ways in varying contexts, and many of them change over time, it is extremely difficult for scientists to identify the precise influence of any one factor. Generations of winegrowers have nevertheless gained the experience to be able to tell very precisely how they should cultivate their vines on different parts of their properties: as my friends in the Hautes Côtes de Beaune tell me, the aligoté should grow on that particular slope, whereas the chardonnay should grow in that area, and the pinot noir must be grown on these sunnier slopes (Figure 8.1). Indeed, one need only taste from the barrel or vat wines made as far as possible in identical ways by a single producer from neighbouring vineyards to begin to have an understanding of the role that the environment has in winemaking.

There is much more, though, to growing grapes for wine than just the 'natural' environment. Vineyards have often been cultivated over very long periods of time and have therefore been changed over centuries by people ploughing them, terracing some slopes, adding fertilisers and pesticides to others, breaking up boulders or introducing irrigation. Vine growers likewise use differing trellising systems and pruning methods to produce fruit with varying characteristics on similar types of land. The assemblages of natural yeasts in the vineyards have also evolved over time. Moreover, organic viticulture enables a different expression of terroir from that created by the use of inorganic fertilisers, pesticides and fungicides. Human activities in the physical landscape have therefore been crucial in shaping the environment in which vines are grown, even before the diverse processes of vinification and maturation are applied to the grapes to turn them into wine. Defining terroir is therefore extremely complex.

The crafting of terroir

Origins

The use of the word 'terroir' relating to wine in the twentieth and twenty-first centuries emerged from this complexity (Patterson and Buechsenstein 2018; see also Teil 2012 and in this book). At its heart is the idea that the wines made in particular places have specific identities. Tracing this usage

Cultures of terroir

Figure 8.1 The winegrowing village of St. Romain in the Hautes Côtes de Beaune, looking out across the Côte de Beaune and the Saône Valley

Source: Author, 2017

is far from easy, but the term appears to have emerged in the early modern period as a fairly derogatory term, '*goût de terroir*', to refer to wines that had an earthiness to their flavour (Parker 2015). In medieval France, 'terroir' typically referred merely to the land belonging to a village (Vérin 2016). As Parker (2015) emphasises, though, terroir subsequently became increasingly associated with negative connotations; the Court of Versailles was intent on eliminating the effect of the earth on flavours, so the best terroir was actually no terroir at all (see also Phillips 2016, 2018).

The underlying meaning of 'terroir', though, expressing the influence of nature on agricultural crops, did not change much before the early nineteenth century. It was an integral part of French regional identity associated with the notion of the *pays*, geographical areas where people had common cultural, economic and social interests (Dutton 2019; see also Dutton and Howland in this book). However, three further factors emerging in the nineteenth century all played important roles in the emergence of modern understandings of wine terroir (Trubek 2008): the *Exposition Universelle* of 1855, at which the famous classification of Bordeaux's wine estates was presented; the arrival of phylloxera, which devastated wine production and contributed to an expansion of wine fraud; and the creation of the French appellation system.

Terroir and the origins of the French appellation d'origine contrôlée system

The Burgundians turned the previous rather negative views of terroir into an advantage. In the early nineteenth century, Morelot was eager to understand why the various wines produced in different parts of Burgundy tasted so different, given that they were made in essentially the same way. His *Statistique de la vigne dans le département de la Côte d'Or* (Morelot 1831) provided the first major attempt to understand the relationship between the physical environment and wine characteristics and was one of the foundations for Lavalle's (1855) much more substantive exploration of the terroirs of Burgundy.

Shortly after the 1855 *Exposition Universelle*, the devastating impact of phylloxera (*Daktulosphaera vitifoliae*) led to winegrowers across Europe concentrating production in areas that were most able to produce better qualities of wine. They also started to put in place the legal apparatuses of demarcated winemaking areas, each with its own legislation and regulatory processes, to try to guarantee quality and authenticity in the face of the growing amount of wine fraud that followed the collapse in production (Pouget 1990). In France, the *Appellation d'Origine Contrôlée* system, eventually enacted in 1936, built heavily on these Burgundian traditions (Lachiver 1988; Demossier 1999, 2018). In essence, the *Institut national de l'orgine et de la qualité* (INAO) created a system that placed terroir at its core and classified the different qualities of wines produced based mainly on the environmental characteristics of the land. This had clear implications for the prices at which the wines could be sold and reflected to varying degrees the local political and economic interests of particular wine producers and landowners.

The distinction between quality and terroir

As this account has emphasised, environmental characteristics, and thus terroir, do indeed influence the flavours of wines at a variety of scales (see also Cappeliez, Fedoul and Overton in this book). However, they do not guarantee quality; they merely emphasise difference. It is this elision between the notions of quality and difference that has caused so much confusion and debate (Unwin 2012; see also debate between Jekel 1982, 1983; Prats 1983; Dickenson 1990). Many other factors, especially the processes involved in vinification and maturation, as well as fashion and pricing practices, also influence what is seen to be 'quality' wine.

Rather than being seen as an important signifier of environmental difference, the word 'terroir' has now become embedded in popular (but also often academic) imaginations as a symbol of quality (see also Crenn in this book). Particular soils, especially those on the gravels of Bordeaux or the limestone rocks of parts of Burgundy, are thus seen by many as being *de facto* indications of quality (Figure 8.2). This, of course, serves the interests of winegrowers in these areas, who naturally seek to promote their advantages by increasing their market size as well as the prices at which they can sell their wines. The trouble is that other excellent wines, grown on entirely different soils above different rocks, taste rather similar to good wines from Bordeaux and Burgundy, and quality is very much in the eye, or taste, of the beholder.

Grape growing and winemaking

The terroir debate has also been heavily influenced by tensions between the relative importance attributed to grape growing (viticulture) and winemaking (vinification). Traditionally, especially in Europe, wine was mainly made by the people who also grew the grapes. There have always been merchants (*négociants* in French; see also Lachiver 1988; Brennan 1997; Guy 2003), who removed a purist sense of terroir by blending wines to be sold to distant customers, but most wine has historically closely reflected terroir through the integration of grape growing and winemaking.

From the nineteenth century onwards, however, an important distinction emerged between scientific, and thus professional, winemaking and the 'peasant' agricultural traditions of grape growing. A view gradually took root that anyone can grow grapes, but it takes someone with a proper education and training to make wine (Unwin 1991). Hence, larger properties began to employ winemakers specifically to create their wines. Likewise cooperatives, which increased significantly in number in the twentieth century, also began to employ 'qualified' winemakers to improve the quality of wines blended from the grapes grown by their many members. The perceived importance

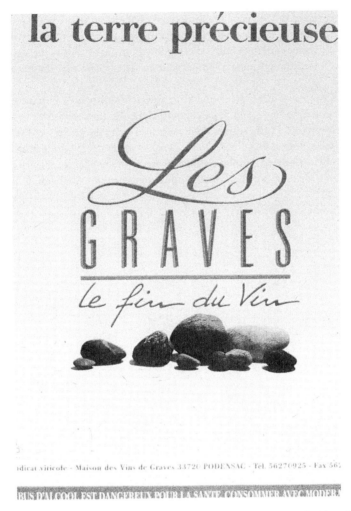

Figure 8.2 Late twentieth-century advertisement for wines from the Graves, emphasising the importance of the precious earth

of the terroir of any particular plot thus declined as winemaking expertise gradually increased in importance at the expense of grape growing, both practically and in terms of status.

Scientific winemaking in California and Australia

This process of status differentiation between 'peasant' growers and 'elite' university-trained winemakers is often seen as coming to the fore, particularly in California and Australia, in the 1960s, when university research institutes such as those at the University of California, Davis, (USA) and Roseworthy College (South Australia) took significant strides forward, especially in understanding the science behind winemaking (oenology) and in training new generations of winemakers. Underlying the emergence of a thriving industry in these 'New World' wine regions was a belief that too many 'Old World' (European) wines were tainted by poor winery hygiene, which could be readily overcome by a modern scientific approach to winemaking. The focus became primarily one of controlling the process scientifically to eliminate flaws and ensure that reasonably good quality wines could be guaranteed. This very much downplayed any sense of the importance of terroir. The emphasis on blending wines to support the bulk brands that came to dominate the wine trade in the second half of the twentieth century also rendered terroir, at least at the vineyard scale, to be rather meaningless, even though some attempts were made to claim that there was such a thing as regional terroirs.

However, there were also many grape and wine research institutes in Europe and former Soviet countries that continued to engage in research and practice in the interests of both viticulture and vinification in their regions. Furthermore, there were also some researchers and winegrowers in the New World (see, for example, Gladstones 1992; Winkler et al. 1992) who continued to champion the role of viticulture in ensuring that winemakers began with the best possible fruit. The distinction between the role of science in New and Old World winegrowing may therefore be less real than is sometimes suggested.

Figure 8.3 Geovino: Terroir tourism above Riquewihr, Alsace
Source: Author, 2019

Figure 8.3 (Continued)

Gradually, most of those involved in winegrowing have come to recognise that different environments (in the fullest sense of the word) do, indeed, lend particular characteristics to the grapes used in winemaking, and a much more nuanced approach to questions of terroir is being adopted (Elliott-Fisk and Noble 1992). This has become increasingly evident as winegrowers turn to organic and biodynamic methods of growing grapes and making their wines (as, for example, with John Williams at Frog's Leap in California). Increasingly, terroir is no longer seen as being synonymous with quality, but rather as being one of many important aspects of the complexity of winegrowing. Terroir has always been used as one of the means by which wine can be 'identified' and differentiated, and it is increasingly being adopted by winegrowers and regional tourist boards with an interest in marketing their products (Figure 8.3).

Terroir: in the mind and in print

Terroir has not only been used by winegrowers, merchants, marketeers and tourist operators, each with their own cultures and interests in the concept, but it has also been used by popular writers and academics as a vehicle for exploring ideas and building their careers. A simple Google Scholar search (14 May 2021) thus reveals some 25,000 publications on wine and terroir (in the English language), most of which have rather low numbers of citations. Although this is a very crude indicator, it serves well to highlight two things that this second section of the chapter briefly explores: the plethora of publications on wine and terroir, and the tendency for people writing about them not to cite the work of others who have preceded them. It delves into the different cultures of writing about terroir, broadly divided into popular and academic cultures.

Terroir in popular wine writing

A recurring feature of much popular wine writing is that it draws on a mixture of individual experience and limited reading of some of the existing literature on the subject. Popular wine writers have many interests in writing about wine: some simply enjoy writing; others do it for the income they generate from wine columns and writing books; and still others do it as part of a wider strategy to raise their personal profiles in the wine world. For all these reasons, the idea of terroir is a useful peg on which to hang their descriptions and ideas.

Most introductions to popular wine books (and tourist accounts) thus continue to have a section on the 'geography' of the region, describing where different places are located, their geology and how terroir shapes the flavours of the various different wines as a result. This is, indeed, fertile ground and helps promote a popular culture about terroir. All too often, though, it oversimplifies. Hinkle (1991: 25), amongst many others, has claimed that '[t]he literal French definition of terroir as we all know, is "soil".' This is, indeed, one cultural understanding of terroir, but as the earlier parts of this chapter have illustrated, it is not one that is now seen as being particularly valid. Likewise, where academics stray into the world of more popular writing, they, too, can fall prey to the temptation to oversimplify and thus create new mythologies and cultures of terroir. As a leading geologist, Jake Hancock, once commented, 'a lot of what is written about geology in wine books is at best misguided and at worst utterly wrong' (Huggett 2005: 239; see also Hancock and Price 1990 and, more recently, Macqueen and Meinert 2006). In reviewing Wilson's popular geology book on terroir, Hancock (1999: 48) thus suggests that Wilson (1998) gives no definition of terroir; he fails to incorporate more recent scientific work on the subject, and '[t]here are extraordinary inconsistencies' in the book (see also Maltman 2018).

Cultures of terroir in academic discourse

Academics, too, have created their own cultures of terroir, largely based on their particular disciplinary backgrounds. Many from backgrounds other than geology continue to fall foul of Hancock's (1999) criticisms noted earlier. As the present book emphasises, wine is an inherently multidisciplinary field of enquiry, but even those academics adept at crossing boundaries still often seek to carve out their own cultures of terroir. Geographers, geologists, anthropologists (Ulin 2013; Muller 2017), sociologists, historians (Conca Messina *et al.* 2019), philosophers, chemists (Cadot *et al.* 2010) and economists (Gergaud and Ginsburgh 2008; Haeck *et al.* 2019) cannot help but be constrained by their own disciplinary backgrounds when writing about terroir. Each refines and redefines the meaning of terroir within their own cultural context.

Academic career progression and thus salaries are highly dependent on publications in leading journals and the number of citations that these receive. Some wishing to build their careers, therefore, find an idea in another body of literature that may not have been much researched in their own discipline and then seek to claim that their research on it is, indeed, novel: what I have previously called the magpie tendency in my own discipline of geography (Unwin 1992). This is all too true of much of the wider recent 'research' on terroir, with many authors unfortunately often failing to trace back the origins of ideas in a sufficiently rigorous and scholarly manner, thereby seeking to claim that their contributions, at least to their own disciplines, are in some way novel (Ulin 2013). These do, nevertheless, sometimes also sow the seed and inspire new traditions of subsequent research on terroir in their own disciplines.

Academic cultures also often obscure as much as enlighten, providing boundaries of language that isolate and protect practitioners in one discipline from the preying eyes of others. This is well reflected in Reckinger's (2019: 213) comments with respect to terroir in a recent historical volume:

> In the didactic realizations of oenophile normativity, emerging from the vector of scientific consolidation, this 'origin' refers in an epistemic way to parcellated vineyard regions which are constructed as terroirs by the interaction of traditional, man-made viticultural techniques and the natural conditions, holding sensory potentials whose sub-text is of a moral order.

Reflections

This chapter has sought to elucidate the great diversity of meanings that terroir has come to have in different contexts and disciplines. It has also sought to shed light on the diversity of interests that have underlain the use of the word, especially as this has burgeoned over the last century. In so doing, I have sought to lay out a map on which readers can situate the various other chapters in this book that use the idea of terroir in their accounts of wine culture. Many chapters in the book thus use terroir as a shorthand for the wide environmental factors that influence the taste of wine (see, for example, Cappeliez, Fedoul and Overton); Taplin overtly refers to it as being an example of the social construction of space. Others, such as Dutton and Howland, highlight its utopian character, with Anderson and Nelgen likewise emphasising its cultural cachet. Above all, these chapters all reflect the diversity and complexity of the ways in which the term has evolved and will continue to do so.

It is important, though, finally to reflect on a set of interests that have also sought to reach an agreed generic meaning for the word, particularly in the legal context of international agreements. A multidisciplinary gathering under the auspices of UNESCO (2005) thus emphasised that it is extremely difficult to translate 'terroir' into languages other than French, but they suggest that the definition proposed by a working group of INRA/INAO could serve to permit a dialogue based on the following common ground:

> *Un terroir est un espace géographique délimité défini à partir d'une communauté humaine qui construit au cours de son histoire un ensemble de traits culturels distinctifs, de savoirs, et de pratiques fondés sur un système d'interactions entre le milieu naturel et les facteurs humains. Les savoir-faire mis en jeu révèlent une originalité, confèrent une typicité et permettent une reconnaissance pour les produits ou services originaires de cet espace et donc pour les hommes qui y vivent. Les terroirs sont des espaces vivants et innovants qui ne peuvent être assimilés à la seule tradition.*[1]

This clearly acknowledges that terroirs are accordingly living and innovative spaces that cannot easily be assimilated into a single tradition. However, it also very definitely emphasises that terroirs are not just about the physical environment, let alone soil, but instead reflect the complex interactions of humans within the 'natural' world that have shaped the character of specific places. These have lain at the heart of 'earth writing' or γεω-γραφία[2] since the origins of European written cultures.

Notes

1 Given this complexity, it is symbolically appropriate to leave the quotation in French. However, for English speakers with no grasp of this language, it may be translated as 'A terroir is a delimited geographical space,

defined by a human community which has through the course of its history constructed it from a set of distinctive cultural traits, knowledges and practices based on a system of interactions between the natural world and human factors. The know-how involved reveals an originality, confers typicity and allows for recognition of the products or services originating in this space and thus for the people who live there. Terroirs are living and innovative spaces which cannot be assimilated to tradition alone'.

2 Geo-graphia – or geography.

References

Angles, S., Veysseyre, J. and Cohen, M. (2013) "Appellations d'Origine Protégée oléicoles, terroirs et territoires méditerranéens: une analyse comparative entre les appellations oléicoles en France et en Andalousie," *Sud-Ouest Européen, Revue Géographique des Pyrénées et du Sud-Ouest*, Special Issue *Identité, espaces, terroirs, territoires et mondialisation* 36, 123–133, https://doi.org/10.4000/soe.489.

Brennan, T. (1997) *Burgundy to Champagne: The Wine Trade in Early Modern France*, Baltimore, MD: Johns Hopkins University Press.

Cadot, Y., Caillé, S., Samson, A., Barbeau, G. and Cheynier, V. (2010) "Sensory Dimension of Wine Typicality Related to a Terroir by Quantitative Descriptive Analysis, Just About Right Analysis and Typicality Assessment," *Analytica Chimica Acta* 660(1–2), 53–62. https://doi.org/10.1016/j.aca.2009.10.006.

Cappelliez, S. (2017) "How Well Does Terroir Travel? Illuminating Cultural Translation Using a Comparative Wine Case Study," *Poetics* 65, 24–36.

Cato, M.P. (1933) *On Farming*, trans. E. Brehaut, New York: Columbia University Press.

Columella, L.J.M. (1941, 1954, 1955) *On Agriculture*, vol. 3, trans. H.B. Ash, E.S. Forster and E.H. Heffner, London: Heinemann.

Conca Messina, S., Le Bras, S., Tedeschi, P. and Vaquero Piñeiro, M. (eds) (2019) *A History of Wine in Europe, 19th to 20th Centuries, Volume II*, Cham: Palgrave Macmillan.

Coombe, B.G. and Dry, P.R. (eds) (2005, 2006) *Viticulture, Volume 1: Resources in Australia*, Adelaide: Winetitles, and *Viticulture, Volume 2: Practices*, Adelaide: Winetitles.

Demossier, M. (1999) *Hommes et vins: Une anthropologie du vignoble bourguignon*, Dijon: Publications de l'Université de Bourgogne.

Demossier, M. (2011) "Beyond *Terroir*: Territorial Construction, Hegemonic Discourses, and French Wine Culture," *Journal of the Royal Anthropological Institute* 17(4), 685–705.

Demossier, M. (2018) *Burgundy: The Global Story of Terroir*, New York and Oxford: Berghahn.

Dickenson, J. (1990) "Viticultural Geography: An Introduction to the Literature in English," *Journal of Wine Research* 1(1), 5–24.

Dutton, J. (2019) "Geographical Turns and Historical Returns in Narrating French Wine Culture," *Global Food History* 5(1–2), 113–131.

Elliott-Fisk, D. and Noble, A. (1992) "Environments in Napa Valley, California and Their Influence on Cabernet Sauvignon Wine Flavors," in H. De Blij (ed), *Viticulture in Geographical Perspective*, Miami, FL: Miami Geographical Society, 45–72.

Gergaud, O. and Ginsburgh, V. (2008) "Natural Endowments, Production Technologies and the Quality of Wines in Bordeaux. Does Terroir Matter?" *The Economic Journal* 118, F142–F157.

Gladstones, J. (1992) *Viticulture and Environment*, Adelaide: Winetitles.

Gladstones, J. (2011) *Wine, Terroir and Climate Change*, Kent Town: Wakefield Press.

Guy, K.M. (2003) *When Champagne Became French*, Baltimore, MD: Johns Hopkins University Press.

Haeck, C., Meloni, G. and Swinnen, J. (2019) "The Value of Terroir: A Historical Analysis of the Bordeaux and Champagne Geographical Indications," *Applied Economic Perspectives and Policy* 41(4), 598–619.

Hancock, J.M. (1999) "Feature Review," *Journal of Wine Research* 10(1), 43–49.

Hancock, J.M. and Price, M. (1990) "Real Chalk Balances the Water Supply," *Journal of Wine Research* 1(1), 45–60.

Hinkle, R.P. (1991) "Just What Is Terroir Anyway?" *Wine & Vines* 72(3), 25–28.

Huggett, J.M. (2005) "Geology and Wine: A Review," *Proceedings of the Geologists' Association* 117, 239–247.

Jekel, B. (1982) "California Wines: The Quality Factors," *Decanter* 7(12), 67–68.

Jekel, B. (1983) "Soil and Wine – the Debate Continues," *Decanter* 8(10), 15.

Lachiver, M. (1988) *Vins, Vignes et Vignerons: histoire des vignobles français*, Paris: Fayard.

Lavalle, M.J. (1855) *Histoire et statistique de la vignes et des grands vins de la Côte d'Or*, Paris: Dusacq.

Lesh, K. and Lally, A.E. (2020) "Contesting Terroir: New Anthropological Imaginations of the Taste of Place," *Anthropology of Food* S14, https://journals.openedition.org/aof/10543.

MacQueen, R.W. and Meinert, L.D. (eds) (2006) *Fine Wine and Terroir: The Geoscience Perspective*, St. John's: Geological Association of Canada.

Maltman, A. (2018) *Vineyards, Rocks, & Soils: The Wine Lover's Guide to Geology*, Oxford: Oxford University Pres.

Marx, K. (1981) *Capital: A Critique of Political Economy, Volume 3*, Harmondsworth: Penguin (first published 1894).

McGovern, P.E. (2003) *Ancient Wine: The Search for the Origins of Viniculture*, Princeton, NJ: Princeton University Press.

Morelot, D. (1831) *Statistique de la vigne dans le département de la Côte d'Or*, Dijon: Victor Lagier.

Muller, R. (2017) "Suffering and the Human Terroir," *Anthropology of Consciousness* 28(2), 156–164.

Parker, T. (2015) *Tasting French Terroir: The History of an Idea*, Berkeley: University of California Press.

Patterson, T. and Buechsenstein, J. (2018) *Wine and Place: A Terroir Reader*, Berkeley: University of California Press.

Paxson, H. (2010) "Locating Value in Artisan Cheese: Reverse Engineering *Terroir* for New-World Landscapes," *American Anthropologist* 112(3), 444–457, https://doi.org/10.1111/j.1548-1433.2010.01251.x.

Perrett, M. (2021) "Groundbreaking Research Proves Existence of Terroir," *Harpers*, https://harpers.co.uk/news/fullstory.php/aid/28350/Groundbreaking_research_proves_existence_of_terroir.html?utm_source=newsletter&utm_medium=e-mail&utm_campaign=Harpers%252Bnewsletter%252BIssue%252B1066.

Phillips, R. (2016) *French Wine: A History*, Oakland: University of California Press.

Phillips, R. (2018) *Wine: A Social and Cultural History of the Drink That Changed our Lives*, Oxford: Infinite Ideas.

Pliny. (1945–50) *Natural History*, trans. H. Rackham, London: Heinemann.

Pomerol, C. (ed) (1989) *The Wines and Winelands of France: Geological Journeys*, London: Robertson McCarta.

Pouget, R. (1990) *Histoire de la lutte contre le phylloxera de la vigne en France*, Paris: INRA.

Prats, B. (1983) "The Terroir Is Important," *Decanter* 8(7), 16.

Reckinger, R. (2019) "Converging Terroir Typicity for Political Usage and Didactic Normativity. The Metonymical Institutionalization of Wine in Luxembourg," in S. Conca Messina, S. Le Bras, P. Tedeschi and M. Vaquero Piñeiro (eds), *A History of Wine in Europe, 19th to 20th Centuries, Volume II*, Cham: Palgrave Macmillan, 213–232.

Strabo. (1949–54) *The Geography of Strabo*, trans. H.L. Jones, London: William Heinemann.

Teil, G. (2012) "No Such Thing as Terroir? Objectivities and the Regimes of Existence of Objects," *Science, Technology and Human Values* 37, 478–505.

Trubek, A.B. (2008) *The Taste of Place: A Cultural Journey into Terroir*, Berkeley: University of California Press.

Ulin, R.C. (2013) "*Terroir* and Locality: An Anthropological Perspective," in R.E. Black and R.C. Ulin (eds), *Wine and Culture: Vineyard to Glass*, London: A & C Black, 67–84.

UNESCO. (2005) *Rencontres Internationales Planète Terroirs UNESCO 2005: Actes*, Montpellier: UNESCO, SC-2007/WS/41.

Unwin, T. (1991) *Wine and the Vine: An Historical Geography of Viticulture and the Wine Trade*, London: Routledge.

Unwin, T. (1992) *The Place of Geography*, Harlow: Longman.

Unwin, T. (2012) "*Terroir*: At the Heart of Geography," in P.C. Dougherty (ed), *The Geography of Wine: Regions, Terroir and Techniques*, Dordrecht: Springer, 37–48.

Urvieta, R., Jones, G., Buscema, F., Bottini, R. and Fontana, A. (2021) "Terroir and Vintage Discrimination of Malbec Wines Based on Phenolic Composition Across Multiple Sites in Mendoza, Argentina," *Scientific Reports* 11: Article 2863, https://doi.org/10.1038/s41598-021-82306-0.

Varro, M.T. (1912) *On Farming*, trans. L. Storr-Best, London: G. Bell & Sons.

Vérin, H. (2016) "Olivier de Serres et son *Théâtre d'agriculture*," *Artefact – Techniques, Histoire et Sciences Humaines* 4, 161–180, https://doi.org/10.4000/artefact.405.

Whited, T.L. (2018) "Terroir Transformed: Cheese and Pastoralism in the Western French Pyrenees," *Environmental History* 23(4), 824–846.

Wilson, J.E. (1998) *Terroir: The Role of Geology, Climate and Culture in the Making of French Wines*, Berkeley: University of California Press.

Winkler, A.J., Cook, J.A., Kliewer, W.M. and Lider, L.A. (1992) *General Viticulture*, 2nd edition, Berkeley: University of California Press.

9
SITES AND SIGHTS OF PRODUCTION

Spaces and performances of winemaking

John Overton

Introduction

In the Colchagua Valley in Chile, visitors to the Viña Montes Alpha winery pass through closed gates and by rows of vines that stretch to the foothills beyond to enter a modern, low-lying building where they find a tasting room, store and fine restaurant (Figure 9.1). There are signs of a working winery nearby, but visitors are ushered to one of the underground cellars, viewed through glass, where some 800 oak barrels are arranged in a tiered semi-circle, reminiscent of a small concert hall, where music plays softly. The music – Gregorian chants – invokes a monastic atmosphere that fits the branding of its premium red wines, such as its Carmenère 'Purple Angel': 'With its moving silence and atmosphere of peace and tranquillity, we believe without a doubt that it is the favourite place of our angels' (Viña Montes n.d.; see also Ross 2006). This is a place of production, one that is tranquil and ordered, constructed and displayed deliberately to promote claims to careful, intensive and time-honoured crafting of high-quality wines.

On the outskirts of Fresno in the Central Valley of California, just north of Highway 80, sits a very large and anonymous industrial estate covering nearly 20 hectares. It has banks of huge steel tanks, networks of pipes and chimneys, extensive truck parks and large buildings, all contained behind security fences (Figure 9.2). To the casual observer, it could be a small oil refinery. There is little or no external signage that reveals the identity or function of the facility, though by one small entrance, there is a small, inconspicuous sign which reads 'E. & J. Gallo Winery Green waste/compost facility'. This is one of several such wine processing 'factories' run by Gallo in California. There is a similar plant in the town of Modesto, the headquarters of the winery where the company identity is more prominent, and others in the countryside – such as a very large industrial estate with hectares of huge tanks lying to the west of Livingston surrounded by fields, where the identity again is almost absent.

These are two of the faces of wine production. One is overtly public (even if public access is controlled), and the other seems to hide its purpose and ownership. But both are essential elements of how wine is made and marketed. This chapter explores the way places of wine production are both 'sites' (locations for winemaking, sometimes linked to vineyards and a rural identity, sometimes more determined by proximity to transport and labour) and 'sights' (displays or not of the activity of winemaking, which may promote qualitative claims about the wine). Although the two examples here present two extremes of winemaking sites and sights, it is important to note that there are variations in between, and the two are linked and, arguably, co-dependent in many ways, just as wine-producing companies may appear in both types of sites.

Sites and sights of production

Figure 9.1 The entrance to Montes Winery, Colchagua, Chile
Source: John Overton

Figure 9.2 A wine-processing facility, Fresno, California
Source: John Overton

The study of the locational geography of wine has sometimes been dominated by viticultural considerations. The underlying concept of terroir (Wilson 1998; Vaudour 2002; Trubek 2008) has focused attention on environmental considerations, such as climate, soils and aspect, as well as human/cultural factors, such as tradition and cultures of grape growing and winemaking (Smith 2015) and the way these influence grape characteristics and, hence, wine quality. Much attention has been devoted to the way wine regions have developed and the ways this have been underpinned by both defined and measurable environmental indices (soil types, rainfall, sunshine hours etc.) and 'constructed' claims to the way terroir is linked to wine quality. (See Chapter 8 on terroir.) Place of origin is used frequently to promote wine (Banks et al. 2007; Bowen 2010; Dinnie 2004), and there is also a strong interest in the way wine regions are seen as idyllic and utopian (Howland 2014; Demossier 2020). What is less well investigated is the way other factors, such as the proximity of labour, investment and tourists, affect the location and growth of wine regions (e.g. Overton 2019). Researchers also have not well explored the reasons for the location of winemaking operations, separate from vineyards, and how these are inter-related. The focus of this chapter is on the siting and character of winemaking (from pressing of grapes to despatch of bottles). It begins by discussing the matter of 'sites of winemaking' – why they are located where they are – then moves to exploring various 'sights of production' – the way production processes are made visible or not – before concluding with comments about the provenance and performance of winemaking. The chapter draws from a range of first-hand observations by the author in wine regions in Europe, North and South America, South Africa, Australia and New Zealand over the past 25 years. These were sometimes the result of single encounters as a casual visitor, and sometimes they involved more in-depth research and interviews. In retrospect, they accord to what Pink (2008) and others (for example, Nakamura 2013; Pennycook and Otsuji 2015) have termed 'sensory anthropology' in that the encounters have drawn on the senses of sight, sound and smell in observing winemaking and selling to understand how these places are constructed and constituted.

Sites of winemaking

Despite well-established romantic narratives of tradition, craft and culture, the making of wine is akin to many other agro-food processing industries. It takes fruit, extracts juice, subjects that to fermentation and other forms of chemical change, then packages the product into bottles before shipping it on down wholesaling and retailing chains. In the processing of grape juice, winemaking requires continual inputs of labour and material, such as packaging, and it produces outputs, whether pallets of wine or waste from crushed fruit. Furthermore, in large-scale operations, such as that described in Fresno, industrial land is needed – a consideration that is important when good vineyard land is at a premium in prestige wine regions.

With these considerations in mind, the siting of winemaking often gravitates towards urban areas and transport hubs, and industrial estates on the outskirts of cities may be well suited, particularly where the scale of operation is large, and wine has to be transported to different markets. Wine in bottles is expensive to transport, and this tends to pull the location of winemaking towards ultimate markets. Such a market-orientated location may also suit some smaller producers, and being close to consumers has been a factor in the development of urban wineries, where winemakers operate and sell their wine in urban neighbourhoods (Barber et al. 2008; Recasens et al. 2016).

On the other hand, the bulk and perishability of grapes means that crushing at least is optimally located near, or even in, the vineyards of origin. Some smaller wineries in particular feel that there are other benefits in being close to the vineyards, especially where winemakers are closely involved in viticultural matters and control over the quality of the grapes. Furthermore, when wineries seek to sell the product and/or promote their identity and quality, having at least some winemaking operations on or near the vineyard can help, as we will see, to associate the terroir of the grapes with the wine in a bottle.

So winemaking can be sited virtually anywhere along the chain between vineyards and markets. Furthermore, in practice, different stages of processing can be split in terms of location so that siting is 'stretched' over multiple locations, even internationally. For example, in New Zealand, one of the main grape-producing regions is Marlborough, but much of the processing and bottling is carried out in Auckland, 760 kilometres distant by road or rail and with a three-hour ferry crossing between the two islands of the country. For several larger wineries, grapes are crushed in Marlborough then transported in tankers to Auckland, where fermentation, sometimes barrel aging and bottling are conducted. In other instances, bulk wine is produced in the country where the grapes are grown (e.g. Chile) and then shipped in large bladders or tankers to a market (e.g. China or the UK) where it is bottled (Charters 2006; Mariani et al. 2012). Wine-producing spaces, then, are highly diverse and differentiated by location, size and character, but they are also often linked in some way, whether by representing different production stages in different places or by being part of large winemaking companies with different production sites in different regions and countries.

Sights of winemaking

The location – the site and sites – of winemaking facilities is but part of how wine is made. Of greater interest in terms of the social and cultural themes of this book, however, is what is made visible of these sites. Wine production has important visceral and sensory dimensions, and these can become important parts of the way wine is perceived and promoted to consumers. Just as a glass of wine can be seen, smelled and tasted, so too does the production of wine involve vision, tastes, smells and the sounds of tanks, pipes, barrels and winemakers going about their craft. There are sounds of machinery, of the hosing down of equipment, of the clanking of tools, of trucks arriving – and even Gregorian chants! There is the smell of spilt grape juice and sometimes of fermentation and cleaning products.

Again, these are little different to a food processing factory or a warehouse. Yet it is the way such sensory experiences are deliberately constructed and selectively revealed to members of the public that alerts us to the way spaces are managed and narratives produced to help sell wine.

A culture of winemaking can be discerned that is in evidence in most winemaking regions around the world, albeit with local variants. This comprises a set of materials (hoppers, presses, tanks, barrels, pipes), sub-spaces where specialist tasks are carried out (particularly the cellars), a multitude of daily practices and a collection of skilled workers. These are presented in ways which instil in the minds of visitors and consumers that such a culture exists, and it is what contributes significantly to the quality of the wine.

Although the majority (by volume) of wine consumed does not see the inside of an oak barrel – or even oak chips – the imagery of barrels is potent, and their prominent display is important to convey the idea that some wine is carefully aged; is given complex flavours; and is, through sampling, blending and monitoring in the barrel, made 'by hand'. The use of French oak also helps establish, for New World wines at least, a link to Old World tradition and quality. Cellars and barrel rooms are prominent in the public displays of winemaking for other reasons, too. They are relatively safe and unhurried places able to accommodate members of the public without too much adaptation, unlike busy and potentially hazardous spaces where grapes are received, crushed and pumped: spaces which are critical in the winemaking process but which remain largely out of sight. Yet cellars also help fix important perceptions of winemaking. They are 'crafty spaces' where wood rather than steel is prominent, and there is a timelessness, almost reverence (as in the Viña Montes cellar), that reinforces notions of careful handling and high quality.

Underground cellars full of barrels of aging red – and even some white – wine may help build the image of craft and tradition in wine, but other winemaking plants can implant alternative suggestions.

Many wineries mix the tradition of barrels and cellars with the modernity of stainless steel tanks and concrete floors. This not only reflects the reality of the way steel tanks are vital for most wine production, but it is also suggestive of cleanliness and, in the case of some fruit-driven wines, the purity of flavours. Markers of difference are also part of this material culture of winemaking. These can be the use of traditional practices such as basket presses or novel techniques such as the use of concrete eggs. These can help construct narratives of novelty and experimentation – even an appealing level of eccentricity – alongside tradition and timelessness.

The prominent display of expensive oak barrels and modern winemaking machinery is sometimes associated with what we have termed elsewhere 'conspicuous production' (Overton and Banks 2015). This involves the heavy investment in winemaking by some individuals who have created wealth in other enterprises or sometimes questionable pursuits but who seek to re-present themselves as winemakers and, thus, associated with craft and tradition and a high-quality product. They may not even seek to maximise profits from winemaking but rather use it to create a new public image for themselves (rather than being primarily associated with arms manufacturing, waste disposal or supermarket retailing). In similar ways, large beverage companies invest and spend heavily on their flagship brands and locations beyond what a simple profit-and-loss calculation might return from a particular production site (a château in Bordeaux or a large, expensive winery building in Mendoza). So sites of production can also be stages for the display of wealth and prestige and exercises in branding.

Another aspect of the staging of wine production is the human element alongside vinicultural equipment. Winemakers, their careers, achievements and personalities have become part of the story of wine and the way it is promoted. Many brands, particularly in more expensive sectors of the market and often with smaller-scale boutique production, identify the winemaker, and they appear on winery websites and labels. Having them visible in the winery, and sometimes available to talk to visitors and customers, reinforces this promotion strategy. It personalises the wine, educates visitors and adds to the narratives of craft. Other workers are also often visible, such as cellar hands or assistant winemakers. Their work appears skilled and unhurried – tasks such as plunging, riddling and racking – which may differ markedly from the (largely hidden) urgency, physicality and noise of harvest and its initial processing.

We can consider these sights of production as performances of craft. They may not be scripted, except by the demands of how and when wine is made, but they are staged in terms of location, access and surroundings. This is not to suggest they are false; far from it, they are all important parts of the production process. Yet what is revealed in these sights is also selective and often deliberate. They convey images and perceptions of wine – craft, care, tradition, distinctiveness – that help increase its desirability and price.

What is opened to view in winemaking, of course, does not reflect the realities of how most wine is produced. Most wine in the lower and middle price ranges cannot be produced in these labour-intensive ways or with the use of expensive oak or lengthy cellaring. Automation, high volumes and short production cycles are more characteristic of industrial approaches to winemaking in order to produce wines that are competitive on the basis of price. Here, visitors are much less likely to see – indeed, as in the case of the Gallo factories, they are rendered invisible – sites of production which have large steel tanks, mechanised pumping and apparently little 'hands-on' involvement by winemakers. Winemaking instead is done more in laboratories, and decisions are made on the basis of chemical analysis. If potential wine consumers were to see such production sites, they would have to subscribe to a very different industrial narrative of winemaking – sterile, impersonal, mechanised and uniform – even if these very characteristics were responsible for making the bottles of wine they consume affordable and of reasonable, predictable quality.

However, the 'unsightly' element of wine production is not just about large-scale wine factories. Nearly all winemaking operations, large and small, use mechanisation, stainless steel and chemical analysis and have areas that are messy, smelly and unsafe for the public. These can be a far cry from the ordered, quiet and crafty spaces that visitors are given access to.

To illustrate these differences, Figures 9.3 and 9.4 portray two different wineries and production spaces in the Okanagan Valley in British Columbia, Canada. One is the barrel room of Mission Hill Winery and the other the winery yard at Summerhill Pyramid Winery. Mission Hill Winery was founded by Anthony von Mandl, who used his wealth to establish a large and impressive winery with apparently little expense spared. Its cellar is open to visitors and described thus:

> At Mission Hill Family Estate, underground cellars have been blasted into volcanic rock. With a capacity of about 800 barrels, the climate and humidity controlled environment is dedicated to the protection, fermentation and careful aging of wine. The architectural philosophy for the space was to edit back to its essential reason and purpose. As tours descend into the caves, a quiet overtakes the group. People speak in hushed, reverent tones almost so as not to disturb the wine.
>
> *(Mission Hill Winery n.d.)*

Summerhill Pyramid Winery, on the other hand, is a small-scale, largely family-run winery and vineyard that uses biodynamic methods to produce its wines. There is a restaurant and tasting room and also a large signature pyramid that is central to the biodynamic and spiritual philosophy of the vineyard and winery. Yet, like any winery, its operations are the scene of activity and the paraphernalia of grape and juice handling, the latter not readily visible to the public, but neither are they hidden from tours.

Figure 9.3   The Barrel Room, Mission Hill Family Winery, Okanagan Valley, Canada

Source: John Overton

Figure 9.4 Winemaking equipment and yard, Summerhill Pyramid Winery, Okanagan Valley, Canada
Source: John Overton

Provenance and performance

These varied presentations of winemaking and associated sites can, in part, be explained in terms of practical considerations, such as health and safety regulations, keeping visitors away from potentially hazardous workplaces or the simple observation that visitors to wineries like to see barrel rooms and some ordered signs of winemaking but are well aware that there is a lot more to the winemaking process than they see. However, the argument here is that the production of wine can also be seen through a cultural lens – in terms of widely practised stages and performances – in ways similar to the examination of cultures of wine consumption (e.g. Demossier 2010; Dutton 2020).

The notion of provenance as it applies to the wine industry is helpful in pursuing this concept of performance. Morgan *et al.* (2006: 185) have explored provenance in terms of food chains in the global economy, and 'provenance', in this sense, refers to 'the spatial and social history of the product'. Provenance is important in the wine industry because, ideally, it gives consumers information about where the grapes were grown and in what year and who produced the wine. Sometimes, there is also information about how the wine was produced – through fair trade or organic certification, for example. This is vital where notions of terroir and vintage are firmly embedded in wine consumption cultures as supposed proxies for quality.

Yet provenance is more than a basic process of the 'facts' of origin of wine; it is also about the way narratives are built to link the facts of place and time with suggestions of quality and claims to price premiums. In this sense, provenance is also a process; acts of 'provenancing' build stories of origin, terroir and production[1]. Places of grape production are promoted, re-imagined and even created as forms of 'fictive place' (Overton and Murray 2016), which, through the regulatory protection of place names, makes place a factor in production: actively crafted, promoted and protected in order to add value to a bottle of wine.

In this light, the performances of production can be regarded as acts of provenancing. They build narratives of craft, of care, of tradition, of patience and of skill in the ways winegrapes are turned into wine. They are linked to terroir-related strategies but build the 'social and spatial history of the product' further, taking the story from the vineyard to the cellar. They use particular stages (vinicultural *matériel* and spaces, especially oak barrels; cellars and small tank rooms) and exclude others, notably the smelly, messy, noisy and busy places and equipment used when grapes are first processed. They employ certain actors, particularly winemakers, to reinforce suggestions of craft, distinctiveness and personality. In many cases, these winemaking performances are reflected in the way the wines are promoted on labels, on websites and in marketing material. The visual is made literal – as with the Viña Montes and Mission Hill websites.

The building of such narratives of production involves but a small proportion of the total wine industry (by volume). It is mainly confined to the boutique sector (Howland 2020) or to brands at the upper end of the market. These wine producers, who may be either large or small in scale of production, seek to use provenancing strategies to claim higher value for their wines by appealing to terroir- or craft-based qualities and origin histories. Thus, conspicuous and narrated winemaking is an important part of the higher-value wine segment of the global wine industry.

Two very different examples of wine production sites were described at the start of this chapter: one open and proudly staged with a clear display of apparently artisanal winemaking; the other closed and anonymous, disguising a large-scale wine factory producing large volumes for a mass market. It is tempting to see these as opposites, evidence of a binary structure in the wine industry: small-scale, boutique, higher-priced and craft production versus large-scale industrial production of a mass commodity competing largely on the basis of low price (Overton *et al.* 2012). In addition, the visible craft-like production of wine may only directly involve a small proportion of wine volume, whereas it is industrial production that dominates the world's wine markets. For example, in 2019, the world's top-selling wine brand was reported to be E&J Gallo's 'Barefoot' label (House 2020). This brand spans several single-variety wines and blends. There is often little or no indication of its provenance, beyond sometimes 'California' as its geographical origin. It does not pretend to have artisanal credentials. The estimated sales of 22.5 million cases (approximately 200 million litres) of this one brand alone is roughly equivalent to the total wine production of Greece and two-thirds of New Zealand in 2019 (Karlsson and Karlsson 2020).

However, whilst high volume cheaper brands might not engage in displays of production and promotion of particular sites of production, they do benefit from the production narratives of expensive brands. The promotion of the latter wines affects public perceptions of wine as a product in total. Wine consumption culture, at least in part, is imbued with ideas of terroir, vintage and craft (Charters 2006; Dutton 2020). These help to differentiate one wine from another and help stratify wines by price. Yet also important for consumer choices is the way it helps distinguish wine from, say, beer or vodka (though we are seeing more 'crafty' narratives being employed by these products as well). Thus, building in the public imagination, through performance and provenance, the idea that wine production involves the use of oak, cellars, skilled winemakers, care and craft arguably helps sell *all* wine to an extent.

This is why many large wine companies hold portfolios of wine brands that often range from cheap labels with minimal provenance to very expensive brands, replete with specifics of region of origin, vintage, a named winemaker, details of aging and use of oak and, should the consumer seek it out, a specific winery with its own sights of production. Thus, the E&J Gallo website (www.gallo.com/portfolio/) lists some 72 wine brands from several different countries and includes, alongside the Barefoot brand, wine such as an Amarone (Allegrini) from a single vineyard in Verona Province, Italy, with a named winemaker, family tradition and a denominated origin (*Denominazione di origine controllata e garantita*, or DOCG) also covering and regulating its specific methods of production.

Such synergies exist at a regional level. A few visible and carefully presented wineries open to the public in a particular region help construct imaginaries of the region as a whole. In the Barossa Valley of South Australia, for example, much of the wine (mainly shiraz and cabernet sauvignon) is produced in large industrial estates on the outskirts of towns such as Angaston, Altona and Nuriootpa – sites with banks of large stainless steel tanks and little, if any, sign of particular wine brands or vineyard origin (as with the large Vinpac winemaking and bottling facility at Angaston). Yet the region welcomes wine tourists to many small wineries displaying on-site winemaking, cellars and barrels and a clearly portrayed link between the vineyard, hands-on winemaking, the cellar and the wines that are tasted.[2] Regional wine clusters (Fløysand et al. 2012), therefore, are interesting in that diverse and competing wine companies can gain from the way some enterprises construct such aspects of provenance that have benefits for all in the region.

Conclusion

Sites of wine production are social and cultural spaces just as much as they are economic ones. The way such sites are constructed and presented or not to public view is diverse, selective and staged. Those sites that are open to view place emphasis on particular winemaking spaces (especially cellars), actors (winemakers) and activities (sampling). They feel unhurried – care, patience, order and tradition are conveyed. They build into processes of provenancing, constructing 'spatial and social histories' of wine – histories of craft and quality – that are deliberate and aim to construct added value in wine. This is a strategy in a competitive market, but it is shared by, or at least benefits, nearly all producers in some way. By performing craft wine production in some sites and shutting from view industrial wine production in others, a desired provenance of wine is created, narrated and reproduced.

Notes

1 I am grateful to Nick Lewis, who alerted me to the potential use of 'provenance' as a verb.
2 An interesting exception is the relatively small cellar door outlet for Penfolds Wines. This is in the town of Nuriootpa and attached to the large processing plant, which has a distinct industrial feel.

References

Banks, G., Kelly, S., Lewis., N. and Sharpe, S. (2007) "Place 'from One Glance': The Use of Place in the Marketing of New Zealand and Australian Wines," *Australian Geographer* 38(1), 15–35.
Barber, N.A., Donovan, J.R. and Dodd, T.H. (2008) "Differences in Tourism Marketing Strategies Between Wineries Based on Size or Location," *Journal of Travel & Tourism Marketing* 25(1), 43–57.
Bowen, S. (2010) "Embedding Local Places in Global Spaces: Geographical Indications as a Territorial Development Strategy," *Rural Sociology* 75(2), 209–243.
Charters, S. (2006) *Wine and Society: The Social and Cultural Context of a Drink*, Oxford: Elsevier.
Demossier, M. (2010) *Wine Drinking in France: An Anthropology of Wine Culture and Consumption in France*, Cardiff: University of Wales Press.
Demossier, M. (2020) "Burgundy's *Climats* and the Utopian Wine Heritage Landscape," in J. Dutton and P. Howland (eds), *Wine, Terroir and Utopia: Making New Worlds*, London and New York: Routledge, 24–41.
Dinnie, K. (2004) "Place Branding: Overview of an Emerging Literature," *Place Branding* 1(1), 106–110.
Dutton, J. (2020) "The Four Pillars of Utopian Wine: Terroir, Viticulture, Degustation and Cellars," in J. Dutton and P. Howland (eds), *Wine, Terroir and Utopia: Making New Worlds*, London and New York: Routledge, 75–92.
Fløysand, A., Jakobsen, S-E. and Bjarnar, O. (2012) "The Dynamism of Clustering: Interweaving Material and Discursive Processes," *Geoforum* 43, 948–958.
House, A. (2020) "Top 10 Best-Selling Wine Brands," www.drinkstrade.com.au/top-10-best-selling-wine-brands, accessed 29 August 2020.

Howland, P. (2014) "Martinborough: A Tourist Idyll," in P. Howland (ed), *Social, Cultural and Economic Impacts of Wine in New Zealand*, Abingdon and New York: Routledge, 227–242.

Howland, P. (2020) "Plain-Sight Utopia: Boutique Winemakers, Urbane Vineyards and *Terroir-Torial* Moorings," in J. Dutton and P. Howland (eds), *Wine, Terroir and Utopia: Making New Worlds*, London and New York: Routledge, 235–252.

Karlsson, P. and Karlsson, B. (2019) "Global Wine Production 2019 Is Returning to 'Normal,' Says Pau Roca of the OIV," www.forbes.com/sites/karlsson/2019/11/03/global-wine-production-2019-of-263-mhl-is-a-return-to-normal-says-pau-roca-of-the-oiv/#1325419e745b, accessed 20 August 2020.

Mariani, A., Pomarici, E. and Boatto, V. (2012) "The International Wine Trade: Recent Trends and Critical Issues," *Wine Economics and Policy* 1, 24–40.

Mission Hill Winery. (n.d.) "The Underground Cellar," www.missionhillwinery.com/estate_winery/architecture/barrelcellars.aspx, accessed 28 August 2020.

Morgan, K., Marsden, T. and Murdoch, J. (2006) *Worlds of Food: Place, Power, and Provenance in the Food Chain*, Oxford and New York: Oxford University Press.

Nakamura, K. (2013) "Making Sense of Sensory Ethnography: The Sensual and the Multisensory," *American Anthropologist* 115(1), 132–144.

Overton, J. (2019) "Rural Idylls and Urban Economies: The Making of Metropolitan of Wine Regions," *Journal of Wine Research* 30(3), 238–258.

Overton, J. and Banks, G. (2015) "Conspicuous Production: Wine, Capital and Status," *Capital and Class* 39(3), 473–491.

Overton, J. and Murray, W.E. (2016) "Fictive Place," *Progress in Human Geography* 40(6), 794–809.

Overton, J., Murray, W.E. and Banks, G. (2012) "The Race to the Bottom of the Glass? Wine, Geography and Globalisation," *Globalizations* 9(2), 273–287.

Pennycook, A. and Otsuji, E. (2015) "Making scents of the landscape," *Linguistic Landscape* 1(3), 191–212.

Pink, S. (2008) "An Urban Tour: The Sensory Sociality of Ethnographic Place-Making," *Ethnography* 9(2), 175–196.

Recasens, X., Alfranca, O. and Maldonado, L. (2016) "The Adaptation of Urban Farms to Cities: The Case of the Alella Wine Region Within the Barcelona Metropolitan Region," *Land Use Policy* 56, 158–168.

Ross, J. (2006) *Where Angels Tread: The Story of Viña Montes*, Santiago: Montes SA.

Smith, S. (2015) "A Sense of Place: Place, Culture and Tourism," *Tourism Recreation Research* 40(2), 220–233.

Trubek, A. (2008) *The Taste of Place: A Cultural Journey into Terroir*, Berkeley: University of California Press.

Vaudour, E. (2002) "The Quality of Grapes and Wine in Relation to Geography: Notions of Terroir at Various Scales," *Journal of Wine Research* 13(2), 117–141.

Viña Montes. (n.d.) "The Room of French Barrels," www.monteswines.com/en/cellar, accessed 28 August 2020.

Wilson, J.E. (1998) *Terroir: The Role of Geology, Climate, and Culture in the Making of French Wine*, London: Mitchell Beazley.

10
WINE ISLANDS
Colonial cultures of the vine

Jacqueline Dutton

Introduction

Islands have a peculiar status in geographical, geological, political, sociological, economic, environmental and cultural history. All these (inter)disciplinary aspects of an island's existence are interconnected and contribute to the specificity of winemaking on islands. Geographical insularity influences climate and topography, and the geological features of islands often include volcanic origins, which have a marked impact on the terroir (Frankel 2019). Politically, islands have been colonised by mainland powers, which leads to sociological determination and economic dependence (Mountz 2014; Baldacchino 2007; McCall 1994). The unique nature and fragile balance of many island ecosystems have distinguished them as environmental laboratories (McCusker and Soares 2011; Greenhough 2011). The cultural consequences of islandness (Vannini and Taggart 2012) are the most interesting of all with respect to winemaking as they encompass viticultural and oenological traditions of production as well as past and present practices of distribution and consumption.

This chapter focuses principally on islands that have been planted with vineyards in the wake of political and cultural colonisation to examine the impact of colonial powers on the resulting wine industries. The very form of the island predisposes it to colonial possession, as 'Islands, unlike continents, look like property' (Edmond and Smith 2003: 1). When a small land mass is surrounded by water, whether viewed from the sea; on a map; or, as technology now allows, from the air, its boundedness is abundantly apparent, bestowing upon it geographical definition and politico-cultural containment. The colonisation of islands therefore entailed taking over a visibly finite place and its people and implanting the colonial culture – especially its language and religion – as well as its agricultural and viticultural practices.

While the island's insularity is an indisputable condition of its identification and subsequent colonisation, its relative isolation can be interpreted in various ways, ranging from a paradise to a hell on earth. Isolation can be a forum for the ideal, as many fictional utopias have been imagined on islands, beginning with Thomas More's founding text *Utopia* in 1516 (Dutton 2020a). It can also be an indicator of social rejection due to illness, such as infamous leper colonies on the Cretan island of Spinalonga and the Hawaiian island of Molokai, or of incarceration in penitentiary colonies like Devil's Island (French Guiana), Norfolk Island (Australia) and Fernando do Noronha, which is now Brazil's most famous eco-island. The presence of vineyards on islands mitigated impressions of excessive estrangement, linking colonisers to home cultures through connection with religious and social rituals of wine consumption. Planting vines and making wines were part of More's imaginary colonial endeavour in Utopia and integral to the 'civilising' mission expounded by both religious and secular colonisers (Dutton 2020a). When religious orders claimed islands to set up their semi-exclusive communities of worship, their self-containment practices usually included viticulture and winemaking for the holy sacraments, as well as domestic consumption and sales. The success and sustainability of these religious winemaking ventures were variable: the vineyards of the Benedictine monks in the Abbey of Mont-Saint-Michel outlasted most of the other plantings in Normandy (Brunet 1996), and the wines of the Cistercian monks in the Abbey of Notre Dame on the Mediterranean Islands of Lérins are famous for having been served to the jury of the Cannes Film Festival and to the G20 heads of government and state in Cannes in 2011 (Abbaye de Lérins 2020). Vineyards and winemaking tended to be less prevalent on prison islands, although, since 2012, the penitentiary on the Tuscan island of Gorgona has been making one of the region's most expensive white wines, with the help of its inmates – and the 700-year-old Marchesi di Frescobaldi winemaking dynasty (Wislocki 2017). Whether islands are considered distant or connected, idealised or damned is determined by the forces that colonise them and the style of society that is installed there, which subsequently influences the presence of vineyards and winemaking.

This chapter suggests that colonial cultures underpin most island winemaking. It begins with an overview of the dependency of wine islands in the Mediterranean before moving on to the extension of viticulture to the Atlantic and Pacific under colonial expansion and concludes by exploring more peripheral wine islands.

Mediterranean wine islands

Since the first evidence of grape wine ferments in Georgia around 6000 BCE, wine spread through the Eastern Mediterranean regions – Iran, Syria, Lebanon, Armenia – and across the Mediterranean with Phoenician traders into the Greek Islands and Sicily by 4000 BCE (McGovern 2003). The Mediterranean islands were therefore some of the first Western territories to be implanted with grapevines and winemaking from the Eastern mainlands, in a practice that endowed small islands with the means to produce an invaluable resource both for calorific and inebriating domestic consumption and for external trade. These initial forays into the Mediterranean did not constitute intentional colonisation but rather a transcultural exchange of produce and practices that was particularly rich in the islands. With archaeological evidence indicating possible winemaking pathways from Egypt through Crete to the Aegean Islands, these islands were sites of experimentation, resulting in innovations like *retsina*: wine to which Aleppo pine resin was added to minimise oxidation (McGovern 2003: 250). As the Minoan civilisation spread from Crete across the Mediterranean from the third millennium BCE so, too, did Cretan knowledge of viticulture and winemaking permeate the islands and mainland Greece.

The emergence of the *polis* or city-states like Athens and Sparta in the eighth century BCE, and their expansion into southern Italy and France, took Greek vines and wines farther afield. Greek settlements in eastern Sicily from around 750 BCE may have complemented or compromised previous winemaking by the indigenous Sicel inhabitants (Nesto and Di Savino 2013: 3). Homer's *Odyssey* contains positive references to Sicily's wines around this time, but they do not apparently measure up to Greece's Maronean wine from Thrace. Archaeological traces of Greek-style amphorae, wine presses and ceramic drinking vessels in Sicily attest to the Sicels' rapid acculturation to the wine ways of Greek colonisers (Nesto and Di Savino 2013: 5). The Greek city-state of Syracuse became the most powerful centre of the Mediterranean under the ruler named Dionysius I (c. 405–367 BCE), and its wines enjoyed an excellent reputation. Its most recognised grape variety there today is Nero d'Avola, possibly brought to the island by the Greeks and initially grown around Avola in the eastern province of Syracuse before being planted in hotter regions of Italy and around the world.

Following the Greek colonisation of the Mediterranean, the Romans began expanding their Republic throughout the Italian peninsula from around 500 BCE, annexing their first *provincia* around 250 years later. Unsurprisingly, these first possessions were islands: Sicily (241 BCE), Sardinia (237 BCE) and Corsica (238 BCE). Sicily's Mamertine wines from the Messina district in the northeast of the island were its most famous export to Rome and beyond, according to the geographer Strabo, and the presence of Tauromenium wines on the best tables in Pompeii were noted in the writings of Pliny (Wilson 1996). In a reverse colonisation of the mainland by the island, the Eugenia vine was transplanted from Sicily to the Alban Hills, southeast of Rome, and Murgentina was sent to Mount Vesuvius to make Vesuvinum, while Amminia from Sicily and the mainland was listed amongst the noble varieties by the Roman emperor Diocletian in the third century CE (Nesto and Di Savino 2013: 7–8). Successive invasions by Vandals and Goths, followed by Byzantine rule, destabilised Sicilian viticulture, but under Muslim domination (878–1061) and then Norman rule, the island's agricultural economy and reputation flourished, along with winemaking. However, from the mid-thirteenth to the mid-eighteenth century, Sicily's status as an island possession to be passed from one European power to another eroded its capacity for stable quality production of wine, and its reputation declined significantly. It was not until another colonial power, in the form of Englishman John Woodhouse, arrived in the eighteenth century that the export potential for the sweet wines of Marsala was unlocked. Marsala then became a cheaper island wine alternative to compete with the highly priced wines of Madeira and the Azores Islands in the Atlantic Ocean.

Sardinia's wines were also subject to the Italian mainland's demands under Roman and Byzantine rule, but Spanish colonisation via the Aragonese conquest in the thirteenth century saw Sardinia become a kingdom until the eighteenth century. Avoiding the degradation that Sicily suffered during this period, Sardinian viticulture was therefore influenced by Spanish colonial culture, including plantings of Spanish varieties like Garnacha, which persist today. Corsica's colonisation was different again, becoming a vassal of Pisa in the eighth century, then of Genoa in the thirteenth century. During the Genovese period, Corsica's most reputed wine was made in the Greek style – like a sweeter Malvasia – that came from Cap Corse, the island's closest point to Genoa. In the nineteenth century, phylloxera decimated the island's vineyards, leading to a mass exodus to the mainland. Recent efforts to strive for quality using grape varieties with more historical attachments to the island – such as Niellucciu (Sangiovese), Sciaccarellu and Vermentino – have been successful in rehabilitating and adding value to Corsican wine reputations (Maurange 2011).

The Christian era saw practically every Mediterranean island planted with vines, making wines not just for the church sacraments but also for the resident population, as well as the mainland, especially when the island climate provided stronger-tasting or better-coloured wines than those produced on the mainland. For Athenians, the ancient vineyards on the terraced hillsides of neighbouring Tinos produced much richer wines than those made on the Athenian plains, so the island wines were used to enhance the quality of the mainland wines. Wines from the island colonies were also sold for export. The Venetians, having promoted the fashion in Europe for a sweet white wine named Malvasia after the Greek port Monemvasia on an island to the east of the Peloponnese (Harding *et al.* 2012), suffered supply problems when their usual sources on the Istrian and Dalmatian coasts were depleted, and the general climate was cooling in the 'Little Ice Age' of the 1300s. But the Venetian republic reached out to their extended empire of islands across the Mediterranean, which included the much warmer climes of Crete at that time. Cretan Malvasia was amongst the most heavily taxed wines of the thirteenth and fourteenth centuries, demonstrating its high price, quality and demand, and Venice drew heavily on its wine island colony for profit (Dutton 2019; Dal Borgo and Riponti 2014).

The Atlantic and the New World

Once the Mediterranean was fully occupied by European powers and its islands were dotted or striped with vineyards, colonial forces began to look outwards to the Atlantic and beyond. With eyes turned towards potential new trade routes to the west, the Canary Islands, the Azores Islands and the island of Madeira became more attractive as both stopovers and settlements for provisioning passing ships. Although Greeks, Phoenicians, Romans and Majorcans had all left traces of their earlier passage on the Canary Islands, whose indigenous inhabitants – the Guanches – were linked to North African Berber peoples, the Castilians officially claimed the Canaries at the beginning of the fifteenth century. They planted the islands with sugar cane for European export, but when Brazilian and Caribbean sugar began to enter the European market at lower prices in the sixteenth century, Castilian colonists in the Canaries pivoted to plant vineyards. The warm conditions produced the sweet white wines still popular in Europe, which were called Malmsey and were made from Malvasia vines brought from Cyprus. They also produced a dry green wine from Vidogna grapes and a sweet purplish wine for three main export markets: the Spanish and Portuguese colonies in the Americas; Portuguese Cape Verde in West Africa; and European markets in France, the Netherlands and England (Unwin 1991: 214–217; Steckley 1980). The culture of these wine islands was completely determined by demand from the relevant metropolitan centres, fluctuating according to Spain's peace or war with England or Portugal, and dependent also on what was happening between these two empires. During the sixteenth and seventeenth centuries, Tenerife's Malmsey wine was in high demand from the English, reaching top prices, but when tariff-free wine trade with Portugal was included as part of Portuguese princess Catherine of Braganza's dowry in her marriage to King Charles II in 1662, Madeira became the island wine of choice for the English, as well as for the Americans.

While the Castilian Spanish claimed the Canary Islands, the Portuguese colonised Madeira and the Azores. With a similar tropical climate, volcanic soils and steep terrain, Madeira's wines were also sweet, based on the Malvasia and Vidogna varieties, supplemented by Bual, Verdelho and Sercial during the eighteenth-century boom in Madeira's transatlantic trade (Hancock 1998). It was an extraordinary colonial dynamic that made Madeira a favourite in British, American and Caribbean drinking circles (Tuten 2005). Although the Portuguese colony of Brazil had already been an export market for Madeira in the sixteenth century, the mid-seventeenth-century Portuguese-British pacts meant that British merchants dominated the island's wine industry, exporting to their own colonies in the Americas and the Caribbean with little to no competition or tariffs. The addition of fortified wine – brandy – to stabilise Madeira's wines for export across the Atlantic improved the quality of the product, and the effects of hotter conditions at sea while crossing the equator helped preserve the wines and were also pleasing to the palate. Indeed, additions and conditions that usually degraded wine from other regions made the composite product from Madeira greater than the sum of its parts.

The Azores Islands have their own distinct wine story, internationally recognised with the UNESCO classification of the Landscape of Pico Island Vineyard Culture in 2004 and, more recently, as the site where the famous grape variety of Verdelho originated from as-yet-uncertain European parentage, with its plantings on Terceira Island being mentioned for the first time in texts dating from the early sixteenth century (Moita Maçanita et al. 2018). With harder volcanic rubble slopes and much windier climes than Madeira and the Canaries, Pico must have seemed impossible to plant, but Friar Pedro Gigante persisted in placing the vines in soil in the basalt crevices and surrounding them with stones. This method succeeded and was developed into larger structures to surround the vines that grow low to the ground without trellising. The walls protect the vines from the wind and also retain the daytime heat to combat cold night temperatures. Their persistence across the centuries and continued use today contributed to the UNESCO classification of this surreal viticultural landscape in 2004. While less renowned than its island neighbour's product, Pico Island's Vinho Verdelho was in direct competition with Madeira wines and sometimes sold as such, perhaps disguising its historical appreciation. Most notably, a bottle of Pico Vinho Verdelho was found in Czar Nicholas II of Russia's cellar after he was deposed and executed (Moita Maçanita et al. 2018).

Travellers on ships sailing farther west had been telling stories of wine islands since Leif Erikson and the Vikings landed in North America around 1000; their discovery of 'Vinland' features in Adam of Bremen's *Descriptio insularum Aquilonis* (c. 1075). Whether or not they really saw an island covered in grapevines for making wine is debatable, but they may well have seen native *Vitis labrusca* on the Newfoundland or New Brunswick peninsulas. Certainly Jacques Cartier and his crew on their second voyage to *La Nouvelle France* (North America) in 1535–36 observed an island in the Saint-Laurent River so covered in grapevines that they called it the 'île de Bacchus' after Bacchus, the Roman god of wine (Dutton 2020b; Cartier 1992). This island, about five kilometres east of Quebec City, is nowadays known as Orleans Island but still has half a dozen wineries, some of which play on the historical links to Bacchus (www.isledebacchus.com).

Farther south, Martha's Vineyard, near Cape Cod off the coast of Massachusetts, has long been a summer vacation colony for the wealthy, who stay in beautiful estates created by the nineteenth-century Boston sea captains with the profits of whaling. The tradition of winemaking on the island is somewhat hazy despite its evocative name. The one vineyard that had produced wine on the island for 37 years – Chicama Vineyards – closed in 2008. An American Viticultural Area designation for Martha's Vineyard and Chappaquiddick Islands was created in 1985 based on 'historical evidence' that viticulture and winemaking had been practised there since 1602. However, historians cannot seem to ascertain definitively whether there really were ever grapevines or who exactly the island was named after. John Brereton's 1602 account of early settlers notes an abundance of 'natural' vineyards – grapevines entwined around trees – that were also observed by subsequent explorers Sir Walter Raleigh and Richard Hakluyt. As English colonists were keen to reduce their dependencies on wine imports from Spain, France and Portugal and build their own viticultural colonies, the notion of the vineyard was appealing on many levels. Martha's Vineyard may well have been named for its promise of paradise, of bounty, of independence from European imports, rather than for its productive reality (Mood 1933).

The islands along the Eastern seaboard of North America stimulated almost every European explorer's imagination as sites for vineyards. The contained terrain, protected from indigenous surprises and often already covered by thriving grapevines, must have appealed as an enclosed haven for the civilisation that wine cultivation represented. The Spanish claimed Santa Elena Island (now Parris Island), and the vineyard they established there in 1568 is likely to have been the first in North America. The Dutch planted a vineyard on Manhattan Island (New Amsterdam) as early as 1642. When the English took over the colony in 1669, an entrepreneurial Paul Richards immediately planted a vineyard on Long Island and was granted tariff-free status, and a Dutch traveller to Coney Island in 1679 saw both wild grapevines and planted vineyards, but wine production still seemed confined to the realms of hope rather than reality (Pinney 1989). In 1524, the Italian explorer Giovanni da Verrazzano saw an island covered in vines that resembled those of his native Lombardy, and it was the same island, Hatarask Island, off North Carolina, where Sir Walter Raleigh's expedition landed in 1584, describing it as covered with a carpet of grapes right down to the sea (Pinney 1989). Mother Vineyard, an ancient Scuppernong vine (*Vitis rotundifolia*) on neighbouring Roanoke Island, has been mythologised as evidence of the 'Lost Colony's' winemaking traditions on the island, but there are few other traces of past or present winemaking there. Today, there are boutique wineries for tourism more than commercial production on the islands in this area. On Hilton Head Island, near Savannah, the Island Winery is owned by the Mortimer family, who also started Westfall Winery in Montagu, New Jersey, in 2000. They have been bringing in grapes and other fruit to make wines on the island since 2006. Silver Dew Winery on Daufuskie Island, also near Savannah, is a tiny winery that has been operating on and off since 1953, housed in an 1883 wick house – a storehouse for wicks, oil and lamps for the neighbouring Bloody Point Lighthouse. Farther north on Wadmalaw Island, near Charleston, Irvin House Vineyard was founded in 2001, transitioning in 2015 to Deepwater Vineyard, which makes wine from its own grapes on its 48-acre vineyard, combined with semi-fermented grape juice from Miramont Estate Vineyards in Linden, California.

Though the English and other European settlers were adventurous in their colonial winemaking on North American islands, the results were very patchy and short lived. Winemaking on these islands in the twenty-first century is heavily influenced by wine tourism and proximity to cities with high tourism appeal on the mainland – Savannah and Charleston. The colonial strategy regarding island wines has shifted but is still present, as these islands provide wine for the temporary colonists from the mainland – the tourists.

Peripheral wine islands

Reunion Island, the most eccentric of any European territory, is also the most peripheral wine island in the world. It was settled in the 1660s by Frenchman Etienne Regnault, who, with 20 other colonists, planted grapevines around their camps at Saint-Denis and Saint-Paul. Around a decade after Regnault's arrival, another French traveller to the island, André Bourleau Deslandes, wrote that the wine produced there was quite drinkable. This tradition continued through the era of slavery and sugar cane until the first *Vitis labrusca* vines were introduced from North America around 1860, and European vines were no longer allowed onto the island due to the outbreak of phylloxera. The *Vitis labrusca*, or Isabella from America, was found to be much more suited to the climate and thrived when planted in the *cirques*, volcanic plateaus 600 to 1,300 metres above sea level, that were traditionally populated by escaped slaves (*marrons*) and poorer communities of farmers. During the nineteenth and twentieth centuries, Isabella wine was bartered or sold on the roadside and at grocery stores. The foxy-candy taste might have turned the French off it, but the Reunionese enjoyed it, traditionally with a plate of lentils, also grown in the *cirques*. Its reputation for causing madness due to methanol toxicity – both the grape variety and the techniques used could have contributed to higher levels of methanol – meant that Isabella wine was banned from 1975, and French grape varieties were reintroduced, including malbec, chenin blanc, and pinot noir. The Reunionese planted these new varieties into their *cirque* terroir at Cilaos, producing wine from the 1980s and forming a cooperative, Le Chai de Cilaos, in 1992. Although French varieties are used, the wines produced are still sweet to please the palates formed by strawberry-like Isabella wines and are the first 'French' wine of the year's vintage (Dutton 2020b). Le '*vin des cyclones*' may have been awarded '*vin de pays*' (table wine) status in 2004 and the Cilaos region an *Indication géographique protégée* (geographical indication) in 2014, but these wines and this terroir subvert French colonial ideals of wine.

Australia and New Zealand also represent peripheral wine islands in relation to the heart of the British empire, even though mainland Australia's size is more like that of a continent, and its geographical and climatic diversity cannot really be correlated to Mediterranean or Atlantic islands' status and experiences. British settlers brought grapevine cuttings with them on the First Fleet in 1788 and planted them in the areas around Sydney. The first governor, Sir Arthur Phillip, reported that his vines were flourishing and laden with fruit in 1791, as were those planted on Norfolk Island. A German ex-convict, Phillip Schaeffer, planted the first productive vineyard around the same time, and Captain John Macarthur – better known for introducing Merino sheep to Australia – was also instrumental in developing Australia's early wine industry with plantings at Elizabeth Farm, then Camden Park, and searching out vine cuttings from Europe to bring back to the colony (McIntyre 2012). The French influence on the development of the Australian wine industry was more important than on North American vineyards, from the co-opting of a few French convicts who knew nothing about winemaking to the development of oenological education and introduction of

French technological advancements (Pierre 2020; Sexton 2011). Until the renaissance of Australian winemaking in the post-1945 years, the country was focused on exporting much of its viticultural product to Britain and the Commonwealth and consequently made wines to correspond to their tastes – mainly fortified wines. Tasmania and Kangaroo Island are the best-known small islands where quality wines are produced, catering to mainland Australian demand for cool-climate wines.

New Zealand was also colonised by the British, and the first grapevines for wine were planted by a Church of England missionary, Samuel Marsden, in 1819. James Busby, who was also highly influential in the Australian wine industry as an originator of the Hunter Valley wine region, produced the first recorded wine at Waitangi in 1836. The industry struggled until the 1970s in this fairly traditionalist British colony with higher consumption of beer and spirits and not enough sunshine to produce the sweeter and fortified wines for export. A Croatian migrant, Ivan Jukić, planted his first vines in 1934 west of Auckland on the North Island and, by the 1960s, had become a commercial producer called Montana with 10 hectares of vineyards. In 1973, Montana planted sauvignon blanc, along with other varieties in the Marlborough region in the northeast of the South Island. It was sauvignon blanc that thrived, producing the quality wines, notably by Cloudy Bay, that made New Zealand internationally famous for the varietal. Pinot noir plantings followed in several regions such as Wairarapa (especially Martinborough), Canterbury and Central Otago, with abundant global recognition and respect.

Conclusion

Colonial cultures clearly underpin island winemaking around the world – both in the past and in the present. The Mediterranean islands where ancient vines and wines took root were passed like possessions from one empire to the next, providing their best wines to the imperial centres which, in turn, dictated desirable styles for production. The Atlantic islands similarly serviced demands from the colonial metropolitan centres, as well as providing wines for mainland colonies in the New World. Preliminary attempts to grow vines and make wines on the Eastern seaboard islands of North America were mostly futile, but colonial dreams have more recently simply been substituted by tourist appetites. Peripheral islands have been most successful in setting their own wine agendas. After initially following colonial customs, they have been able to break away from imperial influences to develop their own distribution networks and markets.

Wine islands must nevertheless still submit to the mainland on many levels. Island wine industries are not usually sustainable without mainland markets or tourism infrastructures. Even Australia, the world's biggest island, produces far too much wine for its own use and exports around 200 million more litres than it consumes (Wine Australia 2020). Wine islands are still like possessions whose fortunes can shift dramatically at the whim of the new 'owner'. Their histories paint pictures of the wider world of wine, telling stories of heritage and innovation, supply and demand on a microcosmic scale. Their relevance and importance are not only political and cultural but also economic and environmental, as mini-markers of mainland pressures and, potentially, forgers of future solutions.

References

Abbaye de Lérins. (2020) "Le Vignoble," https://excellencedelerins.com/en/content/7-le-vignoble.
Baldacchino, G. (2007) *A World of Islands: An Island Studies Reader*, Luqa: Agenda Academic and Institute of Island Studies, University of Prince Edward Island.
Brereton, J. (1602) "A Briefe and True Relation of the Discouerie of the North Part of Virginia," https://quod.lib.umich.edu/e/eebo/A16711.0001.001?view=toc.
Brunet, P. (1996) "Un vignoble défunt: la Normandie," in C. Le Gars and P. Roudié (eds), *Des vignobles et des vins à travers le monde: hommage à Alain Huetz de Lemps: colloque tenu à Bordeaux les 1, 2 et 3 octobre 1992*, Bordeaux: Presses Universitaires de Bordeaux, 183–194.

Cartier, J. (1992) *Voyages au Canada*, Paris: La Découverte.
Dal Borgo, M. and Riponti, D. (2014) "Malvasia: Wine, Legislation, Commerce and the Expansion of the Venetian Republic," in C. Favero (ed), *Venice and Viticulture. Vines and Wines: The Legacy of the Venetian Republic*, Biblos: Citadella, 218–233.
Dutton, J. (2019) "The Wine Merchants of Venice: Outsiders, Foreigners, and Vines in the Lagoon," *The World of Fine Wine* 64, 102–111.
Dutton, J. (2020a) "The Four Pillars of Utopian Wine: Terroir, Viticulture, Degustation and Cellars," in J. Dutton and P.J. Howland (eds), *Wine, Terroir, Utopia: Making New Worlds*, London: Routledge, 24–41.
Dutton, J. (2020b) "Postcolonial Vine and Wine," in E. Achille, C. Forsdick and L. Moudileno (eds), *Postcolonial Realms of Memory*, Liverpool: Liverpool University Press, 373–382.
Edmond, R. and Smith, V. (eds) (2003) *Islands in History and Representation*, London and New York: Routledge.
Frankel, C. (2019) *Volcanoes and Wine: From Pompeii to Napa*, Chicago: University of Chicago Press.
Greenhough, B. (2011) "Assembling an Island Laboratory," *Area* 43(2), 134–138.
Hancock, D. (1998) "Commerce and Conversation in the Eighteenth-Century Atlantic: The Invention of Madeira Wine," *Journal of Interdisciplinary History* 29(2), 197–219.
Harding, J., Robinson, J. and Vouillamoz, J. (2012) *Wine Grapes: A Complete Guide to 1,368 Vine Varieties, Including Their Origins and Flavours Is a Reference Book About Varieties of Wine Grapes*, London: Allen Lane (Penguin).
Maurange, P. (2011) "Vins corses, un vent nouveau sur l'île de beauté," *Revue du Vin de France* 550, 76–86.
McCall, G. (1994) "Nissology: The Study of Islands," *Journal of the Pacific Society* 17(2–3), 1–14.
McCusker, M. and Soares, A. (2011) *Islanded Identities: Constructions of Postcolonial Cultural Insularity*, Amsterdam: Rodopi.
McGovern, P.E. (2003) *Ancient Wine: The Search for the Origins of Viniculture*, Princeton, NJ: Princeton University Press.
McIntyre, J. (2012) *First Vintage: Wine in Colonial New South Wales*, Sydney: New South Books.
Moita Maçanita, A., Santos, R. and Catarina Gomes, A. (2018) "Unravelling the Origin of *Vitis Vinifera* L. Verdelho," *Australian Grape and Winegrower* 24(4), 450–460.
Mood, F. (1933) "Why the 'Vineyard'," *The New England Quarterly* 6(1), 131–136.
Mountz, A. (2014) "Political Geography II: Islands and Archipelagos," *Progress in Human Geography* 39(5), 636–646.
Nesto, B. and Di Savino, F. (2013) *The World of Sicilian Wine*, Berkeley: University of California Press.
Pierre, M. (2020) *"France of the Southern Hemisphere," Transferring a European Wine Model to Colonial Australia* (PhD Thesis, University of Newcastle).
Pinney, T. (1989) *The History of Wine in America: From the Beginnings to Prohibition*, Berkeley: University of California Press.
Sexton, A. (2011) "The French in the Australian Wine Industry 1788–2009," *International Journal of Wine Business Research* 23(3), 198–209.
Steckley, G.F. (1980) "The Wine Economy of Tenerife in the Seventeenth Century: Anglo-Spanish Partnership in a Luxury Trade," *Economic History Review*, 2nd series 33, 335–350.
Tuten, J.H. (2005) "Liquid Assets: Madeira Wine and Cultural Capital Among Lowcountry Planters, 1735–1900," *American Nineteenth Century History* 6(2), 173–188.
Unwin, T. (1991) *Wine and the Vine: An Historical Geography of Viticulture and the Wine Trade*, London: Routledge.
Vannini, P. and Taggart, J. (2012) "Doing Islandness: A Non-Representational Approach to an Island's Sense of Place," *Cultural Geographies* 20(2), 225–242.
Wilson, R.J.A. (1996) "Sicily, Sardinia and Corsica," in *The Cambridge Ancient History, Vol. X the Augustan Empire 43BC-AD69*, Cambridge: Cambridge University Press, 434–448.
Wine Australia. (2020) "Australian Wine Sector at a Glance," www.wineaustralia.com/market-insights/australian-wine-sector-at-a-glance#:~:text=Australia%20exported%20729%20million%20litres,sales%20volume%20in%202019%2D20.
Wislocki, A. (2017) "Gorgona: The Wine Made by Prisoners," *Decanter*, 6 April, www.decanter.com/features/gorgona-tuscanys-island-white-365678/.

11
EXPRESSING SENSE OF PLACE AND TERROIR THROUGH WINE TOURISM ENCOUNTERS

Antipodal reflections from France and New Zealand

Rory Hill and Joanna Fountain

Introduction

In an increasingly competitive global marketplace, expressions of wine regionality and provenance are important tools to differentiate wine and wine regions. These differences are notably articulated and experienced through wine tourism encounters. Speaking to the inherent and revealed qualities of the place of origin is a task which is central to the wine tourism narrative of many wine producers, effected principally through the labelling, exhibition and 'hand-selling' of their product. One of the terms which is used heavily in the discussion and promotion of wine is 'terroir', used to refer to the array of physical and human geographical particularities in a location, from climate and underlying geology to tradition and *savoir-faire* (Pitte 2001; Trubek 2008; Moran 2016: 4–9; see also Chapter 8). While historically, the term has been used primarily to evoke place, its global application reveals the significance of people and culture in the narratives – and products – of diverse contexts, adding to the perceived authenticity of wine from particular regions and cultures (White *et al.* 2009; Murray and Overton 2011; Charters *et al.* 2017). The sharing of these narratives with visitors to wine regions helps establish an emotional connection between the region, the wine and the consumer (Lignon-Darmaillac 2010; Fountain and Dawson 2014; Sigala and Robinson 2019).

The manifestation of differences in expressions and experiences of terroir in wine tourism has been explored only recently. As Fountain *et al.* (2020: 1) argue, '[T]here may be substantial spatial, historical, and cultural influences' in wine tourism itself, which 'preclude easy generalisations'. Mitchell *et al.* (2012) similarly illustrate the way in which cultural systems are manifest in the landscape of wine regions, impacting the visitor experience. And not all wine producers use the term 'terroir' in their evocation of matters of soil, climate, topography, winemaking traditions and heritage. Complementing the other contributions in this section, this chapter draws on interview data with wine producers and industry stakeholders and discourse analysis from recently completed research projects to explore the narratives of place and terroir used in encounters between wine producers and customers in Burgundy, France, and North Canterbury, New Zealand. We argue that, in addition to the varied local articulations of globally valuable wine concepts, it is possible to find clues to wider regional and national culture in the aesthetic and practical experience of wine tourism destinations, particularly at cellar doors. In this way, regionally specific wine tourism encounters both shape and are shaped by precepts of wine culture that may have been developed over centuries or more recently acquired.

There are a number of compelling reasons to compare these two regions. Aside from the fact they are geographical antipodes of each other, it is in Burgundy that the concept of terroir first emerged and where its current use builds heavily on its historical dimensions, symbolised by the ascension of its celebrated sub-region of the Côte d'Or to UNESCO world heritage status. By contrast, North Canterbury is an emerging region in a comparatively young wine producing nation with a traditionally beer-drinking culture (Beaven 1977; Moran 2016). Wine is increasingly important in this region's economic and cultural life, and wine tourism encounters are key sites for the transmission of ideas of local distinctiveness. This is encountered in the maps on display at cellar doors, guided tours of the vineyards with explanations of soil types, winery restaurants marrying local food and wine, and the creation of wine trails that allow tourists to gaze upon vineyards framed by rugged hills (Mitchell et al. 2012; cf. Urry 1990). If North Canterbury is an emergent region of the New World, Burgundy is a self-consciously old part of the Old World. The concept of terroir is mobilised in both regions, but with different inflections, and in North Canterbury, it is just one of several terms employed to promote local distinctiveness. The release of the documentary film *A Seat at the Table* in 2019 brought the concept of terroir and the idea of provenance-driven quality in New Zealand wine to the fore, in direct comparison with the Burgundian winemaking experience and tradition (Nash and Mark-Brown 2019). That film reflects much wider conversations about the comparability of Old and New World wine regions competing and influencing each other at the global scale.

Articulating terroir

The wines of Burgundy have established a reputation and distinctive taste profile over hundreds of years and – notwithstanding more detailed provenance traced by ampelographers – a claim to being the homeland of the pinot noir and chardonnay grape varieties. The differences between Burgundy wines and those of Bordeaux, the Loire Valley or Provence, for example, are constantly rehearsed in producer narratives and tourist encounters; they are compounded in the words of wine critics and wine writers; and they are even repeated in the geographic organisation of wine shelves in many European wine stores and supermarkets. The term 'terroir' and its connotation of uniqueness are central to the rhetorical communication of the value of both wine and region.

For the North Canterbury region of New Zealand, however, neither the grape varieties grown nor the fact of a winemaking tradition is unique to it within the country. North Canterbury competes with Central Otago in the production of pinot noir (red) wine and with Marlborough in the production of sauvignon blanc (white) wine: those two regions 'have awesome brands', felt one producer we interviewed, though 'our region is making equally good wine'. On the one hand, the existence of successful wine tourism elsewhere in New Zealand helps justify the creation of cellar doors, vineyard trails and wine festivals in North Canterbury; on the other, the competition drives the need to establish regional – and, potentially, even internal – differentiation.

Whilst the concept of terroir was familiar to the producers interviewed in North Canterbury, and the term appeared on over half the websites of the region's producers (often in the phrase 'unique terroir'), their use of it in the sharing of narratives when meeting consumers was limited. Its foreignness was keenly felt, with one producer remarking: 'It's someone else's terminology'. 'Why would I use terroir?' asked another; 'I'm . . . not French, and we're not in France'. Its value within fine wine circles was understood – 'I might sort of accidentally throw it in if . . . I'm at a winemakers dinner' – but it was not much used in promoting wine to everyday customers:

> [Terroir] is very, you know, relevant and the French use it quite right . . . and [it] describes things really well. [But] we haven't chosen it in any of our language, generally the language

that we use is . . . it's relatively casual, you know . . . we're trying not to be high falutin' I guess in terms of our choice of language.

This feeling on the kind of language to use in promoting wine is a cultural watermark. 'The best thing New Zealanders do', remarked another producer, quoting a local chef, 'is informality'. Potentially elitist or esoteric language is largely avoided in the country's wider consumer culture when compared to Britain or France, for instance. Foreign terms such as 'terroir', which, as the Oxford English Dictionary put it, is 'not fully naturalized into English' (OED 2015), often reside in those elite or esoteric categories. As the New Zealand poet Tony Ireland remarked in the culinary television series *Kiwi Kitchen* (TVNZ 2006), 'If you call it beef bourguignon, people are intimidated, but if you call it red wine stew [they're not]'. This is quite different from Burgundy, where not only is terroir a native term, but elitism and esotericism in wine culture are also, in fact, widely anticipated. The appreciation of wine's quality is guided through a hierarchical system of *premiers crus* and *grands crus*, in which a certain amount of wine knowledge is assumed on the part of the visitor, and the moral and cultural value of wine is 'venerated' (Gade 2004: 861). In the national context, terroir is known, taught and celebrated as part of France's heritage in domains beyond wine; it is a fundamental part of the 'mythology' of Burgundy wine (Roudié 2007; Laferté 2011). This is not the case in New Zealand.

Beyond the *prima facie* reception of terroir, the concept is meaningful within France as part of renewed discourses of patrimonialisation (Gade 2004; Boltanski and Esquerre 2017). Whether in specifically viticultural and culinary heritage – such as the UNESCO protection of the *climats* (or particular vineyard terroirs) of Burgundy's Côte d'Or, and of the Parisian bistro – or more widely in the landscape, built environment or even literature, terroir is a concept which generates value that can be effectively captured by those selling cultural goods like wine, art or historical real estate (Boltanski and Esquerre 2017). It is easy to arrogate the value of heritage and tradition to that of wine when it is produced in an 800-year-old vineyard or by a family that has made wine for many generations. It is readily accepted that this heritage and value are transmitted through the land – after all, Burgundy's most revered vineyards have legally protected boundaries that have changed little since the late medieval period – and this can be appreciated by wine tourists in the 'winescape', with old stone walls, farm buildings, *oratoires* and so on, as well as in the vineyard and in the wine itself. But what of the sense of place in those wine-producing regions with much more recent foundations? Can terroir reflect and refer to the New World's emerging spaces of wine production?

Sense(s) of place

The term 'terroir' is not always used explicitly in North Canterbury, but elements of place and local distinctiveness nonetheless feature prominently in the promotion of wine and the experience of the winery cellar door. Many cellar doors have a view of the vineyards and towards the Waipara Hills, Banks Peninsula or distant Southern Alps, and some provide outdoor seating to encourage simultaneous consumption of wine, food and winescape. As has been remarked in other regions of Australasia, some wine producers also plant olive trees near their vineyards, benefiting from climatic affordances but also creating an allusion in the landscape to classical, European spaces of cultivation (Schirmer 2006). Contrasting the view of the weathered Waipara Hills enjoyed from their cellar door to the sharper relief of the Remarkables and Dunstan ranges of mountains in Central Otago, one North Canterbury producer remarked:

> I'm getting a bit deep here, but . . . there's certain people who are drawn to living in this particular place rather than Martinborough or Central [Otago]. . . . We really believe in that, the power, that pull of the land . . . and it's the kind of personality you are, some people love really dramatic, intense mountains, other people love the roll out here.

Whilst North Canterbury wine producers cannot refer to multi-generational winemaking history in promoting the distinctiveness of the place, as in Burgundy and elsewhere in the Old World (Banks *et al.* 2007), the matter of time in the promotion of wine is also used alongside space, albeit in different ways. Some producers will refer to their place in the fairly recent timeline of production within the region, with those that started business in the 1980s – planting grapevines on what were previously sheep paddocks – being considered among the pioneers. Some will refer to the age of their vines mirroring their own roots in the region and adding to the flavour and complexity of their wine (in comparable fashion, though with a telescoped timeframe, to the *vieilles vignes* designation sometimes applied to the labels of French wines).

The specificity of each season is also emphasised; one wine producer argued that every vintage is different, encapsulating each 'summer in a bottle', while another remarked that 'annual variation is part of the romance of wine'. Indeed, that producer follows a strategy of cellaring wine for a number of years before releasing it so that it hits the market as 'vintage' wine. Finally, many producers make reference to much deeper geological time, promoting the fact that the region has many areas of soil rich in limestone and fossils, much like the Côte d'Or in Burgundy, and this can serve as the basis for flattering comparisons with the wines from that region (see Moran 2016: 345–349). If the valuable terroir of villages like Volnay, Pommard and Gevrey-Chambertin is based on limestone-rich soils and expressed through the pinot noir grape, goes the implicit argument, the terroir of Waipara has something in common and could attain some of that value. That implicit argument is sometimes rendered explicit in the explanations given to visitors.

Within the New Zealand and specifically Māori context, there is a deeper sense of connection to place found in the term *tūrangawaewae*. This is a term that has recently been adopted by some in the wine industry. As an officially bicultural society, discourse at all levels in New Zealand includes words from the Māori language, but these words cannot be fully understood without their rich cultural context. The concept of *tūrangawaewae* is often translated as 'a place to stand', referring to a sense of belonging and connection to a particular place, but it is a more complex concept than this. One (non-Māori) wine producer described the term as referring to '[the] place, the people, the whole thing'; that 'whole thing', within Māori cultural traditions, incorporates intergenerational relationships to the land, including the long line of one's ancestors (*whakapapa*) and their spirit (or *wairua*) in that place. When mobilised by wine producers, terroir or *tūrangawaewae* can evoke past generations and the imagery of roots both in family and farming terms, even if, in North Canterbury, those past generations were not involved in wine production from the land. One producer remarked that 'when I first heard people using it, I kind of thought it was . . . that some New Zealanders were looking for their version of terroir instead of using the word terroir'. Though our research showed the term is not used in promotional materials like websites as much as terroir, many producers nonetheless recognised its value and its potential to resonate with consumers and visitors to the region:

> I really get tūrangawaewae, I think you need to know where you are, understand the land and yourself, before you can reach out and explain that to other people, or make a truly good wine.

The use of *tūrangawaewae* in the wine industry is contested, however, and likely to be more so if it is used more widely, a point already acknowledged by one producer:

> [I]t's sad to see it used as a catch phrase, you know, by some people who I don't think have provenance to use it probably. Like a big company that draws things from everywhere and batch blends and whatever, because that's a good commercial model for something of that scale.

While some Māori applaud the incorporation of indigenous concepts and words into mainstream New Zealand culture as a signal of greater cultural understanding, others feel the use of such terms by non-Māori is inappropriate. Some *tangata whenua* (Māori with specific rights to the land) have claimed the use of *tūrangawaewae* represents appropriation through language of cultural values, and some wine producers are also cautious about a potential change from its traditional indigenous meaning. Even more problematically, in the context of the wine industry, its use ignores the fact that much of wine industry relies on land dispossessed from *tangata whenua* by colonial settlers in the nineteenth century. This connects to wider issues of alienation from traditional lands and ways of life under, and since, colonial administration, and it has been argued that the European settlement of New Zealand – including the planting of vineyards – has caused intergenerational trauma within Māori communities, as well as changes to how the land is shared and used (Reid *et al*. 2017; McAllister *et al*. 2020). More research is needed in this area: research that recognises, respects and affirms the deep spiritual and ontological connections of Māori to land even after it has formally passed out of their immediate ownership and the 'centrality of lands and water to Māori identity and wellbeing' (Wynyard 2019: 9).

In our research so far, whether terroir, *tūrangawaewae*, or other terms are used, there is a central focus among North Canterbury wine producers on sharing the story of place in the promotion of wine. All this suggests the adoption of different threads in the weaving of a sense of place narrative, given competition from elsewhere, a relatively short history of wine production and a landscape that, although properly unique, has visual and rural economic similarities to many other parts of New Zealand.

Encountering wine and place at the cellar door

Winery cellar doors are particularly important spaces of encounter with wine as they allow the producer (or their employees) to personally promote the wine, to 'hand-sell' it and to share wider information and storytelling about the wine, including the potential reference to terroir. For small wine businesses in particular, this can be an important sales channel and allows the retention of greater profit on wine sales.

In most circumstances, whether in the Old or New World, visitors at a cellar door can taste the wine before deciding whether to buy it. Beyond that, though, the cellar door experiences in Burgundy and North Canterbury tend to diverge. In Burgundy, though some *négociants* and village cooperatives have custom-built visitor spaces (with the former important providers of wine tourism experiences), the cellar doors of many small wine producers are simply an adapted part of an existing house or farm building. Whilst visitors are often welcome, there may not be many amenities or adjustments made from a workspace to a space of hospitality, and the cellar door view may be limited to vehicles parked in a courtyard. This reflects different traditions of wine consumption, hospitality and vineyard tenure, as explored by Mitchell *et al*. (2012). Indeed, the terms 'cellar door' and 'winery', so widely understood in the New World, do not have straightforward translations into French, not least because the built architecture of wine businesses in France often follows a different plan (Johnson 1985: 34–37; Schirmer 2006). In Burgundy, many cellar doors (and, indeed, many wineries) are centrally located in villages because their associated vineyards are spread in fragments throughout the district and often not marked in any obvious way. This is unlike the typical case in North Canterbury, and more widely in the New World, where a winery complex, or sometimes simply the tasting room or cellar door, is surrounded by its own vineyards.

For some producers in Burgundy who identify closely with their winemaking *métier*, hosting tourists at a cellar door can be a drain on time and resources, with one producer interviewed remarking: 'We make wine. We don't make tourism' (Fountain *et al*. 2020: 14). This contrasts with the cellar doors in North Canterbury, which, in many cases, have been purpose built and offer the visitor a view of the vineyards or at least a pleasant outdoor space. The sense of place elaborated by a producer or salesperson at the cellar door can draw on the immediately tangible cultivated landscape usually visible therefrom, so it could be argued, in common with many other wineries in the New World, that 'tourism and direct sales fashion the landscape' (Schirmer 2006: 113, authors' translation). Visitors to North Canterbury cellar doors are encouraged to linger, to sit, to take in the interior or exterior landscape which frames the wine, and this reflects a more significant difference. In Burgundy, it is rare to drink a whole glass of wine at a cellar door. It is a space to enquire, taste, consider and eventually buy wine by the bottle or case; Fountain *et al.* (2020: 15) found that visiting a Burgundian cellar door is traditionally more 'transactional' than experiential. Whilst this happens in North Canterbury, it is also possible in many of their cellar doors to buy a glass of wine and savour it, indoors or outside. This is positively encouraged by some producers – one sought to create an environment in which visitors could get the 'headspace just to relax'; another, perched at the top of a beautiful sloping vineyard, summarised, '[P]eople come up here and they have a great time'. These comments demonstrate a more relaxed approach to the cellar door experience, common to many parts of the New World (Bruwer and Rueger-Muck 2019), and allude to an informal and 'laid-back' culture found in New Zealand more generally. As was suggested in a promotional video for North Canterbury's Pegasus Bay winery and restaurant, 'We want customers to feel relaxed . . . just come out here and have a full experience of the gardens, the food, the wine, [and] my team of staff giving them love'.

In those circumstances in which wine is available by the glass, food is also offered for sale (being a condition of liquor licensing in the country). This varies in North Canterbury from fully cooked meals in a restaurant setting to simpler fare such as toasted sandwiches (Fountain 2021). The encounter with wine at cellar doors in North Canterbury is, whilst potentially an intellectual exercise, also firmly a hedonistic one, and whilst the sense of place that is gathered by a visitor may be drawn out of the wine, it is usually accompanied by a direct aesthetic appreciation of the vineyards and the wider landscape that frames them. For example, one winery has a walkway which begins at the cellar door and proceeds along the edge of several vineyard blocks, with interpretation boards explaining the grapes being grown and how their cultivation takes account of the specificities of place (wind, shelter, direction of the sun, soil properties etc.).

Finally, within the cellar door space itself, the décor, promotional material and items for sale can be eclectic and reflect much wider cultures of wine than solely that of the region. At one cellar door, there are scores of (empty) wine bottles from all over the world, with their colourful labels, foreign typescripts and unusual shapes; in another, there are humorous signs, newspaper cuttings, posters, works of art and wine paraphernalia; in a third, local olive oil is offered for sale alongside the wine. These are commensurate with an atmosphere of fun, hedonism and informality, and they demonstrate something of the expectations and attitudes of tourists who visit (cf. Senese 2010; Bruwer and Rueger-Muck 2019). One producer explained:

> We . . . always have had this goal that [our cellar door be] an unpretentious space, which is really important 'cause we don't understand why there is such high, massive bars and big rafters in some wineries, so it's an unpretentious space. Anyone's welcome, like cyclists, people who've never tasted a glass of wine ever, or complete nerds.

Many cellar doors feature maps, unfolded on the counter or framed and hung on the wall, showing the topography and/or geological bases of the region. Some have fossils and 'soils in bottles to show people, and all that stuff'. These material props are useful and persuasive in the delivery of narratives of place and wine regionality to those visiting the cellar door, particularly for those businesses that are trying to distinguish their offering within the region, which can include selling wines made from grapes grown on individually named vineyard blocks, as in Burgundy. But it is also common to find promotional literature pertaining to other tourism experiences in the region on display at the cellar door, along with an array of wine-related gifts, clothing, home decorations and works of art. Thus, wine tourism is closely connected to other forms of tourism and the wider cultural and economic activities performed in the region (Mitchell *et al.* 2012). Though some elements of this can occasionally be found at Burgundy's cellar doors, there is a great deal more focus on narrating Burgundy's story, and the iconography that accompanies the sale of wine is rarely exogenous in its references.

Many cellar doors in North Canterbury facilitate an encounter with wine, landscape and culture that easily fits within the 'experience economy' theorised by Pine and Gilmore (1998) and many others (e.g. Quadri-Felitti and Fiore 2012; Sidali *et al.* 2015). Given the relative lack of fame enjoyed by the region's wines and the flow of people through the region with no intention of stopping, creating an experience for tourists who may know little about wine, utilising the cultivated landscape to establish a sense of place, seems sensible. Yet it is also interesting to note that whilst Burgundy is steeped in winemaking history and synonymous with elite consumption, it is receiving an increasing number of 'mass tourists' with potentially no knowledge of wine, for whom an organised visit to a winery is just one part of a set of experiences of 'typical France' (Fountain *et al.* 2020: 15). These diverging expectations of wine producers and tourists can create tensions but also opportunities for more commercialised wine tourism experiences.

Conclusion

In this chapter, we have revealed some of the cultural rooting of expressions of sense of place in two very different contexts, as well as the cultural conditioning of wine tourism as an activity. Wine tourism experiences are framed around stories of place and people; in Burgundy, this draws more on the heritage of previous winemaking generations and the inheritance of land with the aptitude to furnish great wines (Hill 2020) and, in North Canterbury, on the pioneers of the 1980s and 1990s, technical accomplishment in making the landscape fruitful, geological and microclimatic features, free associations with older European and Mediterranean culinary cultures, and deep-seated cultural values associated with the indigenous Māori culture. In France, narratives of terroir are legible within renewed processes of patrimonialisation and a widespread geographical culture built on a panoply of GI food and wine (Demossier 2011; Hill 2018). Wine tourism is often seen as providing valuable economic diversification, even as it can be seen to distract from the winemaking *métier* and the elite status of the nation's fine wines (Fountain *et al.* 2020). In New Zealand, meanwhile, encounters at winery cellar doors betray a typically informal and hedonistic engagement with place, coupling wine with café-style dining that allows for tea, coffee and even toasted sandwiches to be enjoyed with a view of the vineyard.

This chapter has elaborated several points of connection and tension between Old and New World and complements the analysis of terroir made elsewhere in this book to take into account the mobilisation of the concept within nationally and regionally variegated wine tourism experiences. This contributes to calls for better understanding of the 'small stories' that make up terroir and illuminate how it is used and what it means in practice (Pitte 2001; Gade 2004; Demossier 2011; Ferbrache 2013) and of how issues relating to wine tourism are expressed 'on the ground' (Fountain *et al.* 2020: 19). Our chapter has revealed significant national, even hemispheric, differences between broad cultures of wine tourism, but it has also revealed nuances within the regions: in Burgundy, the tourism offering is growing to take greater account of wine novices, and in North Canterbury, the drive towards premium market share is seeing growth in boutique wine experiences and more explicit place-based narratives that distinguish the region from its national competitors and make flattering allusions to regions like Burgundy. If it is possible that 'the world's best terroirs have yet to be found' (Jones 2014: 43), could it also be possible that encounters with wine, vines and wine culture at cellar doors might precipitate their discovery?

References

Banks, G., Kelly, S., Lewis, N. and Sharpe, S. (2007) "Place 'from One Glance': The Use of Place in the Marketing of New Zealand and Australian Wines," *Australian Geographer* 38, 15–35.
Beaven, D.W. (1977) *Wines for Dining*, Christchurch: Whitcoulls.
Boltanski, L. and Esquerre, A. (2017) *Enrichissement: une critique de la marchandise*, Paris: Gallimard.
Bruwer, J. and Rueger-Muck, E. (2019) "Wine Tourism and Hedonic Experience: A Motivation-Based Experiential View," *Tourism and Hospitality Research* 19, 488–502.
Charters, S., Spielmann, N. and Babin, B.J. (2017) "The Nature and Value of Terroir Products," *European Journal of Marketing* 51, 748–771.
Demossier, M. (2011) "Beyond Terroir: Territorial Construction, Hegemonic Discourses, and French Wine Culture," *Journal of the Royal Anthropological Institute* 17, 685–705.
Ferbrache, F. (2013) "Knowing 'Terroir': A Sense of Place," *Geography Directions*, http://blog.geographydirections.com/2013/09/10/knowing-terroir-a-sense-ofplace/.
Fountain, J. (2021) "Wine tourism In New Zealand," in R.C. López and G. Szolnoki (eds), *Innovative and Sustainable Wine Tourism*, Almeria: Cajamar Caja Rural.
Fountain, J., Charters, S. and Cogan-Marie, L. (2020) "The Real Burgundy: Negotiating Wine Tourism, Relational Place and the Global Countryside," *Tourism Geographies*. https://doi.org/10.1080/14616688.2020.1713880
Fountain, J. and Dawson, D. (2014) "The New Gold: The Role of Place and Heritage in the Marketing of the Central Otago Wine Region," in M. Harvey, L. White and W. Frost (eds), *Wine and Identity: Branding, Heritage, Terroir*, Abingdon: Routledge, 43–56.
Gade, D.W. (2004) "Tradition, Territory, and Terroir in French Viniculture: Cassis, France, and Appellation Controlée," *Annals of the Association of American Geographers* 94, 848–867.
Hill, R. (2018) "Staging a Nation's Culinary Geography at the Salon de l'Agriculture," *Cultural Geographies* 25, 643–649.
Hill, R. (2020) "Aptitude or Adaptation: What Lies at the Root of Terroir?" *Geographical Journal* 186, 346–350.
Johnson, H. (1985) *World Atlas of Wine*, 3rd edition, London: Mitchell Beazley.
Jones, G.V. (2014) "Climate, Terroir and Wine: What Matters Most in Producing a Great Wine?" *Earth Magazine* 59, 36–43.
Laferté, G. (2011) "The Folklorization of French Farming: Marketing Luxury Wine in the Interwar Years," *French Historical Studies* 34, 680–712.
Lignon-Darmaillac, S. (2010) "Les terroirs viticoles, quels enjeux pour l'oenotourisme?" in J.-R. Pitte (ed), *Le bon vin, entre terroir, savoir-faire et savoir-boire*, Paris: CNRS Editions, 331–337.
McAllister, T.G., Beggs, J.R., Ogilvie, S., Kirikiri, R., Black, A. and Wehi, P.M. (2020) "Kua takoto te mānuka: mātauranga Māori in New Zealand ecology," *New Zealand Journal of Ecology* 43, 1–7.
Mitchell, R., Charters, S. and Albrecht, J.N. (2012) "Cultural Systems and the Wine Tourism Product," *Annals of Tourism Research* 39, 311–335.
Moran, W. (2016) *New Zealand Wine*, Auckland: Auckland University Press.
Murray, W.E. and Overton, J. (2011) "Defining Regions: The Making of Places in the New Zealand Wine Industry," *Australian Geographer* 42, 419–433.
Nash, D. and Mark-Brown, S. (2019) *A Seat at the Table* (film).
OED. (2015) "terroir, n. and adj.," in *Oxford English Dictionary Online*, Oxford University Press, www.oed.com/view/Entry/199605?redirectedFrom=terroir&.
Pine, B.J. and Gilmore, J.H. (1998) "Welcome to the Experience Economy," *Harvard Business Review*, July–August, 97–108.
Pitte, J-R. (2001) "La géographie du goût: entre mondialisation et enracinement local," *Annales de Géographie* 621, 487–508.
Quadri-Felitti, D. and Fiore, A.M. (2012) "Experience Economy Constructs as a Framework for Understanding Wine Tourism," *Journal of Vacation Marketing* 18(1), 3–15.
Reid, J., Rout, M., Tau, T.M. and Smith, C. (2017) *The Colonising Environment: An Aetiology of the Trauma of Settler Colonisation and Land Alienation on Ngāi Tahu Whānau*, Ngāi Tahu Research Centre, University of Canterbury, www.canterbury.ac.nz/media/documents/ngai-tahu-research-centre/The-Colonising-Environment – PDF-final.pdf.

Roudié, P. (2007) "Le Terroir, mythe(s) or réalité(s)?" Actes du Colloque International sur les Terroirs, 9–12 Mai, Aix-en-Provence, 16–18.
Schirmer, R. (2006) "Les paysages des vignobles d'Australie: de l'Arcadie au Jacob's Creek," *Sud-Ouest Européen* 21, 105–116.
Senese, D. (2010) "The Okanagan Wine Region of British Columbia, Canada," in P. Dougherty (ed), *The Geography of Wine*, Dordrecht: Springer, 81–91.
Sidali, K.L., Kastenholz, E. and Bianchi, R. (2015) "Food Tourism, Niche Markets and Products in Rural Tourism: Combining the Intimacy Model and the Experience Economy as a Rural Development Strategy," *Journal of Sustainable Tourism* 23, 1179–1197.
Sigala, M. and Robinson, R.N.S. (eds) (2019) *Wine Tourism Destination Management and Marketing*, Cham: Palgrave Macmillan.
Trubek, A. (2008) *The Taste of Place*, Berkeley: University of California Press.
TVNZ. (2006) *Kiwi Kitchen* (Series One: Episode Four), TVNZ/Gogglebox Productions (TV series).
Urry, J. (1990) *The Tourist Gaze*, London: Sage.
White, M.A., Whalen, P. and Jones, G.V. (2009) "Land and Wine," *Nature Geoscience* 2, 82–84.
Wynyard, M. (2019) "'Not One More Bloody Acre': Land Restitution and the Treaty of Waitangi Settlement Process in Aotearoa New Zealand," *Land* 8, https://doi.org/10.3390/land8110162.

12
WINE, CULTURE AND ENVIRONMENT
A study of the Sierra (Nevada) Foothills American Viticultural Area

Michele M. Tobias and Colleen C. Myles

Introduction

Land(scape) claims can be made through legal mechanisms such as the purchase of private property, through institutional definition and maintenance, through cultural ones such as processes of purposeful identity making or through targeted place marketing. The creation and use of geographic designations such as *Appellation d'Origine Controlée* (AOC) in France, the *Denominazione di Origine Controllata e Garantita* (DOCG) in Italy and American Viticultural Area (AVA) in the United States are apparatuses applied towards such multi-faceted ends. Theoretically, such geographic designations support both environmental and cultural claims, insofar as they lend both legal and cultural credence to grape growers and winemakers in a particular region.

Appellations are used around the world to designate geographic locations that produce a distinct agricultural product for marketing purposes (Dougherty 2012). Wine, cheese, cured meats and more have appellations which indicate to consumers that the product they are purchasing possesses a specific and reliably reproducible suite of characteristics (Trubek 2008). Underlying such geographic designations is the assumption that environmental factors contribute to the characteristics of the product (Unwin 1991). Thus, the factors applied to an appellation must, by definition, be unique to that geographic area, such that the product produced there is unlike similar products produced elsewhere.

The United States has a system of proposing and establishing winegrape appellation called AVA, a process which is overseen by the Alcohol and Tobacco Tax and Trade Bureau (TTB). In the written proposal, petitioners are required to describe features that distinguish the area from others, how those features affect viticulture in that space, and how the space is different from nearby areas (Bureau of Alcohol, Tobacco and Firearms 1980). Petitioners are encouraged to include descriptions of the climate, geology, soils, physical features (such as topography) and elevation (Bureau of Alcohol, Tobacco and Firearms 1980).

The process of designating an AVA in the US is subjective. Petitioners make their case to the TTB, which solicits outside opinions through a public comment process, and the final decision is ultimately made by the TTB. Since TTB decisions are based on individual – though professional – perspectives and the external review process is based on self-selected responses, the outcomes could be subject to bias of various sorts and/or be somewhat arbitrary.

While AVAs can vary in size and character, the Sierra Foothills AVA is especially large and variable. Can a large AVA with such varied topography as the Sierra Foothills AVA truly meet the criteria of being distinct? Approved in 1987, in the foothills of the Sierra Nevada mountain range and covering a large portion of seven counties, the Sierra Foothills AVA currently ranks number 17 (out of 248) in terms of total size by area in the US. It overlaps five smaller AVAs, only one of which, Fair Play, was established after it (Tobias *et al.* 2020). We explore the environmental evidence and discourse around this AVA's claims to being unique.

This chapter uncovers the variety of environmental features underpinning the Sierra Foothills AVA. We use environmental analysis techniques to assess the qualitative cultural claims made by Sierra Nevada winemakers and winegrowers about the seven-county AVA's large size and (presumable) lack of ecological specificity. Data from interviews with regional stakeholders are combined with environmental data such as elevation, temperature, rainfall and soils to evaluate the viability of the Sierra Foothills AVA in comparison to other, co-located AVAs.

Analysis

Federal Rule documents

AVAs are established by the TTB through a specific process through which a petitioner submits a letter and documentation explaining the rationale for the request and the proposed boundary of the AVA. The TTB uses the proposal to write a proposed rule, which is published in the Federal Register. The public can submit comments on the proposed rule for a specified period of time. The TTB reviews the comments and may decline the proposal, ask the petitioner to revise their request or decide to publish a final rule defining the official legal boundary of the AVA (Bureau of Alcohol, Tobacco and Firearms 1980).

From the outset, the Sierra Foothills were not designed to be an area with a consistent and unique set of conditions. In the text of the proposed rule document assembled by the TTB (Bureau of Alcohol, Tobacco and Firearms 1987a), the author describes the proposed Sierra Foothills AVA as containing 'gently sloping foothills . . . segmented laterally by deep river canyons and steep ridges', a wide variety of terrain rather than a specific set of conditions. Vineyards are planted in a 2,000-foot range in elevation, and the description of distinguishing characteristics compares it largely to the floor of California's Central Valley, a low-elevation area very different from the foothill environment (Bureau of Alcohol, Tobacco and Firearms 1987a). The geology and soils of this AVA are also defined rather broadly. The soils range from 'shallow to moderately deep' and consist of 'rocky soils and gravelly to gritty sandy loams' (Bureau of Alcohol, Tobacco and Firearms 1987a).

The final rule document describes two contested areas, the Yuba and Mariposa counties' portions of the final boundary. Both were included because they were seen as similar enough to the rest of the boundary. Yuba was added by the TTB itself, and Mariposa was initially contested by the TTB but was eventually included (Bureau of Alcohol, Tobacco and Firearms 1987b), adding area and variability to the environment within the boundary. The ATF proposed extending the boundary that was originally submitted by the petitioner to include the North Yuba AVA because they said it has many of the characteristics of the proposed area. The North Yuba and Sierra Foothills AVAs had the same TTB author writing the federal documents, Michael J. Breen, which is why he was familiar with the North Yuba AVA and had an opinion. The Sierra Foothills Final Rule from 1987 (Bureau of Alcohol, Tobacco and Firearms 1987b) notes that the ATF questioned the inclusion of Mariposa County and requested more documentation for why it should be included, but eventually decided that section should be added even though some aspects were different from the rest of the boundary, adding to the variability of the AVA overall.

The public comments on the proposed rule indicate that the interested parties viewed this AVA as (too) large and not containing a specific set of conditions. George P. Radanovich supported the proposal and indicated that he was then the only bonded winery owner in Mariposa County. At the time of the proposal, Mariposa County was not an established winegrowing region. The proposal was also supported by Michael F. McCarney, an amateur winemaker, who commented that the new AVA was similar to the North Coast and Central Coast AVAs, both of which are large with complex boundaries. While winery owner Alan L. Ghirardelli supported the proposal, he would also have liked consideration to have been given to designating localised appellation areas within Sierra Foothills. The only new AVA defined in the area since Sierra Foothills was established has been Fair Play in 2001. Opposed to the proposal was James R. Bryant, the petitioner for the North Yuba AVA, which had been approved two years earlier. He opposed including the Yuba County area in the Sierra Foothills AVA, saying 'one catch-all viticultural area would only serve to diminish the values of the designation of specific areas'. He believed that Yuba County had different characteristics from those otherwise found within the Sierra Foothills boundary (Bureau of Alcohol, Tobacco and Firearms 1987b).

Environmental analysis

In general, the Sierra Foothills AVA has more variability and a larger range in measurements, among factors commonly cited as contributing to terroir, than other AVAs in the region. The massive area and variable topography are likely to be the driving forces behind this variation. This variability contributes to a lack of specificity in the boundary; no one factor is consistent across the area.

There is wide variability in elevation, precipitation and temperatures within the boundary of the Sierra Foothills AVA (Figure 12.1). The proposed rule has tables of rainfall, temperature and number of growing days for the constituent counties, which shows how different each part of the AVA is (Bureau of Alcohol, Tobacco and Firearms 1987a). We explored this more with recent datasets. We downloaded 30-second Bio and Elevation data from WorldClim (Bio 1 Annual Mean Temperature; Bio 12 Annual Precipitation; and Elevation, which is based on data from 1970–2000; Fick and Hijmans 2017). We used the Zonal Statistics tool in QGIS to summarise the count, sum, mean, median, standard deviation, min, max and variance for the pixels that fall inside the AVA boundaries overlapping the Sierra Foothills AVA for each environmental layer.

Differences in rainfall between the Sierra Foothills AVA and the smaller AVAs it contains are not quantitatively large, but the range is very different. The Sierra Foothills AVA contains both the highest and lowest areas of precipitation (Table 12.1).

The mean temperature of the Sierra Foothills AVA is not very different from the other AVAs it contains; however, the range in temperatures is much wider than the smaller AVAs (Table 12.2).

The elevation shows a similar pattern to temperatures (and the two measurements are, of course, related). The average elevation measurements among all the AVAs are not very different, but the range of the Sierra Foothills AVA is much larger than the others (Table 12.3).

The important theme that arises from this analysis is that the Sierra Foothills AVA has a much wider range of environmental variables than the smaller AVAs that it shares space with. This range contributes to the lack of specificity within the boundary, meaning it is much more variable than other AVAs, most of which were established before it was. With much more narrowly defined AVAs already approved, what was the advantage of creating this large and variable AVA?

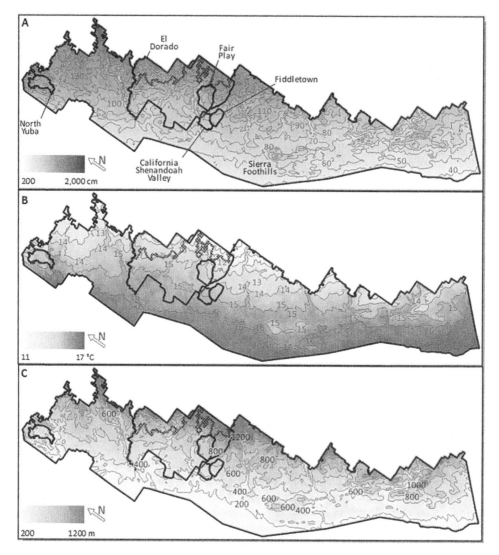

Figure 12.1 (A) Average annual rainfall (cm), (B) average annual temperature (°C), (C) elevation (m)

Source: Fick and Hijmans 2017; California Department of Alcoholic Beverage Control 2020; Tobias *et al.* 2020; OpenStreetMap contributors 2019; Cartography: Michele M. Tobias

Table 12.1 Annual precipitation in millimeters by AVA

AVA	Mean	Standard deviation	Minimum	Maximum
Sierra Foothills	880.0536	258.4981	357	1807
El Dorado	1105.556	188.8185	701	1579
Fair Play	1076.882	94.45604	931	1329
North Yuba	1170.659	71.69839	1007	1382
California Shenandoah Valley	875.6235	53.27509	766	1012
Fiddletown	955.6351	53.91499	834	1086

Source: WorldClim Bio 12 Annual Precipitation; Fick and Hijmans 2017

Table 12.2 Mean temperature (°C) by AVA

AVA	Mean	Standard deviation	Minimum	Maximum
Sierra Foothills	14.94004	1.348754	9.0125	17.21667
El Dorado	13.86742	1.274529	9.625	15.94167
Fair Play	13.94288	0.453122	12.525	14.5625
North Yuba	14.73711	0.419527	13.64167	15.94167
California Shenandoah Valley	15.02564	0.289089	14.40833	15.65833
Fiddletown	14.64302	0.25859	14.00417	15.25417

Source: WorldClim Bio 1 Annual Mean Temperature; Fick and Hijmans 2017

Table 12.3 Elevation (metres above sea level) by AVA

AVA	Mean	Standard deviation	Minimum	Maximum
Sierra Foothills	528.6917	290.9016	57	1648
El Dorado	752.2924	272.3049	214	1528
Fair Play	731.472	116.8511	543	1048
North Yuba	528.7364	96.64765	293	794
California Shenandoah Valley	454.6588	77.26693	287	644
Fiddletown	566.8919	73.7636	389	740

Source: WorldClim Elevation; Fick and Hijmans 2017

Agricultural analysis

Winegrower permits analysis

When the original petition to form the Sierra Foothills AVA was submitted, there were 35 wineries and 150 vineyards (Bureau of Alcohol, Tobacco and Firearms 1987a). This number has grown by 2021. To visualise the physical distribution and quantify the current wineries, we analysed California ABC's winegrower permit (02) for bonded wineries and permits processing grapes, bottling wines and wine tasting (Figure 12.2). We used license data downloaded from the CA ABC database on Wednesday, 5 August 2020, for permit type 2: Winegrower for each county overlapped by the Sierra Foothills AVA – Amador, Calaveras, El Dorado, Mariposa, Nevada, Placer, Tuolumne and Yuba (California Department of Alcoholic Beverage Control 2020). We geocoded the addresses with Geocodio's geocoding service (Geocodio 2020), and the accuracy scores were assessed for quality. Scores of less than 1 seemed to be sufficient for this analysis since we are looking at regional distributions.

Three hundred and fifty-two winegrower (02) permits issued by California's Department of Alcoholic Beverage Control (ABC) were active on 5 August 2020 within the Sierra Foothills boundary (California Department of Alcoholic Beverage Control 2020). The winegrower permits are concentrated in the Fair Play and California Shenandoah AVAs, with other clusters in the El Dorado AVA and one in the Sierra Foothills AVA along the Calaveras-Tuolumne County line (Figure 12.2). The southern part of Tuolumne County and all of Mariposa County have a much lower concentration of permitted wineries than the rest of the AVA. So while the AVA is large, its wineries are concentrated in certain areas, which we demonstrate in the next section.

Grape-growing analysis

The percentage of the total area of land devoted to grape growing varies substantially in the Sierra Foothills AVA area (see Table 12.4; National Agriculture Statistical Service 2016). The California

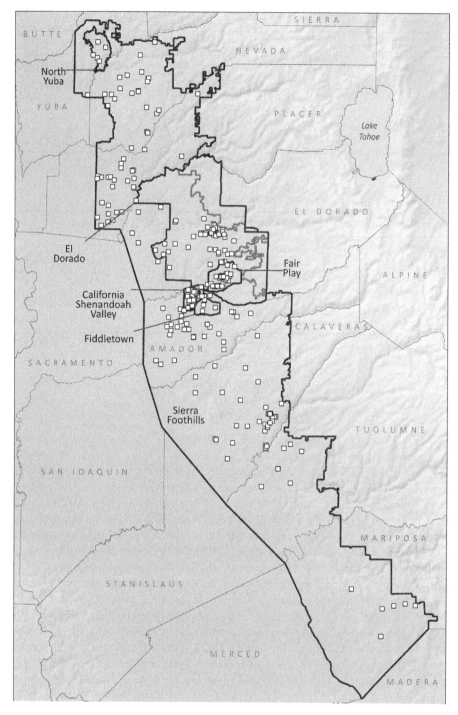

Figure 12.2 Winery permit locations in August 2020 within the Sierra Foothills AVA boundary

Source: Fick and Hijmans 2017; California Department of Alcoholic Beverage Control 2020; Tobias *et al.* 2020; OpenStreetMap contributors 2019; Cartography: Michele M. Tobias

Table 12.4 Area of grape growing by AVA within the Sierra Foothills AVA

AVA	Grape area (km2)	% AVA area in grapes
Sierra Foothills	5.357522913876001	0.000503256066662104
El Dorado	0.14393149848	8.656090894584506
Fair Play	0.011776213512	0.00011158297430424139
California Shenandoah Valley	3.1887369254160003	0.05769427571941573
Fiddletown	0.19692445928400001	0.004026956613738992

Source: National Agriculture Statistical Service 2016

Shenandoah AVA area within the Sierra Foothills AVA has the largest percentage of area devoted to grapes. Overall, the proportion of land area in grapes in the Sierra Foothills AVA is driven mainly by concentrated areas of production in other, co-located AVAs. In fact, large areas of the Sierra Foothills AVA do not show any grape production at all. However, these findings come with one caveat: the data we used to identify the grape-growing areas could have easily omitted smaller vineyards, and, further, these data do not distinguish between winegrapes and other grape types; thus, grape growing may be overestimated in some areas and underestimated in others.[1]

Comparison with Fair Play AVA

The criticisms of the Sierra Foothills AVA uncovered by our analysis do not necessarily apply to all AVAs; to provide a counterpoint and offer an example of an AVA defined with better environmental specificity in the same geographic area, we now briefly examine the Fair Play AVA.

The Fair Play AVA presents a more modern or logical line of reasoning for its petition and uses data to support its claims. In comparison, the Sierra Foothills petition relies on vague statements about environmental similarities, which our analysis proves imprecise. In contrast, the petitioner for Fair Play clearly did his research to demonstrate that Fair Play was, indeed, a unique area. The proposed boundary is based on soil and climate data and specifically states that it is a distinct area within the larger Sierra Foothills AVA (Bureau of Alcohol, Tobacco and Firearms 2000, 2001).

Through the petition process, the Fair Play boundary was eventually revised to include a larger area when soil samples revealed that soils in a nearby area matched those of the proposed AVA (Bureau of Alcohol, Tobacco and Firearms 2014, 2015). The revised boundary expands into the El Dorado AVA – and, of course, the Sierra Foothills AVA – because soil surveys showed evidence that the soils in the proposed addition were more similar to the original area than previously thought. This process reveals the smaller variance in environmental factors (such as soils, topography, climate, growing days etc.) within the AVA, unlike the larger Sierra Foothills AVA within which it is located (Bureau of Alcohol, Tobacco and Firearms 2014). Neither boundary (the original or the revised) for the Fair Play AVA's proposed rules received any opposition during the public comment period.

Qualitative analysis of regional winegrape growers' comments

For this study, we examined the interview data from 60 qualitative interviews conducted in June 2014 to gather comments specifically related to environmental characteristics of the region. Wine industry stakeholders from across the board (growers, winemakers, vineyard managers, tourism officials etc.) were interviewed, but the majority of relevant comments – unsurprisingly – came from the winegrape growers and vineyard managers interviewed. Those comments are reflected here.

Interviewees agreed that the 'core' of the Sierra Foothills AVA is in Calaveras, Amador and El Dorado counties; as one (Interviewee 3, a vineyard manager and winegrape grower) put it, '[T]hey just don't have grapes there' in a lot of the other counties that are included in the large appellation. This large [growing] area produces some challenges, as you might expect. For example, Interviewee 3 said: 'The soil is different [across the AVA], [and] you also have a difference in growing seasons. So being in the [Sierra] Foothills. . . [we] go all the way up and all the way down [the state]. So you have all sorts of different ecologies'. Another (Interviewee 4, also a vineyard manager and winegrape grower) put it this way: '[The] challenges [include] the terrain [and] the distances between everything because the AVA is huge. . . . Say a winery is four miles away, [but those] four miles may take you a half an hour to get there' due to the hilly terrain. As reiterated by Interviewee 3, '[O]ne of the distinct challenges here [is that] everything is more expensive [and] you have to travel [farther]'.

Moreover, increasing the acreage in vineyards in a place such as the Sierra Nevada involves planting in areas more difficult to access and manage, as on steep terrain. One notable grower in the area (as described by Interviewee 3) was said to have 'planted up on the hill'; this vineyard had some vines planted, but they wanted more, so they 'built straight up the hill', which is significantly more difficult – and costly – than in more flat or rolling hills terrain.

The siting of vineyards can be influenced by several factors, as described by Interviewee 1: 'As to the choice of where to put the vineyard, [you] can put it anywhere, in any topography, but it's based a lot on what you have access to, like land [and a] water source'. However, according to Interviewee 3: 'All of the easy land has been developed, and has been developed for a couple of years – outside of a few little parcels that are available'. So now, if people want to plant more vines they need to get creative; growers are:

> pushing the envelope a little bit more than [they] used to have to do. . . . There's no doubt about it, getting back to your question [about] how has the environmental landscape changed: We're planting areas that we thought we could never plant grapes before because there's a return on the investment now and technology, tractors, and irrigation allowed us to do that.
>
> *(Interviewee 3)*

Similarly, according to Interviewee 4:

> The reason why I say we're planting in areas we never planted in before is because a lot of the soils up here in the foothills are really shallow. The reason why they weren't planted before is because it was too steep or there wasn't enough soil there. Now we're planting grapes where there is basically no soil there and we're basically hydroponically growing grapes with drip irrigation and nutrients.

In other words, changes in technology – perhaps, in part, driven by increasing grape values and, thus, increasing production in more challenging environments – make winegrape growing and wine production in the Sierra Foothills (more) viable.

While the vastness of the AVA does cause challenges, growers are not deterred. In fact, the draw is not always just economic; some simply crave a 'wine country' aesthetic. For example, at least one vineyard owner hired a vineyard manager to establish and run the vineyard because 'they just like the idea of having it, but they just don't want to deal with it'. The manager described the landowner's decision this way:

> The customer literally told me. . . [as we] looked out at rangeland, he says, 'Can you imagine looking at this all day every day? I can't stand it. Put a vineyard in there in for me'. He said, 'I don't care if we sell the grapes, I just don't want to look at it. I want to look at a vineyard'. I said 'ok', [but] I was floored. I was totally floored. And then he sold [his

property] and now we have a guy [in there] that actually likes the money from the grapes, so we're leasing [from him] and I sell the fruit. But [the other owner], he didn't want to look at dry grass. 'I want to look at a vineyard'. So we planted a vineyard.

In comparison, the siting choice for a tasting room is based more on 'proximity and accessibility, [having the] "whole package" – shopping, high-end food, trinkets and boutiques, "making a day of it"' (Interviewee 1). Interviewee 1 continues, noting that: 'There are two groups of tourists: One wants to be out in the vineyard . . . the other wants to have "the tasting room experience"'. Interviewee 3 says, based on how essential wine tourism is to the overall viability of the wine industry in the region, that 'people choose to be [in Amador] because [of the] natural flow of [tourist] traffic. If you want to open a tasting room, you'd wanna be on that path. Anything off of the path, you gotta draw people to you'.

However, even with an AVA in place which is designed to demarcate distinction (and thus presumably create economic value), its utility has conflicting social value. For example, winegrape growing in the region is historic in certain places like the Shenandoah Valley in Amador County, which 'is its own AVA, and it has its own notoriety from back forever ago [based on] its zinfandels. That's something Amador has been known for many, many years – and generations, literally' (Interviewee 3). So the utility of the large and largely unspecified Sierra Foothills AVA is less significant in a place like that. Interviewee 3 continues:

> AVAs get so – there's getting to be so many of them, it's almost a pointless thing. An AVA is just a description of a parcel, of an area of land that gives distinct qualities to a wine. So you market on that. . . . There's a number of them here, and each is distinct. It is a value added. . . . If you're [looking] for a raw piece of land, you're going to pay more for having that AVA. . . . So yeah, there's definitely value added to it. [However,] I don't know if they get any more for the bottle of wine with it or not.

Nevertheless, Interviewee 3 sees the greatness present in the Sierra Foothills:

> We're full of characters. . . . It's just a different *terroir*. It's totally different from anything else, from what you're going to get from the Valley and what I call the "West side", you know, Napa, Sonoma, any of those North coast [locations]. Everybody is distinctive in their area and what they bring to their grapes. And we have that. We have very much a distinctive fruit that we get out here, that's different from everybody else's, but still a good quality, a high quality.

And so, despite the challenges, people are (still) planting vineyards in those hills.

Discussion and conclusion

The wine industry is making place in some pretty literal ways in the Sierra Nevada foothills (Myles and Filan 2019). As evidenced by the foregoing analysis, there are people who plant vineyards for the aesthetic value (which vineyard managers in the Sierra Foothills call 'vinescaping'); there are people 'pushing the envelope' in terms of vineyard development since the return on investment is great enough to make more costly and challenging grape growing feasible (plus technological advances in term of hillside machinery makes certain plantings possible that hadn't been previously); and the tourism element of the trade is a major factor in how and when grapes are planted, wineries are established and tasting rooms are opened. In short, the situation for winegrape growing in the vast Sierra (Nevada) Foothills AVA is one of creativity and struggle, but also pride.

AVAs are a cultural construct created in the service of economic aims and marketing goals. Creating an AVA is a legal process that is meant to be based on demonstrated environmental and cultural significance. The Sierra Foothills AVA, however, is based only on vague environmental claims by the petitioner, which were then reified by the TTB staff and, to a limited extent, the people who commented on the proposal during the public comment period. The process of creating an AVA requires that the petitioner make a case for why the area should be designated an AVA, demonstrating both cultural and environmental significance, but, in this case, the process seems to have broken down. The petitioner proposed a non-specific area, and the TTB staff subsequently added an even greater geographic area to the unit, compounding the problem. Dissenting voices from the public review were not taken into account. Thus, the case of the Sierra Foothills AVA is perplexing: its justification is poorly formed, and the impetus behind proposing the boundary selected is unclear. Yet now it is a cultural – and legal – unit just the same. And its presence is itself a driver of cultural creation, of environmental change, of placemaking.

In sum, our analysis leaves us with more questions. This area is generally known by the name 'Sierra Foothills' or some variation, but does that alone warrant the issuance of an AVA? Also, our investigation leaves open whether and when the Sierra Foothills designation is actually applied; we know where the Sierra Foothills AVA designation is appropriate for use but not who is opting to use it. Winegrape growers and wineries in the region could opt to use a smaller AVA designation instead, or they might prefer to apply the relevant county designation if their county is (already) especially well known for a particular variety (e.g. Amador zinfandels). In other words, mapping can quickly indicate which wineries could use a particular AVA, but it will not tell us who actually does. Future research using label collections (such as the ones at the University of California Davis Library) or a survey of wineries within the Sierra Foothills AVA boundary are a good option to investigate these questions. For now, we can say that, by analysing environmental spatial data and qualitative interview data, the Sierra Foothills AVA does not enclose a unique natural or cultural environment – a task that AVAs are meant to do. People have, therefore, questioned the significance of the AVA from the start and can (will?) continue to legitimately do so.

Note

1 We omitted North Yuba AVA from the results because there were no pixels labelled as vineyards, which is probably erroneous.

References

Bureau of Alcohol, Tobacco and Firearms. (1980) "AVA Petition Requirements," Title 27, Part 9 *Federal Register*, 1 April.
Bureau of Alcohol, Tobacco and Firearms. (1987a) "Sierra Foothills Viticultural Area; Proposed Rules," 52 *Federal Register 19531*, 26 May.
Bureau of Alcohol, Tobacco and Firearms. (1987b) "Sierra Foothills Viticultural Area; Rules and Regulations," 52 *Federal Register 44103*, 18 November.
Bureau of Alcohol, Tobacco and Firearms. (2000) "Fair Play Viticultural Area; Proposed Rules," 65 *Federal Register 45739*, 25 July.
Bureau of Alcohol, Tobacco and Firearms. (2001) "Fair Play Viticultural Area; Rules and Regulations," 66 *Federal Register 11537*, 26 February.
Bureau of Alcohol, Tobacco and Firearms. (2014) "Proposed Expansion of the Fair Play Viticultural Area; Proposed Rules," 79 *Federal Register 34474*, 17 June.
Bureau of Alcohol, Tobacco and Firearms. (2015) "Expansion of the Fair Play Viticultural Area; Rules and Regulations," 80 *Federal Register 400*, 6 January.
California Department of Alcoholic Beverage Control. (2020) *Winegrower (02) Permits for Amador, Calaveras, El Dorado, Mariposa, Nevada, Placer, Tuolomne, and Yuba Counties*, CSVs, www.abc.ca.gov/licensing/licensing-reports/licenses-by-county-and-census-tract/, accessed 8 May 2020.

Dougherty, P.H. (ed) (2012) *The Geography of Wine: Regions, Terroir and Techniques*, New York: Springer.
Fick, S.E. and Hijmans, R.J. (2017) "WorldClim 2: New 1km Spatial Resolution Climate Surfaces for Global Land Areas," *International Journal of Climatology* 37(12), 4302–4315.
Geocodio. (2020) "Bulk Geocoder," www.geocod.io/, accessed 23 November 2020.
Myles, C.C. and Filan, T. (2019) "Making (a) Place: Wine, Society, and Environment in California's Sierra Nevada Foothills," *Regional Studies, Regional Science* 6(1), 157–167. DOI:10.1080/21681376.2019.1575764.
National Agriculture Statistical Service. (2016) "CropScape. CLD_2016.tif," www.nass.usda.gov/Research_and_Science/Cropland/metadata/metadata_ca16.htm, accessed 23 January 2017.
OpenStreetMap contributors. (2019) "Norcal-latest-free.shp," https://download.geofabrik.de/, accessed 5 December 2019.
Tobias, M.M., Hart, Q., Brittnacher, T., Jessup, A. and Ensberg, V. (2020) "American Viticultural Areas Digitizing Project," *GitHub*, https://github.com/UCDavisLibrary/ava.
Trubek, A.B. (2008) *The Taste of Place: A Cultural Journey into Terroir*, Berkeley: University of California Press.
Unwin, T. (1991) *Wine and the Vine: An Historical Geography of Viticulture and the Wine Trade*, New York: Routledge.

13
MAKING WINE, MAKING HOME

William Skinner

In a garden in Adelaide's southern suburbs, my father-in-law, Nino, stands amongst his vines. They have been growing for 40 years, ever since he and his wife, Ana, built their house in the new outer-suburban development, her parents moving in on the other side of the street. Together Nino worked with Ana's father, Bepo, to plant the small vineyard on an undeveloped house block – 100 or so winegrape vines (mostly grenache, with some shiraz vines interspersed), plus white and red table grape varieties. Together, over the years, they tended to the vineyard: pruning in winter and, during the growing season, applying sulphur spray to prevent mildew and trimming the canopy to ensure adequate shade and airflow for the ripening bunches. In between the vine rows, Bepo planted potatoes, peas and beans.

At the end of summer, in late February, the grapes are ready for picking. Nino had announced the harvest date around two weeks prior, based on his judgement of how the grapes were ripening. He likes to pick the grapes slightly early, the higher acid levels and lower sugar levels translating into a lighter wine amenable to everyday drinking with lunch and dinner. This is the Dalmatian style, he says. Not too heavy. For his part, Bepo usually likes drinking his wine mixed with water ('bevanda') – a light and refreshing drink, especially in summer. Bepo rarely drinks water on its own; he's been drinking wine since childhood.

When Bepo oversaw the family's winemaking endeavours, he co-fermented the red winegrapes together with the white grapes that grew alongside them. As he got older and less mobile, Nino took over and began separating the ferments, making both a red and a white wine. Even with his eyesight failing him, though, Bepo enjoyed spending time amongst the vines, methodically snipping away wherever the tendrils and leaves were too tangled, pulling out weeds. Nino grumbled sometimes at the seemingly never-ending tasks of vineyard maintenance, the constant worry about maintaining the health of the vines and of the grapes, but after Ana's death from cancer and his own retirement from work, the vineyard seemed to provide a sanctuary for him, too.

The harvest is an annual ritual: the whole family gathers at Nino's house for coffee, breakfast and a shot of rakija, then heads into the vineyard while the morning air is still cool. The picking itself takes a few hours – it's important to find every last grape, hiding in nooks and crannies around the old garden shed, growing on shoots that have poked through fences and wire mesh and from the vines growing across the pergola trellis.

When the picking is finished, there are dozens and dozens of buckets full of grapes sitting under the pergola; a tonne and a quarter, Nino reckons. Now it's time to break for lunch: a spread of cured meats and cheese, some chicken soup, bread, pasta. We dig in, washing it down with a tumbler of

DOI: 10.4324/9781003034711-16

last year's wine. After we eat, we load up the grape buckets onto trolleys, transporting them over several trips down across the street to Bepo's shed. Here sits a big old wooden vat, on top of which is a crusher jerry-built by Bepo (with steel-studded rollers and a hopper made from various timber offcuts, powered by an old washing machine motor). We take turns standing on a table, pouring buckets of grapes through the crusher, the air thick with sticky-sweet grape juice and the noise of the crusher. Once in the vat, the grapes will be left to ferment (to 'cook', as Nino says), yeast micro-organisms present on the grape skins gradually converting sugars into alcohol and carbon dioxide. Nino will plunge down the 'cap' of skins floating on top of the ferment a few times a day to keep it moist, and after a couple of weeks, we will reconvene to press the wine off the skins using a basket press and transfer it into the oak barrel in which it will mature for the next nine months or so, before being siphoned into two-litre flagons and second-hand screw-top wine bottles. Once the wine is pressed off, the fermented grape skins will then be used to distil into rakija, a clear brandy which is drunk neat or used as the base for a range of liqueurs.

After the grapes are crushed and the buckets and equipment are washed, the main tasks of harvest day are complete, and it's time to relax: a cold beer in the heat of the afternoon, then cake and coffee, more cheese and meat, games of cards (*briškula* and *trešeta*). Nino brings his guitar out to play Dalmatian songs.

Nino and Bepo are Croatians who emigrated to Australia from Yugoslavia during the 1960s. Bepo; his wife, Ana; and their two young children, Ivan and Ana, came from the northern island of Cres via an Italian refugee camp, arriving in Adelaide in 1962. Nino, from a village near Zadar on the Dalmatian coast, came at the age of 18, following in the footsteps of older brothers who had come to work in the copper mines at Mount Isa. Both men grew up making wine – the 'old-fashioned way', as Nino says, learned through participating in vintage work with his father and the other men in the village – and wine and winemaking remained integral to notions of their own cultural heritage and patrimony. For them, wine is not a luxury item but an ordinary part of daily life and a crucial part of a meal, not set apart from other daily comestibles but taking its place on the table alongside them. But it is precisely as an ordinary and 'everyday' drink that this homemade

Figure 13.1 The backyard crush

wine is so significant. Making wine is a domestic tradition with deep roots in Croatia (Belaj 2015; Skinner 2019), and for Nino and Bepo, the wine they make aligns closely with their own sense of 'Croatianness'. It is, Nino tells me, 'just who we are'.

The wine world is marked by widespread and interconnected movements of people, knowledge and money, and global wine culture is often discussed in terms of wine's role as both an agro-industrial commodity and a luxury consumer product. To date, significant scholarly attention has focused on the ways an increasingly globalised wine industry shapes and is shaped by consumption practices (Demossier 2010); production technologies (Jung 2016); relations of land, labour and capital (Demossier 2018; Overton 2010; Raftery 2017; Ulin 1996); and, of course, the sometimes-slippery concept of terroir (Dutton and Howland 2019; Patterson and Buechsenstein 2018). Much has also been made of the cultural role that wine plays as a medium for performing distinction (Smith Maguire 2016) and for structuring social and cultural relationships in various other ways (Black and Ulin 2013; Charters 2006). Exceptional vintages from famous vineyards provide opportunity for connoisseurship; cultural capital may be cultivated through wine knowledge, the ability to distinguish fine wines and speaking in the language of tasting and savouring. This chapter, however, highlights a range of other values that wine can hold – values associated with home and homeliness, family and familiarity, longing and belonging. The sort of wine I discuss here is not wine that is bought and sold at all, but wine made and drunk at home and shared with family and friends. Its producers are not professional vignerons but amateurs: migrants and the children of migrants from 'traditional' winegrowing lands across southern Europe who brought their winemaking practices with them and adapted them to their new lives in Australia. The annual 'backyard' vintage is an event familiar not just to many Croatian-Australians but to migrant families from other places where winegrowing is culturally important – Italy, Greece, Malta, Hungary and elsewhere – and throughout my research, many of my winemaking interlocutors have highlighted their own families' background with amateur wine production, describing scenes very similar to that outlined earlier.

As a practice largely unfamiliar to most Australians of British heritage, home winemaking can be a mark of difference and a source of pride: not just in a specific ethnic heritage, but also reflecting a broader modality of migrant Australian belonging. Home winemaking, according to Nino, is 'just part of wog life'. ('Wog' is a general, pejorative term for Southern European migrants, but one which is sometimes used as an expression of self-identification.) 'Wogs' were often subjected to social prejudice and ridicule for their maintenance of traditions that were seen as backward or alien to the British-dominated mainstream culture of Australia (Sala *et al.* 2010). This included food cultures, with their emphasis on homemade produce, cured meats, pickled and fermented vegetables, and, of course, the homemade table wine quaffed by migrant men (James 2004). Wine drinking was normally the province of the privileged classes in Australia, who favoured 'fine wines' (a symbol of social distinction in Australia as elsewhere); most other men drank beer while women might drink sherry. In the homes of many European migrants, however, and at the social and sporting clubs that sat at the centre of their expatriate communities in Australia, wine drinking was the norm.

Throughout the twentieth century, and particularly in the decades following World War Two, many thousands of migrants arrived from southern, central and eastern Europe to seek a new life, bringing with them a range of skills and practices that they could draw upon to help make their new lives. This migration has also been an enormously influential factor in the development of the Australian wine industry. Many European migrants entered the industry as labourers in the vineyard and the winery, and many of these also purchased vineyard land or founded their own wineries. These 'New Australians', as non-British post-war migrants were known, also had a dramatic influence on Australian drinking culture. Until the 1950s and 1960s, this was overwhelmingly dominated by beer, and most winegrapes were used to make fortified sherries and ports or distilled into brandy. It was migrants from Europe who popularised the practice of drinking wine with meals, at home and when dining at restaurants. Partly as a result of these demographic and cultural changes, the Australian wine industry went through a boom period beginning in the late 1960s, with the production of table wines increasing dramatically and numerous new wineries popping up to service this increasing demand (Anderson and Aryal 2015; McIntyre and Germov 2018). Many of these wineries prospered, fostering the economic development of the industry.

According to Gianni, a professional winemaker and the son of Italian immigrants from the Marche region:

> My father started out (in Australia) just making wine for family and friends. When he got together with his provincial friends and played bocce, you know, bowls, it was OK in the summer months because they could drink cold beer, but in the winter they wanted wine! And they didn't want to drink sherry, so my father decided he would start making the sort of wines he had made back home.

Gianni's family's winery began primarily by producing wine for other migrants but soon found a more 'mainstream' customer base as well. Nowadays, they make wines not only from the usual 'staple' grapes of Australian wine, like shiraz, chardonnay and cabernet sauvignon, but also from a range of Italian varieties such as aglianico, barbera and sagrantino.

While some 'New Australians' successfully leveraged their knowledge and skills into winemaking as a business enterprise, others like Bepo and Nino simply maintained winemaking as an amateur practice, in the way familiar to them from their homelands. They planted vines in their back gardens, alongside fruit trees, tomatoes and vegetable gardens, and the wine made from these grapes was incorporated into a broader household economy of home produce, shared with family and friends. For amateur winemakers without access to their own grapes, some wineries also sell already-crushed grape must, to be fermented at home. At one winery, operated by an Italian-Australian family, the sale of *musto* is an important annual occasion. When I visited, dozens of cars were queuing up, and groups of old men milled about, chatting and waiting to fill up their own containers with juice to take away. Yet the event used to be even more popular. As the proprietor of the winery, Roberto, told me:

> You get the Italians, but also all sorts of others – Greeks, Serbs, Hungarians. . . . But the older ones are dying off. There aren't as many as there used to be. They used to get here at four-thirty in the morning to get their spot in line, play cards on the blankets.

In Roberto's view, the declining popularity of home winemaking is very much linked to demographic changes. The Australian-born children of immigrants often do not continue home winemaking. He told me that things are changing 'back in the old country' as well: home winemaking is usually regarded as a relic of the past, out of step with the modern world.

> Wine is cheap, you can get OK wine for not very much money. People don't need to make their own wine usually. But for them [his customers] it's a hobby, it's a way of connecting.

This sense of connection is a significant one for the home winemakers I have worked with. Winemaking, seen as a maintenance of tradition, therefore becomes an arena for the performance and reproduction of an 'authentic' ethnic identity. It is often consciously accompanied by other symbols of ethnicity: the songs that are sung, the food that is eaten, the jokes that are made. This is winemaking as patrimony, interrelated with notions of ethnic and family heritage, cultural tradition and community (Calabresi 1987; Jung 2013). For many migrants, then, home winemaking does not just involve the production of wine but is also a process of making self, a rehearsal and reproduction of identity. Duruz (2004) shows that the ordinary tasks of cooking can evoke memories of past kitchens, a mytho-historical thread linking present to past, mother to daughter. Home winemaking is tinged with the same sort of nostalgia, strengthening notions of ethnic and cultural belonging by reaching across geographic space and time towards a familial homeland, both real and imagined. This is a continuity with a rustic, golden past: although this past was actively left behind in the search for a new and better life in Australia (or, indeed, perhaps because of this fact), home winemaking retains its romantic aura.

Homemade wine can therefore represent a sort of cultural essence for many migrants. Barthes (1972) suggests that, for the French nation, wine is a sort of 'totem-drink', embodying a number of key symbols of Frenchness. The same is true for Dalmatians, who attach to wine an array of highly significant cultural values: it is unpretentious, a mark of home and family, of sociality and commensality (Skinner 2019). Making wine takes patience and hard work and is emblematic of a culture of self-sufficiency – why buy wine when you can make your own? The product of self-reliant and self-directed labour, not tied to regulation and taxation, not bought or sold, homemade wine is autonomous and independent. Wine drinking and winemaking represent, for some, a way to perform cultural identity and resist assimilation to a hegemonic mode of 'Australianness' rooted in British tradition. Here it is important to highlight that, despite the emphasis on heritage, patrimony and cultural continuity associated with a home winemaking tradition among migrants, actual winemaking practices, techniques and technologies do change. Nino's descriptions of vintage work during his youth, for example – the men of the village working together, crushing the grapes in the field into a vat atop a horse-drawn cart – seem a far cry from harvest day in his small vineyard in suburban Adelaide. He was young when he migrated to Australia, though, and learned most of what he knows from Bepo. For Bepo, grape growing and winemaking took place around a whole host of other activities – fishing, growing fruits and vegetables, making olive oil, tending to sheep. Upon moving to Australia, his life as a shepherd and fisherman was replaced by working on the Chrysler production line, but the home gardening and winemaking remained. He was a farmer: it would be wrong to own a block of land and not use it productively. When Bepo was a young man on Cres, people had to be self-sufficient: they made their own cheese, grew their own vegetables, made their own wine.

When Bepo oversaw the family winemaking, he took what would now be called a 'minimalist' approach. There was nothing much added to the fermenting must: fermentation took place via the yeasts extant on the grape skins and without any of the additives like acid, tannin, fining agents and so on that are found in the toolkits of commercial vintners – or even the potassium metabisulfite added to help prevent oxidative spoilage, although a sulphur candle burned in the barrel before filling provided some prophylactic against this. Vintage qualities varied: some years, the wine turned out delicious, other years less so, but Bepo enjoyed the wine nonetheless. Once Nino took control of the vintage, however, he started to explore ways to improve the process. Firstly, instead of fermenting red and white grapes together, he separated them: a barrel of grenache and a smaller demijohn of white wine. More recently, Nino began introducing commercial cultured yeast to the ferments, too. Now, he engages the local brewshop owner in conversation about things like yeast nutrients, temperature control, malolactic fermentation and the use of oak spirals and staves. Nino and Bepo's wine used to mature in an old oak barrel, but this 'went bad'; although Nino subsequently bought another barrel, he now prefers to mature all his wine in large glass demijohns, favouring the neutral, unoaked flavours. Recently, he has also invested in more up-to-date winery gear to replace Bepo's homemade equipment: an Italian crusher/destemmer, a ratchet-operated basket press and large plastic fermentation vats.

Among some amateur winemakers I have worked with, the goal is to produce a wine that is as close as possible to the 'quality' of a good store-bought wine. For them, commercial wines represent a benchmark against which they can judge their own wines. Others, like Nino, however, are not interested at all in making wine that tastes 'like' an equivalent commercial wine. Although he is interested in making good, drinkable wine, he prefers the taste of his own wines, made from his own grapes: 'they are to my tastes; this is what I like to drink'. A preference for homemade wine is a preference for the familiar. As James highlights in her examination of family tomato-sauce making and 'wogginess' among Italian-Australians in Melbourne, for example, the senses of smell and taste are central to cultural production: 'Predilection and delectation, the taste *for* and the taste *of* something are unified cultural truths' (James 2004: 24). As making and drinking wine are, for Nino, a marker of his own Dalmatianness (and broader 'wogginess', set against an 'Aussie' or Anglo-Australian mainstream), the very difference of this wine to that bought at bottle shops and commercial wineries holds value. This is his wine: real, homemade wine.

The sensorial properties of wine emerge from the process of its production – the selection of grapevine varieties and clones, the soils, geology of the vineyard, the climatic and weather conditions, the growing season, the yeasts that are used in fermentation, the techniques and technologies of vinification and so on – innumerable environmental factors and (conscious or unconscious) choices of intervention by the winemaker. This is true of homemade wine just as it is of commercial wine. Materially, then, Nino's wine is not the same as that drunk in the 'old country': the grapes are different, the vineyard is different, the equipment, the process. In its taste, however, is a connection and continuity with Dalmatia. For many migrant winemakers like Nino, their wine speaks of place, but this is not the rooted terroir celebrated in fine wine discourse (see Patterson and Buechsenstein 2018). Instead, their wine reaches across the seas, making present a homeland distant in space and time.

In this chapter, I have focused on a relatively underexamined form of wine: a 'homemade' drink fermented by amateurs outside the realm of commercial production and shared through non-market social and familial networks. Although this sort of wine occupies only a small niche of overall wine production and consumption in many parts of the world, including Australia, its associated cultural and social meanings render it quite distinct. For many migrants, winemaking represents a culturally significant skill and marker of ethnic heritage. Its practice embodies a sense of patrimony and 'authenticity' inherited from previous generations and reproduced in the vintage, even as specific techniques and equipment change over time. Wine produced in this way is valued not for any special physical properties but precisely for its ordinariness as an everyday drink, a manifestation of 'what we've always done'. Home winemaking is a practice, too, that nestles comfortably within an attitude of 'do-it-yourself' productivity and self-sufficiency common to many post-war migrant communities in Australia. Nino and his father-in-law, Bepo, see winemaking as an inalienable part of their own identities as Croatian migrants, an ingrained way of life linked to their personal histories as peasant farmers and gardeners and to a broader sense of community belonging. While it may seem that home winemaking is a gradually waning cultural tradition, taken up by fewer and fewer as generations pass by, it is likely that the values it embodies – differing substantially from, and in some ways opposing, those of commercial wine – will ensure its continuing significance.

References

Anderson, K. and Aryal, N.R. (2015) *Growth and Cycles in Australia's Wine Industry: A Statistical Compendium, 1843 to 2013*, Adelaide: University of Adelaide Press.

Barthes, R. (1972) *Mythologies*, trans. A. Lavers, London: J. Cape.

Belaj, M. (2015) "Family Production and Consumption of Wine and New Forms of Tourism," in N. Santos and F. Cravidão (eds), *Gastronomia e Vinhos do turismo de experiência à experiência pelo turismo*, Coimbra: Centro de Estudos de Geografia e Ordenamento de Território; Edições Minerva Coimbra.

Black, R. and Ulin, R.C. (eds) (2013) *Wine and Culture: Vineyard to Glass*, London: Bloomsbury.

Calabresi, A.T. (1987) "Vin Santo and Wine in a Tuscan Farmhouse," in M. Douglas (ed), *Constructive Drinking: Perspectives on Drink from Anthropology*, Cambridge, New York and Paris: Cambridge University Press, 122–134.

Charters, S. (2006) *Wine and Society: The Social and Cultural Context of a Drink*, Oxford: Elsevier Butterworth-Heinemann.
Demossier, M. (2010) *Wine Drinking Culture in France: A National Myth or a Modern Passion?* Cardiff: University of Wales Press.
Demossier, M. (2018) *Burgundy: A Global Anthropology of Place and Taste*, New York: Berghahn Books.
Duruz, J. (2004) "Haunted Kitchens: Cooking and Remembering," *Gastronomica* 4(1), 57–68. DOI:10.1525/gfc.2004.4.1.57.
Dutton, J. and Howland, P. (eds) (2019) *Wine, Terroir, Utopia: Making a New World*, London: Routledge.
James, R. (2004) "The Reliable Beauty of Aroma: Staples of Food and Cultural Production Among Italian-Australians," *The Australian Journal of Anthropology* 15(1), 23–40.
Jung, Y. (2013) "Cultural Patrimony and the Bureaucratization of Wine: The Bulgarian Case," in R.E. Black and R.C. Ulin (eds) *Wine and Culture: Vineyard to Glass*, London: Bloomsbury Academic, 161–178.
Jung, Y. (2016) "Re-Creating Economic and Cultural Values in Bulgaria's Wine Industry: From an Economy of Quantity to an Economy of Quality?" *Economic Anthropology* 3(2), 280–292. DOI:10.1002/sea2.12057.
McIntyre, J. and Germov, J. (2018) "'Who Wants to Be a Millionaire?' I Do: Postwar Australian Wine, Gendered Culture and Class," *Journal of Australian Studies* 42(1), 65–84. DOI:10.1080/14443058.2017.1410722.
Overton, J. (2010) "The Consumption of Space: Land, Capital and Place in the New Zealand Wine Industry," *Geoforum* 41(5), 752–762. DOI:10.1016/j.geoforum.2010.04.007.
Patterson, T. and Buechsenstein, J. (2018) *Wine and Place: A Terroir Reader*, Berkely: University of California Press.
Raftery, D. (2017) "Producing Value from Australia's Vineyards: An Ethnographic Approach to 'the Quality Turn' in the Australian Wine Industry," *Journal of Political Ecology* 24(1), 342. DOI:10.2458/v24i1.20877.
Sala, E., Dandy, J. and Rapley, M. (2010) "'Real Italians and Wogs': The Discursive Construction of Italian Identity Among First Generation Italian Immigrants in Western Australia," *Journal of Community and Applied Social Psychology* 20(2), 110–124.
Skinner, W. (2019) "'A Gift from God': Autochthonous Grapes and Wine Heritage on the Island of Hvar, Croatia," *Journal of Wine Research* 30(4), 294–311. DOI:10.1080/09571264.2019.1678016.
Smith Maguire, J. (2016) "The Taste for the Particular: A Logic of Discernment in an Age of Omnivorousness," *Journal of Consumer Culture* 18(1), 3–20. DOI:10.1177/1469540516634416.
Ulin, R.C. (1996) *Vintages and Traditions: An Ethnohistory of Southwest French Wine Cooperatives*, Washington, DC: Smithsonian Institution Press.

14
CLIMATS AND THE CRAFTING OF HERITAGE VALUE IN BURGUNDY TERROIR

Marion Demossier

Introduction

On the eve of the prestigious annual wine auction of the Hospices de Beaune in November 2017, it was announced that the Clos de Tart had been sold to the French entrepreneur, François Pinault, for 220 million euros, leaving the world of wine in shock. This was considered a massive sum for only 7.53 hectares of pinot noir, more than 29 million euros per hectare (2.471 acres). This Grand Cru, located in the heart of the Côte de Nuits in Morey-Saint-Denis, had only known three owners in 1,000 years, and François Pinault had fought of stiff competition from Jack Ma, the Chinese founder of Alibaba, who had made a much higher offer. Pinault's triumph was down to the intervention of the French government, who did not want to see this symbolic monopoly fall under foreign ownership. The Clos de Tart is the largest monopoly (singular owner) in the Grand Cru of Burgundy, which reinforces its rarity. This latest acquisition forms part of a series of recent sales which have seen an increase of non-Burgundian financial investments in the region. Such astronomical prices paid for tiny parcels of vineyard by non-winegrowers illustrates a much broader economic phenomenon in global capitalism: that of the progressive 'disengagement of capitalist commodities from their makers at the mercy of market transactions' (Tsing 2013: 22) coupled with what geographers describe as the rise of 'conspicuous production' (Overton and Banks 2015).

The impact of globalisation

The intense globalisation of the world of wine has radically transformed both wine production and consumption, offering, I argue, a unique window into the study of economic markets and the globalisation of cultural commodities. Perhaps more than anywhere else, Burgundy epitomises many of the seemingly contradictory effects of global capitalism with its crafted production, ostentatious consumption and increasing corporate ownership. In the French context, it is also paradoxically characterised by what the sociologist Marion Fourcade (2012: 539) describes as a 'corporatist-conservative logic rooted in privilege, experience and tradition', clashing, at first glance, with the Western liberal political economy. However, this picture is much more complex. The apparent boundaries between 'Old' and 'New World' are, at least in the wine industry, more porous than is sometimes assumed, and, indeed the stereotypical dialectics of tradition and craft versus industry and finance, respectively, need to be called into question (Banks 2013).

Burgundy's acquisition of UNESCO World Heritage status was based on an attempt to claim 'to be the best', which means redefining some of its most prominent global references. Nowhere was this more evident than with the concept of terroir, which has been transformed into *climats*, once again linking place to taste by presenting the site of production as an authentic, historically enduring, trustworthy and reliable place. For producers, professionals and consumers, Burgundy has long been seen to epitomise the terroir model of the designated origin appellations (or AOC system) by which place names became formally recognised as legal mark of production (Fourcade 2012: 528). The concept, which dates back to the 1930s, emphasises the relationship between a given place, its microclimatic characteristics and the local culture incarnated by winegrowers and their production methods. The AOC system helped consolidate the mythical image of an ahistorical terroir producing a wine with a taste unchanged since time immemorial. It also provided a strict geographical definition of the 'high-quality' wine production areas, sometimes down to very small areas (Fourcade 2012: 528). According to the terroir logic, strict rules concerning grape varieties, pruning methods, viticultural techniques and oenological practices govern each AOC through a system of self-regulation concerning what is defined as '*usages locaux, loyaux et constants*' (in accordance with local, fair and consistent practices). The story of terroir seemed to guarantee both the quality and the taste of place and to justify the high price of purchase for this closed gustatory experience.

With the intentional shift to *climat*, Burgundians once again linked place to taste by presenting the site of production as an authentic, stable, trustworthy and reliable place. Central to this whole new visual reconfiguration is the concept of *climats* defined as particular to Burgundy. *Climats* designate a parcel of land dedicated to a precisely delineated vineyard, known by that name for hundreds of years and, therefore, a precise plot, soil, subsoil, exposure and microclimate forming together within a vineyard, characteristics that constitute a personality unique to one terroir and one cru. The local narrative emphasises the prestigious and historic influence of monks in selecting the best parcels and crafting quality wines. The *climats* are presented as Burgundy's own recent translation of the word 'terroir', taking on a different sense to that usually associated with geographical or meteorological conditions. For their advocates, *climats* have been historically created and constitute an exceptional mosaic of vineyards with a hierarchy of wines and an international reputation. Superficially, then, Burgundy might appear to be simply acquiring recognition for its unchanging landscape, tradition and culture (Demossier 2018). From terroirs to *climats*, the same story is perpetually constructed and deployed in different locations, passed from one generation to the next and transmitted throughout the global wine economy, benefiting the whole community. The perpetual search for monopoly rents entails seeking out criteria of speciality, uniqueness, originality and authenticity in each of these realms (Harvey 2002: 100).

I have argued elsewhere (Demossier 2018) that the Burgundian winegrowers have adapted economically to the forces of globalisation and managed change while continuously weaving the terroir story into the seamless unfolding of modernity. For most of the local producers and *négociants* (wine merchants), family business is the defining feature of post-industrial capitalism, and different strategies of land exploitation have sought to preserve the integrity of the domains within the same family. Yet the recent intrusion of external investors, which until recently were in a minority, and the subsequent shift in focus to *climats* pose questions about the extent to which processes of heritagisation, defined as constituting something (like food) as a legacy, creating and recreating cultural and historical meanings and identities such as that represented by UNESCO, contribute to both the creation of added value and the possible disintegration of specific cultural forms and social relations. It must be recognised that juxtaposing these terms – success and disintegration – in the context of the world of wine is likely to generate debate. The world wine industry is supported by a powerful and connected economic, cultural and political edifice which is built on a shared, but also changing, hierarchy of Western values (Herzfeld 2004) as well as more personal social exchange and consumption of the product.

Unlike economists, anthropologists have always emphasised ways in which local histories, cultural norms and socioeconomic institutions concurrently enable and constrain choice for different groups of people at particular times and places (Chibnik 2015). Anthropological approaches to the economy have developed over time, reflecting both theoretical debates and new field settings for ethnographic research. Interestingly, different sub-fields have emerged as part of the cultural turn incarnated by studies of commodities, globalisation and consumption in capitalist societies. Jonathan Friedman (1995), Arjun Appadurai (1990, 1996) and Daniel Miller (2008) are amongst the key thinkers in the field of consumption. As a result of this intellectual shift, production and consumption have been analysed in a specific fashion through their intimate material culture and the work they do in (re)producing the social relationships, identity constructs and social distinction of consumers, although they are often framed in the local-global perspective. There was a clear awareness of world capitalism and its complex local manifestations, but most analyses were limited in their quest for holism or lacked a clear critical stance (Graeber 2011).

Another influential area of debate attached to the commodification of culture and the politics of value has been the concept of monopoly rent analysed by the geographer David Harvey (2002). According to Harvey (2002: 100), monopoly claims – which are at the heart of the Burgundian viticultural system – form the basis of an over-emphasis on micro-location of place and are as much 'an effect of discourse' and an outcome of struggle to preserve the monopoly rent as they are a reflection of the qualities of the product. The claim by Burgundy to be the quintessence of terroir is partially explained by the transformations which have affected 'the economic space of competition which has changed in both form and scale over time' (Harvey 2002: 98). In this example, scarcity has been central to the local strategies by either being played out through micro landownership or being based on an intensive control by the producer of commercialisation. I argue here, in response to David Harvey's question about the future of terroir narrative claim (2002: 100), that the language of terroir and tradition is abandoned in order to develop a new competitive aesthetic and visual discourse embedded in the UNESCO wine landscape narrative which chimes with global concerns.

In this chapter, I propose to engage ethnographically with both 'studying people up' and following wine as an ordinary but also powerful Western cultural commodity and icon of capitalism. Building on a long-term ethnography (Demossier 1999, 2011, 2018) of both the site and the commodity, I seek to engage with both production and consumption theories not only by following wine as a commodity through its life cycle, but also by unpacking the different meanings, symbols, discourses, social practices and values around its production and consumption. I focus on its materiality 'here and there' by seeking to unfold the messy, ostentatious, fussy and irrational social relations shaping the political economy of place. Place and products coalesce in my ethnographic gaze through a complex articulation of politics, social relations and cultural imaginaries. Starting from the way local people understand their economic activities, but also what they see as the core values of their professional group, I argue that the study of such an economically valuable commodity provides a new perspective on the production of value at a global level by individuals and groups through complex reflexive imbrication processes and through both differentiation and hierarchisation. Heritagisation is the latest project in a long line of strategies deployed by Burgundian wine producers in their quest for power, and it is what I discuss here.

Crafting a new wine cultural imaginary

In Burgundy, perhaps more than in any other wine region, place matters. The relationship to place and wine has materialised through an historical landscape, a system of interdependent parcels which idealise a model of viticulture that has supposedly resisted historical changes, ruptures and crises. The Burgundy story has been constructed on the foundations of terroir, while a constant effort to craft authenticity has been led at key points of historical juncture by the local elites. From the development of the AOC and the concept of terroir in the 1930s to the UNESCO campaign and its *climats* in 2015, the same story is being perpetuated and relentlessly told. By becoming a world heritage site and promoting a new reading of terroir through *climats*, Burgundians make sure that they maintain their hegemonic position in the global hierarchy of wine where place, taste and social experience matter (Demossier 2015). But this is also about shifting the environmental agenda and repositioning Burgundy in the global wine heritage landscape. Heritagisation has recently become a competitive field for global power. The act of representation through heritagisation is inscribed in the making and remaking of the place, and the *climats* story adds another layer to the already rich and colourful veneer of the Burgundy story.

However, what was distinctive about the Burgundian campaign for UNESCO world heritage recognition was the major shift from the AOC classification to a new and powerful visual and aesthetic remapping of the site based on the invention of *climats*. Until recently, the AOC system, defined as a set of rules and regulations codified and institutionalised through self-regulation, was often opaque to the international wine consumer. The AOC labels exercised a performative dimension which was read in a more subtle fashion by many French and European consumers who were familiar with this ideological construction of food quality while it remained a list of iconic place names for international consumers who were unaware of the AOC system and relied on marketing and reputation. The very act of naming geographical entities implies a power over them and, more particularly, over the way in which places, their inhabitants and their social function are represented (Harvey 1990: 419). Reputation, traditions, images and tastes were central to the local, national and international rankings of the local producers. In the context of a fluid and postmodern environmental shift, the transition to terroir as text to *climats* as fixed visual and ecological landscape proved to be a trump card in the campaign for UNESCO wine heritage status. The vast orchestration of the mapping and remapping of place as well as creating a new visual and aesthetic imaginary of the world heritage site is inscribed in the long historical development of the hierarchisation of Burgundy and its wines and in the 2016 recognition by the French rural code of the gastronomic and landscape cultural heritage. As part of the broader international reconfiguration of wine landscapes attached to UNESCO sites, the main Burgundian social actors created their own visual imaginary, taking the *climats de Bourgogne* as a pretext to recreate the terroir ideology and to position their vineyards in the new wine global hierarchy as sustainable, symbolic, ethno-active and aesthetic places. By the same token, they reposition Burgundy as an exemplar in the changing wine hierarchy of value.

This new, predominantly visual reconfiguration of terroir relies on a folkloric and naturalised presentation of the productive space anchored in pre-agrarian viticultural techniques and traditional ways of making wines. Most producers have started to engage with the visual narratives of *climats* by creating new (or adapting older) visual stories. The image of horse-drawn ploughing, for example, started to be heavily featured in the local iconography. This digital *mise en scène* of winegrowers represents a major shift in the way in which individual stories are told, and it has repercussions for the global world of wine with its paradoxical values such as capitalism (particularly productionist maximisation) versus artisanship, its constant process of kaleidoscopic imbrications cascading from the local to the national to the transnational and back and forth. The *climats* have become the ingredients of a new story centred around environmentally friendly practices and a return to a more sustainable and picturesque landscape. If winegrowers and *négociants* have started to invest significantly more in the visual production of their own individual landscapes, they are also doing it in parallel with the Burgundy wine board responsible for promoting the wines and also, more broadly, the attractions of the whole region for tourists and wine lovers. In this process, a specific aesthetic category of wine landscape has come to dominate the heritagisation of the site as well as its touristic gaze. What results from the myriad of individual initiatives and inventions is a paradoxical engagement with the site as 'authentic' and invested with a new moral economy. If the concept of terroir stressed the distinctiveness and authenticity of the individual wine (Karpik 2010), *climats* today pushes it further by reconciling the ecological concern with the nostalgia for rural pre-capitalist ways of life.

From taste to vision, 'you can see it, but not drink it'

Against this broader context of creating 'wine landscape' as a new, meaningful category of collective perception and a place-shaping strategy, a wide range of local actors have sought to engage with the new iconography of the *climats de Bourgogne*. The range of visual initiatives attached to the aesthetic and picturesque dimensions of wine landscape fits into the global appreciation of and desire for ordered, cultivated, productive landscapes that point to man's refined enhancement of nature, the environment and place as a sensorial category of perception. The visual largely dominates any other sensorial dimensions, partially replacing the gustative experience of tasting, which has become increasingly rare, other than through the larger *négociants*. Indeed, several producers have discussed this growing paradox on Facebook following complaints from wine lovers. Following the Burgundy campaign for UNESCO world heritage status, I was struck by the range of initiatives developed by the *Association pour la reconnaissance des climats de Bourgogne*. In 2011, it promoted the phenomenally successful *Marche des climats*, echoing other global ecological movements and taking the local population through a walk in the local vineyards. In 2013, it organised the *Climats on the roc 2013* initiative to appeal to younger audiences, referring both to alcohol-drinking culture ('on the rocks' meaning alcohol with ice cubes) and the world of stone masonry, which is an architectural feature of the local wine landscape. More recently, it prepared an exhibition entitled *Paroles Vigneronnes*, a reference to the folkloric and agrarian past, in collaboration with the DRAC Regional Directorate for Cultural Affairs. A modern twist was given to the old terroir ideology. What all these activities have in common is the deployment of the *climats* as a new visual landscape device through which names are relentlessly perceived, seen, learned and experienced.

In his study of the artisans producing the highly coveted *zisha* pottery in the Jiangsyu province of China, Geoffrey Gowlland (2009) discussed the relationship between value and vision in an economy of exchange. According to the anthropologist, visibility and invisibility are part of learning to see value in exchange between artisans and their clients, creating what he called the 'politics of vision' of this Chinese craft. In the case of Burgundy, crafting wine is also governed by the politics of visibility and invisibility, as well as the politics of saying and silencing. In Burgundy, most wine producers are eager to cultivate and preserve an aura of mystery when discussing knowledge and skills (Demossier 1999). The same discretion is applied to the economic sphere, and generally, wine producers are not voluble informers. In his article, Gowlland (2009: 234) refers to both Dilley (2004) and Graeber (1996, 2001) to discuss the role of learning in the acquisition of economic knowledge. Teaching terroir value to wine lovers here forms part of the new politics of vision sustaining the heritage wine politics of the site. Building on Gowlland's discussion, I argue that, for the Burgundians, learning to read the vineyard through the *climats* contributes to the construction of a new regime of value that is associated with the politics of wine heritage, the aestheticisation of wine landscapes and broader ecological concerns. It enables them to circumvent the politics of taste and terroir which has recently become the object of internal criticisms and contestation (Demossier 2011). Yet at its most refined levels, consuming Burgundy wines remains beyond the economic and social capitals of most wine drinkers.

A clear illustration of this emphasis on the visual is revealed by the intense process of deployment and circulation of maps of the *climats* which have accompanied the campaign and are at the heart of the definition of the site. Geological mapping is key to any process of strategies to enhance the value of place (Skinner 2020). Indeed, deciding who is included or excluded from the mapping exercise conducted by the local elites helps determine the economic destiny of wine producers and their families. Yet UNESCO recognition appears to have had dramatic economic repercussions, and the average price of a vineyard in the Côte d'Or, whatever the AOC denomination, has increased by 40% (see www.mns.com/fr-fr/finance/economie/en-bourgogne-les-prix-des-vignes-atteignent-des-millions/ar-BBUFGpC). Heritagisation, it would appear, has undeniably benefited the whole region. The website for the *Association pour la reconnaissance des climats de Bourgogne* is littered with pictures, images and maps. Several publications, originally commercialised in the 1980s and 1990s, came back into fashion such as *Le Vignoble Bourguignon Ses Lieux-Dits* by Marie-Helene Landrieu-Lussigny, which was re-edited recently in collaboration with Sylvain Pitiot (former and now retired manager of the Clos de Tart) and renamed *The Climats and Lieux-dits of the Great Vineyards of Burgundy*. Several domains have since included on their commercial websites maps of their *climats*, fostering this gigantic orchestration of place.

The Clos de Tart offers a perfect example of the multiplication and deployment of maps as well as the great care taken to identify place in greater detail. Several maps are presented from the Napoleonic land survey to recent geological investigations to highlight the organisation of wine production. Interestingly, the remapping involves an attempt to identify precisely the *climats* located at the top of the historical wine classification. Yet little is said about viticultural practices or winemaking, which are both obscured, despite the fact that they are central to any definition of quality in wines. The new mapping is part of the construction of economic singularities, which, for Lucien Karpik (2010), are unique and cannot be understood with the tools of neoclassical economics (in which supply and demand are said to determine prices). Judgement devices, he argues, are produced to help wine lovers gauge the quality and authenticity of the product (Barrey and Teil 2011; Karpik 2010: 44–45). The politics of vision refers to those judgement devices, but it is only one part of the whole economic story.

In parallel with this new politics of vision, oenotourism, which was until recently underdeveloped, has now acquired a new local dynamic. As a result of the acquisition of UNESCO status, sustainable oenotourism has been encouraged to try to reduce the damaging effects of mass tourism already witnessed at other UNESCO sites. A walking trail map as well as a cycling path and the introduction of a pricing policy incentive are amongst the strategies supported by the Association. The local tourist office has already started to promote visits to the *climats*, and the cities of Beaune and Dijon have prepared themselves for an increase in visits. A gastronomic city is under construction in Dijon while its great rival, Beaune, has now decided on a vast exhibition centre dedicated to the *climats*. Overall, the wine profession, especially wine producers, remains extremely worried about the impact of this touristic flow and how it is likely to clash with their use of the land during the grape harvest or at other points in the viticultural calendar. Moreover, the issue of the protection of vines from human disease remains a reality for the producers, and, it might be argued, the protection of the public from the pesticides and other chemical treatments used in the culture of the vines ought to be an added challenge.

Conclusions

For local communities, heritage articulation and recognition not only represent a fashionable trend, but also involve social, economic and political choice (Bessière 1998: 32). Driven by modern capitalism, heritagisation projects tell us as much about global processes as about locality and its transformations. The collective nature of the enterprise remains a decisive factor in the long-term success of Burgundy's *climats* strategy. Much depends on the ways in which different interest groups take hold of the power potentially inherent in this new discourse. It is clear that the UNESCO campaign fostered a sense of collective belonging which was said to be clashing with a general apathy at the regional level (Borin 2015: 112). If often the achievement associated with becoming part of the private club of tangible and intangible world heritage members is a source of pride and joy, the impact of the UNESCO recognition might prove to be more of a challenge for the people living nearby

(Demossier 2020). Often, the communities around World Heritage sites are constrained by these heritage regimes rather than empowered by them (Brumann and Berliner 2016). Yet in Burgundy, the heritage card enables the crafting of more uniqueness and particularity, both of which are crucial to the definition of non-replicable 'special qualities' attached to place (Harvey 2002).

In this context, the *climats de Bourgogne* project calls to mind the wine crises of the 1930s, convincingly analysed by Gilles Laferté (2006) in his discussion of the folklorisation of Burgundy wines. The same ingredients prevail with a group of economic elites often defined by their business profiles leading the heritagisation process. What differs this time is that rather than representing winegrowers as elements of the local folklore and developing a new form of gastronomic hospitality, wine landscapes are the stars in the new globalised cultural imaginary. They are now visually constructed: that is to say, they derive meaning and often even their physical form from the actions and imaginations of people in society. The uniqueness of the site as constructed by local actors moves the focus away from the product – wine – to put emphasis on the material, 'natural', 'authentic', and 'ecological' element of wine production, the *climats*. In the current context of growing concern about the negative impact of alcohol consumption on public health, this makes perfect sense. It seeks to create a stronger and different identification between peoples and places (Tilley 2006: 14). It provides a new and powerful blueprint for the world wine industry in terms not only of terroir wine excellence, but also of food and foodstuffs.

The development and ratification of the UNESCO Intangible Heritage Convention (2003), which broadened the scope of heritage as defined by the earlier Convention Concerning the Protection of the World Cultural and Natural Heritage (1972) by embodying 'a particular understanding and conceptualisation of the nature of both cultural and natural heritage' (Smith and Akawaga 2009: 1), have been highly significant in this case. Moreover, the scope of the UNESCO application goes further by integrating many different heritage dimensions, including wine from historical landscapes (the historical cultural landscape of the Tokaj wine region in Hungary) to cultural sites (Piedmont, Italy) and touristic wine routes (Spain). In 2013, the ancient traditional Georgian winemaking method of *kvevri* was inscribed on the Representative List of the Intangible Cultural Heritage of Humanity. These new forms of heritage politics compete in the development of oenotourism as a distinct form of leisure. At a time of major challenges from climate change to competition against newcomers like China, any trump card seems to be welcome. Heritage value is one of the global strategies used by the 'Old' World to combat the aggressive and often innovative competition coming from the New World, especially China, New Zealand and Chile. Recognising and protecting 'heritage' are important parts of the cultural globalisation processes, which run in parallel with, and in some ways in opposition to, the commodification and branding of cultures by actors in the globalised neo-liberal capitalist economy (Elliott and Schmutz 2016). Yet the pervasive effects of money and power might precipitate the dislocation of specific localities which have gone too far in taking advantage of the game of globalisation. Ultimately, that might be a small price to pay for ensuring that Burgundy remains uncontestably the global symbol of excellence.

References

Appadurai, A. (1990) "Disjuncture and Difference in the Global Cultural Economy," in M. Featherstone, S. Lash and R. Robertson (eds), *Global Modernities*, London: Sage, 109–133.

Appadurai, A. (1996) *Modernity at Large: Cultural Dimensions of Globalization*, Minneapolis: University of Minnesota Press.

Banks, G. (2013) "Between Old Worlds and the New? Transcending Place and Space in the Contemporary Geography of Wine. Introduction," *EchoGéo* 23, http://journals.openedition.org/echogeo/13380.

Barrey, S. and Teil, G. (2011) "Faire la preuve de l' "authenticité" du patrimoine alimentaire," *Anthropology of Food* 8, 12 May, http://aof.revues.org/6783, accessed 31 March 2016.

Bessière, J. (1998) "Local Development and Heritage: Traditional Food and Cuisine as Tourist Attractions in Rural Areas," *Sociologia Ruralis* 38(1), 21–34.

Borin, E. (2015) "Local Participation for the Enhancement of Cultural Heritage: The UNESCO Candidature of the Climats du Vignoble de Bourgogne," The Ecology of Culture: Community Engagement, Cocreation, Cross Fertilization, Book proceedings 6th Annual Research Session ENCATC, 21–23 October, Lecce, Italy.

Brumann, C. and Berliner, D. (eds) (2016) *World Heritage on the Ground. Ethnographic Perspectives*, New York and Oxford: Berghahn.

Chibnik, M. (2015) "Economic Anthropology: Introduction," *American Anthropologist*, https://anthrosource.onlinelibrary.wiley.com/hub/journal/15481433/economic-anthropology.

Demossier, M. (1999) *Hommes et vins: une anthropologie du vignoble bourguignon*, Dijon: Editions universitaires de Dijon.

Demossier, M. (2011) "Beyond *Terroir*: Territorial Construction, Hegemonic Discourses and French Wine Culture," *Journal of the Royal Anthropological Institute* 17(4), 685–705.

Demossier, M. (2015) "The Politics of Heritage in the Land of Food and Wine," in W. Logan, M. Nic Craith and U. Kockel (eds), *A Companion to Heritage Studies*, Chichester: John Wiley, 87–100.

Demossier, M. (2018) *Burgundy: A Global Anthropology of Place and Taste*, New York and Oxford: Berghahn.

Demossier, M. (2020) "Burgundy's *Climats* and the Utopian Wine Heritage Landscape," in J. Dutton and P.J. Howland (eds), *Wine, Terroir and Utopia: Making New Worlds*, London: Routledge, 75–92.

Dilley, R. (2004) "The Visibility and Invisibility of Production Among Senegalese Craftsmen," *JRAI* 10, 797–813.

Elliott, M.A. and Schmutz, V. (2016) "Diffusion and Decoupling in the World Heritage Movement: Exploring Global/Local Tensions in Africa," *European Journal of Cultural and Political Sociology* 3, 152–176.

Fourcade, M. (2012) "The Vile and the Noble," *The Sociological Quarterly* 53, 524–545.

Friedman, J. (1995) "Global System, Globalization and the Parameters of Modernity," in M. Featherstone, S. Lash and R. Robertson (eds), *Global Modernities*, London: Sage, 109–133.

Gowlland, G. (2009) "Learning to See Value: Exchange and the Politics of Vision in a Chinese Craft," *Ethnos* 74(2), 229–250.

Graeber, D. (1996) "Beads and Money: Notes Toward a Theory of Wealth and Power," *American Ethnologist* 23(1), 4–24.

Graeber, D. (2001) *Towards and Anthropological Theory of Value: The False Coin of Our Own Dreams*, New York: Palgrave.

Graeber, D. (2011) "Consumption," *Current Anthropology* 52(4), 489–511.

Harvey, D. (1990) "Between Space and Time: Reflections on the Geographical Imagination," *Annals of the Association of American Geographers* 80(3), September, 418–434.

Harvey, D. (2002) "The Art of Rent: Globalisation, Monopoly and the Commodification of Culture," in Lea Panitch and Colin Leys (eds), *A World of Contradictions*, London: Socialist Register, 93–110.

Herzfeld, M. (2004) *The Body Impolitic: Artisans and Artifice in the Global Hierarchy of Value*, Chicago: University of Chicago Press.

Karpik, L. (2010) *Valuing the Unique. The Economics of Singularities*, Princeton, NJ: Princeton University Press.

Laferté, G. (2006) *La Bourgogne et ses vins: image d'origine contrôlée*, Paris: Belin.

Miller, D. (2008) *The Social Life of Things. Commodities in Cultural Perspective*, Cambridge: Cambridge University Press.

Overton, J. and Banks, G. (2015) "Conspicuous Production: Wine, Capital and Status," *Capital and Class* 39(3), 473–491.

Skinner, W. (2020) "Wine, Geology Mapping and the Value of Place in McLaren Vale," *The Australian Journal of Anthropology* 31(1), 85–100.

Smith, L. and Akawaga, N. (eds) (2009) *Intangible Heritage*, London: Routledge.

Tilley, C. (2006) "Introduction: Identity, Place, Landscape and Heritage," *Journal of Material Culture* 11(1–2), 7–32.

Tsing, A.L. (2013) "Sorting Out Commodities. How Capitalist Value Is Made Through Gifts," *HAU: Journal of Ethnographic Theory* 3(1), 21–43.

15
WINE, DEEP IN THE HEART OF TEXAS

Colleen C. Myles, Kourtney Collins and Christi G. Townsend

The context of wine in Texas

'The future is bright for Texas wine; an emerging wine region on the cusp of something great' (Balter 2019). Farming has always been big business in Texas, with nearly three-quarters of its 172 million acres of land under some type of agricultural production (USDA 2017). The broad range of climates and soil types means that a variety of crops can be produced, which historically have included the large-scale production of cotton, corn, sorghum and orchard crops. Although this is still the case in many parts of the state, the ways in which agricultural landscapes are used are changing, in large part due to changing political, economic, environmental and cultural circumstances. These changes have led, in part, to the rapid emergence of one unique and perhaps unexpected agricultural product: wine. This chapter explores the cultural and environmental transformation of these (now) fermented landscapes (Myles 2020) in the state of Texas; our focus is on the wine industry and how it has changed the culture of the High Plains and Hill Country regions, the two largest and most productive appellations in the state. Through a series of targeted interviews conducted with growers, winemakers and other wine industry insiders, we form a framework for understanding both the historical and contemporary contexts for wine in Texas and outline the major transitional moments of the Texas wine industry.

Texas is not the largest wine producing state in the United States in terms of grape and wine production (California is the leader), consumption (California, by volume; Idaho, per capita) or number of wineries (also California), but the recent growth of the Texas wine industry has nevertheless been astounding. Even though viticulture and winemaking are not entirely new to Texas, the modern industry is relatively young compared to better-known grape-producing states, such as California and Oregon. Industry insiders and affiliates have nevertheless worked enthusiastically to make Texas wine production competitive with other top producing (and consuming) states. Every new year, from budburst to harvest and from fermentation to bottling, renews the industry's energy for improving quality and gaining recognition.

Although eight American Viticultural Areas (AVAs) exist in Texas, the two largest of these dominate the state's wine production (Figure 15.1): the Texas Hill Country AVA (established in 1991) and the Texas High Plains AVA (established in 1993). (For a different AVA context, see Chapter 12 in this volume.) The Texas High Plains AVA is located in north Texas in a region known as the *Llano Estacado*, or 'Staked Plains', and is the location where the greatest quantity of winegrapes are grown.

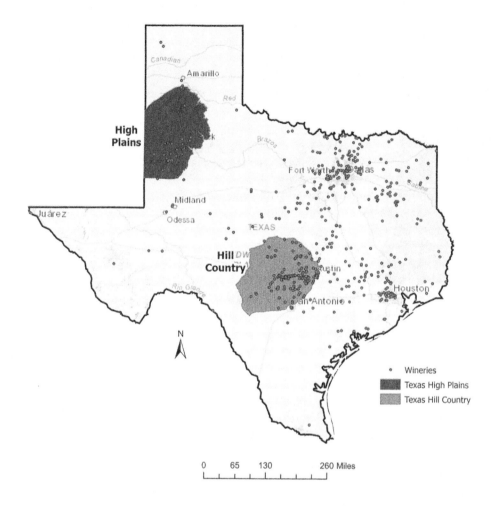

Figure 15.1 Map of Texas wineries with the High Plains and Hill Country American Viticultural Areas
Source: Christi Townsend and Nathaniel Dede-Bamfo, September 2020

The Hill Country AVA is located in central Texas and is where the wineries – and the tourism that accompanies them – are in (relative) abundance.

To compile this narrative of Texas wine, interviews were conducted with growers, winery owners and wine educators who have been involved in the wine industry in some manner over the last decade. Interviewees were selected such that they could offer perspectives of multiple wineries or vineyards. A review of literature was also conducted in an effort to create a timeline delineating the major transitions that have occurred in Texas viticulture and winemaking and to provide a base of reference for interview discussion. The interviews served as a supplement to ongoing participant observation by author Kourtney Collins, who has worked in the wine industry for the past five years.

A geographic history of wine in Texas

Texas has more indigenous grape species than any other location on earth (Johnson and Robinson 2007), and before the arrival of Europeans, indigenous peoples harvested and consumed these grapes, which grew prolifically in many parts of Texas, particularly near rivers and streams where the native vines climbed the trees of the riparian landscape, although there is no evidence that wine was made with these grapes (McEachern 2003; Kane 2009). Wine has, however, been produced to some extent in Texas since the 1600s, with the arrival of Spanish (Franciscan) missionaries, but the first successful attempts at commercially viable viticulture only occurred at around the turn of the twentieth century. By 1919, there were at least 50 working wineries in Texas and 3,000 cultivated acres of vineyards (Kane 2009), although all were forced to cease operation with the ratification of the Eighteenth Amendment to the United States Constitution. The Volstead Act, which ushered in a period known as Prohibition, thus decimated the nascent wine industry (Kane 2009).

Despite that formidable setback, the wine industry did recover and has experienced considerable, almost explosive, growth in the last three decades. Only one commercial winery existed in Texas in 1975 (Morse 1990); in 2008, there were 162 (MKF Research 2008). Today, there are more than 600 (TABC 2020). Since the 1970s, the wine industry in Texas has been focused near the cities of Lubbock, Fredericksburg, Fort Worth and Fort Stockton, areas which are considered to be at a lower risk of Pierce's disease, a plant disease which remains prevalent throughout the state. The disease has contributed to significant losses in many Texas vineyards (Kamas 2000; Townsend 2012). High humidity (a common weather element in central, east and south Texas) and location near a body of water put vines at an enhanced risk, whereas cooler temperatures, higher elevations and aridity are geographic factors which seem to help limit its spread. Despite the challenges presented by Pierce's disease, industry actors were committed to grape growing in the state, and so intensive research began to find the causes of the disease, how it spreads and how to stop it.

Although the early days of commercial sale in the Texas market were not easy, the wine industry has become more established in recent years. Early consumers were perhaps poorly educated about grape varieties, other than those which had gained notoriety *vis-à-vis* the booming California industry (chardonnay, cabernet sauvignon, and merlot, for example). Customers visiting Texas tasting rooms may have wanted or expected a California-style cabernet, for example, and were disappointed to discover that cabernet does not grow in Texas like it does in California. Although the varieties that were introduced to the market in Texas – like Tannat, Mourvèdre and Blanc du Bois – are not new *per se*, they are less familiar to consumers than some other grape types, which means producers have had to work creatively to connect with consumers. As one winery owner said: 'In 2013, at a wine and food festival, you had people who did the tasting part [of the event] who would dismiss Texas wine without even tasting it. 2014 was the tipping point, where[in] people had become warmed to Texas wines' (Winery Owner A, personal interview, 12 August 2020). Texas wine consumers may have warmed to these lesser-known varieties, but this issue will continue to be one of the most important challenges Texas winemakers will need to overcome as they attempt to expand into national and international markets.

In the early 2000s, when the Texas wine industry gained momentum in growth, winemakers would often source fruit from out of the state because the availability or quality of Texas fruit was low, and wineries could not sustain themselves from their own vineyards. Many wineries still hold on to fruit sourcing out of state for their business models, but more and more consumers are wanting to 'taste' Texas when drinking wines at a Texas winery. The phasing out of the use of non-Texas fruit has evolved over the past few years as lawmakers have changed labelling laws that require a wine labelled as a 'Texas wine' to be 85% or more fruit obtained from within the state, and that percentage will increase over a period of a few years. This is adding to the demand for Texas fruit provided by growers from both the consumer and wineries (Figure 15.2). Today, on weekends in the Hill Country visitors

Figure 15.2 Mourvèdre vines at Hoover Valley Vineyards in Marble Falls, nestled in the Central Texas Hill Country

Source: Kourtney Collins, July 2019

flock from far and near who are becoming more educated on Texas wine as the industry pushes a unique identity for Texas, expressing the relationship between growers and wineries.

While more Texas wineries making wines made with grapes grown in Texas is good news for the integrity of the industry in Texas, those wineries that choose to source fruit from out of state still play a large role in the industry in the Hill Country. Cultural activities such as weddings, team-building activities amongst co-workers or friends and family outings make up a large percentage of the clients in tasting rooms. Some wish to enjoy the company they are with over what is in the bottle, giving those wineries a chance to show their Texas hospitality and create a more fun-focused environment for guests. These wineries still promote traffic into the area, giving tourists an opportunity to try something different or enjoy whatever that winery emphasises, such as particular wine styles, food and wine pairings or live music and entertainment.

Given the prevalence of geographical specifications for wines based on the environmental attributes of their places of origin (Wine Origins 2020), over time, Texas vineyards have increased in both number and scale as the desirable characteristics of the Texas environment for growing winegrapes is increasingly recognised. That growth has facilitated an increase in fruit sourcing by wineries in both Texas and other states. Industry insiders expect this trend to continue as wineries begin to see the value of place-based designations and organisational memberships, which help businesses create distinction in the market. An example of such an organisation is the Texas Wine Growers (TWG), which promotes the use of Texas fruit in Texas wine. Thus, the mission of TWG (Texas Wine Growers 2020) is 'to promote and protect the integrity of Texas Wine by making wines solely from grapes grown in the Terroir of Texas'.

Texas winemaking has developed and matured, particularly in the last five years, as the state's grape production and growth of wineries have accelerated. Today, growers, winemakers and winery owners come from many diverse backgrounds, and 'Texas wine' has become a term that encompasses a wide range of different business types, from viticulture and winemaking to restaurants, events and tourism (Esco 2009). In addition, Texas wine consumers have also developed and matured in terms of their demands, and wine producers have been able to meet those demands with higher quality wines. Texas wineries have been able to meet consumers where they are by producing wines that are similar in style to more well-known varieties, but consumers in the state have also demonstrated their willingness to be adventurous as they sample unfamiliar wines, as long as wineries maintain a high-quality tasting experience. Though the industry is still developing, the transition of Texas wine from 'emerging' to 'established' is clear.

Environmental and cultural implications of wine in Texas

Growing winegrapes in the state of Texas is not easy, as so many of those new to the industry are quick to discover. The physical environment in particular makes viticulture extremely challenging, so when Texans first attempted to produce wine on a commercial scale, it was difficult to produce wines containing 100% Texas fruit because vineyard yields were often insufficient or unpredictable. Wineries would instead rely on vineyards in other states for fruit and juice to make their product. However, that trend is rapidly changing.

Winegrape growers throughout Texas must contend with both physical and biological threats, which vary by geographic location. For example, 'Pierce's disease is the number one limiting factor to the production of grapes in Texas' (Appel *et al.* 2010), and vineyards in the Hill Country are more susceptible to this disease, which makes it much harder for wineries in the area to grow their own fruit. The humidity and inconsistent, though often extremely heavy, rainfall and flash flooding in the Hill Country add to disease pressures. In contrast, vineyards in the High Plains are less vulnerable to the effects of Pierce's disease, owing to the drier and cooler climate. However, other natural hazards such as hail and late spring freezes are much more frequent in the High Plains than in the Hill Country.

As the palates of Texas wine consumers have evolved, so, too, has the ability of wine producers to meet their demands with higher-quality wines. The industry continues to mature through targeted efforts in education, a greater investment in higher-quality equipment and an increased focus on crafting a better product. Institutions of higher education, such as Texas Tech University in Lubbock, have expanded their wine and oenology programs to meet the growing needs of the industry. Further, wine equipment retailers and suppliers have found a lucrative market in Texas for their wares as the industry grows and matures. As one winery owner said, 'New methods of winemaking – new vineyard and winemaking technology – and varietal experiments are happening at every level in the industry and continue to improve' (Williams 2020).

However, unforeseen hindrances to industry expansion do still occur. The High Plains AVA in Texas has a large presence of cotton farms, which outnumber vineyards three to one (Williams 2021). Farmers across the country who used the pesticide Roundup are having to switch to other herbicides such as plant-growth regulators (PGR) 2,4-Dichlorophenoxyacetic acid (2,4-D) and dicamba due to the build-up of weeds resistant to Roundup. This affects vineyards because the application method used for PGRs is spraying onto monocrops, such as cotton, and the spray drifts onto nearby vineyards, crippling and killing off the vines. Growers in the High Plains have watched their vineyards deteriorate as a result of exposure to herbicide drift, with little political action taken to resolve the matter (Kennedy 2018). Protocols for spraying PGR consider wind and proximity to vineyards, but sanctions on growers who violate those regulations are minimal. In October 2020, the EPA set out new regulations which had little to no effect on the consequences of vineyard drift, and growers and winemakers remain upset as the Texas wine industry, like that in many other states, struggles to grow.

Of the 170 cases of vineyard drift that were reported to the Texas A&M AgriLife Extension, 165 of them were in the High Plains, the area where winegrowing in Texas is most prominent. This has a large impact on wineries in the Hill Country, which adds stress for a solution from industry members across Texas. Justin Scheiner, a viticultural specialist at the Texas A&M AgriLife Extension, claims 'there is no definitive handle on this in Texas. . . . [I]t was not a compelling research topic prior to the widespread damage. Now we are trying to catch up, and the research moves relatively slow', impeding the development of vineyards in Texas (Williams 2021). Because of this and other obstacles, growers in the High Plains have become hesitant to expand, thus slowing the rate of growth of the industry as a whole.

An increase in land values may be associated with a potential deceleration of wine industry expansion in the near future. This is particularly apparent in the Hill Country, where along Highway 290 near Fredericksburg, land was $40,000 per acre in 2014. That acre now costs between $100,000 and $120,000 (Chalk 2020). Planting a new vineyard or constructing a winery in the Hill Country now demands a much greater monetary investment than it once did. To address these higher costs, winery owners are often faced with choosing between planting a vineyard or sourcing fruit from the High Plains. This is an important factor to recognise as partnerships between Hill Country wineries and High Plains growers increase; they are now leaning on each other more as the price of Hill Country viticulture becomes increasingly unsustainable.

Growers are realising that lesser-known varieties of grapes are growing better than those which were originally planted when Texas first started growing and making wine. As the wine industry has become more mature, so have its consumers. Early consumers were poorly educated about grape varieties and where grapes grow best in certain regions, other than what was being grown in California, which helped growers shift into this lesser-known territory. An important development has been the acceptance of lesser-known grape varieties. Although the varieties being introduced to the market in Texas – such as Tannat and Mourvèdre – are not new, they are less familiar to consumers, which means producers need to focus on bridging the cultural gap with consumers. This will continue to be one of the most important challenges Texas winemakers will need to overcome as they attempt to expand into larger markets. For example, as one of us who has worked in tasting rooms over the past several years notes, there has been a shift in terms of what consumers are asking for; increasingly, they want to know more about specific varieties, which is a recent evolution.

This dynamic adds to the cultural complexity of Texas wine. Those in the industry have had to grow and adapt production to meet consumer preferences; growers and winemakers have had to identify grapes that 'meet the growing conditions of Texas', which is itself 'an ever-evolving process', as well as helping themselves – and their customers – understand 'what's right for them in terms of their tasting profile' (Winery Owner B, personal interview, 11 August 2020).

Texas 'wine country': a tale of two interconnected regions

The previous sections emphasised the vastly different environmental and cultural obstacles, as well as opportunities, that exist in the Hill Country and High Plains wine regions. Although there is a unique set of challenges associated with viticulture in the High Plains, in most years, crop yields are higher and crops less expensive to cultivate than in the Hill Country, and yet the consumer supports for the industry are lacking, both from the local population (access to workers, for example) and from tourism. The Hill Country, on the other hand, is much better positioned when it comes to the consumer side of the industry due to its proximity to the cities of Austin and San Antonio and its well-established hospitality, tourism and retail services. These differing contexts make for a clear Hill Country reliance on High Plains growers to supply fruit, which allows wine-based businesses and operations to flourish in both locales.

The complementary linkages between the two regions are driven not only by the quantity of grapes produced, but also by quality and style concerns; for example, since white winegrapes tend to grow better in the High Plains, sourcing them from there is really the only way to build a viable white wine programme at a Hill Country winery. Similarly, even though the quality of grapes might be superior in the High Plains, there are no consumers to build wine tourism around, so the industry there remains focused on viticultural production. This spatial mismatch between winegrowing and winemaking is akin to other 'unlikely wine regions', such as Arizona (Myles *et al.* 2020), which are also thriving against expectations.

Wineries have made the Hill Country a travel destination, and tourists not only visit the wineries but also stay in the hotels, eat in local restaurants and shop at local retail outlets. Opportunities for outdoor recreation here are also plentiful and include hiking and camping at one of the many nearby parks, hunting at one of the many large ranches in the region and fishing and boating at one of the neighbouring Highland Lakes, a string of reservoirs running roughly northwest to southeast through the centre of the Hill Country. Combined, these opportunities have contributed to an economic boom for the region. The success of the wine sector in this region demonstrates the compounding economic benefits of a thriving fermentation-focused industry (Slocum *et al.* 2018). However, there certainly exist drawbacks to these kinds of fermented landscapes (Myles 2020), such as increased traffic and possible gentrification effects (Myles *et al.* 2020). The potential downsides notwithstanding, the place-based impacts of this fermentation-focused economic development are generally seen as positive overall elsewhere (Myles and Filan 2017), as well as in Texas.

The two regions, while operating with different foci and facing different challenges, are synergistically linked; the consumption focus in the Hill Country enables the production focus in the High Plains and vice versa. The cultural challenges in the High Plains, stemming mainly from a lack of consumers, is complemented and overcome by building a strong consumer base in the Hill Country; conversely, the environmental challenges in the Hill Country related to production are complemented and overcome by a strong production system in the High Plains, which then serves as a reliable source for Texas-grown fruit in the Hill Country. In sum, although there are challenges as well as many opportunities, there is no doubt that there is wine – and it is there to stay – deep in the heart of Texas.

References

Appel, D., Black, M., Labay, A., Lewis, J., Kamas, J. and Morano, L. (2010) *Pierce's Disease Overview & Management Guide*, Texas A&M AgriLIFE, https://aggie-horticulture.tamu.edu/fruit-nut/files/2010/10/Texas-Grape-Growers-PD-Management-Guide.pdf.

Balter, E. (2019) "The Future Is Bright for Texas Wine," *Wine Spectator Magazine*, www.winespectator.com/articles/future-is-bright-for-texas-wine.

Chalk, A. (2020) "The Wine Industry Continues to Expand in the Hill Country," *Wine Industry Network. Press Release*, 14 July, https://wineindustryadvisor.com/2020/07/14/the-wine-industry-continues-to-expand-in-texas-hill-country.

Esco, M. (2009) *Texas Wineries*, Fort Worth, TX: TCU Press.

Johnson, H. and Robinson, J. (2007) *The World Atlas of Wine*, 6th edition, London: Mitchell Beazley.

Kamas, J. (2000) *Management of Pierce's Disease in Texas. Texas Agricultural Extension Service Publication*, Texas A&M AgriLIFE, https://aggie-horticulture.tamu.edu/fruit-nut/files/2010/10/Texas-Grape-Growers-PD-Management-Guide.pdf.

Kane, R. (2009) *The Wineslinger Chronicles: Texas on the Vine*, Lubbock: Texas Tech University Press.

Kennedy, M. (2018) "West Texas Vineyards Blasted by Herbicide Drift from Nearby Cotton Fields," *NPR*, 21, www.npr.org/sections/thesalt/2018/08/21/638588456/west-texas-vineyards-blasted-by-herbicidedrift-from-nearby-cotton-fields.

McEachern, G.R. (2003) "A Texas Grape and Wine History," in *Proceedings of the 10th Annual Oktober Gartenfest, Jointly Sponsored by Texas Cooperative Extension and The University of Texas Center for American History (Dr. William C. Welch, Committee Chairman)*, Texas: Winedale, 2003, https://aggie-horticulture.tamu.edu/southerngarden/Texaswine.html.

MKF Research. (2008) *The Economic Impact of Wine and Grapes on the State of Texas 2008*, Texas Wine Marketing Research Institute, Texas Tech University, www.depts.ttu.edu/hs/texaswine/docs/FINAL_Economic_Impact_TX_2008.pdf.

Morse, S. (1990) "The Growing Texas Wine Industry: Product Distribution Problems and Consumer Preferences of Texas-Produced Wines," *Journal of Food Distribution Research* 21(2), 43–44.

Myles, C.C. (ed) (2020) *Fermented Landscapes: Considering How Processes of Fermentation Drive Social and Environmental Change in (Un)Expected Places and Ways*, Lincoln: University of Nebraska Press.

Myles, C.C. and Filan, T. (2017) "Boom-and-Bust: (Hi)stories of Landscape Production and Consumption in California's Sierra Nevada Foothills," *Polymath* 7, 76–89.

Myles, C.C., Holtkamp, C., McKinnon, I., Baltzly, V.B. and Coiner, C. (2020) "Booze as a Public Good? Considering How Localized, Craft Fermentation Industries Make Place for Better or Worse," in C.C. Myles (ed), *Fermented Landscapes: Lively Processes of Socio-Environmental Transformation*, Lincoln: University of Nebraska Press, 21–55.

Myles, C.C., Tobias, M. and McKinnon, I. (2020) "'A Big Fish in a Small Pond': How Arizona Wine Country Was Made," in M. Pezzi, A. Faggian and N. Reid (eds), *Agritourism, Wine Tourism, Craft Beer Tourism: Local Responses to peripherality Through Tourism Niches*, New York: Routledge, 93–112.

Slocum, S.L., Kline, C. and Cavaliere, C.T. (2018) *Craft Beverages and Tourism, Volume 2: Environmental, Societal, and Marketing Implications*, Cham, Switzerland: Palgrave Macmillan.

Texas Alcoholic Beverage Commission (TABC). (2020) www.tabc.texas.gov/.

Texas Wine Growers. (2020) "Our Mission," www.texaswinegrowers.com/.

Townsend, C. (2012) *An Evaluation of Hazard Awareness Among Viticulturists in Texas* (Unpublished Dissertation, Texas State University).

United States Department of Agriculture (USDA). (2017) "Census of Agriculture," www.nass.usda.gov/Publications/AgCensus/2017/Full_Report/Volume_1,_Chapter_1_State_Level/Texas/.

Williams, M. (2020) "Innovation Leads in the Dynamic Texas Wine Industry," 14 October, www.forbes.com/sites/michellewilliams/2020/10/14/innovation-leads-the-way-in-the-dynamic-texas-wine-industry/#4d32b3c15cfd.

Williams, M. (2021) "Off-Target Herbicide Drift Threatens Vineyards Across U.S.," 12 January, www.winebusiness.com/news/?go=getArticle&dataId=240287&fbclid=IwAR3_uYEtUAj0DU3Mkq4-vn849FDqq0TsISygafiAXgpprA4mQM3sSSEkD5s.

Wine Origins. (2020) "Wine Origins," https://origins.wine/.

PART III

Intermediation and consumption

16

CHARACTERS OF WINE

The cultural meanings of typefaces and fonts in wine labels

Franck Celhay

Introduction

Many studies have shown that wine label designs convey specific meanings to consumers (Boudreaux and Palmer 2007; Celhay and Remaud 2018; Orth and Malkewitz 2008). These designs are cultural artefacts that develop brand narratives and differentiate wines in the marketplace (Celhay *et al.* 2017). Through the choice of design elements, wine labels communicate specific brand values (e.g. sustainable, trustworthy), personality traits (e.g. fun/serious, sophisticated/rough) and suggest a wine's organoleptic properties (e.g. light/heavy, sweet/astringent).

Among the most important design elements of wine labels are typefaces and fonts. This is especially so because all labels present text, and many use only text with a limited range of colours and no illustrations. Compared with other design elements (such as colours, ornaments and illustrations), typefaces present the peculiarity of being the visual transcription of verbal signs (Drucker 1997). Given this dual nature, typefaces are often thought of as the textual or verbal part of packages and are therefore disregarded as a design element. Type designer Gerard Unger (1992: np) astutely observed that when someone is reading, the object of reading tends to disappear:

> The black, printed letters dissolve in your mind like an effervescent pill in a glass of water. For a short moment, all those black signs disappear off the stage, change their outfits and return as ideas, as representations, and sometimes even as real images.

Yet Unger also pointed out that invisible typefaces do not exist and that typefaces endow printed matter with character (Unger 1992). According to several type specialists, this ability to remain hidden in plain sight confers on typefaces a supraliminal power of communication and influence (Hyndman 2016; McNeil 2017). Several studies have indeed demonstrated that typefaces have the ability to convey associations of ideas, set a mood or tone and arouse emotions that subsequently influence consumer buying choices (e.g. Doyle and Bottomley 2004, 2006; Giese *et al.* 2014; Karnal *et al.* 2016; Schroll *et al.* 2018).

Obviously, these observations have to be considered within a given cultural context for at least two reasons: first, different cultures may use different writing systems, and second, typeface meanings are strongly connected to the history of calligraphy, lettering and print techniques in a given cultural area. In the present chapter, we focus on Latin typefaces and their meanings in a Western context. This should not be regarded as a major limitation as the vast majority of wine labels use

Latin characters. Moreover, just because typeface meanings are culturally dependent does not imply that they are 'arbitrary'. In fact, most of the time, the opposite is true. Typeface meanings should therefore be described as 'motivated': i.e. the relationship between the typeface and its meanings is not a pure convention and can be logically explained (Celhay et al. 2020). In some cases, the meanings associated with a specific letterform are historically grounded (e.g. blackletter typefaces mimic the calligraphy of the copyist monks of the Middle Ages and therefore convey meanings of oldness, tradition and craftmanship). In other cases, the meanings attached to a specific letterform are based on its physical attributes (e.g. bold uppercase fonts are big and wide and are therefore connected in the human mind to meanings of strength, robustness and assertiveness).

In this chapter, we present the meanings usually associated with Latin typefaces and fonts and explain their cultural origins. By doing so, we hope to provide winemakers with guidelines to help them choose typefaces and fonts in line with their wine story and its particularities.

In the first section, we clarify the differences between typefaces and fonts, which are commonly taken to be synonyms. We then present the main typeface families that are relevant for wine label design and the cultural origins of the meanings associated with them. Last, we present the differences in meaning that can be produced through font variations.

Typefaces and fonts

'Typeface' and 'font' are increasingly used as synonyms, but type designers make a distinction between these two terms. Among specialists, a typeface refers to a specific design for letters and glyphs that is available in different sizes (12 points, 14 points etc.), weights (light, regular, bold etc.), styles (roman, italic) and cases (lowercase, small caps, uppercase). A font refers to a particular size, weight, style and letter case within a typeface (Garfield 2012; Pohlen 2011). For instance, Ambroise, Acumin and Bickham are three typefaces. Ambroise regular, Ambroise regular italic and Ambroise extrabold are three different fonts (Figure 16.1). Some typefaces are available in a large number of fonts and are therefore more versatile (e.g. Acumin), while others propose a limited number of fonts and are therefore more specialised (e.g. Bickham).

	Acumin extralight	
	Acumin extralight italic	
	Acumin light	
	Acumin light italic	
	Acumin regular	
	Acumin regular italic	
	Acumin medium	
	Acumin medium italic	
Ambroise std light	**Acumin semi bold**	
Ambroise std light italic	***Acumin semi bold italic***	
Ambroise std regular	**Acumin bold**	
Ambroise std regular italic	***Acumin bold italic***	
Ambroise std bold	**Acumin black**	
Ambroise std bold italic	***Acumin black italic***	*Bickham Regular*
Ambroise std extrabold	**Acumin ultrablack**	*Bickham Semibold*
Ambroise std extrabold italic	***Acumin ultrablack italic***	***Bickham Bold***

Figure 16.1 Typefaces variation (horizontally) versus fonts variation (vertically)

Typefaces examples: Ambroise (design: Jean François Porchez), Acumin (design: Robert Slimbach) and Bickham (design: Richard Lipton)

The distinction between typefaces and fonts originated at the time of mechanical printing. When printers used a specific typeface, they needed to possess and stock complete sets of physical letters in different sizes, weights, styles and cases. Each of these sets of movable characters was then called a font.

Now that all the typefaces and fonts are digital and therefore immaterial, the distinction between the two may seem obsolete. This is not the case for two reasons. First, the choice of a typeface and the choice of a font are two different steps in the creative process. Designers usually think first in terms of typefaces, depending on the meaning, tone or mood they want to convey through their design. They then select specific fonts within the chosen typeface, depending on the layout constraints, to reinforce the effect they want to produce or to hierarchise the textual information inside the design. Second, typefaces and fonts are ways to manage the tension between the need for unity and the need for contrast in any design. Most graphic design manuals recommend using a limited number of typefaces in a document in order to preserve design unity and consistency. However, it is then possible to bring some contrast and variation through the use of fonts.

Typeface families and their meanings

Thousands of typefaces are available to designers, with new ones being created every day. Over time, type designers and type foundries have proposed many classifications for these typefaces. Each system has its own number of families and often uses its own terminology. For instance, one of the most famous, the Maximilien Vox classification, has 11 categories (Vox 1954). This classification was later criticised by type designer Jean Alessandrini, who reorganised it into families and subfamilies, renamed some of the families and included five new families that had emerged with the development of digital typography (Alessandrini 1979). Adobe currently offers a classification system based on eight families on its fonts website (https://fonts.adobe.com/), whereas acclaimed type designer Jonathan Hoefler retains only six families to organise his foundry catalogue (www.typography.com/). It seems difficult to claim that one classification is more consensual or more accurate than another. However, it could be noted that most of them are built on the same fundamental distinctions. We therefore borrowed from these classifications and retained two families with seven subfamilies that are distinguished one from the other in most of the systems. First, we distinguished script from non-script typefaces as being the two most inclusive type families. Second, within the script typeface family, we distinguished three subfamilies: the blackletters, the formal cursives and the casual manuals. Last, within the non-script family, we distinguished four subfamilies: the serifs, the sans serifs, the tuscans and the stencils. This classification does not cover every typeface, but it is a useful way to present the typeface families that are most frequently used in wine label design (Celhay et al. 2017).

The script family

The script family regroups all the typefaces that imitate handwriting. Thus, script typefaces are usually associated with meanings of craftmanship and handcrafting. They also communicate human warmth and a sense of intimacy (Liu et al. 2019; Schroll et al. 2018). Script typefaces can be divided into many subfamilies, depending on the style of writing that the typeface mimics. The three most common categories presented in most classifications are the blackletters, the formal cursives and the casual manuals. Each of these subfamilies produces its own meanings.

Blackletters

The blackletter subfamily regroups typefaces that imitate the calligraphy of the copyist monks of the Middle Ages. The design of the letters is usually angular and very elaborate with strong stroke modulation and ornaments for the uppercases. The characters are narrow and look dense and heavy (Pohlen 2011) (Figure 16.2). As they imitate a calligraphic style from the Middle Ages, these typefaces emphasise meanings of oldness, tradition and brand heritage. As they imitate slow and painstaking writing, they also communicate meticulous craftmanship (Blanchard 1998). Not least because of the complexity of this lettering and its connection with monasteries, blackletters can also convey meanings of mysticism, esoterism and the sacred. In terms of taste, their heavy and angular design may suggest a powerful and tannic wine (Velasco *et al.* 2018). For this reason, blackletters are mostly used on red wine labels.

𝔄𝔫𝔠𝔦𝔢𝔫𝔱 𝔚𝔦𝔫𝔢

Figure 16.2 Example of a blackletter typeface: Amador

Design: Jim Parkinson

Formal cursives

The formal cursive family regroups typefaces that mimic handwriting with a dip pen (Figure 16.3). The characters are usually joined together in a flowing manner, slanted and rounded. The design of the letters is usually thin and elaborate with stroke modulations and flourish ornaments for the uppercases (Pohlen 2011). Given their thin, elaborate design and ornamental presentation, formal cursives usually communicate refinement, elegance and luxury. They are also associated with romance and femininity because of their round and delicate shapes. By mimicking slow and painstaking writing, they also convey a sense of meticulousness. For the same reasons, Blanchard (1998) noted that they also show deference to and respect for the reader. According to Cavassilas (2007), the thinness and long curves of these typefaces suggest a wine with a delicate taste and a long finish. Cursives are extensively used in regions specialising in sweet wines (e.g. sauternes) as their roundness suggests a sweet taste and thus makes them relevant for this type of wine (Velasco *et al.* 2018).

Figure 16.3 Example of a formal cursive typeface: Bickham script pro

Design: Richard Lipton

Casual manuals

In contrast to the formal cursives, the casual manual subfamily regroups typefaces that mimic more modern and casual handwriting with writing instruments like ballpoint pens, felt pens and pencils (Figure 16.4). Similar to the other cursives, the characters are usually rounded and slanted and may be joined together in a flowing manner. However, they tend to be simpler and rougher, showing some irregularities in their curves (Pohlen 2011). Moreover, they usually express more speed and therefore suggest quick, informal writing. As a result, casual manual typefaces generally express warmth, simplicity, modesty and familiarity (Blanchard 1998). They do not look luxurious but can emphasise a brand's authenticity. For instance, a typeface from this subfamily would be a choice to communicate the story of a good, simple, honest and down-to-earth farmer's wine.

Casual Wine

Figure 16.4 Example of a casual manual typeface: Professor
Design: Brian Willson

The non-script family

In contrast to the scripts, the non-script family regroups all the typefaces that imitate mechanical writing systems. The design of the non-scripts tends to be more geometric and less organic than the scripts. Non-scripts are usually available in a larger number of fonts than scripts. They are therefore more versatile and can be used in more diverse contexts. They also tend to be more easily readable, especially in small sizes. Conversely to the scripts, they do not convey meanings of human warmth and craftmanship, but rather of seriousness and functionality. The four most common categories in most classifications are the serifs, the sans serifs, the tuscans and the stencils. Each of these subfamilies produces meanings of its own.

Serifs

The first printed books in Western history, such as the Gutenberg Bible printed in 1455, used blackletter typefaces to imitate the most common calligraphic style of that time. In the decades that followed, new styles appeared as printing techniques progressed and spread across Europe (McNeil 2017). Notably, the spread of printing in Italy marked the appearance of the first serif typefaces, such as Nicolas Jenson's typeface (Figure 16.5). Jenson typeface was inspired by ancient Roman calligraphy, but it started a process of simplification in letter design that was better adapted to mechanical printing (McNeil 2017; Pohlen 2011). Therefore, serif typefaces present characteristics that recall their calligraphic origins (the serifs, the stroke modulation) but are simpler in shape and more geometric. Serif typefaces seemed to be more easily readable than blackletters and quickly became the new standard for printing books. As serif typefaces were originally associated with the Italian Renaissance and have remained the most common choice for the text of printed books, they produce meanings of classicism and erudition (Kaspar *et al.* 2015). The characters are straight and built on a serif, conveying a sense of stability and seriousness (Blanchard 1998). By extension, serif typefaces tend to be reassuring and communicate a feeling of confidence. Many styles of serif typefaces have been developed over time. They are usually distinguished by the shape of their serifs and their ratio to stroke modulation. For instance, the didones regroup typefaces that use very thin serifs and strong stroke modulation. The mecanes, on the other hand, regroup typefaces that use a slab serif and slight stroke modulation. Each of these subfamilies communicates distinct meanings, depending on their physical attributes and historical origins. The didones, for instance, communicate refinement and sophistication (e.g. Linotype Didot; see Figure 16.5) while the mecanes communicate strength and solidity (e.g. Questa Slab; see Figure 16.5).

SERIOUS WINE
REFINED WINE
STRONG WINE

Figure 16.5 Examples of serif typefaces
Adobe Jenson Pro (design: Robert Slimbach), Linotype Didot (design: Adrian Frutiger) and Questa Slab (design: Jos Buivenga and Martin Majoor)

Sans serif

The first sans serif typefaces appeared in the nineteenth century and pushed the process of simplification in letter design even further. As indicated by their name, they present no serif, and their stroke modulation is very subtle. The sans serif typefaces are geometric, present straight shapes and are very minimalist (Figure 16.6). The use of these typefaces became popular in the twentieth century, promoted by such artistic movements and graphic styles as the 'new typography', 'Bauhaus' and the 'Swiss style'. As a conjoint effect of their geometric characteristics and their association with modern graphic styles, the sans serifs usually communicate meanings of modernity, simplicity and functionality. They can appear cold and strict but can also communicate elegance and luxury when used in a minimalist design.

MODERN WINE

Figure 16.6 Example of a sans serif typeface: Acumin Pro
Design: Gerry Powell

Tuscans

Tuscan designs have an antique Italian origin, as evidenced by fourth-century Roman stone inscriptions (Morison 1928). According to Kelly, some of the best Tuscan interpretations were produced by Italian engravers in the sixteenth and seventeenth centuries (Kelly 2010). However, Tuscan typefaces became truly popular mostly in the nineteenth century, after being exported to England and from there to America. During the Industrial Revolution, typography became a medium for mass communication and advertising. Foundries at this point were competing to develop new display typefaces that would stand out and catch the eye of consumers (Jubert 2006; McNeil 2017). The time was right for the creation of more exuberant typeface designs, and Tuscans were soon adopted by most type founders in Europe, becoming notably popular in America. The characters of this family can be easily recognised by the following characteristics: bifurcated or trifurcated 'fish tail' serifs, bulging medians and ornamental decorations inside and around the letters (such as drop shadows or outline strokes) (Kelly 2010) (Figure 16.7). Tuscan typefaces propose mainly display, uppercase and bold fonts as they are not easily readable in small sizes. Because this typeface family was very popular in America in the nineteenth century, it is strongly associated in the collective memory with American 'Western' movies and conveys mental associations with the Old West, cowboys and saloons. These typefaces are also frequently used for circus advertising. As a result, and because of their exuberant designs, they also convey meanings of extraversion, fun and craziness and are somehow spectacular.

CRAZY WINE

Figure 16.7 Example of a tuscan typeface: Zebrawood
Design: Carl Crossgrove, Carol Twombly and Kim Buker Chansler

Stencils

The use of stencil lettering developed at the end of the nineteenth century with the rise of international trade (McNeil 2017). This lettering solution was well adapted for marking the wooden boxes, barrels and burlap bags that were used to ship supplies like coffee beans and port wines overseas. The technique consists of using a thin and rigid piece of metal from which the letter shape has been cut and then spray painting through the cut-out holes onto the surface to be marked. The first adaptation of stencil-lettering technic into a typeface is usually attributed to Robert Hunter Middleton in 1937 (McNeil 2017). Bauhaus professor Josef Albers had previously developed a sans serif stencil (Jubert 2006); however, Middleton typeface was a more typical reproduction of the original stencils used to mark packages: bold uppercase letters with narrow and rounded serifs (Figure 16.8). Since then, many stencil variations have been created, including serif and sans serif versions and lowercase fonts. Stencil typefaces can be easily recognised by the discontinuities in their strokes, usually around the letter counter-forms. These discontinuities are produced by the little metallic bridges that maintain the letter counter-forms in the cut-out models which are used to spray the letter shapes. Stencil typefaces propose mainly bold fonts as the technique is not appropriate for reproducing thin letters. They usually present a simple and rough design. During World War II, the US Army used the stencil technique to mark their vehicles and ammo boxes (McNeil 2017). Much later, graffiti artists like Banksy, Shepard Fairey and Blek le Rat brought the technique into new prominence by using it to spray protest messages and subversive images in the streets. Stencil typefaces come from a very basic technique of letter reproduction, initially to mark raw materials. They therefore carry meanings of roughness, robustness and masculinity. By extension, this perceived roughness can also carry meanings of simplicity and authenticity. Their boldness also suggests a strong, heavy taste (Velasco et al. 2018). As stencils have long been used by armies and have more recently been appropriated by street artists, they can produce associations of ideas related to the military (McNeil 2017) or, conversely, to rebellion, street culture and protest (Heller and Vienne 2012), depending on their combination with other design elements. Stencil lettering implies the use of cut-out models but also some handcraft manipulation; stencil typefaces thus stand apart from other non-script typefaces as conveying a sense of craftsmanship (Blackwell 2013).

ROUGH WINE

Figure 16.8 Example of a stencil typeface: Stencil
Design: Robert Slimbach

Font variations and their meanings

Replacing one typeface with another on a label can change the meaning communicated about a wine to the consumer. Similarly, it is possible to communicate different meanings while keeping the same typeface but choosing different fonts inside the chosen typeface. However, it is important to note that non-script typefaces offer more opportunities for font variations than script typefaces. Most script typefaces are not meant to appear in all caps and offer few variations in terms of boldness. They are usually available only in slanted versions and present no Roman (i.e. straight) font. Thus, the font options that we will discuss in the following section concern mostly non-script typefaces.

Uppercase versus lowercase fonts

Except for a few specialised display typefaces, most Latin typefaces are available in two letter cases: lowercase (also called minuscules) and UPPERCASE (also called capitals or majuscules). On a wine label, displaying the brand name in lowercase versus uppercase letters will communicate different meanings. The difference produced by letter case is mostly linked to the difference in size between lowercase and uppercase letters. Uppercase letters are taller than lowercases and will therefore communicate such meanings as greatness, prestige and pretention. Their large size makes the brand looks impressive, confident, even assertive and less approachable. Conversely, lowercase letters will generate the opposite meanings of smallness (a small estate, a small wine company) and modesty (Xu et al. 2017; Yu et al. 2021). By extension, they can signify an intimate wine, known only to a happy few. Their small size makes the brand look less prestigious but also friendlier and more approachable.

humility   GREATNESS

Figure 16.9 Lowercase versus uppercase fonts

Design: Richard Lipton (typeface: Adobe Jenson pro)

Bold versus thin fonts

Typefaces also have fonts that differ in terms of boldness. Boldness refers to the variation in font thickness. Non-professional typefaces (like the default typefaces that are installed on any laptop) are usually available in two fonts: regular and bold (i.e. thicker). However, professional typefaces offer a much wider range of options. For instance, the typeface Acumin Pro is available in nine degrees of boldness, from Acumin thin to Acumin ultra black (Figure 16.1). Displaying a very thin versus a very bold font on a wine label will communicate a different meaning and result in a drastically different brand impression. The differences in meaning are mostly explained by the physical attributes of the fonts. Bold fonts are wider and therefore look heavier. As a result, they usually communicate meanings such as strength and solidity. By extension, they may suggest wines with a powerful taste. Moreover, their massive appearance usually communicates a rough and masculine brand image. Thin fonts, on the other hand, look delicate and lighter. By extension, they may suggest wines with a subtle taste. Their thin shapes leave more room for negative space, which gives them a minimalist aspect (Pracejus et al. 2006). As a result, they convey meanings of modernity and elegance. Their thin designs usually communicate a feminine brand image.

delicate   **POWERFUL**

Figure 16.10 Thin versus extrablack fonts

Design: Robert Slimbach (typeface: Acumin)

Roman versus italic fonts

Last, most non-script typefaces offer straight versus slanted versions. Straight versions are usually called Roman fonts, while slanted versions are called italic fonts. Displaying a wine name in Roman versus italic font may also communicate different meaning. The differences result mostly from the impression of movement produced by italic fonts compared to the stability of Roman fonts. Italic fonts lean towards the right, recalling the movement of a hand tracing letters. In addition, the design of italic fonts is usually curvier and looks more calligraphic than the design of Roman fonts, which looks more rigid and mechanical. The meanings produced by italic and Roman fonts are in line with these observations. Roman fonts will communicate a more serious and stricter brand image, while italics look a bit warmer and friendlier.

Rigidity   *Smoothness*

Figure 16.11 Roman versus italic fonts

Design: Robert Slimbach (typeface: Adobe Garamond Pro)

Conclusion: finding the right typographic mix

In this chapter, we have looked at the cultural meanings usually associated with Latin typefaces and fonts in wine label design. Understanding these associations may provide insights for winemakers as they think about the typefaces and fonts that best transmit their wine story. Depending on the story to be told and the brand values to be communicated, some typefaces and fonts will, indeed, be more relevant, whereas others should be avoided. For instance, to present a wine as prestigious and serious, a winemaker might choose to have the brand name in a serif typeface with uppercase letters, whereas to present a wine as friendly and simple, the winemaker would use a casual manual typeface in lowercase. To emphasise the long history of a wine, a blackletter typeface might be the best option. Typefaces and fonts can be combined on a single wine label, providing further opportunities to communicate complementary meanings through the choice of complementary typefaces. For instance, wine labels frequently show a combination of serif uppercases as the primary typeface and formal cursives as the secondary typeface, thereby communicating prestige, seriousness and craftmanship.

Obviously, knowing something about type history can provide winemakers with a keener sense of cultural context, which, in turn, can help them better consider the choices made by their designers. Such knowledge would undoubtedly facilitate the process of design management and ultimately help winemakers and designers find the right typographic mix for every label.

This chapter does have some limitations, however. First, we presented a classification that does not include every possible type design. Some typefaces are experimental, hybrid in shape and therefore difficult to classify in one of the categories. Thus, knowing the history and cultural meanings of the major typeface families is not always sufficient. For the more peculiar typefaces, it would be necessary to dig into their history and think about how their particular visual attributes affect their potential meanings.

Second, the meanings presented here are potentialities that may or may not be actualised, depending on the articulation of the typefaces with a given label's verbal content and other design elements. Typeface meanings are, indeed, anchored by a label's verbal content (Barthes 1977): textual mentions like 'chateau', 'la vieille ferme', '19 crimes', 'punch', 'loco', or 'dolce vita' are not neutral but instead are likely to guide the interpretation of the typeface meanings in certain directions. Similarly, typefaces interact with other design elements like label colours, illustrations, ornamentation and composition. Notably, the label layout and composition may drastically change the meaning of a typeface. We pointed out that a serif typeface conveys meanings of seriousness and classicism. This is true when the layout is centred on a vertical axis, and the text is aligned on a straight horizontal baseline. However, if a serif typeface is combined with a destructured composition inspired by Dadaist experiments (Drucker 1997) or the punk graphic style (Heller and Chwast 2018), the meaning of the typeface will be completely changed, conveying instead a sense of craziness or subversion.

Last, we should acknowledge that the typeface meanings discussed here may be perceived slightly differently from one consumer to another. Previous research in consumer culture theory (Schroeder and Salzer-Mörling 2006) has shown that the final meaning produced by a communication material emerges from a co-construction between the brand and the consumers. This doesn't mean that typeface meanings change drastically from one consumer to another, but rather that each consumer probably layers their own subjective meanings over the cultural meanings of the typefaces that we have presented.

References

Alessandrini, J. (1979) "Une Nouvelle Classification Typographique : Le Codex 1980," *Communication et langages* 43(3), 35–56.

Barthes, R. (1977) "Rhetoric of the Image," in S. Heath (ed), *Image, Music, Text*, New York: Hill and Wang, 32–51.

Blackwell, L. (2013) *Twentieth Century Type and Beyond*, London: Laurence King Publishing.
Blanchard, G. (1998) *Aide au choix de la typo-graphie*, Reillanne: Atelier Perrousseaux.
Boudreaux, C.A. and Palmer, S.E. (2007) "A Charming Little Cabernet. Effects of Wine Label Design on Purchase Intent and Brand Personality," *International Journal of Wine Business Research* 19(3), 170–186.
Cavassilas, M. (2007) *Clés et codes du packaging: sémiotique appliquée*, Paris: Hermes Lavoisier.
Celhay, F., Cheng, P., Masson J. and Li, W. (2020) "Package Graphic Design and Communication Across Cultures: An Investigation of Chinese Consumers' Interpretation of Imported Wine Labels," *International Journal of Research in Marketing* 37(1), 108–128.
Celhay, F., Masson, J., Garcia, K., Folcher, P. and Cohen, J. (2017) "Package Graphic Design and Innovation: A Comparative Study of Bordeaux and Barossa Wine Visual Codes," *Recherche et Applications en Marketing* 32(2), 1–25.
Celhay, F. and Remaud, H. (2018) "What Does Your Wine Label Mean to Consumers? A Semiotic Investigation of Bordeaux Wine Visual Codes," *Food Quality and Preference* 65, 129–145.
Doyle, J.R. and Bottomley, P.A. (2006) "Dressed for the Occasion: Font-Product Congruity in the Perception of Logotype," *Journal of Consumer Psychology* 16(2), 112–123.
Doyle, J.R. and Bottomley, P.A. (2004) "Font Appropriateness and Brand Choice," *Journal of Business Research* 57(8), 873–880.
Drucker, J. (1997) *The Visible Word: Experimental Typography and Modern Art, 1909–1923*, Chicago: University of Chicago Press.
Garfield, S. (2012) *Just My Type: A Book About Fonts*, New York: Avery.
Giese, J.L., Malkewitz, K, Orth, U.R. and Henderson, P.W. (2014) "Advancing the Aesthetic Middle Principle: Trade-Offs in Design Attractiveness and Strength," *Journal of Business Research* 67(6), 1154–1161.
Heller, S. and Chwast, S. (2018) *Graphic Style : From Victorian to Hipster*, New York: Abrams.
Heller, S. and Véronique Vienne. (2012) *100 Ideas That Changed Graphic Design*, London: Laurence King Publishing.
Hyndman, S. (2016) *Why Font Matters*, Berkeley, CA: Gingko Press.
Jubert, R. (2006) *Typography and Graphic Design: From Antiquity to the Present*, Paris: Flammarion.
Karnal, N., Machiels, C.J., Orth, U. and Mai, R. (2016) "Healthy by Design, but Only When in Focus: Communicating Non-Verbal Health Cues Through Symbolic Meaning in Packaging," *Food Quality and Preference* 52, 106–119.
Kaspar, K., Wehlitz, T., von Knobelsdorff, S., Wulf, T. and von Saldern, M. (2015) "A Matter of Font Type: The Effect of Serifs on the Evaluation of Scientific Abstracts," *International Journal of Psychology* 50(5), 372–378.
Kelly, R.R. (2010) *American Wood Type 1828–1900: Notes on the Evolution of Decorated and Large Types*, Saratoga, CA: Liber Apertus Press.
Liu, S.Q., Choi, S. and Mattila, A.S. (2019) "Love Is in the Menu: Leveraging Healthy Restaurant Brands with Handwritten Typeface," *Journal of Business Research* 98, 289–298.
McNeil, P. (2017) *The Visual History of Type*, London: Laurence King Publishing.
Morison, S. (1928) "Decorated Types," *Fleuron*, 6.
Orth, U. and Malkewitz, K. (2008) "Holistic Package Design and Consumer Brand Impressions," *Journal of Marketing* 72(3), 64–81.
Pohlen, J. (2011) *Letter Fountain: On Printing Types*, Koln: Taschen.
Pracejus, J.W., Olsen, G.D. and O'Guinn, T.C. (2006) "How Nothing Became Something: White Space, Rhetoric, History, and Meaning," *Journal of Consumer Research* 33(1), 82–90.
Schroeder, J. and Salzer-Mörling, M. (2006) *Brand Culture*, London: Routledge.
Schroll, R., Schnurr, B., Grewal, D. and Aggarwal, P. (2018) "Humanizing Products with Handwritten Typefaces," *Journal of Consumer Research* 45(3), 648–672.
Unger, G. (1992) "Legible?" *Emigre*, 23.
Velasco, C., Woods, A.T., Wan, X., Salgado-Montejo, A., Bernal-Torres, C., Cheok, A.D. and Spence, C. (2018) "The Taste of Typefaces in Different Countries and Languages," *Psychology of Aesthetics, Creativity, and the Arts* 12(2), 236–248.
Vox, M. (1954) *Pour une nouvelle classification des caractères*, Paris: Ecole Estienne.
Xu, X., Chen, R. and Liu, M.W. (2017) "The Effects of Uppercase and Lowercase Wordmarks on Brand Perceptions," *Marketing Letters* 28(3), 449–460.
Yu, Y., Zhou, X., Wang, L. and Wang, Q. (2021) "Uppercase Premium Effect: The Role of Brand Letter Case in Brand Premiumness," *Journal of Retailing*.

17

'MAKING THE RIGHT IMPRESSION'

Irish wine culture, c. 1700–present

Charles C. Ludington and Graham Harding

Introduction

So strong is the popular perception of Ireland as a beer- (most notably stout) and whiskey-drinking culture that one can be excused for asking whether Ireland has or has ever had a wine culture. The answer is yes. Indeed, archaeological and eyewitness evidence indicates that Celtic Irish kings and princes regaled themselves and their retinues with French wine, and the eighteenth century, when our survey begins, was the historic pinnacle of Irish wine consumption by volume. For most of that century the Irish – defined as all residents of the island – achieved consumption levels rarely seen among non-wine-producing nations, and Irish merchants on the European continent were deeply involved in providing wine for both home and foreign markets (Murphy 2005: 11–56; Ludington 2019a: 25–44). Most of the nineteenth and twentieth centuries, however, were a different story as Ireland stood at the other end of the wine-consumption spectrum, and for the most part, Irish wine merchants no longer played the innovative role they once had. Yet trends are dynamic, and the downward trend of much of two centuries seems to have turned in the 1980s and 90s, when wine consumption in Ireland once again flourished. Nevertheless, the customer base of committed wine drinkers in Ireland remains relatively narrow. So Ireland does have a wine culture, past and present, but it has always skewed towards the higher end of the social spectrum, sometimes overwhelmingly so. Whether that changes has much to do with Irish government fiscal policy, which currently charges the consumer €3.19 per bottle, the highest in the EU, and an additional 23% VAT (Foley 2019: 40). Thus, one must purchase a €10 bottle to even begin to pay more for the cost of the wine (production, packaging, shipping) than one pays to the Revenue Commissioners. One might ask whether an imported beverage can ever be tightly woven into a nation's cultural fabric. It can, of course, as tea and coffee did, but there are good reasons to imagine that, in the short term at least, habitual Irish wine drinkers will continue to go against the grain.

'Making the right impression': Ireland in the eighteenth century

Writing in the late 1730s, the author and Church of Ireland clergyman Samuel Madden stated that 'Ireland flowed with wine as much as the land of Canaan flowed with milk', although he did so in the context of urging his countrymen to drink somewhat less (Madden 1738: 40). Likewise, Lord Chesterfield, the English Lord Lieutenant of Ireland, remarked in 1746 that the 5,000 tonnes of French wine imported annually helped destroy 'the constitutions, the faculties, and too often the fortunes of those of superior rank' (Cullen 1980: 59). One year later, Chesterfield continued his lament:

> Drinking is the most beastly vice in any country, but it is really a ruinous one in Ireland – nine gentlemen out of ten are impoverished by the great quantity of claret [i.e. red bordeaux], which from mistaken notions of hospitality and dignity, they think it necessary should be drunk in their houses.
>
> *(McConnell 2014: 233)*

Irish society in the eighteenth century was particularly 'pre-occupied with making the right impression'; one way to do that was to serve and consume copious amounts of imported wine, most especially claret, or what Jonathan Swift jokingly referred to in a letter of 1710 as 'Irish wine' (Barnard 2004: xxi; Swift and Ryland 1923: letter VI, 10 October 1710). In this way, the extravagant hospitality of the Gaelic Irish aristocracy, once condemned by the English, was ironically – and frighteningly, for those who were historically aware – practiced by the new Anglo-Irish ruling elite. The performance of wine drinking also required myriad accoutrements. As Tara McConnell, the leading scholar of eighteenth-century Irish wine drinking, writes: 'fashion demanded decanters, a range of drinking glasses, wineglass rinsers, monteiths, cisterns, and wine coolers' (McConnell 2017: 13). Decanters also carried silver bottle tickets and looked best when displayed on mahogany sideboards or tables.

Yet it was not only the wealthy Protestant aristocracy and gentry who drank so much; so, too, did the upper levels of the middling sorts, which included lawyers, successful merchants and the Catholic gentry. Daniel O'Connell, an upper-middling lawyer and a Catholic landowner, enjoyed his claret after work in Cork or at home in Kerry (McConnell 2017: 11). Chesterfield, a concerned observer, believed that the 'affection of drinking wine has even got into the middle and lower ranks of the people' (Murphy 2005: 31). Probably more accurate was the remark by Kilkenny-born George Berkeley, Bishop of Cloyne: '[W]hile in England many gentlemen with £1,000 a year never drank wine in their houses, in Ireland this could hardly be said of any who had a £100 a year' (Murphy 2005: 31). Wine in general, and claret in particular, were powerful social signifiers in Ireland; as Berkeley lamented, people 'often drank [wine] rather for vanity than for health or pleasure' (Powell 2005: 11). It therefore makes perfect sense that those who were striving hardest of all to make a grand impression would drink wine, even if it strained their budget. In Belfast at the turn of the nineteenth century, William Drennan, a middle-class Presbyterian physician and United Irishman, felt compelled to purchase and serve 'a dozen very good claret' when he was visited by 'great men' and then lamented the socially necessary expense in a letter to his sister (McConnell 2017: 10). Down in Dublin, the Catholic Committee complained at the extravagant £100 bill run up by the United Irishmen Simon Butler and Oliver Bond when they were imprisoned in 1793 (Powell 2005: 10). Apparently, Butler and Bond wanted to make the best of their confinement in Dublin's Newgate Prison, but presumably, they were also maintaining their gentlemanly status among fellow inmates.

Of course, we cannot always know the intentions of all consumers. Some who drank wine did so as much for enjoyment and health as for vanity. Indeed, wine was still considered medicine. Swift insisted that his disorders made wine essential to his health, and his fellow Church of Ireland prelate Bishop Edward Synge of Elphin counselled his daughter Alicia in Dublin, regarding a faithful servant who had fallen ill, to 'give him Claret as long and as much as the Doctor pleases' (Legg 1996: 336). Likewise, a gentleman in County Armagh, advised a friend in 1783, that 'It is not fit for you and me at our Time of Life to Drink Water. . . . I beseech you not to drink less than a Bottle of claret in good condition after dinner' (McConnell 2014: 234).

Given the many reasons to drink wine in eighteenth-century Ireland, its consumption would never be limited to the elite alone. The sales records of an anonymous Drogheda wine merchant from 1773 to 1785 reveal a vast social range of clientele, from the landowning Philip Brabazon and John Van Homrigh to the middling Captain Walsh, Alderman Donogh and Reverend Bernard Dogherty to the much more modest Pat Fannin, Owen McTegart, Miss Cheshire and Mr. Hurley of Shopstreet. The wealthiest customers bought their claret, malaga, French white, old hock, tenerife, sherry, frontinac, red port, lisbon, and calcavella by the hogshead, or dozens of bottles; the poorest purchased one or two bottles at a time (National Library of Ireland, Ms. 9540). While the majority of wine in eighteenth-century Ireland was consumed by roughly 2,000 major landowning families with homes in the capital, Dublin's approximately 500 barristers and the wealthiest merchants and manufacturers, there were many others (Cullen 1983: 19).

The Irish abroad

Such strong local demand for wine provided a clear business opportunity. Consequently, Irishmen, often with their families and staff, made their way to Nantes at the mouth of the Loire; to Cadiz, the Spanish Atlantic port; and, most of all, to Bordeaux. While Nantes's Irish colony was bigger than Bordeaux's prior to 1730, and Cadiz's Irish colony was probably the largest over the course of the eighteenth century, Bordeaux's Irish colony was the one most directly linked to the wine trade (Cullen 1980: 51–63; Poussou 2017: 25).

Bordeaux had few Irish merchants in the mid-seventeenth century, but settlement accelerated after the Jacobite defeat in 1691. While butter dominated the earliest Irish trade, Thomas Lynch, a Catholic Jacobite from Galway who arrived in Bordeaux in 1698, began by selling tallow. Soon, the trickle of Jacobites became a flood of Irish merchants whose sole motive was profit. William Johnston, a Protestant from Dublin and Armagh, arrived in 1717, stayed for three years and went home a wine importer. He returned to Bordeaux in 1743 and died there in 1772. Nicholas MacInerheny, a Catholic from Limerick, arrived in 1723 and joined the established firm of William Coppinger from Cork. Thomas Barton, a Protestant from County Fermanagh, arrived in 1725. He was the scion of what became Bordeaux's most famous Irish merchant family and, indeed, Bordeaux's only Irish family to retain its Irish citizenship to this day (Poussou 2017: 1–32).

The names of Irish merchants in Bordeaux, most of whom arrived with the express purpose of being in the wine trade, are far too extensive to list here, but the leading historian of 'British' immigration into eighteenth-century Bordeaux has shown that approximately 95 traders had settled there by 1740 and that its entire 'British' merchant community in 1756 included 234 people, roughly 80% of them Irish (Poussou 2017: 9). Indeed, Bordeaux's 'Irish' merchant community was the largest of all the foreign merchant communities in the mid-eighteenth century (Poussou 2017: 25). These merchants were both pushed from Ireland and pulled by Bordeaux. Irish Catholics had lost most of their land during the seventeenth century, and between 1692 and 1714, the all-Anglican Irish Parliament passed penal laws against Irish Catholics and dissenting Protestants, excluding them from public office and the military and limiting access to the professions. In short, Protestant Irish landowners dominated the largely agrarian Irish economy. Ambitious Irish Catholics, Presbyterians and even landless Anglicans saw commerce as their best or only option. Selling wine to those thirsty Irish landowners and lawyers was one of the best options.

Bordeaux, meanwhile, was more than just a wine region and entrepot. The city in the Catholic kingdom welcomed Irish Catholics. Moreover, an Irish college opened there in 1603, with Irish priests training Irish seminarians (Ó'Catháin 2017: 1–26). Irish Catholics in Bordeaux were abroad but still among their own. Meanwhile, Bordeaux also welcomed Irish Protestants. Officially, Protestantism was proscribed in France in 1685, but it was tolerated because foreign Protestants, such as the small, affluent Huguenot community, stimulated trade and generated tax revenue. Furthermore, the French distinguished little between Irish Catholics and Protestants: they were all Irish and, therefore, not English. They were the acceptable face of Britain, an identity which the French preferred – plus, they spoke English and were British subjects. They knew and had access to the British market, including the extraordinarily lucrative London. Lastly, while the Irish wanted wine and French barrels for making whiskey, the French wanted Irish salt beef for French sailors (navy and merchant marine) and enslaved Africans producing sugar in the French West Indies, which – more than wine – was Bordeaux's greatest source of eighteenth-century wealth (Butel 1974: 24–25).

Bordeaux's Irish experienced a benevolent cycle in the eighteenth century. British wars with France could be economically debilitating, but the business opportunities during good times yielded some Irish fortunes for the Gernons, Galweys, Burkes, Byrnes, Coppingers, McCarthys and many others. The Bartons and Johnstons enjoyed uneven but prolonged commercial success. Generations of Johnstons supplied some of the most elite British customers, including the Irish-born Duke of Wellington (Ludington 2019a: 28). Thomas Barton earned enough to purchase a Tipperary estate in 1751, thus placing his family among the upper Irish gentry. In 1777, he was the second wealthiest merchant in Bordeaux. Abraham Lawton, a Protestant from Cork, arrived in Bordeaux in 1739, married a local Catholic and became the region's leading broker. His specialty was connecting Irish wine buyers with French producers (Ludington 2019a: 28). All three families are still in Bordeaux.

Bordeaux owes no less than the invention of its modern Grand Cru wines to these merchants. Annually, Irish merchants purchased the best wines at a few months old – today's *en primeur* – and shipped them to their Garonne River warehouses in Bordeaux's Chartrons district. They would periodically rack the wine into clean, sterilised barrels; clarify the wine; top up barrels to prevent oxidation or acidification; and, most importantly, cut the wines with Hermitage (syrah) from the Rhône Valley and grenache and mourvèdre from eastern Spain. This well-known process of 'raising' the wines was not remotely scandalous. The French called it 'Travail à l'Anglaise', and it was necessary to prepare the wines for the discerning British and Irish customers. Wines that were not dark, smooth and full-bodied simply would not suffice in the British Isles (Ludington 2019a: 38–40). This blending or cutting was not reserved for lesser wines: quite the opposite. It was done, and at much greater expense, for the very best, such as Haut Brion, Latour, Lafite, and 'Castle' Margaux, the vast majority of which went to London annually (Ludington 2019a: 30–38).

With lower tariffs, Ireland was a major destination and imported more Bordeaux than all of Great Britain. Export figures suggest that in the early 1740s, roughly 300 tonnes of Bordeaux wine went to London, while another 700-odd tonnes went to the rest of England. Scotland imported approximately 2,500 tonnes total, and Ireland imported over 4,000 tonnes. However, the average prices per tonne were 1,500 livres tournois (London), 800 livres tournois (the rest of England), 600 livres tournois (Scotland) and 400 livres tournois (Ireland) (Lachiver 1988: 304). Ireland's price was lowest because it was both 'a mass market for Bordeaux wines and a luxury market', as well as a mostly legal market (Butel 1974: 81). In Britain, and especially Scotland, at least half of the Bordeaux wine was regularly declared for customs purposes to be Portuguese or Spanish (Ludington 2013: 106–113). Keep in mind also that the average price per tonne of Bordeaux wine sold in France or northern Europe was a mere 200 livres tournois. (Archives Nationales, Paris: F.12/1500 (1740)). The English, Scottish and Irish were all drinking at the upper end of claret quality and price; the Irish were just drinking more of it.

A shrinking home trade: early nineteenth to mid-twentieth century

In general, Ireland's landed classes lorded it over the merchant milieu, but wine merchants benefited socially from both their worldliness and the exalted status of their goods. As the meticulously observant and mostly sympathetic English geographer Edward Wakefield wrote in his *Account of Ireland, Statistical and Political* (1812), the 'higher ranks' in Ireland considered tradesmen 'as a distinct class in society; and every business is condemned, that of wine merchant excepted' (Wakefield 1812: II,

804). Success in the wine trade placed Dublin wine merchants like Sneyd, French and Barton among the first families of the kingdom.

Not surprisingly, Ireland's wine trade was its most conservative trade: not only were they importing wine, but they also sold prodigious quantities to the peerage and rich gentry. Consequently, wine merchants shared their major clients' fears that political change could go too far (Cullen 1983: 49). In Dublin, clearly the centre of the trade, Protestants, including French Huguenot families like the Nairacs, dominated, although Catholic merchants thrived in provincial towns and cities. The Lynches, for example, dominated eighteenth-century Galway (Cullen 1986: 198).

But being a wine merchant in Ireland was never easy. Beyond British-French conflicts, simply getting paid could be a problem. Sneyd, French and Barton wrote to the Earl of Courtown's agent Robert Owen in August 1830, seeking payment for wine sold on six months' credit and delivered to the earl's Wexford home during 1826–27. 'If you could lend us any aid in obtaining this money', they pleaded, 'we should be thankful'. After many more pleas and an agreement to drop the interest, the bill was finally paid with a cheque on Messrs. Latouche and Co, the leading Dublin bank, in January 1832 (Trinity College Dublin Library, Courtown Papers, P/30/1/26l; P/30/1/118). Remarkably, such was the pull of serving the aristocracy that Sneyd, French and Barton continued to do business with the Third Earl of Courtown, as well as his son, the Fourth Earl, who was also delinquent in his payment (Trinity College Dublin Library, Courtown Papers: P/30/29/1–45; P/28/2/234–235).

Irish duties on wine imports remained relatively low throughout the eighteenth and early nineteenth centuries, helping explain the higher per capita consumption and dynamism of the wine trade in Ireland relative to Britain. In 1707, the year of English-Scottish Union, British duties on wine totalled over £54 per tonne on French, £25 on Portuguese, £26 on Spanish and over £30 on Rhenish wines. Irish duties were £10 Ir. per tonne of French, £12 Ir. on Portuguese, £15 Ir. on Spanish and £11 Ir. on Rhenish wine. (The Irish pound traded at 0.92 British pounds sterling.) That is, British wine duties were two to six times higher than Irish for the same wine, with French wine reflecting the greatest discrepancy. In 1750, British duties were over £62 per tonne on French and £29 on Portuguese wines, the most popular wine in Britain, while the Irish tariffs on the same were just over £17 Ir. for either.

In the middle of the Napoleonic Wars (c. 1810), British duties were £144 for French and £96 for Iberian wines, while Irish duties were £105 Ir. on French and £70 Ir. for Portuguese and Spanish wines. Rates were converging by 1823, when British duties maintained their 1810 levels while Irish duties rose to over £134 Ir. per tonne on French and over £89 Ir. per tonne on all other wines. In 1826, the Irish adopted the British pound; nevertheless, Irish duties remained just below British duties until 1853, when they were finally equalised.

Demand depends on relative price and income, and for the Irish, who were still on average poorer than the British, the duty increases that began in 1778, especially on French wines, had two dramatic effects. First, port surpassed claret as the leading imported wine in 1780 and fell to second place in 1781 but then regained the lead and maintained it well into the nineteenth century. It is clear that many of the very wealthy, like the banker and MP for Cavan, Henry Theophilus Clements, continued to drink more claret than anything else, but that may have been habit as much as anything else (Trinity College Dublin Library, Ms. 7276). His son, Colonel Henry John Clements, MP for Cavan in the new United Kingdom Parliament, drank much more diversely and, by 1805, was purchasing just as much port as claret, and while the port was less expensive, Clements would not have been inhibited by price (Trinity College Dublin, Ms. 7354/1–7).

Closer to national averages, the detailed sales books (1779–1814) of the Drogheda wine merchant Edward Hardeman show that he began selling more bottled port than bottled claret in 1796, although his sales in barrels still favoured claret. However, by 1798, he sold overwhelmingly more port than claret (Trinity College Dublin Library, Ms. 4798–4812). The second effect of the frequent and steep tariff increases from 1778 to 1824 was to diminish dramatically the social range of Irish wine drinkers. The anonymous Drogheda merchant who supplied both the great and the good in Louth, Meath and Westmeath, as well as the low-ranking military officers, parish priests, gentlemen farmers and shopkeepers from 1784 to 1795, served far more of the former and far fewer of the latter from 1804 to 1810. Apparently, the duty increases hurt his business, which was struggling by 1806 and barely there in its last year on record (National Library of Ireland: Ms. 9541).

The popularity of port over claret and the increasingly rarefied consumer base outlived the Napoleonic Wars because the tariff structure precipitating them continued; duty reductions in 1825 and 1831 made little difference. Irish gentlemen still maintained a reputation within the United Kingdom as claret drinkers; however, as can be seen in a droll depiction of 'British types' by the English caricaturist Henry Heath from 1826. In his print (Figure 17.1) 'The Comforts of Life', the mischievous Irishman (on the extreme left) is represented by claret.

Connoisseurs and men of taste celebrated 'Sneyd's claret' throughout the British Isles and beyond. Robert Peel, Chief Secretary for Ireland from 1812 to1818, purchased his claret from the Dublin firm even after he returned to England and became prime minister. If wine itself was a class signifier, claret had a higher status than port, but port was the more popular drink (Ludington 2013: 121–125).

Tastes change, however, and, as in the rest of the United Kingdom, sherry rose to primacy over both port and claret in the 1840s. Indeed, sherry and port together were the most popular wines in Ireland and throughout the United Kingdom until 1866, when claret surpassed port, and then in 1876, when claret surpassed sherry. But the two Iberian wines were the majority of both Irish wine imports and Irish wine consumption throughout the nineteenth century (Ludington 2019b: 260).

Meanwhile, average consumption declined, signifying wine's increasingly elite status. In 1852, the wine writer and tariff reform advocate Cyrus Redding calculated that Irish consumption had fallen from 3.5 bottles per head in the 1780s to 1.25 bottles per head from the 1780s through the 1840s (Redding 1852: 26). Redding convinced the Chancellor of the Exchequer William Gladstone to reduce duties in the 1860 through 1862 budgets, sparking English but not Irish demand.

Figure 17.1 'The Comforts of Life' by Henry Heath, c. 1826

For example, English wine dealer licenses tripled from 1860 to 1880 to over 4,600, while Irish numbers only rose from around 120 to 150 (Wilson 1940: table 24, 390–393). Irish preference for whiskey (allegedly 'owing to the humidity of the climate') was cited as the reason (*Irish Times*, 13 March 1873: 2). Ireland's eighteenth-century love affair with wine was over.

Alcohol consumption remained high in Ireland nonetheless, and in response, the Irish temperance movement, powerful in the 1830s and 40s, was revived by Father James Cullen in the 1890s. The violence and hardship supposedly caused by excess alcohol consumption concerned Cullen. Reflecting mid-twentieth century on the persistent Irish drinking culture, Maurice Healy, a long-standing teetotaller before his later-life conversion to wine, wrote that a 'deliberately degraded' people found in alcohol their only pleasure, despite the considerable economic and social consequences (Healy 1949: 18). Earlier in the century, concern about women's fertility strengthened the temperance cause (*Belfast Telegraph*, 28 June 1908: 6). After World War I, Republican leaders and the Irish Free State reinforced the temperance message. Measures such as the Licensing Acts of 1924 and 1927, supported by the Catholic Church, further stigmatised alcohol (Ferriter 2015: 6–7). Contemporaneously, the image of wine, called 'new to this country' in a 1930s newspaper report, suffered from stories about Red Biddy, a cheap 'Empire wine' spiked with added alcohol and used as a party drink by young people and reputedly abused by 'habitual drunkards' (*Northern Whig*, 15 December 1938: 7). It was the strong cider of its day.

Wine resurgent, 1950s to present

Between the wars and well into the 1950s, wine consumption was limited. In 1950, wine consumption in the Republic was some 200,000 cases (less than one bottle per head annually). Much of that was liebfraumilch from Germany and off-dry, effervescent rosé from Portugal. By 1970, consumption reached 1.3 million cases and increased dramatically in the 1980s and 1990s, reaching 4.8 million cases by 2000. Sales nearly doubled again by 2007 but have since remained largely static. Growing affluence and European Community membership (1973) have driven recent increases. The latter brought not only reduced duties but also increasing familiarity with Continental European eating and drinking habits (*Irish Independent*, 7 April 1987: 4). Nonetheless, Irish wine consumption has remained low by European standards. The Irish, said a 1988 headline, were the 'dregs in the wine league' (*Dublin Evening Herald*, 2 August 1988: 2). An *Irish Times* article suggested that in Ireland wine drinkers were considered 'either pretentious or weird, and probably both' (*Irish Times*, 18 October 2008: 34–35).

Nevertheless, the increased consumption triggered a slow change in Irish wine-drinking habits. No longer did advertisements focus solely on sherry, port or claret. As the *Irish Independent* wrote hopefully in 1987, 'it may not be long before Australian, New Zealand, and even Chilean wines become relatively common features of the better wine lists in our hotels and restaurants' (7 April 1987: 6). Wine courses and organised tasting sessions such as W. & A. Gilbey's 1990 'sniffathon' attracted attention (*Irish Independent*, 4 August 1980: 10). By 1999, wine appreciation courses were reportedly the 'favourite leisure pastime of the tippling classes' (*Irish Times*, 21 August 1999: A2). Sophisticated articles on wine by writers such as Tom Doorley and the late Tomás Clancy began to appear in Irish newspapers. But, as the famously caustic Kevin Myers put it in 1997, 'Most Irish people do not know whether Chateauneuf du Pape comes from Burgundy, Bordeaux, Loire or the Vatican, and more to the point, do not care' (*Irish Times*, 7 February 1997: 13).

In the first decades of the twenty-first century, the 'wine boom' centred on white wine in general and champagne in particular. From the late 1980s onwards, champagne was the most commonly advertised wine in Irish newspapers, even though it was accepted that the bulk of this consumption was at weddings and public celebrations. From then on, however, in the boom years of the 'Celtic Tiger' (the term given to Ireland during its period of rapid economic growth in the late 1990s), it was marked as a wine of excess and private hedonism, epitomised by the story of one of Ireland's 'new merchant princes' who took his wife in a private jet to Paris to celebrate Valentine's Day. The jet was bedecked in red roses, and the couple bathed together in Cristal champagne before 'renewing their wedding vows' at the cost of a 'cool £1 million' (*Irish Independent*, 6 November 2004: 30). The Irish wine boom was ascribed to various factors, including a switch to home socialising, the greater perceived sophistication of wine, the economic boom and a great deal more holiday travel to southern Europe, from where the taste for wine was brought home. Columnists claimed that 'we have become a nation of wine-lovers like never before', and advertisements and articles for wine picked up again the story of the so-called 'wine geese' or eighteenth-century Irish wine merchants in Bordeaux, Nantes, Cadiz, Madeira and Tenerife (*Sunday Tribune*, 29 April 2001: 70; *Dublin Evening Herald*, 17 December 2008: 32).

Throughout the period from the 1980s onwards, wine was gendered as a drink for women chosen by women. Prosecco was positioned as the cure for a 'bad hair day' (*Irish Independent*, 22 February 2002: 45) whilst men asking for a 'white wine spritzer in the local bar [were] unlikely to draw admiring glances', reckoned the *Dublin Evening Herald* (13 January 1998: 20). However, voices of official caution perpetuating a century of concern over excessive alcohol consumption among women tempered recognition of wine as woman's drink and a woman's choice. In 1989, a female columnist claimed that a clause in a proposed bill to close down wine sections of groceries and supermarkets was 'an anti-women plot' emanating from the 'smoky subconscious of our male legislators' for whom women are 'alcoholics while men are "lads-at-the-bar having a few pints"' (*Irish Times*, 9 January 1989: 12). Much of the concern was directed at the alcohol industry, whose marketing and business practices were creating 'a major public health issue with female alcohol dependence in Ireland' (*Irish Times*, 12 September 2016: 12).

In part this concern reflected a continuing Irish ambivalence over alcohol. In 2010, 20 per cent of the Irish population were said to be teetotallers whilst the same article, headlined 'Is Ireland Falling Out of Love with Alcohol?', claimed that 'half of all Irish drinking occasions are bingeing', concluding 'we don't do moderation well in Ireland' (*Irish Times*, 27 March 2010: B1). By this point, it is possible that both economic choices and demographic shifts were pushing against further wine consumption. The baby boomers, who had led the wine boom of the previous decade, were now in their 30s with families and mortgages, and 2009 was rated the 'worst year' for alcohol sales since the 1990s. (*Irish Times*, 27 January 2010: B1). The ending of the Celtic Tiger boom exposed a shallow pool of frequent and knowledgeable wine drinkers supplemented by a far larger number of special-occasion purchasers whose consumption waxed and waned with the state of the economy.

Conclusions

Anthropologist Thomas Wilson has cogently identified acceptance of a deep-rooted Irish drinking culture (Wilson 2004: paras 4, 17). But, if such a culture exists, does Ireland have a 'wine culture'? This chapter has shown the past importance of wine in Ireland as a marker of social and national differentiation. Irish businessmen in France made a significant contribution to the history of wine with their development of Grand Cru clarets. The champagne boom of the early twenty-first century was an expression of the evanescent success of the newly financialised economy.

Whatever its historical roots, it is clear that contemporary Irish wine culture is stunted. Compared to the rest of Europe, per capita consumption remains low. Though wine 'comfortably remains' second only to beer in the alcohol market, 83% of wine sold in 2019 was in the off-trade sector, and there was little more than slow, partial and begrudging acceptance of wine in Irish pubs: stories of poorly treated stock; inadequate, error-strewn wine lists; and hostility to wine drinkers, male and female, are no longer as prevalent as they once were, but reliance on distributors' advice for pub or restaurant wine lists remains (*Drinks Ireland Wine* 2019: 2; *Dublin Evening Herald*, 1 October 2009: 104). Moreover, wine is a convenient tax base as there is no native industry to lobby against taxation. Indeed, €3.19 per bottle excise tax (in addition to the VAT) discourages anyone of modest means. Taxes are high on other alcoholic drinks, but Guinness, the archetypal stout, has become a critical component of global 'Irishness'. (While both Ireland and Guinness use the harp symbol, the latter trademarked the image in 1876, while Ireland waited until 1922 to adopt it.) Dozens of websites expound the principles and practice of whiskey connoisseurship; the 'Guinness Academy' offers training in the 'six steps' to the perfect pour. There are fewer vinous equivalents to such generalised expressions of connoisseurship.

Irish culture may depend on alcohol, but wine is no longer an expression of Irish identity as claret was during the period from 1700 to 1850. In that sense, there is no Irish wine culture in the way that there is clearly an Irish beer, whiskey or tea culture. In the last half century, Irish women (and men) have used wine increasingly as a marker of individual identity. Wine in Ireland – like other drinks – forms part of the stories that we as individuals tell ourselves about who we are (and who we want to be) and, importantly, how we are different from others. In that sense, there is a wine culture in Ireland (as in every European country). The depth of that culture has changed over time, and it can certainly be disputed. We would contend that it is now relatively shallow by historical and European (even perhaps British) standards. But wine still has a cultural value, a cultural charge – be it positive or negative – in Ireland as elsewhere. Hence, the value of this book.

References

Newspapers

Belfast Telegraph
Dublin Evening Herald
Irish Independent
Irish Times
Northern Whig
Sunday Tribune

Primary sources

Archives Nationales, Paris: F.12/1500 (1740)
Lewis Walpole Library: http://hdl.handle.net/10079/digcoll/.
National Library of Ireland, Ms. 9540; 9541.
Trinity College Dublin Library, Courtown Papers, P/30/1/26l; P/30/1/118; P30/29/1–45; P/28/2/234–235.
Trinity College Dublin Library, Ms. 7276; 7354/1–7.
Trinity College Dublin Library, Ms. 4798–4812.

Secondary sources

Barnard, T.C. (2004) *Making the Grand Figure: Lives and Possessions in Ireland, 1641–1770*, New Haven, CT and London: Yale University Press.
Butel, P. (1974) *Les Négociants Bordelais, l'Europe et les Iles au XVIIIe siècle*, Paris: Aubier.
Cullen, L.M. (1980) "The Irish Merchant Communities in Bordeaux, La Rochelle and Cognac in the Eighteenth Century," in L.M. Cullen and P. Butel (eds), *Négoce et Industrie en France et en Irlande aux XVIIIe et XIXe siècles*, Paris: CNRS, 51–63.

Cullen, L.M. (1983) *Princes & Pirates: The Dublin Chamber of Commerce, 1783–1983*, Dublin: Dublin Chamber of Commerce.

Cullen, L.M. (1986) "The Dublin Merchant Community in the Eighteenth Century," in L.M. Cullen and P. Butel (eds), *Cities and Merchants: French and Irish Perspectives on Urban Development*, Dublin: Trinity College Dublin.

Drinks Ireland. (2019) "Irish Wine Market Report 2019," www.https.ibec.ie/drinksireland/-/media/documents/drinks-ireland-new-website/insights/wine-market-report-2019.pdf, accessed 2 January 2021.

Ferriter, D. (2015) "Drink and Society in Twentieth-Century Ireland," *Proceedings of the Royal Irish Academy* 115C, 1–21.

Foley, A. (2019) *Excise Tax Rates in Europe: How Ireland Compares*, Dublin: The Drinks Industry Group of Ireland (DIGI).

Healy, M. (1949) *Stay Me with Flagons*, London: Michael Joseph.

Lachiver, M. (1988) *Vins, vignes et vignerons: histoire du vignoble français*, Paris: Fayard.

Legg, M.L. (1996) *The Synge Letters: Bishop Edward Synge to His Daughter Alicia, Roscommon to Dublin, 1746–1752*, Dublin: Lilliput.

Ludington, C. (2013) *The Politics of Wine in Britain: A New Cultural History*, Basingstoke: Palgrave Macmillan.

Ludington, C. (2019a) "Inventing Grand Cru Claret: Irish Wine Merchants in Eighteenth-Century Bordeaux," *Global Food History* 5, 1–2, 25–44.

Ludington, C. (2019b) "United Kingdom," in K. Anderson and V. Pinella (eds), *Wine Globalization: A New Comparative History*, Cambridge: Cambridge University Press, 239–271.

Madden, S. (1738) *Reflections and Resolutions Proper for the Gentlemen of Ireland, as to Their Conduct for the Service of Their Country*, Dublin: Printed by R. Reilly, for G. Ewing; Re-Printed.

McConnell, T. (2014) "Ireland in the Georgian Era," in B. Keatinge and M. Pierse (eds), *France and Ireland in the Public Imagination*, Bern: Peter Lang, 223–240.

McConnell, T. (2017) "The Social Meaning of Claret in Eighteenth-Century Ireland," Unpublished Paper Presented at the Irish Community in Eighteenth-Century France: Contributions and Contexts, Conference in Bordeaux, 25 November.

Murphy, T. (2005) *A Kingdom of Wine*, Cloghroe: Onstream.

Ó Catháin, D. (2017) "The Irish College in Bordeaux and Its Connections with the Wider World," Unpublished Paper Presented at the Irish Community in Eighteenth-Century France: Contributions and Contexts, Conference in Bordeaux, 25 November.

Poussou, J-P. (2017) "La colonie marchande irlandaise de Bordeaux au XVIIIe siècle remise en perspective," Unpublished Paper Presented at the Irish Community in Eighteenth-Century France: Contributions and Contexts, Conference in Bordeaux, 25 November.

Powell, M.J. (2005) *The Politics of Consumption in Eighteenth-Century Ireland*, Basingstoke: Palgrave Macmillan.

Redding, C. (1852) *Wine Duties Reduction. An Abstract of the Evidence Given Before the Select Committee of the House of Commons upon the Import Duties on Wines, in May and June 1852, with a Draft of the Chairman's Report*, London: Charles Skipper and East.

Swift, J. and Ryland, F. (1923) *The Journal to Stella, A.D. 1710–1713*, London: G. Bell and Sons.

Wakefield, E. (1812) *An Account of Ireland, Statistical and Political*, vol. 2, London: Longman, Hurst, Rees, Orme, and Brown.

Wilson, G.B. (1940) *Alcohol and the Nation: A Contribution to the Study of the Liquor Problem in the United Kingdom from 1800–1935*, London: Nicholson and Watson.

Wilson, T. (2004) "Globalization, Differentiation and Drinking Cultures, an Anthropological Perspective," *Anthropology of Food*, https://doi.org.10.4000.aof.261, accessed 20 February 2020.

18
WINE AS PART OF POLISH IDENTITY IN EARLY MODERN TIMES

Constructing wine culture in non-wine countries

Dorota Dias-Lewandowska

Introduction

The cultural history of wine is, above all, the history of the circulation of ideas about wine and its consumption as well as their representation (Ory 2004). In this chapter, I will examine how wine was perceived and what role it played in a non-wine country, including the choice of particular wines and taste and the reception of the new trends (e.g. champagne).

The citizens of the Polish-Lithuanian Commonwealth had a unique attitude to imported wines, in particular those from Hungary and France. In the country of beer and vodka, wine not only became a symbol of prestige and elitism but was also closely related to identity. Historically, Polish drinking was defined by occasional, ritualistic and oppressive consumption of alcohol, and rejection of this tradition in the second half of the eighteenth century could be considered an attempt to stand out, a manifestation of otherness or the assumption of a foreign identity. As a result, it was subject to negative evaluation. This period coincides with the decline of the Sarmatian warrior culture and the formation of new consumption patterns, which led to significant changes in the Polish drinking culture. Hungarian wines were symbolically considered 'Polish' while all others, particularly French wines, were viewed as new-fashioned, cosmopolitan and foreign.

Polish identity was created in opposition to the West – countering the absolutist tendencies of western Europe with the Polish nobles' 'golden freedom', which, in the eighteenth century, became a heavily criticised concept. In the mid-eighteenth century, the cosmopolitan nobility shifted towards French wines, which had previously been ignored if not despised, whilst the conservative faction remained loyal to the Hungarian wines, and this shift symbolised the identity schism in the noble community.

Wine as an element of identity was particularly emphasised at the end of the eighteenth century when Poland was losing its independence. On the one hand, foreign wine was blamed for the country's downfall. On the other, consumption of Hungarian wine became a manifestation of nostalgia among both nobles and the middle class.

Thus, one important period for the relationship between wine and identity was the eighteenth century, a time of social change when – initially in a narrow, elite circle – we can observe a consumer revolution. This change in attitudes, aspirations, ways of communication and new consumption patterns spread further, to other social groups. Alcohol and its consumption were used to communicate new attitudes and values.

'Polish wine' and Polish identity

In Poland, the appearance of vineyards and wine was closely related to the adoption of Christianity (Małecki 1894: 421). Most of the medieval vineyards were located in the regions of Lesser Poland and Greater Poland linked to the development of a network of monasteries. Until the thirteenth century, Polish vineyards were few, and Polish wine was not widely consumed. Monastic wine was used for personal consumption in hospitals and in the church (Gołębiowski 1830: 180). In the fourteenth century, however, the church began to lease its property, including the vineyards, for profit. This gave rise to small-scale commercialisation of domestic wine (Kwapieniowa 1959: 385).

The growth of domestic wine consumption was further facilitated by the lack of competition from foreign wines. Wine was imported in small quantities, mainly by the royal court and rich nobles. The quality of domestic wines still left much to be desired, and foreigners believed that the grapes growing in Polish lands were more suitable for eating than for making wine, which was judged to be rather sour (Gintel 1971: 127).

The decline of Polish winemaking was attributed to climate change in the sixteenth century, as well as to the shift of the economic model to a manorial system. The demanding grapevine was replaced by grain, which was easier to grow and more profitable (Jeżowa 1938). Gradual improvement of the quality of roads also made international transport easier, and as a result, domestic wine faced strong competition in the form of foreign, mainly Hungarian products. The latter became a culturally significant factor contributing to the image of the Polish nobility in early modern times.

To understand the important role played by wine in the formation of Polish identity, we must also answer the question of identity itself: who felt a member of the nation and why were other groups excluded from it? In the seventeenth century, the concept of a nation as ethnically homogenous did not exist. Instead, in the political sense, the state comprised only the nobility, who possessed the right to vote and the right to own land. They even used the term 'a Republic of Nobles' denoting their status. At the root of the noble nation was the myth of shared descent from the ancient Sarmatians and the weakness of the other classes, especially the lack of strong townspeople and the servile status of peasants. The narrative of that time developed around two opposing myths: the Sarmatian one, according to which Polish nobles were the heirs of the Sarmatian warriors, and the myth about the rustic origin of the peasants (from the biblical Ham – hence, the Polish reference to peasants as 'hams'). The representatives of townspeople and peasants were a later addition, without their own place in the nation (Paczos 2014).

Sarmatism maintained its dominant position until the mid-eighteenth century (Tazbir 1978), when the unity of the noble nation experienced a major crisis. This was caused by fairly large social inequalities within this privileged group, which included both great landowners and impoverished representatives of the nobility, whose only link to the noble nation was their title and whose lifestyle was closer to that of the peasants or townsmen.

The emblematic drink of the noble nation, until its crisis in the eighteenth century, was Hungarian wine of all kinds. The *Nullum vinum nisi hungaricum* (no wine except Hungarian) principle (Tuwim 1959: 58) testified to its dominant position. The Polish nobility's liking for Hungarian wines was so great that even at feasts at the royal court in Versailles, it was this wine that was served to the Polish deputies (Komaszyński 1966: 46). Similarly, French wine merchants selling to Poland often selected wines similar in taste to Hungarian ones, believing that only such products stood a chance of being purchased by the Polish nobility (Boissonnade and Charliat 1930: 101). This tendency to adjust the taste of wine to the tastes of the consumers has continued for centuries. Even at the beginning of the nineteenth century, when a representative of the Clicquot champagne house was visiting the Polish lands in search of customers, this practice continued. After meeting with merchants and customers of Cracow, Louis Bohne wrote in his diaries that for the local people, wine must be honey sweet like the best Hungarian wines (Bohne 1802–04: 82). This fondness for Hungarian wine and its strong connection to Polish identity was also manifested in the use of the adjective 'Polish' to describe strong and high-quality Hungarian wines (Zawadzki 1963: 229). Hungarian wine was said to have been born in Hungary but formed in Poland – *Hungariae natum, Poloniae educatum* (Carter 1987).

The subsequent success of French wines, including champagne, which pushed Hungarian wine off its pedestal in the mid-eighteenth century, also brought about a change in the drinking culture and the perception of alcohol itself.

The drinking culture – the culture of wine

Defining drinking culture has its roots in the broad definition of culture itself, as proposed by anthropologists. Based on the definition by Dwight Heath (1990), who considers culture to be a 'simplified label covering broad patterns of thought and behaviour as demonstrated by individuals in their daily lives', we can understand drinking culture as a set of practices related to drinking, attitudes towards alcohol and the roles that this consumption plays in society. Therefore, what shaped the culture of wine in a non-wine country such as early modern Poland was, above all, the beverage, the ritualisation of its consumption and the socialising and culture-forming functions of wine.

The drink

What makes wine or beer intoxicating is not the volume of alcohol, but the way, amount and context in which it is consumed, as well as the intellectual, emotional and physical state of the person who drinks it (Withington 2011). Therefore, when analysing the way alcohol consumption was perceived in Poland, it can be assumed that drunken excesses were caused not only by the alcohol itself but also by the way a person was drinking in a given situation. One example of this is the custom of drinking a shot of vodka before breakfast. From the perspective of a Polish nobleman, such behaviour was the norm, and its purpose was to 'flush one's spirits', as dietary treatises defined it (Hercius 1660). To an outside observer, this behaviour seemed proof of widespread drunkenness in early modern Poland. The perception of immoderate consumption of wine and other beverages among the nobility also had its roots in differing perceptions of the role of these beverages. As Philippe Gillet (1985: 44) writes, for the French, Italians and Spaniards, drinking was an activity directly related to eating. While drinking at the table during a feast, a person is also eating a meal, and the purpose of drinking is precisely to satisfy hunger.

For foreigners describing the habits at the Polish table, a feast consisted of two parts: the first part was about eating a meal; the second part started with ceremonial toasts and then serving different drinks one by one. Thus, a distinction was made between activities which, for foreign observers, constituted an inseparable whole. The consumption of wine after a meal separated the act of drinking from the meal itself. In Poland, on the other hand, during a meal, one drank beer (Kitowicz 2003: 219), which was treated as a nourishing drink; wine, as the foreigners observed, was served immediately after the meal.

Socialisation

Reflections on the type of alcoholic beverages drunk over time across Europe and the different ways in which they were consumed was started in the 1980s by Jean-Louis Flandrin (1983). He compared the way opinions about drunkenness changed during the sixteenth and eighteenth centuries. What seems to stand out is the discourse about drunkenness in northern Europe. The inhabitants of this part of the continent were associated with a particularly excessive use of alcohol, as opposed to the inhabitants of the South, who were famed for their temperance. This excessive consumption of alcohol can be illustrated by an excerpt from a seventeenth-century English treatise on cider:

> So at this day the Germans are much given to drunkenness, as one of their own Countrymen writes of them; that they drink so immodestly and immoderately at their Banquets, that they cannot pour it in fast enough with the ordinary Quaffing-Cups, but drink in large Tankards, whole draughts, none to be left under severe penalties; admiring him that will drink most, and hating him that will not pledge them. The Dutch-men are not behind-hand with them; inviting all Comers with a Pail and a Dish, making Barrels of their Bellies. In Poland, he is most accounted of that will drink most Healths and held to be the bravest Fellow, that carries his Liquor best; being of opinion that there is as much Valour to be found in drinking as in fighting. The Russians, Swedes, Danes, and those Northern Inhabitants, exceed all the rest, having made the drinking of Brandy, Aqua Vitae, Hydromel, Beer, Mum, Meth, and other Liquors in great quantities so familiar to them, that they usually drink our countrymen to death. Priests and people, men and women, old and young do so delight in drunkenness, that they are daily early and late found wallowing in the streets.
>
> *(Worlidge 1678: Preface)*

More than 100 years later, at the beginning of the nineteenth century, 'drunk as a Pole' became a popular saying which meant not so much excessive consumption but drinking beyond measure and having a strong head (Moskalewicz and Zieliński 1995: 224).

Drunkenness as a common and socially accepted phenomenon in Poland is already clear from earlier accounts. As early as in the second half of the sixteenth century, Fulvius Ruggieri described this phenomenon in the following way: 'Drinking is a praiseworthy custom among them, an unquestionable proof of sincerity and good manners; sobriety, on the contrary, perceived as coarseness, can sometimes be a sign of secretive character and deception' (Gintel 1971: 140). Drinking was treated as natural behaviour. It was seen as the norm, to the point of getting drunk, which, although criticised and its disastrous effects noticed, was not fully condemned. Whoever drank together with the host and enjoyed his hospitality gained the acceptance of the people around him and inspired trust. This was not the case for those who refused to drink. Refusing to drink was perceived in a negative way. It aroused suspicion and calls for caution. This was particularly evident in the case of forced drinking, in which the host or other guests try at all costs to involve the person refusing to drink in the feast. Alcohol not only accompanied private feasts but was also an essential part of any political event. It also served as a means of persuasion and helped win the hearts of political opponents or secure the favour of some nobles (Aimé-Martin 1833: 12–17). A similar perception of socialising functions was present in early modern Sweden, where toasting and feasting together was proof of loyalty not only to the host but also to the guests at the feast (Sennefelt 2014: 281).

The ritual

The feast, which was itself a kind of spectacle, could not take place without a number of rituals and gestures. In the research on the history of alcohol, the important questions are still those concerning the symbolic role of its consumption, the rituals accompanying it and the factors shaping the level of consumption. The occasional, theatrical consumption of large amounts of alcohol in early modern Poland was called barbaric by external observers and evoked more indignation (Elias 1980) than regular consumption of small amounts of alcohol. Making consumption public and subjecting it to rituals, customs and special rules played a greater role in defining drunkenness than the amount and volume of alcohol consumed.

Feasting was a characteristic of Polish hospitality and made famous by foreigners. Its key elements were ritualisation, the great importance of the gesture (raising a glass, drinking from a single cup etc.) and the special position of alcohol. Maria Bogucka (1983, 1994), writing about the customs of the Polish nobility in the sixteenth and seventeenth centuries, notes that during this period, the gesture served three basic functions: it enabled communication, it expressed feelings and it was also a sign of belonging to a circle of nobles. The importance of gesture during a feast was still observable in the eighteenth century, although this was already a time of gradual abandonment of old practices and customs related to drinking.

One of the central symbols of the old Polish feast was drinking from a single cup, which was mentioned as a characteristic element of the feasting of the Polish nobility. Some observers of Polish customs even described it with aversion. Johann Joseph Kausch wrote that 'he did not enjoy drinking wine after the meal from one cup, shared by everyone one by one, without rinsing it every time' (Zawadzki 1963: 276). Hubert Vautrin (1807: 210), when describing the toasts, observed that at each feast, 'no sooner had the cup that nobody misses been emptied than the next one, in which ten pairs of moustaches have already been wetted, appeared'. This free passing of wine between the guests was considered in Poland as proof of hospitality. In other countries like Denmark, drinking from one cup was included in the catalogue of games and fun activities that accompanied drinking (Van Bruaene and van Bouchaute 2017: 8). The ritualisation of drinking and the importance attached to toasts met with resistance from foreigners. In the eighteenth century, when coffee became popular in Poland, it was used to excuse oneself from drinking: '[I]t was like a privilege of health, that whoever drank coffee could not be oppressed with wine' (Kitowicz 2003: 242). Such an escape, giving a few hours of break from the feast, could also be used when the host offered poor wine.

Responses to the 'barbaric' drinking of the inhabitants of the Republic of Poland also reflected the drinking habits in the observer's country of origin. Matthieu Lecoutre's (2011) study of drinking in France shows that the drinking culture of the French might have, in a sense, been formed in opposition to drinking in northern Europe. The analysis of foreigners' opinions on drinking in Poland and the evaluation of one's own drinking culture and those of others reveal a model of the early modern wine consumer. It is surprising that the progressive cosmopolitanisation of the nobility and the influence of French culture, including the choice of the drink and the manner of its consumption, were barely reflected in the foreigners' accounts, even from the late eighteenth and early nineteenth centuries. This stereotypical view is certainly due to the slower reception of the culture of wine drinking. The more tradition was valued above fashion in a given community, the more hesitant the reception of wine. Furthermore, one can observe a kind of interpenetration of new fashion with the aesthetics of splendour and excess, which, in the case of wine consumption in eighteenth-century Europe, was in decline. According to Stephen Mennell (1985: 32), the eighteenth century was characterised by the shift from quantitative to qualitative consumption. Consequently, drinking wine ceased to be a determinant of one's social status. Drinking quality wine, however, which required knowledge and connoisseurship to admire its properties, became a new way of expressing one's social position.

The culture

Focusing on the difference between an observed foreign culture and one's own experience reveals how often impressions from travel and contacts with strangers made it possible to mythologise one's own culture. Veronique Grappe (2006: 78), researching the phenomenon of drunkenness in France during the *Ancien Régime*, used a qualitative analysis of medical, religious and literary sources related to alcohol abuse to show that excessive drinking in France during this period was not an exotic and rare behaviour. However, such an impression of excessive drinking was given by the descriptions of Polish feasting and alcohol consumption written by French men and women living in Poland in the seventeenth and eighteenth centuries. Foreigners – observers of a feast and its ritualised drinking – became intermediaries between those who crossed the boundary of intoxication and lost control of themselves and the readers indirectly observing that culture. In each case, the observer puts himself in the position of an outsider, describes the sequence of events from the perspective of a non-participant and, at the same time, is aware of the sanctions he may face if he does not take part in the feast.

The consumption of alcohol resulting in intoxication is, as Grappe writes, something more than just giving in to weakness, a moment of euphoria and a sense of community. It is impossible to reduce alcoholic intoxication to the process of the reversal of norms, progressing with every drop of alcohol (Grappe 2006: 82). During the feast, the person refusing to drink with others expresses their unwillingness to belong to the community. By drinking toasts with guests, however, they cross the line between being an outside observer, considered a stranger, and a member of the community.

Hungarian wine, champagne and the national wine – a time of nostalgia

The passing of fashion, the emergence of new trends and the ambivalent attitude to novelty are often accompanied by nostalgia for everything that is well known and familiar. Certainly, this is how the processes concerning wine consumption in modern Poland could be described in a nutshell. In the mid-eighteenth century, goods known until then as exotic and luxurious – coffee, tea and cocoa – became largely mass produced (Welter 1868) and their consumption a sign of good manners and sensitivity (Brewer 1997). The increasing closeness of consumer identity to political identity was manifested through consumer protests. Ritual boycotts of consumer goods such as tea became a manifestation of the struggle for political independence (Breen 2004). In Poland, such manifestations of political and national views were present in fashion and attire. They usually took place on the axis of the self/other and usually involved the boycott of the 'foreign' option (e.g. champagne).

Manifesting political opinions and worldviews by means of clothing, behaviour or drinking behaviour was widespread. The status of Hungarian wine as the national wine among the nobles had strengthened; after all, even though the beverage was produced in Hungary, it was Poland where it took on its final form. The lack of domestic winemaking since the sixteenth century, combined with a strong need to identify with a beverage, resulted in the choice of Hungarian wine as a national drink. The use of Hungarian wines in early modern Polish fiction clearly indicates a strongly emotional association of this wine with national patriotism. For some, Hungarian wine, although imported, was traditionally Polish, while French wine, which was as foreign as the Hungarian, was perceived as culturally alien. The most frequent opposition was the 'good old Hungarian wine', full of value and tradition, and the trivial, even empty, champagne, which had no value whatsoever. This was particularly evident in the nineteenth century. Juliusz Strutyński (1878: 13–14) used this type of opposition in his poem 'Down with the Champagne': 'Crémant! Clicquot! – to hell with it/The old Hungarian – that's the wine'. The issue of the age of wine was particularly relevant in the nineteenth century, and this motif was frequently used in nostalgic discourses about the old glory.

The influence of French culture in Poland in the eighteenth century was strong and manifested itself not just in the popularity of the French language or attire. Not only did French cuisine become popular, but the very concept of French fashion and sophistication was also celebrated (Prunitsch 2011: 79). In this context, Sarmatism as an ideology and a way of life retained core values of national identity on which the Poles would draw over the next century.

Thus, a certain dissonance can be seen in both views and behaviours which manifested themselves in the consumption of wine. Hungarian wines were portrayed as an expression of attachment to tradition, in opposition to new-fashioned customs gaining popularity in the second half of the eighteenth century. Conversely, champagne was identified with cosmopolitanism, following the new fashion and taking delight in the foreign. The very choice of a beverage could therefore be regarded as adopting a certain attitude: traditional, Polish and Sarmatian in the case of Hungarian wines or cosmopolitan, foreign and new-fashioned in the case of champagne (Dias-Lewandowska 2014).

The taste of wines also changed. Alcoholic drinks sent to the markets of the North remained for centuries under the influence of the tastes of the inhabitants of these areas. To ensure its sale, the wine's taste was adjusted to the demands of the recipient. Fascination with wines from France in the mid-eighteenth century was therefore more related to the trend of French culture than to the taste of its wines since most of the champagne coming to these areas, for example, was adapted to the taste of customers by sweetening with sugar or syrup (Lewandowska 2012).

'In the age of the knights food was eaten voraciously, in the 18th century with sophistication; in the 19th century, having broken with tradition, people eat, or at least want to eat in a hygienic way' (Gomulicki 1880: 17). These are the opening words of the chapter about cafes, confectioneries and wine bars of nineteenth-century Warsaw. The voraciousness of the Middle Ages juxtaposed with the elegance and exquisiteness of eighteenth-century consumption can be seen not only on the Polish plate but also in the glass. It is easy to overlook the fact that changes in the food culture were accompanied by changes in the drinking culture. In the century of industrial, scientific and technical development, eating and drinking, once strongly connected, started to follow different paths. The nutritious beer pottages, *kaliszans* (mixes of beer, bread and wine) and vodkas drunk to 'flush the spirits' were increasingly banished from the Polish menu, not only because of the fight against the spread of drunkenness but also because of the strong arguments of scientists that the belief in the nutritious properties of beverages should be treated as a legend rather than used to justify alcohol consumption (Dias-Lewandowska 2017).

This approach illustrates how food was perceived in the past and what values were aspired to at that time. After all, the nineteenth century was a century not only of great political events in the history of Poland but also of life under the partitions, unsuccessful uprisings and repressions carried out by the invaders. The culinary and consumption aspects underwent no less important changes and, unlike the national liberation uprisings, were not necessarily doomed to failure. Such changes focused on the discourse about drunkenness, fostered the return of domestic winemaking and led to changes in the symbolism of wine and identity.

In the context of the criticism of drunkenness in modern times, a discourse that included the wealthy nobility, the magnates and their love of expensive foreign wines predominated. After the loss of independence at the end of the Age of Enlightenment, there was a change of emphasis; the criticism of the nobility drinking their freedom away gave way to the concern for the sobriety of the lower social strata. As a result, the moral and economic decline of peasants was blamed not on wine – which was supposed to have caused the ills of the elites – but on the common *gorzałka* (a distilled spirit produced and sold by the nobility). In the first half of the nineteenth century, the emphasis on the harmful properties of vodka was so great that in the fight against its consumption, one of the ideas was to try to eliminate the strongest spirits by consuming the weaker ones – wine, beer and cider. Beer and cider, in particular, played a major role in this respect as they were not only cheaper than wine but were also domestic drinks, though cider seems to have been less appreciated than beer (Dias-Lewandowska *et al.* forthcoming).

At the end of the eighteenth century, Poland had been annexed and then partitioned by Prussia, Russia and Austria so that it effectively ceased to exist as an independent country in the nineteenth century. Thus, in an era of civilisational, social and cultural transformations in Europe, Poland had to face the loss of independence, oppression on the part of the partitioners, mass emigration and failed pro-independence uprisings. At that time, wine was associated mainly with foreignness, invaders and the drunkenness of the nobility and thus associated with the collapse of the state. In the nineteenth century, we can see a return to the idea of Polish wine, although among the Romantics, the idea of mead as a truly national drink also reappeared. The vineyards opened in 1828 in the Warsaw Botanical Garden were a project that was to begin the process of the modernisation of Polish agriculture that had been dominated by cereal cultivation from the sixteenth century. This idea was promoted by Tadeusz Mostowski, Minister of Internal Affairs and Police. The project did not turn out to be successful on a mass scale. Nevertheless, Warsaw's vineyards became places frequented by the nouveau riche and the new intellectual elite of Warsaw (Włodarczyk 2018).

The association of wine with foreignness, loss of independence and denial of Polish tradition referred primarily to French wines, especially champagne. It was champagne that was contrasted with the good old Hungarian wines, and this narrative became even stronger in the nineteenth century. For many conservatives, champagne, a new-fashioned drink devoid of history and tradition in Poland, could not match Hungarian wine, which evoked memories of the glory of the Republic. It was from this period that the fame and reputation of the Fukier Winery in Warsaw, and especially 'Hetman's cellar', a collection of the best and oldest Hungarian wines, emerged. Although the fame of the Fukier brand was based on the noble tradition of appreciation of Hungarian wines, the long-established trade traditions of the Fukier family contributed to the identity of the Warsaw bourgeoisie during the development of capitalism (Kurczewski 2018). In the nineteenth century, with the development of restaurants and cafes, the Fukier Winery resembled a museum of old customs. Rather than introducing the newly popular champagne or burgundy into its assortment, it stayed faithful to tradition. Visited by the traditionalists, in the capitalist new world, it was a refuge of the old order and a place of nostalgia. Over the years, the legendary Hetman's cellar had been enriched with older and older wines. The journalists, writers and authors of guides who described it gradually moved the vintages of the oldest wines even as far back as to the sixteenth century. In this way, the Hetman's cellar became a kind of wine chronicle of the golden era of the Polish state.

Wine played a significant role in the formation of the identity of not just the noble nation, united by toasts raised with a cup filled with 'Polish' Hungarian wine. The same Hungarian wine, which lost its eighteenth-century popularity among the elite of the Republic of Poland, became appreciated by the bourgeoisie, which, at a time of great economic and social changes, created its identity based on the good traditions of old merchants, symbolised by the Fukier Winery.

Polish local wine competed unsuccessfully with foreign drinks both in the Middle Ages and in modern times. Attempts to revive the idea of Polish vineyards also failed, giving way to the long-established Hungarian wines and the new-fashioned champagne. The true renaissance of winemaking had to wait until well into the early twenty-first century, when new, small vineyards were planted in areas where vines were grown as early as in the Middle Ages. Emphasising local traditions and rediscovering the history of Polish winemaking enabled wine, no longer Hungarian but Polish, to become an important element of the development of culture and landscape (Greinerta *et al.* 2019).

Acknowledgements

The chapter was written as part of research financed by the National Science Centre, application no 2016/20/S/HS3/00107.

References

Primary sources

Aimé-Martin, L. (1833) *Œuvres posthumes de Bernardin de Saint-Pierre*, Paris, Lefèvre.
Bohne, L. (1802–1804) *Deuxième carnet de voyage de Louis Bohne. Second voyage octobre 1802–mars 1804*, Veuve Clicquot Archives 1A 1E 104.
Gintel, J. (1971) *Cudzoziemcy o Polsce. Relacje i opinie 1*, Kraków: Wydawnictwo Literackie.
Gomulicki, W. (1880) *Ilustrowany przewodnik po Warszawie*, Warszawa.
Hercius, S. (1660) *Bankiet*, Kraków.

Kitowicz, J. (2003) *Opis obyczajów za panowania Augusta III*, Wrocław: Zakład Narodowy im. Ossolińskich.
Strutyński, J. (1878) *Poezye Berlicza Sasa (Juliusza Strutyńskiego) i wspomnienia jego wierszem*, Kraków.
Vautrin, H. (1807) *L'observateur en Pologne*, Paris: Chez Giguet et Michaud.
Worlidge, J. (1678) *Vinetum Britannicum: Or a Treatise of Cider and Other Wines and Drinks*, London.
Zawadzki, W. (ed) (1963) *Polska stanisławowska w oczach cudzoziemców 2*, Warszawa: PIW.

Secondary sources

Bogucka, M. (1983) "Le geste dans la vie religieuse, familiale, sociale, publique et politique de la noblesse polonaise aux XVIe XVIIe et XVIIIe siècles," *Revue d'histoire moderne et contemporaine* XXX, 3–16.
Bogucka, M. (1994) *Staropolskie obyczaje w XVI-XVII wieku*, Warszawa: PIW.
Boissonnade, P. and Charliat, P. (1930) *Colbert et la Compagnie de Commerce du Nord (1661–1689)*, Paris: Rivière.
Breen, T.H. (2004) *The Marketplace of Revolution: How Consumer Politics Shaped American Independence*, New York: Oxford University Press.
Brewer, J. (1997) *Pleasure of the Imagination: English Culture in the Eighteenth Century*, New York: Routledge.
Carter, F.W. (1987) "Cracow's Wine Trade (Fourteenth to Eighteenth Centuries)," *The Slavonic and East European Review* 65(4), 537–578.
Dias-Lewandowska, D. (2014) *Historia kulturowa wina francuskiego w Polsce od połowy XVII wieku do początku XIX wieku*, Warszawa: Muzeum Pałacu Króla Jana Sobieskiego w Wilanowie.
Dias-Lewandowska, D. (2017) "Czy alkohol jest używką? Wstęp do badań nad kulturą picia w Polsce w czasach nowożytnych," *Przegląd Historyczny* CVIII (2), 263–277.
Dias-Lewandowska, D., Fenton, L., Goodman, S. and Kümin, B. (forthcoming) "Altered States: Changing Conditions of Excess in European Drinking Cultures," in G. Hunt, T. Antin and V. Asmussen Frank (eds), *The Routledge Handbook of Intoxicants and Intoxication*, London: Routledge.
Elias, N. (1980) *Przemiany obyczajów w cywilizacji Zachodu*, Warszawa: PIW.
Flandrin, J-L. (1983) "Boissons et manières de boire en Europe du XVIe au XVIIIe siècle," in M. Milner and M. Chatelain (eds), *L'imaginaire du vin*, Marseille: Laffitte, 309–314.
Gillet, P. (1985) *Par mets et par vins. Voyages et gastronomie en Europe XVIe-XVIIIe siècles*, Paris: Payot.
Gołębiowski, Ł. (1830) *Domy i dwory*, Warszawa.
Grappe, V. (2006) "L'histoire longue d'ivresse," *Sociétés* 93, 77–92.
Greinerta, A., Kostecki, J. and Vystavna, Y. (2019) "The History of Viticultural Land Use as a Determinant of Contemporary Regional Development in Western Poland," *Land Use Policy* 85, 249–258.
Heath, D.B. (1990) "Cultural Factors in the Choice of Drugs," *Recent Developments in Alcoholism* 8, 245–254.
Jeżowa, K. (1938) "La culture de la vigne en Pologne," *Comptes rendus du Congrès International de Géographie* 4–6, 94–102.
Komaszyński, M. (1966) *Stosunki handlowe między Francją a Rzecząpospolitą za panowania Ludwika XIV*, Katowice: Wyższa Szkoła Ekonomiczna.
Kurczewski, G. (2018) "Teofil Fukier i jego winiarnia," in D. Dias-Lewandowska and G. Kurczewski (eds), *Wino i historia*, Warszawa: SHS, 122–159.
Kwapieniowa, M. (1959) "Początki uprawy winorośli w Polsce," *Materiały Archeologiczne* 1, 353–400.
Lecoutre, M. (2011) *Ivresse et ivrognerie dans la France moderne*, Tours: PUFR.
Lewandowska, D. (2012) "La fraude dans la construction du goût du vin français en Pologne XVIIe-XVIIIe siècles," in M. Figeac-Monthus and C. Lastécouères (eds), *Territoires de l'illicite: ports et îles. De la fraude au contrôle (XVIe–XXe s)*, Paris: Armand Colin, 377–388.
Małecki, A. (1894) *Studyum nad Bullą Innocentego II z roku 1136*, Poznań: Towarzystwo Przyjaciół Nauk Poznańskie.
Mennell, S. (1985) *All Manners of Food: Eating and Taste in England and France from the Middle Ages to the Present*, New York: Basil Blackwell.
Moskalewicz, J. and Zieliński, A. (1995) "Poland," in D.B. Heath (ed), *International Handbook on Alcohol and Culture*, Westport: Greenwood Press, 224–236.
Ory, P. (2004) *L'histoire culturelle*, Paris: Presses Universitaires de France.
Paczos, S. (2014) "Refleksje na temat narodu i państwa w polskiej myśli politycznej," *Historia Slavorum Occidentis* 2(7), 63–89.
Prunitsch, C. (2011) "Sarmacja, Sarmaci i sarmatyzm w encyklopedii Zachodu," in P. Czapliński (ed), *Nowoczesność i sarmatyzm*, Poznań: PSP, 79–90.
Sennefelt, K. (2014) "Wine, Corruption and the Politics of Intoxication in Eighteenth-Century Stockholm," *Past & Present* 222(9), 277–295.

Tazbir, J. (1978) *Kultura szlachecka w Polsce: rozkwit, upadek, relikty*, Warszawa: Wiedza Powszechna.
Tuwim, J. (1959) *Polski słownik pijacki i antologia bachiczna*, Warszawa: Czytelnik.
Van Bruaene, A-L. and S. van Bouchaute, S. (2017) "Rederijkers, Kannenkijkers: Drinking and Drunkenness in the Sixteenth and Seventeenth-Century Low Countries," *Early Modern Low Countries* 1, 1–29.
Welter, H. (1868) *Essai sur l'histoire du Café*, Paris: Reinwald.
Withington, P. (2011) "Intoxicants and Society in Early Modern England," *The Historical Journal* 54, 631–657.
Włodarczyk, W. (2018) *Wino narodowe. O winnicy rządowej w Ogrodzie Botanicznym*, Warszawa: Łazienki Królewskie.

19
THE SHAPE OF LUXURY
Three centuries of the champagne glass in British material culture

Graham Harding

Introduction

Describing a dinner given by the wit and dandy George Bulwer-Lytton in 1832, Benjamin Disraeli wrote to his sister that: '[W]e drank our champagne out of a saucer of ground glass mounted on a pedestal of cut glass' (Disraeli 1887: 42). This is the first unequivocal nineteenth-century reference to the saucer shape of champagne glass that became the fashion in the late 1840s or early 1850s. The *Illustrated London News* wrote in 1851 that the 'old-fashioned long and slender champagne glass [Figure 19.1] seems to be giving way rapidly before its new-fangled rival – the open, saucer-like affair perched upon the top of a thin, straight stem' (*Illustrated London News*, 21 June 1851: 597) (Figure 19.2). This form, usually known as a saucer but sometimes as a coupe, remained the dominant shape of the champagne glass until at least the 1920s.

This chapter explores the intimate link of glass and wine and the significance of this link for the material culture of wine before turning to the chronology of this change to the saucer shape. It reflects on why this shape remained fashionable for so long and considers what its adoption and continued use tell us about British society since the Victorian period.

The histories of wine and glass are, as James and Penelope Shackelford (2017: 1, 8, 39) have rightly noted, 'intricately intertwined' since the discovery of glass-blowing techniques in around 200 BCE and the subsequent wide availability of glass in the Roman Empire. Glass, a chemically inert substance, neither taints the wine nor hides its colour. Though most wine in the medieval period would have been drunk from ceramic vessels, glass continued to be used, as evidenced by Duccio di Buoninsegna's depiction of glasses of red wine on the table in his early fourteenth-century masterpiece, *The Last Supper* (part of the *Maestà* in Siena cathedral) (Young 1999: 239; Varriano 2010: 93–94). By the mid-fifteenth century, Venetian glassmakers had mastered the art of crystal-clear glass, and further advances were made by English glassmakers in the seventeenth century: in particular, George Ravenscroft's discovery that the addition of lead enhanced the sparkle of glass vessels (Jacoby 1993: 86–89; Bickerton 2000: 3–5).

The origin of the saucer form of champagne glass has been linked to the Venetian *tazza* (a shallow bowl on a tall stem), but it is unclear if there was a dedicated shape for sparkling wine in the seventeenth century when sparkling champagne first became popular at the court of Charles II. Albert Hartshorne, the great nineteenth-century collector and glass historian, suggested that a Venetian *tazza* was first used before giving way to taller flute-shaped ale glasses in the middle of the eighteenth century, but there is no definite evidence for this conclusion, and Grant Francis, writing in the

Figure 19.1 'Mr Punch' holding a flute glass
Source: *Punch*, 30 January 1858, 46

1920s, suggested that the taller shape was the norm by 1750 and remained 'fashionable throughout the remainder of the eighteenth century and well into the nineteenth' (Francis 1926: 72; Hartshorne 1897: 293–294). Writing more recently, Leonard Bickerton has claimed that there is no 'proof' that a shallow bowled glass was ever used for champagne in the eighteenth century. He does endorse the claim that the tall glass was dominant by mid-century, though he also pointed out the very considerable similarities between ale glasses and champagne glasses in that period (Bickerton 1984: 14; Bickerton 2000: 135). The earliest extant price list of Whitefriars Glass (1812) makes no mention of specific glass types – except for 'hock', the light white wine from Germany (Evans *et al.* 1995: 10).

Glass historians nonetheless concur that dedicated champagne glasses came into fashion around the mid-1840s (Morris 1978: 81). An 1841 Irish newspaper said of a Chinese vessel with a glass globe on an ivory stem that its shape was 'not unlike our modern champagne glass' (*Wexford Conservative*, 30 January 1841: 4). Writing in 1870, Charles Tovey, the Bristol wine merchant and wine writer, described an 1845 dinner party he had attended. 'The saucer-shaped champagne glasses which are now fashionable were then just coming into use', he wrote (Tovey 1870: 74–75). A Whitefriars Glass catalogue of the 1860s appears to shows only saucer glasses for champagne (Evans *et al.* 1995:

The shape of luxury

Figure 19.2 'Mr Punch' with a saucer glass
Source: *Punch*, 30 June 1866, iii

253–254). By 1880, a column on table decorations in the *Aberdeen Journal* was suggesting that the best use for the 'tall old-fashioned champagne glasses' to be found in second-hand shops was to fill them with 'pretty moss' and use them for table decorations (*Aberdeen Journal*, 20 November 1880:1).

An analysis by the author of *Punch* cartoons between 1850 and 1912 graphically depicts the decline of the flute and the triumph of the saucer. Twenty-eight cartoons show an identifiable bottle of champagne in clear association with a specific glass shape. Five tall 'flute' glasses are shown – but all but one of these date from before 1860. Of the remaining 23, 14 (50% of the total) are saucer shaped with another four bowl-shaped glasses. Lastly there are five tumblers: that is, straight-sided glasses with no stem. The predominance of the saucer shape in the second half of the century is also shown by the Silber and Fleming catalogue of glassware, which was targeted at the middle and upper classes. Silber and Fleming claimed to have the largest stock in the country of glassware, and their 1883 catalogue featured 16 different glass sets or 'services'. All bar one of these services had saucer-shaped glasses. The exception was a slightly deeper goblet shape (Bosomworth 1991: 131–137). The hegemony of the saucer shape lasted at least until the 1920s. Writing in 1926 on the history of English drinking glasses, Grant Francis testifies to the continued dominance of the saucer as the fashionable shape for champagne glasses (Francis 1926: 93–95).

Why did this new glass become so fashionable in the 1840s? The appeal of the saucer – according to the *Illustrated London News* in 1851 – was that:

> In highly-flavoured and effervescing wines no small part of the pleasure of consumption rises from the discharge of the perfumed gas with which the fluid is charged being inhaled and appreciated by the olfactory nerves while in the act of drinking; now, in the shallow, saucer-glasses the discharge takes place with great rapidity and power, in consequence of

the breadth of the surface of the liquid brought into contact with the air, a phenomenon which only occurred to a very limited extent in the long narrow tube-like glass.

(Illustrated London News, 26 June 1851: 597)

In the mid-1840s, champagne itself was becoming more available. There were occasional advertisements in *The Times* for champagne in the 1830s and early 1840s, but it is only from 1846 that the number of advertisements in the key selling month of April rose from two or three to twenty to twenty-five with the first appearance of prominent merchant names such as Hedges and Butler and T.W. Stapleton.

Sparkling wine from Champagne was not, of course, new. Sparkling champagne was introduced to the court of Charles II through the agency of the exiled French aristocrat the Marquis de St. Evremond in the 1660s. The first literary reference to 'sparkling' in the context of champagne dates from Sir George Etherege's 1676 comedy *The Man of Mode, or, Sir Fopling Flutter* when 'sparkling Champaigne . . . quickly recovers poor Languishing lovers' (Etherege 2011, act IV, scene 1: 68). Newspaper advertisements started to differentiate 'sparkling' from 'still' and the lightly effervescent 'creaming' champagne in the 1780s (*Saunders's Newsletter*, 5 February 1782: 1). In 1853, Charles Dickens's *Household Words* brought to a wider, middle-class audience the story that diplomats and solders acquired the taste for sparkling wine at the 1815 Paris peace negotiations. Described as the 'sweetest, most ample revenge the French ever took on us', wines 'foraged out of the cellars of Rheims . . . at about 75 centimes a bottle [were] sold to the English and the Cossacks at about six to ten francs' (Dickens 1853, 7(165): 270–273). What is not always appreciated, though, is that champagne was a wine made by English agency. The story of the champagne saucer is the story of a new glass for a new wine.

Arguably, champagne was both the first wine of the modern era and the last great wine of historic time. Burgundy, bordeaux, tokay, sauternes, Rhine wine, sherry and port were all well established by the early nineteenth century. The wine of Champagne that made its reputation in the British market was not the sparkling style but the still, dry wine of the Sillery region of Champagne, drunk with food by elite men, and the highest-priced wine on the English market from the 1820s onwards. For the wine of Champagne to be truly sparkling rather than gently creaming was an irresistible novelty for nineteenth-century drinkers. This 1845 quotation from William Thackeray (writing under the pseudonym of 'Fitz-Boodle' in *Fraser's Magazine*) indicates its appeal:

> [A]ll gourmands swear and vow that they prefer Sillery a thousand times to sparkling, but look round the table and behold! We all somehow drink it. All who say they like the Sillery will be found drinking the sparkling. Yes, beloved sparkler, you are an artificial, barley-sugared, brandied beverage. . . . You are universally drunken – you are the wine of the world.
>
> *(quoted in London Evening Standard, 22 November 1845: 2)*

This new wine was the result of technological changes in France. The belated adoption of the saccharometer in the 1840s enabled winemakers to measure how much residual sugar there was in the wine and thus control the second fermentation much more effectively. This was coupled with the introduction of newer, stronger bottles that could withstand the often-destructive pressure of the wine. Cellarmen still had to wear masks to protect their eyes, but now makers could deliver the high-pressure wines known as 'saute-bouchon' from their explosive effect on the cork (Figure 19.3).

Neither the new wine nor the new glass conformed to French taste. First, the French continued to prefer sweeter champagne drunk either on its own or with the dessert course. Young British men from privileged backgrounds led the drive to drier wine and so made drinking champagne through the meal possible. Second, the French continued to prefer the flute glass, and English consumers would have known this. Describing the French Exhibition at Earls Court in 1890, the *London Daily*

Figure 19.3 Masked cellarmen
Source: Vizetelly 1882: 163

News (14 August 1890: 6) highlighted the bar of the champagne exhibit where 'champagne may be tasted out of long narrow glasses, just as it is drunk daily by crowds of thirsty travellers at the railway station at Epernay'.

The new saucer shape directly affected the experience of drinking the wine. First, the flute shape accentuated the length of the 'bubble train' rising through the glass but gave larger bubbles on the surface of the liquid; the saucer shape produced both more bubble trains (since there was a larger surface area to produce them) and smaller, closely crowded bubbles on the surface of the liquid, though the larger surface area meant that the aroma (which was carried by the bubbles) dispersed far more quickly (Liger-Belair 2013: 150–154). The Bristol wine merchant and wine writer Charles Tovey (1870: 76) put the advantage of the new shape succinctly: 'pink Champagne ... looked singularly beautiful when poured into them and crowned with its snow-white foam'. The visual sensation was prioritised at the expense of the taste and the aroma, which quickly dissipated in a way which it did not in either the flute or the more modern tulip glass. Today, aroma and taste are central to the evaluation of wine; in the nineteenth century, the priority was on the look, a practice derived from the habit of assessing port in particular by its colour and other visual characteristics (Harding 2022). Second, the saucer glass demanded more physical control and dexterity. As the *Illustrated London News* neatly put it in 1851 (21 June 1851: 596): '[I]t was not so convenient to drink out of, for reasons that will be appreciated by every man who ever sipped his tea out of a saucer'.

Sparkling wine was portrayed more and more as the 'ladies' wine'. For Edmund Dixon, writing in *Household Words* in 1855, champagne was the 'confectionary of wine-making'. Its place, he thought, was at a ball where a 'cavalier' might offer it to his 'lady danceress' and where it 'takes its fitting rank and position amongst feathers, gauzes, lace, embroidery, ribbons, white satin shoes, and eau de Cologne' (Dixon 1855, 11(256): 57). Writing nearly 50 years later, the pioneer restaurant critic Nathaniel Newnham-Davis claimed it was the 'wine of the fair sex' and he opined that 'until we . . . give up taking ladies out to dinner, champagne will be practically the only wine drunk at restaurants' (Newnham-Davis 1899: xx). Champagne bottles were increasingly 'dressed' (to use the industry term) in feminine rather than masculine colours: gold and silver rather than red and black. The vocabulary used to describe the wine was stereotypically feminine – sparkling, elegant, delicate (Harding 2021).

Yet the evolution of the taste of champagne was driven by elite young men in the clubs of London's West End. Their preferences took champagne from around 20 to 30 grams of sugar per litre in 1850s to zero dosage by the mid-1870s. Making the wine dry meant it could become the preferred dinner wine of the elite and the aspiring of British society, even if several good critics suspected that very few men or women actually liked the very dry wine. Though, in 1867, the London agent for the French champagne house of Pommery and Greno, Adolphe Hubinet, had correctly forecast to his principals the coming British trend to very dry wines, by the 1890s, he was convinced that the professed British liking for dry wine was pretence intended to display sophistication. In 1894, he wrote to his principals in Reims of his surprise on his meeting with one of the 'rare' English consumers who truly liked dry wine (Flocquet nd [1950s], 30 January 1894). The consumer press agreed. The *Guernsey Star* described how when:

> the fashion [for dry wine] went to the extremes, [it was] pathetic but amusing also to watch the wry faces of ladies while they sipped wine which they would have confessed to be positively disagreeable if they had spoken out their minds.
>
> *(Guernsey Star, 21 October 1884: 4)*

The saucer shape of glass was particularly difficult for men with moustaches and beards, a trend that took off in the mid-1840s. Dwight Robinson's (1976: 1135–1137) analysis of *Illustrated London News* illustrations has shown that there was 'an unmistakable rise in bearded men by 1850, a trend that peaked around 1870 when about half of the men appeared with full beards'. It has been suggested that this trend of wearing beards might be attributed to a desire to express a masculine authority, a need that was all the more acute since many Victorian males were becoming increasingly sedentary and domestic. Joining the hugely popular Volunteer movement was one way of expressing masculinity and, from newspaper reports, drinking a great deal of champagne (Oldstone-Moore 2005: 11). It has also been suggested that many Victorian men exercised iron self-control as another means of reconciling the need for masculine virtue and authority with their increasingly feminised role (*Household Words*, 7(1777): 560–563).

The idea of control can be extended to control not only of the mind but also of the body. That it was difficult to drink cleanly with a luxuriant moustache was vividly demonstrated by the proliferation of moustache guards and moustache cups and spoons in the nineteenth century. But there are no pictures of equivalent 'moustache glasses'. To drink champagne from a saucer glass demanded control in the face of temptation, both alcoholic and romantic.

Champagne's special virtue at the dining table was that it was a drink that encouraged disinhibition. It was recognised by Victorians as quick to inebriate, and the comments of Henry Vizetelly (1882), probably the most widely read of Victorian writers on champagne, show clearly that its virtue lay in its ability to overcome the reserve of 'more Britannico'. Describing a dinner party of the late 1870s, he observed that it started with 'preliminary glowering . . . in the drawing room' followed by 'icy silence' as his conversation with the 'Gorgonesque' dowager and the 'young lady just out' elicits only monosyllables. But then, he noted, you hear 'the magic word "champagne" . . . and a change comes over the spirit of your vision'. The young lady shows an 'astounding aptness for repartee', and even the Gorgon thaws (Vizetelly 1882: 262).

Champagne gave girls just out of the schoolroom the confidence to shine and to demonstrate their worthiness as social as well as sexual partners. Yet for men and women, to go too far with their repartee, or even to drop food or wine on their clothes, was a faux pas. Hence, we have a disinhibiting drink taken from a glass designed to test physical control.

So why did men in particular not challenge the fashion? There were occasional suggestions of such challenges, but they came to nothing. In the late nineteenth century, champagne was briefly drunk from tumblers, and there is some evidence to suggest that this form was associated with outdoor pursuits: spectators at cricket matches, men in shooting parties, 'Mr. Punch' on the river (*Bristol Mercury*, 24 July 1880: 7; *Punch*, 10 September 1902: 172; *Punch*, 2 July 1913: 11). The saucer or coupe form endured – as the early twentieth-century cartoon in Figure 19.4 shows. I suggest this was because it enabled men to demonstrate their breeding and their physical virtuosity and thus distinguish themselves from their inferiors. Dry wine did much the same thing. In 1881, an 'enthusiast on dry side of fizzies' reported of his 'truly magnificent' Pommery Brut 1874 that he 'had four men to dine with me yesterday, and not one of them could drink it' (*Hampshire Telegraph*, 8 January 1881: 6).

By the end of the nineteenth century, however, the hegemony of the saucer shape was beginning to be challenged. The tumbler shape was, as we have seen, shown in advertisements from the 1880s and was referred to as the 'newest' shape in an 1880 newspaper article (*Nottingham Evening Post*, 9 October 1880: 4). Mrs. Humphry's *Manners for Men* (1897) informed her 'young friends' that 'either a long-stemmed, wine-cupped glass or a small tumbler' might properly be used for champagne (Humphry 1897: 82–83). A 1904 article in an Oxford paper suggested that the saucer shape was going out of fashion (*Oxfordshire Weekly News*, 10 March 1904: 6), but by 1926, journalists were

Figure 19.4 Saucer glass
Source: *Punch*, 17 May 1911: 374

again promoting the saucer shape in coloured or opalescent glass as the choice of 'Miss Twentieth Century' (*Aberdeen Press and Journal*, 23 August 1926: 3). Well into the 1950s, fashion remained with the saucer shape, a shape increasingly linked to femininity and hedonism. Pierre Balmain's 1953 fashion collection, called 'The Champagne Look' in British newspapers, echoed the silhouette of the saucer glass (a look copied by a Florentine designer in 1955) (*Londonderry Sentinel*, 15 August 1953: 6; *Daily Mirror*, 21 January 1955: 6). In the 1964 film *What a Way to Go*, the honeymoon bed for stars Robert Mitchum and Shirley MacLaine was a giant saucer-shaped glass with the bed on top (*Tatler*, 15 July 1964: 139).

By 1965, though, the coupe was beginning to lose its charm. In a libel case brought by Showerings, the makers of 'Babycham', the popular British sparkling perry of the post-war years, the defendant, the wine and food writer Raymond Postgate, claimed that the 'shallow glass' was regarded by the public as *the* champagne glass, though 'top people', according to a contemporaneous article in the *Daily Telegraph* (21 April 1965: 15) preferred the taller flute glass (*The Times*, 2 November 1965: 15). By 1977, the tide had turned. Pamela Vandyke-Price, writing in *The Times* (12 November 1977: 12), was emphatic: 'shallow saucers give a mean measure, flatten the wine quickly and cheat the drinker out of the delectable smell'. Echoing Vandyke-Price's condemnation, wine writers from thence forward were unanimous in their condemnation of the saucer and their advocacy of the straight-sided flute or more curvaceous tulip glass.

But the saucer shape failed to fade away. The mythical story linking the shape of the saucer glass to the bosom of Marie Antoinette first appeared in British newspapers in the 1970s and has been repeated regularly since then (*Daily Mirror*, 11 October 1976: 24; *Daily Telegraph*, 7 December 1986: 107). Explaining his use of 'frosted saucer-shaped Hollywood goblets' at the Atlantic Bar and Grill in London in the mid-1990s, restaurateur Oliver Peyton said simply that they were 'more glamorous' (*Daily Telegraph*, 31 December 1995: 96–97). Glasses modelled on the breasts of Claudia Schiffer in 2008 (by fashion designer Karl Lagerfeld) and Kate Moss in 2014 (sculptor Janet McAdam Freud) were widely publicised. The latter was a promotional exercise by Richard Caring, another restaurateur, but, arguably, both reinforced the linkage of the coupe form to hedonistic luxury and perhaps, too, with the 'romantic frisson' identified by an Irish journalist in 2001. Reporting on the return of the 'totally unsuitable' coupe form to the range of British household store Habitat, he and other contemporary commentators linked the return of the coupe form to the appeal of the retro styles of the hedonistic 1960s or the glamour of the 1920s and 1930s (*Sunday Life*, 23 September 2001: 31; *Sunday Tribune*, 4 July 2004: 76).

Today, the consensus of experts and connoisseurs is that the saucer form is an anachronism which 'simply does not work for champagne' (Burt 2015). The shallow bowl dissipates the effervescence and destroys the aroma, whilst the flute emphasises the 'fizz' at the expense of aroma. The 'tulip glass' with a broad mid-section and narrow aperture is the preferred shape since it allows both bubbles and aroma to develop to the full (Figure 19.5). Riedel, the Austrian glassware specialist, features more than a dozen different lines of champagne glasses, mostly tulip-shaped, and the eleventh generation head of the family firm has declared his ambition to make the flute shape 'obsolete' (Mercer 2013). Nevertheless, the company continues to sell flute glasses since 'there is a commercial demand' from hotels and restaurants, and, as recently as 2014, both Riedel and Dartington Crystal confirmed that the straight-sided flute remained their best-selling champagne glass (Burt 2015).

The relatively limited work to date on the effect of the glass shape on the perception of the wine suggests that whilst the glass shape has some effect on the intensity and appeal of the aroma, there is also a pronounced psychological effect. If consumers associate a specific shape with champagne, then that shape will cue a favourable perception of the wine's aroma (Burt 2015). Until the mid-twentieth century, the saucer glass on the table forcefully displayed the luxurious habit of the consumers; since then, the flute glass has taken over that role. As the grower-producer Cedric Bouchard has said, 'In a restaurant, other tables will notice right away that you are drinking Champagne if it's in a flute' (Goldfield 2014).

Figure 19.5 Riedel Veritas glass
Source: Riedel

The evolution of the glass shape over time, from ale glass to saucer, from saucer to flute and then to the tulip shape, therefore reflects changes in both society and wine appreciation. The Victorian saucer form emphasised the visual sensation of the bubbles, then an extraordinary novelty. Reflecting a society newly introduced to light (i.e. unfortified) wine, the colour and visual appearance of wine were of paramount importance to most Victorian consumers. Little attention was paid in the wine books of the time to aroma and taste (Harding 2022). The Victorian preference for the saucer shape perhaps also reflects the perception that champagne was a 'feminine' wine. References to the use of the tumbler for champagne focus more on male than female consumers and cease to occur after the late 1920s. (For a very late reference, see *Gloucester Citizen*, 25 August 1928: 3.) In the second half of the twentieth century, the flute shape was dominant – despite the marketing attention drummed up by and for Schiffer and Moss. The champagne glasses featured in the great majority of James Bond movies are flute shaped (though a saucer glass was used in the 1965 *Thunderball*). In the first Bond film, *Dr. No* in 1962, the wine is served in a straight-sided flute. After that, the flutes become steadily more curvaceous, culminating in the 2015 *Spectre*, in which Bollinger R.D. 2002 is drunk from a glass that closely mirrors the tulip-shaped 'tasting glass' created for the champagne house ('The new Bollinger glass', Champagne Bollinger 2015).

The continued popularity of the flute – regardless of its organoleptic shortcomings – derives from and speaks to the role of champagne (and other sparkling wines) as a symbol of popular celebration at weddings and public events; it has become a 'commercial' glass suited for use with younger and cheaper champagnes (Krebiehl 2016). The narrow profile allows many glasses to be held on a tray and ensures the wine retains its effervescence longer than other shapes, making it ideal for mass catering.

The saucer or coupe shape may have lost any appeal to those with connoisseurial aspirations, but it retains its power as a visual marker. The cover of the United Nations Development Programme report of 1992 (created long after the coupe shape had been dismissed by the experts) shows its enduring power (Figure 19.6). The shallow bowl of the glass represents the richest 20% in the world who own 80% of the wealth of the world; the poorest 20% at the bottom of the spindly stem have almost nothing. As statistical expert Julian Champkin (2014: 39–40) has observed, the data and the presentation may be problematic, but the image speaks immediately to conspicuous consumption, hedonism and irresponsible luxury (United Nations Development Program 1992). The glass remains – as it has ever been – a metonym for the drink and its social role.

Figure 19.6 Champagne glass effect

Source: United Nations Development Programme report of 1992

References

Bickerton, L.M. (1984) *English Drinking Glasses, 1675–1825*, Aylesbury: Shire Publications.
Bickerton, L.M. (2000) *Eighteenth Century English Drinking Glasses: An Illustrated Guide*, Woodbridge: Antique Collectors' Club.
Bosomworth, D. (1991) *The Victorian Catalogue of Household Goods: A Complete Compendium of Over Five Thousand Items to Furnish and Decorate the Victorian Home*, London: Studio Editions.
Burt, V. (2015) *Does Glassware Have an Impact on the Sensory Perception of Champagne?* London: Institute of Masters of Wine.
Champagne Bollinger. (2015) "The New Bollinger Glass," www.champagne-bollinger.com/en/INT/download/27, accessed 21 August 2020.
Champkin, J. (2014) "The Champagne Glass Effect," *Significance*, 11, https://ezproxy-prd.bodleian.ox.ac.uk:2095/10.1111/j.1740-9713.2014.00726.x, accessed 4 March 2020.
Dickens, C. (1853) "English Milords," *Household Words/Conducted by Charles Dickens* 7(165), 270–273.
Disraeli, B. (1887) *Lord Beaconsfield's Letters 1830–1852*, London: John Murray.
Dixon, E. (1855) "A Bottle of Champagne," *Household Words* 11(256), 51–57.
Etherege, G. (2011) *Man of Mode or, Sir Fopling Flutter*, Early English Books Online Text Creation Partnership, https://quod.lib.umich.edu/e/eebo/a38694.0001.001/77:6.3?vid=106920, accessed 3 March 2020.
Evans, W., Ross, C. and Werner, A. (1995) *Whitefriars Glass: James Powell & Sons of London*, London: Museum of London.
Flocquet, A. (n.d. [1950s]) *Compilation de la Correspondance de Hubinet*, Reims: Archive Pommery.
Francis, G.R. (1926) *Old English Drinking Glasses: Their Chronology and Sequence*, London: H. Jenkins.
Goldfield, H. (2014) "The Tragic Flute: Why You're Drinking Champagne All Wrong," www.bloomberg.com/news/2014-12-15/the-tragic-flute-why-you-re-drinking-champagne-all-wrong.html, accessed 24 August 2020.
Harding, G. (2022) "'The Stock of a Connoisseur?': The Development and Commercialisation of Wine Connoisseurship in the Long Nineteenth Century," in C. Anderson and P. Stewart (eds), *Connoisseurship*, Oxford: Oxford University Press.
Harding, G. (Forthcoming) "My Lady Champagne: Sexuality and Subjugation in Victorian Britain," in E-J. Abbots (ed), *Routledge Companion to Gender and Food*, London: Routledge.
Hartshorne, A. (1897) *Old English Glasses: An Account of Glass Drinking Vessels in England, From Early Times to the End of the Eighteenth Century*, London and New York: Edward Arnold.
Humphry, C.E. (1897) *Manners for Men*, London: James Bowden.
Jacoby, D. (1993) "Raw Materials for the Glass Industries of Venice and the Terraferma, About 1370–About 1460," *Journal of Glass Studies* 35, 65–90.
Krebiehl, A. (2016) "Farewell to Champagne flutes?" *Decanter*, www.decanter.com/learn/farewell-to-champagne-flutes-in-2016-286743/, accessed 11 October 2020.
Liger-Belair, G. (2013) *Uncorked: The Science of Champagne*, Princeton, NJ: Princeton University Press.
Mercer, C. (2013) "My Goal Is to Make Champagne Flutes Obsolete, Says Maximilian Riedel," *Decanter*, www.decanter.com/wine-new/opinion/the-editors-blog/champagne-flutes-will-be-obsolete-says-maximilian-riedel-30992/, accessed 8 August 2020.
Morris, B.J. (1978) *Victorian Table Glass & Ornaments*, London: Barrie & Jenkins.
Newnham-Davis, N. (1899) *Dinners and Diners: Where and How to Dine in London*, London: Grant Richards.
Oldstone-Moore, C. (2005) "The Beard Movement in Victorian Britain," *Victorian Studies* 48(1), 7–34.
Robinson, D.E. (1976) "Fashions in Shaving and Trimming of the Beard: The Men of the *Illustrated London News*, 1842–1972," *American Journal of Sociology* 81(5), 1133–1141.
Shackelford, J.F. and Shackelford, P.L. (2017) *The Glass of Wine*, Hoboken, NJ: John Wiley & Sons.
Tovey, C. (1870) *Champagne: Its History, Properties, and Manufacture*, London: J. C. Hotten.
United Nations Development Program. (1992) *Human Development Report 1992*, New York: Oxford University Press.
Varriano, J. (2010) *Wine: A Cultural History*, London: Reaktion Books.
Vizetelly, H. (1882) *Facts about Champagne and Other Sparkling Wines: Collected During Numerous Visits to the Champagne and Other Vinicultural Districts of France, and the Principal Wine-Producing Countries of Europe*, London: Vizetelly & Co.
Young, C.C. (1999) "Depictions of the Last Supper," in H. Walker (ed), *Food in the Arts: Proceedings of the Oxford Symposium on Food and Cookery, 1998*, Totnes: Prospect.

20
'FOR US AS EXPERIMENTALISTS'
An Australian case study of scientific values in nineteenth-century New World winegrowing

Julie McIntyre

Introduction

In 1858, Walter Scott, the president of the Hunter River Vineyard Association (HRVA) presented his address to the annual meeting of this association in Maitland, a township in the Hunter Valley, north of Sydney in the British colony of New South Wales. Scott's speech drew from a recent publication by British parliamentarian Emerson Tennent titled *Wine, Its Use and Taxation: An Inquiry into the Operation of the Wine Duties on Consumption and Revenue* (1855). This treatise by Tennent, a free trade advocate, argued for the importation of wines from France that were lower in alcohol than those of Portugal. For winegrowers in the Hunter region, Tennent's argument held a different meaning than it did for Westminster parliamentarians debating customs duties: namely, the export potential for Hunter wines. Scott (from an English family, formerly of India) sought to encourage persistence in the region to open a British market for Hunter wines. His encouragement occurred despite the problem that almost 30 years after settler colonials first planted *Vitis vinifera* in the region, Hunter wine volumes were barely sufficient to supply a small consumer base in Sydney.

Some demand for Hunter wine in the British market had been achieved in 1855 when wines produced by founding HRVA chairman James King, a Scottish immigrant, received recognition as novel and promising at that year's Paris International Exhibition. The resulting spike in export could not be sustained, however, due to a lack of wines to sell (McIntyre 2012). In 1857, Henry Carmichael, also a Scottish immigrant and one deeply committed to Enlightenment values of colonial progress and improvement, voiced concern about the complexity of the challenge: 'For us as experimentalists' to create marketable colonial wine (9 May 1857). Hopes for instigating a colonial wine industry in a wholly new place, which had seemed possible a generation earlier, remained out of reach. Scott's speech reflected his determination on behalf of the HVRA, including Carmichael, to continue to turn land in the Hunter region to winegrowing, rather than other purposes, despite failing to capitalise on British demand after the Paris Exhibition. What is of interest to me in this chapter is the role of a culture of faith in science that infused and buoyed aspirants seeking to create profitable Hunter Valley wine enterprises from 1847 to 1858.

Grape science, or viticulture, which historically included winemaking, is a subset of horticultural science. In the nineteenth century, this meant knowledge of a combination of natural laws explaining soil types and management of vines to control yields; other facets of plant biology, such as grapevine requirements for sunlight and water; and the propensity of specific cultivars to ripen, as governed by climatic conditions. Science-mindedness in nineteenth-century New World winegrower organisations is a neglected area of research in studies of wine and culture.

In the cultural history of wine, where 'culture' is taken to be textual and visual portrayals of consumption practices in 'Western civilisation' up to Europe's Middle Ages, the definition of 'science' is limited to medical understanding of the effect on the human body of drinking wine (Varriano 2010). Where 'culture' is defined as tradition or artistry, science may be thought of as separate from, or even in opposition to, culture. Yet scientific research and instruction are human endeavours requiring practices of reasoning through problems, encounters between practitioners and knowledge exchanged in modes of communication from interpersonal to international. Science in its development and application is a form of human culture. Referring to Martin Wiener's exploration of shifts in the English 'industrial spirit' from 1850 to 1980, cultural historian Peter Burke observed that 'A concern with culture . . . offers us a new vision of the whole historical process as driven by values rather than material conditions' (Wiener 1981; Burke 2012: 5). This chapter is concerned with the values of industry science-mindedness as spurs of material change.

The Hunter Valley is a region on the eastern seaboard of New South Wales. This colony was established in 1788 with the arrival in the land of the Dharug first peoples of 11 ships from southern England carrying some 1,400 men, women and children. About half of these voyagers were convicted felons selected from those sentenced in London to transportation from British shores to serve a period of exile in a British colony. The other half of the population of the colonising flotilla were members of the military garrison for New South Wales and their families. During the 1787–88 voyage from England, colonial officials collected many commercial plants at supply ports, including winegrape vines from the Cape of Good Hope. Wine was first made from this imported plant stock as early as 1792. Subsequent attempts to create a wine industry as a small part of the early British colonial project are documented in *First Vintage: Wine in Colonial New South Wales* (McIntyre 2012) and not revisited here. *First Vintage* argues that although winegrowing constituted a very modest proportion of the nineteenth-century economy, its potential to 'civilise' land and the labouring classes maintained official and settler interest in its value (see also McIntyre 2011; Dunstan and McIntyre 2014).

Winegrape stocks from the Sydney Botanic Gardens were planted as early as 1828 in the Hunter Valley (McIntyre and Germov 2018), mainly in the country of the Wonnarua and Worimi first peoples. *V. vinifera* is not native to Australia, and imported cultivars available at this time originated in Spain, mainland Portugal, the Portuguese island of Madeira, Germany and France as well as the Cape of Good Hope. Such diversity in the source of plant stock being acclimatised in the colonies was a hallmark of early Australian winegrowing experiments (McIntyre 2012). Wine was first made in the Hunter Valley in 1832 from grapes harvested and crushed by male convicts at a property operated by the Australian Agricultural Company. This is documented in *Hunter Wine: A History* (McIn-tyre and Germov 2018), which traces evidence for the claim that the Hunter Valley is Australia's oldest continuing wine region (see also McIntyre and Germov 2021).

The HRVA arose in 1847 from differences within the Hunter Valley's community of moderately wealthy settlers. Men such as King and Carmichael and their peers preferred winegrowing over other possible land uses, leading them to break away from the region's agricultural society (HRVA 1854). The HRVA is one of the earliest New World winegrowing organisations in the Anglosphere, preceded in Australia only by a short-lived organisation in the Swan River colony of Western Australia and starting a few years before such associations in the United States (McIntyre 2012).

Members of the HRVA organised themselves to scale up knowledge and opportunities open to individuals through the shared efforts of the group. Moreover, the HRVA co-existed with the emergence of a growing storehouse of scientific knowledge shared across imperial, colonial and national borders. Formed before the shifting of science from broad philosophies on the laws of nature into professional specialisations, records of the HRVA show that this organisation did not seek merely to acquire knowledge from Europe. Some members considered themselves capable of contributing to scientific understanding of winegrowing.

Accessing science-mindedness: methods, sources, context

Cultural history arose in the 1990s to refocus interpretations of the past. Flowing from social historians' statistical and textual analyses of large groups of working-class people who had been written out of history, cultural historians focus on human habits and rituals, person-to-person encounters and relationships. Cultural history may tell us something generalisable about inequalities of power based on race and/or gender, as well as class. Cultural history 'finds room for everyone's ideas', rather than privileging the thinking or action of elite political or intellectual figures and events, structures or institutions. It does so by adopting 'a viewpoint' of individual historical agents and the 'symbolic element' or meaning in their activities (quoted words and phrases from Burke 2012, 7–8). Instead of seeing culture as homogenous, cultural historians are concerned with 'the reception of ideas such as liberty and democracy in different cultures [and] their "cultural translation" or adaptation to local circumstances' (Burke 2012: 8). Hunter winegrowing involved the reception of traditional forms of grape growing and winemaking know-how from European regions and wine business from Britain and the adaptation of these practices in a new place. Tracing scientific-mindedness in the Hunter winegrowing community is a contribution to understanding how the diverse and complex New World of wine emerged through the development and diffusion of knowledge.

The mission of cultural historians to recover the lives of forgotten peoples and portray more culturally diverse representations of the past is also relevant for this chapter because it concerns the emergence of a settler colonial industry. In the 1950s, when Algerians colonised by France battled to expel their colonisers, French philosopher Roland Barthes wrote that 'Wine cannot be an entirely happy substance unless we wrongfully forget that it is also the product of an expropriation' (Barthes 2012: 82). As anthropologists Rachel Black and Robert Ulin observe, pleasurable rhetoric about wine, such as the contemporary emphasis on terroir (a term not used in relation to wine in colonial Australia as it is today) can be a dehumanising diversion. Such rhetoric 'takes us away from the unromantic images of concrete human subjects as they toil in the vineyards, experience harsh living conditions, and even face gender and class exploitation that are quite contrary to how we wish to imagine wine' (2013: 7; see also Grimstad et al. 2019).

Australian cultural historians following British scholar E.P. Thompson's 'history from below' from the 1990s set about recovering the "invisible" stories and agency of Aboriginal people, women, convicts, and multicultural Australians (Curthoys 2015: 26). As male British settler capitalists, members of the HRVA were not forgotten peoples. It is a matter within the ambit of Australian cultural history, however, that the aspirations of Hunter Valley landowners to develop a wine industry was premised on possessing and transforming landscapes that had for thousands of years been managed differently by first peoples. As I have written elsewhere in response to a growing body of scholarship on Aboriginal land management before and since colonisation, 'All Australian plantings of *V. vinifera* are made on land once occupied and cherished by Aboriginal locals' (McIntyre and Germov 2018: 26; see also McIntyre et al. 2019a).

In paying attention to the ethics of inclusion in cultural history, an account is required of the HRVA's British membership when non-British Europeans were also involved in Hunter winegrowing. Membership of the HRVA at no time in its life span from 1847 to 1876 exceeded two dozen men, all of whom were British immigrants or the offspring of British immigrants. Although the HRVA fostered the immigration of labourers from southwestern regions of pre-unification Germany from 1849 to perform labour indentures, it does not appear to have admitted German men who became landowning winegrowers (McIntyre and Germov 2018: 136–157).

Some account is due, too, of the lack of women in the HRVA. Truthfully, only one woman might have qualified to join the association. Maria Windeyer, the niece-in-law of a key member of the HRVA, won awards for wine produced at her property, Tomago, in the 1850s (McIntyre and Germov 2018: esp. 113–114). It is not clear whether Windeyer was not invited to join the HRVA or was invited and refused. The lack of an invitation seems more likely. Her employment of a German winemaker was not a reason to exclude her as HRVA members did not always make the wine associated with their properties and often employed Germans. In considering Windeyer's exclusion from the HRVA, it is worth noting the comparative story of Mary Penfold in the British Australian colony of South Australia in the latter part of the nineteenth century. There is evidence that Penfold, not her husband, instigated the famous Australian wine brand Penfold's. This is overlooked in today's marketing of Penfold's wine. Like Windeyer in the Hunter, Penfold did not belong to the peak viticultural organisation operating in her colony during the years in which she grew grapes and made wine (McIntyre 2019).

There is no original document archive of the HRVA available to historians. Nevertheless, sympathetic reporting of the association's meetings and addresses in the *Maitland Mercury* left an engaging, even endearing, record of the concerns, debates, concordances, initiatives, hurdles and persistence of the HRVA. This record of approximately 1,000 'column inches' of newspaper reportage from 1847 to 1876 is selectively cited in a chapter in *Hunter Wine: A History* (McIntyre and Germov 2018: 102–135) and newly interpreted here. From 1847 through to 1865, the *Maitland Mercury*'s HRVA reports were written by John O'Kelly, an Irish immigrant who appears to have been a general roundsman for the *Mercury* without prior expertise in wine. The international reputation of the Hunter as a wine region in the nineteenth century grew from extensive republication of press reports such as O'Kelly's throughout the Australian colonies and in London more than from Hunter wine itself.

After O'Kelly's death in 1865 (much lamented by HRVA and the wider Hunter community), other unnamed reporters reported on the HRVA in the *Mercury*. Once a domestic wine market developed in the 1860s, the relatively light white and red wines of the Hunter sold well in the populous cosmopolitan cities of Sydney and Melbourne (McIntyre and Germov 2018). The other key primary source for this chapter is the *Historical Summary of the Proceedings and Reports of the Hunter River Vineyard Association: From Its Origination to Its First Annual Meeting in the Year 1853*, printed in Sydney for the Association (HRVA 1854).

The sole book-length history of a viticultural organisation in Australia, *A Vision for Wine: A History of the Viticultural Society of Victoria* by David Dunstan (2013), does not mention the HRVA. Victoria was a British colony of Australia that became independent from New South Wales in 1851. By the 1860s, Victoria's wine industry, along with that of South Australia, exceeded New South Wales in production output even though these other colonies started winegrowing later. The Viticultural Society of Victoria (VSV) met first in 1905 in the Vinegrowers Club in Victoria's capital of Melbourne, considered at the turn of the twentieth century to be one of the great cities of the world. The VSV allowed industry figures to gather to appreciate fine food and wine. Dunstan's history of the VSV focuses on wine business (2013: esp. 85), reflecting the society membership's predominant expertise. *A Vision for Wine* contains no reference to professional grape or wine scientists such as viticultural experts employed by the state to work with the wine industry.

A brief history of the professionalisation of viticultural and oenological science

In Australia, the principles of scientific inquiry received some formal discussion and dissemination with the inauguration in 1821 in Sydney, the capital of New South Wales, of the Philosophical Society of Australasia, an organisation of brief existence. There is every reason to assume that some members of the HRVA, if not already versed in the scientific method of hypothesising, experimenting, observing and recording the laws of nature, became so as part of the small circle of educated colonial elites. Before the formalisation of research and instruction in professional positions funded by Australian government bodies, science travelled through the diffusion of books and newspapers, membership of learned societies, agricultural societies and other forms of word of mouth. (For a comprehensive study, see Pierre 2020.) Formal French higher education in agriculture, including viticulture, dates from the 1840s. French works on grape biology and wine chemistry from the late eighteenth to mid-nineteenth century by Jean-Antoine Chaptal, Jules Guyot and Louis Pasteur were deeply influential in New World wine countries such as Australia as well as in France (Pierre 2020).

By 1847, the Hunter's winegrowers benefited from some publications on winegrowing elsewhere in the colony of New South Wales (McIntyre 2012). None existed for Hunter conditions, however. Nor did colonial publications yet contain scientific rigour on what are now understood as theories of plant biology; the chemistry of soil fertility, yeasts and wine fermentation; and organic decay and wine storage and transportation. The professionalisation of the natural sciences in Australia received a fillip when, in 1852, Australia's first institution of higher learning, the University of Sydney, employed Scotsman John Smith as foundation professor of chemistry and experimental physics. Smith enjoyed a close relationship with members of the HRVA as an enthusiastic consumer of their wines, especially Kaludah Ruby (property and style of wine) produced by James Blake (McIntyre and Germov 2013). There are inferences in the HRVA records that Smith encouraged students to visit the Hunter wine region and conduct experiments relevant to winegrowing.

It is notable that, in 1859, the HRVA received a request from winegrowers in South Australia for advice on Association regulations and other processes, in order to form a 'kindred association' (*Maitland Mercury*, 7 May 1859). As explored by Pierre, the first appointment of a viticultural expert in Australia, a Frenchman, was by the colonial government of South Australia in the 1870s. By this time, South Australian producers dominated the colonial wine industry in output volume, yet Australian production remained comparatively modest in global terms. As a point of reference, French readers of the *Revue Viticole* were informed in 1863 of progress in colonial Australia, during a decade in which Australian wine output of 50,000 hectolitres a year was dwarfed by French production amounting to 50 million hectolitres (Pierre 2020).

American research and instruction in the applied grape and wine sciences began at the University of California, Berkeley, in 1880. This department later relocated to the University of California, Davis, where it continues today (https://wineserver.ucdavis.edu/about/history). Formal instruction in growing grapes and making wine in Australia began in South Australia in the 1880s at Roseworthy Agricultural College, attached to the University of Adelaide (Pierre 2020). A history of grape and wine scientists and educators in Australia, and the transnational nature of their endeavours, is yet to be written. It can be said, however, that no more than three or four men at any one time were employed as viticultural experts across the Australian colonies (later states) from the 1890s to the 1960s.

Carmichael of the HRVA stated in 1852, in his delightfully florid manner of speaking, that Hunter Valley winegrowers might expect 'all blessings consequent' from 'the application of science' (Carmichael, quoted in *Maitland Mercury*, 12 May 1852). Science symbolised hope for Carmichael and his peers before the disappointment of the failed export drive of 1855. Tracing evidence of scientific thinking and practice in ideas circulating between members of the HRVA and beyond begins to address the absence of historical attention to scientific attitudes in histories of New World wine industries.

'For us as experimentalists'

At the inaugural meeting of the HRVA in 1847, members recorded its purpose as 'promoting the culture of the vine, and turning its products to the most profitable account' (HRVA 1854: 3). In seeking to promote winegrowing, HRVA membership was to assemble 'every reputable and intelligent vine-grower in the district' (HRVA 1854: 7). 'Intelligence' meant that which settlers perceived to be a rational and educated or scientific approach to land use, rather than one based on intuition and tradition.

Articles of the HRVA regulations that reinforced the role of various forms of experimentation in Hunter landowners' culture of the vine and its products are as follows:

- VII. It shall be the imperative duty of every ordinary member, at least once every year, to communicate, in writing, to the Secretary some specific information or suggestions, such as to him seem likely to forward the objects of the Association; all such written communications, having the signature of the respective members attached, to be read at the next Annual General Meeting, and to be filed among the transactions of the Association (HRVA 1854: 3).
- VIII. Previous to the Annual General Meeting in each year, each Member shall furnish for the use of the Association, at least four bottles of wine [later two], the produce of his vineyard; besides, at his option and convenience, any additional wine, and such other products of his vineyard or orchard as he may deem as deserving the Society's notice; the wines to be properly labelled, and packed in a box fitted with locks and hinges, and the key to be lodged with the Secretary. Moreover, the wines thus furnished shall be accompanied by a statement specifying the soil, aspect, mode of culture and management of the vineyard, the age of the vines producing them, the sort or sorts of grapes, the manipulation and appliances used in the manufacture, the age of the wines furnished, and the quantities made, disposed of, and on hand, and the circumstances under which any product furnished may have been perfected (HRVA 1854: 4).
- IX. 7. [lastly in the order of business] The wines and other products furnished shall be examined (HRVA 1854: 4).

To draw out another pointed reference to a scientific way of thinking, it may have been King or Carmichael who, in 1848, pronounced that:

> One of the established laws of nature is – that chemical changes are accelerated with a rapidity proportioned to the temperature of the mass subject to such a change; consequently wine in warm climate will naturally arrive at maturity sooner than a cold one and 'cool cellars' preserve wine through protection from heat, rather than from frost as in Europe.
>
> *(HRVA 1854: 8)*

Hypotheses circulated within the HRVA that, as wine must conform to universal laws on the speed of decomposition of organic matter in large mass in a warm climate, it would be more desirable to bottle wine for aging than to leave it in large wooden casks.

Carmichael perceived pests and weather (such as the timing of rainfall) as 'local problems', in contrast to universal laws which could surely be determined for the pruning of dormant grapevines in the winter months (June to August in Australia) through 'sheer empiricism' (*Maitland Mercury*, 5 May 1849). Carmichael's full report to the HRVA is published in the *Historical Summary* and states:

> That there is a perfect mode of pruning the vine, cannot be doubted, depending on the physiological conditions of the plant, taken in connection with the ascertained atmospherical and terrestrial elements concerned in its growth, and it may, perhaps, be reserved for the scientific vigneron of Australia to solve this problem aright, for the guidance in future of all vineyard labourers throughout the world.
>
> *(HRVA 1854: 10)*

Carmichael subsequently referenced the practice of pruning espoused by an English grower of table grapes, a linkage unlikely to be made today by viticulturalists in Hunter, where premium winegrape pruning is a specialist field.

There are further, equally intriguing threads of HRVA scientific thinking to unpack from the historical record, many of which are in line with twenty-first-century practices. HRVA records indicate that the membership's enthusiasm for thinking with scientific concepts echoed the broader optimism of colonial officials and settlers as to the development potential of New South Wales.

Wine tasting played a crucial role in allowing HRVA members to perceive the advance of winegrowing processes. That is, advances in the stages of development along the wine value chain from vineyard to winery and cellar to consumer, as well as changes over time in the quality of wine produced. At first, HRVA members' understanding of wine was based on their experience as consumers before they immigrated to New South Wales and appreciating imported wines once they arrived in New South Wales. In the absence of formalised scientific processes, tasting wines offered an encompassing empirical basis for experimentation.

The origin of competitive HRVA tasting procedures – the examination referred to in Article IX, clause 7 of the regulations – lay in colonial wine judging at agricultural shows. Judging of wines along with other agricultural products began in New South Wales, and therefore Australia, during the 1820s, once British colonial administrators removed restrictions on colonial immigration by free settler capitalists. The arrival of these settlers saw the flourishing of societies in the Sydney district, such as one for agriculture (McIntyre 2012) based on British models of rural show judging.

Comments on Carmichael's Shepherd's Riesling (Semillon), blended from grapes harvested in 1850 and 1851, demonstrated varied levels of expertise on the technical aspects of manufacture and the lack of a lexical precision for tasting.

> It was of a pale colour, and clear, with a fine but rather sweet taste. It was spoken of as the best yet tasted, a fine wine, by far the best, 'there is a bouquet in it', 'there is a strong taste of honey in it'. . . . '[I]t was a ladies' wine', 'it was a jumble of sweetness and bitterness' . . . 'slightly aluminous – the grape was from a heavy soil'. . . . '[I]t was pronounced to be a good, marketable wine'.
>
> *(12 May 1856)*

At the same meeting, association chairman Archibald Windeyer exemplified the spirit of non-competition and collective benefit of the HRVA in insisting, humbly, on 'my small experience not ranging over more than almost fifteen years in a science that has occupied many of the master minds of the civilised world' (12 May 1856). Yet a chorus of fellow winegrowers judged his 'Pineau Noir' to be

> 'largely a good wine', 'I do not think there were any stalks in the wine', 'if there had been they would have improved it, and it would have lasted longer', 'it was sound not altogether palatable'. . . . 'it would sell all over the world' . . . 'wanted tannin for keeping'.
>
> *(12 May 1856)*

This 1853 red, Windeyer explained after the tasting, was fermented with one-third of grape stalks from the total mass of fruit. It had won a gold medal at a Sydney exhibition of agricultural and industrial products.

It was due to correspondence between King and the leading agricultural chemist of the era, Justus Liebig, in Giessen (near Frankfurt in present-day Germany) that members began to grasp a variety of new ideas (HRVA 1854). For example, Liebig returned to King details of measures of the gravity of King's and other colonial wines compared with European wines. As Liebig reported to King:

> The wine [of William Macarthur, a grower near Sydney], Pineau Noir, Tinta, and Pineau Gris, indicates a specific gravity -9920; produces, in 100 volumes, 16.20 of alcohol; the same volumes, .505 free acid, 3.265 dry residue, and .498 of incombustible ashy constituents. The other (white) sort, Irrawang [King's wine], has a specific gravity .940; contains, in 100 volumes, 13. Volumes of alcohol; .660 free acid; 100 volumes yield, by evaporation, 3.313 dry residue, which consists principally of saccharine matter and .563 ashy constituents.
>
> (HRVA 1854: 39–40)

It is evident in later *Mercury* reports that this intelligence from Liebig prompted a shift in the minds of some in the HRVA from describing degree comparisons of wine weight from light-, medium- or heavy-bodied to a more numerical and empirical approach. Liebig compared the New South Wales wines unfavourably but encouragingly with Burgundian pinot noir, Hungarian tokaji and others. He recommended potential international markets for the colonial wines (HRVA 1854: 40). It appears to have mattered little to Liebig that he fostered New World competition with Old World wines in his curiosity about New World wine and what it meant for his scientific understanding. Further study of science-mindedness in other wine regions, and of the historical figures developing grape and wine sciences, may indicate other transnational alliances intersecting with and diverging from wine business interests.

Liebig and King became friends, and their connections with Blake and Frederic Muspratt, a settler with expertise on chemical reactions of wine in storage, are explored by an Australian historian of science and Liebig's biographer (Rae and Brock 2013). Blake later 'proposed that on this point also the members should each experimentalise, and note the results' (9 May 1857), a remark that conjures visions of Blake in conversation with Professor Smith over how to solve problems empirically.

What reinforces the impression that science symbolised hope for the HRVA is members' transparency in their stumbles, disagreements and failures. Irrespective of the profit motive underlying their shared experimentation, their publicising of failure shows they were prepared to allow for the reproducibility of their experiment, which was based on the hypothesis that marketable wine could be made from grapes grown in the Hunter Valley. This is in contrast with the careful management in today's press and other media of narratives about wine firms and regions as brands in wine business marketing.

Returning to the opening vignette of this chapter, Scott stated that 'It must be obvious to all of us that the culture of the vine in this district had not progressed to the extent that we had at one time reason to expect' (*Northern Times*, 8 May 1858). It was at this point that Scott read aloud from Tennent's views on whether Britain could expect to increase its wine imports, in which Tennent infers that there was a limit to the places in the world where grapes could be grown for fine wine. Tennent had stated, 'The finest known wines are the produce of soils the combination and proportions of whose ingredients are extremely rare and exceptional' (Tennent 1855: 81). And Scott continued with Tennent's assertion:

> Art and horticultural science have been applied to extend the limits thus circumscribed by nature; but with such unsatisfactory results that, as a general rule, it may be stated that the higher class wine of any known district has not been successfully reproduced beyond it.
>
> (Tennent 1855: 81)

Scott did not, however, interpret Tennent's description of the eminent suitability of established European territories for fine wine as ruling out hopes for fine wine production in the Hunter or, indeed, any style of wine that might turn a profit. The HRVA president concluded his reading from *Wine, Its Use and Taxation* by seeking to reinvigorate Hunter Valley experimentation. He argued for trialling grape varieties in Hunter soils with lower nutrient richness than the fertile alluvial ground where vines had mostly been planted. According to Scott, 'with a demand for wine exceeding supply, our splendid climate, and great variety of soils, we have every reason, if we continue in the course we have so well begun, to expect to rival some of the famous wines' of Europe (*Northern Times*, 8 May 1858).

By 1860, HRVA members, by now including the famous Henry Lindeman, a medico, were engaged in spirited disagreement about the best principles of aging colonial wine. Comparative experiments were proposed to resolve the issue (*Maitland Mercury*, 3 May 1860). Notably Lindeman did not believe in the possibility of a scientific solution to the problems resulting from unfavourable rainy weather conditions at harvest in the portion of the Hunter where his vineyard lay. This set him at odds with the boosterish faith of King and Carmichael that science could comprehensively explain nature so that it might be harnessed by humankind (*Maitland Mercury*, 7 May 1864). Lindeman proved to be more astute than King and Carmichael at recognizing suitable land for cultivating winegrapes and the limits of scientific intervention.

The HVRA demonstrated enthusiasm for experimentation with new forms of technology as well as science. Immigrating in 1856, geologist William Keene, who had previously owned a vineyard in the French Pyrenees, conducted experiments to find the most suitable saccharometer. In 1864, he introduced a type of this instrument to the HRVA that, by 1866, had become the most important addition yet to the toolkit of colonial New South Wales winemakers (*Maitland Mercury*, 12 May 1866). In 1869, the HRVA began to lose momentum although the wine region was economically viable and the Association appears to have met finally in 1876 (McIntyre and Germov 2018: 132).

It has been argued that the natural and physical sciences in Australia moved from 'the parochial and primitive phase to the professional and national stage' with the foundation in 1887 of the Australasian Association for the Advancement of Science (Hoare 1966). From the late nineteenth century onwards, New South Wales sought to develop viticultural knowledge and expertise. As well as the employment, at the turn of the twentieth century, of a French-trained viticultural expert from Italy, the Department of Mines and Agriculture published the *Agricultural Gazette of New South Wales*, to which this expert contributed, from 1891. The *Gazette's* inaugural edition of 1891 stated that a formal channel was required to foster knowledge exchange from Australia to Europe, as well as that which already occurred from Europe to Australia. This exchange particularly concerned the impact on winegrapes of the vine-feeding insect *phylloxera*, first detected in Australia in Victoria in 1877, and methods of removing and deterring *phylloxera* (McIntyre 2012, see also Pierre 2020). The Hunter, which was and remains free of *phylloxera*, briefly hosted an experimental vineyard for developing *phylloxera*-resistant American *Vitis* rootstocks on which to graft *phylloxera*-sensitive *V. vinifera* (McIntyre and Germov 2018).

Conclusion

Settler colonialism in the British colonies of Australia included plans for exploiting natural resources to develop export as well as domestic markets for luxury goods such as wine (Dunstan and McIntyre 2014). While there has been considerable research into economic perspectives on the nineteenth-century globalisation of wine (Simpson 2011; Anderson and Pinilla 2018), little was known of the culture of grape and wine science in this era. This chapter offers new insight into the creation of a branch of the British colonial wine industry in Australia as informed by scientific thinking and action. Prominent members of the HRVA arrived in New South Wales believing an Enlightenment faith in scientific knowledge provided a pathway to developing commerce and trade. Being British colonists, Hunter Valley winegrowers possessed an intellectual enthusiasm and capacity for scientific experimentation alongside reverence for the European wines they knew well. Members of the HRVA adapted winegrowing to local conditions as a mutual state of becoming, with knowledge systems comprising viticultural science that increasingly travelled the globe. And they did so with an élan characteristic of elite British colonists. It is hoped that this chapter will lead to further study of the reception, adaptation and innovation of New World grape and wine science in places such as South Australia. Although it is the largest of the colonial Australian wine industries, South Australia has been largely overlooked by historians.

It was not until the 1990s that Australian wines posed serious competition in a globalising market (Anderson and Pinilla 2018). Hunter wine production to the present day has been sustained by successive generations of family firms, some of which date to the 1850s, networked into a small to medium enterprise business cluster (McIntyre *et al.* 2013). The wider Hunter region hosts industries in coal mining and export, thoroughbred horse breeding and some agriculture. The Hunter produces less than 2% of Australian wine, and wine tourism is now a larger source of regional income than wine (McIntyre *et al.* 2019b). This is, in part, due to the region's focus on premium wine and its unsuitability for large-scale grape production. The region's contemporary international status, despite the modest size of its output in volume, would surely have pleased Scott, Carmichael, King and their HVRA peers.

References

Anderson, K. and Pinilla, V. (eds) (2018) *Wine Globalization: A New Comparative History*, Cambridge: Cambridge University Press.
Barthes, R. (2012) *Mythologies*, trans. Richard Howard, New York: Hill and Wang.
Black, R. and Ulin, R. (2013) "Introduction," in R. Black and R. Ulin (eds), *Wine and Culture: Vineyard to Glass*, London: Bloomsbury, 1–10.
Burke, P. (2012) "Strengths and Weaknesses of Cultural History," *Cultural History* 1, 1–13.
Curthoys, A. (2015) "History from Down Under: E. P. Thompson's The Making of the English Working Class and Australia," *Historical Reflections* 41(1), 20–39.
Dunstan, D. (2013) *A Vision for Wine: A History of the Viticultural Society of Victoria*, Melbourne: Viticultural Society of Victoria.
Dunstan, D. and McIntyre, J. (2014) "Wine, Olives, Silk and Fruits: The Mediterranean Plant Complex and Agrarian Visions for a 'Practical Economic Future' in Colonial Australia," *Journal of Australian Colonial History* 16, 29–50.
Grimstad, S., Waterhouse, J. and Burgess, J. (2019) "'Creating a Little Bit of La Dolce Vita': Explaining Resilience and Transformation in the Hunter Valley Wine Region, NSW, Australia," *International Journal of Globalisation and Small Business* 10, 359–380.
Hoare, M. (1966) "Adolph Basser Library: Notes on Research – Some Primary Sources for the History of Scientific Societies in Australia in the Nineteenth Century," *Historical Records of Australian Science* 1, 71–76.
Hunter River Vineyard Association. (1854) *Historical Summary of the Proceedings and Reports of the Hunter River Vineyard Association: . . . Year 1853*, Sydney: Printed by W.D. Piddington.
McIntyre, J. (2011) "Adam Smith and Faith in the Transformative Qualities of Wine in Colonial New South Wales," *Australian Historical Studies* 42, 194–211.
McIntyre, J. (2012) *First Vintage: Wine in Colonial New South Wales*, Sydney: NewSouth.
McIntyre, J. (2019) "Penfold, Mary (1816–1895)," in *People Australia*, National Centre of Biography, Australian National University, https://peopleaustralia.anu.edu.au/biography/penfold-mary-29651/text36618, accessed 10 January 2021.
McIntyre, J., Brady, M. and Barnes, J. (2019a) "'They are Among the Best Workers, Learning the Ways of a Vineyard Quickly': Aboriginal People, Drinking, and Labor in the Early Australian Wine Industry," *Global Food History* 5, 45–66.
McIntyre, J. and Germov, J. (2013) "Drinking History: Enjoying Wine in Early Colonial New South Wales," in S. Eriksson, M. Hastie and T. Roberts (eds), *Eat History: Food and Drink in Australia and Beyond*, Melbourne: Cambridge Scholars Press, 121–143.

McIntyre J. and Germov, J. (2018) *Hunter Wine: A History*, Sydney: NewSouth.

McIntyre, J. and Germov, J. (2021) "The Hunter Valley: Historicising a Multi-Form Wine-World in the Grape-Wine-Complex," in S. Lachaud-Martin, C. Marache, J. McIntyre and M. Pierre (eds), *Wine, Networks and Scales: Intermediation in the Production, Distribution and Consumption of Wine*, Brussels: Peter Lang, 199–216.

McIntyre, J., Mitchell, R., Boyle, B. and Ryan, S. (2013) "We Used to Get and Give a Lot of Help: Networking, Cooperation and Knowledge Flow in the Hunter Valley Wine Cluster," *Australian Economic History Review* 53, 247–267.

McIntyre, J., Senese, D. and Hull, J. (2019b) "Fruit Forward? Wine Regions as Geographies of Innovation in Australia and Canada," in A. Van Luyn and E. de la Fuente (eds), *Regional Cultures, Economies, and Creativity: Innovating Through Place in Australia and Beyond*, London: Routledge, 21–44.

Pierre, M. (2020) *France of the Southern Hemisphere: Transferring a European Wine Model to Colonial Australia* (PhD thesis, History, Dual award: University of Newcastle, Australia and the University Bordeaux Montaigne, France).

Rae, I. and Brock, W. (2013) "Liebig's Australian Connection: James King's Scientific Viticulture," *Historical Records of Australian Science* 24, 189–206.

Simpson, J. (2011) *Creating Wine: The Emergence of a World Industry, 1840–1914*, Princeton: Princeton University Press.

Tennent, J. (1855) *Wine, Its Use and Taxation: An Inquiry into the Operation of the Wine Duties on Consumption and Revenue*, London: J. Madden.

Varriano, J. (2010) *A Cultural History of Wine*, New York: Reaktion Books.

Wiener, M. (1981) *English Culture and the Decline of the Industrial Spirit, 1850–1980*, Cambridge: Cambridge University Press.

21
TASTING AS EXPERTISE
Scientific agronomists and sommeliers in France in the first half of the twentieth century

Sénia Fedoul

Introduction

While discourse surrounding wine and the art of wine tasting is part of a longstanding history, the twentieth century has profoundly modified its legacy through the combined effect of two very different factors: on one hand, the need for the total reconstruction of European wine regions after the *phylloxera* crisis (Garrier 1989; Pouget 1990, 2015) and on the other, the rising power of scientific wine expertise (Montaigne 1996). Following the *phylloxera* crisis of the last third of the nineteenth century, the question of flavour in wine became a major economic concern, leading to the need to rebuild the criteria for quality throughout all vineyards. New and badly acclimatised grape varieties, the unreliable development of hybrids, the appearance of 'sophisticated wines' and the uncontrolled use of certain agricultural inputs changed the relationship of producers to consumers, calling for new forms of expertise. The development of the technique of using rootstocks from hybrid varieties (Le Boulc'h 2017) challenged the traditional notion of gustative quality in wine. As early as 1889, the *Loi Griffe* brought about the first official definition of wine 'as product', evidencing the involvement of public powers in the economics of quality, reinforced by the 1905 law on the repression of fraud (Stanziani 2005).

Thus, it was in the context of recovery from a crisis that wine quality control on a sanitary level was implemented, entailing a newly critical vision of what was going on in the cellars of winemakers, wine merchants and restaurants alike. At the beginning of the twentieth century, wines were still transported and sold in barrels, glass bottles not yet being available on an industrial scale (Hamon 2007). Due to this, the management of the sanitary and gustative quality of wines during storage, which required specific technical skills, was of major importance.

The preservation of wine is complex. As a living product subjected to continuous physical and chemical changes, its vulnerability involves a great number of parameters, in particular that of cellar hygiene. This was particularly important in the world of production, as producers had to face the risks of lost product and unsatisfied customers. If the wine was diseased – an expression which recurs frequently in sources from the period – this meant that it could be considered as a doctor would, which is to say that the disease could be 'diagnosed' and that the wine could be 'treated': this was the major aim in rendering wine expertise more scientific.

It is in the context of the wine market's fragility that agronomists trained in techniques of chemical analysis (Jas 2001) in the spirit of the revolution instigated by Pasteur (Loubère 1990; Paul 1996) became agents in the spreading of a new form of technical knowledge aiming to locate diseased wines, conduct a diagnosis and treat them. At the mid-way point between agronomy and pharmacology, oenology came into being as a singular field of exploration within the economy of consumption. This brought with it one major challenge: while chemical expertise on wine made it possible to find the main faults and sanitary risks, it was powerless, given the tools of the period, to identify the subtle qualitative characteristics of wine as a drink: that is to say as a product related to hedonic consumption (Nourrisson 2013).

It was in relation to this interplay of constraints that wine tasting became, in the first half of the twentieth century, the common recourse of each of the stakeholders in the viti-vinicultural industry. Yet its appeal to the senses of sight, smell and taste was not self-explanatory in an age of positivism which was wary of subjectivity in the production of knowledge. How to prevent sanitary risks to consumers while also satisfying their expectations? This was the challenge which, within half a century, forced two different approaches to practice and discourse which, up until then, had been mutually unaware, to face each other and to hybridise. On the one hand, there was the practice of chemical analysis, associated with 'oenological cold discourse' on wine, and on the other, the world of service and luxury, associated with 'oenological hot discourse'. (We have retained the literal meaning of the French terms here. 'Cold' implies a very analytical and technical approach to quality whilst 'hot' is less scientific and more allusive and evocative. 'Hot' tasting tends not to break down the component parts of a wine but rather to taste it as a single entity) (Fischler 1999; Demossier 2007). The 'hot oenological discourse' is hedonistic. This type of discourse comes from both the French gastronomic and terroir discourses, which promote place, territory and hedonism.

In the space of half a century, tasting expertise consolidated its position as the main instrument for the production of a new framework synthesising the myth of place (Parker 2015) and of agro-food rationality: the 'taste of terroir', the basis for identity in French viticultural production and a token of the renewed confidence of consumers in the post-*phylloxera* reconstruction.

Regenerating vineyards, redefining wine

One of the greatest problems of the viticultural sector in the nineteenth century was that of wine storage, already an issue before the *phylloxera* crisis, but worsened by the use in cultivation of new vines and by fraud linked to the tempting prospect of pre-empting markets which were on the way to renewal. Chemists of the Third Republic, commissioned by producers and merchants, identified multiple risk factors: the hygiene of cellars and wine storage containers, the choice of materials for the latter and the management of cellar temperature. Throughout the second half of the nineteenth century and the early twentieth century, manuals geared to winegrowers, sommeliers, merchants and consumers, which popularised technical knowledge about wine storage, began to be published (Jullien 1822; Maigne and Brunet 1903). The president of the *Union des Sommeliers de Paris*, Emile Carme, explained the duty of the sommelier in 1926:

> It is the Sommelier's duty to provide every possible care to wines which enter an establishment, so as to be able to present them to clients with the highest level of quality that they can acquire. To this purpose they must put them through the appropriate operations, such as topping up, racking, fining, and filtering, allowing each one to receive the treatment that is necessary to it so as to ensure proper preservation.
>
> *(Le Sommelier 26, 15 February 1926)*

As the president of the *Union des sommeliers de Paris* explained, sommeliers were fundamentally acting as cellar managers. The cellar manager, or the sommelier acting in that capacity, was present wherever consumption and sales took place: restaurants, cabarets, luxury hotels etc. As the last people to taste the wine before clients, they had to vouch for its quality. Yet the entire strategy of those within the scientific world was aimed at proving that expertise had to be founded on methods of analysis which only technicians trained in the world of the laboratory possessed. Thus, the original relationship between oenology, wine technology and the work of the sommelier was openly understood to be a form of subjection.

Thus, through the contemporary technical manuals, we may observe the way in which a curative oenological technique, based on scientific knowledge in direct imitation of medical discourse, was established. The goal of this process was to identify the symptoms of the diseases present in wines and to implement preventative methods, taking into account cellar hygiene norms. The faults and diseases in wines were numerous, sometimes leading to a loss in production. Technical works took on the objective of drawing up an evolving list of these diseases, with indications about their causes, so as to allow for the earliest possible diagnosis.

At a time when cellar work was based purely on practical empiricism, faults were primarily the result of the aging and storage of wines, but equally the ignorance of preventative wine technology practices. It is, nonetheless, apparent that the names of wine faults and diseases were increasingly borrowed from the lexicon of wine tasting, with references to evaluation using the senses, slipping from 'cold' discourse to 'hot' discourse. A mastery of tasting thus appeared from the nineteenth century onwards as the way to identify faults and diseases in wine. It is particularly in the changing vocabulary of 'bad flavours' that pre- and post-*phylloxera* terms present the most differences.

The example of '*flavours of terroir and farmyard*' allows one to measure how words and representations changed in the socio-technical system of wine. According to chemist and agronomist Raymond Brunet, writing at the beginning of the twentieth century, such a flavour was characteristic of the environment in which the wine has been made and stored:

> Among the different flavours of terroir, there are those that we find to be agreeable, if they are not too pronounced. Such is that of gun flint in the wines of Chablis (Yonne), of Périguère and a fewer other vintages from the *département* of the Haute-Pyrénées. So too is that of raspberry and violet, in a few wines from Bordeaux and the Dauphiné etc. But vines planted in sticky or marshy ground, those that are too often manured or which have been over fertilised are likely to transfer to the plants their unpleasant flavour, such as sludge or muck, used in the area surrounding Paris, as well as those plants known as kelp, which are used on the Ile de Ré and in several vineyards of countries next to the sea, producing wines of which the earthy or brackish flavour is very unpleasant.
>
> (Maigne and Brunet 1903)

Table 21.1 Synthesis of faults and diseases of wine, oenotechnical manuals (1822 to 1903)

Origins and causes	Faults	'Diseases'
Cellar and barrel hygiene	'*Flavours of barrel and mould*'	
Oenotechnical problem	During clarification, fining with egg whites: '*Flavours of spoiled egg; burned and smoky flavours*' During conservation, use of a sulphur wick: '*flavours of sulphur*'	
Foreign bodies, accidents	'*flavours of terroir and manure*'	
Microbial 'disease' which is recognisable upon tasting		*Volatile acidity, bitterness, ropiness, stale, tastes of formaldehyde or rot, musty flavour*

While this flavour was not considered to be dangerous – and while it appears that some consumers accepted it – it does emerge as the product of objective faults in methods of production. To prevent this farmyard flavour, the chemist, and agronomist Professor Vincens advised his readers in 1906 and 1922 to pay attention to the storage of wines and to their containers:

> As wine very easily absorbs every smell, one only needs a badly-stoppered container full of liquid to be placed near an odorous body for the latter to become concentrated within the container. This is the case with stable waste, manure, and fodder, left in the immediate neighbourhood of the cellars.
>
> *(Vincens 1922)*

The agricultural practices of the period were dominated by family-run polyculture, using animals for ploughing as well as for manuring. The specific flavour of the production location was considered recognisable through tasting. At the beginning of the twentieth century, this still had a negative connotation, but it moved towards a positive appreciation of certain local characteristics as time went by. This reversal in judgement was reinforced by the rejection within the socio-technical system of wine of the 'foreign' character of flavours that came from new varieties. In some ways, mourning pre-*phylloxera* wines was necessary to allow, in time, for the full blossoming of the 'taste of terroir'.

Towards a synthesis of 'cold' and 'hot' discourse

In the 1900s, the rise of issues pertaining to hygiene (Afanasyeva 2017; Howard 2006), to fighting against fraudulent activity and to the search for a greater quality of wine via sanitary control led to the necessity of making the vocabulary of flavour standardised and scientific. The aim was to develop a discipline which would go from the winegrower to the cellar manager, focusing on preventative and curative wine techniques. With the idea of transmitting their own 'formal knowledge' (Freidson 1986), scientific agronomists endeavoured to popularise scientific and technical discourse via the creation of a lexicon of 'off flavours', published both in professional vinicultural journals, such as *Le Moniteur Vinicole* (from 1856) and *Le Sommelier* (from 1923), and in journals geared towards gastronomes, oenophiles and professionals in the wine business, such as *La Revue du vin de France* (from 1927). The lack of technical training centres meant that this need for technical wine knowledge and analytical tasting (cold discourse) remained critical.

In 1924, the professional bulletin *Le Sommelier* began a series of articles titled 'Vocabulary of the Sommelier', which was, in fact, a serialised version of the dictionary *Le Maître de Chai*, a decision that demonstrated the increasingly close relationship of cold and hot discourse. The articles provided a lexicon to be used in identifying the faults, diseases and flavours of wines, designed to be of value both in the cellar for curative purposes and on the restaurant floor. It constituted one of the favoured channels for the standardisation of oenological discourse. The example of 'acerbic' flavour allows for an understanding of how the authors of these articles in 1924 combined scientific expertise and qualitative discourse, as it:

> brings together the sharpness and the flavour which characterises vegetable acids. It lacks body, sap (sève), and finesse. It irritates the teeth, and contains an overabundance of tartaric acid, malic acid, etc. It usually originates in grapes that are less than fully ripe, and in bad varieties.
>
> *(Le Sommelier 10, 15 July 1924)*

Here we have a full translation of a chemical characteristic of wine into sensorial terms, leading to a critique of both vineyard production systems and, especially, of the use of hybrid varieties: in this case, the Noah. Wine tasting had become the mediator which allowed for an understanding of wine as a 'complete product'.

Despite all this, this technique was still seen as problematic by scientists trained in experimental methods and legitimated as experts by the Pasteurian revolution. Manuals and treatises published in the first half of the twentieth century bear witness to the debate which surrounded the scientific justification of wine tasting as a tool of expertise. Professor Vincens crystallised the debate in 1906:

> But what, then, is the tasting of wine; what definition can we give of it? I admit that here I feel rather perplexed. Our sensations have a vague and imprecise character; their intensity cannot be measured on scales, with a ruler, or with any other instrument of precision. It follows that we can hardly give a rigorous, scientific, and precise definition of wine tasting.
>
> (Vincens 1922)

A scientific fact may only be proved by instruments of analysis and measurement. As it is difficult to measure sensations, scientific agronomists, wary of being demoted from their role as experts, called upon other branches of scientific knowledge, such as physiology, in their attempt to explain sensorial tasting processes through the mechanisms of mouthfeel, aroma and flavour. For Maigne and Brunet of the *Encyclopédie Roret* in 1903:

> In true wine tasting, the tongue must ensure that the wine is in contact with all the mucous membranes of the mouth. It is the sensations gathered by each of these mucous membranes that allow the taster to determine the qualities and the faults of the wine. The back of the mouth denotes the flavours of terroir, of barrel, of cork, and of bitterness. The glossopharyngeal nerves of the tongue makes out alkalinity; the lingual nerves of the tongue perceive acidity.
>
> (Maigne and Brunet 1903)

The argument of the *Encyclopédie Roret* is that 'cold tasting' might be justified from a scientific perspective by the physiology of the nerves, allowing the chemist to recognise the 'good flavours' of wine without renouncing their place in the world of science:

> Tasters judge bouquet and sap with the nasal cavities. The sap is the aromatic flavour which first hits the pharynx, then once absorbed the nasal cavities. In order to define it, one must therefore not spit out the wine after having tasted it. [This section of the text explicitly states that the English method requires keeping the wine in your mouth to appreciate the taste and smells.] This manner of proceeding is called tasting à l'Anglaise ['in the English manner'].
>
> (Idem)

Through this analysis, Raymond Brunet creates a link with 'hot tasting', as every part of the mouth plays a role in determining both good and bad flavours. The taster, he argued, must call simultaneously upon the senses of gustation and olfaction, leading to different tasting practices, such as the 'English method', in which (he asserted but did not explain) the wine was not spat out, but rather swallowed in order to fully taste all the organoleptic flavours.

The debate surrounding the principle of analytic wine tasting as a scientific tool continued from that moment on, with two purposes at stake: defining the best method and legitimating the most competent protagonists. Professor Laurent Mathieu, a chemist and agronomist, promoted tasting as a scientific fact. His advice was published both in the *Revue des Vins de France* and in the professional bulletin *Le Sommelier*. In 1922, during a seminar of promotion of French wine, he explained:

> To taste well is therefore an art, without a doubt, but it is also partially a science, because it involves engaging our sensorial organs and our brain, the operations of which, if we well understood them, could be directed methodically in order to produce a greater result. . . . Experimental physiology and psychology are relatively recent sciences; the latter has only had laboratories at the Sorbonne for the past few years. . . . Combined with experience, which always plays a preponderant role through the acquired concepts that only experience can bring, this knowledge allows for the rational direction of tasting and, consequently, gives the professional a clear superiority; it reveals to the wine-lover with all the connoisseurial pleasures concealed within a great wine.
>
> *(Mathieu 1922)*

The call to cognitive sciences was thus used in the 1920s to 'rationalise' wine tasting and, in doing so, to legitimate the extension of the sphere of chemical expertise into that of hedonic practices. In spite of this, it was only through words and not in exact calculation that chemists were able to go so far. As another chemist and agronomist, Professor Joseph Dubaquié, admitted in 1934, 'chemistry and tasting represent two different things. It is the second which is, in the end, vindicated, and absolutely so. It is useless to repeat it: wine is made to be drunk'. While chemists wished to be recognised as experts, they could only do so by accepting shared authority over the area of wine tasting.

Indeed, chemists and chemical agronomists occupied a hybrid space between the world of the laboratory and that of the social system of vine and wine. This point was the subject of debate within the world of chemists and chemical agronomists, who no longer made a distinction between expertise and common knowledge, but rather between technique and research. In a 1928 text, Professor Lucien Sémichon differentiated processes of innovation by attempting to describe the different skills at stake with the aim of defining the boundaries of 'oenological science': 'oenology encompasses the study and the knowledge of wine facts. It includes both the application of methods of wine-tasting with which experienced brokers concern themselves, and physical and chemical analysis' (Sémichon 1928). For Sémichon, oenology was a scientific technique which had to be used once the winemaking and aging processes were completed and which operated on a strictly analytical level. It should not be confused with either science on the one hand or brokerage on the other.

As for Professor Dubaquié, he admitted to his difficulties in taking a stance on the role of the chemist in regards to wine tasting in a context which was no longer that of triumphant positivism, but rather that of the inter-war years, which were becoming increasingly marked by nostalgic agrarianism. Thus, for him, 'chemists could do wine a great favour by cleverly contriving never to being seen responsible for it. For the consumer likes a natural product, born of the plant and of generous nature'. Chemists, seen as responsible for the development of 'sophisticated wines' (i.e. wines with chemical additives), could never be seen as legitimate through the symbolic and affective lens of terroir wines. On the contrary, they might be seen as responsible for the 'denaturation' and standardisation of the flavour of wines through the use of oenological additive, and the over-use of pasteurisation (which gave wine a 'cooked flavour'). In the context of prohibitionist and hygienist discourse, only 'natural wines' could appear to be simultaneously good for one's health, for rural life and for the nation, as they were likely to resist the chemical campaign of the scientists. Campaigns aiming to rip up the worst vines and to control hybrid varieties – which were both too productive and produced off flavours – were intended to return to the 'natural' state of the terroirs, as the right grape would supposedly grow in harmony with its soil and produce a healthy beverage.

In spite of this, it would be incorrect to draw the conclusion that chemists capitulated in the face of this collective imagination of natural wine and of the qualitative discourse of hotel sommeliers. Professor Dubaquié wrote in 1934:

> [I]t is less easy to interpret in chemical terms the notes that a taster awards to a fine wine. And even a chemist who is also a taster (indeed, this does occur) would very probably express themselves as everyone else does. That is, he will be wary of associating a number or a chemical with each of the precious qualities identified in the product. Admittedly, a highly practised operator might find the volatile acid content, merely through smell and taste but with a degree of uncertainty. Furthermore a broker, however competent, may mistake a residue of fermentable sugar, which is dangerous in red wine, for praiseworthy qualities such as texture or softness.
>
> *(Dubaquié 1934)*

Yet, all things considered, wrote Dubaquié, science does not lose any ground: 'A chemist who is also a wine taster will judge most soundly'. They will not have the final say, however, for 'they would risk exaggerating the importance of a certain quantity of volatile acid which may yet do well and even very well in an old, well-structured wine, exempt of microbes as well as sugar residue' (*Idem*).

A wine might be good, perhaps even excellent, despite a precarious physical and chemical balance. However, the recurring risk of a disease is all the greater in this case. Only chemists can guarantee the absence of any hidden faults. They must always, therefore, speak first, with non-negotiable control of the foundation of the wine system.

Towards an alliance of forms of expertise

In fact, it was under the control of the scientists of the Republic that sommeliers professionalised and normalised their own practices, most notably through 'fieldwork' in viticultural regions. This was publicised in *Le Sommelier* in 1925:

> It may be interesting to note that this year, the sommeliers' excursion was conducted under the auspices of the government, for this certainly proves that public powers attach more importance to the trips than some among us. And yet, from the greatest to the smallest, from the beginner to the most experienced, we all have something to learn from them.
>
> *(Le Sommelier 24, 15 September 1925)*

In order to do so, the most knowledgeable scientists would be called upon, following the example of Lucien Sémichon during a meeting in Carcassonne the same year:

> Mr. Sémichon first endeavoured to explain to us how the economic conditions which once allowed for a profitable flow of the best wines of Minervois and Corbières towards choice customers, today can no longer be relied on: he proved the important role that sommeliers could play to maintain the customers' taste for good wines, described to us the particular type of each of the wines of the region, and allowed us to perceive his high oenological and viticultural value.
>
> *(Idem)*

The combination of oenological expertise and the art of the sommelier was not an equal one; on the contrary, it took place within an accepted asymmetry which made it possible to accumulate different forms of legitimacy, rather than opposing one to the other.

Chemists, through their mastery of analytical tools, retained their status as the legitimate experts of wine tasting – or, at least, of the criteria of wine tasting. Their expertise found its limits in the interpretation of smells and flavours, assuming that such expertise should confine itself to tasting with a physical and chemical perspective in mind. Furthermore, the language of science could only be translated with difficulty for the winemaker, the broker and even more so the consumer. It must therefore be understood as both a 'translation' and a controlled alternation between cold analysis and hot discourse in a dialogue which was still emerging during this period. Thus, during the 1920s and 1930s, there was a progressive and cautious yet highly important move to go beyond cold tasting, from the standpoint of the chemist's legitimacy, and towards warm tasting and the definition of wine's hedonic qualities, in an alliance with the world of the sommelier that was not yet social and professional but was already semantic and symbolic. Indeed, the role of sommeliers working in luxury hotels and high-end restaurants was to value 'natural' wines, as expressed by the president of the *Union des Sommeliers de Paris*, Emile Carme, in 1926:

> The sommelier has another equally important role, which consists of artfully presenting wines to consumers so as to allow them to be tasted in the most advantageous manner. . . . Then the customer must be guided through their order. . . . In order to facilitate the decision, it is proper to know the menu that has been ordered, so as to associate with the desired foods such wines as should bring out their finer points. It is also necessary to be a bit of a psychologist, for this allows one to rapidly grasp the tastes and the habits of the customer.
> *(Le Sommelier 29, 15 February 1926)*

The voluntary disappearance of chemists from the public eye and the development of the sommelier's theatrical performance within luxury establishments are testaments to the role of 'hot discourse', which appeared to consumers as the framework for quality in wine. Far from a victory of one form of expertise over the other, this represents a single socio-technical system which was in the process of building its legitimacy during this period.

Conclusions

The French passion for defining 'correct tasting' is emblematic of what was at stake in the world of wine in the inter-war period, in deciding between a definition of quality through industrial-type criteria and a definition anchored in practices and representations which put chemistry at the service of hedonic appreciation. It was not merely a question of determining quality, but more one of promoting its recognition in order to fight against the recurring problems of the wine market: lack of control over the product, sanitary risks, hygienist critiques etc. It is within this context that one must understand the attraction for chemists of the legitimation of that which they formerly denounced – the 'taste of terroir': that is to say, the idea of a wine which expresses the qualities of its soil, in this way avoiding any criticism as a 'sophisticated' product potentially harmful to humans on the one hand and to the protection of rural life on the other. Thus, cold discourse surrounding wine meets hot discourse in a delicate and conflicting synthesis operating in the inter-war years, which leads in a highly symbolic way to the law of 1935, which established the system of *Appellation d'Origine Contrôlée* for French wines. Wine tasting represents, in this story, the historical compromise between scientific and socio-cultural definitions of quality, brought to national and international success in the second half of the twentieth century.

Acknowledgement

Translated from French by Sophie Purkis Charters.

References

Afanasyeva, V. (2017) "L'Union des Françaises contre l'Alcool: pour une histoire de l'antialcoolisme (1916–1940)," *Alcoologie et Addictologie* 39(2), 120–127.

Demossier, M. (2007) "Le discours "œnologique" contemporain: Région contre nation au XXIe siècle," in F. Hache-Bissette and D. Saillard (eds), *Gastronomie et Identité Culturelle française, Discours et représentations (XIXe-XXIe siècles)*, Paris: Edition Nouveau Monde.

Dubaquié, J. (1934) "Les fêtes du Vin. Vins Fins et Finesse des Vins," *Le Sommelier* 130, 15 Juillet 1934.

Fischler, C. (1999) *Du vin*, Paris: Edition Odile Jacob.

Freidson, E. (1986) *Professional Power. A Study of Institutionalization of Formal Knowledge*, Chicago: The University of Chicago Press.

Garrier, G. (1989) *Le Phylloxéra. Une guerre de trente ans. 1870–1900*, Paris: Albin Michel.

Hamon, M. (2007) "L'industrie de la bouteille en France au début du XXe siècle. Entre modernisation et concentration," in C. Bouneau and M. Figeac (eds), *Le verre et le vin de la cave à la table, du XVIIe siècle à nos jours*, Pessac: Maison des Sciences de l'Homme d'Aquitaine, 323–336.

Howard, S. (2006) *Les images de l'alcool en France, 1915–1942*, Paris: CNRS Éditions.

Jas, N. (2001) *Au carrefour de la chimie et de l'Agriculture. Les Sciences agronomiques en France et en Allemagne, 1840–1914*, Paris: Éditions des archives contemporaines.

Jullien, A. (1822) *Manuel du sommelier, ou Instruction pratique sur la manière de soigner les vin*, Paris: L. Colas – Imprimeur Libraire, Mme Huzard – Imprimeur Libraire.

Le Boulc'h, A-E. (2017) *Une histoire de la greffe végétale au XIXe siècle et au début du XXe siècle. Enjeux scientifiques d'une pratiques horticole* (Thèse de doctorat en Histoire Contemporaine, Université de Nantes).

Loubère, L.A. (1990) *The Wine Revolution in France. The twentieth century*, Princeton, NJ: Princeton University Press.

Maigne, P. and Brunet, R. (1903) *Encyclopédie Roret, Sommelier et Marchand de Vin*, Paris: Éditions France-Livres.

Mathieu, L. (1922) "Art de bien Goûter les Vins," *Compte Rendu de la Semaine Nationale du Vin*, Paris, 13–18 mars 1922.

Montaigne, É. (1996) "Crise biologique, différenciation des savoirs et mutations des systèmes technique et de production viticoles," Histoire des trajectoires technologiques et filières productives (1870–1970), CTESI Montpellier, Documents et Débats, 6/96, INRA, 40–68.

Nourrisson, D. (2013) *Crus et cuites. Histoire du buveur*, Paris: Perrin.

Parker, T. (2015) *Tasting French Terroir: The History of an Idea*, Berkeley: California University Press.

Paul, H.W. (1996) *Science, Vine, and Wine in Modern France*, Cambridge: Cambridge University Press.

Pouget, R. (1990) *Histoire de la lutte contre le phylloxéra de la vigne en France, 1868–1895*, Paris: INRA.

Pouget, R. (2015) *Le phylloxéra et les maladies de la vigne, la lutte victorieuse des savants et des vignerons français (1850–1900)*, Paris: Edilivre.

Sémichon, L. (1928) "L'état actuel des recherches œnologiques," 1er Congrès Mondial de la Vigne et du Vin, Bordeaux, 21 au 24 juin 1928, Bulletin International du Vin, 3 August 1928.

Stanziani, A. (2005) *Histoire de la qualité alimentaire, XIXe-XXe siècle*, Paris: Edition Seuil.

Vincens, J. [1906] (1922) *L'Art de déguster les Vins*, Toulouse: Imprimerie du Sud Ouest.

22
WINE WRITING AS LIFESTYLE WRITING

Communicating taste and constructing lifestyle in *The Saturday Times* wine column

Ana Tominc and Nikki Welch

Introduction

Since the 1950s, media advice related to wine consumption has evolved and diversified as a result of the increasing availability of wine to the majority of the population in Britain. From the introduction of consumer-focused specialist books and publications in the 1950s (Shapin 2012) to regular columns in British newspapers, such as *The Sunday Times* in the early 1980s (Reichl 2007), popular wine writing offered its audience guidance to help navigate the choice of wines available. At the same time, it defined popular tastes related to wine, in part as a reflection of general changes in lifestyle media. A gradual shift from wine media discourse based more heavily on technical expertise and wine tasting language to a more lifestyle-oriented presentation in the last decades, in which taste and qualities of wine are described using less standardised professional language, can be considered part of the post-modern shift towards taste individualisation and discourse democratisation, defined by Fairclough (1992: 201) as 'removal of inequalities and asymmetries in the discursive and linguistic rights, obligations and prestige groups of people'. The process of mixing established terminology of wine writing and inventing new, *ad hoc* ways to describe wine taste, incorporating various language styles and transgressing accepted boundaries of wine discourse resulted in a hybrid genre that created a unique wine column format with a distinct format, style and genre within the discourse of wine (Machin and van Leeuwen 2003, 2005). In this sense, lifestyle media is not just 'accommodation of the different media products that are centred on ideas of taste and lifestyle', such as the wine columns themselves, but also 'intense proliferation and hybridisation, as well as genre bending and blending' (Bell and Hollows 2005: 9). This is when metaphors, metonymies, onomatopoeia and repetition that are generally thought of as parts of advertising discourse and the advertising genre (e.g. van Leeuwen 2005) become seminal parts of another discourse or genre, as in the case of food writing. In Jamie Oliver's culinary discourse, for example, the more traditional cooking genre that centres on objectivity in description of the cooking process and technically precise description of its parts is no longer at the core. Instead, personifying desserts in terms of people, exaggerating the taste of dishes and framing foods to evoke their eroticism, Oliver's cookbooks and associated media performances build his brand through a combination of various linguistic features that ultimately construct both himself and the food he recommends as approachable, youthful, tasty and sexy (Tominc 2017). Using a language style, then, results not only in discourse construction of lifestyle but also in an increase of cultural capital for those who produce or consume the media (Bourdieu 1984).

In this chapter, we illustrate this shift in communicating taste and constructing lifestyle through a case study of Jane MacQuitty's wine columns in *The Saturday Times* (2000–20). By focusing specifically on figurative language and poetic devices employed in descriptions of wine taste for a non-technical audience, we use MacQuitty's writing as a snapshot of the lifestyle wine media discourse in which expert-driven advice for consumption yields its place to a more informal style of writing for the consumer, putting taste and choice into the hands of the buyers and allowing them to start engaging with taste as a personal preference representative of a lifestyle. Use of figurative language is significant because 'when we signify things through one metaphor rather than another, we are constructing our reality in one way rather than another' (Fairclough 1992: 194). Unlike the professional tasting note, in which taste description is constructed using standardised figurative language with clearly identifiable metaphors, the wine column allows for the 'variability of "subjective" experience in tasting' (Korsemeyer 2007: 3) to come to light alongside the technical language used to designate MacQuitty's expertise and proliferate the elite status of wine.

Popular and professional wine writing

The last two decades in particular have seen significant shifts in popular wine writing, including the increase of metaphoric language analysed in this chapter, especially as the role of traditional expertise, such as that of MacQuitty, gave way to lifestyle writing which, nevertheless, maintains a certain distinction in relation to the 'amateur' reader. This relative distance or subtle hierarchy prevails despite the general trend of seemingly classless omnivorousness in contemporary middle-class taste, in which appreciation of a broad range of tastes is awarded high cultural capital (Johnston and Baumann 2010; Naccarato and LeBesco 2012). The removal of the wine column from the main body of the newspaper to be inserted in the lifestyle section underscores a shift in attitude to consider wine as a lifestyle consumable along with interior design, food and gardening. However, it is unclear whether the inclusion of wine in lifestyle writing indicates an effective democratisation or a simple stylistic adjustment. If wine appreciation seems to be communicated through four frames that suggest accepting a larger range of wines in a more equal manner – transparency, heritage, genuineness and external validation – Smith Maguire (2018) nevertheless reports that 'established hierarchies of taste' that position the Old World more prominently continue to exist. In a similar vein, MacQuitty's wine writing does not represent a successful democratisation of wine, but still remains grounded in the ideas of expertise and distinction with which wine has been associated for so long. As we show in our diachronic analysis of MacQuitty's wine columns from 1982 to 2017 (Welch and Tominc 2021), MacQuitty represents herself as a more traditional expert with a high level of technical knowledge during the late 1980s and early 1990s and subsequently adopts a more lifestyle-focused discourse recommendation. It is the latter period of writing that interests us here in our analysis of communicating taste and constructing lifestyle. Like technical knowledge, 'winespeak' also encapsulates the professional code used to describe a wine's qualities (as in the tasting note that requires learned denotation of taste). While MacQuitty rarely uses the tasting note format in its professional guise, she does present some of the tasting note vocabulary to the readers, thereby offering an opportunity for them to acquire it, while also communicating status and expertise. Her role of the 'everyday' expert, however, is established through complex modes of evaluation, a process in which cultural intermediaries are not only involved in the legitimation of tastes but also 'actively engaged in constructing, and not simply exemplifying, new canons of good taste' (Smith Maguire and Matthews 2012: 559; Smith Maguire 2016).

Professional tasters have long aimed to attribute wine properties that are similar to other foods and non-consumables with an aim to facilitate objective description of its taste. The role of figurative language is integral to both wine writing in general, due to the need to communicate the complexity of sensory experience, and lifestyle writing. Due to its proximity to conversational and advertising discourse (van Leeuwen 2005), metaphor and other stylistic devices play a central role in this analysis due to their ability to present one area in terms of another one. In the traditional tasting note, this helped create a way through which wines can be compared and analysed and constitutes an area of considerable academic attention (Gluck 2003; Lehrer 2009; Silverstein 2004; Caballero 2007; Caballero and Suarez-Toste 2008; Lehrer 2009; Creed 2014). The newspaper wine column, on the other hand, has been neglected as a discourse genre and a place where non-professional wine enthusiasts can learn about new trends and tastes (Silverstein 2004; Bender 2008), despite works such as Fitzmaurice (2017), which demonstrate the role of the wine critic influencing consumer trends, albeit for a more elite audience. By selling more than just taste, wine columns can be seen as a window to people's aspirations as they promise to bring sophistication of palate and glamour. Their rise in the late twentieth century reflects the shifting of the responsibility of choice and taste making from the expert to the consumer through the information communicated between them. In this context, MacQuitty and other wine media writers act as cultural intermediaries: expert guides influencing consumer tastes and positioning wines as fashionable symbols of good quality, the drink of choice for everyone while at the same time still reflecting the notion of high status and complexity that has been attached to wine.

Communicating the taste of wine: between professional standardisation and popular description

Britain has long been seen as a leading market for wine, because of its status as both a non-producer (UC Davis Library 2020), although this is slowly changing with the rise of domestic wine production in the UK (Anderson and Wittwer 2017), and a historic influencer of market trends and politics (Ludington 2013). For many years, its status as a non-producer was particularly important. Without local wine production, all wine was imported, and the variety of wine available was greater and less geographically biased than in a wine-producing region where locally produced wines dominate the shelves. This gave wine writers a wider spectrum of wines to discuss and recommend as there was less likelihood of bias towards locally produced wines (Friberg et al. 2011). In funding a collection of wine writing at the UC Davis Library (2020), Winiarski credits British wine writers with creating a technical and neutral wine vocabulary for winemakers to facilitate their craft because of the diversity of wines they were discussing in both flavour and origin, despite being influenced by the established hierarchy of wine quality and classification (Howland 2013). It can be argued that this neutrality extended to the popular consumer press, where wines from around the world are discussed and recommended.

Whilst Britain's impact on the global wine industry can be traced back through centuries, the attempt to describe a wine's character through its flavour is a relatively modern phenomenon, as noted by Shapin (2009). Even though evaluations of wine existed in Roman times and throughout history in order to identify its medicinal properties or, more latterly, 'goodness', it wasn't until the late eighteenth and early nineteenth century that more than a handful of adjectives, if any at all, were used to describe its taste. The Edwardians and Victorians introduced a poetic form to evoke the character of the wine, epitomised in Englishman George Saintsbury's 1920 *Notes on a Cellar*, which was more likely to compare a wine to a poem than describe or evoke its flavour (Shapin 2009). Description of wine through the use of figures of speech, especially allusion, would have been presented to the public as poetry, rather than in the mainstream media, and therefore, would have reached a far smaller audience than the contemporary lifestyle food media discourse analysed in the continuation of this chapter. The birth of 'winespeak', as we know it, was catalysed by the end of Prohibition in the United States, and by 1937, the *New York Times* had already published its famous cartoon lambasting the pretentious language of wine. Between the 1930s and the 1970s, the majority of consumer wine communication was aimed at enthusiasts and published in speciality wine and, more latterly, home or food and drink magazines, such as *Gourmet* (1940) and *Wine Magazine* (1959). The 1970s and 1980s were also the birth of a significant scientific movement to standardise the description and evaluation of tastes and flavours in both the UK and the US, the development of Anna Noble's aroma wheel in 1984 being perhaps the most significant for wine. New attempts to describe wine objectively in both a technical and amateur way were largely a response to the increasing diversity of wine available to the average consumer, particularly through the supermarkets, and a feature of the post-modern individualisation of choice (Reichl 2007; Lehrer 2009; Lewis 2008). In this context, the role of wine media written to inform and educate consumers became increasingly important.

To illustrate the complexity of wine description through figurative language in lifestyle writing, we will focus on analysing lifestyle wine discourse in MacQuitty's wine columns published in *The Saturday Times* between 2000 and 2020. This period represents the point at which her column moved from the main body of the newspaper to the lifestyle section – indicating the newspaper's new perceptions around the role of wine in the consumer's life. During this period, use of metaphor in text also changes, and description of taste via such language becomes less dependent on professional descriptions used by the industry (e.g. Welch and Tominc 2021). The analysis broadly follows methods of critical discourse analysis as it aims to demonstrate how wine taste is constructed through use of metaphor (Fairclough 1992: 194–195); as a result, it is methodologically positioned in the tradition of qualitative, interpretative data analysis that perceives discourse 'as a form of social practice' that is 'socially constitutive as well as socially conditioned' (Fairclough and Wodak 1997: 258). The numbers following the examples refer to the date, month and year when the column was published in *The Saturday Times* (e.g. 010100 means 1 January 2000).

Wine writing as lifestyle writing: using figurative language and poetic devices to describe taste and lifestyle

Lifestyle can be linguistically constructed through 'co-occurrence of contradictory or inconsistent elements – mixtures of formal and informal styles, technical and non-technical vocabularies, markers of authority and familiarity, more typically written and more typically spoken syntactic forms' (Fairclough 1992: 97). All these constructions appear in the wine columns analysed as we found frequent examples of advertising discourse, direct speech, calls to action and colloquialisms (see also Welch and Tominc 2021). However, one of the most powerful was the use of figurative language to construct a specific lifestyle within the wine column genre. Figurative language, which forms part of much of lifestyle writing, is generally understood to include stylistic devices that transfer meaning, such as metaphors, metonymy and synecdoche; these speak of one thing in terms of something else (Leech 1969). They play an important part in both the technical and the lifestyle descriptions of subjective taste and smell because they suggest that wine tastes and smells similar to other known foods. This is why they make sense to the reader (Silverstein 2004; Caballero 2007; Lehrer 2009; Creed 2014; Caballero and Suarez-Toste 2008). This use of metaphor can also refer to non-consumable tastes and flavours, such as petrol, tar or iodine, which are not found in wines. The connection between the described flavour of the wine and actual taste is, in this case, more abstract. Whilst metaphor is used in standardised wine writing, we explore with our analysis the change in metaphor used in wine columns and its contribution to wine communication not as a metaphor to better describe the qualities of the wine but to invoke the cultural capital of the wine.

Wine as a human and other wine metaphors

Caballero (2007) finds three kinds of metaphors to describe wine in winespeak: anthropomorphic metaphors describe wine through human characteristics; structural or 3D metaphors describe wine in terms of a building or structure; textile metaphors describe wine through the texture or its feeling in the mouth. He also identifies the use of 'manner-of-motion' verbs: that is, when the wine is described in terms of way of moving (e.g. 'tiptoed'). In MacQuitty's writing, wine is commonly personified. Rather than thinking of one thing in terms of something else (a metaphor), cognitive metaphors are about organising one area or conceptual domain in terms of another one. Wine is often described as 'lively' ('A notch above the white, this bold, lively, inky red heaves with seductive, spicy liquorice, raspberry and black pepper-spiked style, complete with a decent 14% dollop of alcohol' (080504)), so the cognitive metaphor WINE/TASTE IS A PERSON constructs wine and wine-related taste as a person with specific human characteristics: for example, being 'lively'. (In the same example, see also liquorice as 'seductive', which is the same cognitive metaphor.) While this cognitive metaphor is also found in tasting notes because 'lively' is used to convey the taste experience of acidity in wine, however, a sensual metaphor such as 'seductive' goes beyond a taste metaphor and instead begins to infer other qualities more associated with the drinker than the drink. Throughout the corpus, these anthropomorphic descriptions of wine are increasingly used to portray wine as a human, as 'jolly' and 'competent' ('this jolly, juicy Aussie wine delivers lots of competent, earthy, spicy, seasonal food-suitable fruit' (021206)) or as a 'charmer' (070516) as demonstrated later in this chapter.

While this is a common way of writing about wine, wine is also constructed in other ways, as for example in (030514), where the cognitive metaphor WINE IS AN AEROPLANE is used ('touched down' and then 'took off again', just like a plane), demonstrating how wine in MacQuitty's columns takes on new frames through which it is talked about:

> British wine buyers are so obsessed with finding the next in-vogue grape variety that already the smoky, minerally assyrtiko from Greece, Japan's shy koshu and even China's mysterious cabernet gernischt are all viewed as old hat. Way before that, Moldova's ancient reds and stickies beloved by the Tsars, India's sultana fizz, Uruguay's tannat, and Romania's curious feteasca whites and red touched down briefly in Britain's wine racks and took off again.
>
> *(030514)*

In early wine columns (see Welch and Tominc 2021), wine is represented more in terms of its qualities using standardised vocabulary and rarely used wider food-related metaphors. The increasing appearance of the informal and intertextual metaphor (and other figures of speech), particularly related to food, suggests a move away from some of the earlier themes, which focus more on educating consumers about the wine industry, to the language of the broader audience for whom food has specific cultural (or indeed, culinary) capital (e.g. Naccarato and LeBesco 2012). The wine is increasingly thought of through a variety of food types and styles outside the technical, defined comparison found in Anna Noble's aroma wheel, which provides a standardised expanding flavour categorisation, starting with basics such as fruit, earthy, spice or vegetable and then expanding to more nuanced descriptions (raspberry, plum etc.). These range from fruits and spices, such as (080504), in which wine is described as 'spicy liquorice, raspberry and black pepper-spiked style', to meat, such as here: 'a beefy, rose-scented, chunky charmer' (070516). In this case, the wine is described as a human, but the 'charmer', in turn, is 'beefy', beef not only reminding the reader of the fleshy texture and taste of (matured) beef but also evoking the physical connotations that meat in Western culture traditionally carries. From its gendered link to masculinity and its stereotypical characteristics, '[r]ed meat has traditionally been widely endorsed as a potent expression of sheer brute power, particularly for "red-blooded" males' (Fiddes 1991: 111), even if, today, its meanings are more complex.

One of the central characteristics that differentiates wine columns from tasting notes in terms of figures of speech, however, is metaphors that use the language of recipes or food descriptions and those in which the aim is to create an atmosphere or occasion: in this case, such descriptions create an overall sense of the wine, rather than just the taste (Caballero 2007; Lehrer 2009). By utilising language more commonly understood by the reader, the writer makes wine drinking a more familiar and approachable subject to the reader. We can see this reference to culinary discourse in the example in (080504), in which MacQuitty uses 'a decent 14% dollop of alcohol' to describe the quantity of alcohol in wine using a measure normally used to communicate a quantity of soft food using a spoon (e.g. a dollop of cream). It could be argued that through this, she speaks of WINE AS FOOD. Throughout the corpus examined, the use of 'dollop of' to refer to wine and its components is frequent, perhaps reflecting a general shift in this word's meaning towards describing something indefinite, large in quantity and liquid in British English (see definition in the *Merriam-Webster* dictionary). Another example of this cognitive metaphor is 'topped up with carmenère and syrah', in which 'topped up' is taken from culinary discourse in order to help the reader to understand the makeup of the wine through ways in which food is normally discussed: 'This burly red, made from one third cabernet sauvignon and merlot, topped up with carmenère and syrah plus a smidgin of *mourvèdre*' (041204).

Such combinations of elements from various discourses (defined as interdiscursivity by Fairclough (1992), with recourse to Foucault) could be an attempt – conscious or not – to position wine in terms of the cultural capital normally associated with food (Naccarato and LeBesco 2012; Johnston and Baumann 2010). This is demonstrated through the likening of wine taste to food outside the established range of vocabulary borrowed from more familiar discourses, as discussed earlier. A more striking example of MacQuitty's departure from established ways of communicating taste in such lifestyle discourse is evident when she likens wine to whole dishes: for example, wine taste components are compared to an ice cream sundae, seemingly because a combination of chocolate, berries and spices might remind readers of ice cream: 'lots of guts, spice and berry fruit, topped with black pepper and chocolate, the vinous equivalent of an ice-cream sundae' (041204). Here, depicting the taste of wine in this way not only communicates gustatory characteristics but also – and possible more importantly – suggests a sense of occasion that the reader is able to build in their mind when thinking of an ice cream sundae: a large ice cream topped with syrup, berries and nuts; a sunny day by the sea; holidays; a dessert; a relaxing day. Of course, the connotations here are endless, although some are culturally shared for both ice cream and its American origins. Such use of figurative language, however, is found throughout the corpus as the author paints a picture of the occasion or lifestyle with which the themes would resonate.

Wine taste and lifestyle discourse through stylistic devices

Apart from figurative language, there are also various poetic devices, such as rhythm, assonance and simile, that perform a similar function to metaphors in the communication of wine taste. They are often used in advertising to add interest, memorability and entertainment to the text, although here, they can also have a different function (Van Leeuwen 2005; Myers 2004). Through this, wine writing overlaps with the discourse of advertising that can be defined through linguistic features, such as more direct language with reference to audience ('you'), disjunctive grammar, figurative language and poetic devices that are used to attract audience attention and increase the memorability of the product advertised (Myers 2004; Leech 1966).

As with metaphor, MacQuitty uses poetic devices to evoke a mood of place and to put the reader in it, therefore attaching a high social value to the wines she mentions later since, as with food, taste and knowledge of a range of destinations displays high capital. In example (030514) discussed earlier, the perception of a number of locations is built through the enumeration of various locations and wines and a sense of tradition and knowledge through allusion ('Tsars'). In addition to this, MacQuitty also describes bad-tasting wine, employing adjectives and simile that suggest its low price (and hence, the associated reference to low quality) and its olfactory and gustatory characteristics while, at the same time, also suggesting the quality of its taste through what such wine does to one's body: it makes you 'burp' and 'nauseatic' ('but it's bland, boring, burp-making and, frankly, often nauseatingly sweet prosecco that's responsible for this boom' (051215)).

The following examples function in a similar manner to advertisements as poetic devices 'are more pleasurable than, for instance, technical descriptions of products' (van Leeuwen 2005: 152). MacQuitty uses overlap with food and recipe, as seen earlier, to explain wine and food interactions. By using a simile such as 'the acidity works like a squirt of lemon' (221208), she normalises a technical aspect of wine and food pairing, bringing it into the readers' lifestyle. In this example ('from the now tiring '06 white French vintage to the young, perky '07s, such as this precocious, peardrop and pineapple-laden, colombard grape-dominant Gascon white' (030508)), the blend of alliteration ('precocious, peardrop and pineapple-laden'), simile and metaphor in both style and flavour descriptions create a wine description for the reader that is not only more memorable, but also pleasurable, thus transgressing the traditional distinction between the educational and entertaining, and even between high and low culture, both of which are characteristic of lifestyle discourse. Wine can now be described much as a young lover, desirable and special: 'young', 'perky', 'precocious', 'Peardrop', on the other hand, for many evokes the notions of childhood, as this reference to one of Britain's popular candies is used to describe wine's sweet, pear-like taste, despite being, at the same time, a technical tasting term.

Conclusion

The interdiscursive relations of these texts with advertising discourse and conversational style construct wine as the everyday choice of drink for the ordinary person, even if there is a parallel tendency to preserve the distinction commonly associated with wine in Britain. In the time of greater reliance on social media than on newspapers, newspaper expert advice is increasingly competing with non-expert lifestyle advice and even the advice of amateur wine reviewers and influencers. This trend is not unique to wine advice, however, as the traditional gate-keeping authority once given to experts (and newspapers) has been diminishing for decades (Hanke 1989). In this sense, MacQuitty's lifestyle wine writing described in this chapter is an illustration of this trend, as her wine columns, heavy in metaphor, intertwine descriptions of wine taste with the expert-backed 'winespeak' language that masterfully merge the need for an expert with an accessible format of wine advice.

With the global reach of the media, the question of wine distinction and its representation – including its symbolism – is no longer obvious, due to its cultural specificity, and new forms of distinction like exoticism take precedence (Naccarato and LeBesco 2012). Thus, the examination of *The Saturday Times* and MacQuitty's columns provides us with a microcosm to examine wine media discourse and its transformations. This analysis may provide a foundation for exploring the forms evolving from the wine column, and it may be that while competing with social media, these traditional genres will not entirely disappear but will acquire new meanings and practices associated with the possible prestige of newspapers that may enable, unlike the fast social media, the potential for a return to 'slow reading'.

Acknowledgements

The authors thank the editor, Jacqueline Dutton, for all her advice, help and patience in the process of writing this article.

References

Anderson, K. and Wittwer, G. (2017) "U.K. and Global Wine Markets by 2025, and Implications of Brexit," *Journal of Wine Economics* 12(3), 221–251.

Bell, D. and Hollows, J. (2005) "Making Sense of Ordinary Lifestyles," in D. Bell and J. Hollows (eds), *Ordinary Lifestyles: Popular Media, Consumption and Taste*, Maidenhead: Open University Press.
Bender, J. (2008) "What the Wine Critics Tell Us," in F. Allhof (ed), *Wine and Philosophy: A Symposium on Thinking and Drinking*, Malden: Blackwell, 125–136.
Bourdieu, P. (1984) *Distinction: A Social Critique of the Judgement of Taste*, London: Routledge & Kegan Paul.
Caballero, R. (2007) "Manner-of-Motion Verbs in Wine Description," *Journal of Pragmatics* 39, 2095–2114.
Caballero, R. and Suarez-Toste, E. (2008) "Translating the Senses: Teaching the Metaphors in Winespeak," in F. Boers and S. Lindstromberg (eds), *Cognitive Linguistic Approaches to Teaching Vocabulary and Phraseology: Volume 6 of Applications of Cognitive Linguistics*, Berlin: Mouton de Gruyter.
Creed, A. (2014) "Wine and Metaphor: Cross-Cultural [dis]Harmony," in W. Midgley, K. Trimmer and A. Davies (eds), *Metaphors for, in and of Education Research*, Newcastle upon Tyne: Cambridge Scholars Publishing, 10–25.
Fairclough, N. (1992) *Discourse and Social Change*, Oxford: Blackwell.
Fairclough, N. and Wodak, R. (1997) "Critical Discourse Analysis," in T. van Dijk (ed), *Discourse Studies. A Multidisciplinary Introduction 2*, London: Sage, 258–284.
Fiddes, N. (1991) *Meat, a Natural Symbol [Electronic Resource]*, New York: Routledge.
Fitzmaurice, C. (2017) "How Rosé Became High Class: Categorical Divestment and Evaluation," *Poetics* 61, 1–13.
Friberg, R., Paterson, R.W. and Richardson, A.W. (2011) "Why Is There a Home Bias? A Case Study of Wine," *Journal of Wine Economics* 6(1), 37–66.
Gluck, M. (2003) "Wine Language: Useful Idiom or Idiot Speak" in J. Aitchison and D. Lewis (eds), *New Media Language*, London: Routledge.
Hanke, R. (1989) "Mass Media and Lifestyle Differentiation: An Analysis of the Public Discourse About Food," *Communication* 11, 221–238.
Howland, P. (2013) "Distinction by Proxy. The Democratization of Fine Wine," *Journal of Sociology* 49, 325–340.
Johnston, J. and Baumann, S. (2010) *Foodies: Democracy and Distinction in the Gourmet Foodscape*, New York: Routledge.
Korsemeyer, C. (2007) "Introduction. Perspectives on Taste", in C. Korsemeyer (ed), *The Taste Culture Reader. Experiencing Food and Drink*, Oxford, New York: Berg.
Leech, G. (1966) *English in Advertising, A Linguistic Study of Advertising in Great Britain*, London: Longman.
Leech, G. (1969) *English in Advertising*, London: Longman.
Lehrer, A. (2009) *Wine and Conversation*, Bloomington: Indiana University Press.
Lewis, T. (2008) *Smart Living: Lifestyle Media and Popular Expertise*, New York: Peter Lang.
Ludington, C. (2013) *The Politics of Wine in Britain. A New Cultural History*, London: Palgrave MacMillan.
Machin, D. and Van Leeuwen, T. (2003) "Global Schemas and Local Discourses in Cosmopolitan," *Journal of Sociolinguistics* 7, 493–512.
Machin, D. and Van Leeuwen, T. (2005) "Language Style and Lifestyle: The Case of a Global Magazine," *Media, Culture and Society* 27(4), 577–600.
Myers, G. (2004) *Words in Ads*, London: Edward Arnold.
Naccarato, P. and LeBesco, K. (2012) *Culinary Capital*, London: Berg.
Reichl, R. (2007) *History in a Glass: Sixty Years of Wine Writing from Gourmet Magazine*, New York: The Modern Library.
Shapin, S. (2009) "Against the Pussyfoots," *London Review of Books* 31(7), 32–33.
Shapin, S. (2012) "The Tastes of Wine: Towards a Cultural History," *Rivista di estetica*, 49–94.
Silverstein, R. (2004) "Cultural Concepts and the Language-Culture Nexus," *Current Anthropology* 45, 621–652.
Smith Maguire, J. (2016) "Introduction: Looking at Food Practices and Taste across the Class Divide," *Food, Culture and Society* 19, 11–18.
Smith Maguire, J. (2018) "The Taste for the Particular: A Logic of Discernment in an Age of Omnivorousness," *Journal of Consumer Culture* 18(1), 3–20.
Smith Maguire, J. and Matthews, J. (2012) "Are We All Cultural Intermediaries Now? An Introduction to Cultural Intermediaries in Context," *European Journal of Cultural Studies* 15(5), 551–562.
Tominc, A. (2017) *The Discursive Construction of Class and Lifestyle. Celebrity Cookbooks in Post-Socialist Slovenia*, Amsterdam: John Benjamins.
UC Davis Library. (2020) "The Power of the Written Word," www.library.ucdavis.edu/alumni-friends/inspiring-stories/the-power-of-the-written-word/, accessed 02 August 2021.
Van Leeuwen, T. (2005) *Introducing Social Semiotics*, London: Routledge.
Welch, N. and Tominc, A. (2021) "Is Wine Consumption in Britain Democratizing? Communicating Class and Taste Through the *Saturday Times* Wine Column (1982–2017)," *Social Semiotics* 31(4), 652–669, https://doi.org.10.1080/10350330.2019.1681069

23
SOME PRACTICAL ECONOMICS OF SELLING WINE AS A CULTURAL GOOD

Ben Christiansen and Denton Marks

Introduction

This is a shop-level study of the monopolistically competitive retail wine market in a large Midwestern city north of Chicago (it was the 39th largest US Metropolitan Statistical Area out of 384 identified in 2019). Especially with the emergence of online selling, wine retailing is intensely competitive wherever governments allow that. Before online competition emerged, competitive differentiation often reflected location advantages from government regulation at various levels that either prohibited or taxed interjurisdictional sales.

Our focus is another type of differentiation. Wine vendors' goals vary. Perhaps most seek only a good living and have chosen alcohol sales because of enjoyment of the product and the reliability of the market, however competitive. Others have a more studied interest in wine and pursue that, with livelihood being a constraint and a by-product of that pursuit, not unlike the motivation to produce wine with profitability a secondary consideration (e.g. Morton and Podolny 2002). Such vendors ask how much to offer what is profitable and how much to offer what is important.

While popularity and profit are important, we distinguish here a special role for cultural goods (e.g. Throsby 1994, 2001), discussed in Chapter 3 in this volume (Marks 2022). In economists' taxonomy of goods, the distinguishing characteristics of cultural goods (CG), following Throsby, include (1) widely acknowledged creativity in production, (2) possession of intellectual property – an embedded identity – in the conceptual if not the legal sense and (3) symbolic meaning. CG buyers will have a developed and evolving taste from a history of consumption. CG sellers follow a persistent motivation to contribute significantly to culture along with their desire to make a living. Such goods embody cultural value – often difficult to quantify – usually in addition to market value.

Fine art, music, dance, film and architecture can provide familiar examples of cultural goods; expanding the category provokes controversy because defining it rigorously is difficult. To focus this discussion, we shall follow Marks's analysis in Chapter 3 and assume that some wine – perhaps at least 'fine wine' – is a cultural good.

Accepting that, the vendors of interest might be 'cultural intermediaries' as described in the cultural studies and related marketing literature (e.g. Smith Maguire 2010; Smith Maguire and Matthews 2012, 2014; Baker, 2012). The term applies to numerous commercial roles, even within wine markets – 'wine promoters, including wine makers, publicists, retailers, distributors, and writers' (Smith Maguire 2010: 2): our focus is retailers, or vendors.

These are neither CG producers nor simply middlemen. Smith Maguire (2010) describes the role of the intermediary:

> They produce symbolic added-value by disseminating, and converting others to their belief in consumer goods and services as legitimate markers of social status and repositories of cultural value. It is this proselytizing aspect of their work that leads Bourdieu (1984: 365) and others to suggest that cultural intermediaries act as the 'transmission belt' of a new consumer morality.
>
> *(2010: 3)*

They convene producers and consumers, especially when that connection is strained or difficult due to distances that are geographic, linguistic and perhaps economic (expensive product, poor consumer) (e.g. Bourdieu 1986; Smith Maguire and Matthews 2014). Just as we cannot draw bright lines between cultural and non-cultural goods or specify degrees of 'culturalness' (like public goods' degrees of publicness), we cannot identify them rigorously. At most, we can document a differentiated way of doing business consistent with the concept.

Suggesting a special place for some wine vendors is consistent with a level of respect that has been granted them historically. For example, in their chapter on Irish wine culture in this volume (Chapter 17), Ludington and Harding (2022) explain that the landed Irish class of the nineteenth century generally disapproved of the merchant class, with the exception of wine merchants who 'benefited socially from both their worldliness and the exalted status of their goods'. They depended on selling to 'the peerage and rich gentry' – targeted marketing which was and continues to be, in its modern form, important to the survival of the business, as we shall see.

By describing how this vendor entered and has developed the business, we will identify markers of cultural intermediation. We begin with the business background and then analyse how the business has evolved, some of its distinctive core activities and practices, its current place in its market and a brief economic analysis of its market behaviour. We close with some highlights of the discussion and directions for further research.

Background

Ben Christiansen's background is academic. Both his parents and maternal grandparents held doctorates which grounded their careers. Unlike almost all his peers, he attended a small, private liberal arts college far from home and specialised in nonvocational subjects (sociology, Chinese). He was drawn to an academic career – though his interests were less scholarly and more managerial – which may help explain why wine's cultural significance attracted him.

He recognised early both his sales skills and his academic-like desire for independence and anticipated a career in university fundraising. After completing a graduate degree in educational administration, his early venture there was unsatisfying. Inspiration for a different career emerged from his parents' love of entertaining. He earned a two-year culinary degree from a prominent Chicago programme and then worked in several prominent Chicago and Milwaukee restaurants.

Hospitality work's long, odd hours were hard on his growing family, so he became the family homemaker in 2005, researching his next career move in the midst of child rearing and freelance cooking. With interests and training in food and hospitality and considerable study of prominent wine writers (especially Hugh Johnson), he opened Waterford Wine Company (later Waterford Wine and Spirits (WWS)) in late 2005 in an old (1893) Milwaukee residence (zoned commercial) in Milwaukee's bustling Eastside. While charming and well located, the retail space was small and lacked parking. Locating there reflected good instincts for location and atmosphere but naivete about a viable long-term site.

When asked about iconic wine shops that guided his vision, Ben cites none of the world's historic or highly respected shops. Instead, he cites a short-lived shop from his hometown – Des Moines, Iowa, the state's capital and another large Midwestern city:

> I loved the experience: the owner greeted customers with wine. He'd ask your interests or the occasion and then recommend wines. Bottles were laid down and identifiable only if handed to you – a 'hand sell' environment. Service was selective and focused on repeat clients and big spenders. Others were on their own.
>
> I loved the environment: making perfect matches and bringing a sense of *joie de vie*. My parents loved shopping there. The business seemed effortless – offering a product you love for people whose company you really enjoy. What can be better?

'Hand selling' was compelling, flowing naturally from the owner's love of wine.

More generally, a business fabric from the threads of food, wine, entertaining and conviviality was emerging.

Why special?

What is unusual about a beverage shop (later two) like WWS in a large Midwestern US city? Unlike most wine vendors in the world's traditional wine regions – primarily Europe – US vendors are less tied to regional products and traditions. Relative to US markets, important US wine regions are isolated (primarily the West Coast). In traditional wine regions, vendors specialise in local products. Familiarity with the world's wines falls rapidly as one ventures farther from the local vineyards. Traditionally, French vendors know little about Italy, Italians know little about Germany, and so forth. Local customers have grown up with local products and the 'wine culture' surrounding them, so, relative to many US vendors, their focus is more on discovering exciting new products and navigating the maze of local wines than on providing wine education.

In contrast, most dedicated US wine vendors must know wines from distant countries with markedly different wine cultures, traditions and rules. Imports into the US have traditionally been a larger share of domestic consumption than for many major markets – three to four times higher than Italy or Spain and 50% or more higher than France (Anderson and Pinilla 2017: Table 55).

Success requires delivering a message that is relatively – often literally – foreign to local consumers. The challenge is even greater with Wisconsin's history of German and Scandinavian working-class immigration. Most Wisconsin residents come from German roots with a culture drawn more to beer and a few wines, not iconic European wine regions. Wisconsin – especially Milwaukee – was the home of major US brewers from German immigrant families like Miller, Pabst and Schlitz (Magee 2014).

Beer and spirits dominate US beverage sales. While proprietary and scarce, we have beverage sales data for a recent six-month period (mid-February–mid-August 2020). Total US alcohol sales of $36.3 billion consisted of 57% beer, 19% spirits and 24% wine. We obtained spirits and wine figures for Wisconsin with market shares of 22.4% and 20.6%, respectively, if we impute the national 57% beer share to the state. Coming from the beginning of the COVID pandemic, these sales may be atypical: beverage sales likely shifted away from on premise, and perhaps (1) overall sales have changed, and (2) market shares by category have shifted. Unfortunately, it is too early to know.

Our beer imputation likely underestimates Wisconsin's recent beer sales and market share as well as total beverage sales. In 2018, average US beer consumption per adult was 99.2 litres, but Wisconsin consumption was 28.2% higher (127.2 litres), sixth highest among the states (USA Today 2019). By contrast, average US per capita wine consumption (litres of ethanol) in 2018 was 1.67 and 1.48 in Wisconsin – 11.4% below average and 26th among the states. Haughwout and Slater (2017) provide older (through 2015) but more comprehensive data that are generally consistent with this, reporting that Wisconsin's 2015 per capita consumption of spirits was 48.1% above the national average. While crude, these estimates indicate the categories' relative importance in the state. Thus, among the three major categories, wine is the least popular in Wisconsin, and, unlike the other two for which per capita consumption is far above the US average, wine consumption is below.

Metropolitan Milwaukee is the state's largest urban area with 1.6 million residents, 27.6% of the state's residents (2019). It is about 145 kilometres from downtown Chicago, a major wine market and the third largest US metropolitan area (approximately 10 million) (2019). While metropolitan area sales data are even scarcer than state data, we expect that the city's purchasing patterns differ from the state's, but we do not know how.

While limited, our best data on the city's purchasing patterns come from two of WWS's major competitors. One (Company A) is a large, locally owned vendor begun as a 'liquor store' in 1961. The other is a national chain (Company B), which arrived recently but has built three large stores in the city. Both competitors appear on winesearcher.com, which calculates vendor 'price lists by region', so we can compare their product offerings with WWS's.

Table 23.1 presents data on each vendor's advertised choices. The round numbers for Companies A and B seem overblown; their websites confirm that consistently only for wine. A's website lists 1,176 beers, 2,201 spirits and 2,576 wines. These numbers may be inflated (e.g. different formats of one product), and stockouts are unknown, but the selection is still considerable.

Table 23.1 Waterford (WWS) and two major competitors

	Waterford	Company A	Company B
Number of beers★	0	1,000	2,500
Number of spirits★	176	2,000	3,000
Number of wines★	2,123	8,000	8,000
Share of **all products** by region (%)★★:			
US	33	44	47
France	27	9	14
Italy	24	8	8
Spain	5	4	3
Germany	★★★	2	2
Portugal	★★★	2	★★★
Argentina	1	★★★	2
Australia	2	2	2
Chile	1	★★★	1
South Africa	1	★★★	★★★
Scotland	2	7	4
Mexico	★★★	4	4
Ireland	★★★	3	1
Canada	★★★	2	2
England	★★★	2	★★★
Puerto Rico	★★★	1	★★★
Sweden	★★★	1	★★★
Other	4	11	10

★ = from website
★★ = from wine-searcher.com
★★★ = 0 or Other

Company B's website lists 1,675 beers and related beverages (e.g. ciders); 3,959 spirits; and 4,916 standard-size (750 ml.) wines. Table 23.1 overstates its beer and wine but far understates spirits.

From Table 23.1 and the preceding discussion, we see:

- Relative to its competition, WWS's clear focus is wine in a market favouring beer and spirits relative to national patterns.
- WWS could likely increase profits by offering full lines of beer and spirits like its competitors, but that is inconsistent with its identity. Without being rigid about it, its success in the products it sells may depend on what it decides not to sell.
- WWS is smaller than its major local competitors.
- Measuring domestic (US) wine listings is difficult in Table 23.1 (e.g. "products by region" include many domestic beers, spirits), but WWS's relative strength is Old World wines.
- WWS's sales profile is closer to an online specialty wine site than a traditional beverage shop.

Aside from deciding not to sell broad categories of other beverages, WWS also exhibits its selectivity through a variety of mailing lists (e.g., "Major", "Insider", "Terroir"). For example, it does not promote all its products to all its customers. While its "Major" promotions are broadcast widely, it limits its "Insider" and "Terroir" promotions to select customers and then offers other more limited products only through personal communication.

A closer look at WWS's sales history reinforces this. We have sales data starting with its first full year of operation (2006). Considering Old World wine sales (primarily France, Italy, Spain and Germany) as a share of total wine sales is more illuminating than simply as a share of gross sales. Figure 23.1 shows that share's upward trend that started at 49.8% and has exceeded 70%, which is approximately the current share. While not smooth growth – especially because of some large, one-time New World sales during 2010–11 – the trend line reflects an implied annual *share growth rate* of 1.2%, which, along with its opening share of 50% of sales, is an indication of WWS's commitment to the appreciation of Old World wines.

Finally, annual data on the average price (after 5.6% sales tax) of each bottle sold from 2006 through 2019 indicate a range of approximately $27 (2006) to $36 (2011), with a median of $30.85. While bottle sizes vary and a few sales are spirits, almost all sales are standard 750 ml. wines. While

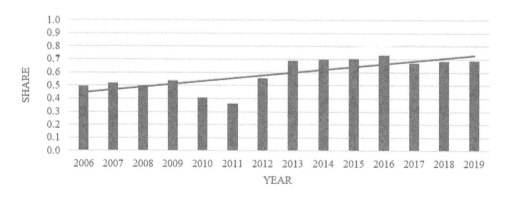

Figure 23.1 Waterford Wine and Spirits sales of Old World wines as a share of total wine sales

no industry standard classification of wine by price segment exists, the marketing data firm Information Resources, Inc. (IRI) uses the following current classifications (IRI 2020):

1. Value <$5.99
2. Popular = $6.00–8.99
3. Premium = $9.00–12.99
4. Super Premium = $13.00–19.99
5. Ultra Premium = $20.00–34.99
6. Luxury = $$35–69.99
7. Super Luxury = $70.00+

Even assuming constant prices, Waterford's average sale has consistently been Ultra Premium. According to the financial news/opinion company 24/7 Wall St., LLC, the current (Feb 2020) average prices of wines bought in Wisconsin (before sales tax of under 6% statewide) are $11.99 for white, $15.99 for red and $11.99 for rosé (no data for sparkling), with an overall average of $13.32. Clearly, WWS has always sold relatively expensive wine.

Waterford's lifetime sales describe a shop that, within its market, focuses on relatively unusual and expensive wines. Its strength has been selling Old World wines in a market where that cultural presence is unusual. It could likely grow more and be more profitable if it expanded into popular beers and spirits and 'commodity' wines – like its major competitors – but that would be inconsistent with Ben's interests, expertise and goals. Preserving that focus is important to a significant share of the customer base: Ben offers what he knows.

We consider now some contributors to these outcomes.

Distributors

Wine distributors (wholesalers) are pivotal in US retailing. The US market is unique in the world with 50 state-controlled alcohol markets subject to underlying federal interstate regulations as a legacy of US Prohibition (1920–33). With very few exceptions (e.g. state retail monopolies such as New Hampshire and Pennsylvania and states where vendors import directly (California)), vendors must purchase from state-licensed distributors within a so-called 'three-tier system' (vendor-distributor-(perhaps) importer).

Because it outlaws transactions that might otherwise occur (e.g., vendors dealing directly with the world's producers) and artificially limits choice, the system creates retail inefficiency. However, in an unregulated market, distributors could still increase market efficiency by exploiting economies of scale in search and distribution for both wineries and vendors, just as most consumers usually prefer dealing with vendors rather than directly with wineries.

WWS benefits significantly from its distributors, which offer global selection in manageable quantities – overall, easier than buying winery direct. In its early years, distributors taught Ben important competitive lessons because they stood to benefit from his studied interest in broadening the varieties of wines available locally and encouraging more serious wine appreciation in the market.

Inefficiency arises because vendors must buy only from their own state's distributors: choices are more restricted, and the (wholesale) prices they pay are higher than if they could buy anywhere. As with consumers, the ideal would be unlimited choice in what and how they buy.

A complication with distributors is that relationships develop over time with more and less favoured distributors (and similarly for more and less favoured vendors): varieties of non-price rationing occur. Prices are not always market clearing, so distributors may favour some vendors for products in short supply, and vendors may pay 'too much' for some product that is not selling well to compensate for past favourable treatment. This practical complication to the simple model of demand and supply is worth highlighting because it pervades wine distributor-vendor transactions. The importance of friendly and supportive relationships is difficult to model formally and test empirically and is likely important in other parts of the market (e.g. between producers and wine experts).

Learning and expanding

An early WWS turning point (2006) was guidance from a distributor drawn to Ben's plans who helped craft a more sustainable business model from Ben's interest in the distributor's finer wines. Working together, they helped WWS popularise wine styles new to the local market (e.g. Old World rosé).

Another turning point was the 2008–09 financial crisis. Luxury markets contracted significantly as wealth shrank: at its worst, stocks and housing values together fell 17.3%. Many of WWS's sales were to collectors ('20% of our customers, 80% of our business') whose demand shrank as they drew from their cellars or other collectors' liquidations. While remaining eclectic, WWS broadened its range of wines to broaden its customer base.

A serendipitous development in 2011 was a group of loyal customers' offer to develop WWS's online marketing. 'Very substantial growth' resulted (cf. Figure 23.1). Ben's knowledge-based motivation attracted volunteer outside help. In that way, work for or with WWS resembled winery work – often fledgling – attracting those drawn to wine culture.

WWS could afford expansion in 2017 after 12 years' experience with the area's demographics and consumption patterns and competitors' locations and behaviour. The flagship served the gentrifying city centre (downtown) market, but a traditionally agricultural area west of the city was attracting executives seeking large residences near local lakes, golf courses and private clubs. WWS expanded to that suburb.

Ben's experience with the two stores (city centre (CC), suburban (S)) over 15 years – with changing regulations, volatile business cycles and market transformations like widespread online shopping – has suggested to him three broad categories of beverage vendors that fall along a spectrum from passive to active interest in wine as a cultural good and how they view their customers:

1. Finders (F): This is the most passive intellectually. The core business is products that 'sell themselves': customers will 'find' these vendors. Selling from this position (e.g. government monopolies, privileged dealing arising from strong loyalties from customers and/or suppliers) requires protection from competition or perhaps extraordinary service and customer coddling since competitors selling the same products threaten survival.
2. Commodifiers (C): This category of vendors sells more actively and opportunistically, relying primarily on volume and traditional and widely used marketing techniques. Conspicuous examples are vendors known for deals, aggressive promotions, emphasis on popular and mass market brands and reliance on 'easy' selling anchors like expert ratings.
3. Developers (D): This category is the most active in educating customers, hoping to broaden and deepen their wine appreciation so that the buyer-seller relationship becomes more culturally symbiotic. The seller may have more market information, but the buyer's enthusiasm and satisfaction – not simply their purchasing power – inspire the relationship. This is closest to WWS.

Vendors tend towards one of these three types. Different types of consumers gravitate towards them, though the experience of any vendor usually blends these three approaches: F, C and D.

In addition, Ben perceives five customer segments and estimates, where possible, his segment shares from the two shops' aforementioned segment-targeted mailing lists – the larger city (CC) lists begun in 2006 (9,741 addresses) and the smaller suburban (S) lists (495 addresses) begun in 2018:

1. *Analysts* are savvy and intellectually engaged (market shares: CC = 10.9%; S = 14.7%). They do homework, form their own choices and disregard recommendations from unfamiliar sales staff.

They follow the retail market closely and know buying options. Good value (e.g. 'quality-price ratio' (QPR)) based on published expert opinion and ratings is a priority. This group buys at WWS in response to both the C and D retailing models, and WWS welcomes its considerable purchasing power.

2. *Everyday devotees* enjoy wine daily, perhaps sharing a mealtime bottle, but are not particularly curious. They like variety and thoughtful pairing but have some favourite labels and a price ceiling. They like WWS's unusually wide variety of value wines and are a large, reliable, relatively low sales-per-capita group that follows C and D retailing.
3. *Executives* have wine industry connections and knowledge but perhaps limited intellectual interest (market shares: CC = 3.1%; S = 1.0%). They expect the owner's attention and exclusive access and can command that; recall Ben's observations about the owner of his hometown wine shop. They drink with peers whose preferences influence their purchases, often towards 'trophies': they fit best with F retailers. Their financial impact can be far reaching. WWS's suburban shop's recent opening and some management turnover may have affected this segment's growth there.
4. *Explorers* are the most naturally curious, adventurous and intellectually engaged (CC = 2.9%; S = 4.8%), often starting naïve but learning rapidly from tastings/classes and then outgrowing them. Good wine becomes art to them, and they can afford WWS's Ultra Premium average price. They reflect best WWS's role as a Developer.
5. *Regulars* – WWS 'groupies' – like to socialise (and learn something) through tastings and buy primarily for social events. They visit for conversation and fun as well as shopping. They seek a wine-oriented lifestyle with a carefree view of what and how much they drink. This segment developed rapidly at the suburban store. Numbers at the two shops are similar; thus, they are a considerably larger share of the smaller suburban market. Its wine bar may matter here as one of the few such local gathering places.

These numbers indicate that WWS considers over 80% of its mailing lists Everyday or Regular customers – a source of steady sales but not the passionate and invested followers that WWS seeks to develop. Executives are critical to profitability, but Explorers are closest to WWS's vision, and they are numerous enough in the city (almost 300) to represent a clear following. That may emerge with time in the suburbs.

One sees parallels here with the six identified consumer categories in Constellation Brands' important study of wine consumers – for example, its 'Image Seekers' (Regulars and perhaps Executives), 'Enthusiasts' (Explorers), and 'Everyday loyals' (Everyday devotees) (https://winesvinesanalytics.com/news/article/134707/Study-Identifies-Wine-Consumer-Personalities).

Just as perceiving 'students as customers' has received considerable attention in higher education research, the WWS experience suggests that perceiving 'customers as students' could be as thought provoking, using established student typologies (Hu and McCormick 2012). Some have more curiosity – perhaps a reflection of greater confidence – and want to ask questions and dig deeper into wine differences and the reasons for them (e.g. effects of vintage). They may have a greater sense of adventure, interest in exploring and economic security. They are more likely to appreciate differences than to avoid them. These are Explorers.

Others (Everyday devotees?) prefer to avoid complications and uncertainty and tend to purchase within a narrow range of products. Vintage differences may represent most of the variety they experience. Still others (Analysts?) may be shopping more for experts than for wine (Ashenfelter and Jones 2013) by conditioning purchases largely or entirely on expert ratings the way students choose courses or specialties based on employment considerations rather than innate interest. Finally, social life is the priority for some, and education simply provides the environment (Regulars?).

Cultivating wine culture: sharing the ongoing search

One hopes that vendors know their products, but generally customers cannot tell. In contrast, Ben's daily wine journey appears on the cellartracker.com website (www.cellartracker.com). Cellartracker.com (CT) allows users to post their tasting notes (TN) as a public record of tasting experience. When vendors post, this resembles Smith-Maguire's aforementioned 'disseminating' by cultural intermediaries.

Ben is among CT's most prolific contributors: over 37,000 notes posted since 2008 (as of August 2020) on over 25,000 bottlings, many of which are multiple vintages of the same wine. About one-third of his TNs are notes on second and subsequent tastings. Among four wines recently tasted, he has posted about five TNs per wine in the last three years. He has averaged about 3,000 posts annually; in recent years, that has risen to between 4,000 and 4,500. He is currently the most frequent CT contributor, with over 58 million global views of his TNs. This in itself attests to the breadth of his experience, curiosity and adventurous business style.

He does not award points and stopped using them long ago: 'Why dumb it down? There is no shortcut to understanding wine' as a cultural good. He tries to avoid using expert ratings in his promotions, preferring instead to say enough about the wine and its origins to compel purchase, but he may provide one or more of a wine's highest ratings as 'critical acclaim' for Analysts. Importantly, he also admits in his TNs that he is having 'a bad tasting day' or 'that's just me', an honest revelation about intrapersonal variation never uttered by popular experts.

Table 23.2 provides the distribution of Ben's TNs since 2008, indicating the number of countries of origin tasted and the share of TNs from his most popular countries – France, Italy and the US, the source recently of about 80% of his TNs. These postings do not fully document Ben's wine experience but represent an unusually comprehensive look at his experience, opinions and interest in sharing. It is probably the most comprehensive collection of publicly available vendor TNs and, more generally, unusual evidence of a vendor's experience with his own products.

Cultivating wine culture: welcoming WWS staff and investors

Morton and Podolny (2002) made a winery-oriented contribution to the vast literature on work and its meaning, some of which explores culture's role (e.g. Rosso *et al.* 2010: 105). It is an early study among others (e.g. Charters *et al.* 2016) that highlight non-financial motivations for owning a

Table 23.2 Tasting Note History as of August 2020 (Source: cellartracker.com)

Year (% of total)	Tasting Notes	Countries	Top 3 (%FR/IT/US)
2020 (to date) (6.6)	2437	22	75.0
2019 (12.0)	4410	27	79.6
2018 (11.7)	4284	21	79.5
2017 (10.7)	3879	22	79.2
2016 (9.8)	3594	19	76.3
2015 (7.7)	2837	18	80.6
2014 (8.3)	3035	19	76.3
2013 (5.3)	1945	21	79.5
2012 (5.6)	2047	17	81.2
2011 (6.9)	2534	17	77.7
2010 (6.9)	2542	15	76.1
2009 (5.9)	2151	17	68.6
2008 (2.8)	1025	14	70.6
Total TNs (100%)	36721		

winery. They study California, which, with 4,138 wineries, has by far the largest state wine industry in the US (www.americanwineryguide.com/regions/states/). Wisconsin residents attracted to the industry are less likely to find opportunities in one of its 81 wineries (*Ibid.*), most of which either import their grapes or focus on more obscure cold-climate varieties.

To our knowledge, no one has studied this phenomenon, but WWS – as a cultural intermediary – may represent the next best opportunity for urban residents to work in the industry in a state with few wineries.

First, numerous 'volunteers' work for WWS. The downtown shop has 2.5 regular employees (because some are part time) and 27 others who spend a variety of hours helping at the shop: filling orders, restocking, helping customers, cleaning, moving rubbish to the bins outside and performing other tasks. The suburban store has one regular employee and about 20 volunteers. Records are unavailable, but dozens more have passed through WWS as an opportunity to participate 'inside the industry' and sometimes work in the industry. Most volunteers have other employment but help at WWS because they enjoy wine, learning about wine and having inside access to the wine market's supply side, albeit only at the retail level.

Related to this, Fattorini (1994: 5) has written critically about '[invariably affluent] professional consumers' in the UK whose apparent emulation of members of the trade – for example, prolonged technical education and certification, engaging in wine tasting (vs. drinking) – appears to reflect a middle-class desire to affiliate with the 'romantic and glamorous' (p. 7) trade without actually entering it. The WWS volunteers may share some of that motivation, but the similarity is not strong. First, while they all want greater understanding of and experience with wine, most of the volunteers are not affluent; they are typically retirees, current university students or recent graduates or young professionals. Also, their time in the shops is spent on unskilled or semi-skilled tasks such as stocking, order filling and cleaning; their reward is access to informal wine tastings and, in most cases, discounts on purchases. Finally, some of the volunteers have gone on to full-time work in the trade based on their experience and motivation; few, if any, pursue formal wine education.

As another form of participation, investing can also have varied motives as suggested by movements such as socially responsible investing, crowdfunding and microfinance. Investors may derive both utility and financial rewards from the allocation of their capital; this may be particularly true for family-owned businesses, a point emphasised by Morton and Podolny.

WWS has selectively offered investing as another way to participate in the industry. While Ben is the primary investor, he has some backers – almost all major customers originally – with the most significant ones joining as he planned the suburban shop. They are silent partners who earn no current return on their investments: earnings are reinvested in WWS so their returns would appear as capital gains if WWS was ever sold or Ben bought their shares. Plans to open a third, more distant store may follow a similar path.

Along with providing a working environment where aficionados can participate in an active retail shop, WWS has investors who have a similar interest in participating in the industry without seeking maximum financial returns on investment. We know of no other shop that offers these opportunities.

More practical economics

The foregoing describes WWS's efforts to differentiate its product as a monopolistically competitive strategy. Other features of the business are unconventional, such as widespread use of volunteer labour and investors with motives other than maximising returns. What else can we observe about the economics of WWS?

By its nature and available supply, relatively more of WWS's inventory is difficult to find elsewhere – certainly in the local off-premise market. Much of its chosen product line – by everyday standards, relatively expensive Old World wines – is available at some distance from its shops (e.g. Chicago) or online, if at all. WWS generally follows a local (and perhaps more widespread) pricing rule of thumb: 33% markup over gross cost. Assuming he likes a wine or expects that his customers will, using this rule and his experience with what his market will pay governs his buying. He does not use the language of substitutes and complements (products that may be purchased, respectively, instead of or along with those he offers), but instinctively, he watches the prices of substitutes by tracking competitors ads and others selling his products on winesearcher.com. He seems less concerned about close substitutes – for example, different comparable quality chateaux from a given Bordeaux vintage – and imputes considerable strict brand loyalty to his customers, particularly the more affluent. He does not perceive much willingness to substitute among his regular customers (e.g. treating Super Tuscans and California Meritages as Bordeaux substitutes).

A recent example was the effect of a 25% US tariff on most European wines in effect since October 2019. This raised Ben's cost to replenish much of his Old World inventory by 25%, and he simply raised his retail prices accordingly (and thus increased his dollar, though not his percentage, margin). He noticed neither a drop in sales of his more expensive wines nor any evidence of increased demand for lower-priced non-European substitutes. He may have seen some reduced quantity demanded at his lower prices. Two caveats to concluding that this simply reflects inelastic demand are that (1) off-premise wine sales have risen considerably during the COVID pandemic (in part, because on-premise sales have plummeted), and this may fade and (2) we have only short-run evidence, and behavioural adjustments may take longer.

WWS also follows various pricing and timing 'rules'. Certain bottle prices 'never work' (e.g. $20.99). Implicit in this must be that the competitive price is around this number, so Ben chooses something a bit higher or lower perceived to be more acceptable (e.g. $19.99). Also, certain days and times are best or worst for releasing online promotions. Ben has adopted these rules of thumb from his 15 years of experience but has no other firm evidence to support them.

Ben gets wholesale volume discounts with many exceptions, often driven by the price elasticity of demand for the wine. Wholesale prices may be non-negotiable, but distributors have other ways of dealing such as adding extra bottles or something else (e.g. spirits, giftware) to his order – a form of bundling. Ben sometimes offers volume discounts – for example, 12-bottle case purchases – but it is difficult to tell how he decides this. It may depend on his inventory and how quickly he needs to move the wine for space or spoilage reasons (e.g. rosés).

The varieties of wholesale pricing strategies challenge simple economic predictions and make testing the economics of the industry difficult. For example, 'iconic' producers may punish any significant discounting. While one would think that vendors could charge whatever they wish, producers punish any 'tarnishing the reputation' of the brand or 'cheapening' it. For popular brands, this could hurt vendors' businesses – unless they have numerous alternatives (substitutes).

While Ben's current sales floors have over 3,000 square feet each, his original shop was about 20% of that, and he priced more aggressively to preserve floor space. He moves regular inventory more slowly now.

Another competitive pressure is that suburban store customers are more likely to be members of licensed private clubs that can buy wines wholesale – especially high-end domestic wines – and undercut Ben's markup. Also, customers order directly from domestic wineries, which can easily ship into the state. Both these alternatives threaten Ben's profit from domestic wines and thus limit what he offers.

Conclusion

We have presented wine retailing with ideas about wine and culture – cultural goods, cultural intermediaries – and discussed how this perspective broadens our approach to the economics of this market. We have highlighted various cultures – higher education, markets, consumers, motivations of employees and investors – in the process and discussed their relevance. Where feasible, we have tried to quantify evidence of the cultural process underway.

Our approach has been inductive, presenting the story of Waterford and extracting general observations from it:

- How appreciation of wine's cultural importance affects the buyer-seller relationship
- How wine's cultural importance can affect its merchants' behaviour
- How appreciation of wine's cultural importance affects employment and investment relationships
- The added complexity of transactions involving cultural goods

We hope that future studies pursue these themes. Of particular interest is better understanding of conditions that lead to the retail characteristics that have been highlighted here – for example:

- Identifying the range of products that fall within a legitimate category of cultural goods. What changes in that are consistent with stated goals (e.g. what if WWS began to offer artisanal beer or spirits?)? What changes would threaten them? Despite its licensed right to sell them, WWS avoids the range of products offered by competitors.
- Identifying owner behaviour that cultivates the market (e.g. customer access, widespread posting of owner experience with their own products (i.e. tasting notes)).
- What business characteristics attract volunteer labour and 'benevolent' investors? Is 'proximity to the owner' a significant consideration?

A related question from this study is how much WWS's sustainable business has depended on any magnetism from Ben's enthusiasm and persistence. Without promising or delivering remarkable financial returns, WWS has built some community beyond its customer base and has managed to attract a considerable number of adherents, including some who volunteer simply to have experience in the wine trade and some willing to back the enterprise financially.

The enduring challenge to studies like this as academic research is their value in getting us closer to truth. Nurturing an appreciation of wine after growing up in a Midwestern city – lovely but not steeped in wine culture – may be an especially valuable lesson here. Those who have lived for generations in a wine culture may be less likely to develop the excitement and sense of discovery that comes from arriving at wine from the outside. One may need that naivete to bring excitement and a sense of discovery to the field that carries with it an ability to excite others. Those who have never known otherwise may be less likely to feel that and share that and may take it for granted.

Acknowledgements and methodological note

We appreciate significant constructive criticism from an anonymous reviewer as well as co-editors Jennifer Smith Maguire and especially Steve Charters.

This study arose from the authors' shared interest in learning from each other about a research question that, to their knowledge, remains largely unstudied – selling wine as a cultural good. It has been an opportunity for academic-practitioner co-production of knowledge. Since neither the idea of wine as a cultural good nor how to sell it is established in the literature, the research was highly exploratory and therefore particularly appropriate for an edited volume. One author designed and implemented the analytic framework, researched the literature, made the methodological decisions and did almost all the writing; the other freely supplied the raw material for analysis. No request for data, history or other information was denied, and much of the description of business operations was verified on site since the 70 to 80 hours of discussion over 18 months occurred at the business, occasionally during business hours. We present one example of the object of study with no evidence that it is particularly representative of such vendors. We do not claim that either the summary findings or the suggested future research is comprehensive or has general application to wine retailing, though we hope and suspect that it does. Nevertheless, the study was rigorously pursued, the data are verifiable and the findings are informative and potentially useful beyond this setting.

References

Anderson, K. and Pinilla, V. (2017) *Annual Database of Global Wine Markets, 1835 to 2016*, Adelaide: Wine Economics Research Centre, University of Adelaide.

Ashenfelter, O. and Jones, G. (2013) "The Demand for Expert Opinion: Bordeaux Wine," *Journal of Wine Economics* 8(3), 285–293.

Baker, S. (2012) "Retailing Retro: Class, Cultural Capital, and the Material Practices of the (Re)Valuation of the Cultivation of Style," *European Journal of Cultural Studies* 15(5), 621–641.

Bourdieu, P. (1986) *Distinction: A Social Critique of the Judgement of Taste*, Cambridge, MA: Harvard University Press.

Charters, S., Walker, B. and Brown, A. (2016) "Passion Over Pragmatism: The Motivation of Australian Winery Owners," *International Journal of Entrepreneurship and Small Business* 29(4), 512–527.

Fattorini, J. (1994) "Professional Consumers: Themes in High Street Wine Marketing," *International Journal of Wine Marketing* 6(2), 5–13.

Haughwout, S. and Slater, M. (2017) *Surveillance Report #108: Apparent Per Capita Alcohol Consumption: National, State, and Regional Trends, 1977–2015*, Rockville, MD: NIAAA, Division of Epidemiology and Prevention Research, Alcohol Epidemiologic Data System, April, https://pubs.niaaa.nih.gov/publications/surveillance108/CONS15.pdf, accessed 10 June 2020.

Hu, S. and McCormick, A.C. (2012) "An Engagement-based Student Typology and Its Relationship to College Outcomes," *Research in Higher Education* 53(7), 738–754.

IRI (Information Resources, Inc.) Personal correspondence (email), 17 August 2020.

Ludington, C. and Harding, G. (2022) "Irish Wine Culture, c. 1700–Present: Making the Right Impression," this volume, chapter 17.

Magee, B. (2014) *Brewing in Milwaukee*. Images of America Series, Charleston, SC: Arcadia Publishing.

Marks, D. (2022) "Wine, Culture, and Economics," This volume, chapter 3.

Morton, F. and Podolny, S. (2002) "Love or Money: The Effects of Owner Motivation in the California Wine Industry," *Journal of Industrial Economics* 50(4), 431–456.

Rosso, B.D., Dekas, K.H. and Wrzesniewski, A. (2010) "On the Meaning of Work: A Theoretical Integration and Review," *Research in Organizational Behaviour* 30, 91–127.

Smith Maguire, J. (2010) "Provenance and the Liminality of Production and Consumption: The Case of Wine Promoters," *Marketing Theory* 10(3), 269–282.

Smith Maguire, J. and Matthews, J. (2012) "Are We All Cultural Intermediaries Now? An Introduction to Cultural Intermediaries in Context," *European Journal of Cultural Studies* 15(5), 551–562.

Smith Maguire, J. and Matthews, J. (2014) *The Cultural Intermediaries Reader*, London: Sage Publications.

Stebbins, S. (2019) "How Much Beer Does Your State Drink? In the Thirstiest, About 40 Gallons a Year Per Person," *USA Today*, 14 September.

Throsby, D. (1994) "The Production and Consumption of the Arts: A View of Cultural Economics," *Journal of Economic Literature* 32(1), 1–29.

Throsby, D. (2001) *Economics and Culture*, Cambridge: Cambridge University Press.

Websites

https://247wallst.com/special-report/2020/02/13/the-average-price-of-wine-in-every-state/, accessed 27 August 2020.

https://adelaide.figshare.com/articles/Annual_Database_of_Global_Wine_Markets_1835-2016/5696275, accessed 15 August 2020.

www.americanwineryguide.com/regions/wisconsin-wineries/, accessed 30 August 2020.

www.cellartracker.com/list.asp?Table=Notes&iUserOverride=53988#selected%3DW3005778_4_K5b1ba93f49fed7debdec7c053ced3d8a, accessed 29 August 2020.

www.nielsen.com/us/en/client-learning/retail-measurement-services/, accessed 26 August 2020.

www.statista.com/statistics/942205/wine-consumption-in-the-us-by-state/, accessed 27 August 2020.

www.usatoday.com/story/money/2019/09/14/how-much-beer-did-the-average-person-drink-in-every-state/40109241/, accessed 27 August 2020.

https://winesvinesanalytics.com/news/article/134707/Study-Identifies-Wine-Consumer-Personalities, accessed 22 February 2020.

24
CHAMPAGNE – A GLOBAL SYMBOL OF CONTEMPORARY CONSUMER CULTURE

Joonas Rokka

Introduction

Champagne, an effervescent wine assembled from the grapes of the Champagne region of France, stands as the quintessential device and symbol for celebration in today's consumer culture. Champagne's unprecedented success story is also an unlikely one, given that it was originally a simple wine grown in a rather mediocre winegrowing area. Centuries of avant-garde marketing practices were required to forge the distinct cultural and symbolic ingredients that we today associate with it – notably, myths about magic, luxury, nation, modernity and terroir (e.g. Rokka 2017; Rokka and Canniford 2016; Smith Maguire and Charters 2020).

Yet, as with all consumption symbols, champagne is subject to active and constant negotiation and meaning making by both marketers and consumers (du Gay *et al.* 1997; Arnould and Thompson 2005; Rokka 2021). Consumer culture, understood from a social-cultural point of view, is an evolving system of meanings shaped by ongoing doings and sayings of people (Hall 1997). Therefore, in order to analyse and understand any single cultural symbol – such as champagne – one should examine how it is articulated by different market actors. One needs to answer how it is represented, what social identities are associated with it and how it is produced and consumed (du Gay *et al.* 1997: 3). This chapter seeks do precisely this and answer these questions: How did champagne emerge as a global symbol of consumer culture, and how do consumers and brands negotiate and express this symbol today?

It is impossible to understand champagne as a symbol today without an insight into the deeply rooted semiotic connections and mythical resources that were woven together centuries ago. Cultural approaches in consumer research have long highlighted the influence of powerful mythologies and compelling narratives associated with consumption and identity construction (Levy 1981; Thompson 2004). Above all, myths have been used to explain the persisting resonance, appeal and iconicity of certain brands (Holt 2004). The myths associated with champagne have even shaped consumer culture in significant ways. For example, they evoked a new kind of celebratory consumption object and ritual that came to define 'modern' consumer subjectivities and collective imaginations linked with taste and class (Rokka 2017).

This chapter advances prior examinations further with an empirical analysis of the contemporary expressions of champagne found on social media (cf. Rokka and Canniford 2016). In doing so, the chapter highlights how champagne is negotiated by brands and consumers in social media postings on Instagram – a leading branding platform of today. Importantly, it is argued that social media makes visible and gives access to broader social-cultural discourses and sense makings that operate in our society – not only on social media. Compared with other social media platforms, Instagram's status-oriented interactions are compatible with the analysis of champagne (e.g. Marwick 2015; Humphreys 2016).

The findings stemming from this analysis can help us better understand how champagne is integrated and assembled in various contemporary consumption identities, desires and everyday representations. While some key symbolic elements from the past will continue to resonate in both consumer- and marketer-made images, new expressions and symbolic associations are also forged. The chapter concludes with a discussion about what we can learn from the unique success story of champagne – as well as about the tendencies for this ever-resonant consumption symbol to continue to scintillate our imaginations.

A brief history of champagne as a cultural symbol

Before moving on to our social media data analysis and findings, the next section maps out the principal elements through which champagne brands have been commonly assembled and constructed over time. The literature on champagne and luxury wine marketing in particular provides a necessary contextual backdrop that allows us to begin assessing the different elements that have made up champagne brands through time. Following an assemblage theory perspective – useful for analysing the constitution of an identity or a brand (Canniford and Bajde 2016; Parmentier and Fischer 2015; Rokka and Canniford 2016) – we define these to include material and expressive/symbolic elements.

Material elements

Any identity assemblage is composed of material constituents at a variety of scales (Roffe 2016). In considering these, we begin with the wider physical terrain that has always been associated with champagne. Viniculture in this geographical area was introduced by the Romans and developed by Benedictine monks experimenting with winemaking practices through the sixteenth century (Guy 2003). Since the 1930s, however, champagne has, by definition, been a product of the *Appellation d'Origine Contrôlée*, a strictly defined geographical designation.

However, further characterising the geographic bodies from which the identity of these wines is composed is the feature labelled terroir, the 'holistic combination in a vineyard environment of soil, climate, topography and the 'soul' of the wine producer' (Guy 2003: 2; see also Chapters 8 and 11). Terroir is often thought to be linked with the 'soul' or spirit of winegrowers who arduously labour on their land to produce the wine of Champagne. Beyond anything else, the identity link to this particular terroir is thought to hold enduring, natural qualities but also transcendent qualities that symbolise French culture and virtues (Guy 2003: 2; see also, Charters and Spielmann 2014; Charters et al. 2017).

As we move down from the broad levels of region and terroir into more localised parts of champagne's material assemblage, we cannot fail to recognise the particular champagne houses and their iconic cellars – the institutional sites of production that litter the region of Champagne. Further still, we can discern the easily recognised champagne bottle, the liquid characters of this bubbly wine and the unique glasses from which champagne is so closely associated as key defining elements of this specific brand and its identity (see Chapter 19). The wine is defined by its characteristic bubbles, perhaps the smallest manifestation of the overall material aspects of the champagne assemblage yet, ultimately, the most recognisable and expressive single element.

All these material elements are commonly emphasised and expressed in champagne's advertising images. It is also agreed that the intrinsic authenticity of these collections of objects cannot involve too many alterations or else their legitimacy may be endangered (Beverland 2005; Postrel 2003). It is of little surprise, then, turning to the visual expression of these material elements of the brand assemblage that, as Beverland (2005) emphasises, the place of origin is one of the key sources of the authentic identity and status of luxury brands.

Expressive elements

A second aspect of any identity assemblage is the expressive qualities linked with assembled material elements (Roffe 2016). In the previous section, we considered the broad-scale material constituents that have ultimately led to the production of this sparkling wine and, finally, that the material manifestation of bubbles is perhaps the most commonly recognised aspect of champagne, often called simply 'bubbly' or 'fizz' in English. Next, we further consider three key expressions of the champagne brand assemblages that contribute to its overall symbolism: heritage, class and magic.

Expressions of heritage

Moët & Chandon (established in 1743), Veuve Clicquot (1772) and Dom Pérignon (1921) are some of the oldest brands in existence (Beverland 2005). The authenticity of many brands is partly established through explicit references to history, historical characters and events as they collectively offer a source of legitimacy and an 'aura' important for brand heritage and its core values (Beverland 2005). In champagne brand marketing, as in the case of many luxury wines (Beverland 2005), images provide an invaluable source of authenticity as they produce a 'connection to time' (Postrel 2003). In fact, many of the 'authentic' brand images are stylised versions of real events and history.

One such historical pathway to have coloured the brand assemblage layer is connected to the unique historical place of Champagne and its wines in the French royal court (Guy 2003), not least due to its presence at the French coronation festivities that traditionally took place in the Cathedral of Reims from the seventeenth century until the French Revolution. Part of its successful image building, however, has always been champagne brands' ability to link 'old' and 'modern' worlds (Rokka 2017). Despite the ancestral roots and key role in the feudal and monarchic systems, towards the twentieth century, champagne managed to emerge as the staple of 'modernity' and an inevitable expression of luxurious and fashionable 'modern life' (Guy 2003), features that connect it with a second cultural expression, namely class.

Expression of class

Even before the French Revolution in 1789, champagne brands sought to symbolise privilege and opulence by portraying charismatic characters in their advertisements and packaging. Claude Moët, for instance, is said to have launched a promotion of champagne in the fashionable soirées of Marquise Madame de Pompadour, mistress to King Louis XV (see Guy 2003: 14–15). After the Revolution, however, the social hierarchies shifted significantly, paving the way for the new aristocracy of the emerging bourgeoisie (Elias 2000). Champagne became a central ritual for this emerging group.

Expressions of magic

Finally, a key distinction of 'regular' brands is the manner in which some brands can assemble charismatic legitimacy and magic that is expressed, for example, through physical/material objects, retail spaces, events and advertising (Dion and Arnould 2011). In many ways, magic, as a sacred quality, matches the notion that brands, like works of art, should possess an 'aura of authenticity', endowing them with qualities of uniqueness, distance or otherness as well as the impression that commercial motivations are not paramount (Beverland 2005; Humphreys and Carpenter 2018).

An essential identity component for champagne brands is thus 'magic' expressed through exceptional charismatic creators, personae or myths (Dion and Arnould 2011; Rokka 2017). The creation myths and charismatic personae (e.g. Veuve Clicquot, Claude Moët, Dom Pérignon) are strong among champagne brands that, since the early days, were marketed internationally not as fine wine but as an enchanting 'magical elixir' (Guy 2003). For example, in 1870, the wine producers' collective decided to revive Dom Pérignon, a monk who had worked at the abbey of Hautvillers, as the official inventor of champagne – a mythical (but not quite true) story that was thereafter used in official documents and advertising, partly to hide the fact that much of the wine's production process was being disenchanted through industrialisation.

How is champagne expressed in social media images?

In the previous section, we established the identity assemblage of champagne as a glamorous and powerful consumption object that serves as 'an integral social marker of status and membership' (Guy 2003: 12). To better understand how this symbol is currently used in contemporary consumer culture, the focus of this section is a qualitative empirical analysis of the most common types of social media images that feature champagne brands and their associated symbolic ingredients.

The study builds on and adapts ongoing research on and analysis of social media images (Rokka and Canniford 2016) in which most popular champagne brands on Instagram are examined. By means of interpretive visual analysis of both official champagne Instagram accounts and consumer-made images, it was possible to examine the re-occurring patterns of expressive and material elements of some of the most well-established champagne brands, including Moët & Chandon, Dom Pérignon and Veuve Clicquot. The analysis offered thus contains two kinds of images: (1) official ones posted by the brand and (2) consumer-made 'selfie' images in which at least one of the studied champagne brands was mentioned or tagged in.

While the images gathered in the first round of data collection are from 2014 (Rokka and Canniford 2016), this chapter complements and compares these data with follow-up study from 2018. Four years is a particularly long time on Instagram – a place that is constantly focused on the here and now, the moments of consumption that people live through and share online. This is why it is valuable to see what kinds of key tendencies characterise the postings concerning the most popular champagne brands and also how those postings may have changed over time.

Method

The objective of this study was to map out and empirically analyse champagne postings related to the most-talked-about brands online. Analysing the dominant brands cited in online visual discourses, it is possible to gain access to and examine the most common meanings linked with champagne in today's consumer culture. Importantly, this does not mean that only these visual discourses exist as there may also be other alternative expressions: for example, those by more specialised and dedicated amateur enthusiasts. Prior consumer culture research has shown the value of analysing what consumers and brands do, say and post on social media, not only because this may influence others' consumption behaviour but also because these media reflect our society, the way we make sense of our identities and our role in it (e.g. Arnould and Thompson 2005; Rokka 2021).

We first built social media queries concerning 19 well-known champagne brands. The list of brands was constructed from members of *Union des Maisons de Champagne* and other lists, including international sales statistics. Finally, the prominence of the brands' mentions on social media was evaluated based on data retrieved from Brandwatch – a social media monitoring tool.

The data gathered from 2014 confirmed our assumption that only a few globally marketed champagne brands command most of the attention, whereas volumes for smaller brands are significantly weaker or peripheral. Notably, three of the top brands combined for 61% of all social media mentions at the time of the study: Moët & Chandon (31% of all mentions), Dom Pérignon (17%) and Veuve Clicquot (13%) – brands owned by the LVMH group. To study and also compare both official brand images and consumer-made images, these three most cited brands were selected for further analysis. The aim was to offer the possibility for a comparison of how popular social media champagne postings may have changed over time. Specific methodological details concerning the visual content analysis used can be found in Rokka and Canniford (2016).

Two sets of images were gathered in the first round of data analysis. The official brand account images of the three studied brands included a total of 1,833 images that had been posted at the time of data collection (through May 2014). The consumer-made image data set, on the other hand, consisting of 6,820 Instagram postings for the three brands, was gathered over the span of six weeks in spring 2014. The Brandwatch social media monitoring tool was used to obtain the data, which represents 'a slice' of common social media postings that can be found for the brands in question. Since a detailed analysis of all images was not possible, a random sample of 600 images was drawn and closely analysed (100 images per brand per image type).

Following Lutz and Collins (1993), we developed interpretive categories for image coding informed by our theoretical concerns. These offer a 'breakdown of imagery that will be analytically interesting and coherent' (Slater 1998: 236). In particular, we examined, categorised and labelled the various material and expressive features in the images. We then engaged in a critical visual analysis by reading and rereading the images in relation to their broader cultural meanings, practices and contexts (Rokka and Canniford 2016). In a second round of visual analysis, we used this framework for a detailed coding of one-fifth of our sample data, allowing us to better illuminate the nature and tendencies in the two sets of images studied. Thus, 20 images per each brand image type were coded. Importantly, for consumer images, we chose to only include images that we labelled 'selfies'. This purposive sampling was considered highly informative for the analysis and illustration of consumers' relationship with the studied brands and how they constructed and arranged various meanings in their images, including hashtags (e.g. Marwick 2015).

A follow-up data collection and analysis was conducted in 2018. Here, the aim was to follow how the consumer-made images of champagne had evolved, if they had. A similar sample of new data was collected corresponding the same period of time – four years after the first data collection. The Instagram dataset is presented in Table 24.1.

Table 24.1 Instagram data used in visual analysis (2014, 2018)

Images	Moët & Chandon	Dom Pérignon	Veuve Clicquot	Total
Brand account images analysed – second round (2014)	20	20	20	60
Brand account images analysed – first round (2014)	100	100	100	300
Brand account images in total (2014)	295	266	1,272	1,833
Consumer-made selfie images analysed – second round (2014)	20	20	20	60
Consumer-made selfie images analysed – first round (2014)	100	100	100	300
Consumer-made images in total (2014)	3,053	2,228	1,539	6,820
Consumer-made selfie images analysed – second round (2018)	20	20	20	60
Consumer-made selfie images analysed – first round (2018)	100	100	100	300
Consumer-made images in total (2018)	47,462	14,109	16,283	77,854

The following sections report findings from the 2014 and then the 2018 data analysis, summarised in Table 24.1. The sections are illustrated by visual artist Maria Federley's hand-drawn renderings and creative interpretations of the data so as to preserve the integrity and essence of common images in a manner that avoids copyright or privacy violations.

'Branded still life': findings from official champagne brand images

It quickly became clear that the studied brand-controlled Instagram accounts echoed typical champagne advertising images in terms of their character and expressions. They commonly depict a 'still life' of inanimate objects, artefacts and scenery, mainly focused on the product close-up – including the brand logo (75% of the images on average), bottle(s) (63%), liquid wine (25%) and bubbles (13%). The images only rarely included people (only 25% of images on average) and especially recognisable faces (13%). Above all, the official brand images seemed to ensure, as one might imagine, that no other brands were present or identifiable in the posted social media pictures (see Figure 24.1).

All attention in these images seems to be directed towards the focal champagne brand, its essential accessories (e.g. bottle, labels, corks, ice, wine coolers) and its principal, historically shaped material and symbolic associations. The 'official' brand images reflect common layers of 'material' constituents

domperignonofficial Rarity has indeed a taste. #domperignon

Figure 24.1 Champagne brands expressed on official Instagram accounts

@moetchandon We're savoring tonight with a flute in the stunning garden of the Trianon on the Moët Estate! #Moet

domperignonofficial The Abbey of Hautvillers, home of absolute #creation

Figure 24.2 Expressions of heritage, class and magic in official accounts

through which champagne brands have been commonly assembled over time. Notably, the circulating iconic images, of various scales, of the terroir, institutional vineyards and wine cellars and other geographical landscape from the Champagne region. The 'expressive' or symbolic elements, on the other hand, echo common mythical references from the past, as outlined in the first part of this chapter. In this sense, the brand accounts most often include implicit or explicit references to 'heritage/tradition' (55%), 'class/status' (45%) and also 'magic' (22%) (see Figure 24.2).

Other common expressive categories that were coded include celebration (27%), special occasion (18%), relaxation (18%), sharing (17%), travel/vacation (13%) and indulgence/taste (12%). While celebration was underlined most by the Moët & Chandon brand, in every second image, on average, it is clear that the historical precedents of the cultural elite and bourgeoisie resonate widely in all the champagne brand imagery. The social spaces of champagne echo a number of contemporary consumption moments, including fine parties, special occasions and milestone life events or various gustatory settings where champagne is commonly paired with expensive meals.

'Microcelebrity living': brand selfies and the quest for attention

Consumer-made images present a sharp and visible contrast to the 'official' brand account images. While the appearance of bottles, wine and bubbles in consumer-made images was as frequent as in the studied official brand images, the most striking feature was that about 40% of consumer-made images were what can be labelled 'brand selfies': that is, self-portrait social media images taken by the consumer of themselves, usually with a smartphone, that feature identifiable brands or brand hashtags.

These 'champagne selfies', which populate much of the analysed data, present above all an excessively large number of human bodies; 95% of selfie images contain a person or persons (1.5 people per image on average), with as many as 53% of these images featuring identifiable face(s). This shift in the immediate focus impacts the overall feeling of the images in significant ways. Notably, the presence of human bodies and identifiable faces breaks the brand's singularity and gives it an often banalised expression.

In addition, on a closer examination, the consumer-made images were not focused on a single champagne brand, but nearly 40% of the images contained or tagged several brands at once. Instead of being focused on the brand, the consumer images were systematically centred on the self and the body, assembled in various representations or 'looks', making the brand necessarily a more peripheral object or a side mention (see Figure 24.3). More often than not, the brand was only mentioned with a hashtag and was not visible in the image.

What emerges from the consumers' champagne images is an incontestable expression of what can be called 'microcelebrity' (see also Marwick 2015; Senft 2013). This highly popular category, constituting 67% of all the consumer-made images, can be understood as a collection of visual practices and strategies that mimic celebrities' postings, aimed to signal fame and attractiveness to others. For example, common images entail 'mirror selfies', 'gym selfies', 'bathroom selfies', 'bikini selfies' and 'party selfies': in other words, 'ordinary' people posing as if they were famous stars. These postings commonly included attention-seeking hashtags such as #follow4follow, #followme, #like4like and #picoftheday (see Figure 24.4).

The desire for social advancement is perhaps comparable with other luxury goods and historical myths around champagne. A potential difference, however, is that the attention-grabbing, sexualised, attractive-looking photos and popular tag words do not necessarily entail any form of ownership over the photographed objects, allowing much greater flexibility in one's self-expressions through social media accounts. Therefore, a remarkable and necessary new skill of consumer microcelebrities is to be able to playfully adopt popular visual tropes and poses from online celebrity profiles (Marwick 2015) or mimic 'snapshots' from fashion magazines and blogs (Schroeder 2013).

Figure 24.3 Brand selfies and aestheticised bodies of various kinds

Figure 24.4 Brand selfies and consumer celebrities

Other popular symbolic and expressive ingredients coded for consumer images – while also closely relevant for the microcelebrity logic – were celebration (60% of images), class/status (58%), look/appearance (40%) and nightclubs (32%). In contrast, the historically formed champagne associations – and top categories in official champagne brand accounts – such as heritage/tradition (only 8% of consumer-made images) or magic (3%) were less evident. While champagne brand account images were often associated with forms of charismatic and magical aesthetic expression – for example, in relation to charismatic people, breathtaking scenery or utopian artistic creations – the consumer images were often far removed from such magical worlds. Instead, they commonly and intentionally violated the sacred and magical experiences by offering alternative spectacles where champagne brands are either banalised or completely removed from established expressive systems through lowbrow aesthetics, poorly made images (technically or otherwise), or novel and out-of-place associations.

In sum, these findings reveal that consumer-made selfies and social media images as a new form of visual self-presentation practice have come to offer alternative constructions of champagne brands with new kinds of material and expressive features. Especially, they indicate that consumers – and the self(ies) – are becoming the nodal point at which official champagne brand images and consumer microcelebrity assemblages intersect. This powerful shift potentially undermines stable, historically built symbolic and material properties of heritage brands and makes visible a profound heterogeneity of alternative and often chaotic brand images – at least, from the point of view of the brand manager.

Through visual content analysis of both official and consumer-made champagne Instagram images, it was possible to begin to understand more specifically the kinds of expressive and material assemblages of identities that social media images construct. This allows us to map out not only the focal elements that consumer-generated images – perhaps unintentionally – reinforce in the 'official' brand expressions and meanings but also those that effectively disrupt and destabilise them.

Consumers' evolving champagne expressions?

A follow-up analysis was conducted in 2018. This allows us to examine the ways in which consumer-made images of champagne have either remained the same or changed further. The data gathered in 2018 matches the period of the 2014 data, allowing a feasible comparative analysis. A follow-up analysis was deemed important due to the fast pace of social media platforms as well as the changes in them. One of the questions was also whether we could still see similar focus on the 'selfie phenomenon', which experienced important hype around 2014, when Google estimated 93 million selfies were taken every single day.

The first striking result is that, at least according to our data collection tool Brandwatch, we witness a more than ten-fold growth of brand mentions on Instagram regarding the three studied brands. There were a total of 77,854 champagne postings in 2018 versus only 6,820 in 2014. Moët & Chandon was mentioned in over 60% of these postings, making it clearly the most cited champagne brand on Instagram and, likely, in the world. While Instagram has solidified its position as the most important social media branding platform in the recent years (growing from 400 million global users in 2014 to 909 million in 2020), it is fair to say that champagne-related postings have been growing at a particularly fast rate.

The second, more general finding was that the share of selfie images among the studied champagne brand mentions has also increased. The share of selfies was 59% in 2018 versus 40% in 2014. This means that even though there may be somewhat less hype around the selfie phenomenon today, selfies continue to be a key feature in the consumer and influencer images around champagne.

A summary of the findings and comparison is presented in Table 24.2.

Table 24.2 Comparison of champagne selfie coding frequencies, 2014 vs. 2018

(%)	Moët & Chandon 2014	Moët & Chandon 2018	Dom Pérignon 2014	Dom Pérignon 2018	Veuve Clicquot 2014	Veuve Clicquot 2018	Total 2014	Total 2018
Material elements								
Bottle(s)	45	60	65	65	55	50	55	58
Wine glass(es)	35	35	20	35	60	40	38	37
Wine	30	30	5	25	50	30	28	28

(Continued)

Table 24.2 (Continued)

(%)	Moët & Chandon 2014	Moët & Chandon 2018	Dom Pérignon 2014	Dom Pérignon 2018	Veuve Clicquot 2014	Veuve Clicquot 2018	Total 2014	Total 2018
Bubbles	15	15	0	15	25	15	13	15
Human(s)	100	100	90	95	95	100	95	98
Face(s)	55	80	40	70	65	65	53	72
Male (vs female)	44	54	64	65	26	60	45	60
White (vs non-white)	76	89	96	93	77	87	83	90
Natural (vs other) background	10	35	5	5	5	5	7	15
Brand logo	35	35	55	70	50	60	47	55
Other brands	50	40	45	60	20	55	38	52
Expressive elements								
(Micro)celebrity	70	65	75	75	55	65	67	68
Class/status	35	50	80	70	60	60	58	60
Look	40	65	40	55	40	45	40	55
Celebration	50	50	70	45	60	55	60	50
Ironic	25	35	25	35	20	35	23	35
Nightclub	20	40	55	30	20	20	32	30
Sharing	35	40	10	20	35	30	27	30
Special occasion	15	25	0	10	35	45	17	27
Happiness	10	10	5	10	15	25	10	15
Relaxation	15	15	0	10	10	20	8	15
Travel/vacation	0	15	10	15	10	10	7	13
Romantic	5	10	0	10	10	15	5	12
Food pairing	0	10	0	10	30	10	10	10
Indulgence	0	5	0	15	5	10	2	10
Heritage	5	5	10	10	10	10	8	8
Work/workout	15	15	0	5	5	5	7	8
Magic	5	5	0	10	5	5	3	7
Escapism	5	5	0	0	0	5	2	3

Stabilised materiality: omnipresent bottle, persisting fizz and focused bodies

Several elements remained stable in consumers' champagne-related postings between 2014 and 2018. One of these is the remarkably stable frequency and consistent presentation of the enigmatic champagne bottle (present in 58% of the selfie images). This iconic symbol is commonly featured on the table in front of the camera or in the lap or hand, with unmistakable attention on the brand's logo, graphics and label (55% of images). Similarly, what remains essentially unchanged in the images is the consistency in ways of showing wine glasses (37%), liquid wine (28%) and bubbles (15%).

In terms of human presence, the selfies continue to be populated by people and bodies. On the average, there are 1.8 people in a champagne selfie (1.5 in 2014). However, what has changed here is an increased focus on consumers' identifiable faces (72% of the images – up from 53% in 2014). This underlines further the increasing attention to the consumer themselves and the fact that often, the champagne is not the focal point of the image (and identity assemblage); the consumer is. Curiously, we can also see a minor increase in male (60%) and white (90%) bodies in the images, although these changes are very small.

Figure 24.5 Assemblages of connected brands

Finally, in terms of the physical visible objects in the consumer-made champagne images, we continue to see a high number of 'other' brands. While official champagne brand and advertising images contain practically no other brands, the consumer images we studied assemble a collection of brands. More than half the champagne selfie images contain or cite at least one other brand. This tendency is stronger than in 2014, and it is most frequent for Dom Pérignon (70% of the images). The assemblages of 'connected brands' in the selfie images are effective in signalling who the person is, what they do and what they are interested in. Equally, it can also give ideas about how consumers conceive and classify brands together – consciously or unconsciously. Examples of commonly cited brands include other champagne brands and beverages (e.g. Grey Goose, Belvedere, Corona, Red Bull) but also clothing (e.g. Hilfiger, Ralph Lauren, Supreme) and status accessories (e.g. LV, Chanel bags, iPhone). Other objects that frequently stand out from the images include expensive-looking watches, sunglasses, cars and tattoos.

On the other hand, as previously, the tendency of showing 'unfitting', 'unexpected', or 'wrong' objects or brands remains. Not uncommon was the continued combination of 'kitschy' aesthetics with champagne, building on the ironic flavour of many of the postings. There was, among others, a frequent presentation of pets sipping champagne, teddy bears, video game consoles, large TV screens, print T-shirts, swimsuits, bananas, ice cream pots, candy, beer pints and water bottles.

'Give me your attention': microcelebrity lives, looks and play amplified

The data from 2018 both confirm and further amplify the 2014 findings regarding how consumers use champagne brands as cultural symbols. Among the studied brands, there is a further shift towards expressions that underline attention-seeking celebrity-like living (68% of the postings), class/status (60%), look (55%), celebration (50%) and irony (35%). Of these, the biggest increase concerns the look (up from 40%) and irony (up from 23%), whereas celebration was slightly less frequent (down from 60%).

All these results support the increasing shift in luxury products towards 'microcelebrity culture' and influencing (Marwick 2015; Rokka and Canniford 2016) – that is, when 'ordinary people' wish

Figure 24.6 Microcelebrity looks and visual play

to mimic the lives of famous people, not least by posing, narrating and posting about their daily occurrences in largely similar fashion. Moreover, the data from 2018 counted more professionalised influencer accounts than before. Yet again, the difference in terms of images was harder to observe, meaning that it was the number of followers that made these accounts different.

While important in 2014 data as well, there was a small increase in the 'special occasions' type of champagne selfies. These included, notably, birthdays, marriages, anniversaries and moving to new home, but also perhaps a broader category of 'special occasions' than earlier. Worthy moments were, for example, meeting family, 'solo' evening, middle of the week 'humpday' or picnic.

A persistent feature was that historically important associations of champagne to tradition/heritage, taste, terroir and magic were all rare. This may raise the question of when and whether there is a time for renewed interest in champagne from the point of view of cultivated, 'amateur expert' consumers that we now begin to see, for example, in the field of craft beer consumption (e.g. Maciel and Wallendorf 2017). This category of consumers is conspicuously absent, at least when it comes to our analysis of the three most talked-about champagne brands online.

Overall, the visual and assemblage perspective on brands adopted in this study helps address common issues in prior theories of branding and champagne marketing specifically. While there is a widening recognition of the reciprocal co-creation of brand meaning and value between consumers and marketer (e.g. Parmentier and Fischer 2015; Humphreys 2016), most of the research on the issue has focused on analyses of textual material and verbal dialogues or narratives, leaving the visual aspects aside. The results presented here clearly show that brand meaning and value are increasingly constructed through visual expression, which is privileged in visually dominant social media such as Instagram. It thus may be that champagne brands and also scholars need to broaden their views on how consumers construct value in several largely new ways. For example, how they use iconic brands to gain the attention of others (Marwick 2015; Senft 2013) and build various kinds of (visual) identity assemblages that they desire (Canniford and Bajde 2016). This challenges, at least in part, the historical constructions of champagne brands that are mostly oriented to signalling class, heritage and magic.

Conclusion

This chapter has sought to examine how champagne emerged – against all the odds – as a global cultural symbol of contemporary consumer culture. The first part examined the foundational historically established meanings, representations and often mythical associations concerning champagne.

We can say that many of these still continue to spark our collective imagination (Rokka 2017; Rokka and Canniford 2016). The second part examined the specific context and new genres of champagne image and meaning making that proliferate on social media. Based on empirical analysis of Instagram brand accounts and consumer-made images, detailed 'snapshots' were drawn of the most common expressive and material elements that make up champagne-related social media images and consumer culture today. The results shed light on the microcelebrity culture and the logics of the visually driven attention economy through which champagne brands are increasingly constructed, consumed and celebrated.

While further research is still needed to advance and extend these qualitative and interpretive insights, it seems that the symbolic value of champagne brands is highly resonant, attention grabbing and even magnetic, while constantly evolving in ongoing negotiations and expressions with consumers. The sheer volume of consumer postings mentioning, depicting or tagging champagne brands – even if they may, at times, not be the main focus of the posting in question – as part of intimate identity assemblages is unquestionable evidence of this.

Acknowledgements

The author wishes to thank artist Maria Federley for her illustration work and permission to reproduce the images used in this chapter.

References

Arnould, E.J. and Thompson, C. (2005) "Consumer Culture Theory (CCT): Twenty Years of Research," *Journal of Consumer Research* 31, March, 868–882.

Beverland, M. (2005) "Crafting Brand Authenticity: The Case of Luxury Wines," *Journal of Management Studies* 42(5), 1003–1029.

Canniford, R. and Bajde, D. (2016) *Assembling Consumption: Researching Actors, Networks and Markets*, London: Routledge.

Charters, S. and Spielmann, N. (2014) "Characteristics of Strong Territorial Brands: The Case of Champagne," *Journal of Business Research* 67, 1461–1467.

Charters, S., Spielmann, N. and Babin, B.J. (2017) "The Nature and Value of Terroir Products," *European Journal of Marketing* 51(4), 748–771.

Dion, D. and Arnould, E.J. (2011) "Retail Luxury Strategy: Assembling Charisma Through Art and Magic," *Journal of Retailing* 87(4), 502–520.

du Gay, P., Hall, S., Janes, L., Mackay, H. and Negus, K. (1997) *Doing Cultural Studies: The Story of the Sony Walkman*, London: Sage.

Elias, N. (2000) *The Civilising Process, Volumes 1 & 2*, Oxford: Blackwell.

Guy, K.M. (2003) *When Champagne Became French*, London: The John Hopkins University Press.

Hall, S. (1997) *Representation*, London: Sage.

Holt, D.B. (2004) *How Brands Become Icons: The Principles of Cultural Branding*, Cambridge, MA: Harvard Business School Press.

Humphreys, A. (2016) *Social Media: Enduring Principles*, Oxford: Oxford University Press.

Humphreys, A. and Carpenter, G.S. (2018) "Status Games: Market Driving Through Social Influence in the US Wine Industry," *Journal of Marketing* 82(5), 141–159.

Levy, S.J. (1981) "Interpreting Consumer Mythology: A Structural Approach to Consumer Behavior," *Journal of Marketing* 45, Summer, 49–61.

Lutz, C.A. and Collins, J.L. (1993) *Reading National Geographic*, Chicago: University of Chicago Press.

Maciel, A.F. and Wallendorf, M. (2017) "Taste Engineering: An Extended Consumer Model of Cultural Competence Constitution," *Journal of Consumer Research* 43(5), 726–246.

Marwick, A.E. (2015) "Instafame: Luxury Selfies in the Attention Economy," *Public Culture* 27(1), 137–160.

Parmentier, M.-A. and Fischer, E. (2015) "Things Fall Apart: The Dynamics of Brand Audience Dissipation," *Journal of Consumer Research* 41(5), 1228–1251.

Postrel, V. (2003) *The Substance of Style: How the Rise of Aesthetic Value is Remaking Commerce, Culture, & Consciousness*, New York: HarperCollins Publishers.

Roffe, J. (2016) "The Concept of the Assemblage and the Case of Markets," in R. Canniford and D. Bajde (eds), *Assembling Consumption*, London: Routledge, 42–55.

Rokka, J. (2017) "Champagne: Marketplace Icon," *Consumption Markets & Culture* 20(3), 275–283.

Rokka, J. (2021) "Consumer Culture Theory's Future in Marketing," *Journal of Marketing Theory and Practice* 29(1), 114–124.

Rokka, J. and Canniford, R. (2016) "Heterotopian Selfies: How Social Media Destabilizes Brand Assemblages," *European Journal of Marketing* 50(9/10), 1789–1813.

Schroeder, J.E. (2013) "Snapshot Aesthetics and the Strategic Imagination," *Visible Culture: An Electronic Journal for Visual Culture 18*, http://ivc.lib.rochester.edu/portfolio/snapshot-aesthetics-and-the-strategic-imagination/.

Senft, T.M. (2013) "Microcelebrity and the Branded Self," in J. Hartley, J. Burgess and A. Burns (eds), *A Companion to New Media Dynamics*, Malden, MA: Wiley-Blackwell, 346–354.

Slater, D. (1998) "Analysing Cultural Objects: Content Analysis and Semiotics," in C. Seale (ed), *Researching Society and Culture*, London: Sage, 233–244.

Smith Maguire, J. and Charters, S. (2020) "Aesthetic Logics, *Terroir* and the Lamination of Grower Champagne," *Consumption Markets & Culture* 24(1), 75–96.

Thompson, C.J. (2004) "Marketplace Mythology and Discourses of Power," *Journal of Consumer Research* 31, June, 162–180.

PART IV

Belief and representation

25
WINE AND RELIGION
Part 1, antiquity to 1700

Mack P. Holt

Introduction

This chapter examines the changing connections between wine and religion from their origins in the ancient world and wine's use in religious rituals in the Middle Ages to the disruptions caused by the Protestant Reformations of the sixteenth century. The focus is primarily on the Near East and Europe, though the chapter ends with a look at wine and religion in North and South America, Africa and Asia.

Antiquity

The origins of wine can be traced as far back as the Neolithic period (8500 to 4000 BCE) from surviving archaeological remains, though we know little of the exact nature of wine's role in religious beliefs and practices until the invention of writing c. 3000 BCE. Yet we can be reasonably certain that wine and religion had long been connected in those areas where wild grapevines were cultivated, especially in the eastern Mediterranean and ancient Near East. About a decade ago, archaeologists from UCLA discovered the first known winery in an Armenian cave dating from c. 4100 BCE, where they found a wine press, storage vats, jars, cups and *Vitis vinifera* vines and seeds. This earliest known winery was discovered in a burial site, making it clear that the wine was used for religious and ceremonial purposes in addition to everyday drinking. This find makes it clear that grapes had been cultivated and harvested for wine for centuries before 4100 BCE. Indeed, it is believed that some of the earliest hominids enjoyed a wild grape wine and that some early societies were 'wine cultures' (Barnard *et al.* 2010; Maugh 2011; McGovern 2007: 16–84, 299–300). To be sure, wine had always been important for everyday drinking, as it made up a significant component of the diet both as beverage and food in this region of the world. But because drinking wine in excess could also lead to an out-of-body experience approaching the spiritual or divine, wine always managed to transgress the fine and sometimes confusing boundary between the sacred and the profane in Western culture (Félice 1970: 9–35, 336–377). In the ancient Near Eastern societies, 'wine's special benefits were traced back to the gods. Wine served to invoke divine assistance and to bridge the chasm between this life and the next' (McGovern 2007: 134). In this sense, wine and religion had always been intertwined.

Once written records became available to supplement the archaeological evidence, it was clear that wine was so important in these ancient cultures that it had its own god. In

New Kingdom Egypt (c. 1550–1070 BCE), for example, the god Asar, better known by his Greek name, Osiris, was called 'The Lord of wine through inundation', referring to the flooding of the Nile River over its banks every summer. Osiris had been killed by his evil brother, Seth, and it was Osiris's wife and sister Isis who gathered his remains and, on the third day, resurrected him. The resuscitation of the dormant grapevines by the inundation of the Nile was thus tied directly to the resurrection of Osiris, and his resurrection was symbolised by the grapevine (McGovern 2007: 234–235). In ancient Greece, the god of wine was Dionysos, subsequently known by his Latin name, Bacchus. The name Dionysos appears in the earliest form of written Greek (c. 1600–1100 BCE). By this time, the worship of Dionysos had become a central part of Greek religion, and festivals honouring him were held every winter and spring. Drinking, singing, dancing, ribaldry and formal dramatic presentations marked these festivals, and a significant part of these celebrations was the tasting of the new wine from the previous harvest. Thus, like the festivals honouring Osiris in Egypt, the ones dedicated to Dionysos marked the bounty and fertility of the earth's harvest. The worshippers at these festivals were thus 'drinking the god' (McGovern 2007: 244–246).

Yet these and other polytheistic religions were rivalled in the ancient Near East by the rise of Judaism, a monotheistic religion that broke away from the polytheistic religions of the Eastern Mediterranean. The Jews trace their origin to c. 1800 BCE and Abraham's covenant with Yahweh, whom they came to worship as the one true god. But it was not until the first millennium BCE that they became organised around a theology written down and increasingly organised in a library of books referred to as the Tanakh and developed a systematic and sacred use of wine in their principal rituals. The Tanakh mentions wine no fewer than 194 times, and this figure includes only specific references to wine, not the numerous references to wine paraphernalia such as grapes, vineyards or winepresses. Most of these were casual references to how common wine was in the everyday life and diet of nearly all Jewish people. However, many of them were explicitly positive references to wine being the bounty of Yahweh's goodness and blessing (for example, Genesis 27:28, Numbers 15:7, Numbers 18:12, Numbers 28:7, Deuteronomy 7:13). Moreover, the very first thing Noah did after leaving the ark after 40 days and nights during the Great Flood was to plant a grapevine (Genesis 9:20). Nevertheless, after harvesting the grapes, Noah also got drunk. Thus, the Tanakh also condemned the overindulgence of wine and inebriation (Leviticus 10:9, Numbers 6:3, Judges 13:4–7, 1 Samuel 1:14 and many more). Wine, therefore, became a staple of most Jewish rituals and feast days. Indeed, wine was a requisite part of many of them (McGovern 2007: 237), and the ancient Israelites constructed a wine culture in which wine was a vital part of their religious celebrations just as it was a significant part of their secular experience.

It is unsurprising, then, that the offshoot of ancient Judaism that became Christianity in the first century CE was also a wine culture. When Christianity eventually replaced the polytheistic Greco/Roman religion starting in 312 CE with the conversion of the Roman Emperor Constantine, this Christian wine culture spread throughout the Mediterranean and into western Europe. In many ways, Jesus performed the role of the wine god of the ancient polytheistic religions, and his death paralleled that of the Egyptian god Osiris. He claimed in the gospel of John to be the true vine:

> I am the true vine, and my Father is the vinegrower. . . . I am the vine, you are the branches. Those who abide in me and I in them bear much fruit, because apart from me you can do nothing.
>
> (John 15:1, 5)

The very first miracle of Jesus mentioned in the gospels occurred at the wedding feast at Cana, where, when the wine ran out, he turned water into wine (John 2:1–11). But Jesus's most significant link with wine was in the Eucharist, the central rite of Christian worship. On the eve of his crucifixion at the Last Supper, Jesus took a cup of wine, offered a prayer of thanks, then gave it to his disciples, saying,

> This is my blood of the covenant, which is poured out for many. Truly I tell you, I will never again drink of the fruit of the vine, until that day when I drink it new with you in my Father's kingdom.
>
> *(Matthew 26:28; Mark 14:22)*

Early Christians believed that this wine not only became Jesus's actual blood but that it was also a sign that drinking this consecrated wine that was Jesus's blood conferred God's grace upon the imbiber, thereby enabling admission into the kingdom of heaven. Moreover, it is also clear that the ritual of the Eucharist – the consumption of consecrated bread and wine – was a part of the liturgy of early Christians from the beginning in the first century CE (Acts 2:42–46; Acts 20:7; I Corinthians 11:23–25). This theology of the Eucharist was consistent up until the Protestant Reformation of the sixteenth century.

The Middle Ages in Europe

The most detailed medieval explanation of the doctrine of Christ's presence in the Eucharist came from St. Thomas Aquinas, who asserted unequivocally that the consecration of the bread and wine by the priest caused the elements to change substance, although the 'accidents' or physical characteristics of the elements remained unchanged. And this explanation of Christ's presence in the bread and wine remained largely unchallenged within the church until Luther, Zwingli, Calvin and other Protestant reformers denied transubstantiation altogether in the sixteenth century (Rubin 1991: 1–63).

Christianity's relationship to wine was increased further when various religious orders began to purchase, or acquire through donation, vineyards in order to help fund their day-to-day expenses. In the province of Burgundy, for example, it was the arrival of Bernard of Clairvaux (1090–1153) at the small abbey of Cîteaux near Dijon in 1112 that dramatically reinforced the relationship between wine and Christianity in western Europe. The Cistercians, named after their founding house in Cîteaux, were one of the new orders that sought cloistered isolation. They had broken away from the Benedictine order in an effort to return to the more ascetic ways of St. Benedict in the sixth century, and they stressed manual labour, especially in agriculture. The Cistercians wore white habits, in contrast to the black habits of the Benedictines, and they sought self-sufficiency in the rural countryside. Their vineyards and the sale of wine after each harvest were among the means by which they generated income for those things they could not produce on their own. The founding house in Cîteaux owned vineyards in Meursault, Beaune, Dijon, Chambolle, Fixin, Gilly, Morey, Vosne and Vougeot. The Cistercians also introduced the practice of expanding whenever a monastery reached about 30 members, with 12 of them leaving to found a daughter house elsewhere. Nearly a dozen such houses were founded during Bernard's tenure at Cîteaux, and by the time of his death and canonisation in 1153, the white monks had founded over 400 Cistercian houses all over western Europe from Ireland in the west to Poland in the east. Moreover, the white monks practised viticulture wherever possible. Some of them, such as the Kloster Eberbach in the Rheingau region of the German lands, became the centre of viticulture in the region there just like Cîteaux in Burgundy. However, the Cistercians were not the only monastic order to become heavily invested in vineyards, as the Carthusians were another new order seeking isolation from civilisation, and they, too, became heavily invested in vineyards and wine production. By the late Middle Ages, it was common for even parish churches, not just monastic orders, to own vineyard land as the church and the aristocracy virtually controlled medieval viticulture (Holt 2018: 96–98; Scott 2002: 95–115).

There was a disruption in the way the rite of the Eucharist was practised, however, by the twelfth century. Traditionally, the laity was given the consecrated bread – the Host – and the consecrated wine – the Blood – just as Jesus provided at the Last Supper. There had always been exceptions for children and the sick, but until the twelfth century, the practice of receiving the Eucharist in both forms was widespread throughout the Christian world, both Roman and Orthodox. By the time of the Fourth Lateran Council (1215) a century later, however, the laity in the Roman church generally only received the consecrated Host, with the celebrating priest alone drinking the consecrated wine as the blood of Christ (Cross and Livingstone 1997: 386–387). Two explanations were given by the church for this change. Theologically, the doctrine of concomitance implied that Jesus's consecrated body, the Host, contained the blood of Christ, so lay Christians were, indeed, consuming Christ's blood as part of the Host even though they were denied the chalice. Practically, the practice of denying the wine to the laity made it less likely that the sacred blood of Jesus might accidentally be spilt during the ritual of the Eucharist. A third reason, though not much publicised at the time, was that reserving the communion chalice for the clergy alone served to elevate the clergy and further separate them from lay Christians. What this change did not do, however, was make wine any less significant for ordinary Christians in the late Middle Ages. Indeed, it had the opposite effect in many ways as lay pressure to restore the wine during the Eucharist pushed back against the change.

First, priests in many parishes ultimately yielded to lay demand for wine during the Eucharist by providing unconsecrated wine to their congregation. This was not the blood of Christ, but it still had solemn meaning for those who consumed it (Bossy 1985: 70). Second, a couple of priests – John Wyclif in England (c. 1320s–1384) and Jan Hus in Bohemia (c. 1372–1415) – and their followers ultimately challenged the doctrine of transubstantiation, and in Bohemia, the Hussites demanded that consecrated wine be restored to the laity during the Eucharist as was the custom in the early church. Thus, the practice of Utraquism, or communion in both kinds, became a key element in the Hussite revolt. Ultimately, these views were declared heretical by the Council of Constance (1414–1418), where Hus was condemned and burned as a heretic. Wyclif's remains were later disinterred and removed from consecrated ground. Nevertheless, a Utraquist church was ultimately established in fifteenth-century Bohemia, separate from the Church of Rome.

The Protestant Reformation

Martin Luther (1483–1546) and Ulrich Zwingli (1484–1531) in the 1520s and John Calvin (1509–1564) in the 1540s all restored wine to the laity during Communion or the Lord's Supper, the Protestant equivalent of the medieval church's Eucharist. While this did bring back a powerful symbol to Protestant ritual and practice, at the same time, Protestants' rejection of the doctrine of transubstantiation meant that the consecrated wine was no longer thought of as Jesus's physical blood. Catholics took literally Jesus's words at the Last Supper, recorded in the gospels 'This is my blood' (Matthew 26:26–28; Mark 14:22–25; Luke 22: 8–20). Most Protestants, however, instead focused on the words that followed according to Paul: drink this 'in remembrance of me' (I Corinthians 11:23–25). So, in Protestant churches, lay Christians did receive the communion wine along with the bread, but it was consumed in memory of Jesus's sacrifice on the cross, not as a literal re-enactment of that sacrifice that changed the substance of the wine into his own blood.

Another reason that the Protestant Reformation tended to weaken wine's bonds with Christianity rather than strengthening them was bound up in the way that so many Protestant churches attempted to limit and restrict the consumption of wine outside the church. Martin Bucer (1491–1551) was a German reformer and contemporary of Luther who was one of the founders of a Reformation in the free imperial city of Strasbourg in the 1520s. Bucer's goal was not just a reformation of the Catholic Church, but a reformation of Christian society. In short, he wished to construct an earthly kingdom of Christ, completely remaking and reforming Christian morals and behaviour. To that end, he wrote a major work on how to do this titled *De Regno Christi* (On the Kingdom of Christ), though it was not published until after his death. The treatise focused explicitly on social and moral discipline. In terms of the consumption of wine and other alcoholic beverages, Bucer went further than simply echoing the Bible's condemnation of drunkenness. He labelled those who consumed too much wine as captives to Satan, and to maintain moral discipline, he insisted that all public inns should be run by godly men (Pauck 1969: 334, 345–348). So Bucer sought to eliminate or at least limit the consumption of wine outside the church unless it conformed to the drinking of wine in the church during the Lord's Supper: that is, as a means of instilling piety.

Bucer strongly influenced the young John Calvin, whom he invited to Strasbourg in 1538 to organise a French refugee church there. Calvin stayed for three years before returning to Geneva to help re-organise the Reformed church there. Many of the reforms that Calvin later introduced in Geneva – especially the institution of the consistory, created explicitly to enforce and maintain moral discipline – can trace their origins to Bucer's influence on Calvin while in Strasbourg (Watt 2020). Like Bucer, Calvin sought to reform inns and taverns. And also like his older mentor, he wanted to do more than simply eliminate drunkenness. Above all, he sought to divorce the drinking of wine from the sociability of consuming it with friends by making it illegal to buy another person a drink, as he instructed in the *Ordinances for the Supervision of Churches*: 'There is to be no treating of one another to drinks, under penalty of three sous. . . . There are to be no carousals [i.e. enjoying oneself with others], under penalty of ten sous' (Reid 1959: 81). It should be stressed, of course, that Calvin, as well as all the other Protestant groups that claimed allegiance to his ideas, such as the Puritans in both England and New England, never seriously attempted to ban the drinking of wine or any other alcoholic beverage. They were much more interested in separating the consumption of it from the sociability and enjoyment of it when shared with companions. Indeed, there were very few Protestant voices at all advocating the complete prohibition of drinking alcohol. Moreover, the voices of complete abstinence never attracted many followers.

Two such voices, nevertheless, were Ludwig Haetzer (1500–1529) and Sebastian Franck (1499–1542), both of whom started as mainstream Protestants but eventually made their way to the more radical fringes of Anabaptism as they found the reformations of Luther, Zwingli and Calvin to be far too conservative for their taste. Haetzer was a young priest who was hired by Zwingli in Zurich for his inclination for reform and for his linguistic skills. In 1525, he published a short treatise against the drinking of any alcohol titled *On Evangelical Drinking* (Haetzer 1525). We do not know how many copies of this tract were printed, but apparently, none have survived to the present. (The Universal Short Title Catalogue lists no surviving copies.) But Haetzer argued that so-called evangelicals in Zurich and Saxony were more interested in drinking together than praying and worshipping together. Thus, he urged that all drinking should be banned in Zurich, and any evangelicals who could not conform should be expelled from the community (Blanke 1949; Goeters 1957).

Sebastian Franck was another radical Protestant who advocated a total ban on alcohol. Much more widely read than Haetzer's short treatise was Franck's *Concerning the Horrible Vice of Drunkenness*, first published in 1529 but reprinted many times over the next 20 years (Franck 1531; Hayden-Roy 1994: 19–25). His main argument was that drinking wine led to sin, and thus, those who drank it were 'heathens and not Christian, who do not show forth the fruits of faith'. Moreover, Franck feared that God would soon punish all humankind for the sins of drinking and that 'boozing, gorging, and drinking are a certain sign of the end times'. For him, the only remedy available was the complete prohibition of alcohol. And anyone who refused to abide by this policy, he reasoned, should be banished from the community. 'One must remove the impure from the community of God. . . . Our destruction is nearer than we believe' (Hayden-Roy 1994: 21–23).

Those few voices demanding total abstinence and temperance had nowhere near the impact on the actual consumption of wine than did the more mainstream reformers of the Protestant Reformation, above all, those of the Reformed tradition of Bucer and Calvin. As noted earlier, Calvin's goal was to try to regulate and moderate the drinking of wine outside the church by separating it from sociability and commensality. So, for Calvinists, drinking for pleasure and socialising with friends and family, even if it did not lead to drunkenness, was strongly discouraged. Thus, the culture of wine was as much an enemy for Calvin and his followers as public drinking houses, inns and taverns, since both were perceived as potential dens of iniquity. Where Calvinists were in control of the political authority – such as sixteenth-century Geneva and seventeenth-century Amsterdam – these sites could be regulated and policed. But even Calvinists were not always in total agreement over how much regulation and oversight of public drinking was necessary.

In seventeenth-century England, for example, the Protestant Church of England was clearly Calvinist in some of its principal doctrines, even if its liturgy, church hierarchy and practices continued to echo the medieval church in other ways. So when a minority of its members began to demand a more radical reformation of the church, it was not just an effort to purify the Church of England of all vestiges of Catholicism; it was also an attempt to construct a more godly society, a kingdom of Christ on earth, as Bucer had initially defined it. And these so-called Puritans took aim at the culture of drink as part of this effort. Thus, according to Richard Baxter (1615–1691), one of the more outspoken supporters of the famous Puritan 'reformation of manners' in seventeenth-century England, not only was drunkenness abhorrent, but strong drink itself was on the wrong side of the spirt versus flesh dialectical divide. 'O careless sinners!' he wrote in his *A Call to the Unconverted to Turn and Live*.

> The Sanctified are conversing with God, when you dare scarce think of him, and when you are conversing with but earth and flesh, Their Conversation is in Heaven, when you are utter strangers to it, and your belly is your God, and you are minding earthly things. Phil[ippians] 3.18, 19, 20.
>
> *(Baxter 1659: A11ᵛ–A12ᵛ)*

Wine was clearly an earthly thing, and more moral discipline was needed to turn away from earthly things to focus on spiritual things. Like so many critics of social drinking, Baxter (1659) tended to link it to sex. He maintained that those who worked in the very worst and most sinful professions – 'publicans and harlots' – could still get into heaven if they converted their lives away from the flesh and towards the spirit (Baxter 1659: 46). Like Calvin a century earlier, Baxter wanted to divorce drinking from sociability and any physical enjoyment.

All these Protestant efforts to restrict and regulate the drinking culture of wine contrast sharply with the ways in which the Catholic Church as an institution, including the changes of the Catholic Reformation, reinforced the culture of wine. Moreover, those who grew and tended the grapes and then turned the grape harvest into wine reinforced Catholicism. In those parts of western Europe where viticulture played a significant role in the local economies, the workers who tended the vines and made the wine were usually at the forefront of those opposed to the Protestant Reformation. In Burgundy, for just one example, it was the vineyard workers who were the staunchest opponents of Protestantism, reacting against Calvin's attack on the sociability and commensality of their livelihood. And the vineyard workers in Burgundy were hardly an exception as throughout western Europe, agricultural workers in general and vineyard workers in particular were among the least likely to be attracted to Protestantism, and most remained staunchly Catholic. Not only were many of the vineyards they worked in owned by local parish churches, abbeys and religious orders in Burgundy, but nearly all the foundation of masses for the dead were funded by payments in the form of wine promised from specific parcels of vines in perpetuity. Thus, in a variety of ways, Calvinism condemned their faith in the Eucharist, the role their wine played in their salvation and the function wine served as the medium between the living and the dead (Holt 2018: 74–79, 145–147).

Wine and religion beyond Europe

Wine also accompanied Christianity as it spread around the globe from Europe to North and South America, Africa and Asia in the fifteenth, sixteenth and seventeenth centuries. Hernán Cortés introduced grapevines into Mexico in 1521 and, three years later, ordered settlers to plant 1,000 vines for every 100 natives on any land granted to them. In 1531, King Charles I of Spain (Charles V as Holy Roman Emperor) ordered that every ship that sailed from Spain carry vines to try to make the colony self-sufficient in wine. That same year, Juan Pizarro defeated the Incas and began planting vines in Peru. The Spanish introduced vines into Chile in 1554 and into Argentina two years later. And the Jesuit Francis Xavier brought wine with him to Japan in 1545. By the seventeenth century, Jesuit missions were among the most important centres of viticulture outside Europe (Dickenson and Unwin 1992; Robinson 2006: 29, 373, 441, and 649–650). However, Protestant states also spread viticulture outside Europe in this period. The Dutch Calvinist Jan van Riebeeck, the first European settler in the Cape of Africa, was sent to the southern tip of Africa to set up a market garden to supply Dutch ships sailing around the Cape to the East Indies with food and wine. And in 1652, he wrote: 'Today, praise be to God, wine was pressed from Cape grapes' (Robinson 2006: 646). Thus, whether intended for the Catholic Eucharist or the Protestant Lord's Supper, wine became a global commodity by 1700.

Other religions around the globe, however, condemned the consumption of wine and all alcoholic beverages. Buddhism was among the first of these in the fifth century BCE; it was founded in India by the Buddha and spread throughout much of Asia. Even more significant was the advent of Islam, founded by the Prophet Muhammad in the seventh century CE. Although some early Muslims pushed back against the complete prohibition of wine, and even though some colonies in the Middle Ages, such as Moorish Spain, allowed viticulture to thrive, by 1700, Islam's prohibition of all alcoholic beverages was accepted as standard orthodox teaching throughout the Muslim world (Robinson 2006: 363–364).

Concluding: the end of the seventeenth century

By 1700, evangelical Protestants were only beginning to make inroads against the wine culture of early modern Europe. Those attacks would increase thereafter with greater ferocity as new evangelical groups emerged in the eighteenth and nineteenth centuries. In any case, by 1700, new ideas in science had already begun to undermine the hold religion had in explaining the natural world, including the growing of grapes for wine. Once both clerics and laymen began to understand the natural world as a mechanical universe, with God setting the laws of nature in motion at the Creation, never to interfere with their unfolding again, it was just a short step to deism after 1700. Thus, when Providence's role in nature came to be viewed as nothing more than that of 'an absentee landlord', religion and science could seem much less incompatible for some (Walsham 2011: 327–394). Nevertheless, the greatest threat to the wine industry in western Europe after 1700 was not religious fervour but *phylloxera*, a microscopic aphid in the natural world. And it would be science rather than religion that would come to its rescue.

References

Barnard, H., Dooley, A.N., Areshian, G., Gasparyan, B. and Faull, K.F. (2010) "Chemical Evidence for Wine Production Around 4000 BCE in the Late Chacolithic Near Eastern Highlands," *Journal of Archeological Science* 38, 977–984.
Baxter, R. (1659) *A Call to the Unconverted to Turn and Live, and Accept of Mercy . . . to be Read in Families Where Any Are Unconverted*, London: R.W. for Nevil Simmons.
Blanke, F. (1949) "Reformation und Alkoholismus," *Zwingliana* 9, 75–89.

Bossy, J. (1985) *Christianity in the West, 1400–1700*, Oxford: Oxford University Press.
Cross, F.L. and Livingstone, E.A. (eds) (1997) *The Oxford Dictionary of the Christian Church*, 3rd edition, Oxford: Oxford University Press.
Dickenson, J. and Unwin, T. (1992) *Viticulture in Colonial Latin America: Essays on Alcohol, the Vine and Wine in Spanish America and Brazil*, Liverpool: University of Liverpool Press.
Félice, P. de. (1970) *Poisons sacrés, ivresses divines: Essai sur quelque formes inférieures de la mystique*, 2nd edition, Paris: Albin Michel.
Franck, S. (1531) *Von dem grewlichenn Laster der Trunckenheit*, Augsburg: Heinrich von Augsburg Steiner.
Goeters, J.F.G. (1957) *Ludwig Haetzer*, Gütersloh: Bertlesmann.
Haetzer, L. (1525) *Von dem Evangelischen Zechen*, Augsburg: Silvan Othmar.
Hayden-Roy, P. (1994) *The Inner Word and the Outer World: A Biography of Sebastian Franck*, New York: Peter Lang.
Holt, M.P. (2018) *The Politics of Wine in Early Modern France: Religion and Popular Culture in Burgundy, 1477–1630*, Cambridge: Cambridge University Press.
Maugh, T.H. (2011) "Ancient Winery Found in Armenia," *Los Angeles Times*, 11 January, www.latimes.com/archives/la-xpm-2011-jan-11-la-sci-ancient-winery-20110111-story.html, accessed 1 May 2020.
McGovern, P.E. (2007) *Ancient Wine: The Search for the Origins of Viniculture*, Princeton, NJ: Princeton University Press.
Pauck, W. (ed) (1969) *Melancthon and Bucer*, Philadelphia: Westminster Press, Library of Christian Classics.
Reid, J.K.S. (ed) (1959) *Calvin: Theological Treatises*, Philadelphia: Westminster Press, Library of Christian Classics.
Robinson, J. (ed) (2006) *The Oxford Companion to Wine*, 3rd edition, Oxford: Oxford University Press.
Rubin, M. (1991) *Corpus Christi: The Eucharist in Late Medieval Culture*, Cambridge: Cambridge University Press.
Scott, T. (2002) "Medieval Viticulture in the German-speaking Lands," *German History* 20, 95–115.
Walsham, A. (2011) *The Reformation of the Landscape: Religion, Identity, and Memory in Early Modern Britain and Ireland*, Oxford: Oxford University Press.
Watt, J.R. (2020) *The Consistory and Social Discipline in Calvin's Geneva*, Rochester, NY: University of Rochester Press.

26
WINE AND RELIGION
Part 2, 1700 to the present

Rod Phillips

Introduction

At the beginning of the eighteenth century, the great majority of Europeans and European settlers in the wider world were at least nominal adherents either to the Catholic Church or to one of the Protestant churches, all of whose doctrinal positions on wine (discussed in the preceding chapter) were by then well established. In the three centuries between the early 1700s and the present, there were some notable shifts in the relationships between religion and wine: a broad movement against alcohol that developed in the nineteenth century often made its case in religious terms; new religious denominations required their followers to abstain completely from alcohol and reconfigured their communion rituals to exclude wine; and in the 1960s, the Roman Catholic Church itself re-evaluated the position of wine in the Eucharist. More recently, outside Europe and the Europeanised world, the 'Arab Spring' of the early 2000s provoked vigorous debates in some majority-Muslim countries about Islamic law on wine and on alcohol generally.

Two general points should be noted. First, for the most part, this discussion of religion and wine refers to doctrinal positions rather than to the practices of the members of the various religions and churches. Despite the teachings of their respective churches, many Catholics and Protestants – clergy and lay members alike – drank heavily. Some ended up before church and secular courts while others were dealt with informally. Second, in many cases, religious doctrines referred not exclusively to wine but to all alcoholic beverages, including wine. In other cases, however, wine was treated differently from beer and distilled beverages and was accorded a degree of tolerance that the other alcoholic beverages were not.

John Wesley and Methodism

This latter position appears in the thinking of John Wesley (1705–1791), an English clergyman who led an evangelical movement within the Church of England before splitting from it to form a Methodist 'Connexion'. (Wesley was reluctant to see it as a 'Church'.) The various branches of Methodism which developed into Churches out of his Connexion became mainstream Protestant denominations in Britain, the United States, Canada and elsewhere and were especially popular among working-class Christians.

Wesley is often portrayed as an abstainer and prohibitionist, but his ideas about alcohol were more complex, and, like many commentators on alcohol, he was more opposed to distilled spirits than to fermented beverages such as wine. Drinking distilled spirits, Wesley thought, was more likely to lead to drunkenness, and the rules for members of Methodist Societies that he wrote in the early 1740s specified that Methodists were to avoid 'Drunkenness, buying or selling spirituous liquors, or drinking them (unless in cases of extreme necessity)' (Simon 1923: 102). Wesley often referred to distilled spirits ('spirituous liquors') as poison, although he did allow that they could be taken for medicinal purposes – which he here referred to as 'extreme necessity'.

It is significant that as Wesley was being ordained in 1725, and for the following two decades, London and other parts of England were experiencing what has become known as the 'gin craze', a period from about 1720 to 1750 when the production and sale of distilled spirits (generically known as 'gin') were deregulated, and gin became a common drink among the working classes and the poor. The actual extent and social consequences of gin drinking at this time are uncertain, but it was reputed to have been a serious problem for women and their families in particular, and Parliament tried to contain it by a series of laws in the 1720s and 1730s (Warner 2003). This was the context in which John Wesley formed his attitudes towards alcohol, especially distilled spirits.

As far as wine was concerned, Wesley took a more positive stance. He praised it as 'one of the noblest cordials in nature' (Wesley 1831, V: 114), but he still emphasised the importance of drinking temperately:

> I cannot but think, if your wine is good in kind, suited to your constitution, and taken in small quantities, it is full as wholesome as any liquor in the world, except water. Yet the grievous abuse of it, which almost universally prevails, might easily prejudice a benevolent man against it; and make him endeavour to prevent the abuse, by forbidding the use of it.
> (Wesley 1831, XIV: 266)

It is an ambiguous position: good wine is nutritious and wholesome (although not as wholesome as water), but it is so commonly abused that a 'benevolent man' might well be in favour of forbidding its consumption altogether. Here, as so often, there is a distinction between the essence of the beverage (good) and the way it is consumed (bad). Even so, Wesley judged wine less severely than distilled spirits, which were 'poison' and might have medicinal benefits only 'in extreme necessity'.

Wesley's general position was not so far from mainstream Christian thinking about alcohol. The doctrines of the Roman Catholic and Protestant Churches looked upon fermented alcoholic beverages – wine and beer, principally – as good in themselves, and they permitted moderate consumption. What they condemned was excessive consumption and drunkenness, which led to all manner of sins. There was also a tendency to think of distilled spirits differently and more critically than fermented alcoholic beverages. But over time, the Methodist Churches adopted a more rigorous position on all alcoholic beverages, and Methodists became key supporters of the temperance and prohibitionist movements in the nineteenth century.

Catholics and wine in the eighteenth century

Wesley's ambiguous attitude toward wine contrasted with the positive attitude of the contemporary Roman Catholic Church. As the preceding chapter shows, the Catholic Church gave a special theological role to wine that Protestant Churches challenged. Although all shared a common religious text in which wine had a special status and a meaning that was intrinsic to the faith, Protestants rejected the doctrine of transubstantiation as a way of explaining Christ's presence in wine and were more explicitly wary of the dangers that drinking wine entailed. Moreover, Protestant parishes did not own vineyards the way that Catholic parishes and dioceses did, and the fact that Protestant Churches had largely rejected the monastic life meant that they did not have the likes of the Cistercians and other wine-producing orders that were prominent in the Catholic world.

In Catholic Europe, the viticultural practices associated with the Catholic Church that had begun 1,000 years earlier continued during the eighteenth century. Parishes were encouraged to cultivate vineyards wherever feasible, to provide not only sacramental wine for the Eucharist, but also wine for consumption by the parish priest and for sale on the market. Throughout Europe, religious houses continued to be major vineyard owners and produced vast volumes of wine they sold both locally and farther afield (Phillips 2016: 49–50).

Parish-owned vineyards were especially common in areas of wine production. During the middle decades of the eighteenth century (1726–1782), the priest of Volnay, now a prestigious wine village near Beaune in Burgundy, kept detailed records of the vineyards belonging to the parish and the wine they produced (Phillips 2019a). As we might expect, his records often reflected his faith. Each year, the priest, François Delachère, summarised the weather conditions and their impact on the grape harvest, but although he described the rain, hail, floods, sunshine and droughts in quite banal ways, he generally explained them in religious terms. In 1748, for example, Delachère wrote that the vines on the slopes of Volnay were 'preserved [from hail] by a favour from heaven'. Twelve years later, when the growing season was perfect, Delachère acknowledged the divine role: 'the Providence of the All Powerful governs and controls the seasons'.

To ensure good growing conditions and a successful grape harvest, Delachère turned to a tiered system of prayers. Because the harvest (whether of grapes, grain or other produce) was the most important event of the year, prayers for good weather must have been said almost daily. But when weather conditions were poor – in years when there was too much or too little rain, for example – prayers were said publicly outside in the vineyards and fields. When weather conditions were more threatening, such as an extended drought, a bishop or other authority could authorise 40 hours of prayers, with each parish church participating in turn. In 1764, the magistrates of Beaune requested the Grands Vicaires to give permission for 40 hours of prayers *Ad petendam pluviam* – an appeal to God for rain.

But when conditions were so critical that the vines were at risk of dying, the relic of Saint Revérien, a bishop of Autun who was martyred and decapitated in the fourth century, could be brought out from a church in Villy-le-Moutier, a village near Beaune, and carried to that city. The relic, a fragment of bone reputed to be from Saint Revérien's skull, was accompanied by a procession of the faithful chanting prayers for rain. This ritual was used only when conditions were dire, and it took place only twice, in 1761 and 1771, during the 57-year period when François Delachère was the priest of Volnay. On another occasion, the priest of the parish where the relic was kept refused a request to bring it out on the ground that conditions were not serious enough (Phillips 2019a).

Parish vineyards such as Volnay's tended to increase in size over time as parishioners donated whole vineyards or rows of vines in order to have prayers said for their souls. Even if there were no great debates about religion and wine during most of the eighteenth century, grapevines and wine retained their strong connection to the Roman Catholic Church. In the New World, Catholic missionaries planted vineyards in many regions and were responsible for founding the wine industries in Chile, Argentina and California. Again, an immediate purpose might have been to provide wine for the Eucharist, but far more was produced than needed for that purpose, and the bulk was consumed in quite secular circumstances.

In areas where grapes did not grow, missionaries simply did the best they could. The Jesuit priest Paul Le Jeune, living in Quebec, Canada, in 1736, reported that some of his colleagues had made wine for the Eucharist from grapes growing wild locally. 'I tasted it, and it seemed to me very good', he wrote (Phillips 2017: 11) – although sacramental wine did not have to taste good but merely needed to be fermented grape juice that had been blessed.

Accounts of priests going to great lengths to make wine, and of priests and parishioners praying and parading relics to ensure good weather for their vines, suggest a level of piety that sometimes sits awkwardly with the fact that from the 1600s, Europeans became increasingly secular. Historian

Michel Vovelle, for example, writes that in Provence, in southeast France, many people turned away from the Church (Vovelle 1977) from the mid-1700s – at the very time that, a few hundred kilometres to the north, François Delachère and the villagers of Volnay were praying and displaying a relic in the hope that God would send rain to their vineyards.

The French Revolution

Secularisation underpinned some important changes in the relationship between Church and wine during the French Revolution (1789–1799). Official religious policies evolved during the decade of revolution, but they began with the creation in 1790 of a state church that was analogous to the Protestant Churches of Europe. This model was abandoned during the Terror (1793–1794), the radical phase of the Revolution, when the government embraced a policy of dechristianisation, intended to rid France of all signs of the Christian religion. After the Terror, from 1795 to 1799, church and state were officially separated, and limits were placed on the activities of the Church and on religious observance.

It was the first of these policies, the creation of a state church, that had a major effect on the association of the church and wine because the government nationalised and sold all church properties that were not needed for strictly religious purposes. Religious orders were abolished, and their houses sold off, along with many parish churches, buildings and land – including all the vineyards and winemaking facilities owned by the church. In regions such as Burgundy, where religious orders, cathedrals and parishes owned vast areas of land planted in vines, the ownership of vineyards was transformed as they were sold to local vignerons as well as to investors in Paris and elsewhere (Phillips 2016: 125–126). This policy interrupted the centuries-long history of wine production by the clergy that had been a major contribution to France's wine supply and had provided vital income to religious houses and parishes.

As well as cutting the ties between the church and wine production, the French Revolution arguably undermined the religious associations of wine. For a number of years, most communities in France had no regular religious services, and the state attempted to create secular rituals such as festivals to take their place. Wine was often a feature of these events, and Revolutionary governments tried to assure a steady supply of good quality at affordable prices (Phillips 2019b). Historian Noelle Plack has argued that wine became symbolic of the Revolution such that drinking wine to celebrate the new regime was a kind of secular communion (Plack 2012).

Temperance movements

Following the French Revolution, it was in the context of the temperance and prohibition movements of the nineteenth century that religion and wine met again. Yet although these movements were often led by Christians, they did not arise simply because of Christian teaching on alcohol. One of the principal arguments in favour of drinking beer and wine for rehydration was that, as a result of fermentation, they were safer than water, which was often polluted. But by the early 1800s, non-alcoholic beverages, such as tea, coffee and chocolate, were being widely consumed, and from the 1830s, cities and towns across Europe, North America and elsewhere began to provide clean, safe water for their inhabitants (Phillips 2014: 187–191). Suddenly, it became feasible to ask people to abstain from alcohol because there was a safe alternative.

The supporters and activists of the anti-alcohol movements were for the most part Protestant women, and their main organisation was the Woman's Christian Temperance Union (WCTU), which was founded in Ohio in 1873 and soon had hundreds of thousands of members in more than 40 countries. The WCTU was eventually eclipsed in the United States by the less explicitly religious Anti-Saloon League, but it remained the leading prohibitionist organisation in many other places.

Members of other denominations and faiths, such as Catholics and Jews, also participated in the anti-alcohol movements of the nineteenth and early twentieth centuries, but they were not nearly as important as Protestants who, as we have seen in the preceding chapter, from their foundation in the Reformation took a more rigorous view of alcohol consumption. Yet although Protestant churches embraced the notion of temperance – moderate drinking had been their doctrine from the start – not all supported prohibition. This entailed a ban on the production and sale of alcoholic beverages of all kinds and, by implication, the disappearance of alcohol consumption. When, later in the nineteenth century, there was a movement to replace wine with grape juice at communion (see later in this chapter), most mainline Protestant churches balked. Differences over wine in communion point to divisions between the doctrines embraced by these Protestant Churches and the practices advocated by many of their adherents.

This division provided a space for the emergence of new Christian denominations that from the outset supported prohibition. They included Seventh-Day Adventists (founded in 1863) and the Church of Christ, Scientist (1879), both of which from the beginning forbade the consumption of alcohol and advocated specific diets for their members. Seventh-Day Adventists used grape juice at communion while Christian Scientists eschewed this form of communion entirely.

Another important church that emerged in the United States during the nineteenth century, the Church of Jesus Christ of Latter-day Saints (generally known as the Mormons) followed a different trajectory in its doctrines regarding wine. In the early years, wine was accepted as a good thing for consumption (in moderation) and for communion, and it was described that way in the Church's sacred text, the *Book of Mormon*. But subsequent divine 'revelations' experienced by Joseph Smith, the church's founder, modified this doctrine. When Smith feared that people hostile to his religion might poison his wine, he received divine instructions that Mormons could drink only wine they had made themselves (Fuller 1995: 507).

In 1833, as the temperance movement began, Smith received a revelation that reflected the times:

> that inasmuch as any man drinketh wine or strong drink among you, behold it is not good, neither meet in the sight of your Father, only in assembling yourselves together to offer up your sacraments before him. And, behold, this should be wine, yea, pure wine of the grape of the vine, of your own making.
>
> *(Fuller 1995: 507)*

Yet although this can reasonably be understood as meaning that Mormons should abstain from wine and other alcoholic beverages except during communion, they continued to drink and only gradually developed a doctrine of total abstinence from alcohol. By about 1906, they began to replace wine with water in the communion service, and in 1951, the General Conference determined definitively that the 1833 instruction meant total abstinence from alcohol (Fuller 1995: 507).

One of the issues that Mormons and other Christian prohibitionists had to confront was the apparent approval of wine in the Bible, where there are more references to grapevines than to any other plant and more references to wine than any other beverage. Not all the references to wine show it in a good light. When Noah's ark settled after the Great Flood subsided, he planted grapevines and made wine. But Noah drank to excess, took off his clothes and was seen naked by his sons. When Lot's daughters wanted him to have sex with them, they plied him with wine. In both cases, wine was associated with sins.

Yet in other cases, wine was shown in a positive context. Jesus's first miracle was to turn water into wine at the Marriage at Cana – and that was a good thing as it enabled the guests at the wedding to continue the celebrations after the wine supplied by the host had run out. At the Last Supper, Jesus tells his disciples that he will not drink wine with them that night – implying that on other occasions he had – but that he would drink wine with them in heaven.

The dilemma facing Christians who condemned wine and all alcoholic beverages was how to reconcile the positive references to wine with their belief that all alcoholic beverages were not only dangerous but sinful. Why would Jesus make wine and drink it? The solution to the problem was found in the 'two-wine theory', which posited that two beverages were mentioned in the Bible: 'unfermented wine' and wine. By 'unfermented wine' (an oxymoron because wine is, by definition, fermented), supporters of the 'two-wine theory' meant grape juice. By 'wine' they meant wine: fermented grape juice that contained alcohol (Woodruff Tait 2011: 14–19).

Having made that distinction, supporters of the two-wine theory argued that when wine was shown in a negative light (such as the stories of Noah and Lot), the beverage was, in fact, wine. But when the beverage was shown in a positive light (such as Jesus making and drinking it), it was not wine but grape juice – that is, unfermented and therefore non-alcoholic juice. This theory was propagated from the 1830s and gained some popularity as the century progressed, especially in the growing Methodist Churches, with their established negative position on alcohol. It was less popular in the Anglican Church and its American counterparts (such as the Episcopalians), who had never subscribed to the more rigorous alcohol doctrines associated with the Calvinists.

For supporters of the two-wine theory, it was not simply a matter of grape juice being preferable to wine because it did not contain alcohol, but because wine was seen as a critical element in a nexus of problems that included indulgence, excitement, immigrants, sensuality and the leisured upper classes. Grape juice, in contrast, was associated with purity, progress, cleanliness, punctuality, order, sobriety and gentility (Woodruff Tait 2011: 14–15).

Some American Jews – there was no correlation with the Orthodox, Conservative or Liberal communities – who wanted to avoid alcohol adopted a similar practice and made 'raisin wine' to use instead of conventional sacramental wine. One recipe read as follows:

> [P]ut the raisins into the demijohn [a large jar] and fill it with water. Tie a rag over the mouth, and place the demijohn near the fire, or on one side of the fire-place, to keep it warm. In about a week it will be fit for use, making a pure, pleasant, and sweet wine, free from alcohol. . . . This is the wine we use on the nights of Passover.
>
> *(Sarna 1988: 270)*

Grape juice was, in fact, a creation of the late nineteenth century: it was not until the 1870s that Thomas Welch, a Methodist dentist, perfected the method of pasteurising grape juice to prevent it from fermenting. Up until that time, grape juice could be consumed for only a short time after the grapes were pressed because it was at risk of quickly attracting ambient yeasts that would start the process of alcoholic fermentation. Once grape juice could be produced commercially – the Welch family started a famous company that still produces juice and jellies made from grapes – the two-wine theory took on new life, and by the 1880s, the Methodist Church recommended grape juice (which it persisted in calling 'unfermented wine') for all religious and personal purposes.

Prohibition and wine

Ironically, national Prohibition was adopted in the United States largely thanks to pressure by religious organisations, but when it came into force in 1920, there was one main exemption to the ban on producing and selling alcohol: when it was needed for religious purposes. That exemption was not in the Eighteenth Amendment, which introduced national Prohibition, but it was included in the Volstead Act, which set out the ways in which Prohibition would be applied. It allowed priests, ministers, pastors and rabbis to administer wine for sacramental purposes, and this permitted some wineries to keep on producing wine and for limited retail opportunities.

While only small volumes of wine were required for the Eucharist and communion in Christian churches – especially in Catholic churches, where only the priest took the wine – Jews needed much more because kosher wine featured in weekly sabbath meals and the many high holiday rituals (especially Passover) within each Jewish household. Rabbis were required to purchase wine on behalf of their congregation – a complicated bureaucratic process that permitted them to buy no less than five gallons at a time – and when they obtained the wine, they distributed it among the households (Davis 2012: 154). The Christian clergy, in contrast, obtained wine that they used in communion – Catholic priests to take on behalf of the laity, Protestant clergy to dispense to communicants.

The religious exemption to the ban on alcohol consumption led to abuses. Many Jews who did not keep kosher or attend synagogue regularly nonetheless decided that wine was essential to their sabbath and high holiday meals. In addition, unlike Christian clergy, the American rabbinate was loosely organised, and it was not difficult for people to forge rabbinical certification and purchase large volumes of wine for non-existent congregations (Davis 2012: 156). Jewish bootleggers provided wine to Jews and non-Jews alike, and such practices contributed to the 'sacramental wine scandals' of the mid-1920s. There were claims that Jews were profiting from Prohibition – a Presbyterian minister in Newark said that 'The majority of the Hebrew race are engaged in the liquor business for money' (Davis 2012: 157) – and the phenomenon reinforced antisemitic sentiments at the time.

Religion and wine in the twentieth century

After prohibition laws in the United States and elsewhere were mostly repealed in the 1930s, the religious world settled into a new equilibrium with respect to wine. The mainstream Christian churches in the Western world and the various Jewish congregations maintained their historic positions on wine – that their adherents could consume it in moderation – but they were now joined, especially in the United States, by a number of denominations that required their members to abstain from wine and all other forms of alcohol. One of these denominations, the Church of Jesus Christ of Latter-day Saints, actively proselytised around the world and gradually increased the number of Christians who embraced a doctrine that drinking wine was sinful. The Church reported its membership as about 750,000 in 1935, soon after Prohibition was repealed; 3.5 million in 1975; and 16.5 million in 2019 (*Statistical Report* 2020).

During the twentieth century, reformers within the Roman Catholic Church began to press for the re-introduction of the Eucharist under both kinds, where not only the clergy but also the laity would receive the sacramental wine. The issue was discussed at the reformist Second Vatican Council (1962–65), and both progressives and conservatives agreed on two issues: 'the need for a return to the sources of the liturgy in the early Church and secondly the need for greater participation on the part of the laity' (Tanner 2001: 48). In terms of wine, the question was whether or not to overturn the twelfth-century practice of denying the Eucharist wine to the laity. A compromise was reached between reformers and conservatives: that bishops should have the discretion to extend wine to the laity at such significant occasions as masses to celebrate the ordination of a priest and the first Eucharist of a new convert to Catholicism, as well as masses said following a baptism. Beyond those particular cases, bishops were empowered to permit communion under both kinds for ordinary masses. In practice, many bishops give blanket approval for priests within their dioceses to celebrate communion this way.

A 2017 Pastoral Letter of Pope Francis seemed to assume that communion was being offered under two kinds because he reminded bishops of their duty to watch over the quality of the bread and wine offered at the Eucharist. The bread must contain gluten, and the wine

> must be natural, from the fruit of the grape, pure and incorrupt, not mixed with other substances. . . . Great care should be taken so that the wine intended for the celebration of the Eucharist is well conserved and has not soured.

Moreover, communicants who for medical reasons could not ingest alcohol could be served grape juice (*Circular letter to the Bishops* 2017).

Outside the spheres of Western religions, there was some discussion of the relationship of Islam to alcohol in the early 2000s. Although a ban on drinking alcohol by Muslims has been in force for many centuries, policies on producing and consuming alcohol in Muslim-majority societies have long varied from place to place (Phillips 2000: 101–106). Today, a number of these countries, such as Turkey, Algeria, Tunisia and Morocco, are wine producers, and laws regarding wine and other alcohol consumption vary from absolute bans to broad toleration. The 'Arab Spring', which began in 2011 as movements for political reform, ushered in more rigorous policies regarding drinking and other forms of personal behaviour in some countries. In Tunisia, for example, there was a drive 'to improve moral character by imposing restrictions on alcohol and profanity and blasphemy' (Alssayad and Massoumi 2012: 33). In Turkey, which has a vibrant wine industry, new restrictions on the sale of wine and other alcoholic beverages were imposed between 2011 and 2013 (*Hürriyet* 2013).

Conclusion

The slightly more than 300 years that have passed since the beginning of the eighteenth century saw significant shifts in the relationship between wine and some of the world's religions. Protestant Churches, which had from the sixteenth century embraced doctrines less positive than the Catholic Church to wine, lost some members to new non-Catholic denominations that condemned drinking outright. One was Methodism, which had split from the Church of England in the 1700s, but others were churches founded in the temperance and prohibition environment of the nineteenth century. The Catholic Church, while maintaining its tight association with wine, largely abandoned communion under one kind, which it had adopted in the twelfth century. In the early 2000s, there was a slight strengthening of Muslim doctrines against alcohol, although policies in Muslim-majority countries remain variable. It is important to remember that with increasing secularisation, especially in Western societies, religious teachings on wine guide fewer and fewer people. Nonetheless, religious authorities continue to define and redefine their doctrines on wine, not only according to the internal dynamics of their particular faiths but also within specific historical contexts.

References

Alssayad, N. and Massoumi, M. (2012) "Religious Fundamentalism in the City: Reflections on the Arab Spring," *Journal of International Affairs* 65, 31–42.

Circular Letter to Bishops on the Bread and Wine for the Eucharist. (2017) https://w2.vatican.va/content/dam/wss/roman_curia/congregations/ccdds/documents/rc_con_ccdds_doc_20170615_lettera-su-pane-vino-eucaristia_en.html.

Davis, M. (2012) *Jews and Booze: Becoming American in the Age of Prohibition*, New York: New York University Press.

Fuller, R.C. (1995) "Wine, Symbolic Boundary Settings, and American Religious Communities," *Journal of the American Academy of Religion* 63, 497–517.

Hürriyet. (2013) "Turkey Adopts Alcohol Restrictions," *Hürriyet Daily News*, 24 May.

Phillips, R. (2000) *A Short History of Wine*, London: Penguin Books.

Phillips, R. (2014) *Alcohol: A History*, Chapel Hill: University of North Carolina Press.

Phillips, R. (2016) *French Wine: A History*, Sacramento: University of California Press.

Phillips, R. (2017) *The Wines of Canada*, Oxford: Infinite Ideas Books 'Classic Wine Library'.

Phillips, R. (2019a) "A Priest and His Wine: Volnay 1726–1776," *The World of Fine Wine* 63: 104–109.

Phillips, R. (2019b) "Living Revolution, Drinking Revolution: Assuring Wine Quality and Safety in Burgundy during the 1790s," Living the French Revolution Colloquium, University of Melbourne, Australia, July. Published on H-France, https://h-france.net/rude/wp-content/uploads/2020/02/08-PHILLIPS.pdf.

Plack, N. (2012) "Liberty, Equality, and Taxation: Wine in the French Revolution," *Social History of Alcohol and Drugs* 26, 5–22.

Sarna, J.D. (1988) "Passover Raisin Wine, the American Temperance Movement, and Mordecai Noah," *Hebrew Union College Annual* 59, 269–288.
Simon, J.S. (1923) *John Wesley and The Methodist Societies*, London: Epworth Press, 102.
Statistical Report for April 2020 Conference [of the Church of Jesus Christ of Latter-day Saints]. (2020) https://newsroom.churchofjesuschrist.org/article/2019-statistical-report.
Tanner, N. (2001) "The Eucharist and the Ecumenical Councils," *Gregorianum* 82, 37–49.
Vovelle, M. (1977) "Le tournant des mentalités en France 1750–1789: la 'sensibilité' pré-révolutionnaire," *Social History* 2, 605–629.
Warner, J. (2003) *Craze: Gin and Debauchery in an Age of Reason*, New York: Random House.
Wesley, J. (1831) *The Works of the Reverend John Wesley*, New York: J. Emory and B. Waugh.
Woodruff Tait, J.L. (2011) *The Poisoned Chalice: Eucharistic Grape Juice and Common-Sense Realism in Victorian Methodism*, Tuscaloosa: University of Alabama Press.

27
WINE AS METAPHOR

Azélina Jaboulet-Vercherre

Introduction

Inspired not only by the complex cultivation of the vine but also by the etiquette and enjoyment of this 'godly' beverage, the discourse on wine is rich. Beyond its materiality, we find indications of a recognition of wine as an embodiment of what is an almost spiritual harmony between the realms of nature, humankind and the divine.

The allegorical power of wine allows multiple interpretations, and several figures of speech emphasise the repeated alliance between faith, intellect and culture. The metaphor, in particular, is a powerful device. From the Greek μεταφορά, it expresses the notion of transfer as it stands for the use of one thing to designate another, implying the idea of displacement, change, motion. In a religious sense, it conveys a promise to penetrate divine principles.

The polysemy of wine peaked in the writings of the Western Middle Ages. This chapter therefore focuses on – but is not restricted to – the use of wine metaphors in medieval sources. Since these texts were kinds of time travellers, it also includes swift journeys to Ancient Greece and Rome (where they took their roots) and the Renaissance (when their successors developed their metaphorical models) to highlight the representation of wine as a paradigm of civilisation.

Grapes are the fruits of the land. They have also been perceived as symbols of desire at least since the Song of Songs, the biblical manifesto of the art of loving. Wine has therefore come to illustrate joy, prosperity, longevity – enticing pretexts for wine lovers to justify their indulgence. More than any other fermented beverage, wine has inspired metaphors enriching the wine lexicon, whose technical terms may not only fail to reflect the delight of wine but may also even serve to desiccate it.

A metaphor is a sophisticated kind of trope (Greek *tropos*; Latin *tropus*, turn, way, manner, style): that is, a figure of speech using a word or phrase to designate another, thereby suggesting a likeness or analogy between them.

The success of a metaphor lies in the connivance between the user and the receiver, who must perceive the kinship of two apparently unrelated items. This is why metaphors often appear more vivid than comparisons since the latter are, as Aristotle put it, 'metaphors requiring *logos*' (i.e. a broader specification), whose length reduces the immediacy of the pleasurable effect and thereby diminishes the satisfaction of the receiver (*Rhetorics*, III, 4, 1407a: 14–15).

Wine metaphors often transcend mere ornamental device, and their rich lexical field compels us to grant the subject its multifaceted character. Essential to the Homeric epic, their use pervades premodern Western poetic thought. Authors found in metaphor a way to reflect on a given experience through a transfer of sense, adding meaning and resonance to simple, concrete words. It therefore aroused emotions and opened the gate towards spiritual thought.

The metaphor started out as a poetic device, by definition reaching a highly selected audience. As its use becomes more widespread, its message loses acuity. By exploring the rhetoric of wine, this chapter investigates how time may transform metaphor in general and wine metaphor in particular.

The metaphor: a perfect wine trope?

> A metaphor is a poetically or rhetorically ambitious use of words, a figurative as opposed to literal use. It has attracted more philosophical interest and provoked more philosophical controversy than any of the other traditionally recognised figures of speech.
>
> *Stanford Encyclopedia of Philosophy*

Since its inception, the metaphor has been accorded a specific value, and this has led many thinkers to provide their own definition. Among the 120 occurrences of the term 'wine' in Homer, the most famous remains the 'wine-dark sea'. It obviously takes us far beyond a mere descriptive indicator: its dark aspect indicates the fragility of human life, rich in obstacles and dangers. After Homer, and for millennia, wine has remained a colourful vehicle for an ever-broadening imagery.

Classic metaphor and the notion of transfer

Coming from the Greek word μεταφέρω (*metapherein*, 'to transfer'), a metaphor is an implied comparison, the poetical device *par excellence*. Aristotle gave it a clear definition in *Poetics* (1457b: 6–9):

> A metaphor is the application of a word that belongs to another thing: either from genus to species, species to genus, species to species, or by analogy.

Developing his explanation, Aristotle tackled the foundational interrelation between metaphor and analogy and, interestingly, took wine as an example:

> [T]he wine bowl is to Dionysos as the shield to Ares: so one will call the wine bowl 'Dionysos' shield', and the shield 'Ares' wine bowl'. . . . This type of metaphor can further be used by predicating the borrowed term while denying one of its attributes: suppose one were to call the shield not 'Ares' wine bowl' but 'a wineless wine bowl'.

By nature, metaphor speaks to a selected audience, the first major difference between a simple analogy and a metaphor. The second difference concerns the longevity of its use: a metaphor may become a common analogy once it is collectively understood and has passed on to a larger audience as a cultural referent. This difference therefore also corresponds to a transformation of the figure itself.

In the *Poetics*, Aristotle asserts that the primary process of art is imitation (*mimêsis*), a human predisposition. We learn by imitating language(s), manners and other skills with increasing sophistication as we grow – the apex being the art of writing. The metaphor then acts to reveal the discourse a given language creates. Aristotle contends that the primary virtue of the metaphor is to bolster the visibility of an event or a thing. By pulling us away from a pure descriptive set of words, it becomes the embodiment of the subject – sometimes at the expense of clarity.

While metaphors were invented within Greek literature, they apply to a number of languages, starting with Latin – the main source language for the present contribution. Focusing on ancient Roman culture, William M. Short demonstrated the 'metaphoricity' of food in Latin (2013: 247–275, esp. 272 for this neologism). For Latin speakers, he argues, communication is built on the model or figure of speech, starting with the first stage: mental elaboration. The structure of a given semantic system builds meaning across the field of preparation, ingestion, digestion of information turning it to thoughts and analysis. Just like alimentary metaphors, some drinking metaphors have progressively entered the common lexicon (flavour, taste and savour belong to the thesaurus of luxury lifestyle), and many of these still indicate quality, appreciation, analysis or consideration.

The success of a metaphor is, by definition, contextual, embedded in the framework of a given society's mindset and thereby disclosing mental representations of a particular time and language. As Short put it, it should be considered as a conceptual structure rather than a mere linguistic or literary artifice (Short 2014: 339–352). Medieval theology subsequently added depth to the process of building metaphors on analogies, blurring the boundaries between the main figures of speech.

Rhetorical qualities also cover social, cultural and intellectual dimensions: we may display a thirst for knowledge, students might gulp down texts or binge on critics when preparing for an exam/interview. Inspirational thought and poetical beauty are designed to provide a feeling of inebriation: such rhetoric structures our thoughts in a coherent way by allowing swings between physical and mental stimuli and instilling images in one's mind, thereby improving one's intellectual resources. The basic nature of some lexical fields makes the transfer easily understood and readily adaptable to a coherent mapping of corresponding concepts. Physicians have used the wine metaphor in both simple and complex ways throughout the centuries.

Medical metaphors

The famous physician Galen (129–200 CE/210 CE) defined nutrition as 'an assimilation of that which nourishes to that which receives nourishment' (*On the Natural Faculties*, I:11). For him, anything actually nourishing or destined to nourish was 'nutriment'; anything that adheres to the organs instead of nourishing them was 'quasi-nutriment'; and he called 'destined nutriment' the rest of the matter contained in the stomach and the veins. Waste matter then underwent what Galen called a 'process of separation' in the veins before being rejected. He compared the kidneys (though not as active as the main organs) to the filters into which wine is poured (*Natural Faculties*, I:15). Galen again relied on wine as a metaphor to explain the generation of humours, in particular the differences between yellow bile and black bile, the latter being akin to lees by reason of its earthiness but sharp as vinegar (*Natural Faculties* II: 9; *De usu partium* 4.3, I: 205–206).

Before examining the main uses of wine metaphors in religious thought, I shall consider an influential example of reversed metaphor: i.e. a transfer used to explain the effect of wine on human beings. In medical literature, wine appears as a source of heat, beneficial to the body if taken appropriately and harmful if taken to excess. Natural philosophers since Aristotle have continuously used the metaphor of fire: just as a fiery source may be engulfed by a bigger fire, the heart's natural heat may be overcome by too much additional heat, causing illness or even death (Niebyl 1971: 351–368). The philosopher thus clearly distinguishes between intrinsic heat, the force of generation and concoction (i.e. ripening), and extrinsic heat, which, in excess, causes decay and 'corruption'. When discussing the way in which external and internal heat affect nutrition, Galen preferred the motif of the lamp to that of a flame. He believed this would better illustrate the constant decline in innate heat, and he compares the body's need for moisture to a wick in an oil lamp. The oil represents the body's natural moisture, and the flame at the end of the wick represents external heat, too much of which drains all the moisture and extinguishes the lamp. Over 700 years later, in the tradition of Neoplatonic philosophers and physicians, Avicenna (980–1037) also used the lamp motif in his exposition of hectic fever (Niebyl 1971: 358–359; Ziegler 1999: 220). At the beginning of his chapter on food and drink, he explained their effects as a result of their quality, material composition and substance. He provided a detailed account of heat's active power to restore the body by transforming nutritive matter into blood (Avicenna, *Canon*, Book I, fen 2, d. 1, c. 15).

Because of its very nature, mankind is particularly well-suited to receiving the pleasures and properties of wine; this led to the crucial analogy between how wine is made and how the human body functions. This is one of the reasons why wine was believed to regenerate blood, the 'treasure' among the four humours. All ancient and medieval medical texts testify to wine and blood's substantial similarity, and even more interesting are the occasions when wine serves as a metaphor for blood.

Wine and blood's inextricable connections

In addition to ancient and medieval writers' observations of wine's mysterious and miraculous powers, wine has long been associated with blood in a metaphorical sense. These two factors, while distinct, are impossible to fully disentangle from a historical perspective.

As wine embodies the domestication of nature, it came to be considered the paradigm of civilisation from Greek antiquity onwards, when wine was poured to replace animal sacrifices and gain the gods' clemency.

From the iconography of ancient sacrificial practices to medieval representations of the Eucharist, many works of art illustrate the relationships between blood, wine and the divine. The idea that wine and meat have the power to strengthen the body and fortify the soul has been expressed in both positive and negative terms. From the very early days of Christianity, religious zealots (and even moderate Christians) proposed bans on wine based on the assumption that it would induce carnal desires. Wine thus became stigmatised for enticing sexual drive, a problem exacerbated by its sister side effects: altered reason and waning self-control (Philo of Alexandria, *Legum Allegoria* 3:138, 145). Likewise, and also because of its heating effects, meat was seen as a primary agent in the inordinate pursuit of lustful indulgence. Both were held to lead to debauchery, which, because of the contagiousness of sin, worsened the 'weighing down' of the soul (Newhauser 2005: 41). The Church fathers and ascetics therefore advocated the search for purity through the avoidance of overindulgence.

Although not everyone was forced to such an extreme, it is essential that a Christian add water to his wine, in various ways throughout life. Baptism is an indispensable premise: pure water is a primary requirement that quenches one's thirst forever; taking wine from the Lord's chalice serves to reassert the Covenant with God and the faithful's consciousness of Christ's passion. Wine here serves as the remembrance of Christ's own sacrifice through a prayer following communion (anamnesis). Thanks to its consideration as divine principle (hypostasis) in itself, wine is the fundamental substance of Christian liturgy, a religious practice allowing theological debates. This takes us far beyond a mere wine metaphor as wine comes to be blood.

Within the semantic field of wine and blood stands the winepress, interpreted as the mystical press in the Middle Ages, in which Christ is crushed like a grape 'because of our crimes' (Isiah, 53: 5). This is the primary image most often depicted in Christian iconography from the thirteenth century on, particularly in northern Europe (Alexandre-Bidon 1990). The mystical body (*corpus mysticum*) initially referred to Christ's body through the Eucharist: the physical sacrament of communion primarily conveys the message of redemption (Bynum 2002). It recalls Christ's mission to take away the sins of the whole world through his passion, which allowed the sacraments to offer Divine Grace to the faithful (Matthew, 26: 27–29). During the last centuries of the Middle Ages, this paradoxical expression of mystical body came to represent the institution of the Church itself: solid and yet invisible to the external senses.

Scriptural imagery

The collective memory contained in the Scriptures offers a rich poetic and philosophical source. From the 'fruit of the earth' to the 'grapes of wrath', wine finds a plethora of echoes in the Bible; it appears some 200 times in the Hebrew Bible and 3,500 times in the Babylonian Talmud.

The vineyard sometimes corresponds to Israel, as in Isaiah's Song of the Vineyard (Isiah, 5:1–7). The covenant between God and his people often appears through the metaphor of the grape harvest and the protection (Judges 8:1–3) – or destruction – of the land; a barren land may represent unfaithfulness (Isaiah 1:8). Oracles following literary patterns of eating and drinking may also illustrate states of the Covenant between God and His people.

The polysemy of wine peaked in the writings of the Middle Ages: any discourse then had to be equivocal to be worthy of any interest. While today we primarily live in a world of univocity, medieval people considered that every object, subject and living being took significance from what it represented more than what it actually showed, the notion of existing being in itself an extension of a deeper reality or a rich set of corresponding realities on which the spiritual sense(s) rest. Hence, the frequent use of the metaphor to foster meaning.

In Muslim Spain, in the course of the eleventh and twelfth centuries, a group of 'courtier-rabbis' adapted biblical drinking feasts, such as Isaiah's 'feast of wines', to a refined literary expression of wine festivals. Four poets – Samuel HaNagid, Solomon Ibn Gabirol, Moses Ibn Ezra and Judah Halevi – stand out from a larger circle of talented creators of the Hebrew Golden Age in Spain. Though the common imagery is very rich and gives the sense of a community, gifted literary creators demonstrated individual expression (Pagis 1991: 5–23). While they assimilated Arabic patterns, rhetoric and traditional categories (formal constraints of courtly prosody, themes) to reflect aristocratic aesthetics and preoccupations, lyricism included, their writings transcend the traditional conventions of literary genres.

Wine parties took place in richly ornamented gardens with flowing water fountains and channels, where harmony was propounded as an aristocratic ideal. Worldly pleasures could then be taken in the setting of night-time revelry, in which the participants could venture into a dreamlike state between consciousness and sleep, surrounded by attractive servants, dancers and singers.

As did ancient (and, later, Goliardic) poets, these courtier-rabbis associated wine poetry with love, taken in a broad sense. Their recourse to metaphors emphasises colours, brightness and fragrances, often in a hedonistic manner. The lovers enjoy both drinks and company, surrounded by birds (especially nightingales) and flowers (most frequently lilies) for the full satisfaction of all senses. Instead of wild debauchery, they depict delicate scenes and idealised settings thanks to rhetorical devices such as metaphors and similes within a larger symbolic imagery. The idea of intoxication from fragrance (smell, perfume), is a *topos* typical of this highly charged love literature.

Connected to love, and already present in the Hebrew Bible, the prevailing image for wine was blood, as Samuel HaNagid suggested when inviting the reader to 'Drink your grape's blood from between my lips' (Carmi 1981: 298). The grieving lover, 'the blood of eyes and heart commingled', recalls the rightful mixture of wine with water, a moral and medical urge (Moses Ibn Ezra 1945: 16) Sometimes, HaNagid portrays such a mixture as an illusory way to heal the pain (Goldstein 1966). Wine is alternately sweet and bitter; like love, it may heal and/or hurt. Wine and love fuse into the flaming cold oxymoron, even igniting debates regarding the use of wine in cures for lovesickness in which a painful – and inadequate – search for forgetfulness would supersede the pleasures of the revelry.

Wine's medical virtues are revisited here in a specific symbolism; it not only 'sweetens all the bitterness of life', but also helps dissolve inhibitions (Cohen 1945). Moses Ibn Ezra advises revellers to 'Immerse your heart in pleasure and in joy/And by the bank, a bottle drink of wine' (Scheindlin 1986: 91). One should note here the metonymy ('a bottle drink'), even though it has travelled the centuries to the point that we barely notice it. In the idyllic context of the wine party, ruby red or golden wine glows in the delicate cup. Both content and container embed the thought of rich textures, which materialise illusionary (or at least ephemeral) comfort in the fragile equilibrium of terrestrial life.

Wine leads the observer/reader to complex, even kaleidoscopic views. A mere dualistic view opposing good and evil, prosperity and poverty, clean and unclean, terrestrial and spiritual oversimplifies the rich imagery of wine. Even when textures, colours or reflections are described, more or less hidden allusions are to be found and connected to higher symbolism that transcends physicality.

Beyond the rhetorical device: spiritual thirst

The perceivable reality cannot suffice; what is apparent does not give a clear image of the actual universe: hence, the power of a metaphorical spectrum to open one's spiritual perspective.

In the Gospel of John, 15: 1–8, which starts with the famous line: 'I am the true vine, and my Father is the husbandman', the reciprocity is clear. God and the faithful have an organic relationship, re-enacted by belief and behaviour, the real fruits of faith.

Origen (c 185 c 254), a Christian exegete and theologian, blended philosophy with theology, making the former ancillary to the latter (*On First Principles* 4.2:4). He elaborated on the various levels of meanings to be found in the Scriptures: literal and spiritual, corresponding to body/flesh and soul/spirit and speaking to persons diversely educated, from the simplest to the most enlightened minds (Origen 1989: 11–12).

Commenting on John, he also refers to the still-famous psalm 104:15, which he presents as essential to the understanding of the Gospel: 'And wine that maketh glad the heart of man'. For John, the evangelist, the spiritual vine holds a higher truth than its material reality. Resting only on what is tangible may lead to idolatry and veil the holy mysteries, whereas divine reason infuses the heart with ecstatic inebriation – the tautology reflects the power of the process: sipping the wine extracted from the 'true vine' cheers one's soul, as does the access to mystical doctrines (*Commentary to John*: 74–75). Metaphors, here again, are reminiscent of a truth more profound than what may be perceived from the visible, superficial world.

Since wine is blood of the grape (Deuteronomy 32:14), Origen declares (*Homily on Numbers*, 16:9) that the real people of Israel (the 'vine stalks') know how to 'drink this blood' from the grape of the real vine, find nourishment from the flesh of God's Word and relish holy inebriation (something we also find in John 6:53).

Immaterial inebriation

The idea of sober intoxication pervades spiritual writings throughout the centuries: Plotinus (204/5–270 CE), the founder of Neoplatonism who was seemingly taught by the same master as Origen, situates this state of superior understanding far beyond mere sobriety. Philo of Alexandria (first half of the first century CE) turned the concept into that influential oxymoron (Philo, 1930: III:148).

The only way to reach this holy state is by reading the Scriptures, a constantly renewed learning experience, as Origen states (*Commentary on the Canticle*, III:9). The magic of inebriation comes to whomsoever has gained access to the Wine of Wisdom (Ecclesiastes, II:3–4): 'I sought in mine heart to give myself unto wine, yet acquainting mine heart with wisdom'. Rabelais turned this quest into a monumental enterprise.

Rabelais's unquenchable thirst

Rabelais (†1553) is one of the prominent figures of the French Renaissance and is integral to the narrative of wine metaphor, as the author of its most significant reinterpretation. No chapter on wine as a metaphor is therefore complete without a brief overview of the way he tackled wine as a Gargantuan figure of speech. To this day, he is often mentioned in French Bacchic reunions, unfortunately in a way that is far too literal to give justice to the extent of his ideas of wine.

Known as a polymath, Rabelais was particularly well versed in ancient and medieval lore. His technical and intellectual familiarity with the body (he was a physician) and the medical literature (the Hippocratic and Galenic collections in particular) allowed him to use metaphors in a rightful yet original way.

Rabelais is a master of rhetorical transfers. Not only does he play with his readers and characters, but he also fuels dialectics with his very own *mots d'esprit*. In his gigantic cultural fresco, he interlocks figures of speech of all kinds – to the point of blurring the traditional boundaries between similes, tropes and allegories. To differentiate between them is a risky task – as much as to separate the terms from the spiritual messages they may hold in his writing. This is particularly difficult for twenty-first-century minds, struggling with signposts that were easily identifiable to sixteenth-century brains. Rabelais helps us take the measure of the loss of mental agility time has entailed, little by little, and triggers our intellects.

Rabelais's wine reflects inspiration and spiritual awakening and is certainly a vehicle to wisdom. Instead of trying to separate the material realm from the spiritual, we shall follow him in his multidimensional project, which will eventually lead us 'beyond the physical realm': that is, to metaphysics. Wine becomes an essential concept, allowing us to step outside human vanities. Rabelais' Bacchic Council itself designates the spiritual adventure, immaterial by nature:

> Now you are not young; and so you are equipped to philosophize – vinously and not vainly, and therefore metaphysically – and so to be raised at once to the Bacchic Council.
> *(Prologue to The Third Book, trans. Weinberg 1972: 281)*

Rabelais's prose is intentionally cryptic and, just like wine, requires initiation: it is a meta-metaphorical world *per se*. As Panurge (Rabelais's crafty rogue) moves to purify his soul in order to properly receive the Word of the Bottle, the readers understand that the reference is to an oracle rather than just any physical bottle. Wine is Dionysian intoxication – i.e. inspiration – which takes us back to the Aristotelian concept of poetry. But Rabelais takes it further by inventing a whole new language. He builds the unity of the writer on an apparent confusion, an overwhelming range of references to which only a few can gain access, provided they are predisposed to searching for true meanings.

Drinking in Rabelais, therefore, has nothing to do with carousal but rather with seeking to quench one's thirst – a lifetime spiritual quest. Rabelais the *panepistemon* (omniscient) scattered signposts throughout his text, everywhere – or nowhere (if one only understands the material meaning of words). The bottle keeps swirling between the lines as an intellectual text which hides subtexts leading Rabelais's 'noble' drinkers to the right path of life (*Gargantua*, lvii: 159). The readers are invited to taste the text and swallow the gloss: reading becomes a fully sensorial adventure by which the holy spirits penetrate the soul from the mouth (*The Fifth Book*, xlv: 882). The gigantic heroes' search for more debauchery is, in fact, a limitless search for knowledge, a hedonism of learning. Nowadays, the mention of a 'Pantagruelic' dinner usually designates an overindulgent meal – but Rabelais, when coining the term 'Pantagruelism', gave it the sense of 'a certain lightness of spirit compounded of contempt for the chances of fate' (*The Fourth Book*, Prologue: 523). Rabelais uses the humble metaphors of eating and drinking to indicate the sublime goal (wisdom), to ascend blithely.

He sets out his major recommendation: 'It is better to write of laughter than tears, since laughter is proper to man' (*Gargantua*, To the Readers: 2). This is no boisterous laughter but healing mirth, an ability exclusive to human beings. He closes the circle when, at the end of book five, he replaces the effect (laughing) with the cause (wine):

And we here maintain that not laughter but drinking is proper to man. I don't mean simple, unadorned drinking because the beasts drink as well. I mean drinking good cool wine. Note well, my friends, that through wine one becomes divine.

(The Fifth Book, xlv: 883, trans. Weinberg 1972: 33)

With this laughter metaphor, wine becomes the core of Rabelais' conception of *libido sciendi* ('thirst for knowledge'). His kaleidoscopic narrative blurring the reading is inebriating in itself: finding clues between the lines (or even between the words) is akin to performing a high wire act – with both the enthusiasm of a child and the circumspection of a venerable philosopher. Such intoxication increases the reader's discernment, enlarging one's path to free will (the Divine Bottle), and inviting to learn accordingly. Wine stands for a vivid, constantly renewable lifestyle.

Wine epitomises Rabelais's reinvention of the notion of *mimêsis*: he invites the reader to ceaseless thinking and writing – instead of simply reproducing. More than a metaphor, wine is life itself, as Gargantua proclaimed instead of giving the newborn's cry (*Gargantua*, vi: 23).

Conclusion: wine, metaphor, and the process of time

Metaphors were originally used to make elements of language more dramatic. This served to promote conversation between the writer and the reader, a performer and the audience, thereby becoming a common reference. When marking the genius of a given author, it may stay historically situated, serve cross-meanings and even become esoteric.

Over time, some metaphors remained; others were slowly abandoned. The dangers announced in the Homeric formula of the 'wine-dark sea' seldom appear in wine tasting discussions but are inherent in the advocacy of temperance – and we now know that wine does not regenerate blood. Apart from the remembrance of Redemption, the blood metaphor has been diluted; the mystical press is not a strong *topos* anymore. Yet our wine lexicon still bears marks of medieval conceptualisation modes: the term 'robe' to indicate a wine's colour seems to stretch from the medieval humanisation of things.

As a wine becomes a living being, the decorum of drinking vessels becomes part of a drinking party: hence, the search for the right wine for the right moment. Rather than the technical, aromatic, basic analogical lexicon, our ancestors wielded subtle reminders of the alliance of material conditions and spiritual aspirations, which helped every person enjoy his own wine – even if it were solely the wine of Wisdom.

I therefore suggest we use history to reconcile materiality and spirituality, wine and literature. Taking wine as a learning tool may transform one's thirst for knowledge from quaffing lines into savouring thoughts. The art of reading is contrary to literary bingeing. It requires initiation, guidance, patience and practice, just as winemaking and tasting do. It demands attention but may provide pleasure. Far from sinful indulgence, proper wine drinking is, in fact, good sense, not a means to the short-term pleasure of oblivion but a lifetime quest.

References

Primary sources

Aristotle. (1996) *Poetics*, ed. and trans. Malcom Heath, London: Penguin Books.
Avicenna. (1507) reprinted 1964. *Liber canonis*, Hildesheim: G. Olms.
Galen. (1916) *On the Natural Faculties*, ed. and trans. Arthur John Brock, Cambridge, MA: Harvard University Press.
Isidore de Séville. (2006) *The Etymologies of Isidore de Séville*, ed. S.A. Barney, W.J. Lewis, J.A. Beach and O. Berghof, Cambridge: Cambridge University Press.

Moses Ibn Ezra. (1945) *Selected Poems,* ed. and trans. H. Brody and S. Solis-Cohen, Philadelphia: The Jewish Publication Society of America

Origen. (1989) *Commentary on the Gospel According to John, Books 1–10,* ed. and trans. R.E. Heine, Washington, D.C.: The Catholic University of America Press.

Origen. (1992) *Commentaire sur le Cantique des Cantiques,* ed. and trans. L. Brésard and H. Crouzel, Paris: Les Editions du Cerf.

Philo of Alexandria. (1929) *The Works of Philo,* vol. I, ed. and trans. F.H. Colson and G.H. Whitaker, Cambridge, MA: Harvard University Press.

Philo of Alexandria. (1930) *The Works of Philo,* vol. III, ed. and trans. F.H. Colson and G.H. Whitaker, Cambridge, MA: Harvard University Press.

Rabelais. (1955) *Œuvres complètes,* ed. J. Boulenger, rev. Lucien Scheler, Paris: Gallimard.

Secondary sources

Albert, J.P. (1991) "Le vin sans l'ivresse. Remarques sur la liturgie eucharistique," in D. Fournier and S. d'Onofrio (eds), *Le ferment divin,* Paris: Éditions de la Maison des Sciences de l'Homme, 77–91.

Alexandre-Bidon, D. (1990) *Le pressoir mystique. Actes du Colloque de Recloses, 27 mai 1989,* Paris: Éditions du Cerf.

Bynum, C.W. (2002) "The Blood of Christ in the Later Middle Ages 1," *Church History: Studies in Christianity and Culture* 71(4), 685–714.

Carmi, T. (1981) *The Penguin Book of Hebrew Verse,* New York: Penguin Books.

Goldstein, D. (1966) *Hebrew Poems from Spain,* New York: Schocken Books.

Newhauser, R. (2005) *In the Garden of Evil: The Vices and Culture in the Middle Ages,* Toronto: Pontifical Institute of Mediaeval Studies.

Niebyl, P.H. (1971) "Old Age, Fever, and the Lamp Metaphor," *Journal of the History of Medicine* 26(4), 351–368.

Pagis, D. (1991) *Hebrew Poetry of the Middle Ages and the Renaissance,* Berkeley, Los Angeles and Oxford: University of California Press.

Scheindlin, R.P. (1986) *Wine, Women and Death. Medieval Hebrew Poems on the Good Life,* Philadelphia: The Jewish Publication Society.

Short, W.M. (2013) "'Transmission' Accomplished? Latin's Alimentary Metaphors of Communication," *American Journal of Philology* 134(2), 247–275.

Short, W.M. (2014) "Metafora," in M. Bettini and W.M. Short (eds), *Con I Romani. Un' Antropologia della Cultura Antica,* Bologna: Il Mulino, 339–352.

Weinberg, F.M. (1972) *The Wine and the Will: Rabelais' Bacchic Christianity,* Detroit: Wayne State University Press.

Ziegler, J. (1999) "*Ut dicunt medici:* Medical Knowledge and Theological Debates in the Second Half of the Thirteenth Century," *Bulletin of the History of Medicine* 73(2), 208–237.

28
NEW WORLD WINE AND THE EVOLUTION OF UNIVERSAL, VERNACULAR, METRO-RURAL AND INDIGENOUS IDYLLS

Peter J. Howland

Introduction

Once when undertaking ethnographic fieldwork on wine production and tourism in Martinborough, New Zealand, I was left gobsmacked by an instruction from the vineyard owner to 'deadhead the daisies'. This was just hours before Toast Martinborough – an annual wine and food festival that attracts up to 10,000 attendees – was to commence, and at the time, we were frantically making 'last-minute' preparations to the temporary wine bars and food tables in a newly erected marquee. These consisted of 'borrowed' hay bales, topped with wooden boards and covered with crisp, white linen tablecloths on which little flower posies were to be placed. I felt a familiar voice of protest arise, one frequently expressed whenever I feel compelled to undertake a senseless task. However, I quickly remembered my researcher status and dutifully followed several of my co-workers in settling into three hours of deadheading two large beds of Livingstone daisies. Later, some of us were sent to 'smarten up' the entrance and vine rows flanking the driveway.

This vignette exemplifies many of the ideals and practices associated with an orderly, pristine, visually appealing and highly romanticised rural idyll that underpins the aesthetic backdrops and moralising contexts of contemporary winemaking in New Zealand (Howland 2008), Australia (Alonso and Northcote 2009), Canada (Senese *et al.* 2020) and elsewhere (e.g. Burgundy – Demossier 2019) in an increasingly globalised wine world. In this chapter, I briefly explore how the evolving modalities of the rural idyll – which originated mostly in the late-settler New World of wine – are recursively and discursively deployed to generate a range of entangled rural idyll tropes: particularly ideal and romanticised, universal, vernacular, metro-rural and (most recently) indigenous. Using New Zealand as the primary case study, I also analyse idyllic wine constructs in Australia, France, Canada, England and Peru. In addition, I have just commenced research into Māori winemakers in New Zealand and the associated potentialities of an indigenous idyll, starting with foundational analysis of their web-based promotions and news reports. My analysis is also comparatively framed by visits to the vineyards, wine cellars and restaurants of indigenous winemakers in Kelowna, Canada.

Rural idylls

Contemporary idyllic imaginaries, narratives and practices – which are both near universal and vernacular – are generated by winemakers ranging from large, industrial-scale producers to boutique, artisanal and family-based enterprises. Moreover, the cult of the idyllic has a range of registers including historical, instrumental, aesthetic, affective, moral, social and cultural. It is readily apparent that these are often intentionally deployed to add positive value to wine as a commodity – especially economic and moral – and thus to obscure negatives such as exploitative labour relations, profit gouging and ecologically unsound practices (Cloke 2006; Woods 2007). Such wholesome 'countrification' (DuPuis 2006: 126) is also apparent in the marketing promotion of various foodstuffs, outdoor clothing, home decorations and events such as weddings and arts-and-crafts or farmers' markets (Bell 2006). Moreover, idyllic imagery and narratives are deployed both to promote cheap, bulk, mass-produced, regionally undifferentiated or otherwise place-opaque wines and to reflect the literally grounded, place-specific, lived rural experiences of small-scale, family-run winemaking enterprises.

The idealisation of rural spaces, people and institutions co-exists with an antithetical interpretation of rustic or backwards rurality, both of which are highlighted by adjacent counter-theses of the idealisation and/or damnation of 'city life'. The rural idyll has an enduring, relentlessly dialectical history that can be traced back to Ancient Greece and Rome and cannot be reduced to economic and commodity value adding alone (Short 2006; Williams 1973). Today, generic and increasingly globalised tropes romanticise and celebrate everything from cohesive rural communities, close-knit family-run farms, pleasurable pastoral aesthetics and bucolic leisure activities to authentic country-folk production, products and work practices (Williams 1973; Cloke et al. 2006). These sensibilities are supplemented by particular or vernacular tropes: for example, the productionist ethos of the New Zealand idyll. Moreover, they act collusively to provide a moral reservoir of idealised rurality that positively frames countries or nations and associated national identities while also affirming the urbane leisure and consumption of touristic 'city slickers'. Overall, the rural idyll gestures towards an innate, non-alienated human condition in which individuals and societies are constructively generated through the intimate, cohesive and enduring interactions of family, community, history, productive enterprise and communion with nature (Schama 1996; Williams 1973).

In the world of wine, rural idyll tropes were first significantly deployed by New World producers from the late twentieth century onwards, partly aligned with changes in rural production and ownership practices. Until the 1990s, there was little home-based or subsistence wine production, and viable commercial New World production typically requires a scale of land use (i.e. five or more acres) most often found in rural spaces. (By contrast, suburban grape growing and winemaking tends to be less land extensive and hobbyist, while city-based grape growing is virtually non-existent). More importantly, models of legal ownership and development of vineyards (particularly in New Zealand and Australia – see Mitchell et al. 2012) actively promoted fencing off large tracts of rural land with collective vineyards, wineries and winemaker residences. Furthermore, many vineyards were developed close to metropolitan areas (Howland 2008; Overton 2019) and with the 'need' (based on small-scale production, prohibitive costs of developing export markets etc.) to develop domestic markets in the first instance. This local initiative/market focus promoted the construction of in-situ wine cellars, where 'estate' wines were made available for public tastings and sale and which were effectively within walking distance of winemakers' residences. Moreover, the 'rural destination'–based modality supported other in-situ commercial activities such as vineyard-based restaurants, tourist accommodation and events such as music festivals (Hall et al. 2009). This differed from the localised sales of French wine, for example, which was historically undertaken by wine merchants in nearby villages, centralised wine cooperatives or wine-producing *négociants* (Mitchell et al. 2012). These were also the first tentative New World steps toward creating the place specificity of grape growing and winemaking only found previously in the appellation and terroir regimes of the Old World, especially in France.

Now rural idyllic promotions – generic and particular, recursive and discursive – are increasingly found around the globe, including amidst Old World stalwarts such as Burgundy (Demossier 2019).

These modalities, together with various appellation, terroir, and geographical indications initiatives (Charters 2010), represent a veritable grab bag of place-of-origin tropes that primarily seek to assert intersections of place, wine quality, production authenticity and sometimes typicity, which are by cartographic, geographic and/or legal definition all 'unique' and thus non-replicable – even when generic in form and globally rendered.

Universal to vernacular idylls

The original arcadia was the lost Golden Age of rurality conjured by Hesiod (c 700 BCE) in his epic didactic poem *Works and Days*, which celebrated the bountiful agriculture, idyllic customs, beliefs, husbandry and trading lives of Greek peasants. Since then, the rural idyll has largely existed as an evolving dichotomous foil to the elations and tribulations of city living: 'City and country are changing historical realities, both in themselves and in their interrelations. . . . This persistence has a significance matched only by the fact of great variation, social and historical, of the ideas themselves' (Williams 1973: 289).

Williams analyses distinct city-country dialectics at pivotal moments of European history, essentially noting that when city living is cast as overcrowded, alienating, polluted and corrupting, then the rural is likely framed as quiet, traditional, picturesque, authentic, moral and socially harmonious. The country becomes an idyllic site of honest folk, toil and produce, harmonious farming families and cohesive community for rural inhabitants; a space of bucolic leisure, recreation and sociability for jaded urbanites; and/or the moral core of ideal nationhood. By contrast, if the city is framed as cosmopolitan, innovative, progressive and democratic, then the rural is condemned as mundane, backward, oppressive, rustic or 'anti-idyllic' (Bell 2006: 15). Williams laments that industrial capitalism and consumer society have reduced this dynamic to superficial 'symbols or archetypes' (1973: 289) in which the rural is expunged of the harsh realities of poverty, labour exploitation, unsustainable resource use, political conservatism and social isolation, while the idyllic is stripped of the poetic, mythical and allegoric elements that characterised its classical, pre-modern renderings.

Much of this is evident in the vernacular rural idyll that early European (mostly English and Scottish) colonisers cultivated in New Zealand from the mid-1800s. Belich (1996) argues that colonisers were motivated to establish a 'Better Britain' that would return a mythical Golden Age of arcadian pastoralism while also initiating a 'Greater Britain' based on the egalitarian deployment of innovative technologies and progressive institutions of business and government. The idyllic imaginaries of the colonists centred around egalitarian and cohesive rural communities, harmonious and close-knit farming families, productionist or yield-maximising agriculture and a relentless and innovative rural work ethic. This was flanked by slow-paced lifestyles; the natural, picturesque aesthetics of green-pastured farms; and the sublimity of the thick 'bush' or native forests that originally covered much of New Zealand, from which the farmlands had been hewn by the extraordinarily 'hard yakka' of pioneers.

This vernacular idyll clearly differs from the universal idylls of eighteenth- and nineteenth-century Britain. First, it does not contain the allegoric or poetic references to ancient Greece or Rome common among Britain's upper classes of the time. Nor does it contain references to ancient rural histories that highlight cultural origins, innovations and/or enduring traditions such as the invention of the plough, fallow farming or the water-wheel (Schama 1996). Second, the colonists' idyll also has a pronounced late-settler productionist ethos typical of New Zealand, Australia and Canada, which celebrates the rational planning, hard work and innovativeness of ever-increasing agricultural yields.

When the modern wine industry in New Zealand burst upon the scene in the late 1970s and early 1980s, this vernacular rural idyll was still pervasive and was drawn upon to morally situate winemakers' productive activities and promote their wines. For example, Martinborough's founding winemakers and owners – of Ata Rangi, Chifney, Dry River and Martinborough Vineyard

(1979–80) – are routinely referred to as 'pioneers' and are lauded for their entrepreneurial, productionist vision in establishing vineyards on unproductive farmland. Moreover, much is made of the idyllic 'rural family' ethos of Martinborough's vineyards, with promotional material routinely depicting winemaking husbands, wives and young children working and sometimes picnicking among the vines. For example, the Ata Rangi 'story' began in 1980 when:

> founder Clive Paton made the bold decision to sell his small herd of dairy cows in order to buy 5 hectares of stony, barren sheep paddock at the edge of the small Martinborough village. . . . Clive was soon joined by his sister Alison who purchased a 2 ha adjoining paddock. . . . Ata Rangi . . . remains proudly in family ownership.
> *(https://atarangi.co.nz/the-story/, accessed 2 September 2020)*

And this is not mere rhetoric. Many wine tourists in Martinborough, attracted by the bucolic order and aesthetics of local vineyards, also emulate the sociality (familial and community-based) ideals of the rural idyll by enthusiastically waving 'hello' to strangers whilst walking between vineyards; by pursuing personalised connections, even friendships, with winemakers and local homestay operators; and by holidaying with friends or intimate others in quaint colonial cottages with open fireplaces and 'baths big enough for two' (Howland 2004: 103).

Similarly vernacular and strategic idyllic tropes are deployed in the newly minted sparkling wine industry in England, where a number of 'destination vineyards and wineries' have been built since the global financial crisis of 2007–08 (Demossier and Howland 2021; Skelton 2019). Again, the emphasis is on the bucolic, pristine, orderly and aesthetically pleasing vineyards flanked by elegant restaurants, luxury tourist accommodation and welcoming cellar doors featuring vineyard wines and associated 'estate merch'. In addition, quasi-historical links to village life, aristocratic countryside pursuits and longstanding county sensibilities mark out a vernacular idyll. For example, Hambledon Vineyard (established in 1952 – 'reborn' in 1999) emphasises its 'heritage' links to the Hambledon Cricket Club, founded in 1750 as a 'social club for local nobility' and avowed as the 'cradle of cricket' (www.hambledonvineyard.co.uk/see-our-heritage/cradle-of-cricket, accessed 2 September 2020). According to local lore, Hambledon became the foremost English cricket club in the late eighteenth century after it introduced a third [middle] stump to the wickets – an initiative commemorated in the near-replica logos of Hambledon Vineyard, Hambledon Cricket Club and the Bat and Ball Inn, a nearby eighteenth-century pub, which, according to the plaque outside, was the 'first headquarters of English cricket'.

Danebury Vineyards, founded in 1988, incorporates stylised images of racehorses on its wine labels, emphasising its planting on a former training yard near Stockbridge, Hampshire, famous for 'its historical racecourse [circa 1839] . . . considered amongst the finest of the provincial racecourses in Victorian times' (www.danebury.com/about-us/, accessed 17 July 2020). Danebury Vineyard wines, which are 'Distinctly English', are also sold under the emblem of a dog rose – the official flower of Hampshire County.

Scaling from local village to county-based to nationalist registers, these promotional discourses are not mere rhetoric. Wine in the UK has long been produced primarily for local markets, particularly vineyard sales, village pubs and local wine merchants (Haydon 1994), whereas county-based allegiances and rivalries have been a quintessential, albeit evolving, aspect of English culture since the Middle Ages (Richardson 2018). Moreover, nationalistic opportunism was evident when Prime Minister Boris Johnson went 'full English' and served *Nyetimber* (West Sussex) sparkling wines at an exclusive 'Brexit Day bash' held at No. 10 Downing Street (Shadwell 2020).

Similar intersections of historical, vernacular and universal idyllic tropes are increasingly found in the Old World. For example, Demossier (2019) argues the application of the *Association pour les climats de Bourgogne* for *Climats de Bourgogne* for UNESCO certification as a World Heritage cultural landscape in 2015 drew heavily on the bucolic, pastoral imagery of their world-renowned vineyards and historic rural villages, symbolically linking these to enduring histories of hospitality, charity and *climat* (Burgundians' unique take on terroir). Demossier notes that such idyllic sensibilities were wholly absent when she lived in the region as a child and similarly missing among local winemakers when she began her research some 30 years ago. Rather, the vineyards, wineries and wine cellars were regarded as instrumental places of agricultural production. By contrast, since the successful UNESCO bid, numerous website promotions feature the sort of imagery in which 'the viewer is transported from a drone, above the autumnal vineyards, zooming in and out of a golden wine landscape, following rows of vines, a tapestry of hilly plots, walls, villages and the beautiful lake of Geneva' (Demossier 2019: 75).

Some 10,000 kilometres away in another old-yet-new world of wine, albeit one with a very long history of winemaking but little contemporary international exposure, is Tacama Vineyard, Peru. Founded in 1540 by Francisco de Carabantes, a Spanish priest, near Ica – an oasis some 300 kilometres from the capital city of Lima – Tacama Vineyard possesses many of the idyllic trappings expected in the contemporary globalised wine world. Features include particularly orderly vineyards, a sophisticated winery, an American Express–welcoming cellar door and a chic restaurant featuring both 'Americano' and Peruvian fare, all based around a beautiful sixteenth-century Spanish monastery. Yet there are at least three vernacular registers that reflect Peru's distinctive history and culture. First, the hacienda is protected by machine-gun-toting guards, reflecting the unrest and brutal inequities that have long marked agriculture in Peru. Second is a promotional emphasis, especially evident on the wine tour, on the hygienic nature of their production techniques, in an effort to distance Tacama wines from the unsanitary, sometimes fatal, production of alcohol by small-scale peasant farmers. Third is the adjacent production of pisco (distilled grape alcohol), a popular national drink first made when the Spanish prohibited the export of Peruvian wines in 1776 (Howland 2019).

Nevertheless – and without anything other than very rudimentary tourist Spanish and the halting tourist English of cellar door hosts, waiters, etc. (although in the company of my Spanish-speaking daughter) – I felt immediately 'at home' at Tacama Vineyard, very comfortable and knowledgeable of the in-situ cellar door context and the expected behaviours and interactions. Clearly a universal wine habitus was prevailing, and I intuitively knew the machine-gun-toting guards were on sentry duty to ensure our idyllic experiences were 'robustly facilitated' (Howland 2019).

Metro-rural idylls

Aside from drawing on increasingly homogenised idyllic tropes to produce what Woods calls the 'global countryside' (2007: 485), entangling these with terroir and other place-of-origin assemblages, the idyllic framing of rural wine production, consumption and tourism is also clearly linked to the metropolitan rise of a 'global middle-class' (Koo 2016: 3). As a result, the city-rural dialogic is again to the fore, albeit in the transnational emergence of the 'metro-rural idyll' (Howland 2008: 77; Overton 2019) – a practice and optic that draws attention to the intersectionality of the metropolitan and the rural with a romanticised ethos firmly focused on the positive.

Since the widespread neo-liberal reforms of the 1980s onwards, the aesthetic consumption of quality wine has firmly emerged as a ubiquitous marker of cosmopolitan refinement for the global middle class. A high-order cohort, the global middle class are as readily defined by shared characteristics as they are demarcated by nuanced difference (Howland 2019). For example, they share a desire for economic affluence, tertiary education, urban(e) residence, cosmopolitan lifestyles, 'white collar' professional and/or creative employment and upward social – and positive geographic – mobility (as professionalised labour and tourists) and are transnationally alert (especially to global consumption, employment, entertainment and leisure trends). However, different tertiary education and occupational trajectories (e.g. IT, economics, social sciences) routinely generate divergent financial and political outcomes, while ethnicity, religion, culture and kinship modalities also habitually differentiate (Heiman *et al.* 2012; Koo 2016; Lopez and Weinstein 2012).

Middle-class urbanites frequently embrace the rural as a site of retreat from city living and as a place where they can intensely experience metropolitan ideals, especially leisure, hedonic consumption, middle-class distinction, agentic individuality and elective sociality (Howland 2008). Ching and Creed argue that 'positive images of rural life often provide ways to talk about improving the city. . . . not as an alternative to the city, but as a moral image to inspire or discipline urban behaviour' (1997: 19–20). Consequently, the rural idyll frequently acts as a moral reservoir drawn on to validate their metropolitan-derived, and often conspicuously performative, pursuit of urbane commodities and activities. For example, wine tourists who left their dependent children behind to holiday in Martinborough with selected adult friends and lovers can appear to be flouting the idyllic sociality of family farms and rural communities. However, they arguably utilise this 'rural sociality' trope to morally sanction and authenticate their personally elective sociality and, in doing so, also accord primacy to their agentic selves and reflexive individuality.

This ethos is also evident in various metro-rural communication flows directed towards the globalised middle class. For example, in 'rustic-chic' décor, homes, gardens and clothing featured in lifestyle magazines (e.g. *Country Life*, UK), rural tourism promotions (e.g. Martinborough has long been part of a 'Capital Country Escape'), literary works (e.g. *A Year in Provence* (1991) by Peter Mayle) and films (e.g. *Under a Tuscan Sun* (2006) directed by Audrey Wells). Or in advertisements 'for a whole host of products and services that trade on positive connotations of the rural' (Bell 2006: 150), including foodstuffs replete with 'natural' goodness promoted under the rubric of the 'supermarket pastoral' (Pollan 2001).

Such rural-based enterprises, which find exemplary practice in the cultivated finesse of boutique winemaking, are also valued for foregrounding the agency of the individuals involved. For example, the New World 'cult of the winemaker' (Howland 2008: 91) in which biographised winemakers (male and female) are cast as exemplary reflexive and agentic individuals who adroitly deploy the best of nature, science, art and aesthetic taste to make fine wine, achieve enviable work-life balance and lead consummate cosmopolitan lifestyles. Reflexive individuality and agency also manifest in wine tourists' personal-place attachments (Santos *et al.* 2017) and in 'self-image congruity' (Pratt 2019: 45) based on their wine and vineyard choices.

Furthermore, fine wine production and appreciative consumption are also valued for generating middle-class distinctions marked by a 'distance from necessity' and 'stylizations of life' (Bourdieu 2010 [1984]: 55–56). By contrast, enterprises lacking in valued middle-class social and cultural capitals, such as the primary production of sheep and dairy farms or the 'naïve', uncultivated provisioning of rural-based services, are brusquely consigned to the backwaters of rusticity and are subject to complaint from visiting metropolitans (e.g. about noisy cows being milked at five a.m.) (Howland 2008; Bell 2006).

Variance is, however, also evident and especially in the omnivoristic consumption practices of middle-class consumers whereby social distinction is primarily generated by how one consumes (e.g. knowledgeably, ironically etc.), rather than necessarily by what one consumes (Peterson 2005). This includes wine experiences, something that segmented wine industries are astutely attuned to. For example, Kelowna, Canada, offers a cornucopia of in-situ wine experiences including the simple, steel shed used by Kalala Organic Vineyard as a combined winery and cellar door for their award-winning ice wines; the funky 'social wines' of Intrigue Winery with labels featuring a vibrant mishmash of wine-adjacent terms (e.g. 'friends', 'harvest', 'moonlight', 'festival', etc.); the pyramidic spiritualism and 'universal truth, love, and gratitude' of Summerhill Pyramid's biodynamic wines; and the imposing stone archway and five-tonne keystone entrance, manicured gardens, 1200-seat outdoor amphitheater, 12-story-tall Bell Tower, gourmet 'locavore' restaurant, vast underground cellars and exhibition room featuring a rare Marc Chagall tapestry at the opulent Mission Hill Winery.

While similar middle-class variety is found amidst the idyllic offerings of Mornington Peninsula, Melbourne, Australia – from the family-farm, rustic chic of Rahona Valley Estate to the 134-hectare Point Leo Estate with its stunning ocean vistas, man-made lake, one– and two–chef's hat restaurants, '4.5-star' architectural cellar door and outdoor sculpture park featuring 60-plus exhibits.

Indigenous idylls

The incorporation of indigenous nomenclature and cultural, moral and ecological values and practices, as well as delineated indigenous winemaking enterprises, is a relatively recent innovation, originating mostly in the New Worlds of wine – New Zealand, Australia, Canada and the United States. These potentially represent a rich new category for analysis in the range of wine idylls. For example, in Martinborough, there are several vineyards with Māori names – Ata Rangi, Te Kairanga and Nga Waka – respectively, 'dawn sky, new beginnings' and the 'land of bountiful food' – while Nga Waka refers to the three upturned 'canoes' of the explorer Kupe that form the nearby Aorangi Ranges. None of the vineyard founders I interviewed revealed any direct kinship or genealogical links to Māori, although said they had consulted local *Kaumātua* (Māori elders) about the 'appropriateness' of their chosen estate names. However, it should be noted that at the time of the vineyards' establishment the local *iwi* (tribe) Ngāti Kahungunu did not have a *marae* (meeting house/grounds) or a strong presence in or around Martinborough. Indeed, the local *marae* (Hau Ariki) that was later established (circa 1997) had a particular pan-*iwi* orientation; thus, the 'appropriateness' of local vineyards' Māori nomenclature is perhaps contestable. In Australia, there are several wine companies with Aboriginal names, such as Alkoomi, Wirra Wirra and Yalumba, and wine labels featuring Aboriginal-inspired dot paintings and X-ray art such as Mad Fish and the 'affordable' Yellow Tail, Australia's most exported wine to the USA, popular in big-box retailers like Costco.

Some registers are clearly genuine attempts to constructively incorporate indigenous ecological, social and cultural practices. For example, in 1997, New Zealand Wine (NZW) introduced its Sustainable Winegrowing New Zealand (SWNZ) initiative, with non-complying wineries excluded from trade shows and exporting wines under the NZW banner. SWNZ has six focus areas aligned with the United Nations Sustainable Development Goals – water, waste, pest and disease, soil, climate change and people – –and is also orientated around similar indigenous Māori values and practices of *kaitiakitanga*:

> Kaitiakitanga is the Māori concept of guardianship and protecting the environment. A kaitiaki is a person or group that is recognised as a guardian by the tangata whenua [indigenous people of the land]. As all New Zealand Winegrowers members are responsible for ensuring the sustainability of the New Zealand wine industry, we can be considered kaitiaki.
> *(www.nzwine.com/en/sustainability/, accessed 9 September 2020)*

Though for habitus-embodied, deep practice of kaitiakitanga, perhaps one should look to Māori winemakers themselves. There are increasing numbers of Māori winemakers in New Zealand – including Tohu, Te Pā Vineyards, Bird Wines, Kuru Kuru Wines, Tiki Wines and Jeff Sinnott Wine – which all but Tohu are private, rather than *iwi*-based (tribal), enterprises. In 2018, Te Pā Vineyards, Bird Wines, Kuru Kuru Wines, Tiki Wines and Jeff Sinnott Wine formed Tuku, 'the world's first Māori winemakers collective' committed to kaitiakitanga ('We are all certified by sustainable wine growers NZ, but we look beyond that'), whakapapa ('our family, our heritage . . . links people to all other living things'), whanaungatanga ('sense of family connection') and manaakitanga ('hospitality/ generosity'). Tuku state their success in producing 'Māori wines' also supports the 'exciting and developing Māori economy. You are buying from people and their families, nurturing growth and success for future generations' (https://tuku.nz/home, accessed 10 September 2020).

Similar values and aspirations are evident among a handful of Native American wineries and grape-growing companies in California, New Mexico, Utah and British Columbia, some of which are tribal-based entities (Willcox 2019). For example, Kitá Wines, founded in 2010 by the Santa Ynez Chumash and located in Santa Ynez Valley, Santa Barbara County, was the first vineyard and winery in the United States owned and operated solely by tribal members.

Kitá translates as 'our valley oak' and highlights the gifts from Mother Earth. . . . The seasons, changes of the land, and language of nature all speak to us. We have to listen; they are a vision of balance between our surroundings and ourselves. The earth is our mother. She nourishes us, that which we put into the ground she returns to us.

(https://kitawines.com/about-kita-wines/, accessed 10 September 2020)

While there is currently only one indigenous wine enterprise in Australia – Gondwana, a majority-owned Aboriginal or Torres Strait Islander business based in Sydney – it, too, is committed to winemaking practices based on holistic, spiritual ancestral-based notions of 'country', which other non-indigenous winemakers are also increasingly adopting as a vernacular alternative to terroir (Swinburn 2020). Founded in 2014, Gondwana produces a McLaren Vale (South Australian) shiraz, with a portion of sales supporting the 'Leading the Way' initiative, which provides innovative training, employment and capacity-building programs for Indigenous Australians. Currently, Gondwana employs Aboriginal people only in sales and promotions, but the vision is to have an indigenous component throughout (Allen 2018, 2020).

Indigenous winemakers appear to constructively embrace and specifically enhance – rather than seeking to overtly decolonise – the metro-rural idyll ethos, seeking to produce quality wines and urbane vineyard experiences with the particular addition of harmonising indigenous ecological practices. For example, Tiki Wines profess 'An eye for adventure. A taste for good wine. As purveyors of fine wines, we seek the finer things found in other aspects of life in a place that offers up endless inspiration for the body, mind and spirit' (https://tikiwine.com, accessed 7 March 2021). While at the Indigenous World Winery in Kelowna, Canada, I experienced a chic, metro-rural cellar door experience and gourmet dining (featuring local foodstuffs such as bison) in their Red Fox restaurant while also being introduced to their ethical winemaking practices that align with the cultural-ecological stewardship and guardianship of the Okanagan Syilx people, the first nation people of Okanagan and Similkameen Valleys: 'Every effort is being made to produce world class wines in a respectful way to the environment and its people' (www.indigenousworldwinery.com/about-us/, accessed 7 March 2021). However, context-rich research is clearly required to determine how indigenous winemaking specifically plays out and how this compares with the Old World modalities of historical winemaking, cultural identities, terroir and so on (see Monterescu & Handel 2019).

Conclusion

There are other global initiatives that could be included within the indigenous idyll, though in the first instance, they are bio-natural and include the use of wild yeasts and indigenous grapes; the 'wilding' of vineyards; and the minimal interventionism of biodynamic, organic and natural winemaking. From an ontological perspective, these are clearly distanced from the moralities of indigenous winemaking, especially as they flirt with the 'shaggy' arcadia 'of primitive panic' (Schama 1996: 517) and represent varying forms of less-tame or even wild winemaking. Together with such innovations as urban wineries and replica wines, they could potentially be seen as threats to the hegemony of carefully manicured and cultivated rural vineyards and artisanal winemakers who craft fine wines in the moral sunlight of the idyllic – universal, vernacular, metro-rural and indigenous.

Yet wine marketers, attuned as they are to provisioning niche products and promotions and validating a wide array of variegated tastes for omnivoristic wine drinkers, will also surely accommodate these evolutions without any unnecessary (or at least unprofitable) disruption to the globalised idyllic framings and practices discussed earlier. Indeed, with the world becoming increasingly urban and aspirationally middle class, the only real, foreseeable threat to the metro-rural imaginings and enactment of idyllic winemaking are, perhaps, the realities of climate change.

References

Allen, M. (2018) "Taste the Wild with Three Indigenous Drinks Makers," *Financial Review* 25 January, www.afr.com/life-and-luxury/food-and-wine/taste-the-wild-with-three-indigenous-drinks-makers-20180117-h0jnb2, accessed 12 September 2020.
Allen, M. (2020) *Intoxicating: Ten Drinks That Shaped Australia*, Melbourne: Thames & Hudson Australia.
Alonso, A.D. and Northcote, J. (2009) "Wine, History, Landscape: Origin Branding in Western Australia," *British Food Journal* 111(11), 1248–1259.
Belich, J. (1996) *Making Peoples: A History of New Zealand from Polynesian Settlement to the End of the Nineteenth Century*, Auckland: Allen Lane.
Bell, D. (2006) "Variations on the Rural Idyll," in P. Cloke, T. Marsden and P. Mooney (eds), *Handbook of Rural Studies*, London: Sage, 149–160.
Bourdieu, P. (2010 [1984]) *Distinction: A Social Critique of the Judgement of Taste*, London: Routledge.
Charters, S. (2010) "Marketing Terroir: A Conceptual Approach," in *Proceedings of the 5th International Academy of Wine Business Research Conference*, University of Auckland, Auckland, 8–10.
Ching, B. and Creed, G. (1997) *Knowing Your Place: Rural Identity and Cultural Hierarchy*, New York: Routledge.
Cloke, P., Marsden, T. and Mooney, P. (eds) (2006) *Handbook of Rural Studies*, London: Sage.
Demossier, M. (2019) "Burgundy's *Climats* and the Utopian Wine Heritage Landscape," in J. Dutton and P.J. Howland (eds), *Wine, Terroir and Utopia: Making New Worlds*, Abingdon: Routledge, 75–92.
Demossier, M. and Howland, P.J. (2021) "Wine GB. Opportunisme à bulles dans le 'Nouveau/Vieux monde'," *Ethnologie Française* 51(3), 601–612.
DuPuis, E.M. (2006) "Landscapes of Desire?" in P. Cloke, T. Marsden and P. Mooney (eds), *Handbook of Rural Studies*, London: Sage, 124–132.
Hall, C.M., Sharples, L., Cambourne, B. and Macionis, N. (2009) *Wine Tourism Around the World*, London: Routledge.
Haydon, P. (1994) *The English Pub: A History*, London: Robert Hale.
Heiman, R., Freeman, C. and Liechty, M. (eds) (2012) *The Global Middle Classes: Theorizing Through Ethnography*, Santa Fe, NM: SAR Press.
Howland, P.J. (2004) "Martinborough's Pinot Pilgrims: Rural Escapism and Monasteries of Consumption," in *Lotto, Long-drops and Lolly Scrambles: The Extra-Ordinary Anthropology of Middle New Zealand*, Wellington: Steele Roberts, 103–111.
Howland, P.J. (2008) "Martinborough's Wine Tourists and the Metro-Rural Idyll," *The Journal of New Zealand Studies* 6–7, 77–100.
Howland, P.J. (2019) "Enduring Wine and the Global Middle-Class," in D. Inglis and A.M. Almila (eds), *The Globalization of Wine: The Trans-Nationalization and Localization of Production, Leisure and Pleasure*, London: Bloomsbury, 151–170.
Koo, H. (2016) "The Global Middle-class: How Is It Made, What Does It Represent?" *Globalizations* 1(1), 1–14.
Lopez, R.A. and Weinstein, B. (eds) (2012) *The Making of the Middle-class: Towards a Transnational History*, Durham, NC: Duke University Press.
Mitchell, R., Charters, S. and Albrecht, J. (2012) "Cultural Systems and the Wine Tourism Product," *Annals of Tourism Research* 39(1), 311–335.
Monterescu, D., and Handel, A. (2019) "Liquid indigeneity: Wine, science, and colonial politics in Israel/Palestine." *American Ethnologist*, 46(3), 313–327.
Overton, J. (2019) "Rural Idylls and Urban Economies: The Making of Metropolitan Wine Regions," *Journal of Wine Research* 30(3), 238–258.
Peterson, R. (2005) "Problems in Comparative Research: The Example of Omnivorousness," *Poetics* 33(5–6), 257–282.
Pollan, M. (2001) "Naturally," *The New York Times*, 13 May, www.nytimes.com/2001/05/13/magazine/naturally.html, accessed 12 September 2020.
Pratt, M. (2019) "The Image of a Wine Tourist and Impact on Self-Image Congruity," in M. Sigala and R. Robinson (eds) *Wine Tourism Destination Management and Marketing*, London: Palgrave Macmillan, 45–65.

Richardson, R.C. (2018) *The Changing Face of English Local History*, London: Routledge.
Santos, V.R., Ramos, P. and Almeida, N. (2017) "The Relationship between Involvement, Destination Emotions and Place Attachment in the Porto Wine Cellars," *International Journal of Wine Business Research* 29(4), 401–415.
Schama, S. (1996) *Landscape and Memory*, London: Fontana Press.
Senese, D., Hull, J.S. and McNicol, B.J. (2020) "Terroir-Driven Tourism and Migration in British Columbia, Canada," in J. Dutton and P.J. Howland (eds), *Wine, Terroir and Utopia: Making New Worlds*, Abingdon: Routledge, 126–144.
Shadwell, T. (2020) "Inside Boris Johnson's Exclusive Brexit Bash with English Sparkling Wine But no Champagne," *Daily Mirror*, 31 January, www.mirror.co.uk/news/politics/inside-boris-johnsons-exclusive-brexit-21401411, accessed 12 September 2020.
Short, B. (2006) "Idyllic Ruralities," in P. Cloke, T. Marsden and P. Mooney (eds), *Handbook of Rural Studies*, London: Sage, 133–148.
Skelton, S. (2019) *The Wines of Great-Britain*, Oxford: Infinite Ideas Limited.
Swinburn, B. (2020) "Deep Terroir as Utopia," in J. Dutton and P.J. Howland (eds), *Wine, Terroir and Utopia: Making New Worlds*, Abingdon: Routledge, 221–234.
Willcox, K. (2019) "Behind the Rise of Native American Wines," *Wine Enthusiast*, 15 November, www.winemag.com/2019/11/15/behind-the-rise-of-native-american-wines/, accessed 12 September 2020.
Williams, R. (1973) *The Country and the City*, London: Chatto & Windus.
Woods, M. (2007) "Engaging the Global Countryside: Globalization, Hybridity and the Reconstitution of Rural Place," *Progress in Human Geography* 31(4), 485–507.

29
NARRATIVES OF SCIENCE AND CULTURE IN WINEMAKING

Ian Malcolm Taplin

Introduction

Throughout the twentieth century, the science behind grape growing and winemaking increased significantly as the dissemination of formal knowledge from university oenology and viticulture programs became widely available (Anderson and Pinella 2018). Technological innovations in various aspects of the production process, from pruning to harvesting, sorting and new fermentation techniques have occurred. The accumulated benefit of such innovations, the more systematic spread of formal knowledge and the codification of informal practices have resulted in the improvement of the overall quality and consistency of wine. Furthermore, putative gains from a more rigorous adherence to the systematisation of scientific practices in winemaking also include some scale economies plus opportunities to limit vintage variation that often accompanies difficult harvests.

In spite of the widespread adoption of such obviously beneficial innovations, it is interesting to note how some winery owners downplay techno-scientific innovations and continue to emphasise the saliency of tradition, enveloping their viticultural activities in a cultural framework that privileges historical continuity. Such a viewpoint has been evident in ongoing research interviews that I have conducted with winery owners in France, where they invoke the accumulated benefits of an historical legacy of humanity's relationship with the land in all its Arcadian splendour. This sentiment is evident amongst winegrowers in Burgundy, who extol the virtues of extant practices that seek to maximise the true expression of the terrain in which vines grow, arguing that they are inherent to the quality of the wine (Phillips 2017). Here, tradition becomes the *sine qua non* of viticulture, with too much technology presumed to result in a homogenised wine that fails to reflect any of the unique characteristics of its location. Whilst not entirely eschewing science and technology as aids in the vineyard, this approach argues that wine's essentialism lies in its site specificity, and the focus of winemaking should therefore be to find ways to express such individuality. This is the epistemological domain of terroir – the idea that soil, climate and topography, together with human interaction and a socio-cultural umbrella, combine to produce a distinctive product that is closely associated with a sense of place (Parker 2015: 5). Terroir is thus a social construction of space in which tradition is seen as sacrosanct and geographical specificity endowed with unique and non-replicable features that give wine its distinctiveness.

Such a position often stands in contrast with the views expressed by their counterparts in California, especially Napa, where they are more inclined to stress the technological efficiency of their production process. My interviews with winegrowers in that region reveal an enthusiasm for adopting new techniques that many saw as crucial to the region's rapid growth in the past half century (Taplin 2021). For them, the land and site are important, but it is how one maximises their potential that is crucial, and that potential is best realised through institutionalised innovation and an operational culture that sees adherence to scientific techniques as prescriptive and normative.

When winegrowers today talk about tradition, especially in Burgundy, they are often using heritage and deference to the past as ways of differentiating their product, capitalising on the value-added potential of an authenticity image. Conversely, many Napa producers have emphasised technological innovation and the thorough application of scientific techniques because they lend credence to their brand identity and affirm their consistent quality. In other words, they have mobilised a scientific narrative to ascribe their quality and status credentials whilst their French counterparts invoke a culture of traditionalism to burnish their own products. Both appear to be using either culture or science to affirm their identity, construct value and even achieve market differentiation.

In what follows, I explore the cultural parameters that have shaped the various discourses and how each has been integral to the pursuit of quality and regional brand identity. Specifically, I examine how, historically, many Burgundian winegrowers were actually enthusiastic about experimentation and embraced an admittedly imperfect science, but did so with a systematic Baconian empiricism. I then show how, in the early twentieth century, some created an idealised version of the past that downplayed technical innovations and reified the uniqueness of the old ways in a developing discourse of terroir. Invoking an image of a notionally pre-industrial, rural economy in which people's relationship with the land was paramount in the creation of wine, they imparted the stamp of authenticity in a progressively urban, cosmopolitan world. This placed heritage firmly in the marketing of wine as well as arguing for the non-replicability of the product – the ultimate affirmation of distinctiveness and status. In recent decades, when regulatory frameworks have institutionalised new practices that achieve more consistent quality, many still articulate a somewhat ambiguous identity that privileges their position based on a notional cultural heritage and the uniqueness of place.

In Napa, where the adoption of a scientific and technological paradigm was crucial to the region's post-1960s growth, brands have been built around variety designations rather than a specific property. The development of consistent quality and identifiable flavour profiles reflects the evolution of winemaking techniques designed to maximise the benefits of cultured yeasts, fermentation innovations and the use of stainless steel tanks – all part of the infusion of technical rigour in the winery and the systematisation of best practices. Yet in recent decades, some ultra-premium wineries in Napa have emerged as forceful advocates of a value-added uniqueness in their product that comes in part from their specific location as well as their technical sophistication. In other words, they have attempted to further differentiate their product and monopolise value claims by notionally identifying vineyard and estate designation. They have built a brand identity that focuses on site specificity and a distinctive qualitative dimension, implicitly recognising notions of terroir but without the socio-cultural legacy that is found in Burgundy.

Burgundy: the mix of science and culture

In many countries, prior to the twentieth century, grapes were often picked unripe or rotted; fermentation and storage were problematic; sanitary conditions in wineries were of dubious standards; and finally, shipment in barrels that were porous, enabling air to enter the wine, meant that wines rarely lasted more than six months (Phillips 2016). Efforts to alleviate these problems were frequent but often lacking in the sort of scientific rigour that we expect today. Yet despite these shortcomings, there were some individuals who were very systematic in their investigations, bringing an elemental empiricism to an otherwise haphazard process. One such person was André Antoine-Pierre Gentil, the Cistercian abbot of Fontenay Monastery in Burgundy who was recognised as a skilled agronomist. In a treatise attributed to him, he methodically set out numerous procedures to help make poor quality wines taste better (Gentil 1802). One such successful endeavour involved experimenting with various ways of adding honey or sugar to the must during fermentation to help preserve the wine. As historian J.B. Gough notes, 'Gentil represents a curious and wonderful mixture of the most technologically progressive strains of both medieval monasticism and enlightenment empiricism' (1998: 99). His Cistercian counterparts also embraced a commitment to quality because of their sacramental and hospitality obligations and had the fortitude and patience to embark upon systematic experimentation.

Outside the monasteries, there were similar eighteenth-century experimental veins in the search for ways to get grapes to ripen properly before harvest. The most successful of these involved (as Gentil had argued) the addition of sugar – a process subsequently known as chaptalisation. Such additives reactivated the fermentation process, increased the alcohol content and improved the final balance of the wine (Gough 1998: 76). Such adulteration was justified because producers could charge more for a better-quality and longer-lasting wine.

Notwithstanding such efforts, much wine remained notable for its unreliability and significant variation in quality, even in Burgundy (Phillips 2016). For much of the nineteenth and into the twentieth century, many small winegrowers (vignerons) in Burgundy were resistant to change, often unwilling to abandon old methods because they lacked the resources to do so or were constrained by normative practices that inhibited innovation. Many, in fact, clung resolutely to procedures that became articulated as 'tradition' – what sociologist Sarah Daynes refers to as cultural closure – in which the emergence of new practices is resisted on a symbolic level (2013: 23). Unlike their Bordeaux counterparts, who appeared more willing to accept science and technology because their consumer market was demanding it and who were on the whole larger and better-capitalised estates (Ouvrard *et al.* 2019), the Burgundians often eschewed innovations (Trubek 2008).

When production changes to improve overall quality were introduced in the 1920s, it was often a result of exogenous pressures designed to impose greater technical rigour. Regulations governing many aspects of wine production were put in place (e.g. limits on chaptalisation), merchants were demanding better quality wine and cooperatives had been established that more effectively (and legitimately, in the eyes of winegrowers) disseminated the benefits of agricultural research: such factors fostered improved quality and the embrace of new ideas. Building on earlier classifications, the passage of the *Appellations d'origine contrôlée* (AOC) law in 1935 identified wines by their geographical origin but also stipulated required practices in the vineyard as well as the varieties that could be grown in a particular area. Yields were regulated as a way that forced growers to concentrate on better-quality crops, audits and inspections became *de rigueur* and research into viticulture was more widely disseminated (Phillips 2016).

This standardisation of practices, albeit not immutable, nonetheless imposed operational mandates that led to an overall improvement in the quality and consistency of wines. Further changes following World War II, as noted by historian Rod Phillips, were far from traditional in their rationales (2016: 267). These included the use of customised yeasts and more efficient calibrated filtering, as well as technical innovations such as micro-oxygenation and reverse osmosis. Arguably, quality improved because of a regulatory framework that introduced new production processes and technical innovations, but it was a framework that was largely accepted by growers because it elevated the status of their wine.

As Burgundy's reputation for producing world-class wine has continued to grow, it is somewhat ironic that such elevated status often remains enveloped in an historical construction of winemaking practices that refers back to the old ways of doing things. Narratives that invoke monks, the soil and cultural history – the latter being an evocation of vignerons as rural artisans in tune with the land – can be seen in industry promotional documents, wine writers' notes and even winegrowers themselves (Phillips 2016). This is the essence of terroir as an expression of place and the people who worked the land. It is what anthropologist Marion Demossier refers to as the social construction of authenticity (2018). Foremost, it is a cultural explanation that infuses land and history into an immutable sense of place, with Burgundy as the original site of the terroir story. But such a characterisation is very much a product of the 1930s, when wine supply often exceeded demand, classification systems (AOC) helped formalise production structure and *négociants* sought a more marketable identification of the region by extolling the virtues of authenticity. Discourses around place specificity emerged as consumer taste became normalised following the growing legitimacy of wine professionals and intermediaries who sold the wine. Together with wine producers, these groups mounted a marketing campaign that pushed to the forefront a culturally mediated nexus of taste, quality and place, the authenticity of which rested not on objective measurement but on intuitive appreciation of the dynamic interaction of these variables.

In some ways, terroir is a product of twentieth-century marketing that rests on a synthesis of cultural tradition and the ecology of landscape. It operates in tandem with institutional changes, particularly the socially constructed classification systems and the *de facto* self-regulation of governance systems developed and imposed by the winegrowers themselves to complement the earlier AOC laws (Zhao 2005, 2008). For example, from the 1970s onwards, many Burgundy producers developed a strategy of reducing supply, reaffirming that lower yields provided a better-value product for which they could charge a price premium (Demossier 2018: 95). The irony is that the dissonance between terroir and technology invariably comes from the growers and winemakers themselves. They continue to embrace the historical legacies of artisanal labour and the mystical links with the land and the past whilst simultaneously accepting scientific and technological discourses that restructure many vineyard practices. Anthropologist Amy Trubek sums this up nicely when she states 'As the organisation of wine production became more analytic and systematic over time, the definition of terroir and its relationship to wine became both narrower and broader than its colloquial usage: it went from local folklore to defined practices' (2008: 64). Framing terroir as a cultural product has been a crucial marketing strategy that enables Burgundian producers to affirm their distinctiveness, control their value claims and justify high prices. It is a human-ecology cultural interface that privileges tradition whilst implicitly acknowledging the benefits of technical efficiency. As academic viticulturalist Mark Matthews succinctly states, 'Today, terroir is primarily a marketing term that mixes extrinsic and intrinsic wine properties; when formalised into laws restricting production, it becomes a system to extract high rents' (2015: 202).

Napa's embrace of science

Spanish missionaries built missions in the late-eighteenth and early-nineteenth-century coastal region of what was then Alta California. The Franciscan missionaries who came to this area had the same need for sacramental wine as their medieval Cistercian ancestors, as well as a need for a beverage whose sale could supplement their operating budget. Such wine was made from what are now known as mission grapes, probably brought originally from Spain in the sixteenth century (Sullivan 2008). Following the 1833 secularisation of the missions, many of the estates were sold to influential settlers. Most expanded the planting of mission grapes as well as trying other *vinifera* varieties. This pattern continued as demand for alcoholic beverages grew after the 1849 Gold Rush and the growth of the population in the San Francisco Bay area. The emphasis, however, was on meeting the demand of a growing but relatively undifferentiated market, and this was best met with high-yield mission grapes.

This focus changed when newcomers with some viticultural experience settled the area after the 1860s (Sullivan 2008). Many recognised that the Sonoma and Napa regions possessed a favourable climate for grape growing and that varieties other than mission grapes could produce a better-quality wine. Appreciation of the latter came in part from state-sponsored reports and studies of winegrowing that were widely disseminated (Carosso 1951; Pinney 1989). Specialists such as Eugene Hilgard, who was appointed professor of agriculture at the University of California in 1875, were also advocates of the introduction of science into winemaking and increasingly condemned producers whose obsession with high yield and quantity was ruining the potential quality that existed with different varieties (Pinney 1989). In addition, recommendations on new fermentation techniques and better temperature control as well as not allowing grapes to excessively ripen were widely circulated.

Capitalising on the growing reputation after several wines from Napa won awards at national competitions during the first decade of the twentieth century, some winegrowers pioneered the prominent display of the 'Napa' appellation on their bottles – an attempt to differentiate their wine by focusing upon geographical origin (Taplin 2021). But the arrival of Prohibition in 1919 ended such ventures.

The California wine industry did not see a significant rebirth until the 1960s when newcomers, some with wine industry experience, acquired land, especially in what was increasingly recognised as prime grape-growing areas such as Sonoma and Napa. During this time, oenology and viticulture programmes at UC Davis developed a formal and rigorous curriculum designed around the science and technology of grape growing and winemaking. This scientific approach systematised knowledge and mitigated many of the flaws that had plagued winemaking in the past (Guthey 2008). Under pressure from some growers, university specialists were encouraged to find ways to maximise consistency and improve overall quality, but the result was often a wine that was technically balanced but possibly lacking in any form of distinctiveness. As John Overton and his colleagues cogently state:

> This strategy is designed to develop customer loyalty because it delivers an affordable and reliable product that can be easily understood (without complicating factors such as what was a good vintage and what was not). Furthermore, through the use of economies of scale, it allows the product to compete on the basis of price and to support mass marketing.
>
> *(2012: 277)*

Starting in the late 1970s, however, other Napa newcomers began searching for sites within the valley that they believed would deliver wines of exceptional quality, on a par with the finest from Bordeaux and Burgundy (Taplin 2021). In one sense, they were resurrecting their late nineteenth-century counterparts' vision of developing a geographical awareness and site specificity and build branding around this. But they also had the benefits of continued scientific understanding of soil and location and how innovative techniques (such as extended maceration and micro-oxygenation) could maximise the vineyard's potential. Consequently, much more systematic attention was focused on the soil/site/vine/quality relationship to complement their technical viniculture skills (Taplin 2016).

Product consistency through technical proficiency might be acceptable and even desirable for wine produced in large volumes. But it is difficult to sell a quality wine on the basis of technology, no matter how excellent it is. Whereas Burgundians conflated climate and identity by turning terroir into a normative construct whilst embracing technical innovations, winegrowers in Napa reaped the benefits of innovations and demonstrated how reason and science could master nature. Alas, mastering nature doesn't resonate as well as working with nature. Those able to make wines of exceptional quality, particularly the emerging category of ultra-premium or luxury wines, needed another narrative if they were to convince consumers of that quality. This was achieved courtesy of wine critics such as Robert Parker and *Wine Spectator*, which provided accolades (high scores which were easily understood by people) for such wines (Taplin 2015). Numerical scores lent an aura of objective, scientific authority, legitimising the wine and the winery and endorsing its excellence. Such influential critics bestowed an official recognition of what such wineries were trying to achieve with the best sites and the most professional vineyard workers. Meanwhile, winegrowers of what came to be known as cult wines used high price as a marker to further distinguish and substantiate their claims of excellence and high status (Zhao 2008). Their evolving status as providing a positional good was further enhanced by the small-production and limited-availability business models they pursued (Taplin 2016).

By notionally embracing terroir as a defining feature of their uniqueness, this subset of wineries has differentiated their evolving brand from their competitors. At a general level, they have capitalised on the geographic identity bestowed by the sub-appellations that were created after the 1981 Napa AVA was established (Taplin 2021). But they have also gone further, demarcating vineyards into distinctive blocks, designating the unique characteristics of each and thus elevating the status of site specificity (in all its ecological dimensions) as a further defining feature behind their wine (Heimoff 2018; Bonné 2013).

The mobilisation of site specificity in Napa lacks the broader cultural and historical features of its Burgundian counterpart or terroir, and Napa producers have been hard pressed to invoke the tradition to which many French wineries cling. But they have been able to extol the virtues of craftsmanship in making wines of exceptional quality based on experimentation and technical innovation. In accomplishing this, they have demystified wine (Taber 2005: 230), firmly placing it as a product whose value is communicated as a seemingly uncomplicated status marker. Unable to invoke the aura of a long history, they emphasise a meticulous attention to detail, a rigorous professional rationality and empirically embedded techniques to realise the full quality potential of their wines and communicate that to consumers. Finally, they rely on expert ratification to send a market signal of their quality and the credibility of their brands. Place and name are important, brand development crucial and continued excellence essential, history and tradition far less so.

Conclusion

In this chapter, I have argued that winegrowers in Napa and Burgundy have embraced innovative technical skills, the remediation of problems through a better understanding of chemistry, plant physiology and disease mitigation and the transfer and embrace of formal plus tacit knowledge. Yet whilst Napa producers have consistently extolled the virtues of science, technology and new technical skills in the evolution of their quality reputation, many in Burgundy have relied on invocations of tradition and the artisanal culture that is often implicit in it to differentiate their product. Both have been the beneficiaries of scientific innovations, but Burgundians have been more likely to develop narratives of terroir as guarantors of quality and the bases for value claims; their Napa counterparts falling back primarily on innovative technical skills and objective evaluations by influential critics to demonstrate their efficacy.

A cultural affirmation of techno-scientific innovations was crucial for Napa producers, especially in the post-Prohibition decades when their quality identity remained uncertain. However, once such approaches were effectively institutionalised and recognised as complementary to a near-perfect climate and geography for winegrowing, articulating further characteristics to substantiate brand identity was pursued by resource-rich niche players. In turn, they have produced ultra-premium and luxury wines based on careful site selection and a rigorous, professionalised production system. Such wine was conceived as being an expression of place, unique and not easily replicable, but also the product of state-of-the-art technology and scientific rigour. In other words, they have synthesised science and site, then relied heavily on the high scores of critics to affirm their status credentials.

Notwithstanding twentieth-century technical innovations and the imposition of a regulatory framework that became prescriptive and normative, Burgundian producers often fall back on a cultural narrative that marginalises scientific advances and relies on the legacies of the past. For them, the social construction of space with a defined agricultural role for the land has resulted in a cultural narrative that envelops wine in the evolution of French civilisation and enables them to firmly differentiate their product. Terroir creates identity and, in turn, is a product of an evolving privileging of rusticity: from the Renaissance, when it was seen in a more derogatory manner to its eighteenth-century role as an edifice upon which a food and wine culture was built to the present, when it is central to the identity of certain regions (Parker 2015). In an increasingly urbanised and industrialised world, rural life is used to signify the nobility of agricultural activities, and wine occupies a central place in this idealised discourse. It is the counterpoint to a standardised and homogenous culture: a product whose excellence is an overt expression of man's continuing interaction with nature.

If terroir is the acculturation of nature, then science can be seen as the manifestation of progress behind the growth of a new wine industry in Napa. The former has clear socio-cultural overtones whilst the latter is emblematic of the cult of science and innovative techniques. Terroir invokes a cultural identity; technology facilitates the realisation of the land's potential in the absence of a longstanding winemaking culture. Winegrowers who use both these narratives have similar goals – to make the best wine possible from the place where the grapes are grown. The difference lies in how they adumbrate this process since both feature in the brand building of iconic wines. One elevates practical knowledge that is embedded in socio-cultural traditions whilst the other views technical knowledge as the residue of formulas. And yet the apostles of terroir for the most part now accept a form of viticultural rationalism in their techniques, even though they continue to evoke the vestiges of the past. From a marketing perspective, it would be churlish to do otherwise. The technological 'rationalists', meanwhile, are pragmatic enough to realise that experience and location matter, although they are often implicitly acknowledged rather than manifestly extolled. Site specificity is important but lacks the socio-cultural expression of place that one finds in Burgundy. For Napa's iconic wineries, status is derived from a contemporary acknowledgement of their capabilities by critics who are perceived as taste arbiters. What matters for them is the present and the future, not the past.

References

Anderson, K. and Pinella, V. (2018) *Wine Globalization*, Cambridge: Cambridge University Press.
Bonné, J. (2013) *The New California Wine*, Berkeley, CA: Ten Speed Press.
Carosso, V. (1951) *The California Wine Industry, 1830–1895*, Berkeley: University of California Press.
Daynes, S. (2013) "The Social Life of Terroir Among Bordeaux Winemakers," in R.E Black and R.C Ulin (eds), *Wine and Culture: Vineyard to Glass*, New York: Bloomsbury.
Demossier, M. (2018) *Burgundy: The Global Story of Terroir*, New York: Berghahn.
Gough, J.B. (1998) "Winecraft and Chemistry in 18th Century France: Chaptal and the Invention of Chaptalization," *Technology and Culture* 39(1), 74–104.
Guthey, G.T. (2008) "Agro-Industrial Conventions: Some Evidence from Northern California's Wine Industry," *The Geographical Journal* 174(2), 138–148.
Heimoff, S. (2018) *New Classic Winemakers of California*, Berkeley: University of California Press.
Krzywoszynska, A. (2016) "What Farmers Know. Experiential Knowledge and Care in Vine Growing," *Sociologia Ruralis* 56(2), 289–310.
Le Gentil, A.A-P. (1802) *Mémoire sur la question proposée par la Société des sciences de Montpellier: "Déterminé, par un moyen fixe, simple et portée de tout cultivateur, le moment auquel le vin en fermentation dans le cuve aura acquis toute la force et toute la qualité dont il est susceptible"*, Paris: AJ Marchant.
Matthews, M. (2015) *Terroir and Other Myths of Winegrowing*, Berkeley: University of California Press.
Ouvrard, S., Remaud, H. and Taplin, I.M. (2019) "The Bordeaux Classified Growth System: A Strong Legacy," in M. Quinn and J. Oliveira (eds), *Accounting for Alcohol*, London: Routledge and Taylor Francis, 206–222.
Overton, J., Murray, W.E. and Banks, G. (2012) "The Race to the Bottom of the Glass? Wine, Geography and Globalization," *Globalizations* 9(2), 273–287.
Parker, T. (2015) *Tasting French Terroir*, Berkeley: University of California Press.
Phillips, R. (2016) *French Wine: A History*, Berkeley: University of California Press.
Phillips, R. (2017) *9000 Years of Wine*, Vancouver: Whitecap Books.
Pinney, T. (1989) *A History of Wine in America: From the Beginnings to Prohibition*, Berkeley: University of California Press.

Simpson, J. (2011) *Creating Wine: The Emergence of a World Industry, 1840–1914*, Princeton, NJ: Princeton University Press.
Sullivan, C.L. (2008) *Napa Wine*, San Francisco: Wine Appreciation Guild.
Taber, G. (2005) *The Judgment of Paris*, New York: Scribner.
Taplin, I.M. (2015) "Bottling Luxury: Napa Valley and the Transformation of an Agricultural Backwater into a World-Class Wine Region," *Luxury* 2(1), 81–100.
Taplin, I.M. (2016) "Crafting an Iconic Wine: The Rise of 'Cult' Napa," *International Journal of Wine Business Research* 28(2), 105–119.
Taplin, I.M. (2021) *Napa Valley Wine: Organizing Excellence*, Newcastle: Cambridge Scholars Press.
Trubek, A. (2008) *The Taste of Place*, Berkeley: University of California Press.
Zhao, W. (2005) "Understanding Classifications: Empirical Evidence from the American and French Wine Industries," *Poetics* 33(3), 179–200.
Zhao, W. (2008) "Social Categories, Classification Systems, and Determinants of Wine Price in the California and French Wine Industries," *Sociological Perspectives* 51(1), 163–199.

30
APPLYING FASHION THEORY TO WINE
A production of culture example

Richard Mitchell

Introduction

Several authors have discussed that there are fads and fashions in wine consumption (Charters 2006; Hall and Mitchell 2008; Wilson 2016), that some wine consumers are more likely to make wine purchases based on wine fashions (Bruwer *et al.* 2002; Hall and Mitchell 2008; Spawton 1991) and that there is a relationship between the wine and fashion industries (Nicholls and Mitchell 2008). Meanwhile, fashion researchers state that clothing is just one focus of fashion theory (Easey 2002; Kawamura 2005; Nixon and Blakley 2012; Petersen *et al.* 2016; Sproles and Burns 1994), with Aspers and Godart (2013: 175) suggesting that 'fashion is a central social phenomenon, mechanism, or process that can be applied to any domain'. Despite this, there has been no attempt to apply the theoretical constructs of fashion to wine, although Inglis and Almila (2019) have recently suggested there is a need for a research agenda to address such a gap.

'Fashion studies' is a relatively new area of study that draws on disciplines as diverse as history, sociology, anthropology, psychology, philosophy, gender studies, cultural studies and media studies (Rocamora and Smelik 2015b). The theorising of wine as culture is also relatively new (Black and Ulin 2013; Charters 2006; Wilson 2005), but, like fashion (Rocamora and Smelik 2015b), wine is loaded with meaning (Charters 2006; Finkelstein and Quiazon 2007; Hall and Mitchell 2008), and there are several theoretical lenses which can be used to explore this meaning.

Fashion studies' interdisciplinarity (Aspers and Godart 2013) presents a multitude of possibilities for deepening our understanding of the production and consumption of wine. For example, recent texts edited by Black *et al.* (2014), Rocamora and Smelik (2015) and Jenss and Hofmann (2019) provide a wide range of theoretical and empirical work that could lead to insights into phenomena as diverse as premiumisation (Craik 2019), the relationship between tradition and innovation in fashionability (Van de Peer 2015) and exploring how digital media has sped up the development and spread of fashions (Rocamora 2013). This is far from an exhaustive list, and, despite the broad potential of fashion studies' interdisciplinarity, there is limited scope for this chapter to go beyond a relatively narrow illustrative example.

This conceptual chapter starts with a brief overview of fashion and wine as material objects to further demonstrate the links between them (fashion as a noun). It then explores the 'fashion process' (fashion as a verb) with a particular focus on a 'production of culture' (Kawamura 2005; Santagata 2004; Schmutz and Miller 2015) perspective on fashion. This approach has been taken as there is a small body of wine literature that uses such an approach (Hall and Mitchell 2008; Jamerson 2010).

The chapter concludes by introducing a 'fashion-thinking' framework (Dieffenbacher 2013; Nixon and Blakley 2012; Petersen et al. 2016) that could be used for applying fashion theory to the wine production system.

Wine and fashion as material objects (fashion as a noun)

As an object, fashion is analogous to clothing, but clothing and fashion are ascribed with different values (Crane 2012; Kawamura 2005; Rocamora and Smelik 2015b). While clothing has primarily utilitarian value(s), fashion has values that are constructed in our imagination and through our beliefs, and it is these alluring values that attract us to a fashionable item (Kawamura 2005). As a result, the materiality of fashion plays an important role in the development and expression of our identity (Crane 2012; Rocamora and Smelik 2015b; Wilson 2003).

Charters (2006) also makes the distinction between wine ascribed largely with utilitarian values – 'bulk wine' – and that which is imbued with symbolic meanings – 'premium wines'. Here, Charters (2006: 51) is referring to two distinctly different product categories: wine 'merely consumed as a beverage' and wine appreciated for its aesthetic/meaningful outcomes. So fashion and premium wines are fundamentally different to clothing and bulk wines because of the meanings attached to them. Indeed, Charters (2006) suggests that premium wine is analogous to haute couture, and bulk wine is like a T-shirt from a discount store. The discussion that follows pertains to the connections between fashion and premium wines as material objects loaded with meaning and symbolism.

According to Lurie (1981: 3), the viewer of another's fashion may not necessarily be able to put into words what meaning they have garnered from that fashion, but the information is registered unconsciously so that 'by the time conversation has started the sender and receiver have already spoken with each other in an older and more universal tongue'. From this perspective, dress can be thought of as a language of signs (Barthes 1983; Lurie 1981), a form of nonverbal communication.

Likewise, wines can communicate much about the consumer even before a word is spoken (Charters 2006). Champagne, for example, the quintessential drink of celebration, sophistication and status, is said to speak the same universal language around the world, transcending nationalities and cultures as a wine able to communicate with everyone (Velikova et al. 2016). Wine may also be interpreted as making a statement about its consumer: an item with which a consumer can make a fashion statement through nonverbal communication (Bruwer et al. 2002).

The encoding and decoding of fashion is heavily context dependent, and different social groups understand and appreciate different fashions in different ways (Davis 1985; Rocamora 2002; Rocamora and Smelik 2015b). Meanwhile, Gusfield (1987: 77) suggests that the consumption of any alcoholic beverage (including wine) can be 'studied as text, that is a statement of language through which a message is being communicated', and Vannini et al. (2010) have presented an account of the somatic/corporeal performance of wine communication at wine festivals.

As with all forms of communication, this is a two-way process between communicator and receiver. The wearer of fashion (or drinker of wine) is just one part of the equation, and those observing the wearing (drinking) play a critical role in the co-creation of meaning of these heavily symbolic material objects (Crane 2012; Storm 1987; Wilson 2003). In relation to dress, perceivers bring unique characteristics to social interactions that influence how appearance is observed and interpreted since each individual has their own experience of cultural forces and socialisation (Kaiser 1997). Demographic variables (e.g. gender, age, social class, occupation and ethnicity) and self-related characteristics (e.g. self-esteem, values, attitudes, interest in clothing) influence the perceiver and the perceived in regard to dress as well as context or situational variables (Kaiser 1997). Likewise, the perception of wine is subjective and can be assessed using comparable criteria (Lockshin et al. 1997, 2001).

Work by Charters (Charters 2006; Charters and Pettigrew 2005) should be used as a starting point for more research on how and what wine consumption communicates. Using fashion literature as a foundation for this work could be highly beneficial. (Several recent edited texts provide excellent starting points: e.g. Black *et al.* 2014; Jenss and Hofmann 2019; Rocamora and Smelik 2015.) In particular, aside from the work of a relatively small number of researchers, wine research has tended to ignore the role of culture in the construction, perception and interpretation of meanings associated with wine consumption, and much could be learned from fashion studies here. These meanings are acknowledged to have significant value for fashion consumers (Kawamura 2005) and wine consumers (Charters 2006; Hall and Mitchell 2008), and these are fundamental to understanding the fashion process and its application to wine production and consumption.

The fashion process (fashion as a verb)

Fashion is fundamentally about change (Aspers and Godart 2013; Easey 2002), and such change takes place within a cultural context that reflects broader social change and the interests, values and motives of a society at a given time (Aspers and Godart 2013; Sproles and Burns 1994). This process of change is driven by a number of things:

- New fashions come from many sources, not just fashion designers (Aspers and Godart 2013; Sproles and Burns 1994).
- New fashions evolve from past fashions (i.e. there is historical continuity) (Aspers and Godart 2013; Sproles and Burns 1994; Wilson 2003).
- Fashions are determined by external forces (culture, societal dynamics, lifestyle, history, economy, production and consumption systems) (Aspers and Godart 2013; Kawamura 2005).

These influences combine to result in a complex process of creativity, adaptation, adoption and decline. Consequently, all fashions have life cycles, and all fashions end (Atkinson 2002; Sproles and Burns 1994). Different clothing fashion trends also exist simultaneously in different groups of the consumer population, and the result is a tension between individuality and conformity (Aspers and Godart 2013). This leads to a high degree of ambivalence, which Kawamura (2005) suggests is fundamental to fashion. A key influence here is that change is driven on the one hand by consumer desire for novelty and the desire to 'fit in' on the other (Aspers and Godart 2013; Kawamura 2005; Rocamora 2002). As some authors have suggested, this is also a tension when it comes to premium wines (Bruwer *et al.* 2002; Dodd 1997; Galloway *et al.* 2008).

Wine consumption and production are also driven by constant change, and several factors influence this change:

- No two vintages are the same, either in taste or quality.
- Wine changes over time – over months or years in the bottle and minutes and hours in the glass.
- Different foods alter the aroma and taste of wine in different ways.
- Our senses are altered by many external factors (e.g. mood, surroundings, allergies etc.), and this alters our perceptions of wine.

While continual change and novelty are important in the consumption of both premium wines and fashion, the value derived from such change is constructed quite differently. Wine relies on change that results largely from natural phenomena (e.g. variations in vintage, oxidation, the volatility of aromatic chemicals etc.), and therefore, minimal intervention in the process of change is valued, and natural phenomena are revered (e.g. terroir and place) and often mythologised (Mitchell 2012). Meanwhile, changes in fashion are manufactured (e.g. new designs each season, innovation and creativity), and therefore individuals tend to be revered (e.g. designers). This is reflected in the nature of iconic brands within each product category, with iconic wines most often associated with place (a single vineyard, appellation or region) and iconic fashion brands most often associated with designers (although there are clearly exceptions).

Notwithstanding these differences, there is value in the application of fashion theory to the understanding of how new wine styles/fashions emerge, are transmitted and may be managed. The next section is not intended as an exhaustive discussion of all relevant fashion process theories; rather, it highlights some potential concepts and frameworks of interest with the view that this might stimulate further research into how fashion theory might be applied to wine.

The fashion process, the 'production of culture' and wine

The production of value is inextricably linked to the 'production of culture' (Kawamura 2005), and our understanding of this is reliant on our understanding of the process of change. Peterson (1976) developed the 'six facets' model that identified a range of external conditions that influence the production of cultural objects (e.g. technological, legal, organisational, industrial, occupational and market structures). These are used by production of culture scholars to explore how cultural objects are 'fabricated, circulated, and evaluated' (Schmutz and Miller 2015: 1). While the approach is not without criticism (Santoro 2008), it has been used to explain a wide range of products including popular music (Peterson and Anand 2004), fashion (Braham 2007; Kawamura 2005; Mears 2011; Santagata 2004), various forms of media (Power and Scott 2004), craft beer (Chapman 2015) and wine (Hall and Mitchell 2008; Jamerson 2010).

Several authors have used a production of culture approach in the study of fashion and the development of an understanding of the 'fashion system' (Kawamura 2005; Mears 2011; Santagata 2004). For example, Kawamura (2005) takes a holistic view that includes exploring the role of designers, producers, image makers (media, photographers, event organisers etc.) and gatekeepers (reviewers, critics, judges etc.), as well as the institutions of fashion and the way in which fashions are adopted and consumed. Hall and Mitchell's (2008) value chain approach to wine marketing has presented a framework to explore wine in this way and a production of culture approach that draws on fashion studies would extend their work even further. For example, Hall and Mitchell's (2008) descriptive discussion of 'brand image agents' (e.g. winemakers, intermediaries, wine media and critics and judges) could be extended to become more explanatory by applying the work of Van de Peer (2015) (Luhmann's social systems), Kawamura (2005) ('fashion gatekeepers') or Crane (2012) (fashion and social structures).

A production of culture approach might also lead to new areas of inquiry, such as:

- Understanding how 'wine fashion systems' mediate the effect of seasonal environmental influences to determine which vintages are perceived to be high quality and which are not;
- Conversely, identifying how wine fashion change is mediated by the natural processes of change associated with wine (e.g. vintage), and how this alters fashion process models;
- Exploring the mechanisms by which a particular wine might become 'iconic', and how a production of culture approach might explain this;
- Identifying the fashion systems at play that make chardonnay sexy one year and ABC (anything but chardonnay) in vogue the next or 'pink the new white' or sherry cool again;
- Understanding what makes some wine styles timeless and others abject failures.

Fashion diffusion models provide a way of thinking about how winemakers (as designers of wine) and researchers might pursue such lines of inquiry. This could add to the work of Dodd (1997) and Atkin et al. (2006) on the diffusion of new wine products and innovations.

Fashion diffusion models

While fashion adoption relates to the individual decision-making process used to adopt a new fashion (Kawamura 2005; Rahman *et al.* 2014; Sproles 1985; Sproles and Burns 1994), fashion diffusion is the means by which fashion spreads through a group (Braham 2007; Kawamura 2005; Sproles and Burns 1994). At the individual adoption level, consumer attitudes, beliefs and motivations interact with demographics to shape fashion decisions (Sproles and Burns 1994), and individual decision making is widely studied in wine research (Beverland 2005; Bruwer *et al.* 2002; Dodd 1997; Galloway *et al.* 2008; Hall and Mitchell 2008).

Fashion diffusion models work at a societal level and explore the social and cultural mechanisms for diffusion. Table 30.1 introduces several fashion diffusion models, distinguishing between models that are primarily temporal and those that are more spatial in orientation. Temporal models generally assume movement of fashion trends between or within social strata (Sproles and Burns 1994) over time and that fashion leaders and followers perform distinct functions at different times in the process (Braham 2007; Kawamura 2005; Workman and Kidd 2000). Spatial models, on the other hand, are more concerned with the relationships within and between groups (as in symbolic interactionism) (Blumer 1969; Kaiser 1997; Kawamura 2005); how some geographical locations become centres of innovation or creativity where fashions emerge (Sproles and Burns 1994); or how more organic, complex (rhizomic) systems are at play (Mackinney-Valentin 2013).

The diffusion of wine styles is perhaps the area where our knowledge of wine consumption is least understood, and there is much to be gained from exploring this using one or all of the theoretical positions outlined in Table 30.1. For example, a temporal approach could be used to develop a more in-depth understanding of how wine fashions are transmitted by wine fashion leaders such as Bruwer *et al.*'s (2002) 'ritual-oriented conspicuous wine drinkers' or Spawton's (1991) 'connoisseurs'. Similarly, it might be used to examine how and when wine fashion followers such as Bruwer *et al.*'s (2002) 'fashion/image oriented wine drinkers' or Spawton's (1991) 'aspirational wine drinkers' are influenced by fashion leaders. To this end, Workman and Kidd (2000) suggest that 'fashion change agents'/fashion leaders, who have a need for uniqueness and opinion leadership (Kawamura 2005), are constantly monitoring fashion followers' behaviour. Fashion leaders reach a tipping point once they observe that they are not distinct from followers, and they seek new fashions, and the whole process of fashion adoption and diffusion commences again.

A spatial approach would take this further, extending the analysis to include the role of designers (Braham 2007) and centres of innovation and creativity (Power and Scott 2004; Sproles and Burns 1994) that are in a complex relationship with fashion leaders. Meanwhile, a production of culture approach acknowledges that others in the value chain (e.g. media, critics, judges, retailers and other gatekeepers) are also important in understanding the spatial processes at play in the diffusion of fashions (Kawamura 2005; Schmutz and Miller 2015). This means that producers of fashion must keep up with developments in the fashion world (e.g. new fabrics) and related fields (e.g. the fine arts), as well as wider social movements (Braham 2007), especially those amongst fashion leaders, commentators, critics and judges. The role of gatekeepers and image makers in setting aesthetic agenda for wine has been acknowledged by some (Charters 2006, 2007; Dalitz 2009; Hall and Mitchell 2008; Smith Maguire 2010, 2013; Smith Maguire and Zhang 2016), and this could be a particularly useful area for future comparative research in wine and fashion.

Wine opinion leadership has also been explored in the past (Dodd 1997; Goldsmith and d'Hauteville 1998); however, the focus of these studies has been largely on consumer innovativeness and not the temporal nature of the processes at play. Similarly, while the role of gatekeepers is also now starting to receive greater attention, few have attempted to explore leadership (or followership) as spatially connected in an integrated system to the extent that it has been in the fashion literature. Fashion literature has also recently begun to introduce approaches that acknowledge the temporality

Table 30.1 Fashion diffusion models

	Description	Leaders	Followers	Fashion example	Wine example
Hierarchical (Temporal) Models					
Trickle-down	Fashion defined by 'upper class' and moves down through the classes	'Upper class' [haute couture]	'Lower classes' [mass market]	Post-GFC pastel colour trend	Rosé Champagne
Bubble-up	Fashion emerges on the 'street' and moves up to the 'elite'	'Street' [sub-cultures]	'Elite' [designers]	Punk-look	Organic wines
Mass-market theory	Fashion is mass produced and mass marketed and diffuses within social strata	Influencers within social strata [various forms of media vital]		Distressed jeans	Australian shiraz or Marlborough Sauvignon blanc
Organic (Spatial) Models					
Innovativeness and collective theory	Fashion radiates from areas/centres where creative or prestigious designers work	Centres compete for adoption by fashion-conscious innovators		Tokyo street fashion	Low-alcohol wine (e.g. Marlborough sauvignon blanc)
Symbolic interactionism	Meaning and value are ascribed and shared through set of two-way interactions	Complex of social interactions within cultures/sub-cultures		Hip-hop fashion	'Anything but chardonnay' movement
Rhizomic	A 'natural', 'subterranean' mechanism that organically 'cultivates itself'	Complex of production, media, distribution channels and consumption patterns		Slow fashion	Orange wine/natural wines

Sources: Hall and Mitchell 2008; Kawamura 2005; Levchuk 2018; Mackinney-Valentin 2013; Nicholls and Mitchell 2008; Partington 2007; Petersen et al. 2016; Sproles and Burns 1994; Wilson 2016) and spatiality of the fashion process (Kaiser 2019; Nixon and Blakley 2012; Rocamora 2013). One such approach is 'fashion thinking' and, as an extension of 'design thinking' (Nixon and Blakley 2012), has much to offer those involved in the wine value chain.

Fashion thinking and wine production

Petersen et al. (2016: 2) suggest that a fashion thinking approach moves fashion studies from a 'centripetal', introspective examination of fashion to 'a centrifugal approach where fashion is also an analytical option for analyzing social and cultural processes'. To this end, the last decade has seen a growing body of research that explicitly takes this outward-looking approach to the study of fashion (Dieffenbacher 2013; Nixon and Blakley 2012; Petersen et al. 2016), which expands on the work of production of culture fashion researchers. A fashion thinking approach reflects Pratt's (2004: 124) call for the application of a production of culture framework to a wide range of cultural products and industries, 'one redefined to take in the whole "cycle" of the making and shaping of cultural commodities', that might redress the imbalance between consumption and production in the study of cultural goods.

According to Nixon and Blakley (2012: 154), fashion thinking provides a framework for 'organisations whose goal is to be creative innovators and leaders in business environments that are volatile, uncertain, complex, and ambiguous'. They continue: '[F]ashion also has an innovation agenda, one that has diffused beyond fashion apparel to a wide range of consumer products' (Nixon and Blakley 2012: 156). They suggest that fashion thinking has several distinct features: it is temporal, spatial and socially discursive; it requires designers to be pattern finders; it provides a way to prioritise the articulation of taste; and it helps designers understand the balance between commercial and artistic innovation (see Figure 30.1). In this way, fashion thinkers become 'tastemakers' (Nixon and Blakley 2012) who use a combination of analytical tools and intuition in the design of new fashions.

Figure 30.1 highlights the fact that Nixon and Blakley's (2012) elements interact with each other to form a complex way of thinking about designing, producing and marketing fashion. Spatial and temporal analyses are combined to provide a framework in which the past provides references/designs that consumers can readily relate to, which are combined with future-focused innovations and concepts from elite fashion design and/or fashions emerging on the street to create fashion that is of the here and now. Maintaining the balance between past and future and the push of the designer and the pull of street fashion is both analytical and intuitive. For wine, this can be seen in the development of innovations such as low-alcohol wines, which reference widely accepted wine styles and employ innovative vinicultural and winemaking techniques to respond to growing demand for lower-alcohol beverages (Arthur 2019). Like any new fashion, these wines must be close enough in style to existing wines so as not to cause any dissonance amongst purchasers yet just novel enough to start a new fashion amongst fashion leaders and image makers (Nixon and Blakley 2012).

Nixon and Blakley (2012: 164) also suggest that 'a large part of fashion thinking entails "pattern recognition" – an ability to discern meaningful clusters of information that can resolve into trends'. In the case of low-alcohol wine, this might include emerging patterns in health-conscious consumption amongst millennials (Arthur 2019) and trends in the development and consumption of low-/no-alcohol beverages in other categories (Altmann 2020), as well as growing consumer demand for production methods that are 'natural' or low intervention (Arthur 2019). These patterns are combined with emerging viticultural and oenological technologies (Eads 2018) that allow producers to develop new products in response to these patterns.

Social discourse between fashion designers and consumers (often mediated by media and other gatekeepers) has accelerated significantly with the advent of social media, and this has created new challenges and opportunities for the production of fashion (Nixon and Blakley 2012; Rocamora 2013). As a result, fashion designers can now easily 'monitor the trends that are developing within their customer base and enter that conversation in a meaningful and timely way' (Nixon and Blakley

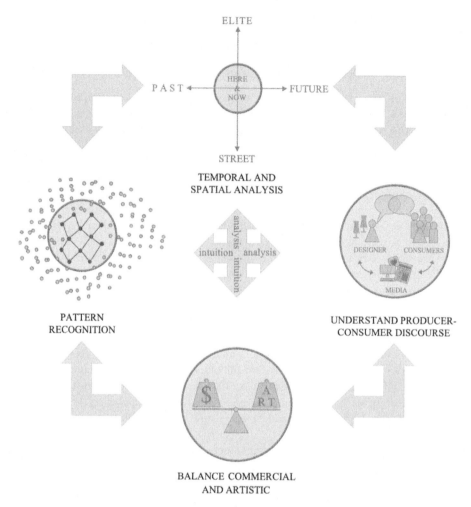

Figure 30.1 Visualisation of Nixon and Blakley's (2012) fashion thinking approach
Source: Author (after Nixon and Blakley 2012)

2012: 163), bridging the space between the 'street' and the design world. For wine, while new fashions may take longer to be developed (because the raw materials are only available once a year and vary with vintage), social discourse between producer and consumer existed well before the advent of social media and continues on several fronts. To this end, wineries and wine drinkers have co-created new fashions in the consumption experience (e.g. new rituals surrounding the opening of screwcaps on bottles) as they can have face-to-face interactions with consumers at the cellar door, restaurants, festivals, shows and the like. For the wine industry, social media is an adjunct to this direct contact, allowing them to discern patterns in the wider marketplace (e.g. discourse around health, low alcohol and other consumption practices).

Like fashion, wine is a commercial activity that involves craft, artistry and an element of self-expression (Charters 2006), and winemakers are constantly balancing the demands of the commercial and the expressive. Nixon and Blakley (2012: 166) suggest that fashion thinking allows companies to manage this as it 'seamlessly encompasses both bottom-line profitability goals as well as overtly fanciful artistry' by embracing the challenge of 'making something unexpected that will sell'. Arguably, this is at the heart of premium winemaking as every vintage is unique and the winemaker must use her/his craft to balance commercial imperatives and the artistry of realising the vintage's full potential.

Conclusion

The fashion and wine industries are cultural systems, and a production of culture approach that is sometimes used in fashion studies can be used to explore the complexity of such systems. To this end, this chapter introduces a selection of fashion theories that can provide insights and systems-level understandings of the cultural processes at play in such phenomena as the diffusion of wine fashions, the spatial nature of the relationships between actors in this diffusion process and how (through fashion thinking) these understandings might be explored as a cultural system rather than as discrete elements within that system.

The value we place on premium wine is the result of a complex cultural process that sees the interaction between consumption (in which consumers attach and share meaning) and production systems controlled by cultural processes of change. As a result, wine provides a fertile ground for the application and adaptation of fashion models to its study and production practices. Nixon and Blakley's (2012) fashion thinking framework provides a useful example of how fashion (production of culture) approaches might be applied to existing understandings drawn from wine research.

References

Altmann, A. (2020, 27 May) "Nonalcoholic Drink Trend Shows no Sign of Slowing Down," *SmartBrief*, www.smartbrief.com/original/2020/05/nonalcoholic-drink-trend-shows-no-sign-slowing-down.

Arthur, R. (2019, 20 March) "New Zealand Winery Helps Carve Out the Lower Alcohol Wine Category: 'Lower ABV is a Feature, not a Compromise!'" *Beveragedaily.Com*, www.beveragedaily.com/Article/2019/03/20/New-Zealand-winery-helps-drive-lower-alcohol-wine-category.

Aspers, P. and Godart, F. (2013) "Sociology of Fashion: Order and Change," *Annual Review of Sociology* 39, 171–192, https://doi.org/10.1146/annurev-soc-071811-145526.

Atkin, T., Garcia, R. and Lockshin, L. (2006) "A multinational Study of the Diffusion of a Discontinuous Innovation," *Australasian Marketing Journal (AMJ)* 14(2), 17–33.

Atkinson, S. (2002) "Designing and Marketing Fashion Products," in M. Easey (ed), *Fashion Marketing*, Oxford: Blackwell, 108–134.

Barthes, R. (1983) *The Fashion System*, trans. M.H. Ward, 1st edition, New York: Hill and Wang.

Beverland, M.B. (2005) "Crafting Brand Authenticity: The Case of Luxury Wines," *Journal of Management Studies* 42(5), 1003–1029.

Black, R.E. and Ulin, R.C. (2013) *Wine and Culture: Vineyard to Glass*, London: Bloomsbury Publishing.

Black, S., De la Haye, A., Entwistle, J., Root, R., Rocamora, A. and Thomas, H. (2014) *The Handbook of Fashion Studies*, London: A&C Black.

Blumer, H. (1969) *Symbolic Interactionism: Perspective and Method*, Englewood Cliffs: Prentice-Hall.

Braham, P. (2007) "Fashion: Unpacking a Cultural Production," in M. Barnard (ed), *Fashion Theory: A Reader*, London: Routledge, 351–372.

Bruwer, J., Li, E. and Reid, M. (2002) "Segmentation of the Australian Wine Market Using a Wine-Related Lifestyle Approach," *Journal of Wine Research* 13(3), 217–242.

Chapman, N.G. (2015) *Craft Beer in the US: A Production of Culture Perspective* (PhD Thesis, Virginia Polytechnic Institute).

Charters, S. (2006) *Wine and Society: The Social and Cultural Context of a Drink*, Oxford: Elsevier and Butterworth-Heinemann.

Charters, S. (2007) "On the Evaluation of Wine Quality," in B.C. Smith (ed), *Questions of Taste: The Philosophy of Wine*, Oxford: Signal Books, 157–182.

Charters, S. and Pettigrew, S. (2005) "Is Wine Consumption an Aesthetic Experience?" *Journal of Wine Research* 16(2), 121–136.

Craik, J. (2019) "'Feeling Premium': Athleisure and the Material Transformation of Sportswear," in H. Jenss and V. Hofmann (eds), *Fashion and Materiality: Cultural Practices in Global Contexts*, London: Bloomsbury Publishing, 214.

Crane, D. (2012) *Fashion and its Social Agendas: Class, Gender, and Identity in Clothing*, Chicago: University of Chicago Press.

Dalitz, R. (2009) "The Multiple Roles of the Australian Wine Show System," *Journal of Wine Research* 20(3), 231–251.

Davis, F. (1985) "Clothing and Fashion as Communication," in M.R. Solomon (ed), *The Psychology of Fashion*, Lexington, MA: Lexington Books, 15–27.

Dieffenbacher, F. (2013) *Fashion Thinking: Creative Approaches to the Design Process*, vol. 14, London: A&C Black.

Dodd, T.H. (1997) "Factors That Influence the Adoption and Diffusion of New Wine Products," *Hospitality Research Journal* 20(3), 123–137.

Eads, L. (2018) "New Zealand Eyes Premium Low Alcohol Wine Sector," *The Drinks Business*, 16 January, www.thedrinksbusiness.com/2018/01/new-zealand-eyes-premium-low-alcohol-wine-sector/.

Easey, M. (2002) "An Introduction to Fashion Marketing," in M. Easey (ed), *Fashion Marketing*, 2nd edition, Oxford: Blackwell, 1–12.

Finkelstein, J. and Quiazon, R. (2007) "Liquid images: Viewing the Wine Label," *Journal of Hospitality and Tourism Management* 14(1), 17–23.

Galloway, G., Mitchell, R., Getz, D., Crouch, G. and Ong, B. (2008) "Sensation Seeking and the Prediction of Attitudes and Behaviours of Wine Tourists," *Tourism Management* 29(5), 950–966.

Goldsmith, R.E. and d'Hauteville, F. (1998) "Heavy Wine Consumption: Empirical and Theoretical Perspectives," *British Food Journal* 100(4), 184–190.

Gusfield, J.R. (1987) "Passage to Play: Rituals of Drinking Time in American Society," in M. Douglas (ed), *Constructive Drinking: Perspectives on Drink from Anthropology*, Cambridge: Cambridge University Press, 73–90.

Hall, C.M. and Mitchell, R. (2008) *Wine Marketing: A Practical Guide*, 1st edition, Oxford: Butterworth-Heinemann.

Inglis, D. and Almila, A.M. (2019) "Inebriation/Participation/Democratization: On Wine, Fashion and Wine Fashions," 9th National Conference in Cultural Studies and 6th National Conference in Cultural Policy Studies, University of Tampere, 13 December, https://events.tuni.fi/kultutkupotu2019-en/.

Jamerson, H.M. (2010) *Wine Tastes: The Production of Culture among Service Workers and Consumers in Napa Valley Wineries* (PhD Thesis, Emory University).

Jenss, H. and Hofmann, V. (2019) *Fashion and Materiality: Cultural Practices in Global Contexts*, London: Bloomsbury Publishing.

Kaiser, S. (1997) *The Social Psychology of Clothing: Symbolic Appearances in Context*, 2nd edition, New York: Fairchild Books.

Kaiser, S. (2019) "Material Subjects: Making Place, Making Time Through Fashion," in H. Jenss and V. Hofmann (eds), *Fashion and Materiality: Cultural Practices in Global Contexts*, London: Bloomsbury Publishing, 21–37.

Kawamura, Y. (2005) *Fashion-ology: An Introduction to Fashion Studies*, Oxford and New York: Berg.

Levchuk, T. (2018). *Trend Diffusion Mechanism in the Modern Fashion Industry* [Master's Thesis], University of Twente.

Lockshin, L., Quester, P. and Spawton, T. (2001) "Segmentation by Involvement or Nationality for Global Retailing: A Cross-national Comparative Study of Wine Shopping Behaviours," *Journal of Wine Research* 12(3), 223–236.

Lockshin, L., Spawton, A. and Macintosh, G. (1997) "Using product, Brand and Purchasing Involvement for Retail Segmentation," *Journal of Retailing and Consumer Services* 4(3), 171–183.

Lurie, A. (1981) *The Language of Clothes*, New York: Henry Holt and Company.

Mackinney-Valentin, M. (2013) "Trend Mechanisms in Contemporary Fashion," *Design Issues* 29(1), 67–78.

Mears, A. (2011) *Pricing Beauty: The Making of a Fashion Model*, Berkeley: University of California Press.

Mitchell, R. (2012) "A Place of Paradox: Champagne as it is Presented to the Outsider," in S. Charters (ed), *The Business of Champagne*, London: Routledge, 53–68.

Nicholls, C. and Mitchell, R. (2008) "Wine as Fashion: Moët & Chandon and Dom Pérignon," in C.M. Hall and R. Mitchell (eds), *Wine Marketing: A Practical Guide*, Oxford: Butterworth-Heinemann, 250–253.

Nixon, N.W. and Blakley, J. (2012) "Fashion Thinking: Towards an Actionable Methodology," *Fashion Practice* 4(2), 153–175.

Partington, A. (2007) Popular Fashion and Working-Class Affluence. In M. Barnard (ed), *Fashion Theory: A Reader*, New York: Routledge, 220–231.

Petersen, T.B., Mackinney-Valentin, M. and Melchior, M.R. (2016) "Fashion Thinking," *Fashion Practice* 8(1), 1–9, https://doi.org/10.1080/17569370.2016.1147699.

Peterson, R.A. (1976) "The Production of Culture: A Prolegomenon," *American Behavioral Scientist* 19(6), 669–684.

Peterson, R.A. and Anand, N. (2004) "The Production of Culture Perspective," *Annual Review of Sociology* 30, 311–334. ProQuest Central, https://doi.org/10.1146/annurev.soc.30.012703.110557.

Power, D. and Scott, A.J. (2004) "A Prelude to Cultural Industries and the Production of Culture," in D. Power and A.J. Scott (eds), *Cultural Industries and the Production of Culture*, London: Routledge, 1–15.

Pratt, A.C. (2004) "The Cultural Economy: A Call for Spatialized 'Production of Culture' Perspectives," *International Journal of Cultural Studies* 7(1), 117–128.

Rahman, S.U., Saleem, S., Akhtar, S., Ali, T. and Khan, M.A. (2014) "Consumers' Adoption of Apparel Fashion: The Role of Innovativeness, Involvement, and Social Values," *International Journal of Marketing Studies* 6(3), 49.

Rocamora, A. (2002) "Fields of Fashion: Critical Insights into Bourdieu's Sociology of Culture," *Journal of Consumer Culture* 2(3), 341–362.

Rocamora, A. (2013) "New Fashion Times: Fashion and Digital Media," in S. Black, A. De la Haye, J. Entwistle, R. Root and H. Thomas (eds), *The Handbook of Fashion Studies*, London: Bloomsbury, 61–77.

Rocamora, A. and Smelik, A. (2015a) *Thinking Through Fashion: A Guide to Key Theorists*, London: Bloomsbury.

Rocamora, A. and Smelik, A. (2015b) "Thinking Through Fashion: An Introduction," in A. Rocamora and A. Smelik (eds), *Thinking Through Fashion: A Guide to Key Theorists*, London: IB Tauris, 1–27.

Santagata, W. (2004) "Creativity, Fashion and Market Behaviour," in D. Power and A. Scott (eds), *Cultural Industries and the Production of Culture*, London: Routledge, 75–90.

Santoro, M. (2008) "Culture as (and after) Production," *Cultural Sociology* 2(1), 7–31.

Schmutz, V. and Miller, C.N. (2015) "Production of Culture," in R. Scott, S. Kosslyn and M. Buchmann (eds), *Emerging Trends in the Social and Behavioral Sciences*, Hoboken, NJ: John Wiley & Sons, 1–14.

Smith Maguire, J. (2010) "Provenance and the Liminality of Production and Consumption: The Case of Wine Promoters," *Marketing Theory* 10(3), 269–282.

Smith Maguire, J. (2013) "Provenance as a Filtering and Framing Device in the Qualification of Wine," *Consumption Markets & Culture* 16(4), 368–391.

Smith Maguire, J. and Zhang, D. (2016) "Shifting the Focus from Consumers to Cultural Intermediaries: An Example from the Emerging Chinese Fine Wine Market," in N. Toulouse, D. Rinalto and R.W. Belk (eds), *Consumer Culture Theory*, Bingley: Emerald Publishing, 1–27.

Spawton, T. (1991) "Wine and the Marketing Mix," *European Journal of Marketing* 25(3), 19–31.

Sproles, G.B. (1985) "Behavioural Science Theories of Fashion," in M.R. Solomon (ed), *The Psychology of Fashion*, Lexington, MA: Lexington Books, xii, 428.

Sproles, G.B. and Burns, L.D. (1994) *Changing Appearances: Understanding Dress in Contemporary Society*, New York: Fairchild.

Storm, P. (1987) *Function of Dress: Tool of Culture and the Individual*, Englewood Cliffs, NJ: Prentice Hall.

Van de Peer, A. (2015) "Niklas Luhmann: Fashion between the Fashionable and Old-fashioned," in A. Rocamora and A. Smelik (eds), *Thinking Through Fashion: A Guide to Key Theorists*, London: Bloomsbury Publishing, 200–214.

Vannini, P., Ahluwalia-Lopez, G., Waskul, D. and Gottschalk, S. (2010) "Performing Taste at Wine Festivals: A Somatic Layered Account of Material Culture," *Qualitative Inquiry* 16(5), 378–396.

Velikova, N., Charters, S., Fountain, J., Ritchie, C., Fish, N. and Dodd, T. (2016) "Status or Fun? A Cross-Cultural Examination of Young Consumers' Responses to Images of Champagne and Sparkling Wine," *British Food Journal* 118(8), 1960–1975.

Wilson, D. (2016) "Flavoured Wine – Fad, Fashion or Trend?" *BIO Web of Conferences* 7, 03008. https://doi.org/10.1051/bioconf/20160703008

Wilson, E. (2003) *Adorned in Dreams: Fashion and Modernity*, New Brunswick, NJ: Rutgers University Press.

Wilson, T.M. (2005) *Drinking Cultures*, Oxford: Berg Publishers.

Workman, J.E. and Kidd, L.K. (2000) "Use of the Need for Uniqueness Scale to Characterize Fashion Consumer Groups," *Clothing and Textiles Research Journal* 18(4), 227–236.

31

SPENDING, TASTE AND KNOWLEDGE

Logics of connoisseurship and good taste in the age of cultural democratisation

Sarah Cappeliez

Introduction

In a New World wine context, how do wine professionals evaluate and understand the ideal consumer for their product? As it circulates in a knowledge-based economy, wine requires very specific skills in a variety of areas in order to consume it competently and confidently (Karpik 2010; Rössel *et al.* 2018: 456–457; Sternsdorff Cisterna 2014: 100). But which consumer skills are considered most legitimate and desirable to wine producers and intermediaries?

This chapter uses a case study of wine professionals' evaluations of consumers in the Ontario (Canada) wine market to outline three key dimensions of ideal consumer connoisseurship in the field of wine: (1) spending sufficiently but wisely, (2) tasting complexity and terroir in wines, and (3) demonstrating knowledge and interest in the details and technicalities of the production and classification of wine. This chapter thus draws empirical attention to the role played by wine professionals in creating cultural norms and conventions of good taste that also help establish them as legitimate, highly regarded professionals in their field. More broadly, it contributes to research on the cultural production of taste by elucidating how the dynamics of homogeneity and difference and of old and new hierarchies function and take shape as wine consumption becomes more popular and democratised.

First, I consider research on taste hierarchies in the wine world and the current tension between democratisation, as wine becomes a popular commodity, and distinction, as strong ties to traditional winemaking status symbols endure. I then examine work that highlights the need to develop consumers' taste for challenging foods like artisanal cheeses or obscure wines and discuss producers' and cultural intermediaries' roles in producing and reproducing shared norms of good taste. To illustrate how wine professionals define consumer good taste, I turn to a case study in the Ontario wine market. Descriptions of consumer taste from this case reveal the ideas of good taste that wine professionals favour, suggesting the contours of producer-oriented taste hierarchies that allow wine professionals to consolidate their positions and careers in the field of wine in times of changing cultural standards and cultural democratisation.

Shifting taste hierarchies in the wine world

In recent decades, cultural sociologists have moved away from Bourdieusian understandings of taste hierarchies as more rigidly organised around highbrow and lowbrow tastes (Bourdieu 1984) and begun to consider taste in more fluid and shifting ways (Bennett *et al.* 1999; Johnston and Baumann 2015; Peterson and Kern 1996; Warde *et al.* 2008). Once associated mostly with elite culture, good taste today includes select popular culture elements as boundaries loosen around the meanings of good taste. Research on this so-called 'cultural omnivorousness' has demonstrated that status hierarchies linked to taste are being challenged through cultural practices like eating authentic and exotic foods (Cappeliez and Johnston 2013; Johnston and Baumann 2015) or listening to classical music and blues (Peterson and Kern 1996).

Evidence of these shifting dynamics of taste hierarchies has also emerged in the wine world (Fitzmaurice 2017; Fourcade 2012; Garcia-Parpet 2011; Howland 2013; Voronov *et al.* 2013; Smith Maguire 2018b) as wine is popularised and commodified as a product and a practice, particularly in new winemaking settings. New World wines are increasingly emerging as legitimate, high-quality wines, comparable to Old World wines. The French term terroir, formerly used to distinguish Old from New World wines and, simultaneously, high- from lowbrow products, now extends to New World wines. Yet New World winemaking continues to rely on traditional conceptualisations of terroir that remain rooted in connecting a wine's legitimacy to established European winemaking culture and practices (Smith Maguire 2018b; Voronov *et al.* 2013), as well as styles and tastes (Fitzmaurice 2017).

Thus, the democratisation of wine tastes appears to develop alongside continued patterns of distinction that maintain the Old World as a reference point. Because the wine world remains stratified and conservative, it provides insight into this tension between the democratic impulses of changing taste boundaries and the enduring undercurrents of distinction. As the broader case of wine shows, hierarchies and status symbols persist, showing that distinction is still very much alive, but these have become harder to pinpoint. While participants in the world of wine are aware of the existence of taste hierarchies, the shape and overall organisation of these taste hierarchies may not always be clearly defined, especially because new knowledge and ideas of good taste frequently destabilise these taste hierarchies (Fitzmaurice 2017; Karpik 2010; Smith Maguire 2018b). What, then, is good taste? And what role do wine professionals (e.g. wine producers and cultural intermediaries) play in defining good taste in wine?

Developing palates for 'challenging' consumer goods

Despite demonstrating the fundamental significance and contested nature of taste practices, sociologists know far less about how norms and 'shared understandings' of good taste are produced and reproduced (Lamont 2012; Smith Maguire 2018a; Warde 2014). To get at this, I focus on the production side of market relations in the wine world and, specifically, on how wine professionals construct their ideal consumers using their own notions of good taste. Recent research on cultural consumption has shifted attention back towards cultural intermediaries' role in cultivating and negotiating the norms of good consumption and taste (Childress 2017; Cronin 2004; Smith Maguire and Matthews 2012). Equally important to consider is how producers of cultural goods construct their ideal consumer and, through this, create and reproduce ideas of good taste that reflect and maintain their interests and positions within the field of wine. Wine professionals do not always make, sell or communicate about wine that will please the most people or produce the most sales. Rather, they sometimes pursue aesthetic goals that align with their own and their peers' shared ideals of good wine, proceeding to locate and mobilise consumers who will appreciate their efforts at a later stage (Smith Maguire 2018a).

Finding these knowledgeable and appreciative consumers can entail actively developing people's palates for wines that may not immediately please them. As producers and mediators of complex products in the wine world, wine professionals are confronted with questions of taste and the ideal consumers of their products at a very practical, everyday level. Consumers can face barriers when it comes to appreciating artisanal foods and drink: cheeses may be stinky (Paxson 2010) or apples misshapen, small or even downright 'ugly' (Jordan 2015). Artisanal products' tastes and appearances may be inconsistent, their cost prohibitive and their moral or ethical 'goodness' undetectable at first glance. In North America, where consumers' tastes may be more attuned to standardised and predictable industrial products, artisan cheesemakers must actively work to convey their cheeses' specific character and added value (Paxson 2010). Even within French food and wine culture, which foregrounds quality and discernment, artisanal producers and tastemakers actively teach consumers how to taste, working to shift consumers from popular to more sophisticated, higher-value options, such as dark chocolate (Terrio 2000) and place-based foods (Leynse 2006). Consumers thus must be taught to become 'good' tasters of complex and less standardised foods. Producers and cultural intermediaries play a key role in defining aspects of these new tastes and subsequently shaping or identifying the audiences for these products. Given this, what attributes of the 'good' consumer do wine producers and cultural intermediaries recognise and uphold? What do they use as a foil to the 'good' consumer in identifying less valued consumer characteristics? And what do these overall perceptions of the ideal consumer tell us about cultural conventions of taste and the shapes of taste hierarchies they suggest?

Defining the 'good' wine consumer

A little over an hour outside Toronto, Canada, sits Niagara, Ontario's largest and oldest viticultural area. Although winemaking in Ontario began in the 1800s (Phillips 2006), the Ontario wine industry dates its true beginnings in quality winemaking to the mid-1970s, when the industry began to adopt European quality standards in an effort to actively change its quality issues and poor reputation in winemaking (Voronov et al. 2013: 611; interview data). Wine quality is regulated by the Vintners Quality Alliance (VQA) Ontario. The Niagara appellations and sub-appellations are part of Ontario's appellation system – the oldest of its kind in Canada. Known globally for its ice wine, Niagara has recently been recognised for wines made from cool climate varieties like chardonnay, riesling, and gamay noir. In the next sections, I use interviews with wine producers and intermediaries, analysis of wine industry websites and field observations at wineries and wine events in Ontario to examine how wine professionals define consumer connoisseurship in three ways: (1) the ability to spend sufficiently but wisely (*spending*), (2) the capacity to taste complexity and terroir in wines (*tasting*), and (3) the demonstration of knowledge and interest in the details and technicalities of the production and classification of wine (*knowing*).

Spending: recognising quality, not just showing off

Wine professionals framed wine consumers' spending behaviours in two contrasting ways. First, the ability and inclination to purchase more expensive wines signalled more highly engaged wine consumers who may also be more experienced and knowledgeable. At the same time, simply spending more on wine could reflect that somebody was a 'know-nothing show-off'.

Looking first at the quality of 'spending sufficiently', wine professionals often clearly differentiated between wines, associating better wines with more engaged wine drinkers who are willing to spend more on higher-quality products. For example, Nathalie (winemaker) distinguished between two levels of wines she produces: both are handmade, but Nathalie considers wine from a delineated 'small lot' section of her vineyard superior in quality to wine blended from different parts of the vineyard and deemed more 'approachable' and 'accessible' for customers. In comparing these wines, Nathalie also describes the types of consumers who appreciate and buy higher-quality wines. The more expensive and exclusive small-lot riesling appeals to those who can afford it and who demonstrate their competence by being 'just a little bit more specific' in their tastes (e.g. have a discriminating palate supported by sufficient wine knowledge to recognise the distinguishing features of these wines).

Wine professionals thus connected consumers' understanding of the price-quality value of premium Ontario wines with more wine knowledge. Premium Ontario wine can appear expensive to consumers, especially when compared to cheaper wines from New World regions like Chile and Argentina or renowned Old World wines whose value is widely recognised. Wine professionals acknowledged that Ontario wines' value and rationale for their higher prices were sometimes difficult to convey, particularly when consumers did not have sufficient education to understand Ontario's position in the broader wine world. Less knowledgeable, 'casual' drinkers might find Ontario wines 'no good or too expensive', as Norman (marketing) indicated, not realising that Niagara's shorter growing season and uneven climate affect wine pricing. By contrast, more experienced consumers can appreciate wines made from varieties like gamay that thrive in Niagara yet are less popular. These consumers understand the price-quality ratio of Ontario wines and specific Ontario wine styles, rather than simply 'trying to get an imitation of Bordeaux here [in Niagara]', as Neil (winemaker) encapsulated.

Although a sign of good taste, buying expensive wine alone was not always an immediate sign of consumer sophistication. Spending sufficiently could demonstrate a higher ability to express specific tastes but could also mean that '[wine consumers] just have more money too', as Nathalie noted. Here, buying expensive wine is less about an educated palate and more about the financial comfort to carelessly consume. Similarly, Nick (winemaker) described certain high-end customers as 'international tasters' with 'their own wine cellars', who nevertheless gravitate to his winery's reserve wine *because* of its higher price and substantial bottle, compared to the longer, narrower, non-reserve bottle. The heavier bottle is intended for those who 'actually probably don't know that much about [wine], but they wanna *feel* like they do'. While some consumers purchase expensive wine because they know more and can recognise quality, others gravitate towards expensive bottles to show off and assert wealth and status. Nick critiques these latter consumers' displays of economic capital as evidence of a lack of cultural capital: they know that wine is viewed as fancy and high class but are easily 'duped' by superficial symbols, like price and bottle shape/size. Nick's winery may cater to these consumers' desire to buy expensive, nicer-looking bottles, but he also appears to scorn this style of wine consumption and consumer. Buying based on high price alone thus emerged as a less refined or knowledgeable way of consuming wine.

Tasting: moving beyond 'yummy' to appreciate complexity and terroir

Consumers' ability to appreciate and taste key aspects of wine emerged as a central way for wine professionals to classify consumers and their wine involvement. There was a clear understanding that unsophisticated consumers prioritise things that are 'yummy', whereas knowledgeable consumers move beyond the obvious sensory pleasures of 'simple wines' to appreciate complexity and terroir. As Tim (writer and educator) indicated, 'complexity puts some people off. They don't want complexity'. Yet in my observations, complexity was precisely the type of taste that wine professionals aspired to produce, sell or promote. A tension thus emerged between trendier, more widely appealing and readily 'delicious' wines – usually understood as sweeter, less tannic, 'easy' wines that were not reputation building for a winery – and wines that wine professionals considered higher in quality and that they described as 'mineral', 'complex', 'elegant' and 'small-batch'. These different tastes and their accompanying descriptors further corresponded to different levels of consumer approachability, as conveyed on Niagara's *Château des Charmes* website, where wines meant for novice drinkers are 'simple' and 'easy/can be drunk now' while wines that are 'complex' and 'age worthy' must be preserved for later enjoyment, which requires knowledge of ageing times and conditions.

Wine professionals further connected wine sophistication to an understanding and appreciation for the taste of terroir. At the broadest level, respondents like Nelly (winemaker) associated more educated wine consumers with a taste for terroir: '[terroir is] something that would engage the top two per cent of wine buyers that are really super keen and are big buyers – they're super engaged in [wine]'. Similarly, Norman recognised that '[terroir] applies to more educated, more serious wine drinkers while 'the average [wine drinker] doesn't have the interest to that extent'. More specifically, wine professionals perceived educated consumers as capable of understanding and enjoying the 'taste from somewhere' that terroir imparts. As Tom (wine writer) described,

> Anyone who's sort of educated themselves about wine will have a better understanding of terroir and understand how it affects wine, whereas someone who doesn't really drink wine might not know how, let's say cool climate will relate to high acid, or that sort of thing.

Wine professionals related the ability to detect the 'taste from somewhere' with the capacity to understand and enjoy terroir's influence on the specificities of taste in wines. For Nate (winemaker), knowledgeable consumers who are 'quite interested in [terroir]' are also consumers who 'have travelled all over the world, and even within the Niagara region'. They appreciate taste in a cosmopolitan sense and can situate Ontario's wines within a global palate of wine tastes by recognising their 'specificity'. Higher consumer engagement and sophistication acquired through travel and tasting experience were thus associated with recognising terroir differences that exist within various viticultural areas of Niagara – understanding 'Niagara within Niagara', as Neil put it – whereas lower tiers of consumer involvement meant simply realising that Niagara produces wine.

Lastly, appreciating specific, terroir-based tastes had price and class implications for wine professionals. Appreciation for complex terroir tastes generally found in higher-priced wines was often contrasted with a less sophisticated taste for simpler, immediately likeable wines with generally cheaper price tags. For Nick, terroir interest mainly occurred in 'the 20 wineries that are on the premium end', whereas 'as a whole, people are coming in a lot of the other wineries and saying, you know, "How much is that merlot?", as opposed to asking about our soil structure and asking about vintage'. Nigel (marketing) agreed, describing terroir's appeal to consumers 'who have spent more than 20 dollars on a bottle at some point in their life', rather than to those who drink 'Maria Christina, or Yellow Tail, or Wolf Blass from southeastern Australia' and for whom 'probably terroir is not something [they're] thinking of; [they're] thinking of pleasure – Is it yummy? Is it not yummy? – and not thinking too much about where it comes from, or how it was produced'. Here, Nigel implicitly values interest in wine that tastes 'from somewhere' and shows specific characteristics. By contrast, consumers who prefer cheaper (usually around $10–$12) blended wines made from grapes that come from vastly different vineyards and are non-vintage are framed as less discerning in their prioritisation of 'yumminess' over 'placeness' and a wine's production methods.

Nick's and Nigel's quotes summarise all three dimensions of terroir taste: 'somewhereness', specificity and premium prices. While these valued taste elements connect to sensory-based aesthetic preferences, they are also strongly associated with consumers perceived as more knowledgeable about wine. Thus, educated consumers display a taste for a wine's complexity and terroir, whereas less sophisticated consumers' taste revolves around simpler, easier to drink, less specific, cheaper blends.

Knowing: appreciating the details of wine production, classification and expertise

Wine professionals also discussed how the sophisticated wine consumer demonstrates extensive knowledge of, and interest in, the details and technicalities of wine. To illustrate this, respondents described consumers' knowledge and appreciation of very detailed aspects of wine related to production methods, appellation systems and sources of expert advice. Wine professionals depicted consumers who were interested in these sometimes very detailed factoids or sources of information and were also keen to learn more about these wine technicalities.

First, consumers' interest in and understanding of production methods signalled higher wine education overall. Nate drew distinctions between the select group of consumers at his small but reputable winery who 'are very knowledgeable about what they want' and are also interested in production techniques 'like [knowing] what kind of yeast [we're] using or what fermentation techniques [we] like' and others 'who've never even tried certain varieties of wine before, you don't have to be as specific [in explaining how a wine is made]'. Pre-existing, precise knowledge of wines is connected here to curiosity about the technical aspects of a wine's production and clearly applies to wine savvy consumers. Nick similarly noted that 'when someone comes in and goes, "Wow, that chardonnay really has a Burgundian style!"', he immediately knows he 'can talk about malolactic fermentation, about grams of acid per litre – about all of these other things'. Higher levels of wine knowledge – recognising a chardonnay that has a 'Burgundian style' – signal familiarity with fairly technical information about a wine's production (e.g. fermentation and acidity details). Inversely, as Nick also observed, 'you can't talk to [novice consumers] about malolactic fermentation because . . . the minute that happens, you've lost them'. Like Nate, Nick clearly distinguishes savvy consumers who grasp technical information about a wine's production from those who will be confused by these aspects.

Wine professionals also associated educated wine consumers with knowledge and understanding of Ontario's appellation system. Born from producers' desire to increase consumer confidence in Ontario wine quality and to legitimate the Ontario wine industry on the world stage, the appellation system defines and ensures authenticity and origin in Ontario wines (VQA website; interview data). Wine professionals frequently expressed reservations about the average consumer's ability to understand the appellation system. Indeed, a recurring theme in interviews was the juxtaposition of less sophisticated wine consumers who do not understand Ontario (sub)appellations with discerning wine tasters, viewed as knowledgeable of the appellation system and its intricacies. For Norman, 'people who are either more educated or more interested in wine will know [the appellation system], and the casual consumer . . . won't'. Tristan (wine writer), who described the appellation system glowingly as 'incredible, extensive', recognised that 'the average consumer doesn't give a crap about [the appellation system], but once you get very serious about wine, you do start to notice things'. Sophisticated, 'serious' consumers are thus understood as capable of grasping the appellation system and appreciating what it brings to wine in terms of wine styles, tastes, authenticity and origin.

Lastly, wine professionals perceived sophisticated consumers as interested in seeking out expert advice when choosing wine. In Norman's words, 'a lot of wine purchases are done by consumers – especially the more interested consumers – based on reviews' from renowned wine critics and wine publications. Tristan similarly compared knowledgeable consumers, who '[go] to their friends who are the wine connoisseurs' for advice to the 'average consumer' who, he noted disapprovingly, tends to rely on sales gimmicks like 'new to watch' stickers, 'stuff on sale' or with 'Air Miles tags', '[trusting] the [Ontario government-run liquor store] to educate them on what's gonna be a good product to choose'. Seeking out expert knowledge was thus viewed as an important characteristic of sophisticated wine consumers, but the best wine consumers were described as possessing sufficient knowledge to navigate the subtleties of wine expertise and avoid emulating wine experts without discernment. For example, Tim described consumers

> who buy a bottle because it got a great score, and they bring it out, and they don't say what it tastes like, they say, 'This is a 97', meaning it got a Parker 97 points, and everyone is supposed to go, 'Woo'.

Here, Tim echoes earlier disapprovals of wine choices guided either by overt class markers (e.g. size, shape or price of a bottle) or by marketing and sale tactics (e.g. special labels or wine scores/awards). Purchasing an acclaimed wine without care or attention to one's own tastes does not reflect wine knowledge but rather status motivations inflected with *nouveau riche* undertones – it is the 'easy' and non-discerning way of choosing wine.

Conclusion

Examining wine professionals' perceptions of consumers in the Ontario wine market sheds light on the construction and conventionalisation of taste from the producers' and intermediaries' point of view. Wine professionals' concern is not just in selling large quantities of expensive wines; it is also very much about producing and promoting wines considered symbolically valuable in the field of wine and then identifying and mobilising an appreciative audience for these wines. Consumers who can identify specifics of Ontario wines demonstrate that they recognise the 'goodness' of these wines, thereby providing legitimacy to the broader project of producing quality wine in Ontario. As this chapter shows, wine professionals view their ideal consumer as recognising and responding favourably to aspects of the best products they make, sell and represent. Thus, wine professionals' perceptions of consumers can help them understand the consumer skills they consider most desirable and necessary to support quality wine production and promotion in fine wine markets, as well as the dimensions of taste hierarchies that help establish and maintain producers' and intermediaries' positions as professionals in the field of wine.

The typology developed here also emphasises some key characteristics of taste hierarchies in today's omnivorous cultural context, in which democratisation exists in tension with moments of distinction. As overt displays of status become less accepted, how people express taste becomes just as important (if not more so) than what people like (Cappeliez and Johnston 2013; Friedman 2012; Holt 1998; Johnston and Baumann 2015; Warde et al. 2008). In the wine world, new taste hierarchies are also organised along more nuanced ways of asserting taste. Once considered an object exclusive to high culture – particularly in a North American context – wine no longer embodies sophistication so straightforwardly. Rather, distinction is achieved through subtler displays of knowledge and connoisseurship. In a time of loosening cultural standards, figuring out the yardsticks of good taste is not an obvious or simple task. Yet specific standards of taste *do* persist, as is patent in the wine professionals' descriptions examined here.

This case study demonstrates that good taste is associated with three logics. First, good taste is associated with informed spending, perceived as understanding higher price points in relation to premium and distinctive goods while avoiding simply spending money on expensive cultural goods. This translates as a willingness of consumers to pay more for higher-quality wine because they understand its value and not just showing off by reaching for the most expensive bottle at a winery. Second, good taste is related to the capacity to sensorially appreciate complex cultural goods that are from *somewhere* and to shun easier-to-like and more generic goods. In the world of wine, this complexity in taste comes mainly from the 'taste of somewhere' that terroir imparts and that reflects many of the broader ideas of authenticity, transparency and craftsmanship associated with good taste today (Johnston and Baumann 2015; Ocejo 2014; Paxson 2010; Smith Maguire 2018b). By contrast, purely 'yummy' wines – generally understood to be sweeter, blended and generic (and, therefore, of inferior quality) – are viewed less favourably. Lastly, good taste involves displaying knowledge of and interest in the details of production and classification of cultural goods. For wine, this means possessing knowledge of and interest in the specificities of a wine's production and also being keen to expand one's wine education by seeking out appropriate expert sources of knowledge, like well-known wine critics or writers. Conversely, buying wines on promotion or to impress friends because they are 'Robert Parker approved' is regarded as pedestrian.

This chapter thus illuminates the attributes of wine professionals' preferred audience for the complex products they make, sell and promote. Products like artisanal cheeses, chocolate or wine require some form of socialisation and taste education to appreciate, making the ability to identify and nurture desirable consumer skills a key practical concern for producers and cultural intermediaries alike. Wine professionals' definitions of the ideal consumer also highlight how producers and intermediaries navigate their own positions and careers in the field of Ontario wine by maintaining distinctions between artisanal, complex and small-scale wines (and the people who can appreciate them) and easier, yummier and more commercial wines (and those who consume them). Adopting an anti-economic logic that favours more 'serious' wines ultimately emerges as a way for wine professionals to establish themselves as reputable in the Ontario wine world while also, incidentally, reinforcing the premium price points of serious wines. Lastly, in a global winemaking context in which emerging wine regions like Niagara still look to external, usually European reference points for winemaking practices and philosophies, identifying an ideal audience and nurturing skills that correspond to one's aesthetic goals (and the production choices that entails) become particularly important. Why? Because developed, mature markets benefit from developed, mature consumers who can taste, pay for and appreciate quality products. Thus, these skills are vital to cultivate for the continued development and success of Ontario wine professionals' long-term project of producing and selling quality wine.

References

Bennett, T., Emmison, M. and Frow, J. (1999) *Accounting for Taste: Australian Everyday Cultures*, Cambridge: Cambridge University Press.

Bourdieu, P. (1984) *Distinction: A Social Critique of the Judgement of Taste*, Cambridge, MA: Harvard University Press.

Cappeliez, S. and Johnston, J. (2013) "From Meat and Potatoes to 'Real-Deal' Rotis: Exploring Everyday Culinary Cosmopolitanism," *Poetics* 41(5), 433–455.

Childress, C. (2017) *Under the Cover: The Creation, Production, and Reception of a Novel*, Princeton, NJ: Princeton University Press.

Cronin, A.M. (2004) "Regimes of Mediation: Advertising Practitioners as Cultural Intermediaries?" *Consumption Markets and Culture* 7(4), 349–369.

Fitzmaurice, C. (2017) "How Rosé Became High Class: Categorical Divestment and Evaluation," *Poetics* 61, 1–13.

Fourcade, M. (2012) "The Vile and the Noble: On the Relations between Natural and Social Classifications in the French Wine World," *The Sociological Quarterly* 53, 524–545.

Friedman, S. (2012) "Cultural Omnivores or Culturally Homeless? Exploring Shifting Cultural Identities of the Upwardly Mobile," *Poetics* 40(5), 467–489.

Garcia-Parpet, M-F. (2011) "Symbolic Value and the Establishment of Prices: Globalization of the Wine Market," in J. Beckert and P. Aspers (eds), *The Worth of Goods: Valuation and Pricing in the Economy*, Oxford: Oxford University Press, 131–154.

Holt, D. (1998) "Does Cultural Capital Structure American Consumption?" *Journal of Consumer Research* 25(1), 1–25.

Howland, P.J. (2013) "Distinction by Proxy: The Democratization of Fine Wine," *Journal of Sociology*, 49(2–3), 325–340.

Johnston, J. and Baumann, S. (2015) *Foodies: Democracy and Distinction in the Gourmet Foodscape*, 2nd edition, New York: Routledge.

Jordan, J. (2015) *Edible Memory: The Lure of Heirloom Tomatoes and Other Forgotten Foods*, Chicago: University of Chicago Press.

Karpik, L. (2010) *The Economics of Singularities*, Princeton NJ,: Princeton University Press.

Lamont, M. (2012) "Toward a Comparative Sociology of Valuation and Evaluation," *Annual Review of Sociology* 38, 201–221.

Leynse, W.L.H. (2006) "Journeys through 'Ingestible Topography': Socializing the 'Situated Eater' in France," in T.M. Wilson (ed), *Food, Drink and Identity in Europe*, Amsterdam: Rodopi, 129–158.

Ocejo, R.E. (2014) "Show the Animal: Constructing and Communicating New Elite Food Tastes at Upscale Butcher Shops," *Poetics* 47, 106–121.

Paxson, H. (2010) "Locating Value in Artisan Cheese: Reverse Engineering Terroir for New World Landscapes," *American Anthropologist* 112(3), 444–457.
Peterson, R.A. and Kern, R.M. (1996) "Changing Highbrow Taste: From Snob to Omnivore," *American Sociological Review* 61(5), 900–907.
Phillips, R. (2006) *Ontario Wine Country*, Vancouver: Whitecap.
Rössel, J., Schenk, P. and Eppler, D. (2018) "The Emergence of Authentic Products: The Transformation of Wine Journalism in Germany, 1947–2008," *Journal of Consumer Culture*, 18(3), 453–473.
Smith Maguire, J. (2018a) "Taste as Market Practice: The Example of 'Natural' Wine," in A. Ventakesh, S. Cross, C. Ruvalcaba and R. Belk (eds), *Consumer Culture Theory*, 19, Bingley: Emerald Publishing, 71–92.
Smith Maguire, J. (2018b) "The Taste for the Particular: A Logic of Discernment in an Age of Omnivorousness," *Journal of Consumer Culture* 18(1), 3–20.
Smith Maguire, J. and Matthews, J. (2012) "Are We All Cultural Intermediaries Now? An Introduction to Cultural Intermediaries in Context," *European Journal of Cultural Studies* 15(5), 551–562.
Sternsdorff Cisterna, N. (2014) "Unexpected Moments and the Wine Experience," *Food and Foodways* 22(1–2), 90–111.
Terrio, S.J. (2000) *Crafting the Culture and History of French Chocolate*, Berkeley: University of California Press.
Voronov, M., De Clercq, D. and Hinings, C.R. (2013) "Conformity and Distinctiveness in a Global Institutional Framework: The Legitimation of Ontario Fine Wine," *Journal of Management Studies* 50(4), 607–645.
Warde, A. (2014) "After Taste: Culture, Consumption and Theories of Practice," *Journal of Consumer Culture* 14(3), 279–303.
Warde, A., Wright, D. and Gayo-Cal, M. (2008) "The Omnivorous Orientation in the UK," *Poetics* 36, 148–165.

PART V

Power and contestation

32
COMPETING AND COMPLEMENTARY UTOPIAS
Towards an understanding of entangled wine ideals

Jacqueline Dutton and Peter J. Howland

Introduction

In the world of wine, there are many competing and complementary ideals that reflect the diverse aspirations, intentions and practices enacted by a large cast of actors – from grape growers and winemakers to promoters and consumers – who generate and evolve the industry. In this chapter, we explore a range of trajectories that co-exist in the intertwined and mutually constitutive fields of place, production and people – firstly, winemaking and terroir, as well as winemakers and wine consumers. There are many other potential pathways and characters who contribute to this intricate network, but the framing theories related to varied utopian ideals of wine and their entanglements encourage a focus on these four areas of influence. After introducing the key concepts and situating the selected trajectories in the frame, we will demonstrate the use value of this approach for analysing apparently disparate and irreconcilable motivations in the wine world.

In the beginning, 'utopia' was a word made up by Thomas More, who wanted a name for his imaginary island, a name which encapsulated both its unrealistic and its desirable qualities. *Ou*-topia means no place, and *eu*-topia means happy place, so More combined the common elements of the two Greek terms to call his island and his book *Utopia*. By the end of the eighteenth century, however, utopia as an ideological concept had flown off the pages and into the fray to inspire the overthrow of the French monarchy in the first truly utopian revolution of 1789 (Bianchi 2017). In the fifth edition of the *Dictionnaire de l'Académie française* (1798), utopia was defined first and foremost as '*Un plan de Gouvernement imaginaire, où tout est parfaitement réglé pour le bonheur commun, comme dans le Pays fabuleux d'Utopie décrit dans un livre de Thomas Morus qui porte ce titre*'. [An imaginary plan of Government in which everything is perfectly regulated for the happiness of all, like in the fabulous Land of Utopia described in a book by Thomas More which takes this title.] The citation ends with the term used in customary context: '*Chaque rêveur imagine son Utopie*' [Each dreamer imagines their own utopia.] (*Dictionnaire* 1798: 710).

This widely accepted usage emphasises the particular ethos, perspective or culture that influences an individual or collective vision of their ideal – place, society, way of being. Yet even though utopia might be 'whatever you want it to be', as soon as individual or collective ideals come into contact with one another, the dilemma of how to reconcile these competing utopian ideals arises and, with it, the challenge of how to bring them into some kind of harmonious or, at least, practically operational frameworks of co-existence.

In the nineteenth and twentieth centuries, a plethora of definitions for utopia as well as its less positive permutations (dystopia, anti-utopia and their critical counterparts) sprang up in academic scholarship. Lyman Tower Sargent's seminal article 'The Three Faces of Utopianism Revisited' provides a much-cited description of 'utopianism' as social dreaming, which echoes more open interpretations of utopia as 'striving towards a better way of being' (Levitas 1990) and 'expressing the principle of hope' (Bloch 1986 [1954]) that helped to rehabilitate utopia from its totalitarian, dystopian connotations in the twentieth century. Levitas also distinguishes between utopias that focus on form (such as literary novels or architectural spaces), content (including political, social, economic and psychological issues) and function.

Around the same time, French theorists of philosophy and literature Gilles Deleuze and Félix Guattari broke through the binaries and categories that placed singular and shared views against or alongside each other. They proposed the rhizome as a metaphor for dynamic thinking that privileges the processes of 'assemblage' and 'entanglement' over adjacent or opposing networks of entities and non-entities (Deleuze and Guattari 1987). Assemblages are 'an ensemble of objects, practices, experiences, and representations that make sense together' (Vannini and Taggart 2015: 70). Entanglements are concerned with flow and flux, processes or lines of becoming and conditions of possibility (Ingold 2008). These dynamic interactions between distinguishable but enmeshed ideas, values and practices are neither hierarchical nor definitive. In contrast to the 'affirmative, transcendent and authoritarian utopias' that Deleuze and Guattari designate 'ignoble', those that emanate from rhizomatic assemblages and entanglements have the possibility of becoming 'immanent, revolutionary, libertarian utopias' (Deleuze and Guattari 1996 [1991]).

Deleuze and Guattari's interpretation of utopia, therefore, prioritises entanglements; erasing boundaries; foregrounding intersectionality; and promoting creative, complex and non-linear relations between and within different perspectives. Their approach enables irreconcilable visions to be considered together, analysed and understood as part of a joined-up, rough but smooth fabric – like felt – without a 'right' or a 'wrong' side (Deleuze and Guattari 1987 [1980]). This makes it a useful frame for considering 'wicked' problems, such as one of the most radical and sensitive examples of such diametrically opposed utopian visions – the rise of Nazism and the Third Reich in Germany and the genocide of Jewish peoples (Mezger 2016).

Wine is one of the world's most unifying and divisive products. It is sacred and profane, revered and reviled, healthy and injurious, made for profit, for love, and sometimes for loss. The global wine industry involves myriads of convergent and divergent perspectives on this beverage: perspectives that, depending on one's role in the chain from production to consumption, may be influenced by region or national identity, cultural capital, economic power, political tensions or, quite simply, by variations in taste. By observing and mapping similar and different wine ideals that co-exist in wine cultures, we are attempting to demonstrate that these entanglements represent competing and complementary utopias that underpin various visions and projects that strive to produce and consume 'better' wines. Most revealing of diversity in utopian wine ideals – that is, where 'better' can be variably interpreted at individual, collective, scientific, cultural, economic, aesthetic or any number of other levels – are winemaking, wine terroir, winemakers, and wine drinking.[1] Examining the co-presence of wine ideals in these densely entangled areas of the industry chain offers opportunities to reconsider how 'better' may be interpreted and enacted by various actors. However, we are not aiming to evaluate, hierarchise or categorise what is good, bad or otherwise. Identifying the co-existence of variable entanglements in wine ideals is our primary objective, while suggesting a foundational understanding of such entanglements is our initial utopian goal.

To illustrate our proposal at both micro and macro scales, we can consider first the entanglements of a family wine business involving a brother and two sisters, who each dreams their own utopia with wine ideals that are enmeshed and yet distinct. We might observe that the sister who is the viticulturalist and winemaker dreams of more sustainable, organic grape growing and winemaking to combat climate change; the other sister, who manages the marketing and sales, wants to make less wine overall and to sell this exclusive product at higher prices; while the brother, who tends to the mixed farming on the property, wants to pull out the labour- and cost-intensive pinot noir vines and run sheep in their place. At this micro level, all three projects can co-exist and represent both competing and complementary utopias. Extrapolated to a collective level at regional or national industry scale, we bear witness to entanglements whose intersectionalities potentially draw in further projects and visions from community interests, environmental groups, legislative bodies and others. Following Deleuze and Guattari, we describe and distinguish ethnographically but do not seek to determine intrinsic or extrinsic value, good or bad, right or wrong, in this analysis.

Utopian winemaking

Since humankind's first foray into winemaking around 6,000 BCE – and in spite of the many technical, technological and other advances since – winemakers everywhere have wrestled with the same innate challenges and opportunities afforded by the cultivation of *Vitis vinifera* grapes. These elemental influences – ever existent[2] in the fundamental physicality, biology and genetics of grape growing and winemaking – lay down intersecting and constantly changing trajectories that all winemakers are compelled to engage if they want to produce wines that are potable, let alone palatable and storable. These include cyclical bursts of weather to climatic change; fluctuations in water, nutrient and yeast availability; and the constant genetic adaptations – seasonal, somatic and reproductive – of grapevines. Indeed grape or winegrowing is subject to these natural forces of vintage variation to such an extent that the 'perfect' wine is never realisable. Winegrowing is, therefore, in the first instance, utopian by nature. Moreover, many of our evolving cultural interventions – from cultivated propagation of vines to trellising, pruning, temperature-controlled fermentations and so on – are primarily enacted to ameliorate and/or constructively enhance this foundational reality to ensure desired outcomes. However, our periodic efforts and the uncertainty of vintage outcome combine with the constant (often progressive – or at least increasingly delineated) evolution of winemaking technologies, grape varieties and consumer tastes and expectations of quality and value, to ensure that contemporary winemaking is also by default utopian. In other words, making the 'perfect' wine is routinely dismissed as an unattainable, although constantly striving for 'quality wines' – and even more definitively, 'better' and/or the 'best' wines – is considered a worthy goal.

Since the rise of modern wine connoisseurship – largely initiated with the seventeenth-century invention of singular (vineyard and vintage-named), bottle-corked, cellarable wines and significantly advanced by a bevy of production codifications discursively disseminated firstly in the early nineteenth century 'golden age' of wine books and then in wine appellations from the 1855 Bordeaux classifications onwards – the pursuit of consistency (or, better still, improvements) in wine quality and varietal typicity has increasingly characterised commercial winemaking. Indeed, the 'spectacular' growth of New World wine production and markets over the past five decades – replete with varietal-labelled, affordable, good-quality wines – effectively cemented a shift away from the Old World production of bulk, unbranded, simple table wines designed for immediate local consumption (Anderson 2020; Howland 2013).

During this time, wine has also – despite wine consumption in the Old World significantly retrenching – transformed from one of the world's least to one of its most traded agricultural items. 'Simultaneously, and largely because of increased competition from the New World, there have been huge improvements in the quality and diversity of wines available to consumers' (Anderson 2020: 827). Wines everywhere are now produced for both local and export markets, which means contemporary commercial winemakers of every scale – large industrial to mid-size, boutique and artisanal – are increasingly compelled by a globalised chorus of wine critics, wine awards and discerning wine consumers to consistently churn out quality wines with desired taste profiles and no obvious faults. Moreover, this is expected across a broad spectrum of branded wine offerings – from inexpensive, non-premium bulk wines sold under faux estate or place-of-origin labels to commercial premium and expensive, super-plus premium, terroir-revered fine wines. Thus – from Paua Cove, a wholly fictious origin-of-place, bulk-produced New Zealand sauvignon blanc to the acclaimed Pavillon Blanc du Château Margaux – producing (or at least asserting via marketing and branding promotions) quality wines is a near-universal utopian goal.

Unsurprisingly therefore, the core competencies required to consistently produce good quality wines are also widely shared, firstly at a structural or ethos level, where the rationalisations of efficiency, calculability, predictability, standardisation and technological control are routinely applied to generate necessary quality-generation practices. Moreover, these practices are routinely codified and standardised via appellation, geographical indication and/or national food/drink safety and hygiene regulations. As a result, the assemblage of competing winemakers also likely shares in core competencies, which largely originated in the New World and are vital to the commercial production of quality wines (Reynaud and Simon 2006). These include seeking out new viti/vinicultural techniques, developing new markets (especially high end and export), fostering upmarket commodity positionings, enhancing brand reputations and the commercialisation of assets (developing merchandise, events etc.).

Yet at the same time, the equally universal and stark stratification of wine quality asserted by producers, critics and consumers results in this utopian goal being rendered as a veritable cacophony of competing (and potentially conflicting) industry-wide entanglements. So which is better – Paua Cove or Pavillon Blanc du Chateau Margaux? The answer largely depends on which *rêveur* you ask. For example, many consumers are excluded and wholly intimidated by the capital costs – economic, cultural and social – of purchasing and aesthetically appreciating a Pavillon Blanc, whereas Paua Cove more than meets their budgetary and taste ideals. While most winemakers will wholeheartedly concede a Pavillon Blanc is a superior quality sauvignon blanc, a shareholder in Paua Cove might bring other, more fiscally orientated ideals into consideration.

Indeed, other competencies and associated utopian strivings also typically differ according to scale. Thus, within large-scale industrial production of grapes and wine, one finds the mechanisation of grape picking and processing, chemical interventions (insecticides and pesticides), contractual and specialised labour, augmented fermentations and widespread economic cost-benefit analyses, all marshalled to realise other utopian goals of maximal yields, minimal costs and increasing shareholder profits, ideally without compromising a given wine's qualities (actual or promotional). Of course, these goals are also constantly shifting – yields can be increased and costs decreased, and profits are potentially unlimited, given that money is the only infinite commodity. As the top ten largest wine companies in the world account for 15% of all wine produced – E&J Gallo (USA) alone produces just shy of 3% of the world's wine (more than Australia and New Zealand combined) – these utopian fiscal dreamings, which are more popularly associated with the rampant productionism of all industrially and/or luxury produced commodities, are significant within the globalised wine world (Anderson et al. 2003).

In contrast, many small-scale artisan winemakers are more likely to pursue making good quality wines for the passion, the reputation and/or the convivial socialities they engender, rather than for profit (Charters *et al.* 2016; Morton and Podolny 2002). Consequently, they are likely to find some large-scale winemaking practices to be dystopian (e.g. mechanised harvesting and hyperbolic promotions) while also sharing in others (e.g. trellising methods and temperature controlled fermentation). Overall, they are more likely to foreground the 'art' of winemaking, with 'economics' a background consideration in their particular utopian pursuit of producing quality wine. Indeed many have little idea of the specific costs incurred in winemaking or how to 'price' a bottle of wine accordingly. We know one small-scale winemaker who suffered a financial loss for most of the 21 years they operated, supplementing their winemaking business with off-vineyard income.

Moreover, just as many knowingly deploy 'costly' production techniques (e.g. hand harvesting, leaf plucking, labour intensive organics etc.) in their pursuit of quality – practices that the accountants or 'grape-counters' of large-scale industrial producers would pre-emptively prohibit in their particular, yet arguably collusive, pursuit of quality wines. Again, which is better depends on who is answering.

Utopian terroir

Terroir has a decidedly utopian flavour, due to the twentieth-century distinction of winemaking linked to singular and noteworthy geographical conditions (Dutton and Howland 2020). Whether considered in its traditional place-based natural-cultural dimensions (OIV 2010) or as a scientific relationship between multispecies ranging from microbial yeasts to vines to plant and animal and human environmental biodiversity (Meinert 2018), terroir now has a positive charge at least and usually a highly idealised connotation.[3] The term 'terroir' is used as a marker of desirability and is very often associated with the word 'unique' in wine marketing to signify the incomparable, inimitable and extraordinary nature of the wine produced from the grapes grown in an identifiable place. However, it should be noted that the state of being unique is essentially a condition, not a quality, and this is arguably how terroir should also be interpreted – as a condition of winemaking rather than a quality marker. Any wine that is made from grapes with an acknowledged and specific source and traceable storyline has 'unique terroir'. So how and why does terroir take on its utopian overtones? Why is terroir wine recognised as good, or even ideal, in contemporary wine culture?

There are three main reasons for the current overwhelmingly positive evaluations of terroir, and each is related to a particular cultural perspective on wine terroir, but they are inherently entangled: the French connection, the Old World-New World dichotomy and the environmental issue. Firstly, the French origins of the term 'terroir' and the luxury status of French wine in many societies – whether justified or not – reference a place-based winemaking tradition that is particularly prevalent in Burgundy. As the exemplar of French terroir, Burgundian wines are prominently marketed and labelled according to their specific classification, provenance and/or appellation *d'origine contrôlée* – ranging from Grands Crus Romanée-Conti, Echezeaux and Corton-Charlemagne to the Villages of Nuits-Saint-Georges, Santenay and Meursault.[4] The use of '*climats*' to designate further specificity in Burgundy's terroir came to the fore during the UNESCO classification of parts of the Burgundian wine region as a cultural landscape in 2015, though there is debate as to whether *climats* are an ancient reference or a (re)invented tradition (Demossier 2018). There is no mention of the dominant grape varieties pinot noir and chardonnay on the labels because, as Thibault Liger-Belair stated at the 2019 Mornington Peninsula Pinot Celebration, he doesn't make 'pinot noir'; he makes Richebourg or Chambolle-Musigny or Corton Les Rognets. Yet as a global benchmark for pinot noir and chardonnay wines, Burgundy is the ideal archetype of French terroir – in conversation and in rivalry with talented producers and the 'unique terroirs' of California, Australia and New Zealand. The prevailing cultural perspective of aligning French wines with both terroir and prestige tends to elevate terroir to a marker of prestige through association with French wines like Burgundy.[5]

The second cultural perspective on wine terroir – Old World terroir versus New World industrialisation – extends the French example in a comparative schema. Although there is no longer such a defined dichotomy between traditional European or Middle Eastern wine-producing communities and regions around the world where winemaking began in the aftermath of European colonisation, there is a lingering perception that the former have closer ties with terroir in family-owned small-scale wineries while the latter are more commercially oriented operations, many owned by massive transnational companies – LVMH, Treasury Wine Estates, Gallo, Pernod Ricard etc. (Banks and Overton 2010).

However, the idealisation of terroir has now transcended geographical and geopolitical boundaries to find its place in boutique-style wineries in the Napa Valley and Martinborough. The family-owned provenance story that denotes trust and tradition in the Old World has been co-opted to foreground knowledge and recognition of terroir in the New World. Links to place through founding origin stories and intergenerational connections to the land have been well articulated by the Australian First Families of Wine (AFFW) (Gow et al. 2021). Such alliances have dissociated themselves from the deterritorialised transnational brands, creating a New World terroir narrative that is both derived from the Old World family-land-tradition-terroir model and authentically Australian. In turn, the boutique wineries bought up by the multinationals have sometimes managed to promote their positive terroir stories more widely through leveraging the networks and support that the transnational backing provides, such as LVMH's worldwide distribution of Cloudy Bay from New Zealand, Cape Mentelle from Australia and Terrazas de los Andes from Argentina.

The implantation of Old World terroir idealism into the New World via human hegemony and grapevine invasion does not just build on the French terroir paradigm; it also foreshadows the third cultural perspective on wine terroir: environmental awareness and terroir. Ecologically sustainable wine production is an ambition for most developed communities, displaying recognition of the interconnectedness of all things, including organic or biodynamic viticulture, land care, climate change, the impact of international transport, chemical interventions and human manipulation (Howland 2021).

Over the last 20 years, the rise in natural, organic and biodynamic wines has been phenomenal, with each producer emphasising that their practices are a portal for terroir to be better expressed in the wine. The goal to be achieved is making wine that directly translates the terroir with minimal human intervention, thus validating the terroir as the ideal place, the utopia, which can only be tasted in the wine it produces (Dutton and Howland 2020). The ideal of a 'pure' or 'unmediated' connection with the terroir resonates with the notion of environmental care and reciprocity – there can be no pleasure taken from the land except that which it is lovingly encouraged to yield (Ascione et al. 2020). Safe and sustainable wine therefore comes from a place that is known, storied, nourished and cherished – terroir.

These utopian entanglements which idealise terroir can be disentangled by predominantly pragmatic commercial considerations. However, it is interesting to note that the economic overlay serves to reinforce – extrinsically – the intrinsic value of utopian terroir in most examples. Comparisons and associations with benchmark French terroir add value to wines made in regions outside France. England's burgeoning sparkling wine region's terroir is traced along geological lines to link up to Champagne's chalky Kimmeridgian ridge; whilst Western Australia's Margaret River soils, climate and prize-winning wine styles are likened to Bordeaux's classic cabernet sauvignon and merlot blends. Such associations inevitably elevate the price of these wines, as does the simple French naming of a standard grenache rosé by Jacob's Creek, called Le Petit Rosé, thereby exploiting financially the idealisation of French terroir. The utopian entanglement disrupting binary divisions between Old and New World winemaking to recognise terroir everywhere is further enabled financially by the value-added proposition of single-vineyard, hand-picked terroir wines, as opposed to budget-priced, mass-produced, non-terroir wines. The Casella family (which is not one of the AFFW mentioned earlier) practices such diversification via their family-owned but non-terroir-oriented enterprise, which produces millions of hectolitres of Yellowtail wine and their investment in prestige terroir wines under the Peter Lehmann label to leverage higher market value. The idealisation of care for terroir as environmental awareness is also validated by commercial valuation as the price point for natural, organic and biodynamic wines is consistently higher than for non-accredited wines.

The utopian entanglements and disentanglements related to terroir, therefore, tend to be in harmony as ideal tropes are reinforced by pragmatic outcomes. There is, however, a fundamental challenge around access to terroir suited to making wines, which is now highly priced and tightly held wherever it is in the world, and the investment in sustainable viticulture and certification can also be prohibitively expensive. These exclusory conditions require further consideration to assess whether the competing and complementary utopias of terroir are inherently positive or not.

Utopian winemakers

Winemakers, like the terroir they cultivate, are inextricably linked to the image of the wine they produce. Their profiles are foregrounded on websites and in marketing material, projecting the personal story firmly onto the product. The positive representations of these people who make the wines are designed to inspire trust in consumers: visible winemakers take responsibility for and pride in their wines, whereas invisible winemakers must, by extrapolation, be suspect and shady, formulaic technicians and unengaged. According to contemporary cultures of wine consumption, 'fine' wines tend to place authorship and authenticity above price and quality (as clearly stated in the *World of Fine Wine* publication).

The winemaker's identity and the identification of the winemaker are generally, therefore, inherently good and are made even more auspicious through association with a series of utopian entanglements. In their idealised versions, winemakers incarnate the spiritual or philosophical guide, the artisanal 'gentleman' farmer and the creative genius. They provide leadership, offer fulfilment, negotiate nature and mediate tastes, all while responding to the desires and drivers of wine consumers.

As a guide, the winemaker is more than simply an instructor on the quality of the wine produced. Since ancient times, the best wines have often been made by spiritual guides – monks and priests – for ritual consumption and noble networking or, in more recent times, by biodynamic gurus and passionate advocates of natural winemaking. Winemakers are also prone to expressing their 'philosophy' of winemaking rather than outlining their methods or practices, rendering them philosophical guides as opposed to practitioners (or parishioners). The abstraction of physical or material acts of winemaking into spiritual and philosophical realms enhances the idealisation of the winemaker's role in illuminating consumers about the essential qualities of the wines produced. These figures can be owner-winemakers, like Nicolas Joly of Clos de la Coulée de Serrant in the Loire Valley or Aubert de Villaine of Domaine de la Romanée-Conti in Burgundy. There are also philosopher-guide consultants, especially from the Bordeaux region, in the wake of Emile Peynaud, like Michel Rolland, Jacques and Eric Boissenot, Stéphane Derenoncourt and Benoît Touquette. Very few women claim such cult status, though Vanya Cullen of Cullen Wines in Margaret River and Celia Welch of Scarecrow Wine in Napa could certainly be considered in this league (Galbreath 2015). The significant and continuing traction of the 'cult of the winemaker' (Horowitz 2012; Howland 2008) reinforces the ideal of a charismatic leader who can draw in followers – both producers and consumers.

The winemaker as artisanal or 'gentleman' farmer corresponds to an idealised connection with or return to the land, with connotations of financial security, potentially earned via professional practices – doctor, lawyer, accountant etc. – or another stable income crop or stock. In the bucolic winemaking areas near capital cities, such as Napa and Santa Rosa near San Francisco, the Yarra Valley near Melbourne and Martinborough near Wellington (NZ), there are many professionals with vineyards who have contributed to the prestige of the wine regions (See Berkowitz 2014; Carter 2014; Howland 2008). In the Yarra Valley, less than an hour's drive from Melbourne, it was a couple of doctors – John Middleton (Mount Mary) and Bailey Carrodus (Yarra Yering) – who relaunched winemaking during the 1960s, followed by James Halliday – Australia's preeminent wine writer – who established Coldstream Hills in 1985. In their wake came what Halliday called 'weekend winemakers' and others labelled 'Fitzroy farmers' – doctors and lawyers from the central city suburb of Fitzroy who set up about 40 new vineyards in the Yarra Valley between 1990 and 2000 thanks to the tax incentives for agricultural entrepreneurship (Carter 2014). The combination of alternative funding resources and professional networks of wealthy wine connoisseurs is a recipe if not for financial success, then for personal fulfilment (Sullivan 2012). The old adage that to make a million in the wine industry, you need to start with two million may well be true, but the idealised status of the artisanal winemaker or gentleman farmer remains relevant today.

The creative genius winemaker is often portrayed as eccentric, as personified by Chester Osborn of d'Arenberg in McLaren Vale, South Australia. His colourful dress and dialogue and outrageous architecturally designed tasting room – the Cube – dramatise the amazing range of wines produced with names that include the Athazagoraphobic Cat and the Laughing Magpie. While Osborn brings in a DJ to play dance music to his fermenting wines, Juan Ledesma of Terroir Sonoro in Chile's Itata region jams with other local jazz musicians and plays the bespoke recordings through speakers in the maturing barrels. Music is one form of viticultural and oenological eccentricity, but sheer poetic personality is another trait of the creative genius winemaker. Anselme Selosse is the capricious 'high priest' of grower champagnes, only allowing certain people to taste his rarefied Jacques Selosse champagnes at the domaine in Avize or at the aptly named hotel-restaurant Les Avisés (the wise ones or those in the know). Jean-Claude Mas of Arrogant Frog Wines fame is equally renowned for his originality and ground-breaking decisions to market cheap Languedoc wines with 'critter' labels for export (Dutton and Normand-Marconnet 2019). From another region in South Australia, Penfolds has just released the Creative Genius Cabernet Sauvignon 2017 to commemorate the scientific prowess of Ray Beckwith, chief wine chemist from 1935 to 1973, whose use of PH technology to stop wine spoiling revolutionised wine ageing and enabled the production of the iconic Grange by Max Schubert. He was a world away from Peter Cargasacchi of Santa Rita Hills, whose antics have been captured in a short film *The Ex-Con, Mad Scientist, Supernatural Winemaker* (2014). Whether visibly flamboyant, musically minded, scientifically gifted or discreetly disdainful, these creative geniuses create their own style of utopian wines and are revered by some, ridiculed by others.

Despite the utopian ideals that these three typologies of winemakers represent, there are clearly fundamental inequalities in the cultures that enable them. Firstly, most of these winemakers are white men from dominant and privileged backgrounds, highlighting the patrifocal, gendered, racially homogenous and commercially pressured environments in which they are working. The utopian entanglements are, therefore, inherently flawed and readily disentangled if considered from a woman's perspective or, indeed, from any variety of 'subaltern' positions.

Utopian wine consumption

In the contemporary wine world, a lot of moral stress is placed on the truth-based 'good' and discursive ethics of authenticity, particularly that embedded in production techniques, product provenance and terroir (Smith Maguire 2018). Yet, as with any profit-empowered industry, wine is awash with fraud, typically aimed at cheating fiscal agencies (e.g. smuggling, tax evasion) or squarely targeted at hustling wine buyers and consumers – including illicit adulterations (e.g. water dilution, flavouring addition), mislabelling and misinformation. The latter – 'consumption fraud' (Holmberg 2010: 108) – is very difficult to discern, especially without benchmarked chemical analysis. This is because distinguishing specific wines through tasting – blind or sighted – is extremely challenging. Indeed, in blind tastings, many expert tasters prefer less expensive wines, whereas blind wines denoted as expensive are consequently rated of higher quality. Thus 'it is unlikely that consumption fraud will be detected through complaints from consumers' (Holmberg 2010: 108), especially so if one personally enjoys a wine.

This brief foray into the dystopian raises (as if often does) some very interesting insights into the utopian vistas of wine consumers everywhere: namely, if one enjoys a wine – including undetected counterfeits, known replicas or appellation certified – then one can only ever be a 'victim' of one's own tastes. Moreover, in the modern wine industry, the tastes and enjoyment of individual consumers are considered sovereign, and the promotion of omnivoristic, niche, eclectic and, ultimately, reflexive consumption is accordingly widespread (Howland 2013). Indeed, research tends to support this proposition with consumer enjoyment or the pleasure inducement bought about by the twinned acts of (often ritualised) drinking and physically consuming wine topping a list of consumer motivations that includes taste experiences (aesthetic and diverse), social lubrication and hospitality, social context generation, conspicuous identity, status and lifestyle management, food enrichment, ritual enactments, intoxication (typically moderate) and relaxation or mood enhancement (Charters and Pettigrew 2008).

Noting that enjoyment or pleasure seeking is a foundational utopian goal is, however, akin to the fundamentalism of noting that wine potability and palatability are equally desired by wine drinkers. Moreover, this is only one ontological step beyond noting that all wine drinkers who are equipped with bio-normal sensory faculties – especially olfactory and gustatory – are minimally able to distinguish the tastes sweet, sour, bitter, salty and umami. This itself is one ontological step sideways from noting that all wine contains taste profiles consisting of acidity, alcohol, tannins, residual sugar and various 'fruit', 'spice', 'floral', 'wood', 'herb' and other flavours and aromas that 'are there for all to recognise' (Smith 2007: 49). The point here is that, like wine production, there are certain utopian trajectories and thresholds that are near universal, and thus shared, between most wines and most (bio-typical) wine consumers. Consequently, '*tastes* . . . are the properties a wine has, and *tasting[s]* . . . an experience which a subject has' (Smith 2007: 44, emphasis in original).

So, at one level, all wine tastes and wine tastings – and their accordant utopian goods – are underpinned by bio-physical universals. Beyond this, however, aesthetic tastes are significantly mediated by various social, cultural and historical influences. Thus, one's ethnic, national, educational, occupational, residential, leisured, consumerist and social (class and status) experiences – let alone one's age and gender habitus – all affect one's wines tastes (Bourdieu 2010 [1984]). Nevertheless, in the commercial world of wine, the conclusive utopia goal still remains happy, pleasure-satiated individual consumers and their doppelgängers, happy, commercially viable wine sellers. However, what is happiness, satiation and joy for one wine consumer will potentially vary for another who hails from a different background. It is not surprising, therefore, that the globalised wine industry also pitches its promotions and products to defined clusters of market-segmented wine drinkers.

There are, of course, many ways to cluster wine consumers which, together, reveal a veritable smorgasbord of adjacent, complementary and competing utopian trajectories. Clustering can be done via the demographics of age, generation, gender, income, education and nationality; differences in wine knowledge, experience, motivations and/or aspirations; lifestyle, consumerist, touristic and other identity/status markers; purchase and consumption settings; quality and consumption frequency; and variations in emotional responses (Calvo-Porral *et al.* 2020). Space precludes a detailed interrogation of the research into wine segmentation, other than noting that findings significantly gesture towards the variability of utopian goods – thus, those most 'involved' in wine (e.g. connoisseurs), most affluent and/or most educated are most likely to consume super-premium wines – and the converse; in the New World, older people are more likely drink premium wines and above (especially red wines) – whereas some of their Old World counterparts likely drink local, often unbranded wines while millennials (born after 1980) are less likely to be actively 'involved' in wine but are just as likely to buy wine, albeit cheaper, 'good value' varieties, to desire convenient, transportable packaging, and 'are more likely to be attracted to wine that is seen as relaxing, sensual, sophisticated, and cool' (McGarry Wolf *et al.* 2018: 186) than baby boomers or generation Xers (in California, at least). Furthermore, a selective list of differently categorised clusters also gives us further insight into the range of utopian wine registers – connoisseurs, enthusiasts, aspirational, basic wine drinkers, ritual-oriented conspicuous enthusiasts, purposeful inconspicuous premium drinkers, enjoyment oriented, price conscious, image orientated, indifferent and the emotionally unattached. So whereas a connoisseur maybe looking for 'classical typicity' and high quality in a wine, a basic wine drinker might be more driven by 'basic' palatability and value for money. Both, however, ideally experience happiness and satisfaction at the bottom of a wine glass.

Yet before we sociologically obliterate the individual wine drinker, we should not overlook that there are thousands upon thousands of wines available to be drunk; unsurprisingly, then, variance in wine knowledge, palate experience and ability to express taste is vast; moreover, wine consumption engages an incredibly complex bio-neural-sensory assemblage of sights, sounds, smells, tastes, ingestion, language, emotion, memories, digestion and intoxication that 'engage[s] more of the brain than any other human behaviour' (Shepherd 2015: 1). This nexus of intersecting factors opens so much space – from the incrementally nuanced to the copiously distinctive – for varied utopian goods, experiences and aspirations and, likewise, in the variability of individual wine consumers. Therefore, in the utopias of contemporary winemaking, the subjective wine drinker remains firmly ascendant.

Conclusion

The contemporary wine world is inundated with competing, complementary, adjacent and sometimes irreconcilable utopias across all its fields of endeavour – including winemaking, terroir, makers and consumption discussed here. Given the immense diversity and constant evolution of grapes – let alone the historical evolution of different grape-growing, winemaking techniques; terroir specificities; winemaker personae; and consumer desires – this is hardly surprising. Indeed, the competitive, stratification logics of a market-based and increasingly globalised wine world only serve to amplify the variabilities of scale of production and product outcomes – and thereby expand the range and variation of utopias.

In this chapter, we have outlined some of the side-by-side, rhizomatic assemblages, entanglements and trajectories that characterise utopian strivings in the contemporary wine world. Some are universal, others particular, some complimentary, others contradictory and so on. All are, in some way, collusive. Firstly, they express and create space for shared and diverse utopian discourses, processes and goals. And secondly, in doing this, they consequently foster an education of hope and desire that manifests in accordant calls for a better way of living and being.

Although it is important to move beyond the foundational outlining of any assemblage variables or influences, including utopian wine assemblages, it is extremely hazardous to attempt to apportion value. In other words, we understand that not all utopias are equal, but it is practically possible to establish which utopias are mutually constructive, which are incommensurate, contradictory or counter-productive; those that are primarily rhetorical or perhaps even false; and those that pursue their utopian goals as 'best practice'. For example, even if all producers and consumers genuinely strive for better wines in taste, typicity and quality, then clearly some will adjudged superior to others. Yet if other criteria are considered equally or even more desirable – such as cost minimisation, profit realisation and associated yield management – then other utopias come to the fore, along with 'good enough' or 'fit for purpose' wines. Finally, if ethical and moral considerations such as accessibility, gender, ethnic and cultural diversity and environmental sustainability are included in a weighted assessment of competing and complementary wine utopias, then the most revered and costly wines cannot be considered utopian, nor can many other wines of the world (Dutton 2020). For this reason precisely, we maintain the significance of firstly understanding entangled wine ideals, rather than assessing them as the conclusion of this chapter. And seek to add that, in the end, *chaque buveur imagine son vin idéal*: each drinker imagines their ideal wine.

Notes

1 There are other areas and actors in the wine industry which potentially express wine ideals and strive towards better or best wines – sales, marketing, distributing, teaching, writing – but all these areas and actors have more nuanced levels of diversity. For example, wine sales will inevitably be striving for better profits, wine teaching for better knowledge etc., whereas striving for better wine terroir is inherently complex due to the

range of factors influencing terroir, and better wine drinking can be approached from several different points of agency.
2 Notwithstanding the recent invention of chemically enabled 'replica wines' (see https://replicawine.com).
3 Terroir has not always been a positive term and was especially pejorative during the nineteenth and early twentieth centuries, denoting a rustic, earthy, 'peasant'-style wine with a 'taste of terroir' (Dutton and Howland 2020).
4 However, industry and expert discourses often privilege the *négociant* or the vigneron as the signifier of quality and confidence.
5 It should be noted that not all French wines are terroir wines; some of the most famous wines, such as champagne, and the popular blended wines like Côtes du Rhône are AOC wines but not necessarily terroir wines. It is also interesting to note that as references to terroir increase in English-language wine publications and marketing, the term 'terroir' is less and less frequently used in French-language wine publications and marketing (Matthews 2015).

References

Anderson, K. (2020) "Wine's Gradual Globalization," in H.L. Meiselman (ed), *Handbook of Eating and Drinking*, Switzerland: Springer Nature, 825–841.
Anderson, K., Norman, D. and Wittwer, G. (2003) "Globalisation of the World's Wine Markets," *World Economy* 26(5), 659–687.
Ascione, E., Belsky, J., Nelsen, M. and Barbato, M. (2020) "Cultivating Activism Through *Terroir*: An Anthropology of Sustainable Winemakers in Tuscany, Italy," *Food, Culture & Society* 23(3), 277–295.
Banks, G. and Overton, J. (2010) "Old World, New World, Third World: Reconceptualising the Worlds of Wine," *Journal of Wine Research* 21(1), 57–75.
Berkowitz, N. (2014) *The Winemaker's Hand*, New York: Columbia University Press.
Bianchi, S. (2017) "Révolution française et Utopie," *Annales historiques de la Révolution française* 388(2), 3–27.
Bloch, E. (1986 [1954]) *The Principle of Hope*, translated by Neville Plaice, Stephen Plaice, and Paul Knight, Cambridge, MA: MIT Press.
Bourdieu, P. (2010 [1984]) *Distinction: A Social Critique of the Judgement of Taste*, London: Routledge and Kegan Paul.
Calvo-Porral, C., Lévy-Mangin, J.P. and Ruiz-Vega, A. (2020) "An Emotion-Based Typology of Wine Consumers," *Food Quality and Preference* 79, 1–11.
Carter, F. (2014). "Yarra Valley: Talk About the Complete Package," *Australian and New Zealand Grapegrower and Winemaker* 609, 40–42.
Charters, S. and Pettigrew, S. (2008) "Why Do People Drink Wine? A Consumer-Focused Exploration," *Journal of Food Products Marketing* 14(3), 13–32.
Charters, S., Walker, B. and Brown, A. (2016) "Passion Over Pragmatism: The Motivation of Australian Winery Owners," *International Journal of Entrepreneurship and Small Business* 29(4), 512–527.
Deleuze, G. and Guattari, F. (1987 [1980]) *A Thousand Plateaus: Capitalism and Schizophrenia*, translated by Brian Massumi, Minneapolis, London: University of Minnesota Press.
Deleuze, G. and Guattari, F. (1996 [1991]) *What Is Philosophy?*, translated by Hugh Tomlinson and Graham Burchell III, New York: Columbia University Press.
Demossier, M. (2018) *Burgundy, a Global Anthropology of Place and Taste*, New York: Berghahn.
Dictionnaire de l'Académie française, 5th edition, Paris: eBooksFrance, 1798.
Dutton, J. (2020) "The Four Pillars of Utopian Wine: Terroir, Viticulture, Degustation and Cellars," in J. Dutton and P.J. Howland (eds), *Wine, Terroir and Utopia: Making New Worlds*, London: Routledge, 24–41.
Dutton, J. and Howland, P.J. (2020) *Wine, Terroir and Utopia: Making New Worlds*, London: Routledge.
Dutton, J. and Normand-Marconnet, N. (2019) "Visual Codes on French Wine Labels for Cross-Cultural Marketing in China and Australia," Proceedings of the 11th Conference of the Association of Wine Business Research, http://academyofwinebusiness.com/2018-2/.
Galbreath, J. (2015) "A Study of Women in Top Business Roles: The Case of the Wine Industry," *International Journal of Wine Business Research* 27(2), 143–158.
Garcia, E. and Termsomket, T. (2014) *The Ex-Con, Mad Scientist, Supernatural Winemaker*, https://vimeo.com/105592626.
Gow, J., Dutton, J. and Grant, B. (2021) "A Recent Development in Wine Classification Systems: Collective Family Ownership," Proceedings of the 12th Conference of the Association of Wine Business Research.
Holmberg, L. (2010) "Wine Fraud," *International Journal of Wine Research* 2, 105–113.
Horowitz, D.M. (2012) "'Cult' Wine?" *Journal of Food Products Marketing* 18(1), 50–64.

Howland, P.J. (2008) "Martinborough's Wine Tourists and the Metro-Rural Idyll," *Journal of New Zealand Studies* 6(7), 77–100.

Howland, P.J. (2013) "Distinction by Proxy: The Democratization of Fine Wine," *Journal of Sociology* 49(2–3), 325–340.

Howland, P.J. (2021) "New World Wine and the Global Evolution of Vernacular, Metro-Rural and Indigenous Idylls," this volume, chapter 28.

Ingold, T. (2008) "When ANT Meets SPIDER; Social Theory for Arthropods," in C. Knappett and L. Malafouris (eds), *Material Agency: Towards a Non-Anthropocentric Approach*, New York: Springer, 209–215.

Levitas, R. (1990) "Educated Hope: Ernst Bloch on Abstract and Concrete Utopia," *Utopian Studies* 1(2), 13–26.

Matthews, M.A. (2015) *Terroir and Other Myths of Winegrowing*, Berkeley: University of California Press.

McGarry Wolf, M., Higgins, L.M., Wolf, M.J. and Qenani, E. (2018) "Do Generations Matter for Wine Segmentation?" *Journal of Wine Research* 29(3), 177–189.

Meinert, L.D. (2018) "The Science of Terroir," *Elements* 14, 153–158.

Mezger, C. (2016) "Entangled Utopias: The Nazi Mobilization of Ethnic German Youths in the Batschka, 1930s–1944," *The Journal of the History of Childhood and Youth* 9(1), 87–117.

OIV – International Organisation of Wine. (2010) "Resolution OIV-VITI 333–2010," www.oiv.int/public/medias/379/viti-2010-1-en.pdf.

Reynaud, E. and Simon, E. (2006) "The Secrets of a Good Winery: Core Competences," *British Food Journal* 108(4), 243–255.

Scott Morton, F.M. and Podolny, J.M. (2002) "Love or Money? The Effects of Owner Motivation in the California Wine Industry," *The Journal of Industrial Economics* 50(4), 431–456.

Shepherd, G. (2015) "Neuroenology: How the Brain Creates the Taste of Wine," *Flavour*, 4(1). DOI:10.1186/s13411-014-0030-9.

Smith, B.C. (2007) "The Objectivity of Tastes and Tasting," in J. Robinson (ed), *Questions of Taste: The Philosophy of Wine*, New York: Oxford University Press, 41–78.

Smith Maguire, J. (2018) "Craft, Labour and the Taste for Authenticity: Reflections from the Field of Wine," in E. Bell, G. Mangia, S. Taylor and M.L. Toraldo (eds), *The Organization of Craft Work: Identities, Meanings and Materialities*, London: Routledge, 60–78.

Sullivan, P. (2012) "Winemaking Lures the Wealthy, But not with Profits," *New York Times*, 25 May, www.nytimes.com/2012/05/26/your-money/winemaking-lures-the-wealthy-but-not-with-profits.html.

Vannini, P. and Taggart, J. (2015) *Off Grid. Re-assembling Domestic Life*, New York: Routledge.

33
THREATS OF PLEASURE AND CHAOS
Wine and gendered social order

Anna-Mari Almila and David Inglis

Introduction

All societies define femininity and masculinity in relation to each other. Examining the one tells us about the nature of the other, as well as the wider gender order. In this chapter, we focus on women's relations with wine, an approach which also informs us about men's relations with both women and wine.

Throughout history, women's relations to all aspects of wine have frequently been significantly different from the typical relations that men have with the same drink. The phrase 'wine, women and song' expresses the widespread idea that females are objects of male power and enjoyment, rather than being active subjects in their own right. Female consumption of wine has, throughout the centuries, often been associated with chaos, and female pleasure in wine has been viewed as a threat to patriarchal social relations, institutions, and cultural formations.

Every socio-historical circumstance is unique, but a mapping of women's engagements with wine and (usually male-dominated) narratives about them reveals various recurring patterns. Women's wine drinking has been subject to markedly more socio-cultural regulation than has men's; it has been surrounded by more and stricter taboos; it has been particularly framed in terms of essentialising gendered stereotypes; the symbolic and physical spaces in which it happens have been more circumscribed; women's wine-relevant agency has been more restricted and more negatively framed; and there have been more dramatic moral panics about female wine drinking. In almost all wine-drinking societies, the phenomenon of women drinking wine was, and still in some ways is, a threatening prospect. Although the evidence about such matters is patchy and geographically biased, we can still set out a broad-brush picture of major tendencies and characteristics concerning women, men, wine and gendered social orders.

Wine and patriarchy

One can plausibly argue that since the beginnings of viticulture and viniculture some 8,000 years ago (McGovern 2003), all societies that have had the making and/or consumption of wine have been patriarchal in one way or another. Patriarchies can be defined as social orders in which, overall, men's interests are prioritised over women's, social relations and institutions involve the subjugation of women in various inter-related ways, and cultural imaginaries present the female as inferior in multiple manners. Patriarchal social orders are rooted in powerful cultural orientations concerning appropriate and inappropriate male and female behaviours, these assumptions animating multiple social spheres which often reinforce each other. Patriarchal notions and practices concerning (supposedly inferior) female biology, psychology, sexuality, fertility and motherhood, medical and psychological vulnerabilities, domesticity, and (non-) participation in public spheres are all inter-related (Walby 1991).

Patriarchal assumptions found across multiple times and places involve claims about women's allegedly essential nature, which is seen to drive their characteristic relationships with wine. Ideas about female differences from men in wine matters are predicated on assuming that male wine practices are the norm. Women's wine relations are commonly presented as a chaos-generating threat to patriarchal order. This is because of wine's alleged negative influences on women, such as the drunken loosening of conventional standards of sexual conduct, heightened by women's putatively lower tolerance of alcohol (Dietler 2006). Wine has frequently been understood as a threat to orderly domestic space, while the presence of wine-drinking women in certain public spaces like taverns has connoted their apparent easy sexual availability (Dragadze 1994; Ho 2015; Ludington 2013; Purcell 1994).

Patriarchal assumptions have informed understandings of women's typical wine preferences – for supposedly lighter and/or sweeter styles – and their wine-tasting abilities and techniques, the latter usually defined as fundamentally different from men's capacities, each gendered disposition said to be rooted in unchanging biology (Almila 2019). Such ideas about women's and men's essential differences continue to inform modern marketing campaigns, which sell specific types of wine to women on the basis that the female market is very dissimilar to its male counterpart (Atkin *et al.* 2007; Barber *et al.* 2006; Johnson and Bastian 2007; Nicolson 1990; Ritchie 2009).

Wine and gender across history

In terms of mythology and religious beliefs and practices, it has often been thought that alcohol in general, and wine in particular, was a gift from the gods (Inglis 2022). Across Eurasia, a notable aspect of alcohol understood as a divine gift has been that mostly 'male gods are credited with having introduced the powerful and enjoyable elixir' (Heath 2003: 148). The powerful male deity Osiris was said to have introduced winemaking to ancient Egypt. The Greek god Dionysos – Bacchus to the Romans – was also male, either depicted as a fulsome boy-child, handsome young man or plump and mature male figure of revelry and debauch (Dalby 2003).

Yet the wild and blood-thirsty Egyptian goddess Hathor, the Mistress of Drunkenness, was also strongly associated with wine, and she could be appeased by temple wine offerings (Poo 1995). Dionysos was regularly presented as sexually ambiguous in nature, his youthful form portrayed as having long hair and dressed in flowing clothes like a woman.

> *He spent his time in dances and with troops of girls,* says [ancient historian] Diodorus of Sicily with a[n] . . . undertone of surprise. Such behaviour was quite abnormal in classical Greece. A young man ought to spend his time with other young men and with younger boys; he certainly ought not to laze around indoors with girls.
>
> *(Dalby 2003: 51)*

As Phillips (2018: 70) indicates, Dionysos 'represented the danger that wine implicitly posed. . . . [He] transgressed rules about drinking, rules about sex, and . . . rules about gender'. Despite his effeminate aspects, Dionysos was presented as seducer of wives and daughters, the figure of the god thereby connecting wine with sexual licentiousness, engaged in by both males and females (Dalby 2003).

Given his feminine associations, Dionysos was pre-eminently a god of both wine and women. The two categories were deeply intertwined in Greco-Roman thinking (Kerenyi 1976), albeit in complex ways (Isler-Kerényi 2014). On the one hand, wives and daughters were strictly excluded from the Greek institution of the *symposion*, the wine-drinking party of elites. The host and guests were men, but the cupbearers, entertainers and prostitutes who were often present were both female and male. When the invited participants raised their wine cups to toast Dionysos's gift of wine to humanity, it was part of a highly patriarchal social ritual (Lissarrague 2016). Conversely, at the annual Anthesteria festival in Athens, which celebrated the new wine vintage, the proceedings were dominated by women because of their special relationship with Dionysos (Nässtrӧm 2003).

The festival-going Athenian women were the socially acceptable female celebrants of Dionysos. Far more distrusted by male society were the female members of the god's cult, the Bacchae (also called Maenads). They are represented by male artists and authors as engaging in female-only wild all-night revelries in celebration of their deity. Although the cult had some male members, it was

> predominantly women that enacted the most striking expressions of the orgiastic side of Dionysian religion. . . . For these women, the Dionysian rites . . . may well have been experienced as a release which contrasted with their customarily restricted way of life . . . a licensed and controllable outlet for frustration [both social and sexual].
>
> (Nässtrӧm 2003: 141)

Although the Bacchae have been widely presented as being drunk on wine at their festivities, there is little evidence to suggest this was the case, strenuous dancing being the more likely method of achieving the state of being possessed by the god (Nencini and Grant 2010).

Nonetheless, the cultural association between wine, women, drunkenness and rumoured sexual abandon remained powerful over time and space. At around the same time as the Bacchae existed in Greece, religious authors in Judea were bemoaning a similar perceived association of wine drinking and female debauchery (Wilson 2012). When the Dionysian cult reached Rome in the second century BCE, the Senate banned its celebrations: it was thought that, scandalously, 'Roman matrons performed obscene rites with their hair undone' (Nässtrӧm 2003: 141). The Bacchae were deemed by upper-class male opinion as particularly egregious, but female wine drinking in general was also condemned. Elite male Romans of the late Republican and early Imperial periods prohibited their womenfolk drinking wine, believing that injunction to be part of an 'ancient code of morality handed down by their venerable ancestors through the mists of antiquity' (Russell 2003: 80). However, archaeologists have found that in earlier centuries, women in Etruscan and Latin cities perhaps took equal part in the wine-centred aristocratic feasting culture of the time. By the time of Christ, with increasingly harsh denunciations of female wine drinking becoming common, the prohibition of female wine drinking was probably 'more than just a petty attempt at social control of women by men' and was 'instead a safeguard to the purity of the Roman state itself' (Russell 2003: 79).

Christianity was born within the Roman empire and subsequently spread throughout its arteries. It was also strongly influenced by the Greek-speaking Hellenistic culture that was pervasive throughout the ancient near East, an important part of which was wine drinking and beliefs about the god of wine. It is, therefore, not surprising that in the early centuries of the new religion, Dionysos and Jesus had – and were seen by contemporaries to possess – some marked similarities. Both figures 'were in some sense bestowers of wine, and consequently wine was an important element in their ritual worship' (Friesen 2014: 234). Jesus was understood as being either synonymous with Dionysos or as a new and rival wine god. In Jesus's first miracle, at the wedding feast in Cana, the Messiah turns water into wine, a feat already associated with Dionysos. Another feature of Jesus's Dionysiac nature was that both cults were particularly associated with female followers. Early Christians had to work hard to persuade friends and foes alike that their cult was free of Dionysiac libidinous female acolytes (Friesen 2014). The Christian communion ritual presented Jesus's body as being present in the wine that worshippers partook of. Today, feminist theologians argue that Jesus's body ceases to be simply 'male' through the ritual, opening up the possibility of a less patriarchal creed than was the case in ancient times (Johnson 2009).

Montanari (2015: 137) probably goes too far in claiming that 'the consumption of wine in the Middle Ages had no gender boundaries'. Nonetheless, as winemaking was preserved and augmented by Christian communities throughout Europe after the so-called 'fall' of the Roman empire, religious establishments run by both men and women engaged in viticulture, viniculture and wine consumption.

During and after the Middle Ages, women in Europe had numerous means of accessing wine: they could be left wine rations in a will (typically their husband's); they could be paid in wine for their labour (such as when working in a vineyard); and they could be given charitable wine gifts. Yet excessive consumption of wine was frowned upon by the Church and laymen alike. Still, even heavy drinking was acceptable if the drinker did not get intoxicated, as was said to be the case with Italian men and women, while French and English women apparently needed to be more careful with their drinking lest they lose their reputations (Martin 2001).

In a story (II.7) in Boccaccio's *Decameron*, the Muslim princess Alatiel is first shipwrecked and then seduced by the nobleman Pericone of Visalgo with the aid of wine. The tale of a woman's loss of a sense of shame due to wine consumption is one that has been repeated and would be repeated time and again across the centuries. In this narrative, it gains particular religio-political significance as the fallen Muslim princess passes from one lover to another across the Mediterranean (Kinoshita and Jacobs 2007).

Wine in medieval and early modern Europe had multiple, intertwined metaphorical aspects, particularly concerning sex, sexuality and fertility. While female wine drinking continued to be associated with licentiousness, intercourse with a husband incapable of sexually satisfying a wife was describable as being like bad wine (Martin 2001). An amorous man could positively liken the bodily liquids of his *inamorata* to wine. Wine was delicious but dangerous, not only for women but for men too, especially when combined with women who might exploit the drunken man financially and otherwise. A man who gave too much power to wine – and thereby to women – risked emasculation. At this time, wine was an unstable product, often travelling and aging badly. Its unpredictability linked it to the perceived inconstancy of women. Gentlemen would praise good wine's 'freshness' and demand both wine and women that were youthful and 'in their prime' (Dolan 2018). While wine's social effects were sometimes defined negatively, its properties were understood positively in medical contexts, as it was believed that wine enhanced female fertility, cured male impotence and worked as a useful treatment during pregnancy and childbirth (Martin 2001). Well into the nineteenth century, it was widely thought that wine could be used to reduce female fatigue and raise women's spirits (Remus 2014).

In winemaking regions, there were (and sometimes still are today) longstanding gendered spatial limitations on female participation. For example, wine cellars have often been out of bounds for women until relatively recently, while menstruating women were considered dangerous for the vines (Bianquis-Gasser 1992). Yet women could become noted wine producers in their own right, most famously the champagne widows, including Barbe-Nicole Clicquot Ponsardin, today renowned worldwide as Veuve Clicquot (Matasar 2006).

The United Kingdom, with a large and longstanding wine trade, is an especially interesting case as regards gendered consumption patterns. Many gendered rules developed there over the centuries. In the fifteenth century, upper-class women were able to enter taverns and drink wine with their menfolk (Colquhoun 2007). But by the eighteenth century, their drinking was strictly limited to home, to small amounts, and only when in their husbands' company (Ludington 2013). Wine buying was an exclusively male domain at that time (Davidoff and Hall 2002). Some domestic drinking practices were strictly homosocial. Port was very much considered a man's drink, and women of the higher bourgeoisie and aristocracy were expected to leave the men alone to drink it after dinner. During the second half of the nineteenth century, women were able to buy port by themselves, but their preferred drinks were more likely to be sherry and champagne, which they by this time they were allowed to consume in small amounts in non-domestic spaces, such as theatres (Ludington 2013). Gendered distinctions between types of wine were not a British peculiarity. For example, some areas in Greece traditionally associated retsina with men and sweet wine with women (Gefou-Madianou 1992).

Wine and gender in the twentieth and twenty-first centuries

By the end of the nineteenth century, new possibilities of female wine drinking arose, at least for relatively privileged women in large urban areas. The United States was a pioneering country in this regard. The social type of the 'new woman' and 'modern girl' – both as real persons and marketing ideals – took root in the 1890s and had become a global phenomenon by the 1920s (Barlow et al. 2005). In big cities like Chicago, new commercialised spaces in places like department stores opened which were aimed at providing safe, comfortable, appealing, and socially legitimate environments for new-style female consumers, who were encouraged to drink alcoholic drinks including wine, either alone or in groups and without any sense of shame (Remus 2014). Novel kinds of spaces for serving alcohol were created, such as tables in cabarets where couples could sit and sip more refined drinks, as opposed to the high tables where male clients stood while drinking spirits and beer (McClellan 2017). Entrepreneurial capitalism also gave women novel drinks offerings. Women were served champagne and other wines, as well as cocktails considered to be suitable for female tastes (Remus 2014).

But the very fact that burgeoning consumerism provided such goods and spaces for women made some commentators suspicious. Public, journalistic, and social-scientific discourses alike 'raised the possibility that the Modern Girl was just a product of clever advertising campaigns in the new commodity culture', thus effectively annulling female agency in the process (Barlow et al. 2005: 245). Just as new freedoms in drinking opened up, patriarchal denunciations of such practices intensified and contributed to Prohibition legislation in the US between 1920 and 1933. Women drinking in public places were sources of particularly juicy moral panics (McClellan 2017). 'Lady tipplers' committed the highly questionable act of consuming alcohol in public locales like restaurants. But as they were seen to be from 'good' and wealthy backgrounds, this caused even more moralising upset. They were seen as seeking alcoholic pleasures for their own benefit. As a consequence, a woman of this sort was often accused of being 'unwomanly, selfish, and reckless with her purse and her body'. Such behaviour was considered to have severe consequences, ranging 'from the decay of home life to the spread of drunken hedonism' (Remus 2014: 753).

From the 1930s onwards, spaces previously considered as male homosocial locales slowly opened up for women. In the United Kingdom, before, during, and after WWII, while 'respectable' women normally did not go to pubs – lest they be thought to be prostitutes – they could still enter country pubs with family members at weekends (Langhamer 2003). Not all rooms of pubs were only for the 'working-class, middle-aged, married [male] breadwinner', as some areas were more communal and meant for mixed-gender activities such as sing-songs (Moss 2015: 140). In such locations, women might drink sherry or port mixed with soft drinks.

In Europe, North America, and some other world regions, in the post-WWII period, it was not enough for women just to have the money and time to go to bars and pubs. They often lacked 'the justificatory sense of deserved personal leisure entitlement exhibited by male drinkers' (Langhamer 2003: 426). Even if women were legally allowed to enter such places, it remained questionable whether such locations would actually have been considered by many women as desirable. However, from the 1980s onwards, a new wave of female-friendly urban drinking spaces developed. Whether designated as 'wine bars' or not, such locations were strongly associated with wine consumption, which now figured as acceptable alcohol consumption for females. A striking example of broader processes comes from Japan, where bars for an affluent urban female clientele have proliferated since the 1990s. In her ethnography of white-collar female workers, Ho (2015: 26) describes a night in a club where a group of three women were entertained for several hours by 'young, able-bodied, fashionably attired' male club hosts. They ran up a bill of over €12,000, mostly by buying champagne, but they considered the price of this experience well worth it.

Throughout the twentieth century, a gradual normalisation of female drinking happened, along with marketing drinks and venues explicitly for women. Yet a distinction between male and female drinking very much survives today. Women are generally expected to drink different beverages than men. While tastes change over time, the fundamental gender distinction in tastes remains (Dragadze 1994; McDonald 1994). Today, across the world, women buy and drink more wine than men. Yet they tend to buy differently from men: making more everyday purchases, handing over special occasion buying to men, and tending to make 'safer' choices (Ritchie 2009). Women may also drink wine at home without feeling oppressed by the old tippling housewife stereotype, this liberation being normalised through popular culture, such as TV programmes, portraying widespread female wine consumption (Kennedy 2017). The social media circulation of memes, jokes and images linked to ideas such as 'wine o'clock' involves women normalising their wine drinking to each other (Almila 2022).

Contemporary female wine drinking intersects with medicine, medicalisation and motherhood in complex ways. State medical authorities typically impose lower alcohol limits on women, problematising wine consumption for women more than men (Almila 2019). The discovery in the 1970s and 1980s of foetal alcohol syndrome demonised alcohol drinking during pregnancy, provoking a series of moral panics (Armstrong and Abel 2000). Women today may even consider their pregnant body as 'naturally' abhorring alcohol (Killingsworth 2006), thus further demonising women who want to, or feel they must, drink during pregnancy. The medicalisation of alcohol use in pregnancy follows the medicalisation of alcoholism, a category long reserved primarily for men (McClellan 2017).

While female wine drinking has been widely normalised in recent decades, this clashes with contemporary notions of responsible motherhood because wine is alcoholic. Yet wine is the preferred drink of many women who are mothers. The 'good motherhood' versus wine drinking contradiction means they have to engage in sometimes tortuous justification strategies. 'I'm drinking wine because I mommed so hard today', says just one of the vast number of memes on the topic to be found online. Post-pregnancy wine drinking often remains a guilty pleasure, spoken of with a conspiratorial tone among mothers. But wine is widely understood as being more motherhood compatible than most other alcoholic drinks. Champagne seems like a particularly justifiable reward for hard domestic and child-rearing work. Wine drinking for a mother of young children can indeed be a form of defiance of social expectations, but it must not become immoderate, lest the women lose her reputation as competent mother and creator of domestic order (Killingsworth 2006).

Moving now from wine consumption to the professional wine world, after the second World War, new kinds of opportunities appeared for women. An early instance here is wine writing. Female wine critics were mentored by benevolent men but faced casual misogyny and gender discrimination, such as being excluded from men-only spaces and events typical of the 'traditional' wine trade. Women could be accused by men both of wearing so much perfume that professional tasting was impossible, and of leaving lipstick smears on tasting glasses, Typically male scents of hair lotion, aftershave and tobacco were conveniently ignored by these male accusers (Vandyke Price 1990: 120). Claims about women using too much perfume can still be deployed today by male customers impugning females' professional capacities (James 2020: 7).

Despite some ongoing misogyny, opportunities for female wine professionals are increasing. Women benefit from the necessity of possessing both academic and professional qualifications to gain entry into professional contexts (Matasar 2006). Wine is nowadays sold and served with more focus than previously on empathetic customer service rather than on wine knowledge alone, the latter traditionally culturally coded as a masculine capacity. Customers are generally less straightforwardly elitist and more varied today. Some argue that women are better at serving such clientele (Almila 2019). Although women may initially join together to avoid feeling isolated in male-dominated environments, they can also win significant benefits through their networking (Ody-Brasier and Fernandez-Mateo 2017). Yet women still face significant career challenges, especially in large corporations (Bryant and Garnham 2014). They may have to make 'flexible' career choices, especially if they have caring duties for children (Brenner 2007). Few today would be able to follow influential wine writer Jancis Robinson's (1997) casual attitude to motherhood in the 1980s as she describes it – taking her baby practically everywhere in her professional life, from interviewing winemakers to shooting TV series.

Conclusion

From ancient times until today, men have been concerned about women's relations to wine. For millennia, women's symbolic relationships with wine were simultaneously stereotyped and problematised, and their practical access to wine regulated, sometimes strictly. Women's wine drinking has been widely felt to threaten disorder in terms of sexuality, domesticity and motherhood. These notions have been framed by religious, political, and medical discourses as well as broad and persisting cultural configurations. Women taking pleasure in wine has also been widely construed as threatening. Over the last century, new possibilities and spaces have opened up for women as wine consumers, makers, and professionals. Patriarchal and misogynist elements persist today, yet women have been able to exercise agency in various ways, and to negotiate challenges that their male counterparts do not face, which those men may indeed help create and reproduce. In the face of entrenched male prejudices, women through the centuries have enjoyed wine and made their distinctive claims upon it.

References

Almila, A. (2019) "Wine, Women and Globalization: The Case of Female Sommeliers," in D. Inglis and A-M. Almila (eds), *The Globalization of Wine*, London: Bloomsbury, 191–212.
Almila, A. (2022, in press) "Wine and the Gendered Self-Gift: Conceptual Considerations," in P. Howland (ed), *Wine and the Gift*, London: Routledge.
Armstrong, E.M. and Abel, E.L. (2000) "Fetal Alcohol Syndrome: The Origins of a Moral Panic," *Alcohol & Alcoholism* 35(3), 276–282.
Atkin, T., Nowak, L. and Garcia, R. (2007) "Women Wine Consumers: Information Search and Retailing Implications," *International Journal of Wine Business Research* 19(4), 327–339.
Barber, N., Almanza, B.A. and Donovan, J.R. (2006) "Motivational Factors of Gender, Income and Age on Selecting a Bottle of Wine," *International Journal of Wine Marketing* 18(3), 218–232.
Barlow, T.E. *et al.* (2005) "The Modern Girl Around the World: A Research Agenda and Preliminary Findings," *Gender & History* 17(2), 245–294.
Bianquis-Gasser, I. (1992) "Wine and Men in Alsace, France," in D. Gefou-Madianou (ed), *Alcohol, Gender and Culture*, London: Routledge, 101–107.
Brenner, D. (2007) *Women of the Vine: Inside the World of Women Who Make, Taste, and Enjoy Wine*, Hoboken, NJ: Wiley.
Bryant, L. and Garnham, B. (2014) "The Embodiment of Women in Wine: Gender Inequality and Gendered Inscriptions of the Working Body in a Corporate Wine Organization," *Gender, Work and Organization* 21(5), 411–426.
Colquhoun, K. (2007) *Taste: The Story of Britain Through Its Cooking*, London: Bloomsbury.
Dalby, A. (2003) *Bacchus: A Biography*, London: British Museum Press.
Davidoff, L. and Hall, C. (2002) *Family Fortunes, Revised Edition: Men and Women of the English Middle Class 1780–1850*, 2nd edition, London: Routledge.
Dietler, M. (2006) "Alcohol: Anthropological/Archaeological Perspectives," *Annual Review of Anthropology* 35, 229–249.

Dolan, F.E. (2018) "Time, Gender and the Mystery of English Wine," in M.E. Wiesner-Hanks (ed), *Gendered Temporalities in the Early Modern World*, Amsterdam: Amsterdam University Press, 19–46.

Dragadze, T. (1994) "Gender, Ethnicity and Alcohol in the Former Soviet Union," in M. McDonald (ed), *Gender, Drink and Drugs*, Oxford: Berg, 145–152.

Friesen, C.J.P. (2014) "Dionysos as Jesus: The Incongruity of a Love Feast in Achilles Tatius's *Leucippe and Clitophon* 2.2," *Harvard Theological Review* 107(2), 222–240.

Gefou-Madianou, D. (1992) "Exclusion and Unity, Retsina and Sweet Wine: Commensality and Gender in a Greek Agrotown," in D. Gefou-Madianou (ed), *Alcohol, Gender and Culture*, London: Routledge, 108–136.

Heath, D.B. (2003) "Alcohol in the Study of Anthropology and Religion," in S.D. Glazier and C.A. Flowerday (eds), *Selected Readings in the Anthropology of Religion: Theoretical and Methodological Essays*, Westport, CT: Praeger, 143–164.

Ho, S.-L. (2015) "'License to Drink': White-Collar Female Workers and Japan's Urban Night Space," *Ethnography* 16(1), 25–50.

Inglis, D. (2022, in press) "On Divine Wine: Wine Gifts Between Gods and Humankind," in P. Howland (ed), *Wine and the Gift*, London: Routledge.

Isler-Kerényi, C. (2014) *Dionysos in Classical Athens: An Understanding Through Images*, Leiden: Brill.

James, V. (2020) *Wine Girl*, London: Fleet.

Johnson, S. (2009) "How is the Body of Christ a Meaningful Symbol for the Contemporary Christian Community?" *Feminist Theology* 17(2), 210–228.

Johnson, T.E. and Bastian, S.E.P. (2007) "A Preliminary Study of the Relationship between Australian Wine Consumers' Wine Expertise and Their Wine Purchasing and Consumption Behaviour," *Australian Journal of Grape and Wine Research* 13, 186–197.

Kennedy, T.M. (2017) "Boxed Wine Feminisms: The Rhetoric of Women's Wine Drinking in *The Good Wife*," in M.A. Goldthwaite (ed), *Food, Feminisms, Rhetorics*, Carbondale: Southern Illinois University Press, 171–180.

Kerenyi, K. (1976) *Dionysos: Archetypal Image of Indestructible Life*, Princeton, NJ: Princeton University Press.

Killingsworth, B. (2006) "'Drinking Stories' from a Playgroup: Alcohol in the Lives of Middle-Class Mothers in Australia," *Ethnography* 7(3), 357–384.

Kinoshita, S. and Jacobs, J. (2007) "Ports of Call: Boccaccio's Alatiel in the Medieval Mediterranean," *Journal of Medieval and Early Modern Studies* 37(1), 163–195.

Langhamer, C. (2003) "A Public House Is for All Classes, Men and Women Alike': Women, Leisure and Drink in Second World War England," *Women's History Review* 12(3), 423–443.

Lissarrague, F. (2016) *The Aesthetics of the Greek Banquet: Images of Wine and Ritual*, Princeton, NJ: Princeton University Press.

Ludington, C. (2013) *The Politics of Wine in Britain: A New Cultural History*, Basingstoke: Palgrave Macmillan.

Martin, A.L. (2001) *Alcohol, Sex, and Gender in Late Medieval and Early Modern Europe*, London: Palgrave Macmillan.

Matasar, A.B. (2006) *Women of Wine: The Rise of Women in the Global Wine Industry*, Berkeley: University of California Press.

McClellan, M.L. (2017) *Lady Lushes: Gender, Alcoholism, and Medicine in Modern America*, New Brunswick, NJ: Rutgers University Press.

McDonald, M. (1994) "Drinking and Social Identity in the West of France," in M. McDonald (ed), *Gender, Drink and Drugs*, Oxford: Berg, 99–124.

McGovern, P.E. (2003) *Ancient Wine: The Search for the Origins of Viniculture*, Princeton, NJ: Princeton University Press.

Montanari, M. (2015) *Medieval Tastes: Food, Cooking, and the Table*, New York: Columbia University Press.

Moss, S. (2015) "Manly Drinkers: Masculinity and Material Culture in the Interwar Public House," in J. Hamlett, H. Greig and L. Hannan (eds), *Gender and Material Culture in Britain since 1600*, London: Palgrave Macmillan, 138–152.

Näsström, B.M. (2003) "The Rites in the Mysteries of Dionysos: The Birth of the Drama," *Scripta Instituti Donneriani Aboensis* 18, 139–148.

Nencini, P. and Grant, K.A. (2010) "Psychobiology of Drug-Induced Religious Experience: From the Brain 'Locus of Religion' to Cognitive Unbinding," *Substance Use & Misuse* 45(2), 2130–2215.

Nicolson, P. (1990) "Gender, Power and Wine Selection: A Pilot Study," *Journal of Wine Research* 1(3), 235–242.

Ody-Brasier, A. and Fernandez-Mateo, I. (2017) "When Being in the Minority Pays Off: Relationships among Sellers and Price Setting in the Champagne Industry," *American Sociological Review* 82(1), 147–178.

Phillips, R. (2018) *Wine: A Social and Cultural History of the Drink That Changed Our Lives*, Oxford: Infinite Ideas.

Poo, M.C. (1995) *Wine and Wine Offering in the Religion of Ancient Egypt*, London: Kegan Paul International.

Purcell, N. (1994) "Women and Wine in Ancient Rome," in M. McDonald (ed), *Gender, Drink and Drugs*, Oxford: Berg, 191–208.

Remus, E.A. (2014) "Tippling Ladies and the Making of Consumer Culture: Gender and Public Space in 'Fin-de-Siècle' Chicago," *The Journal of American History* 101(3), 751–777.

Ritchie, C. (2009) "The Culture of Wine Buying in the UK off-Trade," *International Journal of Wine Business Research* 21(3), 194–211.

Robinson, J. (1997) *Confessions of a Wine Lover*, London: Penguin.

Russell, B.F. (2003) "Wine, Women, and the Polis: Gender and the Formation of the City-State in Archaic Rome," *Greece & Rome* 50(1), 77–84.

Vandyke Price, P. (1990) *Woman of Taste*, London: John Murray.

Walby, S. (1991) *Theorizing Patriarchy*, Oxford: Blackwell.

Wilson, H. (2012) *Wine & Words in Classical Antiquity and the Middle Ages*, London: Bristol Classical Press.

34
WOMEN IN WINE... OCCASIONALLY
Gendered roles in the wine industry

Florine Livat and Clara Jaffré

Introduction

How gender influences wine choice, wine purchase and wine appreciation on the market's demand side has received significant attention from researchers because women have become increasingly important wine consumers (e.g. Remaud and Forbes 2012). However, the pattern of gender roles on the supply side is still an emerging topic in an industry described as patriarchal and/or male dominated (e.g. Bryant and Garnham 2014): the research is limited and relatively recent (e.g. Pavel 2012; Bryant and Garnham 2014; Galbreath 2014, 2018, 2019; Gilbert and Gilbert 2015), an observation shared by other recent researchers (Cesaro 2020: 2). Pavel (2012: 27) has observed that 'Over the wine landscape, women have created a mosaic of acceptance, achievement and influence', and the impression of a patchwork from the mosaic metaphor seems appropriate.

Among economists, the traditional approach here might be to study male/female differentials in compensation, career trajectory and occupational distribution within national wine industries followed by cross-cultural (largely geographic) comparisons. However, we are unaware of data that would allow such an industrywide analysis and so have chosen instead to review the limited literature for a critical look at what has been learned about the role of gender in wine production.

Paoloni *et al.* (2020) argue that at least two developments highlight the importance of learning more about gender roles: (1) increased female entrepreneurship and (2) the specific strategies in female-owned and -managed businesses. Even as a minority in a sector, women influence the way markets function: e.g. champagne (Ody-Brasier and Fernandez-Mateo 2017). We pursue these themes here.

The industry exhibits a pattern of patriarchal and sometimes even patrilineal control in the world's wine regions. However, women are making progress and starting to influence the industry, which may mean increased future female participation. With that said, it is unlikely that generalisations about women's roles apply globally.

Our opening section reviews the literature on gender roles in the industry; we then investigate the place of women in family and non-family wine businesses. Next, we discuss female entrepreneurship and how women network, challenge governance and excel at wine marketing. Then we discuss potential cross-national differences in gender work segregation and entrepreneurship in wine-producing countries. A final section offers conclusions.

Existing research

Research about women's roles in the wine industry is recent and scarce; almost all has appeared within the last ten years. Table 34.1 presents the regions studied and the methodology of the academic articles we reference, which focus on women's roles. It highlights that (1) several prominent wine-producing countries (e.g. Spain, Germany and South Africa) and US states (e.g. Oregon, Washington) are missing from these studies, and (2) qualitative analysis (case studies and interviews) is usually the methodology, reflecting a lack of empirical evidence. As a result, distinguishing between country-specific and global evidence is difficult.

For centuries, a variety of prejudices, traditions, religious practices, superstitions, perceptions of physical characteristics and social stereotypes have propelled gender bias. Matasar (2010) recalls the long-lasting belief that menstruating women might turn wine into vinegar. She also points out that the development of the wine industry by Catholic priests and missionaries in both the Old and New Worlds effectively excluded women. Gendered role differences are therefore entrenched and enduring in many winemaking cultures.

Despite such historic-religious impediments, women have always been involved in agriculture, grape growing and winemaking, though often behind the scenes. Some of the most prominent who replaced their deceased husbands as owners have been called 'wine widows' (Matasar 2010). According to Gilbert and Gilbert (2015: 6), 'the career paths for both female and male winemakers are challenging and demanding, but the fact that the field remains male dominated presents additional challenges to women'. Women have worked to gain authority and recognition because it is often assumed that wine prestige and reputation require a strong male identity (Chauvin 2011; Simonnet-Toussaint 2006).

Table 34.1 Women's roles in the wine industry: Regions and methodologies

Authors (alphabetical)	Country/wine region	Methodology
Alonso et al. (2020)	Chile – Casablanca Valley Argentina – San Juan Argentina – Mendoza	Qualitative analysis
Benedetto and Corinto (2015)	Italy	Case studies
Bessière (2014)	France – Cognac	Qualitative analysis
Bryant and Garnham (2014)	Australia	Case study
Cesaro (2020)	Italy	Qualitative analysis
D'Amato (2017)	Italy – Campania	Quantitative analysis
Escudier (2014a, 2014b)	France	Historic approach
Galbreath (2014, 2018, 2019) Galbreath and Tisch (2020)	Australia – several wine regions	Quantitative analysis
Garcia-Parpet (2000)	France – Chinon	Case study
Gilbert and Gilbert (2015)	US – California	Quantitative description
Le Brun et al. (2019)	France – Gaillac	Case study
Musso and Francioni (2015)	Italy	Three-case analysis
Ody-Brasier and Fernandez-Mateo (2017)	France – Champagne	Quantitative and qualitative analysis
Paoloni et al. (2020)	Several countries	Structured literature review
Pavel (2012)	Romania	Case studies
Santos et al. (2019)	Portugal	Case study

The rapid growth of the industry at the end of the twentieth century and consolidation of family businesses into corporations have opened new opportunities for women (Matasar 2010). Women outnumber men in many viticulture and oenology degree programs, representing sometimes 60% of a cohort (Escudier 2014a). Nevertheless, the impressive examples of women in the wine industry, especially as winemakers or sommeliers, overlooks the gender imbalance in specific occupations. Only about 10% of the lead winemakers in California's 4,000-plus wineries are female; the share is slightly higher in the more prominent Napa and Sonoma regions (Gilbert and Gilbert 2020). Only 28 of the 172 professionals in the US chapter of the Court of Master Sommeliers (CMS) are women (www.mastersommeliers.org/about?wpisrc=nl_lily&wpmm=1). Hulkower reviews the recent memoir of one of them (2020: 125) and concludes that 'her physical and psychological abuses and indignities over the recent past should serve as a cautionary tale reminding us that despite increased opportunities for women in male-dominated professions, attitudes and behaviours remain largely unchanged'. Beyond that personal story, the *New York Times* has covered more extensive sexual harassment at the CMS (Moskin 2020).

It is difficult to disentangle when, how and why differences in culture lead to differences in roles and vice versa; the evolution of roles can change the culture. Due to their traditional exclusion from leadership in the industry, women (and men) in influential roles may, by example and leadership, change the industry and its culture to enable greater diversity.

Women in wine business

Women in family wine businesses

Ward (1987: 252) defines a family business 'as one that will be passed on for the family's next generation to manage and control'. Bessière (2014: 2) also defines family businesses as 'men's and women's business activities . . . entwined with family relations' but notes that these relations 'are ordered according to gender'. Most wine businesses, whether oriented towards production or sales, are small- to medium-size enterprises (SMEs) or family owned. In France, 70% of the family-owned companies operating for 100 years or more are linked to the wine and spirits industry (*La santé de fer des entreprises centenaires* 2015). Globally, an unusual number of wineries, including some very large ones such as Gallo (US), Boisset (France and Canada) and Yellow Tail (Australia), are family firms, not partnerships or public corporations.

When family firms offer favourable opportunities to women, they are usually governance roles (e.g. on the board of directors) rather than management (Songini and Gnan 2009). However, the allocation of household tasks and intergenerational relationships vary across countries (Hakim 1999, 2018) and might explain variations in women's roles in family businesses worldwide (Kagitcibasi *et al.* 2010). Incidentally, exposure to Western culture does not necessarily imply a wider variety of roles for women (Crompton *et al.* 2005).

A preference for males

Family networks dominate the wine industry because these businesses are historically inherited. Parents groom their children for involvement in the family business and the transmission of its legacy. Several studies of French firms highlight the privilege of male heirs. Studying vineyards in Cognac, Bessière (2014) shows that male heirs usually inherit the farm to ensure generational continuity. Families tend to assume that female heirs prefer not to operate the family business and/or are less legitimate to the continuity of the company, so they favour male heirs. Female heirs may operate a family business only in exceptional conditions (e.g. absence or disability of male siblings). Women with partners who require them to leave their family farm (sometimes to live and work on the partner's family farm) also are less likely to become grape growers after their parents. Partners of male farm heads usually take low-skill, low-paying non-farm jobs. Any financial independence and autonomy does not mean that women are disconnected from the farm but rather that they contribute indirectly to the economic continuity of the family business (Bessière 2014).

Studying France, Escudier (2014a) describes a monopoly of men in the transmission of wine knowledge to their son(s). A study of the Chinon appellation (France) concludes that transmitting wine knowledge only from father to son in the name of 'excellence' is inefficient, rigid and old fashioned (Garcia-Parpet 2000). A study from Italy suggests that women who learn from outside the family gain new academic, social and cultural skills that help them innovate, especially in winemaking and wine tourism. They learn to deal better with technological and market uncertainty (Benedetto and Corinto 2015).

Some family companies have provided remarkable opportunities for women, but generally, these are exceptions that support the more pervasive pattern of male dominance. For instance, widows introduced innovations in branding, exporting and marketing in Champagne. Legend claims that Madame Clicquot supplied the Russian army to gain their devotion to her champagne (Matasar 2010). In the 1980s, the absence of male siblings provided opportunities to run prestigious wine estates for Corinne Mentzelopoulos (Château Margaux) and Baroness Philippine de Rothschild (Château Mouton-Rothschild) in the Bordeaux region. Outside France, Mary Penfold (Australia) and Dona Antonia Adelaide Ferreira (Portugal) were gifted women who removed boundaries very early: in the 1840s, Penfold settled in Australia and became a pioneering winemaker while Ferreira led in the cultivation of port and introduced winemaking innovations in Portugal.

Women in non-family wine businesses

Few studies investigate the role of women in non-family wine businesses (e.g. corporations). Bryant and Garnham (2014) studied an Australian multinational in which success was associated with minimal career breaks, especially maternity leaves, suggesting that women's career pattern must conform to men's. Reynolds (2016) reported that, in the Australian wine industry, pregnancy can harm corporate winemakers' careers as they can lose their position and/or be replaced. Some employers ask whether female applicants plan to have children – handicapping those who do and demonstrating a 'very real issue of sexism in the wine industry' (Reynolds 2016: 62).

In their Australian study, Bryant and Garnham (2014) found that men dominated the senior roles in organisations while women were clustered in lower, supportive positions (417). Women are encouraged to take the professional rather than the managerial route so they are more available for home duties. Women are generally considered weaker than men, so bottling tasks and materials handling is usually left to men. Escudier (2014b) also discusses perceived limited strength as a factor explaining gender discrimination in French companies.

Ascent to leadership may be more likely in family businesses, but numerous obstacles still exist when women want to lead. Vertical gender segregation (i.e. unequal dispersion of men and women within an organisational hierarchy) is common in non-family businesses. Corporate culture operates here, and we need more research comparing gender segregation patterns between family and non-family businesses.

Female entrepreneurship

Women and men often have different reasons for starting their own businesses. Women are more likely pursuing a new idea and seeking freedom, self-expression and better working conditions. They usually seek acknowledgement for their work more than men (Startienė and Remeikienė 2008). Growing up in a family business provides an example to children; however, fewer women than men become wine entrepreneurs. In Europe, women are 52% of the population but only 30% of all entrepreneurs; their companies are mainly in the service sector (Langowitz et al. 2005).

Inheriting the family wine estate can, in some cases, be a trap for the aspiring entrepreneur. Studying Lithuanian entrepreneurs, Startienė and Remeikienė (2008) show that women usually receive more financing from their relatives than men, creating financial and organisational obligations because family members tend to impose themselves more on companies that they are financing. Yet Pavel (2012: 26), studying the Romanian wine industry, notes that women who manage to establish an independent reputation have shown an uncanny understanding of marketing and 'deserve to be remembered as experienced employers, with an eye for finding talents, and as perfect entrepreneurs who run their businesses from modest debuts [to] levels of international importance'.

Mentoring and networking

Mentoring is critical for female entrepreneurship (Welter 2004). Prior family business exposure as a form of mentoring can affect entrepreneurial intent (Carr and Sequeira 2007), and Lockyer and George (2012: 188) note that 'the "strong ties" of family and friends not only influence a woman's decision to start a business but also provide the emotional support needed to maintain the momentum with an existing business'. Cesaro (2020) emphasises the critical role of social ties in developing Italian female wine entrepreneurs. Pavel's Romanian study (2012) suggests that inspiring male models can encourage women to become wine entrepreneurs. Indeed, in the context of family businesses, grandfathers and fathers have often provided the guidance and mentorship needed to gain knowledge and know-how. For first-generation women, models have invariably been men. However, Lockyer and George's study of female entrepreneurs in the English West Midlands (2012) stresses that business owners who use networks outside their family and friends are more likely to achieve entrepreneurial objectives.

Commercial and social isolation of various sorts can be both strengthening and threatening. Mentoring and networking can help address the challenges in rural areas distant from multinationals (Beckmann et al. 2021) or neglected by rural media, which overlook the role of women entrepreneurs in agriculture (Alston 2003). Many studies have investigated the role of female farmers in North American professional organisations and show that they are underrepresented, feel isolated and are not taken seriously (e.g. Sachs et al. 2016). A study of the Gaillac wine appellation (southwest France) found that traditional male-oriented professional organisations were not addressing the different priorities of women working there (Le Brun et al. 2019). Consequently, women coalesced and created new networks to challenge professional institutions that questioned their legitimacy. Pavel (2012: 413), commenting in the French context, stresses that '[wine] fellowships have traditionally excluded women from rituals related to wine and tastings, which prevented (female) interaction with people governing the wine industry'. The lack of female mentoring and networking has meant that they are more independent and self-reliant. Women are therefore isolated from some social aspects of the industry but have established their own networks to increase their social capital, defined as the set of resources available to an individual as a result of their personal relationships (e.g. De Janasz and Forret 2008).

Facing such isolation as a challenge encourages women to create networks which can enhance not only their products and enterprises but also the collective reputation of a wine region or appellation. The Women Do Wine association (France), the Diversity in Wine Leadership Forum (North America), the Australian Women in Wine Awards and the Women in Wine Leadership Symposium (US based but international) seek to support and mentor women and to highlight positive female role models and leaders, but they are new and operate in only a few wine-producing countries.

Wine markets can be highly competitive but can also reward cooperation. 'Coopetition' (Crick 2018; Lombardi et al. 2015) can be beneficial for small businesses to increase their life span, manage various risks such as big changes in the industry, decrease learning costs and so reduce trials and failures (Morris et al. 2007). An increasingly globalised and competitive wine industry can also nurture cooperation through the emergence of new networks and groups. Some women define themselves as partner-competitors and say that working together and developing this network enables them to go further than they could individually. These formal, horizontal and inter-organisational networks enhance women's abilities to gain advantages, such as sharing knowledge and experiences or increasing their level of internationalisation, though such benefits are not guaranteed (e.g. Musso and Francioni (2015) studying small Italian wineries). Women also use these networks to communicate unique features of their wines to consumers, narrated in a feminine, cohesive and united voice and supported by a passion for winemaking (Santos et al. 2019).

While networking and mentoring can be helpful, it is not for everyone. It depends on institutional and structural conditions like ease of communication or a critical mass of women in the industry as well as cultural characteristics that can be more or less encouraging (e.g. traditional local rivalries, intergenerational tensions).

Leadership and performance

A limited number of studies have focused on women's influence on leadership and performance. Cesaro (2020) reviews eight studies that conclude that female-run companies perform better than male-run companies in the countries studied (Finland, Italy, the US, Spain, Colombia, New Zealand and an IMF survey of 34 European countries) and other studies that question the relationship (e.g. Denmark, US). In a US-based study, Allen and Langowitz (2003) stress that a feminine style of management highlights mutual empowerment, collaboration, information sharing, empathy and nurturing. In a study of 88 Italian wine firms, D'Amato (2017) found that, compared to high-family-controlled firms (sum of the proportion of family members involved in firm ownership and on the board of directors), women in top positions in low-family-controlled firms affected firm performance negatively.

Most wine industry studies come from Australia. Sheridan and Milgate (2003) find that Australian women seem to promote diversity, whereas men tend to encourage homogeneity and conservatism in selecting members of the board. Studying Australian wineries from 2007 to 2013, Galbreath (2018) found that women represented nearly 13% of CEOs in comparison to only 3% in Australia's largest 500 firms, suggesting that the wine industry is more gender diversified than other industries. He also found that women are numerically underrepresented in Australian wine companies and that the presence of a female CEO increases the likelihood of a female being found in the roles of winemaker and marketing manager. Interestingly, when comparing different wine regions of Australia that exhibit different reputations, prices and involvement in wine research and innovation, Galbreath found no clear differences in the representation rates of women in top roles. On the other hand, Bryant and Garnham's Australian study (2014) found no women in top positions. Men attributed this to a lack of qualified women, whereas women argued that it reflected a 'boys' club' effect that excluded them from boardrooms. In an earlier study, Galbreath (2014) reported that 9% of Australian wineries employed female head winemakers.

The increasing number of women in the industry fosters competencies such as idea generation and innovation. Evidence from Australia shows that women's leadership brings high moral and ethical standards, environmental sensitivity and transformational leadership styles – traits that seems to encourage both competitiveness and a sense of social responsibility in the wine industry (Galbreath 2014, 2019; Galbreath and Tisch 2020).

Existing research on corporate governance also focuses on Australia. We expect that management models vary cross culturally (Schein and Mueller 1992). More inter- and intra-country analyses are needed to allow meaningful comparisons of women's style of leadership and management.

Women winemakers and marketing

The glossy image of elite female winemakers

Media can suggest that women in the industry are no longer subject to gender-based constraints. They may have created the perception that there are far more female winemakers than there actually are: e.g. California (Gilbert and Gilbert 2015). Gilbert and Gilbert (2015: 3) note that 'such perceptions lower the perceived need to encourage women to enter the field and to provide the mentoring and support needed to facilitate their career success'. Acclaim for leading women in the industry can mask the reality of many other women's experiences.

Bryant and Garnham (2014) claim that the media paints a glossy image of elite female winemakers that is decontextualised from the broader wine industry, distorting the actual experience of women in managerial, non-managerial and governance positions. Although increasing numbers appear in senior winemaking jobs in Australia, they find that having women in these positions yields only marginal transformations of organisations' management profiles, inhibiting true structural change in the short or medium term.

Marketing of gendered wines

Wines made by women appeal to consumers and are receiving increasing recognition. Female winemakers in California have received a disproportionate share of recognition (Gilbert and Gilbert 2012). In Portugal, some women producers capitalise on gender by displaying their names on labels, showing affirmation and self-identification (Santos *et al.* 2019). Such a use of gender could become an extrinsic cue for wine. Indeed, wines made by women embed a characteristic that can be used as a differentiation tool. The National Women in Wine Day (California), the Australian Women in Wine Awards, the Italian Women Winemakers tasting event and the South African Women's Wine and Spirits Awards are examples of events showcasing and celebrating wines made by women. In South Africa, Women in Wine claims to be the first wine-producing company owned, controlled and managed by women. Gender-specific wine lists have also appeared in restaurants and wine bars: a London restaurant offers only wines made by women (Shaw 2014), and the Winemak'her bar in New York City offers only wines made by female winemakers or wine estate owners (Aubin 2020).

Cultural differences in work segregation

Nowadays, both Old and New World wine producers feature women in leading roles (Matasar 2010). Our literature review suggests that there are probably some common factors worldwide that enable women to rise in the wine industry. However, if gender segregation, as well as its decline over time, appear to be universal (Gutek 2001), strong cross-national differences remain. Indeed, Chang (2000) and Charles and Grusky (2005) discuss varieties of gender segregation regimes. Socio-cultural norms and characteristics, penetration of egalitarian principles in the society, state interventions and the policy environment, the structure of the educational system and labour market, the level of economic development, and the size of tertiary sector, among other things, can affect occupational segregation by gender (Charles 1992; Charles and Bradley 2009).

Research related to gendered roles in the wine industry remains sparse, especially studying and comparing wine regions exhibiting more or less strong traditions of gender equality. Countries where military service requirements are relatively gender neutral (e.g. Israel) or where there is less influence from male-dominant religious traditions and European settlement might exhibit more gender balance in the industry (and in other male-dominated industries) – for example, Switzerland, which has the UN's lowest Gender Inequality Index (GII) rank (United Nations 2019).

Table 34.2 Gender Inequality Index (GII) rank and women's total entrepreneurial activity (TEA) of the main wine-producing countries

Major wine producers	2018 Wine production (million hectoliters) (OIV 2019)	Gender Inequality Index (rank) (United Nations 2019)	Women total entrepreneurial activity 2018–2019 in % (Elam et al. 2019)
Italy	54.8	14	2.8
France	48.6	6	5.3
Spain	44.4	16	6.0
USA	23.9	46	13.6
Argentina	14.5	75	8.1
Chile	12.9	55	21.2
Australia	12.9	25	9.2
Germany	10.3	20	3.3
South Africa	9.5	93	9.0
China	9.1	29	9.3
Portugal	6.1	17	NA
Russian Federation	5.5	50	3.9
Romania	5.1	61	NA

Table 34.2 presents the GII rank (United Nations 2019) of the most prominent wine-producing countries (here, countries with a wine production of more than five million hectolitres, according to OIV 2019) where 1 is the highest rank, indicating the country with the lowest inequality as measured by the GII – at best, only a crude measure of labour market diversity. Old World wine regions of western Europe rank higher as a group than the others, and Australia and China are the highest among those. Table 34.2 also presents the total entrepreneurial activity (TEA) of women – the percentage of the adult female working-age population (18–64) who are either nascent or new entrepreneurs (Elam et al. 2019). The women TEA indicator is low in some countries ranked high in the GII, and New World wine regions exhibit a higher rate of women nascent or new entrepreneurs than Old World ones. Given the diversity of major wine regions, we wonder about different gendered patterns of occupations and entrepreneurship in those countries and whether they apply in their wine industries.

Conclusion

For years, wine and related industries such as restaurants have been male dominated, patriarchal and sometimes patrilinear, with some examples of remarkable female leadership being the exceptions that highlighted the rule. However, since the beginning of the twenty-first century, women have had a greater presence in the industry, even if gender imbalance remains. Research, which is recent, geographically limited and mostly qualitative, highlights this trend. Being a female winemaker has become an extrinsic cue for wine, and it could also emerge to differentiate wine management models.

Extrapolating reliably from country-specific evidence to global patterns is not possible. Among the few studying gender roles in depth have been Galbreath (2014, 2018, 2019) for Australia and Gilbert and Gilbert (2012, 2015, 2020) for California. We also have single studies and research on gender roles in businesses generally from which we have extrapolated. A strong impression from this survey, aside from variability across wine regions, is that a sense of isolation runs through women's wine culture – isolation from the dominant male leadership traditionally common in business and geographic isolation that reflects the natural geographic dispersion and rural environment of wine production. Set against this is sometimes strong family support – again indicative of the industry – and the emergence of associations encouraging mutual support of women in wine. Aside from the usual risks that go with the territory (e.g. weather, climate change, pests, regulation), the challenging environment can elicit discouragement and failure but also creativity and excellence.

This chapter calls for more research dedicated to inter- and intra-country analyses of both gender cultures and regional wine cultures to allow comparisons. Business culture comparisons are particularly relevant both because, while family businesses have been prevalent, models of family business (and, correspondingly, their gender roles) vary and because corporations have become more important. Catholic religion and European settlement have had a strong influence in many parts of the wine world, and it would be worth examining the situation for women in wine regions that are not subject to these cultural influences (e.g. China). Gendered roles in the wine industry also raise related topics, like how gender, presented through the name or the picture of the winemaker on the label, may influence consumption, or about the role and acceptance of women as wine experts and judges. The gender imbalance among wine economists is another example of persistent imbalance in the profession generally (e.g. Lundberg and Stearns 2019).

Acknowledgements

We are indebted to Denton Marks, who has significantly and tirelessly contributed to the development of this chapter. We would like to express our sincere gratitude. We also thank two anonymous reviewers who provided thoughtful and constructive comments to improve this chapter. Note that, in this chapter, we have assumed that gender is binary. Assuming otherwise introduces an issue of gender roles and discrimination that moves far outside the focus of the chapter and that has attracted even less published industry-related research than the topic addressed.

References

Allen, E.E. and Langowitz, N.S. (2003) *Women in Family-Owned Businesses*, Wellesley, MA: Massachusetts Mutual Life Insurance Company and Affiliated Companies.

Alonso, A.D., Kok, S. and Galbreath, J. (2020) "Entrepreneurial Women in the Wine Industry: A Study in Emerging Economies," *International Journal of Wine Business Research*, ahead-of-print, https://doi.org/10.1108/IJWBR-03-2020-0010.

Alston, M. (2003) "Women in Agriculture: The 'New Entrepreneurs'," *Australian Feminist Studies* 18(41), 163–171.

Aubin, M. (2020) "Winemak'her, un Bar Qui Met les Femmes Vigneronnes à l'honneur à Park Slope," *French Morning*, June 21, https://frenchmorning.com/winemakher-un-bar-qui-met-les-femmes-vigneronnes-a-lhonneur-a-park-slope/.

Beckmann, M., Garkisch, M. and Zeyen, A. (2021) "Together We Are Strong? A Systematic Literature Review on How SMEs Use Relation-based Collaboration to Operate in Rural Areas," *Journal of Small Business & Entrepreneurship* 1–37, https://doi.org/10.1080/08276331.2021.1874605.

Benedetto, G. and Corinto, G.L. (2015) "The Role of Women in the Sustainability of the Wine Industry: Two Case Studies in Italy," in A. Vastola (ed), *The Sustainability of Agro-Food and Natural Resource Systems in the Mediterranean Basin*, Heidelberg: Springer Cham, 73–187.

Bessière, C. (2014) "Female and Male Domestic Partners in Wine-Grape Farms (Cognac, France): Conjugal Asymmetry and Gender Discrimination in Family Businesses," *The History of the Family* 19(3), 341–357.

Bryant, L. and Garnham, B. (2014) "The Embodiment of Women in Wine: Gender Inequality and Gendered Inscriptions of the Working Body in a Corporate Wine Organization," *Gender, Work & Organization* 21(5), 411–426.

Carr, J.C. and Sequeira, J.M. (2007) "Prior Family Business Exposure as Intergenerational Influence and Entrepreneurial Intent: A Theory of Planned Behavior Approach," *Journal of Business Research* 60(10), 1090–1098.

Cesaro, L. (2020) *Female Entrepreneurship in the Wine Industry: Characteristics of the Entrepreneurial Process and the Role of Social Ties* (Master's thesis, Università Ca'Foscari Venezia).

Chang, M.L. (2000) "The Evolution of Sex Segregation Regimes," *American Journal of Sociology* 105(6), 1658–1701.

Charles, M. (1992) "Cross-national Variation in Occupational Sex Segregation," *American Sociological Review* 57(4), 483–502.

Charles, M. and Bradley, K. (2009) "Indulging Our Gendered Selves? Sex Segregation by Field of Study in 44 Countries," *American Journal of Sociology* 114(4), 924–976.

Charles, M. and Grusky, D.B. (2005) *Occupational Ghettos: The Worldwide Segregation of Women and Men*, vol. 200, Stanford, CA: Stanford University Press.

Chauvin, P.M. (2011) "Réputation et Division du Travail," *Ethnologie Française* 41(1), 131–140.

Crick, J.M. (2018) "Studying Coopetition in a Wine Industry Context: Directions for Future Research," *International Journal of Wine Business Research* 30(3), 366–371.

Crompton, R., Brockmann, M. and Lyonette, C. (2005) "Attitudes, Women's Employment and the Domestic Division of Labour: A Cross-National Analysis in Two Waves," *Work, Employment and Society* 19(2), 213–233.

D'Amato, A. (2017) "Do Women Perform Better in Family Firms?" *International Journal of Wine Business Research* 29(3), 299–315.

De Janasz, S.C. and Forret, M.L. (2008) "Learning the Art of Networking: A Critical Skill for Enhancing Social Capital and Career Success," *Journal of Management Education* 32(5), 629–650.

Elam, A.B., Brush, C.G., Greene, P.G., Baumer, B., Dean, M., Heavlow, R. and Global Entrepreneurship Research Association. (2019) "Women's Entrepreneurship Report 2018/2019," www.gemconsortium.org/report/gem-20182019-womens-entrepreneurship-report.

Escudier, J.L. (2014a) "La Résistible Accession des Femmes à l'Acquisition des Savoirs Viticoles 1950–2010," *Pour* 2, 127–134.

Escudier, J.L. (2014b) *Contribution à l'histoire des rapports économiques de genre: application à la viticulture française 1850–2010* (Doctoral dissertation, Perpignan, France).

Galbreath, J. (2014) "Women in Top Roles in the Wine Industry: Forging Ahead or Falling Behind?" *American Association of Wine Economists (AAWE) Working Paper* (150), February.

Galbreath, J. (2018) "A Study of Women in Top Business Roles: The Case of the Wine Industry," in W.T. Ziemba (ed), *World Scientific Handbook in Financial Economics Series, World Scientific* 6, 401–421.

Galbreath, J. (2019) "Drivers of Green Innovations: The Impact of Export Intensity, Women Leaders, and Absorptive Capacity," *Journal of Business Ethics* 158(1), 47–61.

Galbreath, J. and Tisch, D. (2020) "The Effects of Women in Different Roles on Environmentally Sustainable Practices: Empirical Evidence from the Australian Wine Industry," *Australasian Journal of Environmental Management* 27(4), 434–451.

Garcia-Parpet, M.F. (2000) "Dispositions Economiques et Stratégies de Reconversion. L'exemple de la Nouvelle Viticulture," *Ruralia. Sciences Sociales et Mondes Ruraux Contemporains* 7.

Gilbert, L.A. and Gilbert, J.C. (2012) "Evidence of Women Winemakers' Success in a Male Dominated Field," Working Paper, Santa Clara University, Santa Clara, CA.

Gilbert, L.A. and Gilbert, J.C. (2015) "A Case Study of California's Major Wineries: Assessing the Progress and Prospects for Winemakers Who Are Women," *American Association of Wine Economists (AAWE) Working Paper* (178), May.

Gilbert, L.A. and Gilbert, J.C. (2020) "Facts and Figures Gathered in Our On-going Research on California Women Winemakers," Women Winemakers of California and Beyond, https://webpages.scu.edu/womenwinemakers/facts.php, accessed 10 May 2021.

Gutek, B.A. (2001) "Women and Paid Work," *Psychology of Women Quarterly* 25(4), 379–393.

Hakim, C. (1999) "Models of the Family, Women's Role and Social Policy: A New Perspective from Preference Theory," *European Societies* 1(1), 33–58.

Hakim, C. (2018) *Models of the Family in Modern Societies: Ideals and Realities*, Aldershot: Ashgate.

Hulkower, N.D. (2020) "Review: Victoria James, Wine Girl: The Obstacles, Humiliations, and Triumphs of America's Youngest Sommelier," *Journal of Wine Economics* 15(1), 122–126.

Kagitcibasi, C., Ataca, B. and Diri, A. (2010) "Intergenerational Relationships in the Family: Ethnic, Socioeconomic, and Country Variations in Germany, Israel, Palestine, and Turkey," *Journal of Cross-Cultural Psychology* 41(5–6), 652–670.

Langowitz, N.S., Minniti, M. and Arenius, P. (2005) "Global Entrepreneurship Monitor: 2004 Report on Women and Entrepreneurship," University of Illinois at Urbana-Champaign's Academy for Entrepreneurial Leadership Historical Research Reference in Entrepreneurship, https://ssrn.com/abstract=1509263, Accessed 26 April 2021.

"La santé de fer des entreprises centenaires" (2015) EcoRéseau Business, 2 July 2, https://www.ecoreseau.fr/entreprendre/enquete-entrepreneuriale/2015/07/02/2436-la-sante-de-fer-des-entreprises-centenaires/, accessed 10 May 2021.

Le Brun, C., Guétat-Bernard, H. and Annes, A. (2019) "L'Emergence de Collectifs Féminins en Viticulture: Vers un Renouvellement de la Structuration de la Filière?" *Interrogations? Revue Pluridisciplinaire de Sciences Humaines et Sociales* 29.

Lockyer, J. and George, S. (2012) "What Women Want: Barriers to Female Entrepreneurship in the West Midlands," *International Journal of Gender and Entrepreneurship* 14(2), 179–195.

Lombardi, R., Manfredi, S., Nappo, F. and Russo, G. (2015) "A Primary Study on Inter-Company Collaboration in the Wine Business Sector: The Coopetition Perspective," *Piccola Impresa/Small Business* 2, 86–99.

Lundberg, S. and Stearns, J. (2019) "Women in Economics: Stalled Progress," *Journal of Economic Perspectives* 33(1), 3–22.

Matasar, A.B. (2010) *Women of Wine: The Rise of Women in the Global Wine Industry*, Berkeley: University of California Press.

Morris, M.H., Koçak, A. and Ozer, A. (2007) "Coopetition as a Small Business Strategy: Implications for Performance," *Journal of Small Business Strategy* 18(1), 35–56.

Moskin, J. (2020) "The Wine World's Most Elite Circle Has a Sexual Harassment Problem," *The New York Times*, 29 October.

Musso, F. and Francioni, B. (2015) "Agri-food Clusters, Wine Tourism and Foreign Markets: The Role of Local Networks for SME's Internationalization," *Procedia Economics and Finance* 27, 334–343.

Ody-Brasier, A. and Fernandez-Mateo, I. (2017) "When Being in the Minority Pays Off: Relationships among Sellers and Price Setting in the Champagne Industry," *American Sociological Review* 82(1), 147–178.

OIV. (2019) "2019 Statistical Report on World Vitiviniculture," https://www.oiv.int/public/medias/6782/oiv-2019-statistical-report-on-world-vitiviniculture.pdf.

Paoloni, P., Cosentino, A. and Iannone, B. (2020) "Investigating the Female Role in the Wine Sector: Business Administration Perspective on a Decade of Research (2010–2019)," in P. Paoloni and R. Lombardi (eds), *Gender Studies, Entrepreneurship and Human Capital*. IPAZIA 2019. Springer Proceedings in Business and Economics, Cham: Springer.

Pavel, S.M. (2012) "Women's Entrepreneurship: The Rise of Women in the Global Wine Industry," *Cross-Cultural Management Journal* 14(1(25)), 21–28.

Remaud, H. and Forbes, S.L. (2012) "The Influence of Gender on Wine Purchasing and Consumption: An Exploratory Study across Four Nations," *International Journal of Wine Business Research* 24(2), 146–159.

Reynolds, E. (2016) "Women in Wine: It's a Sexist Award, It Needs to Be," *Australian and New Zealand Grapegrower and Winemaker* 624, January, 62–64.

Sachs, C., Barbercheck, M., Braiser, K., Kiernan, N.E. and Terman, A.R. (2016) *The Rise of Women Farmers and Sustainable Agriculture*, Iowa City: University of Iowa Press.

Santos, G., Marques, C.S. and Ratten, V. (2019) "Entrepreneurial Women's Networks: The Case of D'Uva – Portugal Wine Girls," *International Journal of Entrepreneurial Behaviour and Research* 25(2), 298–322.

Schein, V.E. and Mueller, R. (1992) "Sex Role Stereotyping and Requisite Management Characteristics: A Cross Cultural Look," *Journal of Organizational Behavior* 13(5), 439–447.

Shaw, L. (2014) "First Female-Only Wine List Launched," *The Drinks Business*, 3 December, https://www.thedrinksbusiness.com/2014/12/first-female-only-wine-list-launched/, accessed 22 March 2021.

Sheridan, A. and Milgate, G. (2003) "'She Says, He Says': Women's and Men's Views of the Composition of Boards," *Women in Management Review* 18 147–154.

Simonnet-Toussaint, C. (2006) "Le Vin sur le Divan," in *Des Représentations Sociales aux Représentations Intimes*, Bordeaux: Féret.

Songini, L. and Gnan, L. (2009) "Women, Glass Ceiling, and Professionalization in Family SMEs: A Missed Link," *Journal of Enterprising Culture* 17(4), 497–525.

Startienė, G. and Remeikienė, R. (2008) "Gender Gap in Entrepreneurship," *Engineering Economics* 60(5), 95–103.

United Nations. (2019) "Gender Inequality Index (GII)," http://hdr.undp.org/en/content/gender-inequality-index-gii#:~:text=It%20measures%20the%20human%20development,major%20areas%20of%20human%20development, accessed 1 February 2021.

Ward, J.L. (1987) *Keeping the Family Business Healthy*, San Francisco: Jossey-Bass.

Welter, F. (2004) "The Environment for Female Entrepreneurship in Germany," *Journal of Small Business and Enterprise Development* 11(2), 212–221.

Websites

www.mastersommeliers.org/about?wpisrc=nl_lily&wpmm=1

35
SUSTAINABLE WINE
The discursive production of sustainability in the wine field

Gianmarco Navarini and Lorenzo Domaneschi

Introduction

'What is sustainability in the wine world?' A recent article bearing this title answers the question through an interesting and well-documented cross-country analysis of the frameworks used to assess and guide the implementation of sustainability programmes in South Africa, Australia, New Zealand, the US, Chile and France (Flores 2018). The frameworks are described and compared on the basis of four elements: the type (main goal), the territorial scale (national or regional, in terms of design and implementation), depth (how and to what extent the protocol is organised to process the data and information) and learning potential. The last aspect 'reflects the ability of the proposal to promote learning and improvement in practices, which can occur, for example, by comparison with other analysed stakeholders, continuous improvement requirements for next cycles or availability of guides, examples and best practices' (Flores 2018: 2306). Based on previous research (Flores 2015), according to which 'specialists and wine growers have described sustainability as a concept that evolves over time and point out that to be sustainable requires continuous improvement', the learning potential becomes an assessment tool for the various frameworks (high, medium or low). Therefore, for South Africa, there are two high frameworks and one low; New Zealand is medium; Australia and California (US) are high; Chile is medium; and France is high. Despite the author's strictly analytical intentions, the final result of this kind of study is a hierarchical list of requisites needed in order that specific wines or wineries can be defined as 'sustainable'. All in all, this analytical process represents a clear example of how the sustainability discourse continuously reproduces new classifications – in the form of rankings – which shape a new field of cultural competition, where the battle to be recognised as 'sustainable' wines (or wineries) is played out.

This chapter attempts a sociological reading of emerging sustainability discourses as they generate a normative field, supported by the search for empirical evidence, scientific indicators and other forms of objectivity, with the aim of analysing the field as a space of differences in which a new form of cultural competition for the wine sector is taking shape. We argue that the social origin of the concept of sustainability will show how such a competition is primarily of an interpretative kind. Being a concept that has varied over time, its definition always depends on the convergence or clash between similar, complementary and different ways of dealing with and resolving the issue.

Then the chapter illustrates how sustainability can be understood as a competitive discursive field with specific cultural histories and discontinuities, endowed with a comparatively enduring set of conventional dominant definitions and deploying a cluster of instruments in order to 'empirically' measure, evaluate and, hence, legitimate such classifications (in relation to other 'types' of wine, such as organic wines). Therefore, we engage with the analysis of what we have called 'certification work' to show how such tools as labels, reports, indicators and, mainly, certification schemes operate worldwide as discursive devices in the fields of wine. In the conclusion, we turn to winegrowing practices to illustrate the ambivalent effects of 'certification work' in the everyday process of wine production and the respective practical management of such institutional contradictions. Finally, critical discussion on the 'culture of sustainability' and on the directions of a future research agenda will be proposed.

A history of the discursive device

Although the concept of sustainability has a long history which began during the sixteenth century, the word first appears in forestry handbooks in the 1650s (Warde 2011, 2018). Nonetheless, it is commonly believed that its first official definition was launched by the 1987 Brundtland Commission's Report. The latter is a publication released in 1987 by the World Commission on Environment and Development, chaired by former Norwegian Prime Minister Gro Harlem Brundtland, that introduced the notion of 'sustainable development' and framed how it could be achieved. In theoretical terms, the Report of the World Commission on Environment and Development (1987) was clearly an important text from which other sustainability discourses emerged. From the late 1980s, the definitions it proposed began to generate a common belief following the theory of the 'effects of truth' (Foucault 2001). Similarly, in contemporary literature, the text is also treated as a founding myth (Barthes 2009). In fact, it was through specifically drawing on this consecrated text that the two most important discursive formations for interpreting and resolving the issue of sustainability originated.

The first concerns the word 'sustainability', articulated in the form of an adjective that characterises the kind of development that must be promoted. In fact, the report did not define sustainability, but rather 'sustainable development' as a kind of 'development that meets the needs of the present generation without compromising the ability of future generations to meet their own needs' (WCED 1987: 43). In this regard, two key concepts were foregrounded: first, 'the concept of "needs", in particular the essential needs of the world's poor, to which overriding priority should be given' and second, 'the idea of limitations imposed by the state of technology and social organisation on the environment's ability to meet present and future needs' (WCED 1987: 43).

The second discursive formation – supported by the thesis that the report 'changed sustainable development from a physical notion to one based on social, economic and environmental considerations' (Borowy 2014, I) – concerns the so-called three pillars of sustainability: economic, social, environmental. In much contemporary literature, these are called 'dimensions' (Flores 2018; Mariani and Vastola 2015), as if they are essential ways of seeing or analysing sustainability, while the report actually conceives them as pillars: that is, requirements for the pursuit of sustainable development. Yet they are not the only pillars. In fact, the necessary requirements encompass seven systems which, in turn, must be developed:

> a political system that secures effective citizen participation in decision making; an economic system that is able to generate surpluses and technical knowledge on a self-reliant and sustained basis; a social system that provides for solutions for the tensions arising from disharmonious development; a production system that respects the obligation to preserve the ecological base for development; a technological system that can search continuously for new solutions; an international system that fosters sustainable patterns of trade and finance; and an administrative system that is flexible and has the capacity for self-correction.
> *(WCED 1987: 65)*

It is interesting to note that among these seven requirements, which seem to confirm the hypothesis that global societal transformation is one central element of the sustainable development concept (Hopwood et al. 2005), those relating to a change in the financial, administrative or political systems are rather absent in the dominant conception of the three pillars of sustainability. This elimination has contributed to the growth of a critique of the general discourse on sustainability: a discourse that would take place in 'unsustainable structures', and for this reason, it would be nothing more than a new device by which the neo-liberal ideology and economic practices continue to operate (Jacobsson 2019).

Given such a genealogy, the first impact of the sustainability discourse launched by the report in the world of the wine industry was ambivalent. On the one hand, considering that wine is largely a hedonistic product which can be tasted for intrinsic or social pleasure, the focus on the objective of satisfying essential human needs, on the rebalancing of relations with poor countries and on a development which must be sustainable in order to address the problem of the large number of people who live in absolute poverty has made the report's imperative strategies not easy or straightforward to apply to the world of wine. Yet, on the other hand, among the various industrial sectors called into question by the general issue of sustainability, the wine industry had already proven itself to be the most sensitive to what we can call ethical pressures. In fact, organic and biodynamic viticulture, for example, have made wine the most able to effectively address important issues such as limiting environmental degradation within both the industrial and agro-food sectors.

Still, this ambivalence has been strengthened in the 20 years following the mythologised report, especially since a series of official documents and resolutions published by the International Organisation of Vine and Wine (OIV) provided a specific yet significantly divergent definition of sustainable viticulture (OIV 2004), together with related guidelines (OIV 2008). Interestingly, compared to the Brundtland Report, the discourse created by the OIV puts the global issues of poverty into the background, bringing the care of essential needs back to various themes (such as solid waste, energy use and water management, air quality, wastewater, neighbouring land use etc.). Nevertheless, it draws more on the second discursive formation – that of the three pillars – by adding never previously considered immaterial topics such as heritage, history and culture. In this way, the foundations are laid for a discourse specifically committed to the wine field within which sustainable development determines a new field of competition.

Sustainability discourse as a competitive field

In order to understand the boundary lines generated by the sustainability discourse within the wine sector, we need to consider the first definition submitted by the OIV. In its 2004 resolution, sustainable viticulture is defined as a:

> Global strategy on the scale of the grape production and processing systems, incorporating at the same time the economic sustainability of structures and territories, producing quality products, considering requirements of precision in sustainable viticulture, risks to the environment, products safety and consumer health and valuing of heritage, historical, cultural, ecological, and landscape aspects.
>
> *(2004: 2)*

It is evident that the two discursive formations illustrated earlier have been translated into a comparatively long list of brand-new requirements. Understandably, given the heterogeneity of such requirements, responding to one of them potentially leads to not being in the position to fulfil other demands. In short, as with other agro-food fields (Constance et al. 2018), sustainability discourse engenders a lot of contradictions and contestations, in both the fields of production (Pullman et al.

2010; Szolnoki 2013; Signori *et al.* 2017) and consumption (Delmas and Grant 2014; Sogari *et al.* 2015; Pomarici and Vecchio 2019). Also, it is true in the distribution and sales sector, including that of alternative retailers where the actors are dealing with a 'norm-shaping work' with which they 'negotiate what is right and desirable' (Forssell and Lankoski 2018: 46).

Accordingly, as the result of such discursive formations, the sustainability concept in the field of wine is a highly normative idea in which competing interests between different needs and demands can be found. For example, while the political arena, drawing from time to time on one or another requirement, has increasingly taken up the term 'sustainability' to justify various actions (Ortega-Cerda 2005), the scientific discourse has been mostly addressed to only one specific pillar over the others (Christ and Burritt 2013; Sacchelli 2016). According to a recent study, 'international political actors primarily produce discourses on sustainable development in agriculture and on sustainable agricultural intensification. Scientists tend to emphasise issues of environmental management' (Janker *et al.* 2018: 1). Furthermore, between these two competitive positions there are discursive gaps 'that have the potential to hinder the systematic operationalisation of "sustainable agriculture", such as the integration of a social dimension of sustainable agriculture' (2018: 1).

The contradiction between these two sustainability discourses can be partly traced back to their underlying ethical perspectives: while the 1987 Brundtland Commission and other political organisations stand for an anthropocentric worldview, environmental scientists assign a similarly inherent value to the environment. Thus, while the international political discourse aims to achieve development politics and, therefore, focuses on economic growth and human rights, agrarians have largely developed farming systems in harmony with nature, so their products are not typically suitable for the global trade system addressed by political discourse as their products – starting with wine – would be quite diversified (Alonso 2010; Janker *et al.* 2018).

Finally, an even more specific area of contestation includes the discursive definitions of different winegrowing practices. The various documents published by the Food and Agriculture Organization of the United Nations (FAO) and the OIV assert that 'organic' (or 'biodynamic') and 'sustainable' are by no means synonymous. Indeed, to be sustainable, it is not necessary to be organic. Yet while various practices in viticulture – for example, organic and biodynamic winegrowing – have long intercepted some principles of what the Brundtland Report called 'sustainable' development, this sharing of some principles (for example, the defence of plants from diseases using only organic products) was put in place only for what concerns the management of the environment and, even in this case, matches only a small part of the environmental criteria suggested by the report (WCED 1987). As this difference has been maintained, if not increased, in the subsequent developments of the international discourse in agriculture and viticulture (OIV 2008; Christ and Burritt 2013), the development of the discourse on sustainability leads to the establishment of a new field of cultural competition between the meaning of 'sustainable', 'organic' and 'conventional' wine (Goode and Harrop 2011; Baird and Hall 2013; Preston-Wilsey 2015).

Ultimately, this means that a farm that operates only organic viticulture will not be able to obtain the label 'sustainable' while the label can apply to a farm with traditional viticulture that fulfils the norms of sustainability. All in all, this means that there are a series of devices (Foucault 2001) at work within the wine sustainability discourse, in the form of assessment reports (Higgins and Coffey 2016), guidelines, indicators (Ortega-Cerda 2005), certifications schemes and labelling procedures, that constitute precisely that work through which the sustainability discourse is materialised. Also, the scientific discourse on sustainability cooperates in structuring this space of differences when focusing on the analysis of the actions adopted by wineries, providing models that help classify wineries' orientation in terms of sustainability (Casini *et al.* 2010). Mostly, it happens through the detailed analysis of the so-called 'drivers and barriers of sustainability' (Santini *et al.* 2013; Mariani and Vastola 2015).

In the end, therefore, an actual field of cultural competition is generated between different certifications, evaluations and labelling procedures, which leads, eventually, to a competition between wine producers to win the best sustainability ranking (Flint and Golicic 2009; Zucca et al. 2009; Carmichael and Senese 2012; Gilinsky 2016). Winning this sort of competition means obtaining a symbolic prize, which is also assumed to have material effects. This 'price' is as desirable as a certain discursive translation of the concept of economic pillar is believed to be true: the belief that sustainability, as new form of *innovation*, is a successful lever in market competition(Nidumolu et al. 2009).

Certification (at) work

Although the question of food and wine sustainability is controversial and has even been contested (Constance et al. 2018; Sautier et al. 2018), the discourse that defines it as an 'imperative' issue (Janker et al. 2018) has become increasingly dominant, assuming hegemonic tones (Warde 2018; Pires Vieira da Rocha and Nodari 2020). Yet such definitions are, in fact, observable and materialise through specific application procedures. The empirical interpretation of sustainability – of its requirements and demands – sees various actors in the field, from supranational institutions to national and local ones (Moscovici and Reed 2018; Merli et al. 2018), from scientific researches to debates in wine companies (Mariani and Vastola 2015; Signori et al. 2017; Martins et al. 2018), from agencies that deal with drafting programs, guidelines or protocols to subjects that may constitute their targets (territories, companies and, finally, the wine or the single bottle labelled a 'sustainable' product).

Thus, the concept of frameworks (Flores 2018) is usually deployed to define the national or regional variants of these empirical applications on a first discursive level which connects the documents of supranational institutions with national or regional programs. Such frameworks, therefore, are nothing more than practical fallout of the discourse which, by framing some general meanings attributed to sustainability, transforms them into norms and rules to be followed in practice. Finally, the application of these rules is the subject of a complex work that takes place on successive levels, the last of which ends with the single bottle of wine placed on the market and available to consumers, eventually certified or labelled 'sustainable'.

In order to understand the role of these particular 'effects of truth' (Foucault 2001) produced by the sustainability discourse through the 'certification work', we can look at how they are described in a recent volume dedicated to natural and sustainable winegrowing:

> It's all very well for growers to claim that they are working sustainably, but if this is to mean anything to consumers, then some form of certification is needed. Without certification, anyone would be able to call himself or herself "sustainable," even if he or she weren't making the required changes to practices. With certification, there is a chance that winegrowers will reap some benefit if consumers become sufficiently aware of the issues that they are prepared to pay a premium for wine that has been grown and made in a sustainable, more natural way.
>
> *(Bergstrom 2011: 88)*

Here, the process of certification becomes 'boundary work' (Lamont and Molnar 2002) in which a system of classification is set, a situation emulated similarly to what has happened in the ranking classification of quality wines (Zhao 2005; Diaz-Bone 2013). Likewise, every certification scheme works establishing a particular set of indicators in order to measure the sustainability level and accordingly ranking every wine or winery (Pomarici et al. 2014; Moscovici and Reed 2018; Flores 2018). As illustrated in Table 35.1, where the main actual 'sustainability' certification schemes are listed, each of them works on the basis of different numbers and kinds of indicators, yet in each instance, these are exclusively considered the best tools to measure the sustainability level of

Table 35.1 Certification data by region and date established (adapted and updated from Moscovici and Reed 2018)

Name (Label)	Location	Year	Indicators	Ranking Thresholds
NZ Sustainable Winegrowing	New Zealand	1997	biodiversity, soil, air, water, energy, chemicals, by-products, people and business	• 62 benchmarks
Oregon LIVE	Oregon	1999	125 for wineries – 189 for vineyards	• Issues checklists
Lodi Rules	California	2005	101 standards across 6 management chapters: business, human resource, ecosystems, soil, water and pests	• at least 85% of the grapes used in the bottle • at least a 50% score per chapter and a minimum of 70% of total possible points over six chapters
Vignerons en Développement Durable	France	2007	4 fundamental pillars and 12 commitments	• a 1000 point scoring methodology based on the PDCA: "Plan, Do, Check, Act"
SIP (Sustainability in Practice)	California	2008	1000-point scale to assess Requirements and Management Enhancements	• 70% of total available points from Requirements and ME are required to attain certification
CCSW (Certified California Sustainable Winegrowing)	California	2010	32 for wineries – 50 for vineyards	• self-assessment practices on the basis of 15 chapters and 191 best management practices
IPW (Integrity and Sustainability)	South Africa	2010	27 criteria for vineyards – 31 criteria for wineries	• Farms must achieve a minimum of 162 out of 270 points • Wineries must achieve 93 points or more out of 155
Sustainable Australia Winegrowing	Australia	2011	soil health, pest management, biodiversity, water, waste, social relations and economic sustainability	• Blue (highest), Green, Yellow and, Red (lowest) (*No Pass or Fail*)
Wines of Chile – Sustainable	Chile	2011	**Green Area:** Vineyard. Includes own fields and long-term grape suppliers (2 years or more).	• Self-Assessment of Critical Points (PC) for each area • Each PC has a minimum passing score, highlighted in colour

Name (Label)	Location	Year	Indicators	Ranking Thresholds
			Red Area: Process. See the winery, bottling plant and other facilities related to wine production. **Orange Area:** Social. It applies to the company, including its fields, offices and facilities.	• the certification is obtained with 100% of the critical points
Long Island Sustainable Wine Growing	New York	2012	18 Core Criteria (contains at least 136 separate vineyard management issues)	• passing scores on all criteria
FAIR'N GREEN	Germany	2013	150 criteria	• businesses have to reach 50% of the points
VIVA Project EQUALITAS SQNP COSVI (Vineyard Sustainability Committee)	Italy	2011 2015 2016 2021	4 categories: air, water, vineyard and territory	• no minimum access criteria • a national law currently under discussion in parliament is examining the creation of a wine sustainability committee and the establishment of a single national standard certificate
Certified Sustainable Austria	Austria	2015	online tool with 343 activities including 2191 sustainability assessment criteria to achieve 61 quality objectives	• traffic light score with red (unsustainable) and green (sustainable)
Viticulture Durable en Champagne	France	2015	3 areas: Biodiversity footprint; Carbon footprint; Water footprint	• No ranking
Sustainable Winemaking Ontario	Ontario	2017	environmentally sound, economically feasible and socially sustainable practices	• voluntary and confidential self-assessment tool
Sustainable Wines of Great Britain	UK	2019	Vinegrowing and Winemaking guidelines	• Scoring from: "prohibited", "minimum standards", "best practices"

the particular wine or winery analysed. For example, the IPW scheme in South Africa requires a threshold of at least 93 points out of a total of 155 to assign the sustainability certificate to a winery; in the Australian case, on the other hand, based on indicators built on other criteria, a ranking by colour is developed that produces wines with different degrees of sustainability, from blue (highest) through green, yellow and red (lowest). Each of these certifications, in fact, involves meticulous work by wine producers, who must compile registers, answer questionnaires and monitor checklists. Through such practical – basically secretarial – work, depending on the results, 'sustainable wines' are matched against various thresholds of sustainability.

As a result, a multiplicity of rankings with highest and lowest sustainability wines is generated: while such devices are legitimised by the main sustainability discourses promoted by international political organisations and scientific discourses, the very same devices receive support back through generalised discourses of sustainability while also materialising it through empirical applications.

Yet, once again, since the sustainability certification is a work of norms production, it reproduces the contradictions and contestations that we have illustrated here. On the one hand, the production of certification schemes of wineries by public or private organisations based on 'objective' indicators gives such organisations 'the right to hold a sustainable discourse' (Ortega-Cerda 2005: 4), which, in turn, excludes others from asserting such a privilege. In other words, the sustainability schemes have the effect of legitimising new organisations and institutions in the wine field (Corbo 2014; Sautier et al. 2018). On the other hand, the work of certification contributes to creating new 'sustainability objects', both in the sense of fabricating new cultural objects in the shape of a plethora of top and bottom 'sustainable wines' or 'sustainable wineries' competing with each other and in the sense of creating another competitive field of 'sustainability knowledge' in the shape of new codebooks, guidelines and principles and an ongoing renewal of indicators to be applied within the ever-evolving schemes.

Conclusion

Although founded on sound concerns, such as climate change, the protection of the planet's environment and the necessity to guarantee the needs of future generations, the discourse on sustainability has created a space of differences designed to reproduce itself over time, with consequences that currently are not easy to identify. From a research perspective, an attempt in this direction can be made, considering that the symbolic power of certifications – and their constant reproduction – firstly establishes the difference between who is (or will be) capable and who is not (and will not be) able to be sustainable. Small farmers with a 'traditional' production system, for example, whose products were often considered better than the so-called 'industrial' ones, could lose their advantage to larger certified companies with more industrial features. Unlike the latter, the former may not have the economic, organisational and/or bureaucratic means or the ability to invest in technology necessary to fulfil the requirements that sustainability, translated into indicators, parameters and certifications, requires of them. Thus, it becomes clear that the objectives are as different as the interests of the discourse stakeholders. Yet, while such contradictions can be interpreted as a manifestation of power asymmetries between the global North and the global South (Janker et al. 2018: 12), a major consequence of such heterogeneity of brokers and positions is the structural paradox between, on the one side, the practical necessity of a local differentiation of standards of sustainability measurement and, on the other side, the institutional requirement of a standardised global scheme of sustainability.

This issue points towards another, perhaps even more significant, at least in terms of cultural research. As we have seen, the certification work ultimately consists of measuring the degree of sustainability of a wine company, a measurement that is made both by means of parameters and indicators and on the overall ability of the company to generate a process of continuous improvement. Measurements of this kind therefore require two main activities. On the one hand, they require a control in the form of continuous and periodic monitoring carried out by institutions or agencies legitimated as competent, the so-called 'certifiers'. On the other hand, they require the data on which the measurements and control of the parameters are carried out. Here, it is important to note that the data relating to sustainability parameters must be produced by farms and wineries, which are thus increasingly involved in administrative activities (data collection, compilation of forms and registers, drafting of reports etc.). Does this mean that the bureaucratic nature and administrative pressure, already dominant in various areas, will transform the daily life and culture of the wineries of the future? All in all, while the transition towards sustainability by itself does not intend to support such a transformation, it does seem to be already underway throughout the 'certification work'. In fact, the sustainability discourse, as long as it is framed as a development process – that is, a process of societal transitions towards better conditions – it is automatically a normative process. As a consequence, the meaning of sustainable viticulture and its products constantly remains in question and in need of clarification: in other words, defining what can be called 'sustainable wine' is an ongoing accomplishment, a competitive discursive field.

In addition to deepening global developments of the new field of cultural competition, of which we have illustrated the principles in this chapter, research on how companies are reacting to the exponential rise in administrative work is needed to understand how and to what extent the culture of sustainability will change the practices of wine growing and winemaking.

References

Alonso, A.D. (2010) "How 'Green' Are the Small Wineries? Western Australia's Case," *British Food Journal* 112(2), 155–170.
Baird, T. and Hall, C.M. (2013) "Sustainable Winegrowing in New Zealand," in C.M. Hall and S. Gössling (eds), *Sustainable Culinary Systems. Local Foods, Innovation, Tourism and Hospitality*, New York: Routledge, 223–240.
Barthes, R. (2009) *Mythologies*, London: Random House.
Bergstrom, J. (2011) "Sustainable Winegrowing," in J. Goode and S. Harrop (eds), *Authentic Wine: Toward Natural and Sustainable Winemaking*, Berkeley: University of California Press.
Borowy, I. (2014) *Defining Sustainable Development for Our Common Future. A History of the World Commission on Environment and Development (Brundtland Commission)*, London: Routledge.
Carmichael, B.A. and Senese, D.M. (2012) "Competitiveness and Sustainability in Wine Tourism Regions: The Application of a Stage Model of Destination Development to Two Canadian Wine Regions," in P.H. Dougherty (ed), *The Geography of Wine: Regions, Terroir and Techniques*, New York: Springer, 159–178.
Casini, L., Corsi, A., Cavicchi, A. and Santini, C. (2010) "Hopelessly Devoted to Sustainability: Marketing Challenges to Face in the Wine Business," Proceedings of the 119th EAAE Seminar 'Sustainability in the Food Sector: Rethinking the Relationship between the Agro-Food System and the Natural, Social, Economic and Institutional Environments, Capri, Italy, 30 June–2 July.
Christ, K.L. and Burritt, R.L. (2013) "Critical Environmental Concerns in Wine Production: An Integrative Review," *Journal of Cleaner Production* 53, 232–242.
Constance, D.H., Konefal, J.T. and Hatanaka, M. (eds) (2018) *Contested Sustainability Discourses in the Agrifood System*, London: Routledge.
Corbo, C., Lamastra, L. and Capri, E. (2014) "From Environmental to Sustainability Programs: A Review of Sustainability Initiatives in the Italian Wine Sector," *Sustainability* 6, 2133–2159.
Delmas, M.A. and Grant, L.E. (2014) "Eco-Labeling Strategies and Price-Premium: The Wine Industry Puzzle," *Business & Society* 53(1), 6–44.
Diaz-Bone, R. (2013) "Discourse Conventions in the Construction of Wine Qualities in the Wine Market," *Economic Sociology the European Electronic Newsletter*, Max Planck Institute for the Study of Societies 14(2), 46–53.
Flint, D. and Golicic, S. (2009) "Searching for Competitive Advantage Through Sustainability: A Qualitative Study in the New Zealand Wine Industry," *International Journal of Physical Distribution & Logistics Management* 39(10), 841–860.
Flores, S.S. (2015) *Vitivinicultura sustentavel no contexto do Brasil: uma proposta de abordagem*, PhD dissertation, Universidade Federal do Rio Grande do Sul, Porto Alegre, Brazil, e Universite de Bourgogne, Dijon, France.

Flores, S.S. (2018) "What is Sustainability in the Wine World? A Cross-Country Analysis of Wine Sustainability Frameworks," *Journal of Cleaner Production* 172, 2301–2312.

Forssell, S. and Lankoski, L. (2018) "Shaping Norms. A Convention Theoretical Examination of Alternative Food Retailers as Food Sustainability Transition Actors," *Journal of Rural Studies* 63, 46–56.

Foucault, M. (2001) *The Order of Things: An Archaeology of the Human Sciences*, London: Routledge.

Gilinsky, A., Newtona, S.K. and Vegab, R.F. (2016) "Sustainability in the Global Wine Industry: Concepts and Cases," *Agriculture and Agricultural Science Procedia* 8, 37–49.

Goode, J. and Harrop, S. (2011) *Authentic Wine: Toward Natural and Sustainable Winemaking*, Berkeley: University of California Press.

Higgins, C. and Coffey, B. (2016) "Improving How Sustainability Reports Drive Change: A Critical Discourse Analysis," *Journal of Cleaner Production* 136, 18–29.

Hopwood, B., Mellor, M. and O'Brien, G. (2005) "Sustainable Development: Mapping Different Approaches," *Journal of Sustainable Development* 13, 38–52.

Jacobsson, D. (2019) "In the Name of (Un)Sustainability: A Critical Analysis of How Neoliberal Ideology Operates Through Discourses About Sustainable Progress and Equality," *tripleC* 17(1), 19–37.

Janker, J., Mann, S. and Rist, S. (2018) "What is Sustainable Agriculture? Critical Analysis of the International Political Discourse," *Sustainability* 10(12), 4707–4726.

Lamont, M. and Molnar, V. (2002) "The Study of Boundaries in the Social Sciences," *Annual Review of Sociology* 28, 167–195.

Mariani, A. and Vastola, A. (2015) "Sustainable Winegrowing: Current Perspectives," *International Journal of Wine Research* 7, 37–48.

Martins, A.A., Araújo, A.R., Graça, A., Caetano, N.S. and Mata, T.M. (2018) "Towards Sustainable Wine: Comparison of Two Portuguese Wines," *Journal of Cleaner Production* 183, 662–676.

Merli, R., Preziosi, M. and Acampora, A. (2018) "Sustainability Experiences in the Wine Sector: Towards the Development of an International Indicators System," *Journal of Cleaner Production* 172(20), 3791–3805.

Moscovici, D. and Reed, A. (2018) "Comparing Wine Sustainability Certifications Around the World: History, Status and Opportunity," *Journal of Wine Research* 29(1), 1–25.

Nidumolu, R., Prahalad, C.K. and Rangaswami, M.R. (2009) "Why Sustainability is Now the Key Driver of Innovation," *Harvard Business Review* 87(9), 56–64.

OIV. (2004) "Resolution CST 1/2004," www.oiv.org/public/medias/2074/cst-1-2004-en.pdf, accessed 16 August 2020.

OIV. (2008) "Resolution CST 1/2008. Guidelines for Sustainable Vitiviniculture: Production, Processing and Packaging of Products," www.oiv.int/public/medias/2088/cst-1-2008-fr.pdf, accessed 16 August 2020.

Ortega-Cerda, M. (2005) *Sustainability Indicators as Discursive Elements. 6th International Conference of the European Society for Ecological Economics*, Lisbon, 14–17 June, https://ent.cat/sustainability-indicators-as-discursive-elements/?lang=en, accessed 3 August 2020.

Pires Vieira da Rocha, C. and Nodari, E. (2020) "Winemaking, Environmental Impacts and Sustainability: New Pathways from Vineyard to Glass?" *Historia Ambiental Latinoamericana y Caribeña* 10(1), 223–243.

Pomarici, E. and Vecchio, R. (2019) "Will Sustainability Shape the Future Wine Market?" *Wine Economics and Policy* 8(1), 1–4.

Pomarici, E., Vecchio, R. and Verneau, F. (2014) "A Future of Sustainable Wine? A Reasoned Review and Discussion of Ongoing Programs Around the World," *Quality – Access to Success* 15(S1), 123–128.

Preston-Wilsey, L. (2015) *Toward a Sustainable Wine Industry: Green Enology Research*, Boca Raton, FL: CRC Press.

Pullman, M.E., Maloni, M.J. and Dillard, J. (2010) "Sustainability Practices in Food Supply Chains: How is Wine Different?" *Journal of Wine Research* 21(1), 35–56.

Sacchelli, S., Fabbrizzi, S. and Menghini, S. (2016) "Climate Change, Wine and Sustainability: A Quantitative Discourse Analysis of the International Scientific Literature," *Agriculture and Agricultural Science Procedia* 8, 167–175.

Santini, C., Cavicchi, A. and Casini, L. (2013) "Sustainability in the Wine Industry: Key Questions and Research Trends," *Agricultural and Food Economics* 1(9), 1–14.

Sautier, M., Legun, K.A., Rosin, C. and Campbell, H. (2018) "Sustainability: A Tool for Governing Wine Production in New Zealand?" *Journal of Cleaner Production* 179, 347–356.

Signori, P., Flint, D.J. and Golicic, S.L. (2017) "Constrained Innovation on Sustainability in the Global Wine Industry," *Journal of Wine Research* 28(2), 71–90.

Sogari, G., Corbo, C., Macconi, M., Menozzi, D. and Mora, C. (2015) "Consumer Attitude Towards Sustainable-Labelled Wine: An Exploratory Approach," *International Journal of Wine Business Research* 27, 312–328.

Szolnoki, G. (2013) "A Cross-National Comparison of Sustainability in the Wine Industry," *Journal of Cleaner Production* 53, 243–251.
Warde, P. (2011) "The Invention of Sustainability," *Modern Intellectual History* 8(1), 153–170.
Warde, P. (2018) *The Invention of Sustainability: Nature and Destiny, c. 1500–1870*, Cambridge: Cambridge University Press.
WCED. (1987) *Our Common Future*, Oxford: Oxford University Press.
Zhao, W. (2005) "Understanding Classifications: Empirical Evidence from the American and French Wine Industries," *Poetics* 33(3–4), 179–200.
Zucca, G., Smith, D.E. and Mitry, D.J. (2009) "Sustainable Viticulture and Winery Practices in California: What Is It, and Do Customers Care?" *International Journal of Wine Research* 2, 189–194.

36
THE TRIUMPH OF THE HOLY TRINITY

Terroir, typicity and quality anchoring the AOC model in the second half of the twentieth century

Olivier Jacquet

Introduction

Despite criticism and competition, the French *Appellations d'Origine Contrôlée* (AOC) model, widely imitated by Italy, Spain and, more recently, Brazil (Tonietto and Falcade 2018), remains a real economic success (Mérel *et al*. 2020). This success, however, cannot be separated from its meaning and cultural value. Tasters around the world have adopted this 'French idea' (Parker 2017). They enthuse about the organoleptic characteristics conferred by this or that terroir, and they celebrate the complexity of a Grand Cru and the flavours it possesses compared to those of the neighbouring plot. Their identification of the geographical expression of the typicity of each AOC and their gustatory familiarisation with the subtle hierarchies inscribed in the territories are all cultural concepts internalised by many oenophiles and consumers. This internalised relationship between AOC, terroir and quality derives firstly from a consistent policy throughout the implementation of AOCs of considering the physical elements of the terroir and its links to the grape variety as the main determinant of the quality of the wines. This discourse, more and more prevalent during the judgements delimiting the appellation boundaries from the end of the 1920s onwards, became the norm after the 1935 AOC law, when the experts consulted on the delimitations were essentially geologists and agronomists (Humbert 2018). Secondly and contemporaneously, the long-term consecration of geographers as privileged narrators of French wine culture (Dutton 2019) and their role in the discourse on the 'human' origin of the reputation of terroirs also established the idea that AOC areas derive their quality not just from their land but also from their human history (Schirmer 2011). However, recent research has underlined other explanations for the triumph of the AOCs. For example, Joseph Bohling explains the role of macroeconomic, social and political factors during the years 1960 through1970 (Bohling 2018). But other underlying and yet essential factors are at work. Thus, this chapter seeks to show that during this period, a range of normative, scientific, technical and cultural processes were equally decisive in the development of the AOC wine model.

In 1945, France already had 187 wine AOCs. Most of them owed their origin to a succession of regulations promulgated between the beginning of the twentieth century (Wolikow 2018: 121–134) and the decree law of 30 July 1935 founding the AOCs. However, these delimited and controlled wines were not necessarily recognised as quality products. For the consumer at the end of the 1940s, an appellation wine (i.e. from a delimited terroir) was by no means synonymous with a great wine.

The taste of terroir remained pejoratively associated with a rustic flavour, as it had been at the end of the nineteenth century (Parker 2017). This belief, which was deeply culturally rooted, was translated economically into a very limited take-up of AOC wines which, in the 1960s, only represented on average 8% of French consumption, with branded and table wine constituting the majority of national consumption (Jacquet 2018). Although more positive, export figures also remained quite low. In the 1960–61 fiscal year, AOC wines still represented only 25% of French wine exports.

The cultural valorisation of AOC wines and the promotion of a positive conception of wine terroir mainly took place during the period known as the 'Trente Glorieuses', which ran from 1945 to the middle of the 1970s. A regulatory process, initially dictated by economic considerations but supported by a new emphasis on taste, consolidated a new conception of wine based on a quality-driven vision of AOC wines. This positive image derived from three main elements: the regulatory consecration of hierarchies, the definition of a scientific framework of terroir accompanying its intellectual rehabilitation, and a collective process of development and characterisation of the quality of the products.

Towards a hierarchical AOC vineyard

Wine hierarchies within a given territory existed long before the AOCs (Garcia and Labbé 2011: 345–372, 2019). Many examples can be found in descriptive literature of the eighteenth and nineteenth centuries (Lavalle 1855), and André Jullien's *Topographie de tous les vignobles connus*, first published in 1816, is a perfect illustration of this (Lavalle 1855). In Bordeaux and Burgundy, such hierarchies became official during the nineteenth century and were transcribed, respectively, in the classification of Grands Crus Classés du Médoc et du Sauternes of 1855 (Markham 1997) and in the 'plan of 1860' developed by the Comité d'Agriculture de Beaune et de Viticulture de la Côte-d'Or (Jacquet 2007: 85–96). However, these classifications, although recognised, had no regulatory value in terms of appellations. A classified château in the Bordeaux region was part of a collective appellation – Pauillac or Saint-Julien, for example – but its reputation was linked to the private domain. The same was true in Burgundy where, if one spoke of Grand Crus to identify a Montrachet or a Corton, the delimited area remained 'horizontal', and the pyramid that has now become the norm had no official reality. Indeed, at the beginning of the twentieth century, the *négociants* produced the wine and, crucially, had a monopoly on blending, maturing and sales. (The winegrower just provided the grapes, the must or sometimes the wines.) For the *négociant*, there was no strict geographical distinction between the crus. A Gevrey-Chambertin could be made with grapes from the Gevrey but also with grapes from neighbouring communes, provided that each year, it corresponded to a standard taste for a brand. Later, with the laws on AOCs, this was no longer possible, and the strict geographical separation between the crus and villages led to a vertical vision of the vineyard and the wines. But neither the law of 6 May 1919 on appellations of origin nor the decree-law of 30 July 1935 on AOCs provided for specific hierarchies. Regardless of whether some vineyards had better reputations and more expensive wines than others, they did not officially have a different classification. In other words, in law, Romanée-Conti was not superior to a 'village' designation. The hierarchical system of AOCs was only effectively established for the first time in the very particular economic context of the Second World War.

Standardising the hierarchies

The Second World War provided a unique context for standardising the hierarchies proposed by the emerging AOCs. During the Second World War, French people lived under a controlled economy. The prices of goods were fixed by the public authorities while, at the same time, certain production facilities (for wine and food products, for example) which had been captured by the German occupiers were assigned to supply the armed forces and the population (Lucand 2017). Due to shortages and a growing demand from the Germans, successive regulations brought more and more AOC wines into this tax system.

From then on, to avoid receiving only the lowest level price set by the authorities and also what was termed 'taxation', the vineyards producing the wines most in demand by the occupying forces decided to take action. They very quickly asserted that the high quality of some of their vintages justified their receiving a higher price. Thus, by 1942, certain wines had been excluded from the official supply chain, such as the great Bordeaux châteaux from the 1855 classification, which initially, despite their prestige and price, were logically assigned to the sub-regional Bordeaux AOCs and received the 'standard' price. Champagne also benefited from this exemption (Lucand 2017). On 4 April of the same year, a list of Bordeaux wines drawn up by wine merchants was presented to the National Committee of Appellations of Origin (CNAO). This listed by price the Bordeaux wines that should benefit from a more advantageous taxation due to their reputation. It was largely based on the 1855 classification but also included a series of properties not classified but identified as being of similar quality and generally sold at prices equivalent to those of the 1855 crus. More than 170 wines were included. The list of these wines, published in the decree of 14 October 1943, focused on the 1855 crus but also included many sweet wines from Sauternes and outlying areas such as Saint-Croix-du Mont, Cérons, Loupiac and Monbazillac, as well as several Saint-Emilion and 32 Pomerol (Humbert 2011).

On 9 February 1943, this system of price control was extended to all AOCs, and it became urgent for some owners to free themselves from this unattractive position. The National Committee then became responsible for 'establishing the classification of the great growths of Bordeaux and Burgundy which must themselves be taxed' (Humbert 2011: 541). In Burgundy, the response was similarly organised. In order to escape the minimum price level trap, the first growths were 'invented'. Since the commission defining this list accepted that the nineteenth-century classifications had evolved, it focused, above all, on the selling prices of these 'first growth' wines.

Finally, on 14 October 1943, the *Journal Officiel* published the list of the premiers crus and grands crus of Burgundy, as well as the list of the crus and châteaux of Bordeaux that could escape the official minimum price, and officially established, for the first time, a legal hierarchy of AOCs. These provisions, of purely economic origin, profoundly changed the landscape and established a new cultural perception of appellations by setting in stone the principle of wine hierarchies. But, from a cultural point of view, their formalisation also derived from the political context of the period. These hierarchies were established thanks to the Vichy regime and its preponderant Ministry of Agriculture, which was very close to the CNAO. This recognition of the elites resonated completely with the principles of the National Revolution defined on 11 October 1940 by Philippe Pétain, which 'consist[ed] in reaffirming the "social hierarchy" according to the "aptitude to serve", in order to revive "the true elites"' (Vigreux 2012, 2018).

Establishing a standard

Pandora's box was now open, and other vineyards rushed to participate in the new system of classification. Such was the case with the definition of the Crus classés of Provence in April 1943 (Moustier 2018). After the war, the movement was amplified. Saint-Emilion obtained its classification in 1955 and 1958 and Graves in 1953 (completed in 1959). The classification of the Crus classés of Saint-Emilion was determined by professional tasting. On the other hand, the selection of wines to be classified as Saint-Emilion Premier Grand Cru Classé (INAO 1954: 451), as well as the entire list of Graves wines, was based on a procedure similar to the one adopted during the Occupation to establish the hierarchy of the premiers crus of Burgundy. The list of designated crus was essentially based 'on the prices of wines on the markets over a long period of time' (INAO 1953: 287). Finally, in a less precise and less systematic way, other areas imposed a hierarchical system. In 1955, the winegrowers of Brouilly wanted to be able to add the name of a *climat* of origin or the term 'premier cru' to certain Côte de Brouilly wines with a minimum alcohol content of 11 degrees. The same year, the AOC Coteaux du Layon, recognised in 1947, formalised its own hierarchy by establishing seven communal appellations, such as, for example, the AOC Coteaux du Layon Saint-Lambert du Lattay. The same principle was followed in the Rhone Valley with the promotion of a whole series of communes explicitly associated with the Côtes du Rhône appellation, such as Côtes du Rhône Gigondas (1951) and Côtes du Rhône Vacqueyras (1955). The objective of this process of developing areas by differentiating them from the regional AOC was to create a pyramid system, a principle that was also taken up by the Alsatian winegrowers with the recognition of their grands crus in 1975.

The establishment of hierarchies within the vineyards was not without consequences. On the one hand, the idea was established that, apart from wines for everyday consumption, each social group could find its place as a consumer in the AOC sphere and thus exploit to the full the mechanisms of social distinction (Bourdieu 1979). On the other hand, a new way of apprehending wines and the terroirs from which they were made began to take shape. No delimited space is equivalent to another, and each one therefore has, for the taster, a different value, a socially and economically efficient reputation (Chauvin 2010). The positive remobilisation of the notion of terroir from the 1960s onwards reinforced this idea of the existence of places that are characterised by and dedicated to the elaboration of great wines.

The winegrowing terroir as a political and administrative space

Ideological vicissitudes of the terroir concept

Under the Vichy regime, the discourse on terroir aimed at justifying a nationalist, racist and elitist political ideology. 'L'enseignement du terroir' (Faure 1989) valued the terroir as the guarantor of a supposed immutability of the French race, of a return, through folklore but also through agriculture, to the traditions and moral values carried in the countryside by the peasantry. It served the 'myth of national identity' (Meyran 2009), and therefore, like the ground itself, it asserted that the terroir cannot lie.

This transcendental ideology around the terroir pre-existed Vichy. We find traces of it in the nineteenth-century literature by agronomists (Yengue and Stengel 2020; Parker 2017). At the end of the nineteenth century and the beginning of the twentieth, it was essentially part of a literary current of reasserting folklore (Laferté 2006), peasant traditions and the 'immutable order of the fields' (Roupnel 1932), a current that was in complete harmony with Vichyist thought. Without necessarily possessing the same reactionary political sense, this vision of terroir successfully infiltrated the domain of vine and wine. Surprisingly, however, the study of the first delimited areas during the inter-war period shows that the process of defining production areas remained far removed from the ambient agrarian and 'terroirist' discourse. Often it took second place to other criteria such as grape variety or economic considerations. Whether as an instrument of negotiation, an argument of legitimacy and/or a backdrop of territorialised social tensions between professional unions, merchants, cooperators, state agents (from 1935 onwards) and scientists, the definition of good terroir fluctuated according to changing economic, administrative and legal interests (Jacquet 2009).

During the 1950s, the 'Vichy Syndrome' (Rousso 1987) diminished for some time the return of a 'terroirist' discourse in France, especially in the worlds of vines and wine. However, the remobilisation of terroir in the 1960s brought this concept once again to the forefront and finally identified it fully and positively with the AOCs (Garcia and Jacquet 2020: 43–69). Indeed, the positive relationship between quality and terroir stems, particularly in France, from a political will for official certification that was developed and consecrated during the twentieth century (Valceschini and

Torre 2002). In this context of remobilisation and rehabilitation, the National Institute of Appellations of Origin (INAO) became the main architect of the concept of terroir, helped by a revival of agronomic sciences.

The INAO, agronomic expertise and soil science: the return of 'good' terroir

After the war and under pressure from critics who accused it of accepting too many unknown appellations or, conversely, of refusing to protect quality wines with a local reputation, the INAO undertook to set up a standardised framework and, by doing so, to better define the notion of origin (CNAO 1946). As illustrated by the lists of experts consulted by the INAO, these specialists were sometimes oenologists, but principally geologists and agronomists. This last discipline was at that time considered to encompass many skills: study of plant material, cultivation processes, climate, oenology (the agronomist is also a chemist), geography and soils. According to the definition given in 1974 by M. Sébillotte, agronomy is

> the study of the relations between a cultivated plant cover and the conditions of its environment resulting from the states of the physical (soil and climate) and biological (flora, fauna, parasites) environment transformed by human action, with the aim of establishing the laws of functioning of this plant cover.
>
> *(Sébillotte 1974: 3–25)*

This agricultural multi-disciplinarity positioned these agronomists as experts capable of overseeing all elements involved in the AOC concept. For example, Jean Bordas, a regular expert for the INAO and director of the Avignon Agronomic Station began his career as a fraud control chemist, yet his work attests to his close relationship with the pedological (or soil science) side of agronomy. His 'Essai d'agronomie méditerranéenne' (Bordas 1946) was prefaced by one of the founders of French pedology: Albert Demolon (Boulaine 1997: 141–151). These worlds are intertwined, all the more so because of the bridges built in the end of the nineteenth century between agronomy and pedology, which were further developed after the Second World War (Boulaine 1992). Moreover, geologists regularly came to support them in the vineyards.

The influence of these disciplines on the definition of AOC designations appeared to be decisive in the evolution of methodological discourse. Thus, in Alsace in 1959, the expert committee in charge of the delimitation of the regional AOC emphasised that technical and historical practices ('usages' in the French law), which had been approved nine years earlier, were not sufficient to qualify for appellation status. They especially emphasised the 'geological factors of the soil, microclimatic and even climatic factors' (Boch 1959: 238). The example of the complicated delimitation of the Chablis appellation area confirms this 'terroirist' orientation in progress. Since the 1920s, a number of producer groups had been fighting in the courts. Some of them wanted to reduce as much as possible the appellation area to the 'Kimmeridgian' subsoils while others wanted to extend the perimeter of the appellation to the very similar geological areas of the 'Portlandien à facies kimmeridgien'. However, from the 1940s to the 1970s, geological data really became the main element in this debate, now arbitrated by the INAO. The other criteria applied during the delimitations, such as historical or economic uses, for example, were no longer considered at all. Terroir had become a mainly agronomic and geological concept.

The 1960s and the development of standardised delimitation expertise

This epistemological change in the scientific approach to terroir, under the then-predominant influence of French pedology represented, in particular, by Albert Demolon and his principles of soil characterisation, strongly attached AOCs to their terroir of origin (Cornu *et al.* 2018: 53). Thus, the agronomist, a key scientist in the process of delimitation during the 'Trente Glorieuses', was the artisan who shaped the labelled territories and consecrated terroirs as legitimate. It is, therefore, hardly surprising that the first major conceptualisation of the link between origin and quality came at the beginning of the 1960s in the writings of an agricultural engineer, Georges Kuhnholtz-Lordat, professor of botany at the Ecole Nationale d'Agriculture de Montpellier and the appointed expert for numerous AOC delimitations affecting south and southwest France. In 1963, he published a book titled *La Genèse des Appellations d'origine des Vins* (The genesis of the appellations of origin of wines) (Kuhnholtz-Lordat 1963). The then-president of the INAO, Pierre Le Roy, who wrote the preface of the book, was emphatic that Kuhnholtz-Lordat's (1963) book would become a true *Vademecum*, an essential text for those wishing to be appointed as experts by the INAO (Schirmer 2011: 91–92). In summary, Georges Kuhnholtz-Lordat argued that there are elite nuclei, the hearts of appellations, and that increasing distance from such nuclei would lead to a decline in the quality of the wines. He gave several examples, such as Cognac, Côte de Duras and Pécharmant. His analysis, which was based on experience and undoubtedly shared with other experts over several years, in particular the omnipresent agronomists, remained very agronomic. Soils and subsoils explained and shaped these landscape hierarchies, even though Kuhnholtz-Lordat remained very much influenced by Vidalian human geography (Schirmer 2011: 92): i.e. a geography highlighting the physical specificities (soils, climates etc.) of the regions and their influence on people and their practices.

As a result, Kuhnholtz-Lordat proposed a general method to better standardise the principles of delimitation and to try to link origin and quality as closely as possible. His work also provided a solid analytical framework for the movement towards a hierarchy of terroirs that had begun during the war and, as we have seen, continued with the establishment of numerous communal appellations or classifications during the 1950s and 1960s. Finally, this work was positioned as an instrument of 'legitimisation and reaffirmation of the specificity of the AOC system' (Humbert 2018), particularly in the context of the ongoing construction of Common Market regulations in which the French system, despite its international aura, was felt to risk losing part of its soul.

This work, published in 1963, set a scientific precedent and took a decisive place in the doctrines of the INAO, particularly in the 20 years or so following the publication of the work (Humbert 2018). Kuhnholtz-Lordat's study sometimes even gave rise to reinterpretation, validating, in the 1980s and 1990s, the ideology of the primacy of 'natural' terroir among many professionals. Laurence Bérard and Philippe Marchenay even speak of a shift from an elite core to a 'hard core' of wine identity: i.e. a 'boundary delimited by its physical characteristics and, for this reason, immutable' (1995: 153–164).

In any case, the terroirs, their classification, their hierarchical distinctions and their intrinsic influence on the quality of AOC products were concepts that completely imposed themselves on the wine-consuming public in the 1970s and 1980s. Moreover, this model was imposed in a general cultural, economic and political context of revitalisation of the concept (Garcia and Jacquet 2020). First of all, after 1968, there was a desire to return to nature, to revalorise agricultural work and heritage, expressed as a return to the roots (Léger and Hervieu 1979; Rouvière 2015). This process often went hand in hand with the growing appeal of ecology, a trend which began in the late 1960s and has continued to develop to the present day. The pioneering spirit of the 1970s corresponded more generally to the emergence of a new ecological political discourse. In the vineyards, this movement was largely imbued with an ideology of enhancing the value of local products thought to be more 'natural'. Thus, the link to origin and place propounded by the INAO appears to have been a decisive element in the recognition of AOC wines, and fine wines in particular.

In order to be fully recognised as quality products, these AOC wines, now hierarchically ranked and derived from unique and recognised terroirs, were validated by their organoleptic characteristics. This technical and sensory quality definition process was created during the 'Trente Glorieuses'.

The triumph of the 'good' taste of terroir

The crucial issue of quality for AOC wines

The issue of the quality of delimited wines, as we have seen, remained largely in abeyance during the inter-war period. With the implementation of the technically more restrictive system of AOCs in 1935, hopes were high for a profession whose members agreed to comply with these constraints to save an industry threatened by sluggish sales, fraud and unfair competition. But to guarantee good wine, it was not enough simply to adhere to the specifications of the 1935 AOC Decree Law, which detailed maximum yields per hectare, minimum alcohol level, grape varieties from recognised terroirs and sometimes cultivation and vinification practices. Fraud or catastrophic vinification could discredit any wine of origin. In this respect, the development of sales at the property, made possible by the development of AOCs, propelled many winegrowers into the world of winemaking, maturing and bottling, activities previously devolved mostly to *négociants*. However, these new requirements demanded technical skills that many winemakers did not necessarily possess. Moreover, with the war, shortages and black market trade, there was a resurgence of bad practices, frauds and the sale of wines from sometimes undrinkable appellations. It was this painful situation that, on 20 October 1943, during a meeting of the steering board of the National Committee of Appellations of Origin (CNAO), led the president of the institution, Joseph Capus, to propose an addition to Article 23 of the AOC Decree Law of 30 July 1935. He wished to add the following text as a condition to the right to the appellation: 'providing it [the wine promoted to the AOC] presents the substantial qualities characteristic of appellation wines'. This amendment explicitly aimed at introducing tasting into the quality control of AOC wines and, at the same time, ensuring a minimum quality of production. This addendum to the 1935 Decree Law was not immediately ratified by the INAO supervisory ministry, and it was not until the European decree of 19 October 1974 that this principle became mandatory. In the meantime, on a voluntary basis, a double process was organised in many vineyards to take these new principles into account. On the one hand, we can see the establishment of professional and technical networks aimed at improving work in the vineyard and in the cellar and, on the other hand, the progressive development in almost all the AOC regions of a systematic approval of wines through tasting.

The dissemination of new techniques to enhance the quality of wines

Very quickly, the producers and the INAO, supported by new organisations, such as the Technical Institute of Wine and INRA, and oenology faculties and research centres began a process to improve the quality of AOC wines. The aim was to impose technical protocols on producers, based on scientific and oenological knowledge that was fully recognised by the academic world. (The National Diploma of Oenology dates back to 1955.) From then on, each vineyard undertook to improve its winemaking. Pushed by INAO agents, Beaujolais inaugurated, for example, the first systematic and reliable controls of grape and must maturity, essential for making balanced wines. Volatile acidity, which in large doses can give wine acetic aromas and tastes, even nail polish or acetone, also became a highly controlled element (Jacquet 2021). Almost everywhere, the cellars became cleaner, and winemaking courses were opened up to winegrowers. They were taught how to reduce oxidation phenomena, manage fermentation temperatures, carry out malolactic fermentation (Peynaud 1995) and control racking, fining, maturing etc. (Jacquet 2021). In short, the objective was to produce consistently better wines regardless of the sometimes complicated variability of the vintages.

The invention of modern tasting: typicity as an asset for terroir wines

In addition to this technical monitoring, there has been unprecedented development of tasting control practices, an operation carried out by the producers' unions and the INAO. From the 1950s onwards, numerous professional organisations were involved in this process, and all wines had to undergo a tasting session to assess their distinctive quality in line with the standards of their AOC before being labelled and put on sale. This organoleptic analysis was also used in a pioneering way in classifications such as Saint-Emilion (INAO 1948: 9) and in the context of problematic delimitations such as Chablis (Vincent and Jacquet 2015: 91–103) in 1947 and Beaujolais in 1949. Each time, the specific character of each terroir of the wines presented had to be verified.

Despite this progress, the vocabulary used during these tastings – either to verify the qualities of the AOC wines sold or to establish a delimitation – remained very summary and lacked precision and consistency. Due to the highly varied character of the French AOC wines, the tasters – trade unionists, brokers or technical agents of the INAO – struggled to define the typical characteristics of the wines with much precision, the difficulties exacerbated by the fact that, at that time, the exercise was neither regulated nor standardised. From one vineyard to another, from one tasting to another, the criteria used and assessments made lacked homogeneity.

In reality, the analyses made available to these experts continued to be characterised by pre-war tasting methods initiated in the nineteenth century and consisted of a rather limited vocabulary (Shapin 2012: 49–94) which was essentially based on mouthfeel. Before the development of appellations of origin, what counted for a marketable wine was not the specificity given by its geographical origin, by its terroir. The focus was instead on the 'loyal' (i.e. conforming to type) and commercial character of a wine, then resulting from various blends, an entirely accepted and legal process at that time. It was then mainly a question of adapting the taste of the wines to the clientele. The process used to test this quality mainly gave rise to descriptions linked to the mouthfeel of the wines.

The terms used just after the Second World War, therefore, did not allow for a characterisation of typicity. The vocabulary was simply no longer appropriate to the AOC paradigm. The historian Steven Shapin (2012: 49–94) explains very precisely the evolution of the successive changes of tasting vocabulary with reference to the changes over time of the social status of wine and consumers. In addition to these aspects, however, it is also essential to note the decisive role of regulatory anchoring processes as drivers of innovation. This is shown by the exhaustive study of the archives of the INAO, the winegrowers' trade unions and the various scientific entities working in this field in France. Though English-language scholars and practitioners, led by the University of Davis, were contemporaneously developing standardised forms of tasting to expand the wine trade, the modern renovation of tasting vocabulary was initially the work of the INAO and its professional and academic networks. For the Institute, it was a question of standardising tasting and broadening its vocabulary, particularly in terms of smells and aromas (Jacquet 2018). The objective, which was vital for the profession, was to create the tools to define, wine by wine, what this same institution was later to call 'the link to the terroir'. Building on the work of *négociant* and scientist Jules Chauvet (Jacquet 2014: 261–270) and his technical agents, the INAO developed new frameworks for tasting. Giving priority to the bouquet and aromas, these principles called upon collective sensory references to distinguish the wines (aromas of flowers, fruit, tobacco, leather etc.). This new vocabulary was a more suitable tool that could be used to distinguish between wines and appellations that were nevertheless very similar.

In 1972, this research led to the publication of an 'Essai sur la dégustation des vins' (Vedel *et al.*) and the concomitant birth of the INAO glass, the first official glass adapted to olfactory tasting. These new ways of approaching wines, taken up by all the influential new tasters from the end of the 1970s (oenologists, sommeliers, critics) (Fernandez 2004), made it possible to define the relationship between the product and its terroir of origin. It was a question of stipulating the characteristics of each appellation and of considering, even if the word is late to appear, the typicity of each wine, a term first in the work of Vedel *et al.* in 1972 to designate an AOC wine. This term was widely used first by wine writers and then, from 1980, by wine lovers. Henceforth, typicity was perceived as a guarantee of quality and no longer simply as the guarantee of respect for a geographical delimitation. The terroir of wine – or rather the 'taste of the terroir' – became a central element in consumers' quality assessment. As the 1980s progressed, more and more consumers began to appreciate these wines, thus economically consecrating the triumph of the AOC system.

Conclusion

Undeniably, these different initiatives had a direct impact on the AOC wine market. Whereas in 1970, only 12% of the wines consumed in France were labelled as AOC, this number almost doubled in ten years, reached 40% in 1990 and exceeded 50% in 2000. The share of AOC wines in exports doubled from 1960 to 1970, going from 25% to 50%. Of course, other important factors were at play in this 'sober revolution' (Bohling 2018), such as the increase in the purchasing power of Western populations during the 'Trente Glorieuses'. But the craze for AOC wines, like their democratisation, is also part of a much deeper process. Contemporary acceptance of the positive gustatory values of the terroir, the linking of typicity to hierarchies and delimited areas and the idea that a wine of origin has an intrinsic quality due to its typicity are all decisive factors in this triumph. They are partly the result of the successful incorporation of a cultural perception of wine and its qualities among wine lovers. However, the economic, technical, regulatory and, finally, cultural anchoring of this model are the result of a complex historical process, in which the few decades between the Second World War and the 1980s were a key moment. Certainly, since the 1990s, French producers have been protesting against the AOC standards and are trying to revise or remove this regulatory framework, which they consider restrictive. For some of them, as with many foreign competitors, it would be more relevant to allow more freedom in winemaking practices and grape varieties. For others, the AOC has become a misguided, over-standardised system. But this standardisation of viticultural hierarchies in the AOC system, the scientific and ideological remobilisation of terroir and the collective invention of typicity were the most efficient way to assert this model economically but also culturally. Despite criticism and international attempts to unravel it (Roger 2010), this holy trinity of 'terroir, typicity and quality' is now perceived as a guarantee which will determine the basis of an efficient model of the viti-vinisphere for at least a few more decades.

References

Bérard, L. et Marchenay, P. (1995) "Lieux, temps et preuves. La construction sociale des produits de terroir," *Terrain* 24, 153–164.
Boch, M. (1959) "Réflexion sur les travaux de délimitation du vignoble à appellation d'origine 'Vins d'Alsace'," *Les vins d'Alsace* 56, 238.
Bohling, J. (2018) *The Sober Revolution. Appellation Wine and the Transformation of France*, Ithaca, NY and London: Cornell University Press.
Bordas, J. (1946) *Essai d'Agronomie méditerranéenne. Comment aménager un domaine agricole dans la Région du Bas-Rhône*, Avignon: Imp. Ruillères Frères.
Boulaine, J. (1992) *Histoire de l'Agronomie en France*, Paris: Lavoisier.
Boulaine, J. (1997) "Histoire abrégée de la science des sols," *Etude et gestion des sols* 4(2), 141–151.
Bourdieu, P. (1979) *Critique sociale du jugement*, Paris: Éditions de Minuit.
Chauvin, P-M. (2010) *Le marché des réputations, Une sociologie du monde des vins de Bordeaux*, Bordeaux: Féret.
CNAO. (1946) Registre n°1, PV de la séance du Comité Directeur du 12 novembre.
Cornu, P., Valeschini, E. and Maeght-Bournay, O. (2018) *Histoire de l'INRA entre science et politique*, Versailles: Quae.

Dutton, J. (2019) "Geographical Turns and Historical Returns in Narrating French Wine Culture," *Global Food History* 5(1–2), 113–131.
Faure, C. (1989) *Le projet culturel de Vichy*, Lyon: Presses Universitaires de Lyon – Ed CNRS.
Fernandez, J-L. (2004) *La critique vinicole en France. Pouvoir de prescription et construction de la confiance*, Paris: L'Harmattan.
Garcia, J-P. and Jacquet, O. (2020) "Le terroir du vin: trajectoire historique d'un objet multiforme en Bourgogne," in J-L Yengue and K. Stengel (eds), *Le terroir viticole. Espace et figures de qualité*, Tours: Presses Universitaires François Rabelais de Tours, 43–69.
Garcia, J.P. and Labbé, T. (2011) "Le goût du lieu: la mise en place du discours sur la nature des sols comme référence du goût des vins en Bourgogne," *CHVV* 11, 145–157.
Garcia, J.P. and Labbé, T. (2019) "La singularité des vins de qualité par le lieu: les climats viticoles en Bourgogne," in J. Pérard and C. Wolikow (eds), *Vignobles et vins singuliers: de l'unique au pluriel*, Dijon: Centre Georges Chevrier, 355–372.
Humbert, F. (2011) *L'INAO, de ses origines à la fin des années 1960: genèse et évolutions du système des vins d'AOC* (PhD Thesis, Université de Bourgogne).
Humbert, F. (2018) "Une formulation de la relation du vin au lieu: les noyaux d'élite de l'INAO," *Crescentis* 1, http://preo.u-bourgogne.fr/crescentis/index.php?id=345.
INAO. (1949) *Procès-verbal du Comité Directeur de l'INAO du 7 Juin 1948*, 9.
INAO. (1953) *Registre n° 3 des délibérations du Comité National, séance du 14 janvier*, 287.
INAO. (1954) *Registre n° 3 des délibérations du Comité National, séance du 6 mai*, 451.
Jacquet, O. (2007) "Le plan de 1860: élément de normalisation du paysage viticole de la Côte-d'Or," *Cahiers d'Histoire de la Vigne et du Vin* 7, 85–96.
Jacquet, O. (2009) *Un siècle de construction du vignoble bourguignon. Les organisations vitivinicoles de 1884 aux AOC*, Dijon: EUD.
Jacquet, O. (2014) "Les sciences de la dégustation au XXe siècle: la consécration de l'odorat," in S. Lavaud *et al.* (eds), *Vins et vignobles. Les itinéraires de la qualité (Antiquité – XXIe siècle)*, Bordeaux: ISVV-ADESS-Cervin, 261–270.
Jacquet, O. (2018) "Le goût de l'origine. Développement des AOC et nouvelles normes de dégustation des vins (1947–1974)," *Cresentis* 1, http://preo.u-bourgogne.fr/crescentis/index.php?id=271.
Jacquet, O. (2021) "La question de la définition et du contrôle des vins d'appellation d'origine au XXe siècle," in O. Serra and S. Wolikow (eds), *Des appellations d'origine aux indications géographiques: un siècle de protection des réputations (1919-2019)*, Rennes: PUR.
Kuhnholtz-Lordat, G. (1963) *La genèse des appellations d'origine des vins*, Mâcon: Buguet-Comptour.
Laferté, G. (2006) *La Bourgogne et ses vins: Image d'origine contrôlée*, Paris: Belin.
Lavalle, J. (1855) *Histoire et statistique de la vigne et des grands vins de la Côte-d'Or*, Paris: Dusacq.
Léger, D. and Hervieu, B. (1979) *Le Retour à la nature. "Au fond de la forêt . . . l'Etat"*, Paris: Seuil.
Lucand, C. (2017) *Le vin et la guerre. Comment les nazis ont fait main basse sur le vignoble français*, Paris: Armand Colin.
Markham, D. (1997) *1855: histoire d'un classement des vins de Bordeaux*, Bordeaux: Féret.
Mérel, P., Ortiz-Bobea, A. and Paroissien, E. (2020) "How Big is the "Lemons" Problem? Historical Evidence from French Wines," Working paper SMART-LERECO 5.
Meyran, R. (2009) *Le mythe de l'identité nationale*, Paris: Berg International.
Moustier, F. (2018) *Les mutations du vignoble provençal au XXe siècle* (PhD Thesis, Université d'Aix-Marseille).
Parker, T. (2017) *Le goût du terroir. Histoire d'une idée Française*, Tours-Rennes: PUFR-PUR.
Peynaud, E. (1995) *Œnologue dans le siècle, Entretiens avec Michel Guillard*, Paris: La Table Ronde.
Roger, A. (2010) "Constructions savantes et légitimation des politiques européennes. La circulation des savoirs sur la vigne et le vin," *Revue française de science politique* 60(6), 1093–1115.
Roupnel, G. (1932) *Histoire de la campagne française*, Paris: Grasset.
Rousso, H. (1987) *Le syndrome de Vichy*, Paris: Seuil.
Rouvière, C. (2015) *Retourner à la terre. L'utopie néo-rurale en Ardèche depuis les années 1960*, Rennes: Presses universitaires de Rennes.
Schirmer, R. (2011) "Le géographe et l'expertise dans le domaine des vins," in S. Wolikow and O. Jacquet (eds), *Territoires et terroirs du vin du XVIIIe au XXIe siècles – Approche internationale d'une construction historique*, Dijon: EUD, 92–96.
Sébillotte, M. (1974) "Agronomie et agriculture. Essai d'analyse des tâches de l'agronome," *Cahiers Orstom, Série biologie* 3(1), 3–25.
Shapin, S. (2012) "The Tastes of Wine: Towards a Cultural History," *Rivista di Estetica* n.s 51, 49–94.

Tonietto, J. and Falcade, I. (2018) "Indicações Geográficas de Vinhos do Brasil," *Territoires du vin* 9, http://preo.u-bourgogne.fr/territoiresduvin/index.php?id=1570.

Valceschini, E. and Torre, A. (2002) "Politique de la qualité et valorisation des terroirs," in J-P. Sylvestre (ed), *Agriculteurs, ruraux et citadins: les mutations des campagnes françaises*, Paris: Educagri.

Vedel, A., Charnay, P., Charles, G. and Tourmeau, J. (1972) *Essais sur la dégustation des vins*, Mâcon: INAO.

Vigreux, J. (2012) *Le Clos du maréchal Pétain*, Paris: PUF.

Vigreux, J. (2018) "La terre ne ment pas: le terroir viticole à l'épreuve de la Révolution nationale de Vichy," *Crescentis* 1, http://preo.u-bourgogne.fr/crescentis/index.php?id=282.

Vincent, E. and Jacquet, O. (2015) "Statut de l'expertise et enjeux sociaux dans le processus de délimitation de l'appellation Chablis (1920–1978). L'invention d'un terroir: le Kimméridgien," *Cahiers d'Histoire de la Vigne et du Vin* 12, 91–103.

Wolikow, C. (2018) "Le Wait and See Bourguignon," in S. Wolikow and O. Jacquet (eds), *Bourgogne(s) viticole(s). Enjeux et perspectives historiques d'un territoire*, Dijon: EUD, 121–134.

Yengue, J.L. and Stengel, K. (2020) *Le terroir viticole. Espace et figures de qualité*, Tours: Presses Universitaires François Rabelais de Tours.

37
WHAT CAN WINEMAKERS' BUSINESS MODELS TELL US ABOUT THE CULTURAL TRAITS OF WINE REGIONS? A COMPARATIVE ANALYSIS

Jean-Guillaume Ditter, Paul Muller and Corinne Tanguy

Introduction

The global wine industry has undergone unprecedented changes in recent decades, not only through the emergence of new wine producing countries (including the USA, South Africa and, more recently, China) in competition with traditional European wine producing countries, but also through the displacement of major geographical centres and new consumption patterns. A remarkable aspect of new producing countries is that the development of their wine industries has been based on a scientific approach aimed at meeting the expectations of international markets (Giuliani *et al.* 2011). This was a major shift compared to traditional producing countries, for which production strategies were supply driven, with an emphasis on the territorial dimension or even that of 'terroir' as a sign of differentiation and of quality (Brunori *et al.* 2004; Charters and Michaux 2014; Ditter and Brouard 2014).

Still, to the best of our knowledge, the literature documenting the emergence of new producing countries only highlights explanatory factors of a technological and strategic nature. Other dimensions, such as social organisation or culture, have been overlooked. Moreover, a hypothesis underlying these analyses considers producing countries as homogeneous blocks, both in terms of the strategies adopted and their cultures and social organisations. This leads to ignoring the diversity of strategies and cultures that can occur between different winegrowing regions within the same country.

This chapter aims to address these limitations by appraising the influence of regional cultural traits (in the sociological sense of the symbolic aspects of a human society) on the way wine producers operate. To this end, we mobilise the concept of the business model. Generally speaking, it is defined as a cognitive device through which strategic decisions are evaluated, adopted and economically reified (Chesbrough 2006). It provides a better understanding of the processes by which companies' key resources and competencies are mobilised and recombined to create and capture value (Zott *et al.* 2011). As business models are determined by their environment (Osterwalder *et al.* 2010), an inter-regional comparison of wine producers' business models allows us to better understand the influence of cultural traits on organisations. In so doing, we present results from an international cross-comparison between different wine regions, two in France (Bordeaux and Champagne) and one in the USA (California).

The Business Model Canvas

We apply the Business Model Canvas (BMC) framework (Osterwalder *et al.* 2010) for analysing estates in the three regions under consideration. The BMC aims at describing how companies create, distribute and capture the value associated with the products and/or services they offer to their customers. By reporting on how a company's strategy is implemented, BMC allows better understanding of how it structures its offering and customer interactions.

We base our analysis on the assumption that business models are shaped by their environment (legal, economic, technological but also cultural), which constitute both constraints and resources to be exploited (Zott *et al.* 2011). This makes it possible to highlight regularities and possible variations, both at the level of each wine region and between them. The cultural component thus contributes to and is reflected in the business models of companies, and this is precisely captured by the BMC.

The BMC is used to design and evaluate the organisation of companies' activities. It describes the business model based on nine descriptive blocks, grouped into four groups (Figure 37.1):

- The value proposition is central to the model. It is the set of the company's products and services creating value for customers.
- Value creation activities are the key production activities for the good or service, as well as the key resources and key partners they require.
- Value transmission and capture activities describe the company's customer segments, its relationship with these customers and its distribution channels.
- The last block assesses the company's economic viability with, on the one hand, its cost structure and, on the other hand, its structure of revenue.

Each wine company was analysed using the BMC method, providing a common basis for comparison. We focus our analysis on the three first groups of value proposition, value creation and value transmission and capture activities, for which we have extensive data.

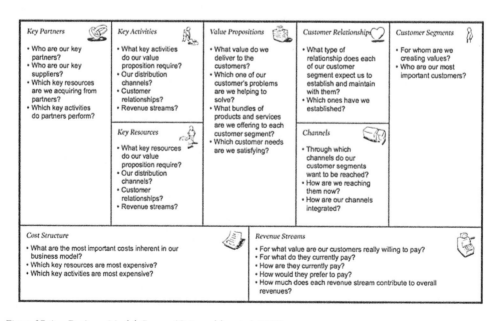

Figure 37.1 Business Model Canvas (Osterwalder *et al.* 2010)

Methodology and data sources

We build on the multiple case study method (Yin 2009), that helps 'predict similar results or produce contrasting results but for predictable reasons' (Johnston *et al.* 1999: 206). All firms' business models were analysed by applying the BMC methodology (Osterwalder *et al.* 2010). A visit was made to each wine company, which led to the design of its business model canvas. The visits were spread over several one-week periods between 2015 and 2019. Primary data obtained in our visits were supplemented by secondary data from specialist newspaper articles and companies' websites. Historical data pertaining to wine regions were obtained from the extant literature on the topic.

The Bordeaux, California and Champagne regions were chosen for different reasons. First, their size and worldwide reputation for quality are such that they are driving forces for the evolution of the wine industry and, especially, of quality wines at the global level. For instance, the three of them account for 6% of world wine exports in volume. Furthermore, and this is the second reason for our choices, their histories are very different, giving rise to distinct cultural traits, which we can find in the economic model of local producers. The origin of Bordeaux's oldest vineyard dates back to antiquity. It is also one of the first to have set up a classification of its wines in 1855. In Champagne, winegrowing emerged in the Middle Ages and became a world leader and model for the production of sparkling wines at the turn of the twentieth century. Its worldwide fame is such that it is one of the biggest contributors to French foreign trade. The Californian vineyard is more recent. However, it has become the fourth leading wine producer, after France, Spain and Italy. It experienced rapid development from the 1930s to the 1970s, before the 'Judgment of Paris' of 1976 recognised the quality of its wines. From that date on, it became a competitor of French wines, including those from Bordeaux. Moreover, this region has established the model of the winery that has since then spread among 'New World countries'. Our sample is made up of 11 Champagne houses of different statuses (*grandes maisons*, independent growers), 11 châteaux and 1 merchant in the Bordeaux region and 11 Californian wineries and estates.

Business models and cultural traits in three wine regions

Bordeaux: beyond tradition, a diverse and evolving range of business models

Resulting from economic exchanges with England (fifteenth century) and the Netherlands (sixteenth century), the nowadays world-famous region of Bordeaux includes all the vines of the Gironde department in the southwest of France. With 117,200 hectares of cultivated area and an annual production of around six million hectolitres, Gironde is the third largest winegrowing department in France in terms of overall production volume and the first for appellation (PDO) wines. Bordeaux wine is mostly red (80%), based on Merlot, Cabernet-Sauvignon and Cabernet Franc. Sauvignon, Semillon and Muscadelle are used for white wines. The region is divided into seven districts (Médoc, Blayais, Côtes-de-Bourg, Libournais, Entre-deux-Mers, Graves and Sauternais), with more than 6,000 estates, called 'châteaux', and 50 different PDOs. One merchant and 11 estates were analysed in our study, of which 7 belong to large groups in the wine, luxury or finance businesses.

The economic model of Bordeaux producers and the relationship with their customers are shaped by the history of the region and the cultural particularities stemming from it (Brand 2017). Two particularly striking dimensions are the 'aristocratic model' of wine development and the marketplace commonly known as the 'Place de Bordeaux'.

Compared to other winegrowing regions in France, the Bordeaux region is unique in that it is named after a port city (Bordeaux) and not a production region (Burgundy, Champagne), which gives its name to the wine region. This particularity reflects the importance of the 'Place de Bordeaux', established in the seventeenth century. Three types of players operate within this system: brokers (*courtiers*), merchants (*maisons de négoce*) and producers, called châteaux. The châteaux, which produce from their own harvest, generally do not sell their wines directly to individuals or to distribution channels, but to merchants, which are commercial companies distributing them in France and in the rest of the world. The 300 wine merchants account for about 70% of Bordeaux's total sales and 80% of its exports.

Brokers connect producers and merchants. They fulfil three missions: to make each party aware of the other's conditions, to advise the parties in question and to try to reconcile their possibly diverging interests. They are divided into so-called 'countryside' brokers, whose role is to sample and make offers of estate or bulk wines to the merchant, and 'city' brokers, who are more specialised in the trading of Bordeaux grands crus. The 80 brokers in the region are involved in 75% of trades.

As early as the eighteenth century, the Bordeaux region was made up of large bourgeois and aristocratic estates whose products were generally related to the estate of origin, without any name, except for the term 'cru'. An 'aristocratic model' (Croidieu and Monin 2011), which still characterises the Bordeaux (and also the Champagne) estates, developed at the end of the nineteenth century. In this model, merchants try to extend their control over the industry, by vertically integrating along the value chain (winemaking, maturing, marketing), in order to create or capture added value at the expense of the owners, who merely sell them their must and, sometimes, wines.

According to this model, the development of the product is therefore essentially ensured by wine merchants, as wine is generally sold *en primeur*: that is to say, it has barely begun its maturing in barrels in the cellar of the château. Wine communication builds on an 'aristocratic and family' repertoire. Longevity is seen as a guarantee of the merchant's good reputation and, consequently, of the perceived quality of the wine among consumers. This repertoire includes the use of family surnames, the reference to a lineage or to a date of foundation and the perpetuation of a first name. The reference to the château appears to be the most expressive and probably the oldest established form of domain (Ulin 1995). It persists even though many estates are currently owned or controlled by large individual and institutional investors (Réjalot 2013).

However, the role of merchants has varied over the course of history. Initially central when wines were sold under their brands, it reduced with the emergence of the châteaux and the establishment of PDO systems, which gave winemakers back control over their production (Brand 2017). The recent emergence of so-called 'New World' wines, which rely on brands (Giuliani *et al.* 2011), has enabled them to reposition themselves at the heart of the industry (Brand 2017). In addition to marketing the wines produced by the châteaux, one of their functions is to regulate the market, in order to stabilise it and enhance consumer loyalty. There are many quality signals, be it the appellation of the wine, the estate or the château and its classification, or even the name of the merchant for certain wines sold by the latter under their own brand name.

Interviews conducted in Bordeaux highlight the impact of this structure on the economic model of producers: direct sales, whether from the estate or to distributors, are limited, with only two of the ten estates involved. Producers market most of their wine, sometimes up to 95% of the volume, through wine merchants. The latter, together with brokers, are frequently cited as essential partners by the estates. Following recent crises, however, direct sales have gradually developed in the Bordeaux region as producers see it as an additional source of income.

Consequently, wine tourism at the estate level is not very developed. Estate visits are most often a side activity for the owner and are organised on fee-paying basis. Their main purpose is to showcase the estate's heritage and products to potential prescribers rather than to directly sell wines. The estate can also be made available to individuals or companies for specific events, generating ancillary revenues.

This results in specific communication strategies: while websites are increasingly used as communication channels, few estates have developed their own online shop or regularly post on digital social media (Facebook, Twitter, Instagram). Trade press and gastronomic guides remain the most frequently cited communication channels.

Customers targeted by the various estates included in our study are diverse, yet with a dominant profile: they are often well-to-do clients. Still some producers in our sample also seek to reach a younger clientele, made up of occasional consumers looking for new experiences. Their motivations range from non-ostentatious hedonism to the search for differentiation and identification with the upper classes through the consumption of a luxury product. The positioning of the wines reflects this variety of clientele: each estate tends to develop a 'vertical range' of products, from classified cru to generic wines, including châteaux and branded wines.

There are also many ways of horizontal differentiation, reflecting the rich history of the region. About 50% of the estates studied are positioned as luxury wines, which are in line with its aristocratic image, but a significant number also refer to the terroir, a concept specific to the typical 'grower' model of Burgundy (Laferté 2006). Although the region is known for long lagging behind as far as the development of organic wines is concerned (Célérier 2015), several producers also claim they use biodynamic or sustainable agriculture to promote their wines to younger customers.

Champagne: innovating for attracting new consumer profiles

Champagne covers nearly 34,000 hectares, or just over 4% of the French vineyards, and produces about 302 million bottles, but it accounts for 33% of French wine exports in value. The production, elaboration and marketing of champagne is based on more than 16,000 small growers who cultivate the vast majority of the region (90%), 132 wine cooperatives and 320 wine merchants (*maisons de champagne* or champagne houses) (Comité Champagne 2020). The latter are at the root of the reputation and prestige of Champagne wines, especially for export. The analysis is based on the description of the economic models of six *surligné par paul mais sans commentaire* and of five family estates. Their size and strategies are very different, with production ranging from 20,000 to several million bottles for '*grandes maisons*'.

Since the beginning of the nineteenth century, champagne houses have sought to develop exports, relying in particular on the networks they had built up in the textile trade. The region specialised in sparkling wines, which were the most in demand, particularly in the German and British markets (Guy 2003). Houses then adopted a strategy of increasing the quality of the product in order to better penetrate these external markets. They also set up a communication strategy via their decorated labels bearing the names of the brands (poster, painting, music, newspaper advertising). The luxury image of champagne thus dates back to this period (Guy 2003). At the same time, the distribution of roles in the sector was settled, between growers who produced the grapes and sold them to merchants and the latter, who carried out the blending, created the sparkling wine and marketed it. The relationships between champagne houses and the growers are still today mostly organised on a long-term basis. However, houses also own vineyards, particularly in the most prestigious areas (crus). Even though most of the production is sold to merchants, growers, for their part, often market bottles under their own name and brand.

It was also during the nineteenth century that many legal protection procedures were undertaken, leading to the creation of the Champagne AOC (PDO) in 1936. The recognition of the appellation consecrated the specificity of this collective heritage and contributed to the establishment of champagne as a luxury good. For this type of good, as can also be the case for a perfume, the value not only derives from the manufacturing cost, but also encapsulates, creativity, culture, image and heritage (Barrère 2007), as well as specific localisation resources and know-how (Smith Maguire and Charters 2021). The ownership and promotion of this historically acquired heritage, which cannot be relocated, is an essential asset of these businesses which, even if they are luxury products, can be manufactured industrially by companies owned by financial groups such as LVMH, the world leader in the luxury industry.

These heritage aspects are thus highly valued and maintained through communication and event strategies, particularly by champagne houses (Smith Maguire and Charters 2021). The most important ones offer paying visits and host a large number of visitors, while other houses and estates only organise visits and tastings for professional customers. Visits for the general public focus on historical aspects and tours of the vineyard, winery and cellars. Other types of events are also organised: polo games or cruises, contemporary art exhibitions, food and wine tastings in the prestigious hotels and restaurants owned by the houses. These events can be offered as wine tourism services, but they are considered more for high-end houses as designed to welcome guests who will play the role of product prescribers and brand ambassadors. Specialist magazines and guides (*Bettane+Desseauve*, *Guide Hachette*) play an essential prescription role for all interviewed estates and houses. In terms of wine tourism, champagne houses place greater emphasis on the 'champagne' product and its luxurious symbolism, while growers put greater value on the terroir, which may cause tensions in the collective definition of what the heritage of champagne is and actions for promoting it (Gatelier *et al.* 2014; Smith Maguire and Charters 2021).

If the biggest houses producing several million bottles per year sell in supermarkets and massively export their production, other actors put emphasis on traditional channels (hospitality, wine boutiques) and direct sales (with a reservation system in some cases), but above all export (from 40% to 75% of their production). Digital communication is relatively limited and is rather the focus of the biggest champagne houses, which have dedicated staff for these tasks. There is generally no sale via houses' and growers' websites but rather through specialised sites (e.g. La Champagnerie, Lavinia, Idealwine, Carré des vins).

It is this now less clear-cut differentiation between champagne and sparkling wines that partly explains their (relative) loss of competitiveness. Indeed, since the 2008 crisis, the champagne industry has suffered from declining shipments while, during the same period, the sparkling wine market has grown very significantly in volume (France Agrimer 2019). Champagne growers have been the hardest hit by this competition from sparkling wines produced in France (Crémants from Alsace, Burgundy, Loire), and also abroad (Prosecco from Italy, Cava from Spain) (Ringeval-Deluze 2019).

Our interviews show a recent evolution in the business models of champagne vintners. First, there is an evolution in the supply of champagne produced in organic agriculture or even biodynamic agriculture. This proportion of organic certified champagne is still low compared to other regions (only 2.9% compared with 12% for France overall), and many producers claim the right to treat if necessary (and therefore not to be certified) while having changed their cultural practices (e.g. limiting herbicides, grassing plots, tillage). In this perspective, champagne houses display various certifications such as Sustainable Viticulture in Champagne, HEV (High Environmental Value), ISO 9001 and 14001. One house claims to offer the first eco-citizen champagne, a juxtaposition of sustainable development approaches, including viticultural practices as much as the reduction in the weight of bottles or the use of labels printed on recycled paper.

Furthermore, the search for new, younger customers is one of the strategies pursued, especially by the houses. This strategy involves developing product innovations (Cuvée Bulles d'argent, small format for consumption through a straw or directly from the bottle, different glass shapes), processes, distribution channels (online sales sites) and consumption times and methods (night clubs or bars, cocktails). New players may also emerge. Some companies break with the luxury and heritage image of champagne: a different process, an original and offbeat back label or the use of new technologies such as augmented reality.

In today's highly competitive sparkling wine market, there is a heterogeneity of profiles, with some houses seeking to develop new activities (wine tourism) and to rejuvenate their consumer targets (product innovations, in terms of marketing), while others continue to present themselves as houses whose high-end champagne is dedicated to connoisseurs. Among the growers, there are also different profiles, from the producer seeking to offer a terroir champagne with a good quality/price ratio compared to that of the houses, to the estate that offers a top-of-the-range champagne from a limited number of *cuvees*.

California: a focus on a community-based customer relationship management

The Californian region produces more than 1.5 million hectolitres of wine, which represents more than 80% of total wine production in the US and 90% of its exports. More than 5,900 growers and winemakers are involved in grape production. Mainly family owned, estates vary in size from small family farms of a few hectares to industrial mega-wineries, such as E&J Gallo, which annually markets 900 million bottles of wine.

California's vineyards cover 244,000 hectares, scattered throughout the state from north to south, from the coast to the Sierra Foothills. There are currently 139 AVAs (American Viticultural Areas) in 30 counties, spread across six regions: Far North, North Coast, Inland Valleys, Sierra Foothills, Central Coast and Southern California.

Californian wine regions benefit from very diverse conditions, both in terms of soils and climatic conditions. More than 110 varieties of winegrapes are cultivated in all three colours, still and sparkling, with a specialisation in cabernet sauvignon, merlot, pinot noir and zinfandel for red wines and chardonnay, pinot gris and sauvignon blanc for white wines (Wine Institute 2020).

As early as the eighteenth century, the cultivation of the vine to produce wine was introduced in California by missionaries to meet their ritual needs. However, commercial viticulture did not develop in northern California until the mid-nineteenth century.

Traditionally, California specialised in the production of cheap table wines for local consumption. This trend was reversed in the 1950s. First, the industrial winery model, based on the development of wines with a strong brand name and meeting consumer expectations, became dominant. Its development relied on the application of modern marketing techniques. Second, the practice of varietal wines developed in addition to an emphasis put on quality (Pinney 2005). In this way, Californian wines gained worldwide recognition in 1976, following the Judgment of Paris.

Our analysis is based on the business models of a sample of 11 wineries located in the Napa Valley and Sonoma Valley, as well as 1 urban winery located in San Francisco. The choice of these two wine regions is justified by the fact that they are the most famous in California (Hira and Swartz 2014). Although not representative, our sample is diversified, with wineries and estates of varying sizes, selling between 8,000 and 120 million bottles, positioned in various market segments (basic, premium, ultra premium, icon) and types of structure (family estate, independent structure, subsidiary of international groups).

Globally, our results show the importance for local estates of creating a community relationship with the customer. This can be seen along three dimensions: marketing channels, wine tourism services and communication on social networks. Concerning marketing channels, in spite of the three-tier distribution system, a distinction can be made according to the size of wineries. While wineries selling more than one million bottles favour national and international distribution channels (mass retailers, hospitality industry), wineries and estates of more modest size value direct sales. Constituting an authorised exception to the three-tier system, this can take two forms: through direct sales at the estate or through a wine club. The latter corresponds to a subscription system, giving the right to the regular allocation of a predetermined assortment of bottles. Several wineries indicated that they offer certain wines exclusively marketed for direct sale, thus indicating the special attention paid to them. Another indication of this specific attention is the form of wine tourism services.

In most of the estates under study, wine tourism, for which a fee is charged, goes far beyond the mere organisation of a wine tasting. Some estates offer ludic activities such as 'make your own wine'. In addition, events are organised in parallel with estate visits. They focus directly on the wines of the estate (presentation of new vintages) or on a wine-related theme (gastronomic events). Finally, they often offer the facilities for the organisation of private events (family celebrations, weddings, professional events). Facilities are framed according to themes related to the identity and values of the estate, without the decoration being necessarily directly related to wine: an English club smoking room to convey a perception of luxury and tradition or a decoration reminiscent of the gold rush to recall the old heritage of the estate. Even though they do not fully reflect historical reality or agricultural practices, these staging efforts contribute to a search for authenticity in the product (Peterson 1997).

Globally, wine tourism services are aimed at customers characterised by heterogeneous levels of knowledge and ease, with wine consumption being an important social marker (Hisano 2017). Customers seeks first to satisfy hedonism and leisure needs rather than deepening wine knowledge. Customers are looking for an entertaining experience. Therefore, the staff are mostly trained in hospitality. It was noticed that the reception staff generally had limited oenological knowledge. Their main task was to ensure customer satisfaction and a relaxed atmosphere corresponding to the identity of the estate.

In addition to a website offering the possibility of buying wines online, wineries maintain a regular link with their customers through the use of social media such as Twitter and Instagram. In the majority of cases, these are fed on a monthly or even weekly basis. The use of YouTube is most often limited to a few videos presenting the domain. Beyond being a communication tool, the use of social media aims at increasing the level of customer engagement with the domains and, in doing so, at developing a community identity linked to the product (Capitello *et al.* 2016; Chen and Lin 2019; Thach *et al.* 2016).

Discussion and conclusion: towards an hybridisation of French cultural models with California?

The analysis of business models from different regions confirms that each has some specific characteristics, building on local economic and cultural heritages: i.e. the aristocratic model in the Bordeaux and Champagne regions or a communitarian relationship management with customers in the Californian region. Our results also show a phenomenon of hybridisation in business models in the Bordeaux and Champagne regions. They tend to evolve towards a model taking up some of the characteristics developed in California. This is particularly visible in their approach to and their relationship with customers, which end up in some kind of 'desacralisation' of wine. This trend is particularly visible in the evolution of the practices developed both in wine tourism and in consumption.

Firstly, wine tourism practices in the two French regions studied get closer to those observed in California. First developed in California, wine tourism gives rise to the organisation of events and activities whose main purpose is to promote wineries and their wines by following a playful approach, as well as a careful staging of emblematic places with the modern architecture of wineries, the decoration of tasting rooms etc. Secondly, a more hedonistic and relaxed approach to wine consumption is promoted. This is particularly visible through the promotion of new formats of champagne bottles, allowing consumption through a straw.

Thus, an important lesson of this comparative study lies in the fact that the cultural representation of wine in Bordeaux and Champagne has evolved towards the Californian. Indeed, the marketing strategies in these two regions were based on the promotion (and also, partly, the reconstruction!)

of folklore and a centuries-old tradition of excellence in wine production (Beverland 2005; Guy 2003; Ulin 1995). Nevertheless, changes in consumption profiles, combined with specific strategies implemented in new producing countries, have questioned the relevance of these strategies (Giuliani et al. 2011), which have led them to copy practices from California. However, despite the presence of several domains claiming direct links with France (e.g. Californian domains belonging to the French Boisset group, French domain managers), our results do not show a reciprocal phenomenon.

Overall, this chapter has made two contributions to the literature on culture and wine. Firstly, from a methodological point of view, the mobilisation of the Business Model Canvas methodology allows the identification of some of the cultural elements specific to a wine region through the observation of regularities within it. As a result, the Business Model Canvas provides a complementary tool to sociological (Jamerson 2010; Smith Maguire 2017) or marketing (Hisano 2017) studies for identifying cultural traits. It also allows a better understanding of how wine companies integrate cultural elements into their operations and innovate in their business models. Secondly, as our comparative study has shown, the analysis by the Business Models Canvas helps identify the dynamics of innovation and hybridisation occurring between regions and how some of them adopt cultural characteristics that are dominant in other places (Foss and Saebi 2017).

However, this piece of work also raises questions that can pave the way for further investigations. First, it would be interesting to extend our analysis to cover other regions, characterised by other cultural trajectories. Historically, the regions of Bordeaux and Champagne have the particularity of having been traditionally very open to the outside world. This may end up diluting their cultural characteristics due to the possible assimilation of external influences. It would be interesting to include in our comparative study regions whose culture is rooted in traditions and folklore, whether historical or reconstructed, such as Burgundy (Laferté 2006). Conversely, due to the structure of our sample, we have not identified any process of cultural hybridisation from European countries to new producing countries. In particular, it would be interesting to include places such as Oregon, which claims a terroir strategy inspired by Burgundy (Dougherty 2012; Marlowe and Bauman 2019).

Another avenue of extension relates to the recent COVID-19 pandemic. The period of lockdown and measures to restrict public access may contribute to questioning certain cultural characteristics specific to each region. For example, cancellations of or restrictions on attendance at folkloric events may jeopardise their sustainability. In the same way, it will certainly become necessary to reconsider hospitality conditions in the frame of wine tourism. Further, the use of digital technologies and social media may be reconsidered: can it be considered an acceptable substitute to hospitality services or remain a complement to it? The cultural impact of these recent developments need evaluation. A longitudinal study would thus allow us to improve our knowledge on this issue.

References

Barrère, C. (2007) "Luxury Industries: Heritage Industries?" Économie Appliquée: Archives de l'Institut de Science Économique Appliquée.

Beverland, M.B. (2005) "Crafting Brand Authenticity: The Case of Luxury Wines," *Journal of Management Studies* 42, 1003–1029.

Brand, S. (2017) *L'analyse institutionnaliste du rôle du négoce vitivinicole: De la filière au mesosystème* (Thèse de doctorat, Université de Bordeaux).

Brunori, G., Galli, M. and Rossi, A. (2004) "Competing Wine Regimes: Some Insights from Wine Routes in Tuscany," in J.S.C. Wiskerke and J.D. van der Ploeg (eds), *Seeds of Transition: Essays on Novelty Production, Niches and Regimes in Agriculture*, Assen: Royal Van Gorcum, 319–340.

Capitello, R., Agnoli, L. and Begalli, D. (2016) "Online Communication Approaches and Social Networks in Traditional Wine Regions: A Case Study from Italy," in G. Szolnoki, L. Thach and D. Kolb (eds), *Successful Social Media and Ecommerce Strategies in the Wine Industry*, New York: Palgrave Macmillan, 30–54.

Célérier, F. (2015) "La viticulture bio dans le vignoble bordelais, les liaisons dangereuses," *Pour* 3, 259–266.

Charters, S. and Michaux, V. (2014) "Stratégie des territoires viti-vinicoles, clusters, gouvernance et marque territoriale: Des concepts aux situations réelles, quels enseignements?" in S. Charters and V. Michaux (eds), *Stratégies des territoires vitivinicoles: Clusters, gouvernance et marque territoriale*, Paris: EMS, 13–37.

Chen, S.C. and Lin, C.P. (2019) "Understanding the Effect of Social Media Marketing Activities: The Mediation of Social Identification, Perceived Value, and Satisfaction," *Technological Forecasting and Social Change* 140, 22–32.

Chesbrough, H. (2006) *Open Business Models*, Brighton, MA: Harvard Business Press.

Comité Champagne. (2020) www.champagne.fr/en/homepage, accessed 26 August 2020.

Croidieu, G. and Monin, P. (2011) "Châteaux contre garages. Mouvements sociaux et identités collectives à Saint-Émilion," *Revue Française de Gestion* 217, 93–116.

Ditter, J.G. and Brouard, J. (2014) "The Competitiveness of French Protected Designation of Origin Wines: A Theoretical Analysis of the Role of Proximity," *Journal of Wine Research* 25, 5–18.

Dougherty, P.H. (2012) *The Geography of Wine: Regions, Terroir and Techniques*, Dordrecht: Springer.

Foss, N.J. and Saebi, T. (2017) "Fifteen Years of Research on Business Model Innovation: How Far Have We Come, and Where Should We Go?" *Journal of Management* 43(1), 200–227.

France Agrimer. (2019) *Ventes et achats de vins effervescents – Bilan 2018 (No. 54)*, Paris, France: Ministère de l'Agriculture et de l'Alimentation.

Gatelier, E., Delaplace, M. and Barrère, C. (2014) "Le développement de l'œnotourisme en Champagne," *Mondes Du Tourisme* 163–201.

Giuliani, E., Morrison, A. and Rabellotti, R. (2011) *Innovation and Technological Catch-Up: The Changing Geography of Wine Production*, Cheltenham: Edward Elgar.

Guy, K.M. (2003) *When Champagne Became French: Wine and the Making of a National Identity*, Baltimore, MD and London: Johns Hopkins University Press.

Hira, A. and Swartz, T. (2014) "What Makes Napa Napa? The Roots of Success in the Wine Industry," *Wine Economics and Policy* 3, 37–53.

Hisano, A. (2017) *Reinventing the American Wine Industry: Marketing Strategies and the Construction of Wine Culture* (SSRN Scholarly Paper No. ID 2966758), Rochester, NY: Social Science Research Network.

Jamerson, H.M. (2010) *Wine Tastes: The Production of Culture among Service Workers and Consumers in Napa Valley Wineries* (PhD Thesis, Emory University).

Johnston, W.J., Leach, M.P. and Liu, A.H. (1999) "Theory Testing Using Case Studies in Business-To-Business Research," *Industrial Marketing Management* 28, 201–213.

Laferté, G. (2006) *La Bourgogne et ses vins: Image d'origine contrôlée*, Paris: Belin.

Marlowe, B. and Bauman, M.J. (2019) "Terroir tourism: Experiences in organic vineyards," *Beverages* 5, 30.

Osterwalder, A., Pigneur, Y. and Clark, T. (2010) *Business Model Generation: A Handbook for Visionaries, Game Changers, and Challengers*, Hoboken, NJ: Wiley.

Peterson, R.A. (1997) *Creating Country Music: Fabricating Authenticity*, Chicago: University of Chicago Press.

Pinney, T. (2005) *A History of Wine in America: From Prohibition to the Present*, Berkeley: University of California Press.

Réjalot, M. (2013) "Difficultés d'adaptation à la mondialisation des marchés: le cas du négoce des vins de Bordeaux," *Annales de géographie* 3(3), 312–331.

Ringeval-Deluze, A. (2019) "Le vigneron champenois dans sa filière. État des lieux, évolutions et enjeux économiques," *Economie rurale* 368, 95–105.

Smith Maguire, J. (2017) "Wine and China: Making Sense of an Emerging Market with Figurational Sociology," in J. Connolly and P. Dolan (eds), *The Social Organisation of Marketing: A Figurational Approach to People, Organisations, and Markets*, Cham: Springer International Publishing, 31–59.

Smith Maguire, J. and Charters, S. (2021) Aesthetic Logics, Terroir and the Lamination of Grower Champagne," *Consumption Markets & Culture* 24, 75–96.

Thach, L., Lease, T. and Barton, M. (2016) "Exploring the Impact of Social Media Practices on Wine Sales in US Wineries," *Journal of Direct, Data and Digital Marketing Practice* 17, 272–283.

Ulin, R.C. (1995) "Invention and Representation as Cultural Capital," *American Anthropologist* 97, 519–527.

Wine Institute. (2020) Https://wineinstitute.org/news/press-room/, accessed 26 August 2020.

Yin, R.K. (2009) *Case Study Research: Design and Methods*, 4th edition, Thousand Oaks, CA: Sage.

Zott, C., Amit, R. and Massa, L. (2011) "The Business Model: Recent Developments and Future Research," *Journal of Management* 37, 1019–1042.

38
REPUDIATION NOT WITHSTANDING
Critics and the case for hybrid grape wines

Connor Fitzmaurice

A complicated case for unconventional grapes

For centuries, the European grape *Vitis vinifera* set the standards for global taste in wine. Today, however, the increasing emphasis on 'local' provenance as a standard of good taste – across a range of consumer goods (Johnston and Baumann 2010; Carfagna *et al.* 2014) – has made matters complicated. Some locations are simply inhospitable to the production of *vinifera* wines, making local wines with 'authentic' winegrapes all but impossible.

In regions with challenging climates, hybrid grapevines have proven adaptable. While many grape varieties bred by crossing different European varietals are referred to as hybrids (e.g. Pinotage), the grapes at the centre of this chapter are hybrids in the strictest sense of the word, botanically speaking. That is, they are *interspecific* crosses descended from *Vitis vinifera* and any of a number of North American grape species. Initially created in response to the *phylloxera* outbreak of the nineteenth century, hybrid grapes also proved to be incredibly cold hardy and broadly disease resistant.

These are impressive qualities and would be a bright spot on any plant breeder's CV. But, in the world of wine, these grapes remain of uncertain value. Critics play key roles in processes of categorisation and the construction of worth (Bourdieu 1996). Yet when categorising hybrid grape wines, critics face a puzzle, pulled between two opposing logics. On the one hand, there are the established Eurocentric hierarchies of wine value (Smith Maguire 2018) and the near universal acceptance of particular *vinifera* grapes as the benchmark of quality (Fourcade 2012). On the other, there is the more recent cultural valorisation of local goods, which would seemingly necessitate non-*vinifera* wines in some regions.

This chapter examines the critical response to hybrid grapes in the American Northeast. There, critics have paid attention to these minor varieties and worked to classify their value, likely in part because winegrowers in the region (with access to major US markets) have, at times, only been able to grow these grapes. How do critics challenge conventions to make room for such innovative – not-yet-legitimate – grapes? I find that they don't.

Based on a discourse analysis of 162 years of *New York Times* wine coverage, I show that the emergence of 'the local' as a powerful aesthetic value does not give critics license to usher these novel grapes into the fold. While the local may be considered 'authentic', so, too, is the historic – and that would include *vinifera* grapes (Johnston and Baumann 2010). Perhaps if *vinifera* grapes could grow everywhere, wines from the American Northeast would cause less trouble. But nature has limits, as do the strictures of good taste. Faced with this opposition, critics effectively bracket hybrid grapes off, preventing direct comparisons with noble varietals. Where *vinifera* grapes cannot be grown, hybrids can be framed as distinctive expressions of place – much as noble grapes are. However, wherever *vinifera* grapes can survive, they remain the hallmark of true wine growing skill and commitment. Indeed, choosing not to grow *vinifera* is framed as a sign of crass profit seeking – even if growers face tremendous risks in the harsh, unpredictable climate of the Northeastern US. Far from broadening criteria of acceptability, critics negate any threat the local might pose to the legitimacy of more longstanding categorisations of taste by essentially classifying hybrid grapes as 'an exciting last resort' for challenging climates.

A brief history of hybrids

During the European *phylloxera* crisis, which began in the 1860s, hybridisation offered a promising solution. *Phylloxera* was a North American pest, and the native grapes of the Eastern United States – which co-evolved with the louse – displayed resistance. Plant breeders used interspecies hybrids to confer this resistance onto European grapes (Beard 1951). However, the North American *Vitis labrusca* used in the hybridisation process has a distinctive flavour and aroma – more grape jelly than wine, with musky undertones. These grapes were faulted as 'foxy' (Beard 1951: 116; see also Pinney 2007: 6). These faults were reduced or eliminated in the new hybrids; nevertheless, the grapes had utterly new sensory characteristics compared with the noble varieties they were created to potentially replace.

However, grafting (growing susceptible vines on rootstocks with North American lineages) made replacement unnecessary. With hardier roots, grafted plants thrived in *phylloxera*-infested soils. And the customary varieties were not lost: a grafted vine still yields the same variety of grape – the same pinot noir, the same riesling – as an un-grafted specimen. With the success of grafted vines, standalone hybrids became practically obsolete. In fact, with a few exceptions, they were ultimately outlawed in much of Europe (Prial 1978a).

Where hybrids did not become obsolete was in Eastern North America. Initial attempts to grow *vinifera* in the US had all failed (Pinney 2007: 94). Unbeknownst to early growers, *phylloxera* may have played some role in these failures, but more importantly, there were climate troubles. Humid summers encouraged rampant outbreaks of mildew; brutal winters proved too much for the vines (Pinney 2007). In the wake of Prohibition, hybrid varieties gave the Eastern US the opportunity to produce wine with a more European character than anything previously made using the native labrusca grapes. With uncertain commercial prospects, hybrids were a risk, but a handful of growers jumped at the opportunity to produce 'wines that taste like wine' (Prial 1997: B7).

Categories, oppositions and a taste for hybrid wines

These novel grapes raised questions for wine experts. Are hybrids 'real' winegrapes? Are they any good? At the core, these are question of classification.

Classification is a social process that is central to taste, identity and the functioning of markets (DiMaggio 1987; Zuckerman 1999). Even for novel goods, we must first recognise what category a thing belongs in before we can understand how it differs (Zuckerman 2016). Classificatory schemas are especially important in markets in which quality is difficult to evaluate or compare (Karpik 2010). In art markets, for example, what category a work belongs in can have a dramatic effect on value (Khaire and Wadhwani 2010).

This is also true in wine: in an inherently variable agricultural product, category expectations have been demonstrated to play an outsize role in sensory perception (Zhao 2005). Classifications allow for commensurability to be established because categories function to 'simultaneously bound competition, reducing the number of comparable others, and act as a legitimation device establishing comparability with similar others' (Weber *et al.* 2008: 547; see also Fourcade 2012). Critics play a key role in this: they circulate and normalise the logics of classification that undergird our often preconscious judgements of taste (Smith Maguire 2018).

Oppositions are one way to mark the boundaries of categories, establishing criteria of inclusion and exclusion (Weber *et al.* 2008). In the case of hybrid grapes, an oppositional identity would provide a simple solution to questions about their place in the wine world. Given their historic role in wine production, *Vitis vinifera* grapes could be considered 'authentic' (Johnston and Baumann 2010). Critics could easily construct an oppositional boundary around the *vinifera* as the *only* winegrape – excluding hybrids and all other grapes from the legitimacy their judgements confer.

However, other logics complicate such a straightforward classification of grape varieties as either 'authentic' winegrapes or pretenders: namely, the emergence of the local as a powerful source of worth. The 'local' has become a predominant frame with which goods – particularly in the gastronomic field – are valorised as authentic (Johnston and Baumann 2010). Omnivorous consumers use the geographic specificity of goods as a basis for distinction (Johnston and Baumann 2010), and the eco-habitus evinced in the practices of many high-cultural capital consumers makes local products all the more salient (Carfagna *et al.* 2014). Yet there are biological limitations to simply transposing European wine culture – rooted, as it is, in the European *vinifera* grape – into new local contexts. 'Authentic' winegrapes simply cannot find local expressions everywhere as they will not grow wherever our cultural logics would have them.

Here, then, is our problem. We have a world where the logics of good taste would seemingly demand that wine be locally produced everywhere bumping up against a demand that great wines only be made from one species of grape – a species decidedly difficult to grow in places like the Northeastern US. As a result, critics classifying hybrid grape wines are forced to 'thread the needle' between seemingly irreconcilable oppositions (cf. Fitzmaurice and Schor 2019).

Faced with competing oppositions, efforts at classification may yield no acceptable objects (Fitzmaurice and Schor 2019). Yet critics have praised hybrid grapes and the wines they produce. Have they succeeded where others have failed? In what follows, I show that critics tend to praise hybrids when they pose no real threat to the superiority of the *vinifera* – that is, only where the *vinifera* literally cannot grow. Far from discursively resolving the tug of war between *vinifera*'s hegemony and local sustainability, critics' commitments to more omnivorous and ecological logics of taste seem less robust than more entrenched classificatory standards.

Methods

This chapter is based on a qualitative discourse analysis of wine writing in the *New York Times*, a high-status newspaper recognised by previous research into the gastronomic field as an important tastemaker (Johnston and Baumann 2010; Jordan 2007). This is justifiable, given a weekday circulation of over 363,000 and a Sunday audience of over 840,000, along with a median household income among subscribers of over $100,000 (Standard Rate and Data Service 2020). Additionally, the *New York Times* is archived and searchable from 1851. This continuity extends a decade before the *phylloxera* crisis in Europe, allowing me to sample the entire history of critical appraisal of hybrids. Finally, while hybrids have been grown in various regions of the United States, they have played a central role in the development of wine production in the Northeastern US. As a result, the *New York Times* provides a site of discourse with cultural authority, widespread reach and continuity, with a regional focus on a geographic region where hybrid grapes have long been important.

A search for '"hybrid" AND "winegrapes"' yielded 162 years of coverage, spanning from 1857 to 2019 (the last full year of articles available). This produced a sample of 237 articles. The search term 'hybrid' proved reliable, given that it both is the technical term for such grapes and was in use as early as 1857, before such grapes were even available to growers. It is unlikely the search criteria failed to capture articles using specific hybrid varietal names since every article in this sample that named cultivars always parenthetically explained that they were 'hybrids'.

Each of the articles was inductively analysed and open coded for themes, making use of a narrative analytic approach. Narrative analysis is particularly suited to uncovering underlying ideologies in the stories we tell about the world, discursively unifying often contradictory realities into a coherent narrative project (Josselson 2011). As the following section will demonstrate, the discourse surrounding hybrids has been tumultuous. Straddling categorical oppositions, critics have variously turned to – and turned on – the hybrids. Beneath the seeming tumult lies a lasting commitment to the European *vinifera*.

Comparison without negation

The (not too) sweet taste of necessity

The opposition which defined hybrid grapes at the outset was with North America's native labrusca grape. Grapes like Concord, Delaware and Catawba were widely grown and popular as wine. Indeed, Henry Wadsworth Longfellow wrote an ode to the native grapes of America, comparing adulterated European imports with the pure, native Catawba (in Goldberg 1986). As a later critic cast them, these native grape tipples were 'the wine equivalent of a savory hotdog' (Goldberg 1986: SM30): enjoyable wines with mass appeal.

Critical palates were unconvinced. The first article in the sample was less about hybrid grapes and more about hopes for them:

> Every horticulturalist, of any distinction, is now looking for the great desideratum in the new seedlings and hybrids that are claiming attention. They have no expectation of success, either from European vines or from our old wild natives. As a class these latter vines are worthless, and the vine dresser is sure to lose his labour who plants them.
>
> *(New York Daily Times 1857: 5)*

Yet the New York wine industry ended up based on native grapes: 'American varieties that bear no resemblance to the grapes usually associated with fine table wines' (Prial 1973: 49). Popularity did little to temper critical disdain. Describing New York wines, one critic noted, 'until very recently most true wine lovers would not touch any of it, even at their third cousin's wedding' (Prial 1973: 49).

It took many years for the promise of hybrids to bear fruit. But by 1954, it seemed inevitable to critics that French-American hybrid grapes would define East Coast wine. Even the fabled Catawba was at risk because French-American hybrids 'combine quality with the hardiness the eastern American climate requires' (Nickerson 1954: 23). Growers who were reticent to rip out native varieties were lambasted for holding back the industry. Even if the expense of vine conversion was recognised, winegrowers were framed as 'scorning' the hybrids in favour of an outdated regional style based on native varieties (Prial 1976: 28). With the advent of hybrids, to grow native grapes was to play it safe: putting profit above quality (Prial 1979).

Critics hardly pretended these new grapes were the same as those of Europe. They produced wines that made 'no pretension to greatness' (*New York Times* 1955: 12), but critics were willing to concede that they were 'interesting in their own right' (Claiborne 1965: 38). Eventually, critics would even compare some of these wines favourably to European examples: 'these are not the sweet, grapey wines you used to associate with New York State. These are dry, often elegant table wines, fit to grace any table . . . made from French-American hybrid grapes' (Prial 1978b: C1). Describing a specific red wine, the same critic noted, 'it was better than most of the doctored Beaujolais

Nouveau the French send us' (Prial 1978b: C1). Hybrids were embraced as a basis for new regional wine industries, and that was a point of pride (Reed 1975). Hybrids may not have been great grapes, but they were good grapes. What's more, they seemed like a necessity: the best the Eastern United States was capable of.

Suffering to be exceptional

The acceptance of hybrids as good grapes for the Northeastern US was short lived. Dr. Konstantin Frank, a Ukrainian-born, German agricultural scientist, immigrated to New York and was shocked when he learned of the widespread belief that *vinifera* vines would not grow in that climate. He took a job at Gold Seal Vineyards in the Finger Lakes region, a winegrowing area in Western New York. Here, he set out to prove that *vinifera* grapes on hardy rootstocks would survive. At first, critics treated the idea of New York State *vinifera* as a novelty, uncertain if the vines would survive in the long term and, even if they did, if the effort would be worth the risk (Prial 1979).

But as more New York growers began planting European varieties, critical appraisal started to shift. The arrival of *vinifera* in the New York wine industry unsettled previous classifications of hybrid grapes. As critics grappled with what to make of them, specific wines made from hybrid grapes continued to earn praise. Critics borrowed the frame of *vin de pays*, or country wines, to make sense of the hybrids. These were wines that sold well locally at the winery, rendering them little known but potentially pleasurable. But even this framing reproduced a hierarchy topped off by well-known *vinifera* dominating global taste.

More telling, the 'superior' sensory qualities of the hybrids (in contrast with native varieties) were no longer suggested as the reason for their local influence. No longer were hybrids framed as a miracle match for the state in terms of climate, disease resistance and style. Instead, hybrids were framed – like the native grapes before them – as simply lucrative: 'for economic reasons more than anything else, most of these new *vinifera* fans are committed to some hybrids for the foreseeable future. Hybrids are the money makers; some produce six times the grape tonnage of vinifera vines', (Prial 1979: SM14). These were 'debt-paying wines because they are cheap to produce, easy to sell and help finance their more ambitious projects' with *vinifera* grapes (Asimov 2011: D1).

Vinifera growing, in comparison, was serious. The grapes themselves were framed as inherently more nuanced and subtle. To explain why Finger Lakes (hybrid-based) wines did well at a New York State wine competition, one article suggested that while all the judges were 'food and wine professionals', the 'easy appeal' and 'candy-like flavors' delivered by hybrid grapes could have overwhelmed more 'disciplined, complex chardonnays, merlots and cabernet francs' (Goldberg 1997: LI1).

What's more, *vinifera* grapes were 'cultivated only with great difficulty' (Robards 1982b: SM82). Critics deftly deployed logics of struggle, hard work and the pursuit of quality over profit to explain why *vinifera* grapes were worth the effort in an unforgiving region. Such logics have long been a feature of high-cultural capital systems of classification, demonstrating distance from necessity (Bourdieu 1984). Entire harvests could be lost after particularly cold winters – and they were. Faced with such losses, 'rumors circulated that many New York wineries would abandon the vinifera and return to their more traditional – and more reliable – varieties. But virtually all producers have continued to cultivate chardonnay, riesling, and other vinifera types, which yield *superior* wines' (Robards 1982a: SM82, emphasis added).

Once revolutionary, hybrids were reframed as beginner grapes. 'It's natural that states in the earliest stages of their vineyard development should rely on the grapes that are easiest to grow' (Asimov 2006: 32). Hybrids were transitional (Prial 1985). When *vinifera* was thought impossible, the adaptability, hardiness and vigour of the hybrid vines were their greatest selling points. But if the *vinifera* had even a chance of survival, the hybrids seemed too easy.

In the wake of that transition, hybrids became as *déclassé* as the labrusca grapes they replaced: 'the industry is retreating from sweet wine made from native labrusca grapes and dry wines made from French-American hybrid grapes. Most lovers of premium wine dislike both types' (Goldberg 1988: C16). After a tasting of New York State wines, one critic acknowledged that while they once felt the neglect of hybrids was an 'injustice', they had since changed their tune: 'At their best the hybrids rivalled some vinifera. More routinely, they produce unimpressive wines' (Prial 1983a: C12).

When readers complained about the treatment given to the New York wine industry, another article was printed in response – this time praising the promise of *vinifera* in the state:

> It would be dishonest and ultimately unfair to the New York wine makers to suspend judgment and ignore the past. Besides, some of the vinifera wines, the chardonnays and rieslings, were excellent. Should there be two standards when judging New York wines?
>
> *(Prial 1983b: C11)*

For critics, two standards – one for hybrids and one for *vinifera* – proved untenable.

The illusion of co-existence

Throughout the 1980s and 1990s, even when faced with excellent hybrid wines, the stories critics told about the Northeast wine industry as a whole were remarkably stable. Hybrid grapes were either transitional or they were cash cows, and they surely weren't part of the industry's future. An article from 2011 noted 'the continuing hold of the hybrid market has caused some tension, as some leading vinifera producers believe that the reputation of the region has been held down' (Asimov 2011: D1). Remembering the life of a hybrid grape pioneer, we are told 'He was right about labrusca grapes; they had had their day. But the hybrid grapes he championed were transitional, too' (Prial 2001: F7).

When praising hybrid wines, critics tended to shift the focus from the qualities of the grape onto the skills of the winemaker. A 2006 story about the Finger Lakes noted:

> [T]asting what some of these same [New York] vintners are doing with labrusca, a native American grape species, as well as hybrids can be absolutely eye-opening. . . . I had lyrical wines from such varietals as Cayuga, Niagara and Vignoles that could stand proudly in an international field.
>
> *(Cecchini 2006: F44)*

Describing a winemaker working with the seyval blanc hybrid, we learn he had 'so mastered this fairly complex, underappreciated French-American hybrid grape that connoisseurs could confuse his wine with an exceptionally lean Macon chardonnay' (Goldberg 2000: WE22).

Despite these examples of 'good' hybrid wines and skilful winemaking, when critics evaluated hybrid wines from Vermont, hybrid grapes' marginality was reimagined as a result of a lack of skill in the past: hybrids were never given a fighting chance because no one gave them the care they deserve.

> For wine lovers conditioned to appreciate the best expressions of [noble grapes], the notion of drinking wines made from hybrids . . . feels like trading in your chauffeur-driven Bentley for a bus pass. . . . Wines from hybrid grapes can often be dull and dreary. Rarely are they grown or vinified with care. . . . But what if hybrids were farmed as carefully and conscientiously as the finest vinifera grapes in a venerable vineyard?
>
> *(2015 Asimov: D1)*

The result, we are told, are wines 'so soulful and delicious, they challenge crucial assumptions long taken for granted' (2015 Asimov: D1).

Rendering hybrids non-threatening

How do we reconcile these tensions and contradictions in the treatment of hybrid grapes? It helps to consider where that 'soulful' hybrid wine is being produced: Vermont.

A 2017 article about the Finger Lakes noted that the focus there on riesling and cabernet Franc is refreshingly 'motivated more by sound viticultural reasons than by commercial concerns'. Yet: 'Even so, the region still has many acres of hybrid and native American grapes' (perfectly adapted to the region, I would note) that are cast as mere legacies of the region's history 'both as a producer of cheap, fortified wines and of small wineries that did the bulk of their selling directly to visitors' (Asimov 2017: D11). Yet in Vermont, hybrids were praised for their ability to 'thrive' in a 'daunting' climate and produce spectacular wines (Asimov 2015: D1).

'Daunting' is exactly how the climates of Eastern states like New York were described before *vinifera* proved growable. At least in their early years, hybrid grapes appeared to successfully thread an oppositional needle in these places: sandwiched between the rarefied *vinifera* and the disreputable native grape varieties. In actuality, the French-American hybrids, by the limitations of climate and agronomy, were lodged in a sort of non-compete agreement with the 'true' *vinifera* winegrapes – bracketed off from direct comparisons. Since *vinifera* grapes could not exist in same time and space with the hybrids, be grown in the same soil or produced from the same vintage – in the same terroir – they could never really be compared (cf. Fourcade 2012). Thus, classifying hybrids as 'good' in comparison to European grapes was a bit of a farce. It was a comparison with no threat of negation: no challenge to the singular virtue of the *vinifera*.

Instead, critics only needed to agree that the hybrids were better than their native grape forebears. Any comparisons to European grapes and wines were shallow at best: a specious comparison of apples and oranges in which the most one could say is 'at least both are fruit'. But once *vinifera* proved viable, hybrids could not co-exist. It was only when newer, even more cold-hardy grapes were introduced – and hybrids planted in places like Vermont – that critics seemed willing to praise them again: in a time and place where the threat of negation, in regard to the *vinifera*, was impossible.

Hybrid grapes are caught between two competing, oppositional logics. On the one hand, a logic of localism suggests that local products are always superior, politically and aesthetically. On the other, there is an entrenched canon of good taste rooted in Eurocentric histories and flavours. Far from reconciling these competing logics or espousing a bigger tent, the ways critics have praised hybrid grapes reveal the lasting power of the latter.

Deirdre Heekin, the Vermont winemaker whose treatment of hybrids so impressed the critics, described hybrids as 'uniquely American, a melting pot' (in Asimov 2015: D1). Only in the absence of *vinifera* can such an assessment stand. In a changing climate, *vinifera* may march northward once more, and the soulful hybrids Heekin grows could once again come to seem unrefined. Given the persistent Eurocentrism of 'good' taste, if a less hospitable climate were to make hybrids necessary in Europe (and not just on the winemaking periphery) then, perhaps, genuine strategies of reclassification may need to be marshalled in the hybrids' defence.

Place is central to taste, with goods taking on different symbolic meanings in diverse contexts (Jordan 2007). The case of hybrid grapes suggests that one reason this may be the case is that place shapes the types of comparisons that can be made. Hybrid grapes – which are often much better adapted to difficult climates – might make better wine than *vinifera* grown under similarly taxing conditions, challenging *vinifera*'s dominance. Only in regions where *vinifera* will not grow can hybrids make 'good' wine without threatening established classifications. Far from a straightforward valorisation of the local, the case of hybrid wines shows the difficulty truly locally adapted goods face gaining acceptance. Instead, critical discourse reveals a clear preference for mere local instantiations of elite culture.

References

Asimov, E. (2006) "A Young Industry, Hints of Possibility," *The New York Times*, 19 November, 32.
Asimov, E. (2011) "Deep Lakes, Icy Climate, Great Wine," *The New York Times*, 12 October, D1.
Asimov, E. (2015) "Soulful Wine from a Hearty Hybrid," *The New York Times*, 2 September, D1.
Asimov, E. (2017) "Cabernet Franc Adds Its Signature," *The New York Times*, 9 November, D11.
Beard, E. (1951) "The Grape Harvest: Franco-American Hybrids Introduced to Public," *The New York Times*, 11 February, 116.
Bourdieu, P. (1984) *Distinction: A Social Critique of the Judgment of Taste*, Cambridge, MA: Harvard University Press.
Bourdieu, P. (1996) *The Rules of Art: Genesis and Structure of the Literary Field*, Palo Alto, CA: Stanford University Press.
Carfagna, L.B., Dubois, E.A., Fitzmaurice, C., Laidley, T., Ouimette, M., Schor, J.B. and Willis, M. (2014) "An Emerging Eco-Habitus: The Reconfiguration of High Cultural Capital Practices Among Ethical Consumers," *Journal of Consumer Culture* 14(2), 1–21.
Cecchini, T. (2006) "New York Uncorked," *The New York Times*, 24 September, F44.
Claiborne, C. (1965) "Winegrowing Is a Serious Hobby for Maryland Couple," *The New York Times*, 24 June, 38.
DiMaggio, P.J. (1987) "Classification in Art," *American Sociological Review* 52, 440–455.
Fitzmaurice, C. and Schor, J.B. (2019) "Homemade Matters: Logics of Opposition in a Failed Food Swap," *Social Problems* 66(1), 144–161.
Fourcade, M. (2012) "The Vile and the Noble: On the Relation Between Natural and Social Classifications in the French Wine World," *Sociological Quarterly* 53, 524–545.
Goldberg, H.G. (1986) "The New World vine," *The New York Times*, 6 July, SM30.
Goldberg, H.G. (1988) "New York's Wineries Chart Their Move Toward Vinifera," *The New York Times*, 29 June, C16.
Goldberg, H.G. (1997) "How Significant Are Medals Awarded in Wine Competitions?" *The New York Times*, 7 September, LI1.
Goldberg, H.G. (2000) "Wine Under $20: From the Hudson Valley," *The New York Times*, 17 September, WE22.
Johnston, J. and Baumann, S. (2010) *Foodies: Democracy and Distinction in the Gourmet Foodscape*, New York: Routledge.
Jordan, J.A. (2007) "The Heirloom Tomato as Cultural Object: Investigating Taste and Space," *Sociologia Ruralis* 47(1), 20–41.
Josselson, R. (2011) "Narrative Research: Constructing, Deconstructing, and Reconstructing Story," in *Five ways of Doing Qualitative Analysis*, New York: The Guilford Press.
Karpik, L. (2010) *Valuing the Unique: The Economics of Singularities*, Princeton, NJ: Princeton University Press.
Khaire, M. and Wadhwani, R.D. (2010) "Changing Landscapes: The Construction of Meaning and Value in a New Market Category – Modern Indian Art," *Academy of Management Journal* 53(6), 1281–1304.
New York Daily Times. (1857) "Government Folly," *New York Daily Times*, 1 September, 5.
New York Times. (1955) "Rockland Wines," *The New York Times*, 5 September, 12.
Nickerson, J. (1954) "Pink Wines Gaining Favor – France Offers Several Fine Ones," *The New York Times*, 29 June, 23.
Pinney, T. (2007) *A History of Wine in America: From the Beginnings to Prohibition*, Berkeley: University of California Press.
Prial, F.J. (1973) "They Labour Well in New York's Vineyards," *The New York Times*, 18 April, 49.
Prial, F.J. (1976) "State's Smaller Vintners Press for Changes," *The New York Times*, 25 February, 28.
Prial, F.J. (1978a) "The Hybrid Solution," *The New York Times*, 5 March, SM17.
Prial, F.J. (1978b) "Thriving, Surprising Hudson Valley Wine," *The New York Times*, 29 November, C1.
Prial, F.J. (1979) "The Upstate Upstarts," *The New York Times*, 5 August, SM14.
Prial, F.J. (1997) "Philip M. Wagner, 92, Wine Maker Who Introduced Hybrids," *The New York Times*, 3 January, B7.
Prial, F.J. (1983a) "Good News and Less-Good News About the Bottlings from the Finger Lakes Area," *The New York Times*, 3 August, C12.

Prial, F.J. (1983b) "How Valuable Are All Those Bottles Hidden Away in Closets with Old Bowling Trophies?" *The New York Times*, 17 August, C11.
Prial, F.J. (1985) "How New York Wine Makers Foiled the Bugs and the Frost," *The New York Times*, 20 February, C13.
Prial, F.J. (2001) "A Farewell to the Baron of Bully Hill," *The New York Times*, 2 May, F7.
Reed, R. (1975) "The Wine-Making Revolution Keeps Growing and Growing," *The New York Times*, 5 October, 64.
Robards, T. (1982a) "State's Vineyards Report a Huge Crop," *The New York Times*, 22 September, C1.
Robards, T. (1982b) "The Possible Dream," *The New York Times*, 7 February, SM82.
Smith Maguire, J. (2018) "A Taste for the Particular: A Logic of Discernment in an Age of Omnivorousness," *Journal of Consumer Culture* 18(1), 3–20.
Standard Rate and Data Service. (2020) *The New York Times*, www.srds.com, accessed 22 January 2021.
Weber, K., Heinze, K. and DeSoucey, M. (2008) "Forage for Thought: Mobilizing Codes in the Movement for Grass-Fed Meat and Dairy Products," *Administrative Science Quarterly* 53, 529–567.
Zhao, W. (2005) "Understanding Classifications: Empirical Evidence from the American and French Wine Industries," *Poetics* 3, 179–200.
Zuckerman, E. (1999) "The Categorical Imperative: Securities Analysts and the Illegitimacy Discount," *American Journal of Sociology* 104(5), 1398–1438.
Zuckerman, E. (2016) "Optimal Distinctiveness Revisited: An Integrative Framework for Understanding the Balance Between Differentiation and Conformity in Individual and Organizational Identities," in *Oxford Handbook of Organizational Identity*, New York: Oxford University Press.

39

IF IT'S FAMOUS, IT MUST BE GOOD

The social construction of brand value in the US wine market

Gregory S. Carpenter and Ashlee Humphreys

Introduction

Two hundred years after the US declared its independence from its Old World rulers, a panel of distinguished wine experts met at the Intercontinental Hotel in Paris to taste and rate wines from Napa Valley and France in a blind tasting that has come to be known as the Judgement of Paris. To everyone's surprise, the panel of exclusively French judges declared two Napa Valley wines as winners. The judges' decisions sparked debate on both sides of the Atlantic about the true potential of California wines. While the debate raged, some French wine producers began quietly buying Napa Valley vineyards. Among them was famed Bordeaux winemaker Christian Moueix, who purchased the Napanook Vineyard in Yountville, California.

Like other Napa Valley vintners, Moueix began producing a wine based on cabernet sauvignon from his legendary vineyard. Unlike other California producers, however, Moueix rejected winemaking methods popular in California and, notably, refused to cater to consumers. How does he think about consumers when making wine? 'I don't', he says. 'I make what pleases me'. After Moueix's first vintage of Dominus Estate in 1983, critics praised it. Moueix's unique approach had, however, produced a wine they described as neither typically French nor typically Californian. Was it more French or more Californian, and was it really worth $40? they asked. Five years later, a new perspective emerged that Christian Moueix was rewriting 'the definition of a Napa Valley reference point wine', according to wine's most influential critic (Parker 1997). With each vintage more critics agreed, and today a single bottle of Dominus Estate can command over $300.

How do wine producers like Christian Moueix succeed so remarkably when consumers have thousands of excellent options below $300? We explore that question, drawing on our ethnographic analysis of the US wine market (Humphreys and Carpenter 2018). In our analysis, we consider brands from both the consumer and producer perspective. From the firm perspective, we describe logics by which wine producers create brands. We find that some producers explicitly dismiss the preferences and tastes of consumers and reject financial gains as a measure of success. These artisanal firms can create high-status brands, but generating the resources necessary to sustain their operation is more elusive. Other firms cater to consumers and seek financial gain using a commercial logic. These firms, which could be described as market oriented, rarely create high-status brands, though they can enjoy greater financial stability.

Our analysis reveals that some firms play a status game. These firms create brands that achieve high status and enable firms to enjoy commercial success. At the same time, some consumers are drawn to high-status brands, which shape their preferences and enable them to signal their status to other consumers, building their own cultural capital. Such consumers seek out certain wine brands and pay premium prices for them. For the firms that own them, high-status brands are valuable commercial assets. In this chapter, we describe the social process through which firms play and win the status game. We explore the implications of our findings for research on market orientation and on status (e.g. Kohli and Jaworski 1990; Jaworski and Kohli 1993; Benjamin and Podolny 1999; Merton 1968; Washington and Zajac 2005).

The artisanal logic

Firms that embrace an artisanal logic start with a creative vision. Financial gains are secondary. 'We're not here to make big money in the short term', one winemaker told us. For firms that embrace an artisanal logic, wine offers a canvas for creative expression, originality and achievement. 'I want to make something unique, something different', a French winemaker told us. 'It's not by using recipes. I want to do something more, something exceptional'. Many consumers find such brands appealing, of course. This logic has elements of both the artisanal and artistic. One the one hand, producers explain at length how winemakers craft the product in a non-standard, non-industrialised way, improvising on the raw product of the grape and its origin. On the other hand, many producers also describe how the winemaker is an artist, conforming to a logic of creating a unique product to please oneself without regard to consumer tastes.

Winemakers

The actual production of wine, however, starts with the source of wine: the natural environment. Lorenzo, an executive with a centuries-old Italian wine producer described his firm's approach:

> We don't create wine starting from the consumer need. . . . Wine is basically a product of nature. . . . [W]e cannot change the product only because a certain market is asking for this product. We start from the terroir, the vineyard, and we have to try to market the product that specific vineyard is able to give us.

Grapes are an agricultural product, but some people see them as ingredients in a creative endeavour. Like a chef, an artist or even a musician, a winemaker can be guided by a vision to create something original or exceptional. A French winemaker, Yves, described it succinctly:

> You have your own vision, your own interpretation. It's like a musician. It has been written before us; the soil has done it. You can interpret it a little faster or a little slower with your own style, your own touch.

This artistic perspective has a strong aristocratic ambition, an intellectual, artistic pursuit with little role for consumer input. Yet this vision creates a paradox: how can winemakers create status – symbolic value – through the fermenting of grapes?

Critics

Critics play a powerful role in the US wine market. Karen MacNeil, Jancis Robinson, *The Wine Spectator*, *Wine Enthusiast*, *Wine and Spirits*, Vinous Media and *The Wine Advocate*, among hundreds of others, review wines, assign scores and publish reviews. Robert Parker, founder of *The Wine Advocate*, is one of the most powerful critics. One additional point from Parker can generate €2.80 of revenue per bottle (Ali *et al.* 2008). Given the power of critics, some producers engineer wines to satisfy a critic and earn a high score. But for those pursuing an artisanal logic, doing so is out of the question. As Lorenzo said,

> We have never produced a wine in order to get a rating, never. I wouldn't say [the winemakers] don't care. Of course, we're happy when we receive good ratings, but we have never been influenced by ratings during the production of the wine.

Distribution and retailing

Most producers rely on a small number of distributors who provide access to a broad network of retailers to reach consumers. Distributors select the wines to sell on a national or statewide basis. Phil, a wine distributor who selects a portfolio of wines for distribution, described the intensity of the competition:

> Oh my God, the threat of substitution in the wine business, you know how high it is? I mean it's staggering and the amounts of Chardonnays that can fill in at twelve dollars. You know these buyers have choices so there's got to be a point of difference in how you break through that clutter.

Like distributors that limit access to retailers, large retailers exercise power by providing access to consumers. Gaining distribution and retail availability is challenging for artisanal producers, especially smaller ones. As a result, many smaller artisanal producers sell direct to consumers through a mailing list and a small number of restaurants.

Consumers

From the perspective of an artisanal logic, consumer tastes are not a pivotal consideration when crafting a wine. If, as Bourdieu (1993) suggests when considering the autonomy of the art world, winemakers are creating great works of art, the perspective of those who consume the art are not important – and, in fact, may hinder true artistic production (Hirschman 1983). And yet despite this lack of concern on the part of the producers, some consumers express a need for elevation, the social and symbolic distinction that wines offer. They value wine, but they value it for its ability to help them navigate social worlds and develop cultural capital that can be mobilised throughout life. Many consumers seek this distinction as they become adults. Matthew describes his introduction to wine:

> And I didn't really get into wine, until I started working. At least that's what I remember. So, the first project that I was on as a consultant, there were some team dinners that we would go to, and that's sort of when I, one of my managers introduced me to gin, so I was a big Tanqueray fan for a while. And then wine was sort of the during dinner beverage consumed by the team. So, there were some people that were fairly knowledgeable about wine, and at one point I was sort of handed the wine list and asked to make a selection. And that's always for like, you know a new consultant. Like, that's the moment when you realize okay, I sort of need to know a little bit more about this.

Like many others, Matthew describes one of his first experiences with wine as associated with being adult. Wine plays a pivotal role in consumers' recognising and marking this life-stage transition. As Michele Lamont and others have noted, these types of symbolic boundaries can be important in marking one person from another and a former self from a current self (Kleine, Kleine III and Allen 1995; Lamont and Molnár 2002).

Wine and the status embodied in the wine send social signals related to a consumer's identity. Debra described that what a person drinks reveals something about that person in a very public way:

> People assign the characteristics of a wine to themselves. . . . It's like the girls go around saying oh, I smoke cigars, I drink scotch, I do masculine things. You need to drink what you like – I think, I think people would look at that [an instance she described about a man asking for Riesling] as being strange. Like it's not manly to drink white, especially sweet Riesling.

Consumers often use brands to signal identity or social status (Arsel and Bean 2013; Holt 1998; Elder and Krishna 2010; Hoegg and Alba 2007). Wine is no exception. Among wine consumers, collectors sit atop the status hierarchy. Hosting dinner parties and charity events, collectors generously share their wine with friends and family, demonstrating their sophistication, knowledge about wine and resources. For example, Onathan, a collector from the West Coast, describes an event he hosted:

> I actually started this charity event because of my obsession. One year I realized I had no more space in my house. . . . So I came up with the idea: How can we drink a lot of wine and do something really good with it in one evening? So, we started this thing in my house. I call it the wine charity event. Basically invite a lot of friends and family from around here. I open as much wine as anybody can drink and when everybody is sufficiently intoxicated people propose what charity all the money is going to go to. So, it initially started as something really light-hearted, but then we realized that sometimes we had ten or fifteen different proposals of charities, so we developed a voting system. And we've donated so far tens of thousands of dollars to different, mainly local charities and the only criterion me and my wine put on it is that all the money goes to one charity and that 100% of the money goes to charity.

By sharing wine with a large group of friends, Onathan gains status among the group (Mauss 1925/2000). Just as with sharing potlatch practices, plenitude – 'as much wine as anybody can drink' – and disinterestedness – that it be for charity or some other non-instrumental goal – are important.

Consumers use high-status wine brands as a way to cultivate cultural capital, building distinctions that both build community and distinguish themselves. Wine consumers distinguish themselves through their knowledge of wine. The cultural capital associated with knowledge is more than the knowledge of wine itself or the language to express that knowledge. Cultural capital is a disposition towards non-economic or instrumental parts of life, 'a sort of withdrawal from economic necessity' (Bourdieu 1984: 54). Indeed, echoing Veblen (1899/2007), Bourdieu explains that cultural capital signals one's removal or distance from economic subsistence. Those with cultural capital are admired by others for their unique knowledge and for their ability to appreciate the finer things removed from material existence. In short, the high-status brands created through the artisanal logic enable consumers to build cultural capital.

Success

Firms that embrace the artisanal logic succeed by achieving their vision and, through that vision, affecting how others think about wine. Satisfying consumers and commercial success are secondary.

One California winery states their ambitions simply: 'We're not here to break even, we are here to break the rules, break records and break through'. For some, commercial concerns are a sign of insufficient devotion to the creative endeavour. For the artists, achieving their vision and gaining recognition for it comprise the essence of success, and the success of firms enables consumers to gain distinction and build cultural capital using the brands firms create.

Employing an artistic logic to gain status is a well-worn path. For a poet, disinterest in commercial success builds symbolic capital – or status – the degree of recognition, 'prestige, consecration or honour' bestowed to an individual (Randal Johnson in Bourdieu 1993: 14; see also Holt 1998: 3; Bourdieu 1984; Lamont and Lareau 1988; Veblen 1899/2007). 'The underlying law of this paradoxical game is that it is to one's interest to be disinterested: the advantage always falls to those who seek none' (Bourdieu 1993: 154). These two perspectives are, of course, apparently incompatible. 'The artist can triumph on the symbolic terrain only to the extent that he loses on the economic one, and vice versa' (Bourdieu 1993: 169). In this sense, wineries that embrace an artisanal logic reject commercial success. They must, however paradoxically, find the resources to sustain the business.

The commercial logic

For many producers, wine is a business first and foremost. Robert, a California wine executive, expressed it simply: 'Everybody gets into this business because it's a lot of fun. Making wine is a lot of fun. After a couple of years, you end up with a warehouse full of cases and you [realize] it is a tough business'. Another executive, Rachel, described the primacy of the commercial view:

> The market's so competitive. There's been a lot of consolidation. . . . And so, for us to get our unfair share of attention, we need to add value in some way. Either the wines need to be so hot that they're just flying off the shelves. . . [or] we also have people on the street managing those distributors and working the street every day trying to sell the wine.

For firms like these, commercial success is a top priority.

Winemakers

In the commercial logic, firms monitor trends, and the firms' winemakers develop products in response. For instance, Clark, an executive at a large firm, describes the development of a very successful, high-volume red wine:

> And so [our firm] decided they would create – they would create something to go against [a successful red wine], and they created a concept. They created a concept but then a lot of focus was done on the product because it was different. It needed a heavy mouthfeel. It needed a big mouthfeel but still needed to be incredibly smooth. It needed an elevated sugar because that's just what people like. And then at the same time they really did a lot of work that was smart to make sure that the wine style itself matched the label. So, the expectation was very clear.

For firms like Clark's, winemaking is similar to developing consumer products, classically market driven.

Critics

If consumer tastes are hard for wine producers to understand, critics have more clearly defined, consistent preferences. Producers may disagree with critics, but rather than battle powerful critics, winemakers craft wines to please critics and earn high scores. According to Avery, the owner of a Napa winery, 'winemakers are trying to please the critics . . . with the idea being that the critic then influences the end consumer'. Firms have even emerged that, as one wine critic described, 'actually engineer wines for people. And they'll say well actually, if we make this style of wine, you'll get a higher score'.

Distribution and retailing

Distributors and retailers are powerful forces in the market, as noted earlier. Both are customers. Because there are so few distributors, they are especially powerful. Satisfying the trade buyer is critical to gain access to retailers and restaurants, according to the commercial logic, and ultimately to consumers. As one chief marketing officer told us,

> We are primarily focused on the trade. . . . So there's an expression that I think I mentioned that we often have to sell the wine three or four times before it even gets to an end consumer. . . . So we are keenly focused on those people that are between us and the consumer first because they are integral to our success, and in many cases they are the evangelists and they hand sell or recommend or get excited about it which helps consumers get excited about it.
>
> *(Barbara)*

Distributors specify characteristics of the wines they will consider. As one executive told us: 'It's really all about providing a product that is, from a price-value relationship consistent with other competition and checking boxes'. Without distribution and access to retailers, producers struggle to even catch the attention of consumers.

Consumers

Seeking commercial success, firms focus on understanding customers, but consumers' understanding of wine may be limited. Seeking to understand wine consumers can be frustrating. As one executive remarked, 'People don't know what they're drinking, basically'. Consumers may readily admit a lack of expertise. One consumer, Susan, described her experience in a wine class:

> I started attending a [wine class], got embarrassed because they poured the wine [and asked us to discuss the colour, aroma, taste]. I happened to get aroma for that wine. . . [but to me it] just smells like wine. . . . It was fun. I had nothing I could say. I was like – it tastes like, it smells like wine. And he [said] you should try when you get like cherry, bright fruit, dried fruit, cooked fruit. I'm like I don't.

To learn more about wine, consumers often attend tastings. Hosted by a wine shop or producer, tastings are opportunities to promote specific wines, including new releases, or to introduce the winery to consumers. For consumers, tastings are an opportunity to sample an old favourite or try something new. Tastings also provide consumers with a rich social and personal experience to enhance their wine expertise and knowledge. As one consumer described, wine is

> overwhelming, and I can't process that so this was really cool to actually sit in a room and go, okay, these 11 wines are all from the same place. . . [so] at least you had some foundation that was the same and I, I felt like, oh, good I can process this because I can do 'one of these things is not like the other'. Like I – but if you hand me a glass of wine and say 'Taste

this. What do you think it is?' I couldn't tell you. I can make guesses, but nine times out of ten I'm not right in that department, but if you tell me these four wines are all Bordeaux or these four wines are all cabernet from California or from wherever, I can compare and contrast them for you and pick out the differences.

(Allison)

As Allison describes, a tasting is a setting in which she can explore a range of wines and gain knowledge about her own judgements. Although firms may see consumers as having well-established preferences, research suggests that consumer judgements depend on the context and the field of alternatives (Ariely 2008; Bourdieu 1984). Consumers use tastings to help navigate that complex array of situations and contexts. Given the complexity created by thousands of options, consumers may enjoy exploring wine through tastings and curated retail experiences. However, most consumers remain inexpert and lack well-defined tastes, posing a challenge to commercially driven firms that try to align their products with those tastes.

Without clear guidance from consumers, firms look to trends for insight about consumer tastes. 'There's a lot of following what's hot, varieties, segments, regions that are robust and hot', said one executive. By following trends, firms often develop similar rather than distinct wines. A wine executive, Aron, summarised a view we heard from many others: 'The top 15 chardonnays all look exactly the same'.

Overwhelmed with the number of similar choices, consumers rely on experts. Critics are especially influential. Critics review wines and typically score them on an easy-to-understand 0-to-20 or 0-to-100 scale. According to Chris, a critic himself, 'What we've done by making [Robert] Parker the most influential critic in the world for anything, we have basically created an objective opinion'. Despite questions about the objectivity of these scores, critics do nevertheless influence consumers. As Clark, a retailer, said: 'People sometimes buy only on ratings' and ignore the description or tasting notes that typically accompany the score.

Success

According to the commercial logic, firms seek to understand consumers, select target customers and develop wines to meet their needs. Firms also produce wines to appeal to critics and satisfy price points established by a small number of powerful distributors, which produces a sea of similar wines. For many consumers, the array of choices is confusing, creating fear and frustration. Some consumers navigate the options through tastings, wine clubs and direct purchase from wineries, gaining status as they gain knowledge about wine. From this process, a small set of successful brands emerge as appealing and distinct from competitors. For producers, the measure of success is consumer acceptance and financial returns.

Socially constructing brand value

The differences between the artisanal logic and the commercial logic create tension within firms. The two logics differ in term of the motivations of firms; the roles of winemakers, critics and retailers; and even how firms measure success. Table 39.1 summarises these differences.

Rejecting the artisanal as impractical, some firms produce wine using a commercial logic; the wines they make are often described by critics as industrial. Other producers reject the commercial logic and embrace the artisanal approach. Our analysis suggests that some firms pursue a third option, seeking to satisfy both logics simultaneously by playing status games. For example, Mike, a California wine executive, described the tension between the commercial and artisanal aspects:

Table 39.1 Artisanal logic and commercial logic in the US wine market

Commercial	Dimension	Artisanal
Commercial enterprise	*Vision*	Creative expression
Well-defined, consistent, discoverable preferences	*Consumer tastes*	Lack expertise, mercurial
Engineers	*Winemakers*	Artists
Screen products, identify high-quality wines	*Critics and media*	Interpret wines and convey meaning
Powerful customers and gatekeepers	*Distribution and retail*	Powerful with buyers, a stage to reach consumers
Consumer acceptance and financial success	*Success*	Achieving a vision with impact

'Naturally we want [our winemaker] to produce wines that are the best in the world. So, we don't want to put a lot of financial constraints on the winemaking team, yet we're a business'.

Given that the logics are contradictory and inconsistent, seeking to satisfy both logics is a challenging path. As Pablo Picasso remarked, 'It is often said that the artist should work for himself, for the love of art, and scorn success. An artist needs success. Not only in order to live but primarily so that he can realize his work' (Muniz et al. 2014: 71). How can a firm satisfy consumers while ignoring them and become financially successful if doing so compromises the firm's legitimacy?

First, firms playing the status game begin with a vision. Crafted without input from consumers, the vision becomes the primary road map for the firm and for the education of consumers. As Alain, an executive said,

> One has to be a visionary to succeed in the wine industry because one has to see what other people don't see. . . . You have to see 5, 10, 25 years down the road. . . . I'm not going to be asking the market what it wants because they don't know what they want until I'm going to show them.

Winemakers invoke their magic, crafting wines to reflect their vision and sharing them with the world.

Second, rather than seeing critics as judges or as customers to be satisfied, firms playing the status game view critics as potential allies. Winemakers cultivate relationships with critics, sharing their knowledge and persuading critics of the wisdom of the winemaker's vision. As one executive told us, 'Education is essential for the success of wine in the market'. More than just rating wines, critics provide consumers with a language to understand and describe the sensations of consuming wine. Critics establish benchmarks and provide language and structure to enable consumers to develop preferences (West et al. 1996).

Relatedly, some winemakers attain celebrity status, allowing them to wield influence much like critics. As Alain recounted,

> Listening to a winemaker is basically like listening to an artist; once the work has been released, whether this is a painting or book or a bottle of wine, it's all about what's behind the work of art. What's your intent? How did you do it?

The goal, as Alain describes, is to 'help the consumer discover the soul' of the wine. Through experiences and conversations, firms shape how critics and the press interpret a wine, and critics and the press shape how consumers understand and interpret wines.

Third, the winery and retail stores provide opportunities for firms to advance their vision and bring their magic to life. In tasting rooms, consumers visit, taste and purchase wines and attend seminars and events. During these events, the winemaker takes centre stage, shares his or her vision of the wines, offers a broader perspective on wine in general and conducts a tasting. A wine executive, Alain, describes his approach:

> Backstage we study in minute detail our sales in each of our key markets to focus and scale our marketing efforts in the most efficient manner, but on-stage we look immune from marketing. We are the proud artisans of great wines not a financial institution or a money machine. . . . Like a successful recording artist, an iconic wine needs to come to life in 3D once in a while to entertain its magic and stir the heart of its worshippers.

Thus, some firms use retail stores in the same way theatre directors use the stage: as a platform on which they can advance their unique vision not only to retail staff but also to consumers, both those new to the brand and those devoted to it.

Winners and losers emerge from these status games. Winners can define categories, set benchmarks within categories, and influence consumers' price sensitivity. Consumers covet high-status brands and pay premium prices for wines from a lauded producer. The price difference between a low- and high-status win can be substantial (Beverland 2005). With strong demand and high prices, high-status producers thrive financially, satisfying both the commercial and artisanal logics.

For winners of the status game, success can be remarkably enduring (Beverland 2005; Merton 1968; Washington and Zajac 2005). Unlike product features that can be copied, status must be earned, making it difficult to duplicate. Some high-status producers retain their advantage for decades or longer – while rejecting consumer input and feigning disinterest in financial success.

Conclusion

Our results suggest that rather than a single logic reflected in the concept of market orientation, some firms pursue multiple institutional logics, which can create tension and conflict within the firms. Status, however, can play an important role in resolving conflicts in organisational logics and become the basis for a firm's valuable brand. Our results differ from previous work on status in three ways. Scholars have examined the process through which firms influence the structure of markets (e.g. Humphreys 2010; White 1981) and how producers signal status through affiliation (Benjamin and Podolny 1999). Our results suggest that firms rely on status to build relationships with retailers, distributors, critics and consumers, influencing the structure of the market itself. By doing so, firms create a hierarchy of brands that influences the choices of consumers and the flow of resources through the system in fundamental ways. Second, research on market orientation suggests that firms can create competitive advantage through shaping consumer thinking, but empirical support has been lacking (e.g. Jaworski et al. 2000). Our study provides empirical evidence about how firms use status to shape consumer thinking, ultimately building valuable, high-status brands. Third, based on the concept of institutional logics (Thornton et al. 2012), scholars identified that firms often pursue multiple logics simultaneously (e.g. Besharov and Smith 2014). Research is beginning to explore how firms resolve inconsistencies in logics (e.g. Gümüsay et al. 2020). Our results suggest that status can be an effective mechanism to resolve inconsistencies between commercial and artistic logics. Here, we see how the market provides a space for the mutual shaping of consumer tastes and market offerings. As a result, the interrelation of wine and culture can be used to better understand how both firms and consumers in the market behave and change over time.

References

Ali, Héla Hadj, Lecoq, Sébastiaien and Visser, Michael (2008) "The Impact of Gurus: Parker Grades and En Primeur Wine Prices," *Economic Journal* 118, 158–173.

Ariely, D. (2008) *Predictably Irrational: The Hidden Forces That Shape Our Decisions*, London: Harper Collins.

Arsel, Z. and Bean, J. (2013) "Taste Regimes and Market-Mediated Practice," *Journal of Consumer Research* 39(5), 899–917.

Benjamin, B.A. and Podolny, J.M. (1999) "Status, Quality, and Social Order in the California Wine Industry," *Administrative Science Quarterly* 44(3), 563–589.

Besharov, M.L. and Smith, W.K. (2014) "Multiple Institutional Logics in Organizations: Explaining Their Varied Nature and Implications," *Academy of Management Review* 39, 364–381.

Beverland, M.B. (2005) "Crafting Brand Authenticity: The Case of Luxury Wines," *Journal of Management Studies* 42(5), 1003–1029.

Bourdieu, P. (1984) *Distinction: A Social Critique of the Judgement of Taste*, Cambridge, MA: Harvard University Press.

Bourdieu, P. (1993) *The Field of Cultural Production: Essays on Art and Literature*, New York: Columbia University Press.

Elder, R.S. and Krishna, A. (2010) "The Effects of Advertising Copy on Sensory Thoughts and Perceived Taste," *Journal of Consumer Research* 36(5), 748–756.

Gümüsay, Ali Aslan, Smets, Michael and Morris, Timothy (2020) "God at Work: Engaging Central and Incompatible Institutional Logics Through Elastic Hybridity," *The Academy of Management Journal* 63(1), 124–154.

Hirschman, E.C. (1983) "Aesthetics, Ideologies and the Limits of the Marketing Concept," *Journal of Marketing* 47, 45–55.

Hoegg, J. and Alba, J.W. (2007) "Taste Perception: More Than Meets the Tongue," *Journal of Consumer Research* 33(4), 490–498.

Holt, D.B. (1998) "Does Cultural Capital Structure American Consumption?" *Journal of Consumer Research* 25(1), 1–25.

Humphreys, A. (2010) "Megamarketing: The Creation of Markets as a Social Process," *Journal of Marketing* 74(2), 1–19.

Humphreys, A. and Carpenter, G.S. (2018) "Status Games: Market Driving Through Social Influence in the US Wine Industry," *Journal of Marketing* 82(5), 141–159.

Jaworski, B.J. and Kohli, A.K. (1993) "Market Orientation: Antecedents and Consequences," *Journal of Marketing* 57, July, 53–70.

Jaworski, B.J., Kohli, A.K. and Sahay, A. (2000) "Market-Driven Versus Driving Markets," *Journal of the Academy of Marketing Science* 28(1), 45–54.

Kleine, Susan Schultz, Kleine III, Robert E. and Allen, Chris T. (1995) "How Is a Possession 'Me' or 'Not Me'? Characterizing Types and an Antecedent of Material Possession Attachment," *Journal of Consumer Research* 22(3), 327–343.

Kohli, A.K. and Jaworski, B. (1990) "Market Orientation: The Construct, Research Propositions, and Managerial Implications," *Journal of Marketing* 54, April, 1–18.

Lamont, M. and Lareau, A. (1988) "Cultural Capital: Allusions, Gaps and Glissandos in Recent Theoretical Developments," *Sociological Theory* 6(2), 153–168.

Lamont, Michèle and Molnár, Virág (2002) "The Study of Boundaries in the Social Sciences." *Annual Review of Sociology* 28(1), 167–195.

Mauss, Marcel (1925/2000) *The Gift: The Form and Reason for Exchange in Archaic Societies*, New York: W.W. Norton.

Merton, R.K. (1968) "The Matthew Effect in Science: The Reward and Communication Systems of Science Are Considered," *Science* 159(3810), 56–63.

Muniz Jr, A.M., Norris, T. and Fine, G.A. (2014) "Marketing Artistic Careers: Pablo Picasso as Brand Manager," *European Journal of Marketing* 49(1/2), 68–88.

Parker, R. (1997) "Dominus," *Wine Advocate* 114, December.

Thornton, P.H., Ocasio, W. and Loundsbury, M. (2012) *The Institutional Logics Perspective: A New Approach to Culture, Structure and Process*, Oxford: Oxford University Press.

Veblen, Thorstein (1899/2007) *The Theory of the Leisure Class*, Cambridge, MA: Oxford University Press.

Washington, M. and Zajac, E.J. (2005) "Status Evolution and Competition: Theory and Evidence," *Academy of Management Journal* 48(2), 282–296.

West, P.M., Brown, C.L. and Hoch, S.J. (1996) "Consumption Vocabulary and Preference Formation," *Journal of Consumer Research* 23(2), 120–135.

White, H.C. (1981) "Where Do Markets Come From," *American Journal of Sociology* 87(3), 517–547.

PART VI

Change and the future

40
INTERNATIONALISATION OF WINEGRAPE VARIETIES AND ITS IMPLICATIONS FOR TERROIR-BASED CULTURAL ASSETS

Kym Anderson and Signe Nelgen

Introduction

How internationalised have vineyards' winegrape varieties become since wine globalisation accelerated from the 1990s? Have each country's vineyards also become more diversified in their varietal mix? What are the implications for terroir-based cultural assets in the countries of origin of each variety and in the countries planting them? How have economic growth and globalisation simultaneously altered beverage consumption cultures in those countries and in non-wine-producing countries? This chapter addresses these questions with the help of two recently revised, expanded and updated global databases, one covering wine production, consumption and trade (Anderson and Pinilla 2018, 2020) and the other on winegrape-bearing areas by variety and region (Anderson and Nelgen 2020a, 2020b).

The chapter begins with reviews of the link on the supply side between culture and terroir and of cultural changes on the demand side in the wake of income growth, urbanisation and globalisation. It then draws on the new global databases to see the net effects of those forces empirically. The final section draws out implications, particularly for cultural assets.

Supply-side links between terroir and culture

In both French and English dictionaries, the word terroir has at least two definitions. The narrower definition equates terroir to soil, while the broader one is closer to the English word 'territory' and refers to all the natural and human characteristics of a delimited area of land. The geologist James E. Wilson (1998) emphasises the former even though the subtitle of his seminal book also mentions climate and culture. Anthropologist Amy Trubek (2008) emphasises not only place but, like Parker (2015), also taste. The geographer Warren Moran (2001) emphasises much more the human factor in both winegrape growing and winemaking, which includes cultural dimensions. Patterson and Buechsenstein (2018) provide an overview of many authoritative definitions of terroir and find the view expressed by Moran (2006) the most holistic. These views from New World countries may be less appealing, though, to Europeans, who are more likely to view their relationship with nature as harmonious and to give more weight to historical traditions. Cappeliez (2017) seeks to bridge this gap by suggesting a distinction between elements of this cultural idea that are connected to place, which are more likely to change as the term 'terroir' travels, and those more capable of remaining stable when the term travels across diverse cultural contexts.

Natural and human (including cultural) characteristics of a region affect the choice of grapes planted and the way their growth is managed, the way wine is made from them, the pride in the region and the promotional or commercial advantages of those characteristics (which may be enhanced by legal recognition via geographical indications). In turn, those features become part of the region's culture.

Thus, a region can have cultural as well as natural capital assets, and the cultural assets can be tangible (e.g. terraced vine rows, distinctive buildings or winemaking equipment or harvest celebrations) and intangible (e.g. the unique specific skills of the vignerons within that region, homage to families who pioneered there). This bundle of cultural and natural assets defines the terroir that yields a flow of services in wine regions that generates economic, social and cultural benefits, some of which have a public-good characteristic (Throsby 2001, 2015).

If in each region the natural assets (e.g. soil, climate, aspect) did not change over time, nor did the technologies of grape and wine production or regulations affecting production, nor the preferences and incomes of local wine consumers, and if each vigneron had no access to cuttings from exotic vines and was so small as to produce wine for no more than own-home consumption and sale within the growing region, then one might presume that the winegrape varieties in that region and the wine blends produced from them also would not change over time. The varietal mix, production methods and wine styles of the region would thus be confined to the region's culture.

In practice, of course, almost no winegrape-growing region is so static or insular. As Scienza and Imazio (2019) make clear, migration, conquest and peaceful cross-cultural exchanges have influenced the historical mix of winegrape varieties in each region. Indeed, that has occurred for millennia, but mostly on the Mediterranean shores and hinterlands until the middle of the previous millennium when two things coincided. One was the settlement and colonisation by Europeans in the so-called New World and the viticultural and winemaking knowledge that came with them,[1] and the other was the emergence of a culture of economic development and growth specific to early modern Europe that laid the foundation for scientific advances and pioneering inventions that instigated explosive technological and economic development (Mokyr 2016).

Changes in climate also have affected the extent and varietal mix of each region's winegrape vineyards over the centuries – as they are doing again this century. The impacts (such as higher temperatures, lower water availability, more extreme weather events) on the quality of winegrapes, their ripening periods and their vineyard yields are becoming better understood. Adaptation strategies by vignerons include switching to warmer-climate or more resilient grape varieties and relocating to a region at a higher latitude or elevation to retain the firm's current mix of grape varieties. Especially in the New World, where regions are still trying to identify their comparative advantages and where regulations and traditions do not restrict varietal choice, winegrowers are continually on the lookout for attractive alternative varieties that do well in climates similar to what they expect theirs to become in the decades ahead.

Meanwhile, ongoing investments in research are altering grape and wine technologies and creating new hybrid varieties; changes in regulations and technical standards are altering production costs; falling information and communication costs are speeding technology transfers and marketing skills between regions; and declines in trade costs are altering the inter-regional (including international) tradability of grape juice and wine and, thus, the competitiveness of each region's producers.

Demand-side influences on beverage consumption cultures

Demand-side forces add to those supply-side influences on the total area and mix of winegrape varieties in each wine region. As incomes rise, so, too, does the demand for luxury products, including higher-quality wines and a broader range of styles and varieties. In addition to rising incomes, reduced costs of transport, information and communication ensure that (1) local wine consumers become increasingly exposed to and interested in exotic varieties and styles that now compete with locally produced varieties, (2) the demands of wine consumers in other regions and countries also now influence local winegrape demand and, hence, prices and (c) more consumers take an interest in wine cultures elsewhere.

These changes in demand conditions have accelerated thanks to globalisation, particularly with the emergence of large multinational wine corporations and retail supermarkets and the growth of international wine tourism (Anderson and Pinilla 2018). They have potential implications for terroir-based cultural assets. For example, if higher-quality wine comes from grape varieties best grown in cool climates (e.g. pinot noir), might the area of vineyards in cool regions grow faster than that in hot regions as global incomes and temperatures rise? And if the global diversity of winegrapes is converging on the best-known varieties (often referred to as 'international' varieties), how is that impacting the cultural assets of the regions of origin and destination? Johnson and Robinson (2013: 8) note that vignerons are beginning to react by reverting to neglected local varieties in the Old World and by exploring or revisiting alternatives to the main 'international' varieties in the New World (and in Italy – see D'Agata 2014).

Globalisation of the world's wine markets over recent decades has been associated with huge changes in national beverage consumption (Anderson and Pinilla 2018, 2020). In the traditional wine-producing countries of France, Italy and Spain, as well as in Chile, per capita wine consumption today is only one-third of its inter-war level, and it has fallen also, by about half, in Portugal, Argentina and much of Eastern Europe. With production in those countries falling far less, surpluses arose, and much was disposed of via exports. Meanwhile, rising incomes in the West and the emergence of large retail supermarkets created a demand for a product in between the quality of fine/super-premium and bulk/non-premium wines: namely, commercial premium bottles of approachable, homogenous quality at a scale large enough for supermarkets to advertise their availability nationally. That coincided with low real exchange rates in Southern hemisphere commodity-exporting countries, resulting in a market-driven wine export boom from temperate parts of New World countries starting in the 1990s.

Consumption per capita rose greatly from low bases in beer- and spirits-consuming countries, from less than 5 litres per capita in the 1960s to more than 20 litres per capita in such countries as the United Kingdom, Ireland, most northwest European countries, North America, Australia and New Zealand (Holmes and Anderson 2017). More recently, grape wine consumption has taken off from a very low base in East Asia to 0.8 litres per capita per year in South Korea and Taiwan to more than a litre in China to more than 2 litres in Japan and Singapore and to greater than 3 litres in Hong Kong (Anderson 2020).

Cultural changes by consumers are normal consequences of disruptions such as rapid income growth, urbanisation, greater openness to international trade and migration and increased labour force participation by women (Giuliano and Nunn 2017; Giuliano 2020; Bernheim et al. 2021; Voth 2021). The latter, when combined with the supermarket revolution and the boom in exports from the New World of accessible wines, resulted in wine purchases becoming a normal part of food shopping for many women for the first time in the late twentieth century. More generally, wine consumers are becoming more knowledgeable about the product, its producers and its regions of origin.

A major facilitator of these changes in beverage demand has been the rising share of global wine consumption that is imported, from below 15% pre-1990 to above 40% (Anderson and Pinilla 2020). Consumers in most countries have never enjoyed such a diversity of wine styles, qualities/prices and winegrape varieties and blends used by winemakers. Contributing to this diversity has been the development of new wine regions, including cool ones in response not only to global warming but also to an increasing preference for the more refined wines that cool regions are capable of supplying.

Both opportunities and competitive challenges abound for vignerons seeking to attract consumer interest by differentiating their product or, alternatively, by emulating the most successful producers. One strategy for producers has been to display names of (especially popular) grape varieties on wine bottle labels. Its success, particularly for lower-priced New World wines, has led to demands in the European Union for liberalising labelling laws to allow such labelling there also. The recent decision by Aldi to organise the shelving of wine in its UK supermarkets according to variety instead of region of origin will strengthen that demand.

As well, producers in the New World are increasingly realising the marketing value of going beyond country of origin to regional labelling as another form of product differentiation – something that has long been practised by Europe's traditional producers, for reasons made clear in Patterson and Buechsenstein (2018). At the extreme is a greater use of single-vineyard labelling, emulating what has long been the practice for the best of Burgundy wines.

These forces could, on the one hand, lead one to expect winegrowing countries to import more exotic varieties to diversify their plantings, especially in the relatively unconstrained growing environment in New World countries and particularly from the largest and most successful winegrowing countries of the Old World (especially France). On the other hand, if vignerons still experimenting with their terroir in the New World and in Eastern Europe felt that emulating the most successful Old World producers was the most reliable and profitable strategy, one might expect to see new plantings dominated by the most popular varieties and blends from the most famous wine regions (e.g. the global proliferation of Bordeaux blends). The overall effect of these supply push and demand pull forces on the location of wine production and consumption should be to disrupt the traditional associations of certain wines with certain cultures, but tracking that remains elusive. What is more tangible is the measurement of significant shifts in varietal plantings, which might lead to future inferences about wine-cultural changes, especially in the new destinations.

What has been the net impact of these various forces this century on the diversity of winegrape varietal plantings globally and in key wine-producing countries? And, in particular, how much has wine globalisation been accompanied by the varietal mix in national vineyards becoming more 'internationalised' since the 1990s?

Empirical evidence from vineyard plantings

To address those question, we draw on a new global database by Anderson and Nelgen (2020a, 2020b) that covers all winegrape plantings by variety in the world's wine regions in recent decades. It is based on vine-bearing areas in hectares and includes various shares and indexes for each of 53 countries involving 700-plus wine regions that account for 99% of the world's winegrape vineyard area. More than 1,700 DNA-distinct 'prime' varieties[2] are in the winegrapes database, covering 2000, 2010 and 2016 as well as more limited data for 1990. Each prime variety is linked to its country of origin and to its synonyms, as nominated by Robinson et al. (2012) or otherwise JKI (2019).

The extent of varietal concentration in the world's vineyards increased non-trivially between 2000 and 2016. Half the world's bearing area of vineyards were accounted for by the top 21 prime varieties in 2000, but, by 2016, it took just the top 16 varieties to get to half (Figure 40.1). This increasing concentration occurred almost entirely in the New World: both it and the Old World needed almost the same number of varieties to reach half their bearing areas in 2000, but by 2016, the New World needed just 9 varieties compared with 18 in the Old World. Increasing concentration is evident as well in the data on individual varieties: for all but 2 of the world's top 30 varieties, the number of countries growing them is higher in 2016 than in 2000. And in three-quarters of the countries with available data, the share of the nation's top 10 varieties in their total bearing area is higher in 2016 than in 2000 (Figure 40.2).

Internationalisation of grape varieties

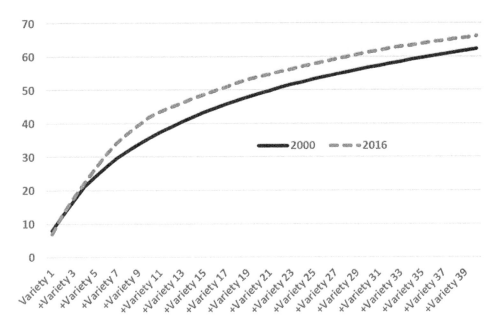

Figure 40.1 Cumulative varietal shares of global winegrape area, 2000 and 2016 (%)
Source: Based on data in Anderson and Nelgen (2020b)

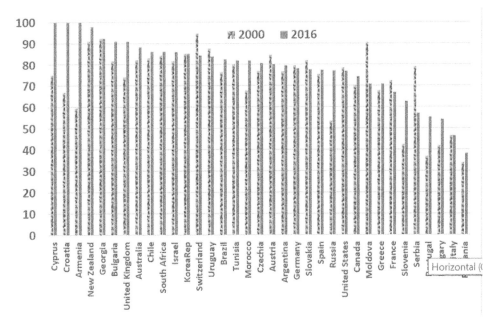

Figure 40.2 Share of nation's top 10 varieties in national winegrape area, 2000 and 2016 (%)
Source: Based on data in Anderson and Nelgen (2020b)

This reduced diversity of the world's vineyards is summarised in the index of similarity between national and global varietal mixes, reported in Figure 40.3. (This index is like a correlation coefficient that ranges from 0 (no similarity) to one (identical mix) – see Anderson 2013; Anderson and Nelgen 2020a.) It reveals that the varietal mix of less than one-quarter of countries became notably less similar to the global mix between 2000 and 2016. That is, since the new millennium, a strong majority of winegrape-producing countries have become more similar to the global average in terms of the mix of grape varieties in their vineyards.

Yet at the same time as the varietal mix is becoming less diversified nationally and globally, it is also becoming more internationalised. The extent of that necessarily varies hugely across countries, given that the share of national area that is planted to own-country prime varieties varies from zero to 100%. But note from Figure 40.4 that only 17 of our 53 countries have more than one-tenth of their winegrape bearing area in own-country prime varieties.

A way to gauge the extent of internationalisation is to examine the share of global bearing area of prime varieties that is outside their country of origin. More than three-quarters of countries of origin saw their varieties' aggregate share of the global bearing area rise between 2000 and 2016 (Figure 40.5).

Another way to gauge the extent of spread of prime varieties beyond their place of origin is to divide the share of prime varieties originating from that nation in the global area of winegrapes by the share of that country in the total global area of all winegrapes. This index of internationalisation of prime varieties is reported in Figure 40.6. Only one-third of countries of origin saw that index of internationalisation of their prime varieties fall between 2000 and 2016.

Even so, from a global viewpoint, this internationalisation is predominantly due to the greater adoption in many countries of French varieties. Between 1990 and 2016, the share of plantings of French prime varieties nearly doubled, rising from 21% to 39% globally. Varieties from Greece and Portugal increased their shares by one-sixth and one-seventh, respectively, but only to 3% each,

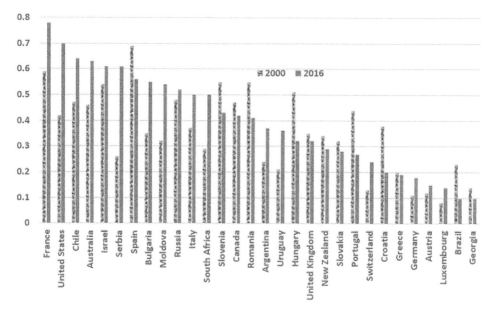

Figure 40.3 Index of similarity between national and global varietal mixes, 2000 and 2016

Source: Based on data in Anderson and Nelgen (2020b)

Internationalisation of grape varieties

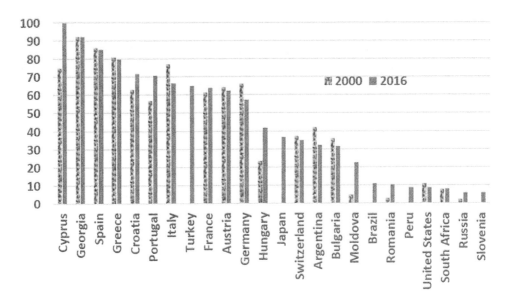

Figure 40.4 Share of national bearing area that is planted to own-country prime varieties, by country of planting, 2000 and 2016 (%)

Source: Based on data in Anderson and Nelgen (2020b)

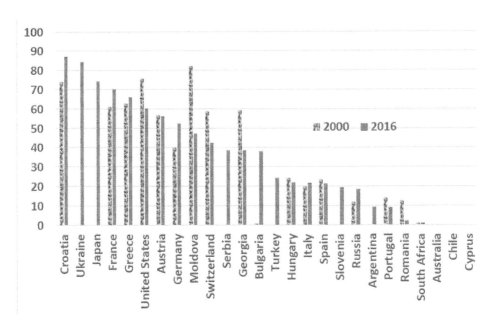

Figure 40.5 Share of global bearing area of prime varieties that is outside the country of origin, by country of origin, 2000 and 2016 (%)

Source: Based on data in Anderson and Nelgen (2020b)

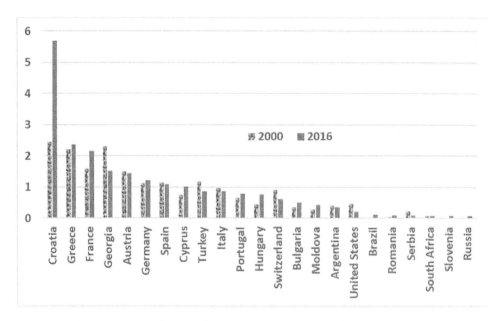

Figure 40.6 Index of internationalisation of prime varieties, by country of origin, 2000 and 2016
Source: Based on data in Anderson and Nelgen (2020b)

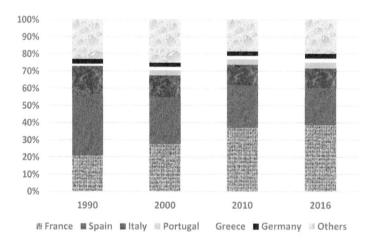

Figure 40.7 Shares of global winegrape-bearing area by varietal country of origin, 1990 to 2016 (%)
Source: Based on data in Anderson and Nelgen (2020b)

while the shares of Italian and Spanish varieties in the global vineyard each fell by roughly one-third. The net effect of these changes on the distribution of prime varieties, shown in Figure 40.7, is that the combined share of the big three wine countries remained at around 70%, but France gradually replaced Spain in first place while Italy's share in third place also shrank.

The apparent paradox of reduced diversity and greater internationalisation in the world's vineyards is partly explained by changes in national bearing areas. Between 1990 and 2016, Spain, on the one hand, had by far the biggest fall in its winegrape-bearing area, by 515,000 hectares or 35%, shrinking its share of global plantings from 18.2% to 12.5% (Anderson and Nelgen 2020b). On the other hand, the countries whose bearing areas expanded most from 1990 to 2016 were Australia, Chile, the United States and especially China, all four of which now have a much higher proportion of their area under French varieties than any other country except France itself.

What about consumers?

The claim earlier in the chapter that the world's consumers have never before had such a wide range of wines to choose from is not inconsistent with reduced varietal diversity in the world's vineyards. The main reason is that two of every five bottles crosses a national border before being consumed now, compared with less than one in seven pre-1990. Greater openness to trade in any product leads to increased specialisation in production and simultaneously increased diversity of consumer choice. In the case of wine, that happens in terms of styles, qualities and prices, as well as the range of winegrape varieties used either on their own or in myriad blends.

As for the quality of the wines produced and consumed, that depends on many factors, of course. But one indicator that wine quality globally may have risen is provided by the change in shares of the global winegrape-bearing area of what are arguably some of the most iconic varieties. The top varieties from Bordeaux (cabernet Franc, cabernet sauvignon, merlot and sauvignon blanc), Burgundy and Champagne (chardonnay, pinot meunière and pinot noir), Germany and Alsace (pinot gris and riesling) and the northern Rhône (syrah and viognier), plus the top one now in Argentina (côt) and Spain (tempranillo), have seen their combined global share rise from 12% to 37% between 1990 and 2016 (Figure 40.8). By contrast, the combined share of the six most-widely planted prime varieties as of 1990 (Airén, Garnacha Tinta, Mazuelo, Rkatsiteli, Sultaniye and Trebbiano Toscano) has fallen from 33% to 13%, and arguably, they are on average of lower quality.

Implications for cultural assets

These results reveal that vignerons are choosing to narrow their winegrape varietal mix on average: they are becoming less diversified as many countries converge on growing the major

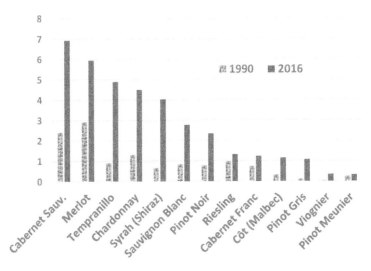

Figure 40.8   Shares of premium varieties in the world's total winegrape-bearing area, 1990 and 2016 (%)
Source: Based on data in Anderson and Nelgen (2020b)

'international' varieties, especially French ones. Yet this is not inconsistent with wine consumers enjoying ever-wider choices because of far greater international trade in wine thanks to the current wave of globalisation. Nor is that trend inconsistent with a strengthening vigneron interest in 'alternative' and native varieties in numerous countries, including Italy (D'Agata 2014) and Australia (Halliday 2018; Higgs 2019). That interest in minor varieties stems in part from a desire by many individual vignerons to diversify their varietal mix to differentiate their offering, as well as to hedge against increasing weather volatility. It just happens that in recent decades, the latter centrifugal forces are dominated by the centripetal force of embracing the most popular noble varieties. Nonetheless, the scope for any vigneron to return to varieties their ancestors grew has never been greater, with far more consumers available via trade outside their own region or country. As for consumers, both the quality and range of the currently available mix of varieties and styles of wines are substantially greater than what were on offer in the 1990s. That diversity for consumers is likely to continue to increase in the decades ahead, even if the diversity of varieties in the global vineyard does not.

What does this say about terroir-based cultural assets? Unless we preclude it by definition, terroir is certainly not a static concept, at least in terms of the winegrower's varietal mix choices in a particular place. Ongoing climate change may even lead to faster changes in the total area and mix of winegrape varieties in each region from now on (and lead to the development of new, cooler-climate wine regions). The global spread in the use of the term 'terroir' has no doubt been in part because of its commercial cache. This is especially so with the spread of geographical indications (GIs) to more and more non-European regions and countries. The conferring of UNESCO World Heritage status on more than a dozen of the world's wine regions so far this century (four in France, three in Italy) has further enhanced the commercial value of a long history of place and taste. A tension that will remain, however, is how finely to delimit a place in order to define its terroir: current GIs versus sub-regions within them versus single vineyards (Demossier 2018a, 2018b). Burgundy has chosen to explicitly emphasise the diversity of its vineyards with its 1,247 *climats* (Demossier 2019), but no other region is likely to commercially justify this degree of subdivision in the foreseeable future.

Notes

1 The key 'New World' countries producing winegrapes are Argentina, Australia, Chile, New Zealand, South Africa, the United States and Uruguay. Brazil, Canada, Mexico and Peru also produce wine but in far smaller quantities. We refer to the 'Old World' wine-producing countries as encompassing all of continental Europe, the former Soviet Union and the Levant. China and the few other Asian countries that grow winegrapes, and the United Kingdom, are included in our 'New World' grouping for completeness of global coverage, but they have a miniscule influence on the 'New World' bearing area averages quoted in this chapter.
2 Winegrape varietal names of DNA-identical varieties can differ across countries for historical reasons. In their effort to ensure the diversity of varieties is not exaggerated, Robinson et al. (2012) nominated one of those names to be the 'prime' variety and called all other DNA-identical varieties synonyms. Their nomination is based on the name used in what they believe to be the country of origin of that variety.

References

Anderson, K. (2020) "Asia's Emergence in Global Beverage Markets: The Rise of Wine," *Singapore Economic Review* 65(4), June, 755–779.
Anderson, K. (with the assistance of N.R. Aryal) (2013) *Which Winegrape Varieties Are Grown Where? A Global Empirical Picture*, Adelaide: University of Adelaide Press. Freely, www.adelaide.edu.au/press/winegrapes.

Anderson, K. and Nelgen, S. (2020a) *Which Winegrape Varieties Are Grown Where? A Global Empirical Picture (Revised Edition)*, Adelaide: University of Adelaide Press. Freely, www.adelaide.edu.au/press/winegrapes.

Anderson, K. and Nelgen, S. (2020b) "Database of Regional, National and Global Winegrape Bearing Areas by Variety, 2000, 2010 and 2016," https://economics.adelaide.edu.au/wine-economics/databases.

Anderson, K. and Pinilla, V. (eds) (2018) *Wine Globalisation: A New Comparative History*, Cambridge and New York: Cambridge University Press.

Anderson, K. and Pinilla, V. (with the assistance of A.J. Holmes) (2020) *Annual Database of Global Wine Markets, 1835 to 2018*, Wine Economics Research Centre, www.adelaide.edu.au/wine-econ/databases/global-wine-history. Summarised in a Compendium by K. Anderson, S. Nelgen and V. Pinilla that is available as a free e-book at www.adelaide.edu.au/press/titles/global-wine-markets.

Bernheim, B.D., Braghieri, L., Martínez-Marquina, A. and Zuckerman, D. (2021) "A Theory of Chosen Preferences," *American Economic Review* 111(2), February, 720–754.

Cappeliez, S. (2017) "How Well Does Terroir Travel? Illuminating Cultural Translation Using a Comparative Wine Case Study," *Poetics* 65, December, 24–36.

D'Agata, I. (2014) *Native Wine Grapes of Italy*, Berkeley: University of California Press.

Demossier, M. (2018a) *Burgundy: A Global Anthropology of Place and Taste*, New York and Oxford: Berghahn.

Demossier, M. (2018b) "Terroir, Wine Culture, and Globalisation: What Does Terroir Do to Wine?" *Europe Now* (20), 5 September.

Demossier, M. (2019) "Burgundy's *Climats* and the Utopian Wine Heritage Landscape," in J. Dutton and P.J. Howland (eds), *Wine, Terroir and Utopia: Making New Worlds*, London: Routledge.

Giuliano, P. (2020) "Gender and Culture," *Oxford Review of Economic Policy* 36(4), December, 944–961.

Giuliano, P. and Nunn, N. (2017) "Understanding Cultural Persistence and Change," NBER Working Paper 23617, Cambridge, MA, July. Forthcoming in Review of Economic Studies (published online at https://academic.oup.com/restud, accessed 27 December 2020).

Halliday, J. (2018) *Varietal Wines: A Guide to 140 Varieties Grown in Australia and Their Place in the International Wine Landscape*, London: Hardie Grant Books.

Higgs, D. (2019) *Rare Ozzies: A Hundred Rare Australian Grape Varieties*, self-published in Williamstown, Victoria, www.vinodiversity.com/rareozzies.html.

Holmes, A.J. and Anderson, K. (2017) "Convergence in National Alcohol Consumption Patterns: New Global Indicators," *Journal of Wine Economics* 12(2), 117–148.

JKI (Julius Kühn-Institut). (2019) *Vitis International Variety Catalogue*, Institute for Grapevine Breeding, Federal Research Centre for Cultivated Plants, Geilweilerhof, www.vivc.de.

Johnson, H. and Robinson, J. (2013) *The World Atlas of Wine*, 7th edition, London: Mitchell Beasley.

Mokyr, J. (2016) *A Culture of Growth: The Origins of the Modern Economy*, Princeton, NJ: Princeton University Press.

Moran, W. (2001) "Terroir – the Human Factor," *Australian and New Zealand Wine Industry Journal* 16(2), March–April, 32–36.

Moran, W. (2006) "You Said Terroir? Approaches, Sciences and Explanations," Keynote Address at Terroir 2006, a Symposium at the University of California, Davis CA, March.

Parker, T. (2015) *Tasting French Terroir: The History of an Idea*, Berkeley: University of California Press.

Patterson, T. and Buechsenstein, J. (2018) *Wine and Place: A Terroir Reader*, Berkeley: University of California Press.

Robinson, J., Harding, J. and Vouillamoz, J. (2012) *Wine Grapes: A Complete Guide to 1,368 Vine Varieties, Including Their Origins and Flavours*, London: Allen Lane.

Scienza, A. and Imazio, S. (2019) *Sangiovese, Lambrusco and Other Vine Stories*, Trowbridge: Positive Press.

Throsby, D. (2001) *Economics and Culture*, Cambridge and New York: Cambridge University Press.

Throsby, D. (2015) "Terroir-based Economies as Economic and Cultural Assets: Value, Valuation and Sustainability," Paper presented at the International Conference on The Heritage Value of Terroir-based Economies as a Model of Human Development, Paris, 18–19 February.

Trubek, A. (2008) *The Taste of Place: A Cultural Journey into Terroir*, Berkeley: University of California Press.

Voth, H.-J. (2021) "Persistence: Myth and Mystery," ch. 9 in *The Handbook of Historical Economics*, Cambridge, MA: Academic Press, 243–267.

Wilson, J.E. (1998) *Terroir: The Role of Geology, Climate and Culture in the Making of French Wine*, London: Mitchell Beazley.

41
CULTURAL HERITAGE AND MIGRATION IN THE WINE WORLD

Chantal Crenn

Introduction

A little over 20 years ago, anthropologist Guille-Escuret (1988: 12) demolished the conservative image that the French wine world strives to project, combining: 'nature and culture . . . while grapes are often presented as a gift from heaven or nature, in contrast, wine is the food into which our civilisation most faithfully transposes its taste for hierarchy, natural prerogatives, and historical legitimacy'. To the extent, he added, that 'the wine world resembles a society composed of old-stock aristocracy, gentry, and rootless commoners. A society set in stone that imposes customary law as immutable'. Guille-Escuret was warning us not to be anesthetised by discourses about wine that mask its basely material components and only express the 'pure marriage of natural grapes and history in the cellar: to them, an authentic winemaker is a craftsman, not a peasant' (Guille-Escuret 1988: 13). At the time, he wondered why the wide range of publications included very little on vats, wines and wine tasters. Since then, the gap has been filled by extensive research in the social and human sciences, covering almost every aspect of wine.

While the transformations of local wine communities have been studied (Ulin and Black 2013) in the context of globalisation (Demossier 2018; Inglis and Almila 2019), the subject of migration has been neglected. Indeed, investigating the relationship between vineyards, wines and migration is a heuristic means to comprehend transformations in the wine world. Thus, a combined study of migration and globalisation on the European wine scene, particularly in the Bordeaux region, offers an opportunity to break away from the essentialised representations of this product and discourse about quality. Indeed, as Pierre-Marie Chauvin (2019) concluded, Bordeaux no longer holds the monopoly on 'good wine', yet it has managed to benefit from globalisation, locally and nationally, in constructing a 'good reputation'.

What is the influence of migration on this process of cultural hybridisation in a large network of stakeholders, as described by Demossier and Chauvin? What influence has it had on transformation in the wine world? What trends do migratory phenomena in the rural world reveal? These questions require us to take a broader perspective and move beyond issues such as migrant integration, focusing our analysis on the anthropology of food and agriculture (Guille-Escuret 1988; Ulin and Black 2013). I propose to start by retracing how the extension of monoculture and the industrialisation of wine production after World War II, followed by decolonisation, brought about profound transformations in rural societies to the east of Bordeaux. I will show how, since the 1950s, several migratory waves have shaped the history of this winegrowing region, highlighting the invisible ties between migration, 'heritagisation' and wine. In the southwest of France, there has been a long tradition in agriculture and viticulture of recruiting temporary workers from Spain and Portugal. Italians have also contributed, especially during the period when they escaped fascism. From the end of the Second World War, the French state has sought to organise the local workforce recruitment (through the ONI National Immigration Office) by targeting its former colonies (Morocco, Algeria and Tunisia) to move into a monocultural intensive national wine production.

Drawing on long-term ethnographic fieldwork conducted in the Bordeaux region, between St-Emilion and Bergerac, since 2004, I will investigate the often-hidden story of migration of Moroccans, Tunisians and Algerians who came to France in the 1970s to work in the vineyards and of Spaniards who joined them later, following the economic crisis of 2008. Analysis of property purchases, the movements of temporary workers, the precarity experienced by these migrants and competition among the various localities will provide insight into the mechanisms enlisted to project 'authenticity' and permanence. According to a survey conducted by Caf, MSA and INSEE in 2011, the small towns of Castillon-La-Bataille and Sainte-Foy-La-Grande belong to the somewhat caricatural 'poverty belt' that extends from the Médoc region to the city of Agen. In both towns, 29% of the population depend on welfare benefits (Crenn 2017: 54).

Modernisation, a single motto in wine production between Saint-Emilion and Bergerac

> After the War, we wanted to modernise, to expand . . . the vineyards, we didn't have that much. . . . It was in addition to the rest, a few cows, cereals . . . mostly white wine. We soon understood there was an opportunity, so my brother and I started to plant . . . then the first tractors arrived. . . . I also recall the Spanish workers we used to pick up at the station in Libourne for the grape harvest.
>
> *(Louis, 91 years old, Eynesse, July 2020).*

It is important to stress that the wine world is inextricably linked with the history of European agriculture (Roudié 1994), which requires no further description as it is well documented elsewhere (Deléage 2013; Berlan 1986 etc.). The Bordeaux wine world was closely bound up with the history of colonisation, initially attracted by the prosperous markets and later offering a haven for *pieds noirs* (French nationals) repatriated from North Africa, as well as employment for former colonials (Bohling 2018). The immediate post-war period, according to Joseph Bohling's *Sober Revolution*, witnessed one of the numerous facets of French modernisation, in a context of decolonisation, Europeanisation and market globalisation. 'The identity of French wine, thanks to the denomination of origin system, contributed to restoring the national identity' (Taveau 2019: 1). At the time, it was considered important to compete with cultural Americanisation and assert the French identity on the international stage since this had become a yardstick of good national governance.

Thus, as the historian Philippe Roudié (1994: 296–299) argued, from a purely winegrowing perspective, once the war was over, everything in the Bordeaux area had to be rebuilt. The Chambers of Agriculture, suppressed during the Vichy period, were re-established, as were winegrower and merchant associations; legislation on denominations of origin was reinstated, and wine classifications were published for Saint-Emilion and Graves. Wine cooperatives were once again in the vanguard in Gironde, with eight new cooperatives opened in 1952 alone (Roudié 1994). As Jacques, a retired winegrower, recalls, tractors brought motorisation to the vineyards. Roudié noted a rapid expansion in tractor ownership, thanks to loans from the Crédit Agricole bank, fuel tariff cuts and an increasing rural exodus. 'Motorisation that transformed work in the vineyards was accompanied by major changes in viticultural techniques, accentuated by the replanting of the vineyards following the severe 1956 frost' (Roudié 1994: 329), which pushed some farmers into bankruptcy and selling their land. Simplified vineyard management focused on three grape varieties: merlot, semillon, and cabernet Franc. The planting of high-trained, widely spaced vines also facilitated mechanisation. It would take too long to list the regions that refused these changes, but in Saint-Emilion, for example, mechanisation was held up as the new system was contrary to the denomination specifications (Roudié 1994), while it was widely adopted in Sainte-Foy-La-Grande. As Philippe Roudié remarked, this difference in vineyard management marked the division between high- and low-ranking denominations.

However, the changes in this area were not only technical. The area around Sainte-Foy-La-Grande, Pellegrue and Castillon suffered from rural exodus, with winegrowers' children increasingly attracted by city life. Italian immigrants who had fled from fascism were able to buy wine estates, especially those with no successors. In addition, former colonists from Algeria reshuffled the cards by purchasing large vineyards, thanks to loans from the Crédit Agricole bank and their own savings (Crenn 2017), and 'rapidly upgrading their independent wine production outside the cooperative movement' (Roudié 1994: 355). At that time, according to the memories of local inhabitants, the first farm labourers arrived from the former colonies, either accompanying their repatriated employers or at the local owners' request. 'France entered the age of industrialised agricultural production thanks to the government's creation of the ONI and seasonal contract visas, combined with the Marshall Plan and the generalised use of tractors' (Decosse 2017: 184). As Decosse demonstrated, it is clear that, after World War II, 'the recruitment of seasonal labour from the ex-colonies was the result of negotiations between the French state, determined to regulate foreign immigration and collect their social security contributions' (Decosse 2017: 190), and employers, keen to increase production. Mechanisation, chemical fertilisers and immigration were all tied together at that early stage.

The history of invisible migration in Bordeaux wine production

> I was recruited in Morocco. My boss came to pick me up at Bordeaux station and I worked for him all my life, until I retired. . . . Growing grapes was my whole life. . . . I've done everything: cane pruning and removal, suckering, cleaning vats. . .
> *(Mohamed, 70 years old, farmhand, Massugas, March 2020)*

Decolonisation brought a huge wave of repatriated colonists from Algeria, accompanied by 'Harkis' (the term used to refer to Algerians who 'chose' France at the time of independence). Algerian immigrants also found employment via ONI contracts on the numerous farms in need of a workforce, due to local labour shortages. They worked in orchards and fruit-processing factories when the annual vineyard work was over. Their polyvalence in agriculture enabled them to find full time employment all year round. They were soon followed by Moroccans and Tunisians, who replaced the Spanish and Portuguese as seasonal labourers, while the latter purchased land, left for other jobs in the cities or, later, returned to their countries of origin after the fall of their respective dictatorships. Christophe Drot (2007) reported that in the Bordeaux region alone, there were 6,000 North African seasonal workers in 1968 and 15,000 by the mid-1970.

The workers I interviewed in the Bordeaux region had arrived in the early 1970s (Crenn 2015, 2017). The men came first, directly from their villages on ONI contracts, mostly from the Gharb region, but sometimes from Oujda or Marrakech in Morocco. Some arrived illegally, via southeast France. Most of them told me they were 'regularised' by the Mitterrand administration in 1981. The migratory flow from Morocco to Bordeaux had only just begun. In the late 1980s, wives came to join their husbands, thanks to the 'family reunification' procedure, while French border controls tightened. Young male workers kept arriving on Office des Migrations Internationales (OMI) contracts or even tourist visas, and family networks facilitated employment in the vineyards. In the late 1990s, still more Moroccans arrived, with the aim of finding employment and a better life. One strategy was to marry a French cousin. 'The ONI, created in 1945 to end the employers' control that prevailed in the inter-war period, had a theoretical monopoly on bringing foreign labour to France. Following the freeze on permanent labour immigration, enacted in 1974, this institution, renamed Office des Migrations Internationales (OMI) in 1988, was reduced to recruiting seasonal workers from countries that had signed a labour agreement with France' (Morice 2008: 61).

Bénédicte Michalon and Swanie Potot (2008: 88) highlighted two factors responsible for the arrival of workers from Eastern Europe later in the 1990s. 'Firstly, French employment legislation, particularly concerning foreign workers, had been considerably modified in the previous few years, due to EU enlargement and French and European labour immigration policies. Secondly, workers' origins had diversified since the early 1990s.' The internationalisation of the wine market forced almost all employers to look for cheap labour. Thus, the farm labourers who had come from Morocco on permanent contracts suddenly found themselves in competition with Polish workers or other Moroccans arriving from Spain, as well as Portugal after the 2009 crisis, and migrants from Morocco, as well as Saharans from refugee camps in Algeria. Temporary work through agricultural contractors became widespread, together with a rise in illegal employment, a reality that anthropologists cannot deny, now denounced by some agricultural unions. Although research in such circumstances is difficult, fieldwork conducted with illegal farm workers in food aid outlets has confirmed this trend.

Mechanisation, with the widespread use of grape harvesters since the 1990s, encouraged by the collective ownership system, as well as the use of chemical pesticides, have reduced the need for foreign labour, particularly in less-renowned areas like Sainte-Foy-La-Grande while, in contrast, internationally famous vineyard areas (like Saint-Emilion or Médoc) hire increasing numbers of foreign seasonal workers for pruning and harvesting, via agricultural contractors who provide personnel according to tasks and needs. The situation of foreign seasonal workers is not the whole story: precarious seasonal employment also involves 'native' people. 'Salaried farm workers, particularly seasonal labour, form a little-known, heterogeneous population, including rural people, farmers' children, foreign workers resident in France or under OMI contracts, French and foreign students, gipsy families, housewives, factory workers seeking additional income, job seekers, workers on reintegration programmes, poor farmers, retired people, illegals etc. It is difficult to measure the proportion of each category (Darpeix 2013: 284)'. As Aurélie Darpeix reported in *La main d'œuvre salariée en agriculture, histoire d'une invisibilité* (Salaried workers in agriculture, a tale of invisibility) since the 2000s, seasonal employment has been increasing due to labour outsourcing and demand from winegrowers, especially those aiming for 'high-quality' production (Darpeix 2013: 284). Could the quest for quality be responsible for the expansion in precarious employment?

Behind the 'authenticity' myth of Bordeaux wine: precarious employment and financial exploitation

You see, we cannot compete with people who have vast amounts of money. . . . They come from other industries. . . . They bought a property in Argentina to make upmarket wine. Investors from overseas make alliances with owners of prestigious chateaux in Pomerol or Saint-Emilion.

(Richard, 73 years old, cellarmaster, Saint-Emilion, 2009)

I waited for the boss to call me back; last year he told me I did a good job, but he never called me again, so now I have to take a very early bus every day to go and work in the Medoc. . . . It's quite far. . . . It's tiring.

(Haléma, 37 years old, vineyard worker, Sainte-Foy-La-Grande, 2013)

Over the past few years, the globalisation of wine (Demossier 2018; Inglis and Almila 2019; Crenn *et al.* 2004) and increasing international market competition between the numerous 'quality' wine-producing areas throughout the world have caused major restructuring at wine estates and, more widely, in winegrowing societies. For instance, Marion Demossier (2018) described how the fame of Burgundy wines was established on the use of the term 'terroir', which is supposed to guarantee stability while, at the same time, major changes were disrupting grape-growing and winemaking methods. Wine marketing now focuses on heritage, with winemakers replacing terroir as the key element, along with landscapes, tourism and gastronomy (Sánchez *et al.* 2018).

The quest for quality, the growth of financial investments (Corrado *et al.* 2017) in the international agro-food trade, the European Union CAP reforms, the dominance of the agro-food industry, mass distribution (Corrado *et al.* 2017) and wine merchants over winegrowers are increasingly pushing producers to export their wines. These factors encourage the employment of a cheap, flexible workforce. As several authors have pointed out, foreign labour meets the requirements of current agricultural economies in competition with each other in international markets, seeking 'quality' combined with large-scale productivity, which requires large amounts of manual labour. Indeed, temporary, precarious labour has no power to demand higher wages (Berlan 1986) yet justifies the marketable slogan 'hand-crafted'. Paradoxically for wine producers in this region, growing high-quality grapes requires intensive labour and, consequently, dehumanisation of their agricultural workers (Chivallon 2018). Notwithstanding the fact that these same wine producers argue for solidarity and an economy respectful of the environment.

Why do winemakers, elected officials, public institutions, sociologists, journalists, tourism professionals and wine-producing communities, as well as winegrowers' associations and trade unions, ignore the presence of foreign workers? It might be explained by the French nationalism, authenticity and purity attached to terroir. The dominant narrative is one of quality, especially when discussing Bordeaux wines. Ixchel Delaporte (2018) illustrates in her book *Les Raisins de la misère* (The Grapes of Poverty) this complete invisibility of foreign workers in French viticulture. This applies not only to the lack of consideration shown by wine industry leaders, particularly the wealthiest, towards this subservient population, but also to the lack of debate surrounding their well-being and health when working in the vineyards. Delaporte revealed the sponsorship by large wine companies of the Bergonié Cancer Institute in Bordeaux, which raised issues concerning the objectivity of research on cancer and pesticides as illustrated in the local and regional press.

The French model, including the Bordeaux vineyards, is strongly influenced by two apparently contradictory phenomena: the Republic and colonial experiences. While defending a raceless model (Fassin and Fassin 2006), the French Republic remains trapped in its colonial history, reflected in its vocabulary. In Saint-Emilion, the universal story told to tourists betrays induced evolutionism. Saint-Emilion tells the story of the human race as seen by Europeans, moving from the antique vineyards to Christianity and then on to the French Revolution, the ultimate model of civilisation according to my winemaking contacts, to the exclusion of all others, labourers from ex-colonies, who are thus placed outside humanity in set colonial categories. This viewpoint may be related to the historical legacy of slavery in Bordeaux, which has been hardly acknowledged in the wine industry (Chivallon 2005; Roudié 1994).

This recontextualises the presence of foreign vineyard labourers, who now seem 'all too visible' as they congregate in impoverished rural town centres. They are under suspicion for their foreignness[1] in the very places where wine production claims its French 'authenticity' (Crenn 2015). Since the 2000s, the word 'invasion' has been in use; an elected representative of Sainte-Foy-La-Grande even said: 'It's Marrakech, here!' Consequently, the 'Arabs' became suspect, like anywhere else in France. In the impoverished villages living in the shadow of Saint-Emilion, the wine shop co-exists with the halal butcher. What is the significance of spatial heritage of unequal value in the Bordeaux vineyards? As mentioned previously, owning vineyard Saint-Emilion, Côtes-de-Castillon,

Sainte-Foy-Côtes-de-Bordeaux or Bordeaux Supérieur does not confer the same prestige. These areas are only a few kilometres apart, even adjacent in places, and yet they do not yield the same financial or reputational benefits. Each vineyard area classified by the National Institute for Origin and Quality (INAO) occupies a different level in the hierarchy, as well as in the historical and contemporary development of the wine industry on local, national and global levels. The current transformation of once-prosperous rural wine towns into poor neighbourhoods with high-density immigrant populations has stirred up racism and discrimination against foreign populations regarded as outsiders.

Indeed, the enhanced reputation of the Saint-Emilion denomination is due to two major actions: first, establishing the list of 'Grands crus classés', similar to the Medoc classification, in the post-war period and, secondly, the campaign for **UNESCO** World Heritage recognition (1999) of the Saint-Emilion vineyards. This has had the effect of pushing all other forms of presence, such as makeshift dwellings or urban housing estates, particularly those inhabited by North Africans, outside the designated area. The contrast is striking between the excessively beautified Saint-Emilion vineyards, where ancient, yellow-stone mansions stand proudly next to newly renovated wine cellars, and the impoverished towns of Castillon-La-Bataille and Sainte-Foy-La-Grande, only a few kilometres away, where run-down blocks of subsidised flats and old town houses provide accommodation for immigrant workers and their families. Worse still, diverse categories of people, including migrants, illegals, and the homeless, sleep in tents or mobile homes in the vineyards, waiting for informal contract work, off-the-books jobs or legal paperwork. Vineyard workers with French nationality harvesting grapes in the Libourne area described the uncertainties facing illegal foreigners. One French female worker (my fieldwork in Libourne, 2018) was probably exaggerating somewhat, considering the limited resources available to labour inspectors, when she described a helicopter from the Agriculture Ministry flying over the vineyards looking for illegal workers. She said she had helped a Moroccan woman by lending her social security card during inspections, to avoid deportation.

Saint-Emilion, more than Saint-Foy-La-Grande or Castillon-La-Bataille, is a peripheral zone where ethnic and spatial processes of exclusion co-exist alongside oenological tourism and globalisation, grands crus and French nationalism. Encouraged by both the global economy and nation-state control, particularly related to designations of origin, winegrowing areas aim for and advertise their authentic identity and publicise the careers of individual winegrowers, as distinct from those of local and foreign vineyard workers, wine merchants and consumers. Today, organic production emphasises the 'border zone', with the visible, almost aged presence of manual workers and draft horses along the roads of Saint-Emilion contributing to this image of 'authenticity' and a traditional, French winegrowing culture while remaining engaged with local, national and global challenges relating to identity and economics, thus generating instabilities.

The quest for meaning and 'quality' has oriented the winemaker-terroir-global market trio exclusively towards individualised consumer relationships and total denial of the existence and living conditions of vineyard workers, particularly 'foreigners', in both the world-famous territory of Saint-Emilion and lesser-known Sainte-Foy-La-Grande. Vineyard contractor G told me that 1,200 'Moroccan' labourers, mostly from Morocco or Spain, were employed during the 2015 harvest, as compared to 200 year-round employees. They are now in competition with 'Saharans'. Chinese, British and Russian investors, as well as international groups like François Pinault's, among others, also occupy a central place in the wine economy. The new Chinese owners have kept the vineyard website made by the previous owners, presenting the history of the Sainte-Foy-la-Grande area, to reassure customers about the authenticity and quality of their wine. They actually asked me how they could integrate themselves legitimately in local history. By opening up international markets and purchasing wine estates as financial investments, they exert an indirect influence on asymmetrical inter-ethnic relations. According to a 2016 interview of an employee of the Agricultural Social Security (MSA), a wine producer in Sainte-Foy or Castillon earns an average of €600 per month and has trouble selling their property. In Saint-Emilion, despite a very different financial situation, vineyard owners who want to retire also sell their land to foreigners when their own children have chosen more prestigious careers in the cities. Beyond the heritage-based communication of wine professionals, it appears that most human experiences in the Bordeaux vineyards, and particularly Saint-Emilion, are at once local and global, due to the development of the wine world's networked society. The various stakeholders are caught up in a dual movement of cultural homogenisation and differentiation. The life stories of Saint-Emilion winemakers reveal that these people, who have been engaged in winemaking for a long time, consider themselves 'heirs' and think they have played a key role in developing winemaking and the regional economy. Yet now they feel they are in competition with a handful of 'new owners from international finance' (Richard, cellarmaster, 73 years old) or the agro-food industry (Crenn and Montagne 2010).

According to my informant, Richard, it is impossible to compete with these 'financiers'. The new owners, 'global winemakers', at the interface of local and world markets, care little about national concerns. In reference to Zygmunt Bauman (1999), the members of this globalised elite are protected within their own cultural, economic and even political networks and do not engage with the local wine world. I noticed that the Chinese I have met, as well as the British and Japanese, move among globalised cities structured by large companies and transnational markets. They employ vineyard managers from California, use contract labourers and make permanent employees redundant, sometimes in ignorance of French law, and own other vineyards elsewhere in the world. They believe that neo-liberal market regulation is the best model. The most shocking phenomenon in local opinion is the disastrous impact two major Chinese groups have had on local vineyards. 'Out of the 6,150 wine enterprises in Gironde, 90 have Chinese owners. The Chinese distribution group Dashang owns 181 large shopping centres throughout China with 12 billion euros in turnover, and the Haichang Group is involved in activities ranging from maritime transport to oil products and real estate. The latter business was sued by the Chinese government for misappropriation of public money for the purchase of French vineyards' (*Le Monde*, 30 May 2012). According to some of my contacts who are employed by these groups, they have bought 25 Bordeaux wine estates and sometimes let the châteaux fall into disrepair, much to the despair of their French employees, some of whom have attempted to raise their awareness, via Chinese interpreters, of the value of this 'historic heritage' (Bernard, 65 years old). Likewise, these owners arouse their employees' consternation when they refuse to pay housing taxes and, fearing inspections by the French tax office, they remove all traces of occupancy from their luxurious houses after sumptuous, yet ephemeral gala dinners (Bernard, 65 years old).

In substance, these ethnographic observations reveal the paradox of permeable borders, an expression coined by John and Jean Comaroff (2010: 94) in South Africa to describe the 'contradiction between national protectionism and the division of labour at international level and migratory European policy.' It also illustrates the situation described by Jean-Pierre Berlan (1986): the confrontation of different ideologies within the French government system on immigration and labour issues, alternating between neo-liberal and interventionist approaches, aimed at defending all workers' rights.

Conclusion

My work is part of a broader movement in France to update anthropology of rural worlds or, at least, recognise the need to investigate the position of these peripheral territories, far from major urban centres (Chauvier 2011). It highlights the agricultural economy's role in producing precarious workers, dependent on economic strategies developed in the global wine business, in particular, as well as national social policies. Along the lines of works by Noiriel (1994) and Hubscher (2005), I revealed the longstanding links between the agricultural world and migration in the Bordeaux area. A more specific contribution consisted of integrating the theoretical frame of interethnic relations for a clearer understanding of wine worlds and revealing the development of new urban social contexts in rural wine areas, where ethnicity plays a role today.

In conclusion, this research revealed the entanglement of economic and symbolic approaches in the wine world, where foreign workers are both economically integrated and kept invisible in the streets of the famous wine towns, as well as tourist brochures and heritage festivals but, at the same time, ethnicised in the peripheral towns. It also describes their contribution to the globalised agricultural system by providing cheap, anonymous labour where authenticity is marketed at very high prices. In the vineyards and chateaux, this is sometimes described as 'domestic offshoring'.

Acknowledgements

Translation by Christine Rychlewski and Isabelle Téchoueyres.

Note

1 The foreignness of migrant workers in the vineyards was reinforced because as Muslims they were associated with the terrorist attacks in New York from September 2011 onwards.'

References

Bauman, Z. (1999) *Le coût humain de la mondialisation*, Paris: Hachette.
Berlan, J.P. (1986) "Agriculture et migrations," *Revue européenne des migrations internationales* 3, 9–32.
Bohling, J. (2018) *The Sober Revolution. Appellation Wine and the Transformation of France*, Ithaca, NY and London: Cornell University Press.
Chauvier, E. (2011) *Contre Télérama*, Paris: Allia.
Chauvin, P-M. (2019) "Globalization and Reputation Dynamics: The Case of Bordeaux Wines," in D. Inglis and A-M. Almila (eds), *The Globalization of Wine*, London: Bloomsbury.
Chivallon, C. (2005) "L'usage politique de la mémoire de l'esclavage dans les anciens ports négriers de Bordeaux et Bristol," in P. Weil and S. Dufoix (eds), *L'esclavage, la colonisation et après. . .*, Paris: PUF.
Chivallon, C. (2018) "Mémoires du corps animalisé en contexte colonial: le faux débat de la modernité, de l'humain et du non-humain," in L. Aje and N. Gachon (eds), *La mémoire de l'esclavage. Traces mémorielles de l'esclavage et des traites dans l'espace atlantique*, Paris: L'Harmattan, 17–48.
Comaroff, J. and Comaroff, J. (2010) *Zombies et frontières à l'ère néolibérale. Le cas de l'Afrique du Sud postapartheid*, Paris: Les Prairies ordinaires.
Compadre, C. (2015) "La Saga Castel," *Sud Ouest Le Mag*, 13 June, 11–17.
Corrado, A., de Castro, C. and Perrotta, D. (2017) *Migration and Agriculture, Mobility and Change in the Mediterranean Area*, London and New York: Routledge.
Crenn, C. (2015) "Ethnic Identity Power, Compromise, and Territory: Locals and Moroccans in the Sainte-Foy-Bordeaux Vineyards," in J. MacClancy (ed), *Alternative Countrysides: Anthropological Approaches to Rural Western Europe Today*, Manchester: Manchester University Press, 61–81.
Crenn, C. (2017) "Wine Heritage and the Ethnicization of Labour: Arab Workers in the Bordeaux Vineyards," in A. Corrado, C. de Castro and D. Perrotta (eds), *Migration and Agriculture: Mobility and Change in the Mediterranean Area*, London and New York: Routledge, 42–57.
Crenn, C., Demossier, M. and Téchoueyres, I. (2004) "Wine and Globalisation: Foreword," *Anthropology of Food*, http://journals.openedition.org/aof/308.
Crenn, C. and Montagne, K. (2010) "Le petit monde de Saint-Emilion, entre localisation et globalisation, une mise en tension?" in J.C. Hinnewinckel (ed), *La gouvernance des terroirs du vin*, Bordeaux: Editions Féret, 291–302.
Darpeix, A. (2013) *La main-d'œuvre salariée en agriculture: histoire d'une invisibilité*, Montpellier: Demeter.
Decosse, F. (2017) "Persistent Unfree Labour in French Intensive Agriculture; An Historical Overview of the 'OFII' Temporary Farmworkers Programme," in A. Corrado, C. de Castro and D. Perrotta (eds), *Migration and Agriculture, Mobility and Change in the Mediterranean Area*, London and New York: Routledge, 183–197.
Delaporte, I. (2018) *Les raisins de la misère. Une enquête sur la face cachée des châteaux bordelais*, Rodez: Éditions La Brune au Rouergue.
Deléage, E. (2013) *Agriculture à l'épreuve de la modernisation*, Paris: Quae.

Demossier, M. (2018) *Burgundy. The Global Story of Terroir*, London: Berghahn Books.
Drot, C. (2007) "Histoire et mémoires des immigrations en Aquitaine," www.criaquitaine.org/pdf/Histoire_et_memoires_des_immigrations_en_Aquitaine.pdf.
Fassin, D. and Fassin, E. (2006) *De la question sociale à la question raciale: représenter la société française*, Paris: La Découverte.
Guille-Escuret, G. (1988) *La souche, la cuve et la bouteille: les rencontres de l'histoire et de la nature dans un aliment: le vin*, Paris: Editions de la MSH.
Hubscher, R. (2005) *L'immigration dans les campagnes françaises (19e-20e siècle)*, Paris: Odile Jacob.
Inglis, D. and Almila, A-M. (2019) *The Globalization of Wine*, London: Bloomsbury.
Michalon, B. and Potot, S. (2008) "Quand la France recrute en Pologne," *Études rurales* 182, 87–102.
Morice, A. (2008) "Quelques repères sur les contrats OMI et ANAEM," *Études rurales* 182, 61–68.
Noiriel, G. (1994) "L'immigration étrangère dans le monde rural pendant l'entre-deux-guerres," *Études rurales* 135–136, 3–35.
Roudié, P. (1994) *Vignobles et vignerons du Bordelais (1850–1980)*; 2nd edn Paris: Editions du Centre Nationale de la Recherche Scientifique.
Sánchez, M.J., Torres Pérez, F. and Yoldi, I. (2018) "Introducción," in M.J. Sánchez Gomez and F. Torres Pérez (eds), *Transformaciones productivas, inmigración y cambios sociales en zonas vitivinicolas globalizadas*, Mexico City: Universidad Nacional Autónoma de México, El Colégio de la Frontera Norte, 9–39.
Taveau, V. (2019) "Joseph Bohling," *The Sober Revolution. Appellation Wine and the Transformation of France, Crescentis: Revue internationale d'histoire de la vigne et du vin*, Recensions, http://preo.u-bourgogne.fr/crescentis/index.php?id=1001&lang=en.
Ulin, R. and Black, R. (2013) *Wine and Culture: Vineyard to Glass*, London and New York: Bloomsbury Academic.

42
THE CHINA WINE MARKET
How wine is gaining cultural value in Chinese culture

Justin Cohen, Larry Lockshin, Armando Corsi, Johan Bruwer, Carl Driesener and Richard Lee

Introduction

China has long been an interest of sociologists, anthropologists and those in other social science disciplines. Since China began to open to the world in the 1980s, it has changed significantly and has become a focus of business practitioners. In less than half a century, it has risen to become a global leader in manufacturing. With the rapid advancement in their economy, China is now also a major player in terms of consumption, having pulled the majority of its population from poverty into the middle class.

Pundits consistently report on the uniqueness of Chinese culture and how this impacts Chinese consumer behaviour in general. Specifically, there is significant discourse within the wine sector that reinforces this mindset. Therefore, this chapter aims to dispel some myths about China and illustrate that wine is becoming a mainstream category, no longer only relevant to the wealthy. It is more useful to categorise what is happening in the broader Chinese wine market in terms of consumption behaviour at an aggregate level than to fixate on the customs and behaviours of the very small number of oenophiles compared to a typical category buyer. A range of research projects on the China wine market will be used to document behaviour as well as to explore wine culture.

This chapter will first document the history of wine in China to show this is not a brand-new beverage and show what is known about its cultural influence. It will then document the current purchase behaviour in China using data obtained from one of the largest academic studies on wine buyer behaviour executed. This will provide context for where wine is purchased and how wine is distributed. Understanding the reasons people enter the wine category to purchase will then be explored. Next, we will explore how Chinese wine drinkers talk about wine, sharing research that investigates sensory descriptions and the opportunity to utilise Eastern flavour descriptors that have been validated as substitutes for conventional Western terminology. Finally, ethnocentrism and involvement, two constructs that can be used to explain behaviour using a cultural lens in China, will be discussed.

History of wine and wine culture in China

Wine made from grapes or using grapes as a fermentation starter for other alcoholic beverages in China can be traced back to 9000 BCE using archaeological evidence uncovered at Jiahu in Henan (Kupfer 2018). Residues of fermented beverages containing traces of grape, honey, grain and spices show grapes were used in a similar fashion to those found in alcoholic beverages in the Near East during similar time periods (McGovern *et al.* 2005). Most of the grapes used were wild grapes, of which China has more than 40 species. Evidence from about 2000 BCE shows the development of bronze workmanship used for ceremonial alcohol drinking as part of Chinese culture (Kupfer 2018).

What is more interesting and pertinent for this chapter is evidence of a drinking culture in the Xia dynasty (twenty-first through sixteenth centuries BCE), which utilised specific drinking vessels. During the Shang dynasty (sixteenth through eleventh centuries BCE), it has even been suggested that the downfall of the dynasty was due to dissolute life and binge drinking (Kupfer 2018). The Zhou dynasty, which followed the Shang, established rules on the production and consumption of alcohol including grape-based alcohol (Li 2010). This indicates that grape wine was a part of formal court culture as far back as the tenth century BCE (Kupfer 2018). Alcohol was perceived as a gift from heaven, and a specific alcohol ministry was developed during the Zhou dynasty which oversaw the use and rituals connected to consumption (Li 2010). By the time of Confucianism, the central concept of the 'virtue of alcohol' was developed (Kupfer 2018).

The earliest written documents attesting to grape wine come from the western Han dynasty around the second century BCE (Kupfer 2018). The famous ambassador Zhang Qian brought back *vinifera* vines and experienced vintners from the Ferghana Valley in central Asia, decedents of Alexander the Great's expeditions, which led to large vineyards planted around the palace at Chang'an (Kupfer 2018). By the time of China's first united empire, the Qin (221–206 BCE), there were strong trade routes along the Silk Road where goods, including grapevines and wines, were exchanged from both East and West. A highly sophisticated wine culture developed, attested to by the finding of glass cups in tombs of high officials, and the earliest poem praising grape wine drunk with friends was written by Lu Ji around 300 BCE, which included references to glass goblets (Kupfer 2018).

From the end of the Han dynasty in 220 CE, China went through various complex political changes which split the country into the south, where brews made from rice, wheat and millet were popular, and the north, where grape wine was esteemed and grown. The Tang empire reunited China and had a strong focus on grape wine, as evidenced by Wang Han's famous poem, 'The Song of Liangzhou', which references the drinking of grape wine from glass cups. There is evidence of precious wine-drinking vessels during this time and even wine being imported from the West. Recent discoveries in tombs near Xuanhua northwest of Beijing show evidence of red wine, grape seeds and stems from about 1000 CE. By the time of the Mongolian dynasty (1279–1368 CE), there are writings from Western visitors (Wilhelm von Rubruk and Marco Polo) about large-scale vineyards and industrial wine production. These were mainly in western China along the Silk Road. The Yuan dynasty followed with grapes now planted in warmer southern areas around Changjiang, Hangzhou, Nanjing and Yangzhou. There was a huge demand for grape wine at court, and during this period, the Chinese established quality control and classification systems for grape wine and special cellars for aging (Kupfer 2018). So there is a strong history of wine culture in China.

Wine culture and production declined dramatically during the Ming and Qing dynasties (1368–late 1800s CE). However, red grape wine was first praised for its health benefits during this period rather than as a ceremonial beverage. It wasn't until 1892 when millionaire Zhang Bishi started Changyu Winery that modern viticulture and wine production returned to China. French Catholics and Japanese investors set up wineries through the 1920s and 1930s (Li *et al.* 2018), believing there would be growth and development of Westernised wine consumption. But it was Chairman Mao, who instructed China to put more effort into the wine industry to reduce the consumption of Baijiu (rice spirits) in 1956, who started the modern move to planting more vineyards and building more wineries (Su 2003). This led to foreign firms, such as Pernod Ricard, establishing grape growing and winemaking as commercial operations, in this case Dragon Seal Winery (Li *et al.* 2018).

The current state of the China wine market

China is now a market of great interest to the global wine sector due to it being the world's most populous nation, its rapidly emerging middle class and its thirst for imported goods. However, it is a challenge to do business there for a number of practical reasons. It is largely impenetrable, and it's difficult to understand anything about how the market really operates, specifically how wine integrates into Chinese culture, if you don't speak the language. Most of the initial views on the usage of wine and how it is perceived by the Chinese have been formulated by those lucky enough to conduct wine business or research on the China wine market. The challenge is that this interaction is skewed towards heavy buyers in the category who are highly involved and not representative of the broader wine market. Cohen and Lockshin (2017) point out the challenges of cultural blindness in understanding how wine is consumed in China amongst both foreign and Chinese actors in the industry. Due to the scale of the country, it is easy for an observer, even a local Chinese, to be misled. It is, therefore, useful to have an evidence-based understanding of market structure in the wine market as a starting point to understand the role of wine in Chinese society.

Tables 42.1 and 42.2 contain data from a survey of 2,440 wine buyers aged 18 to 65 who earn over RMB 4,000 (around US$600) per month, collected across 15 cities of strategic interest to the imported wine category in July 2019.

Table 42.1 Self-reported (n=2440) six-month penetration (percentage of people buying) of alcohol subcategory buying in China (July 2019)

Alcohol Subcategory	Penetration (%)
Chinese beer	64
Chinese grape wine	63
Imported grape wine	61
Imported beer	38
Chinese spirits	30
Champagne	27
Alcoholic cider	21
Craft beer	19
Imported spirits	21
Wine coolers	15
Sparkling wine	14
RTDs	12

Table 42.2 Self-reported (n=2440) six-month channel penetration of wine buying in China (July 2019)

Sales Channel	Penetration (%)
Wine/alcohol retailer	45
Wine distributor	35
Luxury supermarket	26
Wine-specific eCommerce	24
Hypermarket	22
JD.com	20
TMall	20

(*Continued*)

Table 42.2 (Continued)

Sales Channel	Penetration (%)
General eCommerce	18
Western restaurant	17
Cash and carry	13
Supermarket	14
Chinese restaurant	12
TaoBao	11
Bar	12
Convenience	10
KTV	6
Traditional retail	4
Weidian (Wechat store)	3

This data illustrates that wine buyers are broad alcohol category consumers. However, it is interesting to note that only just under a third of these surveyed wine buyers in China purchase Chinese spirits (i.e. Baiju), which suggests that this dominant alcohol subcategory in China is likely more relevant to lower-income Chinese, less-developed cities and rural areas. To further amplify these findings, we also note a prior study looking at a sample of alcohol category buyers (n = 1004), which showed that imported wine buyers have a larger subcategory repertoire size (number of subcategories purchased) than non-imported wine buyers and that their incidence of buying across alcohol subcategories is higher than non-imported wine buyers (Cohen et al. 2018; Driesener et al. 2018). This suggests that what makes an imported wine buyer unique in China is not their level of acculturation, but rather, these are just heavier alcohol category consumers, of which wine is just one subcategory. Table 42.2 documents channel buying penetration in China to illustrate where buying is happening.

These data illustrate that wine is bought in China over a large range of sales (brick-and-mortar, online and hospitality) channels. Wine/alcohol retailers have the largest customer base. Wine distributors are the second-largest channel in terms of buyers due to a lack of restrictions in China from buying direct from a distributor. These distributors organise lots of tasting events, and due to the heavy role social media plays in China, there is a lot more marketing activity aimed at consumers by these operators than you would see in other markets. Luxury supermarkets and hypermarkets are other significant brick-and-mortar channels. Wine-specific eCommerce, JD.com and Tmall are leading online channels. Whilst buying does occur in the on-premise channel across both Western and Chinese restaurants, bars and KTV (karaoke bars), this happens less than some might think. This is largely due to limited distribution of wine and the significant mark-up in these venues.

To add further context to the penetration data reported earlier, Table 42.3 shows data from a retail audit of the wine category reporting the average number of wines available across a broad range of brick-and-mortar retail channels in Beijing, Guangzhou and Shanghai from a sample of 140 stores.

These data show the scale of the availability of wine in China. Retail channels that have initially had significant foreign involvement such as luxury supermarkets, cash and carry and hypermarkets typically range hundreds of specific wines. Luxury supermarkets predominantly sell imported wine, as would cash and carry. Cash and carry, however, sells a number of imported wines that mimic the branding of well-known imported wine brands, suggesting that this channel services a less sophisticated wine buyer than luxury supermarkets. Hypermarkets and supermarkets, which exist for the growing middle class in China, have a significant portfolio of Chinese-produced wines. There is great variation in the types of wines available in specialty alcohol stores. Convenience stores, which are located everywhere in major Chinese cities, have a smaller selection of prominent entry-level

Table 42.3 Average number of stock-keeping units in brick-and-mortar retail

Channel Type	Average number of SKUs
Luxury supermarket	693
Cash and carry	520
Hypermarket	391
Supermarket	91
Specialty alcohol store	42
Convenience store	29
Gas station	12
Traditional retailer	8

imported brands from the main imported wine countries due to their limited floor space. Gas stations and traditional retailers typically have a range of wines that are predominantly Chinese produced.

This section has demonstrated that wine is readily available for purchase and consumption in leading cities in China. There is significant availability of wine of varying quality, both domestically produced and imported across a wide range of sales channels. Buying across hospitality sales channels is less than most would imagine. This is due to there being limited distribution of wine in restaurants outside of five-star hotels, expensive restaurants and bars and those located in areas that are favoured by expatriates and foreign tourists. The wine category is growing in China, but its limitation is more fighting for availability in consumers' minds than on retail shelves. The next section will delve into this important area and explore how wine fits into the lives of Chinese consumers.

Why people buy wine in China

Understanding the effect of consumption occasion on choice was a research area as early as Belk (1974) and evident in a wine context since Quester and Smart (1998). A number of studies regarding wine consumption occasions in China already exist. Liu and Murphy (2007) used qualitative research to generate insights on what types of wines were suited for a few consumption occasions. Corsi *et al.* (2016), using a three-year cross-sectional survey approach, demonstrated an increase in at-home consumption of imported wine whilst investigating key consumption occasions. Corsi *et al.* (2017a) used a discrete choice experiment to investigate how these occasions affected consumer preference. Common limitations of these studies in wine are that the researchers typically only investigate a few key occasions, and the decision about what occasions to study are typically generated by those heavily engaged in the industry and can lead to a culture and heavy buyer bias, as documented by Cohen and Lockshin (2017).

There is, therefore, a need for research to quantify key occasions on which Chinese consumers would buy wine. One way is generating category entry points (CEPs) based on Romaniuk and Sharp (2016). A two-stage methodology can be employed using consumers to elicit occasions and then quantify the importance of the key occasions in which someone might enter the wine category (Hogan *et al.* 2016). Cohen, Lockshin *et al.* (2019) and Cohen, Driesener *et al.* (2019) document the elicitation stage of this process for wine buying in China. Figure 42.1 contains self-reported monthly penetration of category entry point data (percentage of people buying for that occasion) from a survey of 1,093 wine buyers aged 18 to 65 who earn over RMB 4,000 per month, collected across 12 cities of strategic interest to the imported and domestic wine category in May 2019 from the second stage of this methodology.

This data is useful for understanding how wine fits into Chinese culture. Focusing on imported wine, it is most commonly purchased for romantic and high-class occasions and when consuming

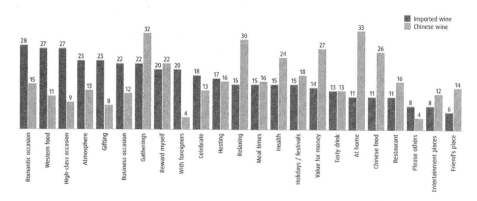

Figure 42.1 Self-reported (n = 1093) monthly penetration of category entry points for imported and domestic wine buying in China (May 2019)

Western food. It is also commonly bought when wanting to create an atmosphere and for gifting and business occasions. Just like in other wine markets, notable occasions are a driver of wine consumption. Wine is also used as a conduit for interacting with foreigners. The penetration of imported wine buying by category entry point drops for more common occasions and those more closely related to Chinese culture, such as Chinese meals and everyday consumption.

The purchase of Chinese wine happens most often for gatherings, relaxing occasions, health reasons, at-home consumption with Chinese food and when looking for value for money. Early qualitative research on wine in China about the importance of health benefits as a prevalent driver of consumption clearly is more relevant for Chinese wine.

If the availability of wine increases in Chinese restaurants and other out-of-home venues and an effort is made to build associations between wine and Chinese food consumption, we may see wine consumption with Chinese food become more prevalent. At this stage, wine is becoming more common in urban environments. Whilst it is purchased for consumption at key occasions in Chinese culture such as holidays, festivals, weddings etc., it is likely still not viewed as emanating from Chinese culture itself despite the long history of wine in China as described earlier. In the next section, we will discuss how wine is described in China.

How wine drinkers taste and talk about wine in China

Another key factor for a more comprehensive understanding of Chinese wine culture and how it might evolve is relative to the terms people use to describe the sensory properties of wines. Until recently, the approach in China had been to adopt the same terms used in a Western context (e.g. strawberry, blueberry, blackberry etc.) to describe the taste of wines to Chinese consumers. This approach, however, is fundamentally faulty because it is known that the more an individual has been exposed to a substance and has had a long-lasting connection between an odour and its name, the more they are able to identify a substance (Cain 1979).

Therefore, if a person has had little to no exposure to the fruits, vegetables, spices and food typical of a Western culture (e.g. strawberry, capsicum, bacon etc.), how can the wine industry expect them to be able to taste those flavours in a wine and use this language effectively to communicate about it? The approach began to change about ten years ago when Master of Wine Jeannie Cho Lee published a book titled *Mastering Wine for the Asian Palate* (Cho Lee 2011). The book suggested what fruits, vegetables, spices and food typical of an Asian context could replace their Western equivalents. For example, instead of saying that a wine has a taste of strawberry, one could say to a Chinese consumer that a wine has a taste of *yangmei*; instead of blackberry jam, one could say a wine tastes of dried Chinese hawthorns. The book, however, had a limitation: the generation of those suggested equivalences was done by one person, albeit a highly knowledgeable wine expert. Corsi et al. (2017a) decided to validate those suggested equivalences using a three-part study based on qualitative, quantitative and sensory research.

Focus groups were first conducted in Shanghai, Guangzhou and Chengdu to identify a list of common terms Chinese consumers use to describe a wine. The second stage of the research was used to select a range of Australian wines available in and representative of the major wine styles exported to China. This was done through a sensorial characterisation by the Australian Wine Research Institute (AWRI). The final stage of data collection quantitatively measured the most common terms Chinese consumers use to describe wines, testing whether Chinese consumers prefer to use Chinese terms to describe wines or their Western equivalents and verifying the equivalences Jeannie Cho Lee proposed in her book. This last stage of the experiment took place in the same three cities mentioned earlier, with an average of 85 consumers in each city tasting the wines selected during the second stage of the research. Due to space limitations, we cannot report all the details of the experiment in this book chapter, but we invite the interested readers to consult the article by Corsi et al. (2017b).

We report here the main results of the third stage of the research:

- Generic terms (e.g. astringent, sour, mellow, lingering etc.) are used by Chinese consumers approximately three times more often than specific terms (e.g. strawberry, *yangmei*, lemon, kaffir lime etc.).
- The use of Chinese or Western descriptors does not lead to a statistically significant difference in likeability, willingness to buy or perceived price point. In addition, while Chinese fruits are associated more than their Western equivalents, savoury tastes are best suited for Western descriptors.
- The equivalence of specific descriptors was verified for 11 out of 20 descriptors for white wines, sparkling wines, and a moscato wine, and 8 out of 14 descriptors for red wines and a South Australian tawny wine.

These findings indicate that wine culture is in its nascency in China. Typical wine drinkers are three times more likely to use generic terms over specific ones, and therefore, communications regarding taste should be more general. At this stage, there is no effect on preference or willingness to purchase when using Western or more culture-specific Chinese terms. Not all the equivalences have been verified, but there does now exist a good base of Chinese terminology that wine educators, sommeliers and the wine trade can use as they try to engage with Chinese who are less likely to have spent time overseas and therefore are less exposed to Western culture and food items. Cohen *et al.* (2014) used these terms as part of their wine education research to investigate their relevance in wine education among new wine drinkers using recently arrived students. However, more research is required to understand how language, Chinese culture and food items can be utilised to improve the impact and relevance of wine communication in China.

Ethnocentrism and involvement in wine

With the world fast becoming a much smaller 'place', particularly from the increase in free trade and the associated accessibility of markets' perspectives, consumers often directly associate product quality with country of origin (COO) (Cilingir and Basfirinci 2014). While COO cues have generally been expressed through 'made-in labels', consumer ethnocentrism (CET), a construct conceptualised and used to explain consumer behaviour in the context of the choice between local and foreign (imported) products, has long stood out as a major determinant of consumer behaviour with strong application in international marketing (Shimp and Sharma 1987).

From a definitional perspective, CET is 'the beliefs held by consumers about the appropriateness, indeed morality, of purchasing foreign-made products' (Shimp and Sharma 1987: 280). Essentially, CET is the tendency to favour the meanings and objects of one's own culture(s) over those of other cultures. The consequences of strong CET include underestimation of imported products, overestimation of domestic products and preference for and a moral obligation to buy domestic products (Sharma et al. 1995). Ethnocentric consumers therefore tend to prefer domestic products (Rice and Wongtada 2007).

Product involvement which essentially measures the importance a product has to a person in terms of its perceived relevance was also increasingly applied to explain consumer behaviour such as purchase decision making (Bruwer et al. 2017). Not surprisingly, because of their apparent symbiotic and/or relational nature, studies have examined the relationship between CET and product involvement on COO effects (Cilingir and Basfirinci 2014). What follows provides some insight into the relationships between CET, involvement and the purchase of wine in China.

An online survey was used to collect the desired information from a sample of 1,165 wine consumers in China. The qualification criteria for participation in the survey were people of legal drinking age (18 years and older) who had, in the six-month period preceding the survey, at least once purchased wine which either originated from foreign countries and/or the home country, China. The use of an online survey had the advantage of sampling across China and a range of Tier 1 and Tier 2 cities. The study achieved a representative sample of the wine-buying population (47% males, 53% females; average age = 41 years; married = 79%; average monthly household income RMB 16,248).

Because limited research has been conducted to examine the role of CET on consumer behaviour in China, we used the original 17-item 7-point Likert-type CETSCALE of Shimp and Sharma (1987), which yielded excellent results in terms of internal reliability (Cronbach alpha = 0.963; $F = 81.965$, $p = 0.000$). Product involvement was measured using five items adapted from the Likert scales of Dholakia (2001) after first adjusting them to the wine product context. The scale also yielded good results in terms of internal reliability (Cronbach alpha = 0.877; $F = 24.431$, $p = 0.000$).

It was found that 52% of the consumers are low on ethnocentrism, with this sub-group comprising females (58%) and males (42%) with an average age of 40 years. Highly ethnocentric consumers are males (59%) and females (41%), with an average age of 41 years. This result in China contradicts research findings of studies done in developed countries such as the USA and the UK, which found that females are generally more ethnocentric than males (e.g. Sharma et al. 1995). In the case of the respondents' involvement with wine as a product, the majority (54%) of consumers are in the low-involvement category, and there are slightly more females (51%) in the high-involvement category than males (49%).

Given the fact that COO perception is generally influenced by both CET and product involvement (Cilingir and Basfirinci 2014), we examined if these also prevail in the context of consumers in China buying imported or locally produced wine. Table 42.4 shows that consumers who are highly ethnocentric buy significantly more ($F = 15.738$; $p = 0.000\star\star$) locally produced than imported wine in China. Similarly, significantly more consumers ($F = 4,613$; $p = 0.032\star$) who have a low involvement level with wine buy more local (Chinese-produced) wine than buy imported wine. Moreover, there is a significant positive correlation (Pearson = $0.173\star\star$; sig = 0.000) between product involvement and the purchase of imported wine by consumers in China.

With China being a transitional economy and its wine culture at a relatively early stage of development, some observations and implications of the aforementioned findings are appropriate. It should be noted that these findings are country specific. The levels of ethnocentrism (high) and

Table 42.4 Consumer ethnocentrism (CET) and product involvement: purchased imported vs. local (May 2019)

Variable	Purchased imported	Purchased local	F	Sig
Low CET	73.8%	82.6%	2.386	0.123
High CET	61.8%	86.3%	15.738	0.000**
Low Involvement	64.8%	83.4%	4.613	0.032*
High Involvement	71.3%	85.4%	0.694	0.405

CET: consumer ethnocentrism; ** p = <0.001; * p= <0.05

involvement (low) were strong predictors of the purchase of locally produced wine. However, this could have been caused by the non-availability of imported wine in certain sales channels and/or by other factors, such as income level. Future research should examine these aspects.

Limitations, future research and conclusion

It is clear from the research in this chapter that wine culture in China is still developing and changing compared to Western countries. Further research will be necessary to document both the changes and the reasons for them if marketers want to utilise wine culture to improve their offerings and communications in China. We have shown it is not enough to survey regular wine drinkers because changes in wine culture will occur as new drinkers enter the wine market and substantially grow the total number of wine consumers. Wine research should always include enough alcohol consumers who buy wine once in a while to understand how this group is adopting and consuming wine. Otherwise, we will be left with a picture of regular wine drinkers, who are the minority of consumers. Along with surveys, qualitative interviews of both heavy and light wine drinkers would be useful to understand how they view wine as part of their overall consumption of alcoholic beverages and how this is impacted by their cultural practices.

A limitation of this research is that it only focuses on urban Tier 1 and Tier 2 cities. Future research could explore alcohol consumption in less-developed cities and more rural areas. Wine culture in China is a new research area. Hopefully, the descriptive results of channel buying, the insights into the category-buying occasions among representative category buyers and the emphasis on needing to achieve category growth by reaching non-wine buyers can help future researchers prioritise their research to decompose the influence of culture in the most prevalent wine-buying and consumption scenarios. This is an important guide for future research into consumption, buying and culture in the China wine market as the OIV (2020) reports a decline in wine consumption in China.

References

Belk, R.W. (1974) "An Exploratory Assessment of Situational Effects in Buyer Behaviour," *Journal of Marketing Research* 11, May, 156–163.
Bruwer, J., Chrysochou, P. and Lesschaeve, I. (2017) "Consumer Involvement and Knowledge Influence on Wine Choice Cue Utilisation," *British Food Journal* 119(4), 830–844.
Cain, W.S. (1979) "To Know with the Nose: Keys to Odor Identification," *Science* 203(4379), 467–470.
Cho Lee, J. (2011) *Mastering Wine for the Asian Palate*, Hong Kong: Asset Publishing and Research Ltd.
Cilingir, Z. and Basfirinci, C. (2014) "The Impact of Consumer Ethnocentrism, Product Involvement, and Product Knowledge on Country of Origin Effects: An Empirical Analysis on Turkish Consumers' Product Evaluation," *Journal of International Consumer Marketing* 26(4), 284–310.
Cohen, J., Corsi, A.M. and Lockshin, L. (2014) "China: 'Writing to Learn' or 'Learning to Write': Is There a Place for Self-Reported Reviews in Wine Education?" *Wine & Viticulture Journal* 29(2), 71–73.
Cohen, J., Driesener, C., Huang, A., Corsi, A.M. and Sbalchiero, F. (2018) "We Need to Be Thinking About All Alcohol Drinkers in China," *Wine & Viticulture Journal* 33(2), 60–61.

Cohen, J., Driesener, C., Huang, A., Lockshin, L., Corsi, A.M., Bruwer, J. and Lee, R. (2019) "What Brings a Chinese Alcohol Drinker into the Category," *Wine & Viticulture Journal* 34(1), 67–68.

Cohen, J. and Lockshin, L. (2017) "Conducting Research with Impact in China: Guidelines for Design, Execution and Dissemination," *Wine Economics & Policy* 6(2), 77–79.

Cohen, J., Lockshin, L., Driesener, C., Huang, A., Bruwer, J., Lee, R. and Kilov, K. (2019) "Understanding the Category Entry Points for Wine," Presented at the 11th Academy of Wine Business Research Conference, Cape Town, South Africa, 14–16 January.

Corsi, A.M., Cohen, J. and Lockshin, L. (2016) "The China Wine Barometer: A Look into the Future," http://research.wineaustralia.com/completed_projects/the-china-wine-barometer-cwb-a-look-into-the-future/.

Corsi, A.M., Cohen, J. and Lockshin, L. (2017) "How Consumptions Occasions Shape Consumer Preferences: A Discrete Choice Experiment Approach," Paper presented at the 10th International Conference of the Academy of Wine Business Research, Rohnert Park, USA, 25–28 July.

Corsi, A.M., Cohen, J., Lockshin, L. and Williamson, P. (2017) "Testing Lexical Equivalences for Wine Flavours in Emerging Markets: Do Hawthorns Taste Like Blackberries?" *Food Quality and Preference* 62, 296–306.

Dholakia, U.M. (2001) "A Motivational Process Model of Product Involvement and Consumer Risk Perception," *European Journal of Marketing* 35(11/12), 1340–1362.

Driesener, C., Cohen, J., Huang, A. and Corsi, A.M. (2018) "The Danger of Relying on Anecdotal Information in China," *Wine & Viticulture Journal* 35(4), 71–72.

Hogan, S., Romaniuk, J. and Faulkner, M. (2016) "Comparing Approaches to Elicit Brand Attributes Both Face-to-Face and Online," *International Journal of Market Research* 58(1), 57–78.

Kupfer, P. (2018) "Amber Shine and Black Dragon Pearls: The History of Chinese Wine Culture," Sino-Platonic Papers 278, University of Pennsylvania.

Li, H., Wang, H., Li, H., van der Lee, P., Xu, Z., Fortunato, A. and Yang, P. (2018) "Worlds of Wine: Old, New and Ancient," *Wine Economics and Policy* 7(1), 178–182.

Li, Z. (2010) *Chinese Wine*, Cambridge: Cambridge University Press.

Liu, F. and Murphy, J. (2007) "A Qualitative Study of Chinese Wine Consumption and Purchasing: Implications for Australian Wine," *International Journal of Wine Business Research* 19(2), 98–113.

McGovern, P.E., Underhill, A.P., Fang, H., Luan, F., Hall, G.R., Yu, H., Wang, C-S., Cai, F., Zhao, Z. and Feinman, G.M. (2005) "Chemical Identification and Cultural Implications of a Mixed Fermented Beverage from Late Prehistoric China," *Asian Perspectives* 44(2), 249–275.

OIV. (2020) "State of the World Vitivinicultural Sector in 2020," www.oiv.int/public/medias/7909/oiv-state-of-the-world-vitivinicultural-sector-in-2020.pdf.

Quester, P.G. and Smart, J. (1998) "The Influence of Consumption Situation and Product Involvement Over Consumers' Use of Product Attribute," *Journal of Consumer Marketing* 15(3), 220–238.

Rice, G. and Wongtada, N. (2007) "Conceptualizing Inter-Attitudinal Conflict in Consumer Response to Foreign Brand," *Journal of International Consumer Marketing* 20(1), 51–65.

Romaniuk, J. and Sharp, B. (2016) *How Brands Grow: Part 2*, Melbourne: Oxford University Press.

Sharma, S., Shimp, T.A. and Shin, J. (1995) "Consumer Ethnocentrism: A Test of Antecedents and Moderators," *Journal of the Academy of Marketing Science* 23(1), 26–37.

Shimp, T.A. and Sharma, P. (1987) "Consumer Ethnocentrism: Construction and Validation of the CETSCALE," *Journal of Marketing Research* 24(3), 280–289.

Su, Z. (2003) "Grape Cultural Exchange between Ancient China and Western Countries," *Yanshan University Journal: Philosophy and Social Sciences Edition* 6, 25–31.

43
BEYOND WHITE
On wine and ethnicity

David Inglis and Hang Kei Ho

Introduction

Wine is intimately bound up with ethnicity. This chapter provides a socio-historical survey of the complex relations between winemaking and drinking on the one side, and ethnicity, ethnic groups and their identities, relations between ethnic groups, and forms of ethnic bias and racism, on the other (Douglas 1987; Wilson 2005).

We are primarily focused here on 'ethnicity', dealing with 'race', racism, and racialisation issues as they arise within particular topic areas. We understand 'ethnicity' in terms of how people categorise themselves and others into different groups, as defined by shared culture, language, history and so on. When an ethnic group is subject to 'racialisation' processes, they are imagined by those defining them as being part of distinct 'races' of people. These can supposedly be identified by physical signs, especially skin colour. We define racism as the prejudicial treatment of some ethnic groups by others on the basis of socially constructed categories of 'race' (ASA 2020).

The chapter proceeds by examining the following inter-related themes. Wine has for millennia been bound up with colonialism. Ethnic and religious groups have often used wine to signify collective identities, including modern national identities. The global spread of winemaking by European colonists continues to shape where and by whom wine is made and how it is presented, including through presentations of ethnic heritage. Wine today is very much dominated by white people, in terms of imagery, consumers and (higher-level) personnel. Much of the hard labour in the vineyard may be carried out by non-white workers, subjected to various forms of exploitation. These phenomena have started to become issues of greater public concern, recently augmented by the Black Lives Matter (BLM) movement's framing of racism and white privilege. The rise to prominence of some East Asian locations as major centres of wine trading and consuming has also created some important new dynamics involving wine and ethnicity.

Wine and ethnicity in the 'Old World'

Winemaking began about 6000 BCE in the Caucasus, spreading westward over the next several millennia (McGovern 2003). In ancient Greece and Rome, wine was a powerful ethnic marker: 'civilised' people made and drank wine, watering it to dilute its dangerous potency. Barbarians were seen to drink un-mixed wine or were ignorant of wine altogether (Lissarrague 2016). The Romans especially regarded the introduction of vineyards to conquered lands as an essential aspect of these being rendered civilised (Purcell 1985).

Christianity arose within a context of widespread Greek, Roman and Jewish wine production and consumption. Jewish practice stipulated that wine was kosher if not touched by gentile hands during production (Horowitz 2016). Christianity came to have the strongest connections with wine of all the major world religions. The ritual of communion intimated to believers that the imbibed wine was, indeed, the blood of Christ (Biale 2007). Winemaking followed the widespread dispersal of Christian practices throughout what is now called Europe, including in such subsequently celebrated regions as Burgundy, thereby creating what would later be called the 'Old World' of wine. The Islamic ban on wine, and alcohol more generally, stands in apparently stark contrast to Christianity's embracing of wine, but actual practice across Muslim territories has varied considerably (Honchell 2015). The official antipathy to wine production remains today a live issue in Muslim countries with extant winemaking traditions, including Turkey (Pitel 2015).

In sixteenth- and seventeenth-century Europe, increasingly clearly defined national identities were the products of nation-building processes. Strong centralised states imposed defined modes of national symbolism and affiliation throughout their territories (Gellner 1964). Notions of what it meant to be 'English', 'French' etc. crystallised and became increasingly taken for granted. Wine played a role here. Even in a country with no significant winemaking activity like England, wine could operate as a strong signifier of identity. In the later eighteenth century, the drinking of port, from politically neutral Portugal, became a strong marker of middle-class English identity, juxtaposed against the unpatriotic act of drinking the wine of the French enemy. The embrace of 'patriotic port' also took root in hitherto Bordeaux-quaffing Scotland (Ludington 2013).

In France, wine played an even more important role in symbolising the nation (Heath 2014; Bohling 2018). By the 1950s, Roland Barthes (2013: 58) could plausibly claim that wine 'is felt by the French nation to be a possession which is its very own, just like its three hundred and sixty types of cheese. . . . It is a totem-drink'. French culture:

> calls anyone who does not believe in wine by *names* such as sick, disabled or depraved. . . . Conversely, an award of good integration is given to whoever is a practising wine-drinker: knowing *how* to drink is a national technique which serves to qualify the Frenchman, to demonstrate at once his performance, his control and his sociability. Wine. . . [is] a foundation for a collective morality.
>
> *(Barthes 2013: 59)*

Consumption of all types of alcohol fell in France from the 1970s onwards, with a marked shift away from wine to beer and branded spirits, and away from old-style anonymous table wines towards branded wines, provoking ongoing crises in the French wine industry (Sulkunen 1989). Since the 1980s, foreign investment in and ownership of French wine production has greatly increased (Curran and Thorpe 2014). Nonetheless, wine remains integral to French national identity (Demossier 2010). Wine is marketed around the world as the quintessence of sophisticated, aspirational Frenchness, thereby masking the complexities of contemporary France and its fractious ethnic divides. This includes the dominance of white people in its wine world and the exploitation of ethnic minority vineyard workers in some regions (Crenn 2015).

France is also the country that has seen the most dramatic disputes concerning wine and nationhood in recent times. 'Mondialisation', the French term for the English phrase 'globalisation', is seen by both the political left and right as striking at the cultural heart of France, its putatively traditional terroir-based agriculture. The winemaker stands as either tragic or heroic figure, depending on how successfully they combat the destructive forces of globalised markets and predatory foreign capital (Demossier 2010). Anti-globalisation has sometimes involved direct, sometimes violent, actions in the southern French countryside (Smith 2016). The case of the failure of the large Californian company Mondavi to set up a winery in the village of Aniane in the Languedoc became a *cause célèbre* in the early 2000s and was brought to wide international attention by Jonathan Nossiter's 2004 polemical documentary *Mondovino*. The events in Aniane were markedly more complex than suggested by journalistic narratives (Barthel-Bouchier and Clough 2005). There were subtle misunderstandings on both sides as to what terroir is and how it is to be respected (Trubek 2004). Since then, the globalisation of French wine has continued in ever more complex ways, further problematising the relations of wine and French nationhood (Dutton 2020).

Colonial legacies in the 'New World'

We now turn from the so-called 'Old World' to the 'New World' of wine. With the expansion of European empire building from 1500 CE, wine moved into a new and literally 'global' situation, with manufacture and consumption now happening across oceans and continents. The creation of the 'New World' – primarily encompassing the Americas, what is now South Africa, and Australasia – was a direct result of 'Old World' imperialism (Inglis 2019). The upshot was both massification and diversification in worldwide wine production (Pinilla and Ayuda 2002).

Dutch settlers in southern Africa started producing wine in the later seventeenth century. Wine from Constantia enjoyed a high reputation in Europe throughout the eighteenth century, an early instance of a prestige wine from a peripheral area. Spanish Jesuit priests began wineries in Peru in the seventeenth century, and Franciscan monks did the same in Mexico and California in the late eighteenth century (Colman 2008). The primary motivations were to meet the needs of communion rituals. Wine as a profit-making entity arose with trans-oceanic mass migration in the second half of the nineteenth century. A significant number of European migrants drank wine in their countries of origin, taking their tastes with them. Some also took winemaking skills, including those Spanish, Portuguese, Italians and others fleeing poverty or persecution who migrated to perceived lands of opportunity, like Argentina, Chile and the USA (Unwin 1991).

Ancient Greco-Roman ideas about the wine/civilisation nexus were applied to colonial contexts. In locales like California, making and drinking wines were important 'tactics for transforming landscapes and for propagating a particular worldview of cultivation and control' over supposed virgin territories (Hannickel 2013: 15). Similar ideas were at work in Australia in the early decades of the nineteenth century. British administrators regarded the colony as a source of wine that would allow the mother country to circumvent reliance on French imports and wean the colonists off hard spirits. Europeans with winemaking knowledges were imported to pioneer the Australian industry (McIntyre 2012).

Regarding ownership of vineyards and wineries, colonialism could sometimes mean, as was the case in nineteenth-century Argentina, the introduction of peasants with their own small wine businesses selling wine to nearby cities, mirroring the European situation in regions like Burgundy (Simpson 2011). Their descendants were forcibly thrown into the unforgiving globalised wine markets of the 1980s in a pan–Latin American wave of agricultural neo-liberalisation (Pont and Thomas 2012). Some less high-profile regions settled by European winemaking immigrants, as in Brazil and Uruguay, are today becoming increasingly globally recognised (Nossiter 2009).

Colonialism also stimulated the massification of wine production. Just as the Romans had set up North Africa as a massive source of wine, so too did the late nineteenth-century French cultivate Algeria (Pinilla and Ayuda 2002). With the local peasantry thrown off the land in favour of a small number of large industrial wineries owned by big French companies, wine production hugely increased. Algeria for a time was the biggest wine-producing country in the world (Simpson 2011). As Barthes (2013: 61) noted, 'wine cannot be an unalloyedly blissful substance, except if we wrongfully forget that it is also the product of an expropriation', of subject people and their lands.

Wine marketing today often emphasises the ethnic, especially Italian, heritages of winemakers in New World locales like California and Argentina. Italian migrants arrived *en masse* after Italian unification in the 1860s, partly due to economic restructuring of rural areas in Italy, and partly due to the devastation wrought to vineyards by the *phylloxera* pest. An influential group in California were immigrants from Piemonte, who used winemaking to create a distinctive socio-economic niche for themselves in the ethnic tapestry of Northern California (Cinotto 2012). They persuaded Italians from other areas to work for low wages. They also exploited the expanding Asian and Hispanic workforces, a situation mirrored in other parts of the Americas (Peck 2009).

The display and performance of ethnicity has today become an important feature of selling wine. This includes in New World locations, which cannot rely, as many of their European counterparts can, on the customer making the assumption that the current winemaking operation is imbued, in direct and virtuous ways, with putatively longstanding traditions (Tiefenbacher and Townsend 2019). Performing one's 'true' ethnicity is a central facet of presenting to buyers a sense of 'authenticity', along with apparent adherence to tradition, family heritage, and respectful stewardship of the land (Beverland and Luxton 2005).

Thus, winemakers in Northern California can present themselves and their wines as genuinely 'Cal-Ital'. This is framed as combining distinctively 'New World' ('Californian') and Old World ('Italian', often Piemontese) features, brought together in a hybrid form presented as unique (Helzer 2001). Self-presentation can have material effects: the widespread belief in the uniqueness of Cal-Ital ethnic heritage and stylistics has motivated the planting of central and northern Italian grape varietals like Sangiovese and Barbera and lesser-known regional Italian varieties (Helzer 2001). Beliefs as to the ongoing power of inherited and authentic ethnicity animate constellations of 'Italian' people, vines and wines, sold as truly 'Italian', even if rooted in soil located tens of thousands of kilometres away from the assumed mother country. Ethnic wine authenticity can sometimes be presented as being preserved over time precisely because it is *not* located in the (nowadays allegedly corrupted) mother country (Peace 2006).

Ethnically divided wine worlds

The presentation of ethnic heritage in winemaking usually implies, assumes and presents the Europeanness of winemakers and, by extension, their ethnic 'whiteness', too. The preponderance of white people in the contemporary globalised wine landscape is one of its most notable features. The visuals of wine marketing often present idealised representations of attractive, affluent, young, white people as supposedly typical drinkers of wine. A scattering of people of other ethnic groups, just as attractive and well-groomed as their white counterparts, may be added to such representations, usually in a tokenistic manner (Thach *et al.* 2016; Thach and Olsen 2016).

The cultural industry surrounding wine – involving mass-market books, magazines, courses for non-professionals, tours and vacations – ideally sells wine to typically white, higher-class consumers as part of a broader presentation of cultural authenticity in food and travel, often involving imagery of idyllic rural settings (Pont and Thomas 2012). Wine tourism has become an increasingly lucrative field, often centred around notions of timeless winemaking heritages in rural paradises (Meneley 2007). Wine tourism presents the winery as a site of attractive pleasures rather than of mundane labour and techno-scientific manipulation. This presentation may disguise local social tensions, including inter-ethnic ones, the presence of large-scale agribusiness, and the exploitation of labour, including ethnic minority or indigenous workers (Peace 2006). Both visitors and on-site personnel will, in most cases, be understood by participants to be 'white', perhaps more obviously so in Europe and North America, but also in Latin America and in Black-majority South Africa, too. In wine promotion for tourists and consumers, internationally recognisable French, Italian or Spanish words like 'chateau', 'domaine' and 'bodega' operate as globally reproducible signifiers of noble, quintessentially 'European' and, by implication, ethnically and racially 'white' wine heritages (Gade 2004).

The cultural 'whiteness' (Ahmed 2007) of much wine marketing and tourism imagery is mirrored in participation at wine events around the Developed World, where non-whites are usually very much in the minority. The great majority of wine industry personnel are ethnically white. Many hold university qualifications in wine management from a relatively small number of institutions in major wine-producing countries (Inglis 2019). These offer broadly identical curricula, usually in English – global business's *lingua franca* – which express convergent assumptions about how wine should be made and marketed (Roger 2010): that is, primarily to white people and, more recently, to richer and aspirational East Asians.

If higher-level wine work is done mainly by whites, then the back-breaking labour of grape picking and other physical activities in vineyards is often carried out by non-whites, who can generally expect low pay and poor treatment (McLaughlin 2013). For example, North African workers in Bordeaux face various forms of discrimination by their managers and the suspicion of local people (Crenn 2015). Semi-feudal relations between white owners and indigenous workers are characteristic of some wine-producing areas in Latin America (Howland 2019). The most discussed case today of troubled ethnic relations in wine production is that of South Africa (Moseley 2008). The rapid and disruptive neo-liberalisation of the industry there from the 1990s onwards has entailed serious consequences for rural Black communities. As grape-growing and winemaking enterprises shifted markedly from domestic to export markets, increased precariousness for labourers followed, and a rural lumpen proletariat was created, living hand to mouth outside the safety net of white paternalism (Ewert and du Toit 2005). South African labour conditions have recently become a matter of concern for filmmakers, journalists and concerned industry buyers, including those from the Nordic state alcohol monopolies, which may have ethical purchasing as part of their remits. Whether Fairtrade wine initiatives benefit Black employees or not has recently become a contentious public issue (Herman 2019).

Such debates are gaining visibility with the recent wave of controversy about racism and ethnic inequalities in the wine world stimulated by the BLM movement. US-resident wine professional Miguel de Leon (2020), of Filipino ancestry, echoes the views of many other ethnic minority wine professionals when he demands wine's 'de-colonization':

> [t]raditional wine tasting grids and wheels are biased to Eurocentric flavours, and crucial wine vocabularies can centre on foods completely foreign to. . . [the typically] Asian [p]alate. . . . Wine is rooted in Europe and its white adjacencies, themselves products of colonial and imperialist histories. From Chile to California, we feel the impact of how winemaking was affected by the conscious, hegemonic spread of Christianity. . . . The wine world does not take into account current experiences of its BIPOC [Black, Indigenous, and People of Colour] and LGBTQ+ members. It is steeped in a language that is coded and arcane, tied up with legal jargon and French techniques that only the privileged, monied few are able to decipher.
>
> *(De Leon 2020: np)*

An important recent initiative to democratise the wine world on ethnic grounds is the HUE Society (HUE Society 2021). It promotes the development of, and networking for, African American individuals and wine businesses. Its motto of 'Assimilation Not Required' sends out a powerful signal that the time has come for the wine world to be 'de-colonised'. The media and internet buzz around the BLM movement has helped stimulate the growing online presence of groups supporting BIPOC people interested in wine as professionals and connoisseurs, especially in the US and South Africa (Beckett 2020). The exclusion of non-whites from higher-level wine industry positions has already for some years been tackled by South African initiatives to involve more Black people in professional roles, such as sommeliers (Govender-Ypma 2018). But whether such developments can meaningfully happen outside primarily English-speaking wine-producing and consuming countries remains to be seen (Robinson 2020).

Enter East Asia

Just as ethnic dynamics are today shifting within more established wine locations, so too does the rise of East Asia as a major locus of wine trade and consumption and, to some extent, production, create novel interplays of wine and ethnicity. Within the last two decades, East Asians have entered the wine stage as significant individual and collective actors in various ways. During the global credit crunch of 2007–09, the luxury wine sector was severely hit in Europe and North America, but it was significantly kept afloat by collectors and investors in East Asia, both in China and in surrounding states (Ho 2019).

The burgeoning mainland Chinese liking of wine – primarily but not only red and French – and the creation of new wineries in Chinese regions, including those endowed with spectacular mock French chateaux, is well documented in journalism, film documentaries and academic analyses (Capitello *et al.* 2016; Howson and Ly 2020; Kjellgren 2019). The development of a capitalist economy in the 2000s created new social elites in the People's Republic, ranging from business billionaires to upper-middle-class professionals, for whom wine has become increasingly prominent. Collecting and drinking wine allows projection of prized Western forms of sophistication and discernment. While seeming highly culturally legitimate on home turf, such practices often seem vulgar to non-Chinese observers (Smith Maguire and Lim 2015) and redolent of *nouveau riche* self-aggrandisement (Smith Maguire 2019).

Meanwhile, attempts to legitimate the fast-growing sectors of viticulture and viniculture in China face the problem of persuading Chinese and non-Chinese audiences alike that both good mid-range and fine wines can be made on Chinese soil. Producers struggle to mount convincing arguments that China has appropriate terroirs that will yield sufficiently sophisticated and valorised wine to meet rising consumer expectations (Smith Maguire 2018). The latter are based on imaginings of the nobility of classic European winegrowing regions, raising the vexing question of how wines can be 'Chinese' and world-class simultaneously (Zheng 2019).

Beyond Shanghai and Beijing, the former colonial hubs of Hong Kong, Singapore and Macau are where much East Asian wine world innovation has taken place. These locations have variously maintained, drawn upon and transcended the drinking practices of the British, Portuguese and (during WWII) Japanese former colonial rulers (Justin 2015).

In the 1960s, cognac became a popular status symbol among affluent Hong Kong Chinese, consumed at business meetings, parties and banquets (Smart 2005). Major brands like Martell and Rémy Martin were advertised on television in the 1980s and 1990s, with famous Hong Kong film stars seen receiving hospitality in France. Inter-ethnic harmony was stressed as cause and consequence of wine-spirit drinking.[1] The rise of cognac helped stimulate the assumption that 'Chinese' alcohols must be lower quality, less sophisticated and less worthy of elite consumption than their Western counterparts. This was the cultural background for wine to move in the 1990s from its hitherto marginal position to become a sought-after and socially aspirational beverage, demonstrative of cosmopolitan sophistication and global savvy. Marketing iconography has developed to appeal to upwardly mobile young people (Ho 2015, 2019). As elsewhere in East Asia, high-end Bordeaux reds, and French wines generally, predominate because they represent refinement in taste and lifestyle (Ho 2019, 2021).

Hong Kong and other East Asian states have developed wine trades with similar characteristics – low-tax regimes oriented to high-cost, prestigious imports – but each has its own particularities.

Macau's casino-driven economy pushed the government to abolish wine import taxation in 2008, greatly stimulating the import industry. Hong Kong and Singapore have rapidly become among the most important wine-trading and auction hubs in the world. As in Macau, wine import duty was withdrawn by the Hong Kong government in 2008. Most wines imported into Hong Kong are then exported to the Chinese mainland, along with ideas about wine as a status symbol and object of appreciation (Ho 2021). The Singapore trade operates a different taxation regime. Duty on alcohol, including wine, is levied on a formula which primarily affects lower-cost beverages; low taxation on prestige products has led to buoyant sales and increasing consumer numbers (Ho 2019).

Many non-Asian wine world actors have welcomed the entry of East Asians into the global wine game. But there have been ethnically based tensions, too, some verging on racism. Acts of apparent sacrilege, like East Asians drinking expensive wine mixed with ice cubes or soft drinks, are circulating tropes in journalism and social media (Topping 2011). The entry of, and possible resistance to, young East Asian females in wine professional roles will be increasingly important research topics in the future (Xiaojin 2019). Resentments among nationalistically minded observers have been fostered by East Asian investors buying vineyards in France (Booth 2010). East Asian collectors and speculators apparently driving up the prices of fine and rare wines has also been a point of contention (Mustacich 2015). Such friction-laden dynamics are likely when large numbers of actors enter cultural fields that previously had little or no participation by people of their ethnicities.

Conclusion

Wine today remains strongly influenced by the drink's long history of entanglements with imperialism, nationalism, and forms of ethnic exploitation and racialised injustices. Ethnic equality in wine world participation remains a remote prospect. Even the recent appearance of relatively privileged East Asians does not change the fact that white people still predominate. Non-white ethnic groups often do the back-breaking work, are marginalised in multiple ways, or are absent altogether. Nonetheless, one may hope that recent controversies about racist assumptions and ethnically based exploitation can help bring about progressive trends. The Court of Master Sommeliers, Americas, has recently announced dropping the title 'Master' from its qualifications, given its racist connotations. Such moves could be seen either as tokenism or as genuine attempts to alter, symbolically and practically, the operation of wine worlds as bastions of white ethnic power, privilege and racism, tacit or otherwise (Morales 2020). What happens next regarding ethnic participation will be a major issue for everyone involved with wine over the coming decades.

Note

1 Some examples of such advertisements can be found online. For example: Martell Gold Medal Advertising, 1991, available at: www.youtube.com/watch?v=wmxKw4DgeMk [Viewed 7 February 2020].

References

Ahmed, S. (2007) "A Phenomenology of Whiteness," *Feminist Studies* 8(2), 149–168.
ASA (American Sociological Association). (2020) "Race and Ethnicity," www.asanet.org/topics/race-and-ethnicity, accessed 8 February 2021.
Barthel-Bouchier, D. and Clough, L. (2005) "From Mondavi to Depardieu: The Global/Local Politics of Wine," *French Politics, Culture and Society* 23(2), 71–90.
Barthes, R. (2013[1957]) "Wine and Milk," in *Mythologies*, New York: Hill and Wang, 58–60.
Beckett, F. (2020) "It's Time the Wine Industry Stopped Taking Safe Stances to Keep Its Primarily White Audience Comfortable," *The Guardian*, 3 July, www.theguardian.com/food/2020/jul/03/it-is-time-the-wine-industry-stopped-taking-safe-stances-to-keep-its-primarily-white-audience-comfortable, accessed 8 February 2021.

Beverland, M. and Luxton, S. (2005) "Managing Integrated Marketing Communication (IMC) through Strategic Decoupling," *Journal of Advertising* 34(4), 103–116.
Biale, D. (2007) *Blood and Belief*, Berkeley: University of California Press.
Bohling, J. (2018) *The Sober Revolution: Appellation Wine and the Transformation of France*, Ithaca, NY: Cornell University Press.
Booth, R. (2010) "Bordeaux Vintners Raise Their Glasses to China's Wine Buffs," *The Guardian*, 2 April, www.guardian.co.uk/lifeandstyle/2010/apr/02/bordeaux-wine-china, accessed 8 February 2021.
Capitello, R., Charters, S., Menival, D. and Yuan, J. (2016) *The Wine Value Chain in China: Global Dynamics, Marketing and Communication in the Contemporary Chinese Wine Market*, Amsterdam: Chandos Publishing.
Cinotto, S. (2012) *Soft Soil, Black Grapes*, New York: New York University Press.
Colman, T. (2008) *Wine Politics*, Berkeley: University of California Press.
Crenn, C. (2015) "Ethnic Identity, Power, Compromise, and Territory," in J. MacClancy (ed), *Alternative Countrysides*, Manchester: Manchester University Press, 61–81.
Curran, L. and Thorpe, M. (2014) "Whose Terroir is it Anyway? Comparing Chinese FDI in the French and Australian Wine Sector," AAWE Working Paper 168.
De Leon, M. (2020) "It's Time to De-Colonize Wine," *Punchdrink.com*, https://punchdrink.com/articles/time-to-decolonize-wine-sommelier-racism-restaurants, accessed 8 February 2021.
Demossier, M. (2010) *Wine Drinking Culture in France*, Cardiff: University of Wales Press.
Douglas, M. (ed) (1987) *Constructive Drinking*, Cambridge: Cambridge University Press.
Dutton, J. (2020) "Wine in Houellebecq: Cultural Transgression or Literary Device?" *French Cultural Studies* 31(1), 73–90.
Ewert, J. and Du Toit, A. (2005) "A Deepening Divide in the Countryside: Restructuring and Rural Livelihoods in the South African Wine Industry," *Journal of Southern African Studies* 31(2), 315–332.
Gade, D.W. (2004) "Tradition, Territory, and Terroir in French Viniculture," *Annals of the Association of American Geographers* 94(4), 848–867.
Gellner, E. (1964) *Thought and Change*, London: Weidenfeld.
Govender-Ypma, I. (2018) "How BLACC is Changing the Game in South Africa," *Wine Enthusiast*, June, www.winemag.com/gallery/black-cellar-club-blacc-south-africa, accessed 8 February 2021.
Hannickel, E. (2013) *Empire of Vines*, Philadelphia: University of Pennsylvania Press.
Heath, E. (2014) *Wine, Sugar, and the Making of Modern France*, Cambridge: Cambridge University Press.
Helzer, J.J. (2001) "Old Traditions, New Lifestyles: The Emergence of a Cal-Ital Landscape," *Yearbook of the Association of Pacific Coast Geographers* 63, 49–62.
Herman, A. (2019) "Asymmetries and Opportunities: Power and Inequality in Fairtrade Wine Global Production Networks," *Area* 51(2), 332–339.
Ho, H.K. (2015) "Hong Kong," in S.C. Martin (ed), *The Sage Encyclopedia of Alcohol: Social, Cultural, and Historical Perspectives*, Thousand Oaks, CA: SAGE Publications, 701–703.
Ho, H.K. (2019) "The Globalization of the Wine Industry in Hong Kong: A Local and Global Perspective," in D. Inglis and A.M. Almila (eds), *The Globalization of Wine*, London: Bloomsbury, 133–150.
Ho, H.K. (2021) "Why has wine consumption become popular in Hong Kong? Introducing a new sociocultural paradigm of traditional, aspiring and creative drinkers," *Asian Anthropology*, 20(4), 248–268.
Honchell, S. (2015) "The Story of a Drunken Mughal," *Social History of Alcohol and Drugs* 29, 4–28.
Horowitz, R. (2016) *Kosher USA*, New York: Columbia University Press.
Howland, P. (2019) "Enduring Wine and the Global Middle Class," in D. Inglis and A.M. Almila (eds), *The Globalization of Wine*, London: Bloomsbury.
Howson, C. and Ly, P. (2020) *Adventures on the China Wine Trail*, New York: Rowman and Littlefield.
HUE Society. (2021) "Home Page," *HUE Society*, https://thehuesociety.com, accessed 8 February 2021.
Inglis, D. (2019) "Wine Globalization: Longer-Term Dynamics and Contemporary Patterns," in D. Inglis and A.M. Almila (eds), *The Globalization of Wine*, London: Bloomsbury, 21–46.
Justin, C. (2015) "Singapore," in S.C. Martin (ed), *The SAGE Encyclopedia of Alcohol: Social, Cultural, and Historical Perspectives*, Thousand Oaks, CA: Sage, 1159–1160.
Kjellgren, B. (2019) "Fluid Modernity: Wine in China," in D. Inglis and A.M. Almila (eds), *The Globalization of Wine*, London: Bloomsbury, 115–132.
Lissarrague, F. (2016) *The Aesthetics of the Greek Banquet*, Princeton, NJ: Princeton University Press.
Ludington, C. (2013) *The Politics of Wine in Britain*, Basingstoke: Palgrave.
McGovern, P. (2003) *Ancient Wine*, Princeton, NJ: Princeton University Press.
McIntyre, J. (2012) *First Vintage: Wine in Colonial New South Wales*, Sydney: NewSouth.
McLaughlin, J. (2013) "The Hands Behind the Harvest: Migrant Workers in Niagara's Wine Industry," in M. Ripmeester et al. (eds), *The World of Niagara Wine*, Waterloo: Wilfrid Laurier University Press, 109–124.

Meneley, A. (2007) "Like an Extra Virgin," *American Anthropologist* 109(4), 678–687.
Morales, C. (2020) "Prestigious Wine Organization Drops Use of Term 'Master'," *The New York Times*, 22 June, www.nytimes.com/2020/06/22/us/wine-master.html, accessed 8 February 2021.
Moseley, W.G. (2008) "Fair Trade Wine: South Africa's Post-Apartheid Vineyards and the Global Economy," *Globalizations* 5(2), 291–304.
Mustacich, S. (2015) *Thirsty Dragon*, New York: Henry Holt.
Nossiter, J. (2009) *Liquid Memory*, London: Atlantic.
Peace, A. (2006) "Barossa Slow: The Representation and Rhetoric of Slow Food's Regional Cooking," *Gastronomica* 6(1), 51–59.
Peck, G. (2009) *The Prohibition Hangover*, New Brunswick, NJ: Rutgers University Press.
Pinilla, V. and Ayuda, M-A. (2002) "The Political Economy of the Wine Trade: Spanish Exports and the International Market, 1890–1935," *European Review of Economic History* 6(1), 51–85.
Pitel, L. (2015) "Turkey Wine-Making Tradition Under Threat from Islamic-Rooted Government's New Alcohol Laws," *The Independent*, 25 December, www.independent.co.uk/life-style/food-and-drink/news/turkey-wine-making-tradition-under-threat-from-islamic-rooted-governments-new-alcohol-laws-a6786201.html, accessed 8 February 2021.
Pont, P.C.A.M. and Thomas, H. (2012) "The Sociotechnical Alliance of Argentine Quality Wine," *Science, Technology, Human Values* 37(6), 627–652.
Purcell, N. (1985) "Wine and Wealth in Ancient Italy," *Journal of Roman Studies* 75, 1–19.
Robinson, J. (2020) "The Many Hues of Wine talent," *Jancis Robinson*, www.jancisrobinson.com/articles/many-hues-wine-talent, accessed 8 February 2021.
Roger, A. (2010) "Scholarly Constructs and the Legitimization of European Policies," *Revue Française de Science Politique* 60(2), 1–22.
Simpson, J. (2011) *Creating Wine*, Princeton, NJ: Princeton University Press.
Smart, J. (2005) "Cognac, Beer, Red Wine or Soft Drinks?" in T.M. Wilson (ed), *Drinking Cultures*, Oxford: Berg, 107–128.
Smith, A. (2016) *Terror and Terroir*, Manchester: Manchester University Press.
Smith Maguire, J. (2018) "The Taste for the Particular: A Logic of Discernment in an Age of Omnivorousness," *Journal of Consumer Culture* 18(1), 3–20.
Smith Maguire, J. (2019) "Media Representations of the Nouveaux Riches and the Cultural Constitution of the Global Middle Class," *Cultural Politics* 15(1), 29–47.
Smith Maguire, J. and Lim, M. (2015) "Lafite in China: Media Representations of 'Wine Culture' in New Markets," *Journal of Macromarketing* 35(9), 229–242.
Sulkunen, P. (1989) "Drinking in France 1965–1979," *British Journal of Addiction* 84(1), 61–72.
Thach, L. and Olsen, J. (2016) "Melting Pot or Blended Wine: Does Ethnicity Still Matter in Understanding Consumer Wine Behaviour?" *Academy of Wine Business Research*, http://academyofwinebusiness.com/2016-2, accessed 8 February 2021.
Thach, L., Olsen, J. and Chang, K. (2016) "Mixed Race and Blended Wine: How Important is Ethnicity in Wine Marketing?" *Winebusiness.com*, www.winebusiness.com/news/?go=getArticleanddataid=167091, accessed 8 February 2021.
Tiefenbacher, J.P. and Townsend, C. (2019) "The Semiofoodscape of Wine, I" in S. Brunn and R. Kehrein (eds), *Handbook of the Changing World Language Map*, Cham: Springer.
Topping, A. (2011) "Bordeaux Vineyards Acquire Taste for Chinese Buyers," *The Guardian*, 25 March, www.guardian.co.uk/lifeandstyle/2011/mar/23/bordeaux-vineyards-welcome-chinese-buyers, accessed 8 February 2021.
Trubek, A.B. (2004) "Incorporating *Terroir*," *Gastronomica* 4(3), 90–99.
Unwin, T. (1991) *Wine and the Vine*, London: Routledge.
Wilson, T.M. (ed) (2005) *Drinking Cultures*, London: Bloomsbury.
Xiaojin, R. (2019) "Women Sommeliers Bring New Zeal to Wine Tasting," *China Daily*, 3 March, www.chinadaily.com.cn/a/201903/08/WS5c81e57fa3106c65c34ed885.html, accessed 8 February 2021.
Zheng, X. (2019) "Narrating *Terroir*," *Food, Culture, Society* 22(3), 280–298.

44
CLIMATE OR TECHNICAL CHANGE IN WINE?

Confronting climatologists' and winegrowers' analyses

Geneviève Teil

Introduction

Winegrowing[1] has spread consistently since the mid-twentieth century and is a major source of income, especially in areas which, due to mountainous topography, particularly stony soil or a relatively arid climate, are not suited to other crops. In the scientific literature, wine is said to be one of the most vulnerable crops to temperature increases and rainfall decreases. The climatologists publishing these claims have multiplied warnings about climate change, for which each new forecast is more drastic than the last. They have recommended changes in grape varieties (Shaw 2012; Jones 2007), geographical relocation (van Leeuwen and Darriet 2016; Moriondo *et al.* 2013; Hannah *et al.* 2013), increased flexibility of grape supply (Mosedale *et al.* 2016; Hayes and Battaglene 2006) and so on. The debate is primarily focused on protected designation of origin wines (PDO), which are subject to constraints in terms of zoning, grape variety and terroir quality.

Simultaneously, over the last twenty years or so, other researchers have been concerned with the preparedness of winegrowers (Pincus 2003; Belliveau *et al.* 2006; Hadarits *et al.* 2010; Battaglini *et al.* 2009; Alonso and O'Neill 2011; Lereboullet *et al.* 2013; Lereboullet *et al.* 2014) and of farmers in general (Weber 1997; Holloway 1999; Buys *et al.* 2012). Their research has yielded somewhat surprising results. While about two-thirds of the general population feels concerned about the ongoing climate change (Lorenzoni and Pidgeon 2006), more than half of all winegrowers appear to be indifferent to it. The result is identical in all the countries studied: in Europe, Australia, Chile and North America. While farmers seem more 'sensitive' to climate issues than the rest of the population, the percentage of those who do not think that climate change is underway remains the same, despite accelerating changes: 'During discussions, several producers were unwilling to attribute recent climatic phenomena to any trend in current conditions' (Lereboullet *et al.* 2013: 278). They argue that the extreme events that climatologists interpret as foreshadowing future events are little more than repetitions of the extraordinary weather events that have occurred throughout history. Some criticise the idea of global warming and emphasise changes in precipitation rather than rising temperatures.

Yet vine growers, like all farmers, are front-row observers of meteorological conditions and are at the forefront of climate change anticipation. Some authors therefore carried out vast questionnaire surveys in an effort to understand 'hurdles' to the development of 'awareness' and attitudinal adjustment (Johnson *et al.* 1993; Patt and Schröter 2008; Weber 2010). They wanted to establish whether the 'obstacles' were psychological, ideological or social forms of resistance; a lack of training or information; or perhaps 'misperceptions' about climate and risk (Peretti-Wattel [2003] 2000; Duclos 1987). Others (Hansen *et al.* 2004; Holloway 1999) have used in-depth interviews with stakeholders to better understand how they were or were not integrating climate change into their activities. Again, the main finding was indifference.

When they eventually were confronted with the warnings of climatologists, farmers showed a kind of *a priori* rejection of scientists' knowledge and previsions, the key elements of which were the unreliability of weather forecasts (Hansen *et al.* 2004) and the difference between the scientific elaboration of a form of knowledge that is general and the very local knowledge of farmers embedded in everyday experience (Holloway 1999). These studies have the merit of highlighting the peculiarities of scientific knowledge: namely that, as with any knowledge, it is the result of a production process that is not solely the work of scientists (Lave and Wenger 1991; Chaiklin and Lave 1996). Still, scientific knowledge has to comply with particular constraints regarding reference (Latour 1987), veridiction (Latour 2013) and, most of all, reliability. On this basis, can we posit that winegrowers' own knowledge production process leads them to different conclusions to those of scientists?

In an effort to answer this question, I conducted an in-depth interview study on climate change with people involved in wine production, particularly winegrowers. My first objective was to see whether the previously evidenced scepticism still persisted to this day and, if so, to better understand how these actors did or did not take note of and analyse changes in their vineyards. The study thus aimed to understand these stakeholders' 'perceptions', not as those of an external 'reality' of climate change but rather, following Holloway (1999), as a process of observation and analysis within the broader activity of managing a farm, a union, a company or such.

Methodology

This study looks at the differences between climatologists' and winegrowers' accounts of reality and requires thus some methodological precautions. To avoid scientism, which considers science as the only source for truth, the social study of knowledge (Knorr-Cetina 1981; Bloor 1984) analyses knowledge not as a more-or-less true statement but as a construction process. Still, the interpretation of the knowledge produced by winegrowers as a 'social' or 'cultural' construction transforms it into a symbolic emergence, unable to account for the particular strengths of scientific knowledge. To avoid this relativism, Callon and Bruno (1992) generalised Bloor's symmetry principle, arguing for a withdrawal from realism's ontological premises: that is, from a nature/society or nature/culture divide. The winegrowers' accounts gathered in this study are thus analysed as the results of a particular production process involving objectives and constraints, observations, experimentations, results comparisons and critical discussions, without making any *a priori* distinction between nature and culture.

The interviews were conducted from July 2012 to February 2015 at winegrowers' places of operation or in the office or shop of sales staff, personnel from certification institutes, independent oenologists, retailers and so on. The winegrower interviews lasted from one to over two hours, often followed by a visit to the vines and tasting session. The subsequent analysis of these interviews aimed to shed light on winegrowers' different ways of observing, thinking and conducting their activity. On such complex issues, interviews grant the possibility to gather detailed yet very diverse information. Though a broad 'structure of analysis' or 'way of doing' may emerge from the corpus, in-depth interviewing fosters diverse and even idiosyncratic answers. Therefore, methodological rigour precludes quantitative estimations and allows only very broad indications on the shared character of some claims or analyses.

Interview samples are always constrained by who is willing to respond. In Alsace, one of the two fieldwork regions, it was difficult to meet wine cooperative members. In order to avoid excluding

Table 44.1 Interviewees

Code	Interviewees	Paris (Paris)	Anjou (Anjou)	Alsace (Al)
V	Independent vine-grower and winemaker/grower		19	16
Coop	Cooperative members or employees			5
PI	Producers' interprofessional organisation		3	2
WT	Wine trade	3		2
CPDO	Certification (PDO syndicate, National Institute of the Denominations of Origin, certification firms)	3	2	2
R, OE	Research and technical advice, independent oenologists		1	4
J	Journalist			1
	Total	6	25	32

them from the analysis, I relied on stakeholders who worked with or represented them, such as heads of associations, cooperatives or PDO management bodies. The results presented here are based primarily on those who provided detailed descriptions of their ways of working, their goals and the indicators they used to determine whether they were on the right track or whether they needed to change their way of thinking. This study, therefore, gives a voice mainly to the most reflexive stakeholders, winegrowers especially. This is undoubtedly an important difference with questionnaire surveys. This does not mean that less talkative interviewees lacked a structured vision of their action, but it may be more intuitive and, therefore, more difficult to communicate in interviews. This methodology similarly sidelined those who refused to participate. These limitations of interview studies are well known yet remain difficult to overcome.

The choice of respondents was designed to reflect the diversity of production structures. Table 44.1 shows the range of the 63 interviewees. Half the winegrowers held or had held responsibilities within PDO associations, professional representation or technical support organisations or even several professions related to vines and wine.

Choice of study sites

The study focused on two French wine-producing regions: Alsace and Anjou. Alsace's production is characterised by white wines, with a few red wines. As in many northern regions, the variability of the vintages is reflected in a greater or lesser degree of sweetness of the wines. From this point of view, Anjou is comparable to Alsace; its main difference is that Anjou predominantly produces single-variety wines, with chenin grapes for white wines and cabernet Franc for red wines. In Anjou, I focused on the small white-wine vineyards of Savennières in order to encompass a diversity of 'perceptions' of climate change in the same appellation. Extending the interviews to a few winegrowers in Anjou ensured that the survey area was not acting as a lens and focusing the analysis on a local characteristic.

It could be argued that choosing two northern regions may be detrimental to the study. This is unlikely. Studies conducted in Chile (Hadarits et al. 2010) and Spain (Alonso and O'Neill 2011) show no greater degree of concern than in Germany or Alsace. With regard to climate, detailed small-scale climate analyses of vineyards (Quénol et al. 2008; Quénol 2014) allow us to extend this argument further, showing that from a temperature point of view, the northern character of the vineyards in the Loire Valley is limited: both average temperatures and averaged-out minimal and maximal temperatures are lower in Alsace than in Anjou. Much like the Languedoc, the winegrowing areas of Alsace and Pays de Loire have less rain than others, which is favourable to vine growing. Still, rainfall is more abundant during summer months in Alsace, whereas in Angers, it is concentrated more in winter.

Most climate studies predict increasing aridity in southern regions. Some, with Jouzel et al.'s report (2014) being less assertive on this point, forecast increasing summer drought over western Europe, including the Loire area, without any extension of the Mediterranean climate towards the north (Quénol 2014). In addition to warming, increasing aridity is therefore not peculiar to the southern vineyards; northern ones are also faced with worsening prospects. It remains possible, however, that irrigation and water scarcity issues may emerge with greater acuity in southern vineyards.

The chapter reports on how winegrowers analyse changes in vine growing while underlining differences with climatologists' views. To preserve the anonymity of interviewees, names are coded according to their occupational categories, their region of activity and an arbitrary interview number. For example, 'V-Al10' is a winemaker from Alsace; 'JandOE-Al1' denotes a journalist and oenologist from Alsace.

Winegrowers' analysis of change

The vines' annual development cycle structures winegrowers' work. Many of them keep a logbook in which, throughout the year, they regularly record the state of physiological development of their vines and elements of meteorology, rainfall, temperature, frost and so on. Some of them have accumulated detailed records of meteorological observations in their vineyards over generations, sometimes for more than 100 years.

They are hesitant when it comes to climate change and wary of 'Intergovernmental Panel on Climate Change (IPCC) alarmism'. The cyclical nature of major weather events emerges from the interviews, echoing Holloway's findings (1999). Even among those who recognise climate change and are committed to slowing it, I notice a wavering between the 'IPCC's assertions' – particularly the increase in temperatures – which 'do remain forecasts' and their own observations. This hesitation goes hand in hand with a sense of critical hindsight, which precludes hasty association of meteorological variations with climate change: there have always been cycles, hot or cold decades, and this continues, with or without climate change.

> In the 1970s, there was one great vintage per decade. There were 2–3 vintages that were decent. There were 3–4 vintages that were mediocre. And 3–4 terrible vintages. In the sixties, '62 was not good, '63 was terrible, '65 was undrinkable, '68 was undrinkable, '69 was mediocre. There was '61 that was great, '64 was not always, because it had rained. . . . In Bordeaux, half of the grapes had been harvested before the rains, those were extraordinary. The ones that were harvested after the rains were a disaster. And '66 was okay, '67 very average, '68 undrinkable, '69 undrinkable. Those were really tough years. And the '70s were no better.
>
> *(V-Al10)*

Yet all note a change that occurred in the 1980s. After this decade, wines would no longer be the same. They were generally much better:

> [After the '70s], that started to change. I think climate change started in the early '80s. It became clear in '88. There was a boom in the '80s. And I remember, at the end of '83, the meteorologists, the great specialists said, 'In the future, you should expect to have one or two vintages of this nature per decade'. Except we haven't seen one since.
>
> *(V-Al10)*

V-Al10 is one of the few winegrower respondents for whom climate change is a reality. Yet he is still unsure on some points. They had been told that summers like the beautiful hot and dry one of 1983, that made that year's vintage so unforgettably good, were going to become more frequent. Instead, he refers to the 2003 vintage as far too hot, the worst in 30 years. Of course, radically new events do happen: 2003, of course, but also 1998 before that:

> I've seen it, climate change. In '98. I was a consulting oenologist. . . . The old man took me to see the vineyard. He said, 'Look at this. . . . I've never seen this!' It was sun-baked grapes.
> (JandOE-Al1)

These exceptional, isolated, single events do not, however, explain the changes in the wines. And in the end, climate change is not of much interest, except as an opportunity to ripen the grapes better.

Open climate scepticism, understood as the refusal of the very idea of global warming, is nevertheless rare. It was only expressed by two or three people in the entire sample spread across different occupational groups. What, then, is the change that all the respondents had noticed in the wines?

From effects to causes, 'an equation with many unknowns'

Winegrowers are fairly unanimous in their diagnosis of recent changes in the wines, and this diagnosis converges with the changes that climatologists associate with climate change: harvests come earlier; grapes' sugar levels, and thus wines' alcohol levels, are rising; and the balance between sugars, acidity and tannins is more difficult to strike. Other changes noted, such as decreasing acidity or certain modifications in wine aromas, are the subject of more debate. However, with the exception of two Alsatian winemakers in the sample, most do not associate global warming to the changes they note in vine development and grape quality.

The arguments they put forward to explain them are both logical and cautious:

> There are four main reasons. Since 1960, the INRA [French National Institute for Agronomic Research] has only done research on increasing degrees. . . . There is the decrease in yields, due to our French system. In Alsace, it was 100 hectolitres per hectare in the '80s. We're at 60 hectolitres, or 55. . . . There is the elimination of grape varieties that gave low degrees. And climate change, which has super-accelerated since 2006.
> (WT-Paris2)

What climatologists interpret as effects or indicators of climate change, interviewees interpreted as the result mainly of multiple other changes – sometimes commercial but more often technical – that have occurred since the 1980s and to which they sometimes add climate change, albeit always as a secondary cause.

Wine production is not a monotonous or repetitive activity. Winegrowers do not live in a stabilised and predetermined world in which climate suddenly introduces additional, easily recognisable variations. Weather conditions change every year, and winegrowers adjust their vineyard management to the particularities of each vintage and to other diverse and ongoing changes. Market competition has changed with the arrival of 'new' producing countries that export a large part of their production. Consumers' tastes have changed, and new markets have opened up. Yields have fallen sharply as a result of reinforcing quality objectives in wine production policies within the PDO framework. Winemaking techniques are also changing through new vine-growing and oenological resources. Finally, winegrowers are great experimenters, testing new vine-growing techniques in relation to the protection of terroirs and the environment or trying out old, rare or even terroir-foreign grape varieties. As one Alsatian winegrower (V-Al9) commented: to draw the link between the changes observed and their possible causes is to solve an equation with many unknowns.

A significant drop in yields

In Alsace and Anjou alike, of all the changes that interviewees mentioned, it was technical change, and specifically the progressive tightening of yield control in PDO winemaking over 30 years, that was systematically cited to explain transformations of vines, grapes and wines.

The winegrowers believed that the spectacular two- to three-week advance in the date of harvest, which is so often presented as 'evidence' of global warming, is rather the result of the drop in the grape load, which allows the bunches to ripen better and faster. Lower yields combined with better ripeness also raise sugar levels.

While common across all French vineyards, the most spectacular drop in yields has certainly taken place in Alsace: 'between 1980 and the early 2000s, we went from 130 to 80 hl/ha' (CPDO/V-Al6). This also affected the Pays de Loire region, albeit less drastically:

> It's not just climate change. I really think we have to stay very lucid. We've all lowered our yields, not necessarily deliberately, but through our practices. . . . So the average yield on Savennières is 35 hectolitres per hectare. . . . And so it has obviously increased concentration and therefore sugar.
>
> *(V-Anjou8)*

Earlier harvests also lead, in turn, to problems of 'maturity discrepancies': a loss of synchrony between the ripening of tannins, which remains a slow process, and the production of sugars and aromas, which is accelerated during hotter summers.

Finally, these winegrowers argued that while the climatic conditions are certainly new, the shifting of the ripening phase of the grapes towards the summer, with its hot and rainy storms which favour the development of the fungi, was probably the cause for some surprising new aromatic notes in the wines, in addition to the overly early and accelerated ripening of the grapes.

A welcome change

Although the decline in yields concerns everyone, it is uneven. Yields can roughly double or even triple from one winegrower to the next, depending on their production projects and strategies. Generally speaking, however, few complain about it: red wines are better, and adding sugar to white wines to raise their alcohol content (chaptalisation) is no longer needed. The German technique of sugar water addition, which dilutes acidity while raising alcohol content, is no longer used in Alsace. In this region, grand cru regulation has also banned chaptalisation.

> If I had to choose between the climate of the '70s and '80s and the climate of today, I'd sign up for today's straight away. . . . That's the paradox. . . . I studied in the late 1970s. And, when we tasted wines from the '70s, be it Burgundy or Bordeaux . . . most of the time, we would look at each other, like, 'is this really the job we want to do?' . . . They were really dreadful wines.
>
> *(V-Al10)*

This winemaker concluded that the change had been brought about by technical developments and winegrowers' enhanced skills.

> When I plant vines, I hope that they will last 50 or 60 years, so we're not going uproot and replace them because of the change.
> Interviewer: If you were to plant a plot today, would you reason differently to when you did so 20 or 30 years ago?
> No. I mean, differently, not because of the climate. Yes, certainly, in relation to the goal, but the qualitative and commercial goal. That's for sure, but not in relation to the climate.
>
> *(V-Anjou1)*

In Alsace and Anjou alike, a certain serenity transpired regarding climate change. The wines are changing, but they are tending to improve, and technical support allows winegrowers to expect continuous progress in winemaking know-how. In Alsace, producers highlighted the leeway they have due to large numbers of grape varieties and diversity of terroirs:

> People like the INRA people here, or the people from the ITV [technical institute for vines and wine], have always said in meetings, 'beware, global warming. . . . [D]isaster is coming. . . . [I]t's around the corner and we're not prepared'. We're lucky to have a lot of room to manoeuvre, because we're dealing with neither a unique product nor a unique terroir.
>
> *(CPDOandV-Al6)*

In comparison with winegrowers' various tools to anticipate and rapidly respond to many sorts of changes, climate appears as a tremendously difficult cause to manage: hence, perhaps, the alarmist tone of climatologists' warnings.

Salespeople are the only participants who are a little reluctant; they complain about the increase in alcohol content in particular, regardless of the region. 'For a dry Anjou to be ripe, it's at 14%. But a dry Anjou is no longer pleasant at 14%. . . . That's brandy'; 'there's no pleasure left in it' (WT-Paris2). Wine merchants find it difficult to explain the increase in alcohol content to customers who ask for drier wines without residual sugars and lower-alcohol wines.

Why do winegrowers who have intentionally reduced their yields not backtrack to mitigate the drawbacks of early maturation? Probably because these issues seem rather rare and do not affect all winegrowers equally. Those who have reduced their yields the most have often done so in a quest for quality. Many of them have also leaned more towards agroecology, or even adopted biodynamic practices, in an endeavour to be more 'respectful' of the plant and its development. They have developed other ways of managing the vine, and yield control is not their only lever of action.

Back to climatologists' claims

Much like the farmers interviewed by Holloway (1999), the interviewees note the same effects as scientists but do not infer from them that climate change is intensifying or having any effect because they take into account a broad range of possible causes.

When asked why, unlike climatologists, they do not associate the changes they observe with global warming, some of them cite cycles that they claim mislead scientists. Above all, most speak of differences in scale between the meteorological variations observed: how could they, in their daily experience as winegrowers, perceive an average warming of two degrees over a few decades when year-to-year variations are so much greater than this average rise? The anticipated rise of a few degrees seems rather trivial in comparison with the annual variations to which they must adapt, and climate change is far from being the most important change they have to take into account.

Therefore, rather than challenging climatologists' interpretations, they emphasise how their framing of experience, selection and processing of data and constraints on interpretation differ from those of researchers. They only have meteorological data from their vineyards and do not conduct sophisticated statistical analyses. One would add that their interpretations fit ordinary logics and do not need to comply with model convergence constraints, nor accurate enough prevision. Nevertheless, the range of aspects they take into account to analyse their activity is beyond the scope of climatologists, and the richness and inventiveness of their practices in vine development exceed anything that climatic modelling can account for.

Conclusion

This study confirms the paradoxical results obtained in previous surveys: winegrowers do not seem very concerned about climate change. Yet one should not hastily conclude that either climatologists or winegrowers are wrong. The conclusions that they draw from their experience and experiments notably depend on the way in which they pre-structure their experience and interpretations. Contrary to models, the world of the interviewed stakeholders is not an exogenous, stable and uncluttered whole to which a new and foreign cause – or 'externality' (Holloway 1999) – suddenly applies. It is a world of perpetual production of itself, traversed by changes that stakeholders constantly accompany, reorient, enhance or, on the contrary, stifle, and where action is fundamentally situated (Suchman 1987; Lave and Wenger 1991). The changes noted by winegrowers emerge from a broad experience of the world in which they act to produce and steer desirable changes, where meteorological data is only one of many variables shaping activity. And, to the conclusion reached by Mosedale *et al*. (2016), that 'viticulture illustrates how agreement about the biophysical consequences of climate change does not imply agreement about the need or strategy of adaptation', one could add that this schism is due not only to the range of opinions regarding the practices to be implemented but also to the diversity in ways of framing the problem of climate change.

In the cases of climatologists and the interviewed stakeholders alike, both the perceived obviousness of changes and their interpretations of causes and effects vary according to their approach. Winegrowers nevertheless put their finger on an essential difficulty in analysing the effects of climate change: the complexity and richness of winegrowing practices, which maintain vital interactions between plants and all the beings contributing to their development, are difficult to integrate into models.

The difference in reasoning should, therefore, be interpreted not as proof of climate scepticism in the wine world – as Alonso and O'Neill (2011) suggest – but rather, as Holloway would argue, as evidence of a divergence in methods used to format and analyse observations and knowledge. Similarities between this research and that of Holloway (1999) nevertheless mask an important difference. In 1999, US farmers seemed to be pondering questions about climate change for the first time during the course of interviews. Fifteen years later, climate change is not novel: the winemakers in this study have thought about its impacts, based on their intimate knowledge of practices and estimates of its complex effects that they derive from their repeated, though never similar, experiences from one year to the next.

Acknowledgements

I deeply thank all the interviewees and colleagues in the Laccave interdisciplinary project from which this study is drawn, as well as the ACCAF metaprogram which funded it.

Note

1 I use this contraction of vine grower and winemaker to translate the French 'vigneron', which includes both activities.

References

Alonso, A.D. and O'Neill, M.A. (2011) "Climate Change from the Perspective of Spanish Wine Growers: A Three-Region Study," *British Food Journal* 113, 205–221.

Battaglini, A., Barbeau, G., Bindi, M. and Badeck, F.-W. (2009) "European Winegrowers' Perceptions of Climate Change Impact and Options for Adaptation," *Regional Environmental Change* 9, 61–73.

Belliveau, S., Smit, B. and Bradshaw, B. (2006) "Multiple Exposures and Dynamic Vulnerability: Evidence from the Grape Industry in the Okanagan Valley, Canada," *Global Environmental Change* 16, 364–378.

Bloor, D. (1984) "A Sociological Theory of Objectivity," in S.C. Brown (ed), *Objectivity and Cultural Divergence*, Cambridge: Cambridge University Press, 229–245.

Buys, L., Miller, E. and van Megen, K. (2012) "Conceptualizing Climate Change in Rural Australia: Community Perceptions, Attitudes and (in)Actions," *Regional Environmental Change* 12, 237–248.

Callon, M. and Latour, B. (1992) "Do Not Throw Out the Baby with the Bath School," in A. Pickering (ed), *Science as Practice and Culture*, Chicago: Chicago University Press, 343–368.

Chaiklin, S. and Lave, J. (1996) *Understanding Practice: Perspectives on Activity and Context*, Cambridge: Cambridge University Press.

Duclos, D. (1987) "La construction sociale du risque: le cas des ouvriers de la chimie face aux dangers industriels," *Revue française de sociologie* 28, 17–42.

Hadarits, M., Smit, B. and Diaz, H. (2010) "Adaptation in Viticulture: A Case Study of Producers in the Maule Region of Chile," *Journal of Wine Research* 21, 167–178.

Hannah, L., Roehrdanzb, P.R., Ikegami, M., Shepard, A.V., Shaw, R., Tabor, G., Zhi, L., Marquet, P.A. and Hijimans, R.J. (2013) "Climate Change, Wine, and Conservation," *Proceedings of the National Academy of Science* 110(17), 6907–6912.

Hansen, J.W., Marx, S. and Weber, E. (2004) The Role of Climate Perceptions, Expectations, and Forecasts in Farmer Decision-Making: The Argentine Pampas and South Florida," report to International Research Institute for Climate Prediction, 142.

Hayes, P. and Battaglene, T. (2006) "Regulatory Response to Climate Change," *Bulletin de l'OIV* 79, 697–708.

Holloway, L. (1999) "Understanding Climate Change and Farming: Scientific and Farmers' Constructions of 'Global Warming' in Relation to Agriculture," *Environment and Planning A: Economy and Space* 31, 2017–2032.

Johnson, E.J., Hershey, J., Meszaros, J. and Kunreuther, H. (1993) "Framing, Probability Distortions, and Insurance Decisions," *Journal of Risk and Uncertainty* 7, 35–51.

Jones, G. (2007) "Climate Change: Observations, Projections, and General Implications for Viticulture and Wine Production," in E. Essick, P. Griffin, B. Keefer, S. Miller and K. Storchmann (eds), *Whitman College – Economic Department Working Paper*, vol. 7, 16, Walla Walla, WA: Whitman College Economic.

Jouzel, J., Ouzeau, G., Déqué, M., Jouini, M., Planton, S. and Vautard, R. (2014) "Le climat de la France au XXIe siècle," Volume 4 Scénarios régionalisés: édition 2014 pour la métropole et les régions d'outre-mer, report to Ministère de l'Écologie, du Développement durable et de l'Énergie, 64.

Knorr-Cetina, K.D. (1981) *The Manufacture of Knowledge: An Essay on the Constructivist and Contextual Nature of Science*, New York: Pergamon Press.

Latour, B. (1987) *Science in Action, How to Follow Scientists and Engineers through Society*, Harvard: Open University Press.

Latour, B. (2013) *An Inquiry Into Modes of Existence: An Anthropology of the Moderns*, Cambridge, MA: Harvard University Press.

Lave, J. and Wenger, E. (1991) *Situated Learning: Legitimate Peripheral Participation*, Cambridge: Cambridge University Press.

Lereboullet, A.L., Beltrando, G. and Bardsley, D.K. (2013) "Socio-Ecological Adaptation to Climate Change: A Comparative Case Study from the Mediterranean Wine Industry in France and Australia," *Agriculture, Ecosystems and Environment* 164, 273–285.

Lereboullet, A.L., Beltrando, G., Bardsley, D.K. and Rouvellac, E. (2014) "The Viticultural System and Climate Change: Coping with Long-Term Trends in Temperature and Rainfall in Roussillon, France," *Regional Environmental Change* 14, 1951–1966.

Lorenzoni, I. and Pidgeon, N.F. (2006) "Public Views on Climate Change: European and USA Perspectives," *Climatic Change* 77, 73–95.

Moriondo, M., Jones, G.V., Bois, B., Dibari, C., Ferrise, R., Trombi, G. and Bindi, M. (2013) "Projected Shifts of Wine Regions in Response to Climate Change," *Climatic Change* 119, 825–839.

Mosedale, J.R., Abernethy, K.E., Smart, R., Wilson, R.J. and Maclean, I.M.D. (2016) "Climate Change Impacts and Adaptive Strategies: Lessons from the Grapevine," *Global Change Biology* 22, 3814–3828.

Patt, A.G. and Schröter, D. (2008) "Perceptions of Climate Risk in Mozambique: Implications for the Success of Adaptation Strategies," *Global Environmental Change* 18, 458–467.

Peretti-Wattel, P. ([2003] 2000) *Sociologie du risque*, Paris: Armand Colin.

Pincus, R. (2003) "Wine, Place, and Identity in a Changing Climate," *Gastronomica: The Journal of Critical Food Studies* 3, 87–93.

Quénol, H. (ed) (2014) *Changement climatique et terroirs viticoles*, Paris: Lavoisier.

Quénol, H., Planchon, O. and Wahl, L. (2008) "Méthodes d'identification Des Climats Viticoles," *Bulletin de la Société Géographique de Liège* 51, 127–137.

Shaw, T.B. (2012) "A Climatic Analysis of Wine Regions Growing Pinot Noir," *Journal of Wine Research* 23, 203–228.

Suchman, L.A. (1987) *Plans and Situated Actions: The Problem of Human Machine Communication*, Cambridge: Cambridge University Press.

van Leeuwen, C. and Darriet, P. (2016) "The Impact of Climate Change on Viticulture and Wine Quality," *Journal of Wine Economics* 11, 150–167.

Weber, E.U. (1997) "Perception and Expectation of Climate Change: Precondition for Economic and Technological Adaptation," in M. Bazerman, D. Messick, A. Tenbrunsel and K. Wade-Benzoni (eds), *Environment, Ethics, and Behavior: The Psychology of Environmental Valuation and Degradation*, San Francisco: New Lexington Press, 314–341.

Weber, E.U. (2010) "What Shapes Perceptions of Climate Change?" *Wiley Interdisciplinary Reviews: Climate Change* 9999, n/a.

45
WINEGROWING, CLIMATE CHANGE AND A CASE FOR BIODYNAMIC VITICULTURE

Robert Swinburn

Introduction

This chapter explores the intersection between winegrowing, climate change and a method of agricultural production known as biodynamics. Biodynamic agriculture is a complex field, on the boundaries of science and mysticism and subject to contested ideas (Chalker-Scott 2013; White and Krstic 2019). In winegrowing, biodynamics – with its focus on rebuilding soils using minute amounts of micro-organisms applied at a time directed by the movement of planets – is used increasingly and by some of the better-known wine producers around the globe. Not everyone, however, embraces it. One critique has suggested that biodynamics is based on the same pseudoscience that climate change deniers use to argue that there is no such thing as man-made climate change (Dunning 2020). What are the possibilities for, and limitations of, biodynamic agriculture for the wine industry, notably at current environmental crossroads, an industry that is not only a victim of climate change but that is also partially to blame for it? As Demossier points out: 'wine offers an incredible platform to think critically about capitalist societies, nature and culture, science and empirical knowledge' (2018: viii). Using the anthropological technique of self-reflexivity to ground this contribution, this chapter examines this question, and the various challenges involved in thinking about climate change through wine, by combining not only relevant literature in the field but also my own experiences and observations as a winegrower and winemaker over the past 30 years.

I planted my own vineyard in the Geelong region of coastal southeastern Australia. While listening to reports of the first Gulf War on the radio, I tended the young vines on the two-hectare site overlooking the Barwon River estuary. My research into viticulture then suggested that too much vigour in my grapevines might be a problem. Excessive vine growth caused shading, the results of which were unwanted 'green' flavours in the wine. As a result, I chose a rocky, exposed paddock on our family farm for the vineyard to make the vines struggle. I also planted a non-vigorous clone of pinot noir and managed those vines on a trellising system that enabled half the vine shoots to be directed downwards, again to reduce vigour. This was a system developed by a retired Californian rocket scientist, Scott Henry, in the 1980s to address excessive vigour in his own Oregon vineyard. In the southeastern Victorian climate of the 1990s, the system worked well. Together with a regime of leaf plucking during the growing season, enabling the sun to reach the grape bunches, the quality of grapes I produced was satisfactory.

Writing this chapter almost 30 years later, significant changes in climate have affected my vineyard choices. Since 1989, harvest dates have steadily moved forward more than a day a year on average, from a date rarely earlier than late March to current harvests in February. All the vine shoots are now trained upwards to get maximum growth. Leaf plucking, if done at all, is done sparingly. The dams that once trapped surface runoff for irrigation have been dry for 20 years. Some vines have died, and cropping levels have more than halved. The quality of grapes has declined because of heat and stress on the vines compounded by lack of water. In 2019, southeastern Australia had its hottest December day on record, with temperatures in the north of the state reaching 48 degrees Celsius. Catastrophic fires 800 kilometres away blew down smoke when the wind turned to the north, changing the colour of the sky to an eerie orange. A local music festival was cancelled because the authorities doubted their ability to evacuate large numbers of people in the case of fire in the surrounding bush. The Australian Bureau of Meteorology added the forecast of 'mud rain' to the outlook when the rain that did arrive was mixed with the dust from the drought-stricken inland. Weather records were broken at such a rate that they often failed to warrant mention on the evening news.

Over the course of the past 20 years, most local vineyards have implemented strategies to deal with the gradual changes in climate. Some growers have grouped together to pipe 'grey water' from sewage farms for their vines, despite the high salt content. Covering the vineyard floor with mulch to preserve moisture is another strategy. New grape varieties, suited to hotter climates, are being planted. Trellising systems have been designed to provide extra shade for the fruit. Grapes are being sprayed with clay-based products which act as sunscreen. In extreme cases, winegrowers looked to establishing vineyards on cooler sites nearby, and even in cooler districts, to hedge their bets about the future.

Not all strategies are available equally to all winemakers to address these climatic effects. For instance, I cannot access the recycled water for my vineyard. As a result, my vines now are stunted. This is exacerbated by exceedingly hot days. Further, lack of rainfall after the previous season's harvest restricted the amount of energy stored in the vines before they shut down for the winter, resulting in a poor bud-burst in the spring. I wonder whether my vineyard, once vigorous and strong, is succumbing to the environmental conditions posed by climate change.

Climate change

It took longer than it might have for me to realise that not only am I the victim of climate change; I am also part of the problem. For a start, wine is a luxury product made from grapes grown in vineyards that are environmentally unfriendly monocultures. Further, an audit of Australian shiraz consumed in the UK reveals that a litre of wine requires 21 megajoules of primary energy, uses 363 litres of water and generates 1.25 kilograms of CO_2, taking into account transportation costs. Globally, wine accounts for 0.3% of the greenhouse gasses produced from anthropogenic activities (Amienyo et al. 2015: 7). Even wines that are not exported have a significant carbon footprint, not only from packaging, electricity and fuel but also through the use of agrochemicals (e.g. pesticides, fungicides etc.) and fertilisers.

These associated and additional environmental impacts are sometimes overlooked in growing industry discussions on the topic of climate change. One widely read industry journal, *Australian and New Zealand Grapegrower and Winemaker*, dedicated its January 2020 issue to the topic of climate change. The environmental impacts addressed included the strategy of using sunscreen to protect grapes from sunburn, how to measure and account for smoke taint and compressed vintage timelines, as well as finding workers who are willing to labour in increasingly difficult conditions. Despite this, there has been a relative under-acknowledgement of the complicity of the industry in anthropogenic climate change. Only one article in the journal listed here acknowledged the complicity of the industry. In that article, an industry consultant listed a number of possible strategies the industry might employ to mitigate winegrowing's carbon footprint. These included capturing CO_2 from ferments and reusing it, harnessing alternative sources of electricity in the winery and rethinking wine packaging and transport (Smart 2020: 17–19).

This relative under-acknowledgement of its own contributions to climate change reflects an underlying tension within the industry. Not all winegrowers are convinced that what we have witnessed in the past 30 years is more than cyclical variation. For example, in the same journal, a West Australian winegrower argues vehemently that discussions of climate change are a political conspiracy. He adds that warmer is better anyway and concludes that if it did become a problem, 'man' the 'engineer' will adapt as he always has (Happ 2020: 19–22). This view is not uncommon among winegrowers in southeastern Australia, most of whom have moved from successful careers in the city to forge something new in the rural periphery (Swinburn 2020, 2013). This may be because of the shortened timeframe from which they have experienced the 'on ground' rural environment or because one of the attractions of moving into an arena such as small-scale viticulture and winemaking is precisely to get away from the constraints of their previous professions.

Mostly, however, the industry overall does not ignore the statistics. Vineyards have been labelled the canary in the coal mine when it comes to climate change (Smart 2020). It comes as no real surprise to most that recent analysis of 664 years of harvest dates in the French region of Burgundy shows that, despite a wide variation, the dates over the past 30 years demonstrate that the change we are currently witnessing is without precedent (Labbé et al. 2019). For example, in Burgundy, harvest dates prior to 1988 shifted from an average picking date of 28 September to an average of 15 September. Those who cling to the notion that climate change is not real would, I suggest, do well to examine other statistics, too. Research demonstrates that the expansion of the global capitalist economy based on fossil-fuel technologies takes the problem beyond climate change and includes ocean acidification, ozone depletion, global fresh-water use, interference with the nitrogen and phosphorus cycles and biodiversity loss (Danowski and Viveiros de Castro 2017: 9). If one statistic stands out, it is that 'since 1970 we have managed to kill off 60% of the world's wildlife by destroying their habitats' (McKibben 2019: 210). This alone should make sceptics sit up and take notice.

To acknowledge that climate change is real, as most people now do, is one thing. It is another to take on board its full implications. In a book focusing on the catastrophic potential of climate change, philosopher Déborah Danowski and anthropologist Eduardo Viveiros de Castro (2017), borrowing a term from Isabelle Stengers, have identified a coming barbarism as people fight for resources in an age of increasingly savage climate change caused by world capitalism (Danowski and Viveiros de Castro 2017: 3). With estimates of potential climate change refugees alone being spoken of in the hundreds of millions, the potential disruption cannot be overstated and will leave the disruption caused by the current COVID-19 pandemic in its wake. In a haunting statement, Danowski and Viveiros de Castro suggest:

> It is one thing to know that the Earth and even the entire universe will disappear come billions of years, or that, long before that but in a still indeterminate future, the human species will become extinct. . . . It is another, rather different thing to imagine the situation . . . that the next generations will have to survive in an impoverished sordid environment: an ecological desert, a sociological hell. In other words, it is one thing to theoretically know that we will die; it is another is another to receive the news from our doctor, test results in hand, that we are suffering from a terminal disease.
>
> (Danowski and Viveiros de Castro 2017: 17)

This sociological hell might see us as 'even *more* defenceless than so-called "primitive man" found itself before the power of Nature' (Danowski and Viveiros de Castro 2017: 17): worse off because we will not be 'protected, and to a certain degree emancipated, by the protective cushion of (our) dreams' (Levi-Strauss, cited in Danowski and Viveiros de Castro 2017: 17).

Danowski and Viveiros de Castro refer to the act of 'subviving' rather than surviving these times. The difference between surviving and subviving is important here. According to Hage (2017), the very notion of 'survival' lacks reflexivity, even when used with recognition of the importance of the ecological crisis such as in a formulation such as 'Can we survive the Anthropocene?'

> The usage of the prefix 'sur' which denotes the capacity to transcend, to rise above, etc. . . . is so full of that very macho sense of omnipotence over 'Nature' that got us where we are in the first place that the usage of this 'sur' is no longer adequate. While 'vive' we must, we can forget about 'surviving'. It will be wonderful if we can manage to subvive given all that is stacked against us. The prefix sub does not only reflect being 'under' but also the capacity to be content with 'imperfection', with a diminished state of being.
>
> *(Hage 2017)*

It is within this generally catastrophic sense of the future that alternative options have to be seriously considered.

Biodynamics

What are the options available to small-scale winegrowers in southeastern Australia, northwestern California or Portugal? In Australia, there are three ways that winegrapes are produced. Conventional viticulture is based on the same principles as other forms of industrial agriculture. Technology, much of which was born out of war-time developments, did much to move agriculture into its industrial phase. The ability to synthesise nitrogen from the atmosphere for the production of explosives meant that nitrogen-based fertilisers became widely available. The rapid development of armoured tank technology fuelled a developing tractor industry, and the chemistry involved in the production of chemical weapons for trench warfare helped pave the way for the production of insecticides (Schilthuis 1994: 37).

However, a large number of winegrowers actively seek to reduce the environmental impact of their operations by using only organic fertilisers and chemicals, signalling another way that winegrapes are grown. These organic products are often sourced off-farm. Weeds are controlled mechanically or with the help of grazing animals, and fungicides are usually limited to elemental copper and sulphur. There are various organisations by which these 'organic' producers can be certified. The Australian Certified Organic (ACO) certification is an ISO9001-certified company accredited by the Department of Agriculture and Water Resources Australia and is the country's largest certifier for organic and biodynamic produce. It covers biodynamic certification as well.

The focus of the remainder of this chapter is on a third group known as biodynamic producers. Organic and biodynamic producers make up less than half a percent of total wine production in Australia, and only 7% of that is sold with a biodynamic certification. Significant growth is, however, evident, with a 34% increase in production from 2016 to 2019. Exports of the same period increased by over 50%, and in the biodynamic sector, wine exports by value increased by 70% (Boys 2019). Regarded with suspicion by many, they make up the smallest cohort but, interestingly, some of the better-known producers of premium wine, both here and overseas. In June 2020, *The Age* newspaper in Australia named its top 50 wine producers in the country. At number 1 was Cullen's biodynamic winery in the Margaret River region of West Australia (Hooke 2020). And one of the world's best-known burgundy wines, Domaine de la Romanée-Conti, produces many of their wines biodynamically, including the renowned La Tâche with a current vintage that sells for A$2,700 a bottle.

The ideas behind biodynamic agriculture come from a series of 1924 lectures by Austrian philosopher Rudolph Steiner (1958), who is better known in Australia and elsewhere for a series of educational ideas and practices on which Steiner schools operate. For Steiner, the farm itself is regarded as a living organism. Ideally, the biodynamic farm is mixed type, producing both crops and livestock. It should be a closed system, producing its own fertiliser from its animal manure. Nitrogen for plant growth should come only from the atmosphere via leguminous plants (Schilthuis 1994: 32). Soil health is the central idea behind Steiner's agricultural thinking. Steiner believed that soil containing proper amounts of humus produced plants that were resistant to parasites and disease. So, too, were the animals that fed on them and, by extension, those people who consumed those plants and animals (Tompkins and Bird 1992: xviii). A central idea for biodynamic farmers is that while production levels may not match those of modern agriculture, the inputs are also limited, with subsequently fewer costs. Further, biodynamic proponents argue that when economists calculate the efficiency of modern agriculture, they fail to take into account the real cost that will be eventually borne by the environment and, subsequently, the people of the world. They also point out that prior to the invention of artificial fertiliser and chemicals, farming production was sustainable, as an examination of European monastery records of hundreds of years adequately demonstrates (Podolinsky 2004: 18).

Steiner and his biodynamics are not without their critics. Steiner himself has been labelled a pernicious racist – even for his time – and an anti-vaxxer, and his biodynamic methods have, it is suggested by some, failed scientific scrutiny (Dunning 2020). Although some aspects of biodynamic agriculture/viticulture make sense from a scientific point of view, many push the boundaries. At the heart of biodynamic farming methods is the addition of 'preparations', the best known of which is preparation 500. This preparation is made by filling cow horns with cow manure and burying them in the earth over the winter in order to breed up micro-organisms. The manure, or the product of the process, is then extracted and mixed with warm water using specific mixing vortices. The final mixture, or 'preparation', is then sprayed on the soil in tiny quantities to promote the growth of favourable soil micro-organisms. These operations take place with an eye to the lunar cycles and to the movement of the planets.

While some of Steiner's ideas might be challenging to a Western-trained mind, Steiner himself pre-empted modern microbial research by four decades by describing the crucial role played by soil fungi in accessing desirable soil nutrients. This idea is crucial to the modern regenerative agriculture movement, which is attracting mainstream – and sometimes controversial – attention today (Massy 2017: 218–222).

Biodynamic production and certification are important to ensuring that Steiner's ideas are suitably enacted and regulated. One key certification is Demeter, founded in Germany in 1928 and brought to Australia in 1967 by the not-for-profit Biodynamic Research Institute. This research institute, linked with the Biodynamic Agricultural Association of Australia, practices an 'Australian Demeter-standard' method, developed by Alex Podolinsky, a Ukrainian refugee to Australia, in the 1950s. Podolinsky took it upon himself to modify European systems of biodynamics for a different Australian climate, particularly because the extra sunlight in Australia makes some of the European systems of silica-based preparations too powerful under Australian conditions. Podolinsky was linked to Steiner through Ehrenfried Pfeiffer, one of Steiner's students who took biodynamics to America. Pfeiffer struck resistance in America because of some of Steiner's claims of cosmic, telluric and spiritual influences on soils and plants, which some saw as tantamount to witchcraft (Tompkins and Bird 1992: 2). After Steiner's death, Pfeiffer worked to develop the various preparations numbered from 500 to 508. The number '500' came from Pfeiffer's estimate that an ounce of treated cow horn manure contained 500 million microbes. The other preparations – mostly compost teas – were numbered sequentially from there. Taking into consideration the specific climate conditions in Australia, Podolinsky developed another preparation known as 'prepared 500', which contained some of these other preparations. Most Australian biodynamic producers use limited types of preparations, an exception being Cullen's Vineyard in West Australia. Again, from his connection with Pfeiffer, Podolinsky learned that resistance to Steiner's claims were likely to come in reaction to Steiner's claims of cosmic, telluric and spiritual influences on soils and plants and therefore maintained that there was no witchcraft or magic in biodynamics: that it was 'absolute, actual science' (Podolinsky 2004: 60).

Notes from the field

For this project, I undertook a limited number of visits to winegrowers who embraced biodynamic principles. Space limits all but a cursory discussion of one field trip. I was particularly keen to speak with one biodynamic winemaker and farmer from Tarrington in western Victoria. My interest was piqued by the fact that he was also a medical doctor, and I was interested in the nexus between biodynamics and science.

I met John on the gravel patch in front of his cellar door on the shortest day of the year. We discussed the readings on biodynamics I had studied on his advice. We stood and talked about biodynamics, mostly going over the work of Alex Podolinsky. At the centre of the biodynamic argument, John explained better than most, is that good soil requires both microbes and worms, and for these to prosper to depth requires a soil profile containing more cavities than solid matter. The microbes turn organic matter into humus colloids, which take a form between a solution and a suspension, like jelly or butter. These colloids hold elements in a water-soluble form, making them available to plants and stopping them from leaching out of the soil or evaporating. These colloids hold 75% of their volume in water.

To demonstrate, John took me out into a nearby paddock. He said, 'Feel how soft the earth is under your feet'. Indeed, it did feel soft. We stopped, and he plunged a fork into the soil and lifted out a clod of earth. We both bent down to examine the soil. I looked closely at the rich red-brown soil with gaps of air and a labyrinth of pasture roots. The soil easily crumbled in my hand but still maintained its fundamental structure. It smelled fresh, and the grass growing in it was a deep green. John reiterated many of the points we had discussed earlier. He insisted that feeling good was not a reason to be in biodynamics. The method had to work. And he latched on to my interest in climate change, saying that much soil carbon had been released into the atmosphere by modern farming practices, and he pointed out the potential for sequestering carbon in the top half metre of soil with biodynamic practices. He pointed out how his soil never became waterlogged when his neighbour's paddocks ran with water after heavy rain. This was because of the water-holding capacity of the humus. He suggested that both the carbon and water-holding capacity of biodynamic soils had been proven scientifically but this had not attracted interest because most agricultural/viticultural research was directed to, and funded by, those who had a vested interest in high-input industrial production.

John said that he regarded biodynamic agriculture as a practical method. He despaired at those who overplayed the mystical aspects highlighted by the Anthroposophy school in Europe, but at the same time, he had no problem with how the moon at least influenced plant and soils life. And he adhered to the idea that the preparation should be activated by mixing, using a process of defined vortices. As a result, John did not dismiss some of the ideas that had not been proven scientifically. In the past 15 years, his farm has had no inputs except some rock phosphate – approved by Podolinsky as a medicine to treat damaged soils. As an experienced farmer, I walked away from my meeting with John (and other biodynamic winegrowers) thinking that nothing that I had been told during my visit seemed to me to be an unreasonable proposition.

Conclusion

The wine industry, especially small-scale wine production, is better suited than most agricultural and horticultural pursuits to adapting to difficult times as both a mitigator of climate change and one able to 'survive' an uncertain future. There is, however, a tension: it is that the science that demonstrates that climate change is real and will have catastrophic consequence is the same science that questions many aspects of biodynamic viticulture.

While there are those producers who speak of biodynamics in terms of religion, many, like my informants, have a more pragmatic view. Nigel Greening of New Zealand's biodynamic Felton Road Vineyard has criticised those biodynamic producers who are gleefully anti-science and argues that the idea that some principles are sacred is unhealthy (Greening 2019). He is not alone. An article written by English-born Italian wine producer and anthropologist Katia Nussbaum thoughtfully examines a possible future for biodynamics not bound by dogma. Drawing on new information regarding 'communication' among plants through subsoil fungal networks and pheromones (see Wohlleben 2016), Nussbaum suggests that we need to rethink how we view nature. She points to a misunderstanding regarding Darwin's notion of natural selection, amended later and popularised with the term 'survival of the fittest' by Hubert Spencer. This coincided with the time of the emergence of industrial capitalism and associated regimes of relentless competition and violent conquest. Consequently, a new interpretation of the notion of 'the survival of the fittest' became a way of justifying the pursuit of wealth, and the natural world came to be understood as one of competition rather than a range of strategies with a heavy emphasis on cooperation and collaboration. This misunderstanding has raised several questions: what if nature is more cooperative than competitive? How would that work as a mirror for human nature? How could that work as a business model? (Nussbaum 2019).

We might instead modernise biodynamics, building on some of the original ideas of Steiner but taking on what we now know about plant communications, ecosystems, biomes and other areas of modern science. Following Nussbaum (2019), might we reframe the original notions of biodynamics, with its emphasis on the interconnected nature of the universe, and create new practical frameworks for creating sustainable agriculture, a less cut-throat business culture and mutually beneficial social networks? This would be to build a forward-thinking biodynamics in which man is not seen as the model of the universe and where he does not reign supreme over other beings and the environment. This would be compatible with Steiner's own ideas: it was Steiner himself who suggested to the attendees at his initial lectures that the benefits of his ideas needed to be able to be demonstrated in the field, and he called for experiment rather than dogma (Paull 2010: 33).

The biodynamic practices that I have come across during this project have all been family-based. The producers, their vineyards and their wineries seem to nestle more comfortably into the environment than most. There seems to be a sensibility that moves easily from the vineyard where the grapes are grown to the winery where the wine is made. Winegrapes have almost the perfect balance of sugar and acid, which means the process requires few if any additions when wine is made. It is possible to take winegrapes propagated by the winemaker; crush them; use the natural yeast on the skin to ferment the sugar into alcohol; for some wines, use wild bacteria to change the harsh malic acid into soft lactic acid; and make a very good wine. If wine is sold locally and in reusable vessels, you have a product that has a minimal impact on the environment. This is especially true if strategies such as the use of solar power, the gravity transfer of wine, electrically powered vehicles and early-morning harvesting to reduce refrigeration, among others, are embraced. Indeed, I have witnessed all these strategies during this project. As is the case with Cullen's wine-producing operation in West Australia, the business can even be made carbon positive. The more I look at it, as an anthropologist and as a farmer, the more that much of what I see in biodynamics, freed from its quasi-religious cloak, is simply good farming that is sustainable and gentle.

References

Amienyo, D., Camilleri, C. and Azapagi, A. (2015) "Environmental Impacts of Consumption of Australian Red Wine in the UK," in L. Preston-Wilsey (ed), *Towards a Sustainable Wine Industry: Green Ecology in Practice*, Oakville: Apple Academic Press.

Boys, C. (2019) "It's Only Natural: Millennials Send Organic Wine Sales Surging," *Good Food Guide*, www.goodfood.com.au/drinks/wine/its-only-natural-millennials-send-organic-wine-sales-surging-20190405-h1d798, accessed 20 November 2020.

Chalker-Scott, L. (2013) "The Science Behind Biodynamic Preparations: A Literature Review," *HortTechnology* 23(6), 814–819.

Danowski, D. and Viveiros de Castro, E. (2017) *The Ends of the World*, Cambridge: Polity Press.

Demossier, M. (2018) *Burgundy; A Global Anthropology of Place and Taste*, New York: Berghahn.

Dunning, J. (2020) "The Problem with Biodynamics: Myths, Quacks, and Pseudoscience," *Word on the Grapevine* blog, 4 June, https://wordonthegrapevine.co.uk/biodynamic-viticulture-pseudoscience, accessed 1 September 2020.

Greening, N. (2019) "Biodynamics beyond Harry Potter: A Reply to Biodynamics – A New Approach Needed?" *Jancis Robinson's* blog, 18 April, www.jancisrobinson.com/articles/biodynamics-beyond-harry-potter, accessed 1 September 2020.

Hage, G. (2017) "The World-(that's)-to-come(-to-an-end): A 'Subvival' Guide," *Hage B'aa*, 3 April, http://hageba2a.blogspot.com/2017/04/the-world-thats-to-come-to-end-subvival.html?spref=tw, accessed 1 September 2020.

Happ, E. (2020) "A Common Sense Approach to Climate Change," *The Australian and New Zealand Winegrower* 672, 19–22.

Hooke, H. (2020) "Here's Cheers: Australia's 52 Top Wineries," *The Age – Good Weekend*, 13 June, www.smh.com.au/national/here-s-cheers-australia-s-52-top-wineries-20200505-p54pul.html, accessed 1 September 2020.

Labbé, T., Pfister, C., Brönnimann, S., Rousseau, D., Franke, J. and Bois, B. (2019) "The Longest Homogeneous Series of Grape Harvest Dates, Beaune, 1354–2018, and Its Significance for the Understanding of Past and Present Climate," *Climate of the Past* 15(4), 1485–1501, https://doi.org/10.5194/cp-15-1485-2019.

Massy, C. (2017) *Call of the Reed Warbler*, St Lucia, QLD: University of Queensland Press.

McKibben, B. (2019) "How Extreme Weather is Shrinking the Planet," in S. Montgomery (ed), *The Best American Science and Nature Writing*, Boston: Houghton Mifflin Harcourt.

Nussbaum, K. (2019) "Biodynamics – A New Approach Needed?" *Jancis Robinson's* blog, 11 April, www.jancisrobinson.com/articles/biodynamics-new-approach-needed, accessed 1 September 2020.

Paull, J. (2010) "Biodynamic Agriculture: The Journey from Koberwitz to the World, 1924–1938," *Journal of Organic Systems* 6(1), 27–41.

Podolinsky, A. (2004) *Biodynamic Agriculture: Introductory Lectures*, vol. 1, Crows Nest: Gavemer Publishing.

Schilthuis, W. (1994) *Biodynamic Agriculture*, Edinburgh: Floris Books.

Smart, R. (2020) "Towards a Sustainable Future: How the Australian Wine Sector Could and Should Help Mitigate against Climate Change," *The Australian and New Zealand Winegrower* 672, 17–19.

Steiner, R. (1958) *Agriculture: A Course of Eight Lectures (George Adams trans., 1958 ed. of 1924 course)*, London: Biodynamic Agricultural Association.

Swinburn, R. (2013) "The Things that Count: Rethinking *Terroir* in Australia," in R.E. Black and R.C. Ulin (eds), *Wine and Culture: Vineyard to Glass*, London: Bloomsbury.

Swinburn, R. (2020) "Deep *Terroir* as Utopia: Explorations of Place and Country in Southeastern Australia," in J. Dutton and P.J. Howland (eds), *Wine, Terroir and Utopia: Making New Worlds*, Oxford: Routledge.

Tompkins, P. and Bird, C. (1992) *Secrets of the Soil*, Arkana: Penguin.

White, R.E. and Krstic, M. (2019) *Healthy Soils for Healthy Vines: Soil Management for Productive Vineyards*, Clayton South: CSIRO Publishing.

Wohlleben, P. (2016) *The Hidden Life of Trees*, Carlton: Black Inc.

CONCLUSION

Graham Harding and Steve Charters

Introduction: our approaches to interrogating wine and culture

As we noted at the beginning of this *Handbook*, our aim has been to produce an interdisciplinary work which brings together a range of academic perspectives on the relationship of wine to culture and how cultural actors engage with it. It is worth noting at the outset of this conclusion, however, that there is substantial disciplinary overlap, which both justifies our approach and shapes its outcome. Many of our contributors began in one discipline but now publish and work in other fields. Some of the contributions mirror this cross-disciplinarity, with authors from two disciplines working together to explore a specific topic. At the same time, it is also clear that certain disciplines have a richer tradition of studying the relationship between wine and culture. Sociology and anthropology feature widely throughout as the disciplinary contexts, history and business a little less, economics and geography less still. This is, perhaps, symptomatic of how culture is currently perceived in those fields, or perhaps, it is merely reflective of the willingness of academics in those fields to consider wine as a significant cultural artefact.

It is also important to underline the range of methodological approaches used by our contributors. Traditionally, studies of culture relied very heavily on ethnography, with extended fieldwork at their core. There are examples of that in this collection and even one autoethnography. Other contributors use ethnographic methods but would not claim that their research is pure ethnography. Others again use more conventional qualitative methods, relying on interviews and case studies. Some use documentary research and even quantitative methods to explore precise cultural issues and measure behaviour and outcomes. We see the multiplicity of research methods as a strength of these varying investigations of wine and its cultural contexts.

The stories of wine and cultural entanglement

Wine is a complex artefact. It has been around for 8,000 years of history (see, for example, McGovern 2003; McGovern 2019), longer than most other human products, in which time it has been imbued with a range of multifaceted meanings. Additionally, it encompasses cultures of production, consumption and mediation. Production itself features primary (agricultural), secondary (manufacturing) and – usually – tertiary (service) components, each with its own cultural framing.

Tim Unwin, in the Introduction, noted the complexities of defining culture. Clifford Geertz's dictum that culture is the 'stories people tell themselves about themselves' is perhaps a valid starting point in this conclusion (Geertz 1973: 448). Language shapes our understanding of the world. Dutton's opening chapter on 'Text, wine and culture' and Jaboulet-Vercherre's work on metaphor demonstrate that our languages are infused with wine. The range of these stories – from the Epic of Gilgamesh to the Christian Bible and from Sufi love poetry to Japanese manga comics – shows the extent to which our cultures have been inspired and informed by wine. All the cultures in this book draw on the ancient, deep and persistent symbolic power of wine. In sum there is a profound 'entanglement' (Dutton and Howland) of wine and culture.

Some of these associations have persisted for millennia; others are newly fermented as wine spreads beyond its Old World roots into new territories. Wine has consistently (probably always) been linked to altered states of consciousness, whether in the domain of organised religion or individual alterity (McGovern 2003, 2019). Yet wine is also inextricably linked to the practice of hospitality. The sacred and the sociable came together in ancient times in the Hellenistic concept of 'xenia' that permeates Homer's *Odyssey*: the duty of hospitality and the offer of wine enforced by the possibility that the unannounced guest might be a deity in disguise (see Papakonstantinou 2009). This tradition has lasted to the present day. The fervent nineteenth-century temperance campaigner Sir Wilfrid Lawson accepted that 'there was no hospitality unless wine or other drink was offered' (*Carlisle Patriot*, 29 December 1871: 6). With hospitality come conviviality and sociability (Dutton and Howland). In the contemporary world, boosting confidence, strengthening friendship and bonding families are endorsed in popular culture as the 'social benefits' of wine (*Reader's Digest*) (www.readersdigest.co.uk/food-drink/drinks/the-useful-social-benefits-of-drinking-wines).

Less stressed in the past but now increasingly valued – and promoted – are other attributes of wine. The idea that wine expresses a specific place or specific pieces of land (or *terroir*) has been revalorised and eagerly promoted by winemakers and merchants (see Unwin; Overton) whilst the link between the production of wine, rurality and the beauty of landscape is increasingly stressed (Howland). Linked to these is the heavily promoted (though much-contested) belief that wine is an expression of nature in its purest form, summed up in the 2002 title of the Wine Institute of New Zealand's publication *The Riches of a Clean Green Land* (Wine Institute of New Zealand 2002; Egoz 2000). Meanwhile new wine 'places' are being invented and imbued with value (Tobias and Myles). In some cases, as Myles *et al.* show, this creation has the power to interact with a wider (traditionally non-wine) culture and even to shape political discourse.

The stories of wine change not only because humans are shaped by the cultures they inhabit but because they themselves shape culture – both materially and symbolically, as shown by the reinventions and re-imaginings explored in this book (Livat and Jaffré). Norbert Elias used the metaphor of the 'dance' between individuals and society to explain the process of change in behaviour and attitude (Elias 2000: 482). The interplay of wine and culture is similar (see, for instance, Skinner; Almila and Inglis) – though one might ask if there is an unchanging strand of wine 'DNA' at the centre of this perpetual dance. In some cases, the changes arise from the idiosyncratic choices of individuals, in others from the deliberate actions of the many intermediaries who shape the world of wine.

Materially, human action has shaped wine for millennia. As McGovern notes, the Palaeolithic domestication of the grapevine demands human intervention and human shaping of the terrain (McGovern 2003: 13–14). The tavern owner Siduri, who serves wine to the Sumerian hero Gilgamesh (second millennium BCE), is perhaps the earliest intermediary known to us by name, and her business implies a range of other occupations: not just those who made the wine but those who traded and distributed it (Kovacs 1989). By the fourth century BCE, merchants were trading oil and wine in amphorae in networks stretching from Greece to the Black Sea (Sarris *et al.* 2002: 184). The encounters of such intermediaries – between cultures, between people of different sorts – are, as Peter Burke argued, the fuel for cultural change (Burke 2012). The networks of knowledge developed by nineteenth-century Australian winegrowers and their European correspondents (McIntyre) are their more recent descendants (see also Teil). Yet whilst wine may be an agent for change, it is also a very strong marker for continuity, maintaining roots and guarding a sense of the history which has shaped us. This is exemplified in very different ways (and with very different wines!) in Swinburn's study of Croatian migrants to Australia who seek to preserve a link to their origins by making their own wines and Demossier's chapter on how *climats* in Burgundy are taking producers back to a (mythic) past.

Symbolically, the dancing 'entanglement' of wine and culture (Dutton and Howland) shapes societies. Because drink – like all foods – is, as Appadurai put it, a 'highly condensed social fact', it also functions as a 'marvellously plastic form of representation' (Appadurai 1981: 494). The switch to wine from other forms of alcohol is, in many modern societies, a typical sign of increasing prosperity and class stratification. The adoption of wine in general and claret and champagne in particular in mid-Victorian society (Harding; Dias-Lewandowska) was driven by a newly prosperous middle class. Similar dynamics can be observed in developing world economies today (Cohen *et al.*; see also the chapter by Anderson and Nelgen).

Yet this dance is not merely driven by consumers. Intermediaries are also critical, not just in the commerce of wine but in the manipulation and management of the cultural symbols of wine (Mitchell). These cultural symbols, which tell the stories of wine, may be quite abstract (the notion of terroir) or concrete (see Celhay's chapter on typeface and Harding's piece on glass shape). Multiple contributions to this volume reinforce this process of manipulation and management in the modern world (Fedoul; Fitzmaurice; Tominc and Welch). It also appears that, with the rising influence of social media, this manipulation of the stories is increasing in pace (Rokka).

Partly in response to the increasing influence of these intermediaries, drinking cultures are homogenising globally (Anderson and Nelgen); wine is taking share in communities and societies traditionally dominated by beer or spirits (Christiansen and Marks), and beer is taking share in wine countries such as France and Italy (Gordon *et al.* 2012: 8). The challenge for the wine industry is to maintain and increase 'share of throat'. To facilitate and drive these changes, new stories are created for new consumers. As many of the contributors to this *Handbook* (e.g. Cappeliez; Carpenter and Banks; Overton; Rokka) demonstrate, these stories exploit the symbolic values of wine to 'sell' consumers new drinks or new habits. Overton's chapter on 'provenancing' and Rokka's on the new power of social media in particular illustrate how stories and texts are created, managed and manipulated by actors in the wine space. Yet drinking cultures, like all other 'cultures', are in a process of constant negotiation and reconstruction (Cappeliez; Cohen *et al.*), and as Rokka has suggested, the power of the consumer in that process may be increasing.

Such renegotiations can contribute to homogenisation but also to differentiation. Stories (and societies) can be shaped to divide as well to unite (Dias-Lewandowska; Ludington and Harding). In Poland in the eighteenth century, Hungarian wine was the drink of the nobility. Champagne's appearance was seen as an attempt to dilute the national identity. In Ireland in the late twentieth century, women saw legislators' attempts to control female (wine) drinking as an example of patriarchal attitudes in a male-oriented drinking culture (see also Almila and Inglis).

Cultural tensions in wine

Wine has consistently been an instrument of distinction and differentiation. Historically, it has divided by class and, more recently, by gender. As wine *qua* wine has expanded its global and socio-demographic reach, so there has grown a need for greater specificity, for a more distinct 'ladder of brands' to enable consumers to signal their cultural and economic resource. Bourdieu's continuing influence in the field of contested taste is apparent in many chapters of this book (Carpenter and Humphreys; Cappeliez; Jacquet). Increasingly, wine has become an instrument of cultural rather than socio-demographic identity in the global west. Yet beyond this, the geography of wine is also creating a series of stresses.

In the East, as exemplified by China, consumption is still driven by emergent elites and new middle-class consumers (Cohen *et al.*), who not only draw upon the existing reservoir of symbolic value but also add new properties – for example, the power of the colour red. In parts of the New World, Howland suggests, the traditional European views of rurality are being reinterpreted as a 'metro-rural idyll' and – at the same time – as an indigenous idyll in a challenge to the dominant colonial meanings (which, as Hill and Fountain suggest, may then be appropriated by the dominant settler culture to help reshape their own meanings of place). Yet at the same time in Australia, some migrants have responded to the prevailing ideas of what wine should represent with a 'return' to an artisanal European approach to production to give a very specific response to the processes of acculturation. Thus, in myriad ways, wine continues to renew its symbolic power.

The result of the foregoing – that the stories of culture may be divisive as well as uniting, that wine is not just a uniting and cohesive artefact but also an instrument of distinction and differentiation, that symbolic meaning is constantly in course of regional recreation – is that the product is riven by a range of tensions. These tensions are played out in the stories told about wine, and each is underpinned by cultural norms and expectations. Some of these tensions have already been noted, such as the use of wine as a marker of being inside a group or of being excluded – which could, for example, be based on gender (Almila and Inglis), ethnicity (Inglis and Ho) or connoisseurship (Cappeliez). Wine economies are rooted in specific cultures, but in turn, the cultural and the economic may live in tension as the producer tries to make something which is authentically rooted yet will also sell. Increasingly, cultural conventions – such as the assumption that hybrid varieties cannot make high quality wines – are being challenged (Fitzmaurice). These challenges mean also that regional wine cultures are being forced to re-evaluate meaning and representation and either rework it to underline its heritage and tradition (Demossier) or learn from other cultures and modify their own understandings accordingly (Ditter *et al.*; Hill and Fountain). This returns us to the notion of intrinsic and instrumental culture (Charters), understanding a culture as a means to comprehending its engagement with and use of wine or understanding a culture in order to glean some other benefit – especially the ability to manage or market more effectively. As the chapters by Teil and Swinburn suggest, this is increasingly being brought to a head with the test of climate change, which requires producers, intermediaries and consumers to reassess what 'correct' wine should be (for example, terroir driven or aesthetically valuable or 'natural') in order to have something sellable, marketable or drinkable. Carpenter and Humphreys interpret this as a tension between artisanal production and commerce-led or market-driven production.

Meanwhile, there are other internal threats to the meaning of wine. Traditionally, consumers have seen wine (compared with 'industrial' beer and spirits) as being a natural drink (Charters 2006), yet that idea now faces a threat from inside the world of wine itself, with the natural wine movement. The value of wine, or of some wines, is questioned due to their inauthentic or 'industrial nature'. There is a recognition that wine can do harm; it has its dark side or 'hidden worlds'. Beyond this, the wine industry itself is divided about viticultural change (Anderson and Nelgen; Fitzmaurice), oenological necessity (Navarini and Domaneschi; Taplin) and the already-noted tensions imposed by the drive for profitability (Christiansen and Marks).

Many of the cultural tensions about wine's meaning are longstanding. The sacred character of wine or its banal or profane use (Belk *et al.* 1991) and the distinction – even conflict – between them are probably about as old as wine itself (Holt; Phillips). The tension between science and tradition (Taplin; Fedoul) has been with us for centuries (see, for example, Paul 1996). Others may have longstanding roots but emerge more recently, such as the tension between wine as a class-signifying product and as a lifestyle drink. (Cappeliez; Tominc and Welch). There is also the tension between the idea that wine should be globally inviting – and thus open to cultural change (Cohen *et al.*; Dutton; Inglis and Ho) – or locally protected (Jacquet; Demossier), which tends towards protecting traditional wine cultures. Most recently, with the growing influence of social media, there is an increasingly overt tension over whether wine's meaning is determined by those who make it, by intermediaries (Carpenter and Humphreys; Tominc and Welch) or by those who drink it (Rokka).

These tensions exist between cultural actors, such as the arguments about the relevance of terroir as a concept (Hill and Fountain; Unwin), but they also exist as internalised tensions for the actors themselves (as exemplified in the chapters on climate change by Teil and Swinburn). Producers, intermediaries and consumers struggle with what they 'ought' to be making, promoting or drinking. Thus, however much they may have one specific cultural starting point, the growing interaction among regions and countries, the different categories of actor and the burgeoning sciences of viticulture, oenology, economics and business all pull those actors in different directions. Studying wine underlines that these cultural tensions are messy, intertwined and not neatly resolved, for individuals, for regions or for the global wine industry (Dutton and Howland).

Are we at an inflection point?

It is clear that the wine industry is facing a series of challenges whose implications are neither fully realised nor fully foreseeable and which will affect both consumers and producers. There is no single inflection point. The COVID-19 crisis of 2020–21 has had significant impacts whose effects on consumption, the marketplace and the human relationship with the natural world will form the subject of much future analysis and research. Demographic shifts will also affect the wine industry profoundly.

There are three interrelated trends to consider. The first is the industrialisation of wine, which embraces packaging, the increasing incidence of 'engineered wine' and the emergence of new players in the commercial landscape. The second is changing global demographics, and the third is the tensions between the 'human' and the 'natural' in the world of wine production and consumption.

The industrialisation of wine is hardly new. The transformation of wine into a packaged product by companies such as E&J Gallo (as illustrated in the *Handbook* by Overton) is not new, but we are beginning to see linked changes in production and packaging. A steady narrowing of clonal diversity accompanies DNA manipulation of grape types. Grapes are being picked later, with rehydration to compensate for the attendant dehydration of late-picked fruit. Technology such as reverse osmosis reduces alcohol in wine, and there is the suggestion that we are moving towards the 'fine wine equivalent of a supermarket tomato', defined as 'perfect yet soulless and contrived' (and possibly tasteless to boot) (*Wine Spectator*, 7 February 2017, www.winespectator.com/articles/matt-kramer-engineered-wine-and-tomatoes).

GMO (genetically modified) wine is another issue. There is the potential for benefits for both consumers (e.g. no-hangover wines) and producers (e.g. resistance to powdery mildew). Engineered yeast may also change flavour profiles and production technology – again to the benefit of larger producers (Molina-Espeja 2020). But will consumers embrace or resist such changes? Research is needed.

Packaging changes also favour larger-scale businesses. The cork 'dinosaur' may be replaced by the ring-pull and the bag-in-box tap. Canned wine could alter not just the places and occasions of consumption but the structure of the industry. Smaller sizes fit the millennial tendency to drink less. Cans also fit an increasing focus on sustainability, taking less energy to make and transport than glass bottles and benefiting from a recycling rate which – by some estimates – is 20% higher. At the time of writing in 2021, the dominant players in canned wine were Molson Coors and Anheuser Busch, both previously known not for wine but for beer (https://conmetric.com/2020/03/10/canned-wine-in-the-media-the-democratisation-of-the-grape). By their 2019 purchase of Babe Wine, the New York–based producer of canned rosé, Anheuser Busch signalled their intent to disrupt the traditional rules, the traditional 'culture' of wine; it is interesting that the key companies engaged in this are from the beer industry (https://beveragedaily.com/Article/2019/07/01/Anheuser-Busch-acquires-remaining-stake-in-Babe-Wine).

Changing global demographics may also affect the consumption (and, ultimately, culture) of wine. Though the global population is still growing (12% increase is the UN forecast for 2030), this growth is concentrated in markets that are currently non–wine drinkers, such as India. The age profile is rising rapidly, and overall household sizes are shrinking as a consequence of both an aging population and later age of family formation as women take a steadily greater economic role. These changes have the potential for significant impact on the wine industry.

The evidence suggests that older demographics tend to spend less and consume less. Amongst those who do consume wine, the importance of women as purchasers and consumers is tending to rise, particularly in countries where there is a less-developed wine culture (note here the chapter by Livat and Jaffré). This will probably affect the presentation, taste and packaging of wine with consequent changes to marketing. Responding to female preference may favour lower-alcohol wine with fewer chemical additives and perhaps higher sugar levels (see Wine Australia, 16 October 2018; https://wineaustralia.com/news/market-bulletin/issue-129), although some would say that this stereotypes female consumers – and cultural variation could be crucial here as in many other areas of consumption change. Higher female influence and smaller household sizes are likely to favour smaller, non-traditional packaging formats and closures. The generational shifts linked to the maturing of 'Gen Z' and the imminent arrival of Generation Alpha into the alcohol market may reinforce these changes. Younger consumers appear to be drinking less overall, and wine is in competition with a host of other beverages, both alcoholic and non-alcoholic. None of these changes to wine is certain, but all have the potential to change the culture of wine.

Will the COVID-19 pandemic of 2020 create an inflection point in wine distribution? The CEO of Naked Wines has shifted the company to an 'online pureplay' in both the US and the UK, arguing that 'I believe the crisis will likely serve as an inflection point for consumer migration online for wine purchase' (www.linkedin.com/pulse/naked-wines-hits-inflection-point-nick-devlin/). Such a shift away from physical distribution – if followed by other major players – will further threaten the traditional culture of wine. But is that a bad thing or a good thing?

The changes outlined here link to the third trend noted: that of the tension between the natural and the technological and the human interface between the two. For decades, the equity of the natural world has dominated wine marketing. The 'authorship and authenticity' that Dutton and Howland identify as key to success in the fine wine market depend on a defined place and (frequently) a known winemaker. The marketisation of terroir over the last decades has given 'place' an ideological hegemony over the world of wine, sometimes perhaps at the expense of the role of the producer. Even in Burgundy where, as Demossier shows, the 'old story' of tradition and terroir has been abandoned in favour of a new focus on *'climats*, landscapes and labour' the sense of place remains the dominant force. The 'essentialism of site specificity' (Taplin) continues to overshadow the technical innovations that have greatly contributed to making great burgundy the force that it is in the contemporary market. In Burgundy, terroir has merely found a new (and highly visual) marketing expression in *climats* to help fight off New World competition.

Yet this focus on site specificity appears at odds with the demands of younger consumers for wine that is easier to understand and easier to access. The success of E&J Gallo's Barefoot brand (the global bestseller of 2019) relies on 'introducing new friends to wines that are fun flavorful, and approachable' (www.barefootwine.com/story). There is no mention of place but rather a focus on its position as the 'world's most loved wine brand' and on conviviality. Visuals on its website show not vineyards but consumers drinking from cans and screw-top bottles. Yet easy-drinking wines for a world 'where everyone belongs' are not so simple to produce. The demand for wine that is sweeter yet has fewer carbohydrates implies contradiction and compromise; a can may be easy to open and easier to recycle, yet it is far from any definition of 'natural'. Producing such wines demands the technical and industrial sophistication that Overton's chapter underscores.

In practice, fine wine producers in New World areas such as Napa have 'emphasised technological innovation' but realise that, as Taplin puts it, 'mastering nature does not resonate as well as working with nature'. Hence, the construction of what Howland terms an idealised and romanticised rural idyll designed to appeal to an emerging middle class that is both metropolitan and global. Brand names such as Echo Falls, Turning Leaf and Blossom Hill tap into the desire for 'communication with nature' that signals a 'non-alienated human condition'. To go barefoot invokes not merely a communion with nature but also a spirit of freedom and liberation.

Thus, in both these sectors of the wine market, nature has been invoked for marketing purposes by human innovators who have mastered the historic quest for consistent high-quality wine. Yet human ingenuity faces a challenge from the natural world. The consensus is that the gathering climate change visible over the past 50 years is the consequence of human actions. Most observers would accept the IPCC view that 'human' factors account for as much as 90% of the effects noted by Teil in her work with winemakers in Anjou and Alsace and by Swinburn in his autoethnographic piece on southeast Australia. Climate change may be human made, but weather is a natural phenomenon that affects winemakers differentially every year. Teil's winemaker interviewees express confidence in their ability to manage the yearly weather variations; Swinburn is less confident. He is fearful about the future of his own vineyard and increasingly clear that the wine industry is not only a 'victim of climate change but also a culprit'. The industry contributes to CO_2 emissions firstly through fermentation and secondly through the shipping of wine around the world in heavy glass bottles. An increasing pace of climate change will pose further, deeper problems for wine producers and wine drinkers and may yet spark further changes to the historical culture of wine.

Meanwhile, the tension between the natural world and human influence is also being played on in the debate about natural wines. These low-intervention wines are sold as a 'return to traditional winemaking' and the representation of a more authentic wine. Yet even here, we find conflict and uncertainty. Natural wines, with a focus on how the wine is made, tend to blur differences of origin (terroir) and even grape variety. These wines may reflect Howland's rural idyll and (especially) Taplin's notion of working with nature but they conflict with the place-based notions of the natural. Beyond this, whilst they respond to a particular cultural turn in Western production and consumption behaviour, they can be seen to conflict with one of the key expectations of many cultures: namely, that their society will advance in its management of nature and development of technology. This is not universal; it is known that some agricultural societies can be conservative, and viticultural enterprises may resist the conclusions of science and the imposition of technology (Paul 1996), but as Holt and Philips note, the history of wine is, in part, the history of greater control and more precise scientific and technological aid; the story of wine is the story of making 'better' wine. To that extent, the claims of the natural wine movement, whilst undoubtedly responding to perceived needs, represent a rupture with previous wine culture(s).

Beyond this, associated with the natural wine movement we can also note the recent trend in the West for 'glou glou' – easy-to-drink and undemanding wine (not necessarily low quality), especially popular with younger drinkers. This can be equated, perhaps, with the traditional French *vin de soif* – wine designed to quench thirst rather than provoke debate and a return to the way that most wine has been consumed in Mediterranean societies for most of the time of its production. This wine, even more, separates itself from a strict focus on the significance of place and downplays the traditional aesthetic appreciation (or connoisseurship) often associated with drinking. This may be a natural drink (however defined), but the key criterion for appreciating it is not a producer-imposed categorisation but a consumer-driven search for something accessible.

Can wine be a force for good?

Much of this chapter highlights wine culture's changing conditions and unsettled questions. Wine and the cultural issues around health have not been covered in this book, which is a gap; however, the dangers of wine are not merely those of poor health. We have also noted issues of discrimination, exclusion, introverted vinous 'nationalism' and the imperial power (and subsequent colonial legacies) of wine, amongst others. Yet we want to underline the positive side of wine: the moves toward democratisation and sustainability, an emphasis on conviviality rather than elitism and challenges to the narrow existing views about how wine should be made and what grapes should be used. Wine is also a key part of the movement to strengthen and sustain communal, local and regional identities and cultures in the face of increasing globalisation.

Can wine be a force for good? Defenders of this proposition tend to focus on its 'power to banish care' (Johnson 1989) and its role as a social 'glue'. Jancis Robinson cites wine's important role in raising money for 'Room to Read' (Robinson 2017), which supports education in the developing world, and, in an earlier article, referred to it as a 'force for good' (Robinson 2010), though a later discussion piece on her site by Richard Hemming also terms it an 'utterly superfluous luxury' (Hemming 2019). These points certainly have some weight, but they are not unique to wine. We do not need wine to investigate art or scientific development or history – and wine is not essential to conviviality, even if it is one of its main catalysts. Thus, the negatives of wine (health, social disfunction) could be seen to outweigh these potential benefits.

What is more, wine can cause environmental problems. It is a greedy consumer of water. According to most estimates, it takes around 120 litres of water to produce a single glass of wine, though this is less than the 'water footprint' of almond milk and coffee and much the same as apple or orange juice (www.waterfootprint.org). The impact of irrigation (although not merely for vineyards) on the ecosystem of Australia's Murray-Darling river system is now close to catastrophic. Much more could be done by recycling and using grey water, yet the wine industry has been very slow in pursuing these and other solutions.

Nor is water the only item on the charge sheet. Although wine production is not a major source of CO_2 emissions compared to industries such as civil aviation (10 to 15 times worse), the emissions are not minor. Most of these derive from the process of packaging and transporting wine in glass bottles (an outdated seventeenth-century form of packaging, according to viticultural consultant Richard Smart). Such forms of packaging account for over 60% of total carbon emissions from the wine sector and could be reduced by using aluminium cans, cardboard packaging and the like (Robinson 2019). Glass bottles, in Smart's opinion, should become a 'dinosaur'. Furthermore, the wine industry should not treat the earth's atmosphere as a 'sewer' by releasing the surplus CO_2 fermentation gas. In short, there is much that the industry could do to improve its performance.

Yet we would argue that wine can, nonetheless, be a force for good in combating climate change. It can be, perhaps, one of several canaries in the coal mine that alerts the world to the effects of climate change. The wine industry preserves a remarkable data series that shows how grape harvest dates have changed in the last 750 years. The Beaune series of harvest dates covers the period since 1354. The dates show that between 1354 and 1987, grapes were picked on average from 28 September onwards. From 1988 to 2013, the harvest began some 13 days earlier (Labbé et al, *Climate of the Past*, 2019). Furthermore, this most recent period of 25 years dominates the records of extreme climatic events. Not only could the wine industry change its practices to preserve water and minimise its carbon footprint and CO_2 emissions, but it could also publicise the impact of climate change on wine – a threat to which might galvanise consumers all across the developed and developing world (see the chapter by Teil).

Beyond the specific environmental advantages wine may offer, the idea that wine can be a 'canary' in broader cultural terms may also have value. Amongst the chapters in this book are those which reveal changes in gender roles, attitudes to colonial histories and current appropriation of indigenous culture, attitudes to ethnicity, the evolution of fashions and new ways of understanding place. In many ways, wine as a product is at the forefront of these changes, and its investigation may reveal much about how such changes are likely to evolve. The wine industry's communication power could be used to sensitise and energise consumers worldwide.

For this reason, in conclusion, we want to extend a heartfelt invitation to others to join us in the focus on wine and its cultural contributions. As is clear from this volume, wine offers a medium to investigate a wide range of cultural factors, artefacts and dynamics, but there is much still to be learned. It is also a convivial field – the researchers involved in the area are generally collegial, friendly and interested in understanding culture beyond strict disciplinary boundaries. And the invitation may go beyond just sharing a research focus to include enjoying a glass together from time to time.

Acknowledgements

With the advice and support of all the co-editors Unwin, Charters, Demossier, Marks Dutton, Harding, and Smith Maguire.

References

Appadurai, A. (1981) "Gastro-politics in Hindu South Asia," *American Ethnologist* 8(3), 494–511.
Belk, R.W., Wallendorf, M. and Sherry, J.F. (1991) "The Sacred and the Profane in Consumer Behaviour: Theodicy on the Odyssey," in R.W. Belk (ed), *Highways and Buyways: Naturalistic Research from the Consumer Behaviour Odyssey*, Provo, UT: Association for Consumer Research, 59–101.
Burke, P. (2012) "Strengths and Weaknesses of Cultural History," *Cultural History* 1(1), 1–13.
Charters, S. (2006) *Wine and Society: The Social and Cultural Context of a Drink*, Oxford: Butterworth-Heinemann.
Egoz, S. (2000) "Clean and Green but Messy: The Contested Landscape of New Zealand's Organic Farms," *Oral History* 28(1), 63–74.
Elias, N. (2000) *The Civilizing Process: Sociogenetic and Psychogenetic Investigations*, Oxford: Blackwell Publishers.
Geertz, C. (1973) *The Interpretation of Cultures: Selected Essays*, New York: Basic Books.
Gordon, R., Heim, D. and Macaskill, S. (2012) "Rethinking Drinking Cultures: A Review of Drinking Cultures and a Reconstructed Dimensional Approach," *Public Health (London)* 126(1), 3–11.
Hemming, R. (2019) "Unpalatable Truths: Is Wine a Force for Good?" www.jancisrobinson.com/articles/unpalatable-truths-is-wine-a-force-for-good, accessed 31 May 2021.
Johnson, H. (1989) *The Story of Wine*, London: Mitchell Beasley.
Kovacs, M.G. (1989) *The Epic of Gilgamesh*, Stanford, CA: Stanford University Press.
McGovern, P.E. (2003) *Ancient Wine: The Search for the Origins of Viniculture*, Princeton, NJ: Princeton University Press.
McGovern, P.E. (2019) "The Dawn of Wine," in M. Karam (ed), *Tears of Bacchus: A History of Wine in the Arab World*, London: Gilgamesh Publishing, 24–78.
Molina-Espeja, P. (2020) "Next Generation Winemakers: Genetic Engineering in Saccharomyces Cerevisiae for Trendy Challenges," *Bioengineering* 7(4), 128, https://doi.org/10.3390/bioengineering7040128, accessed 31 May 2021.
Papakonstantinou, Z. (2009) "Wine and Wine Drinking in the Homeric World," *L'Antiquité Classique* 78(1), 1–24.
Paul, H. (1996) *Science, Vine and Wine in Modern France*, Cambridge: Cambridge University Press.

Robinson, J. (2010) "At Last – Wine is a Force for Good," *Financial Times*, 21 May, www.ft.com/content/e597fdf4-645e-11df-8cba-00144feab49a, accessed 15 May 2021.

Robinson, J. (2017) "Wine Helps to Spread Literacy," www.jancisrobinson.com/articles/wine-helps-to-spread-literacy, accessed 9 June 2021.

Robinson, J. (2019) "Carbon Footprints, Wine and the Consumer," www.jancisrobinson.com/articles/carbon-footprints-wine-and-consumer, accessed 25 May 2021.

Sarris, A., Athanassopoulou, E., Doulgeri-Intzessiloglou, A., Skafida, E. and Weymouth, J. (2002) "Geophysical Prospection Survey of an Ancient Amphorae Workshop at Tsoukalia, Alonnisos (Greece)," *Archaeological Prospection* 9(4), 183–195.

Wine Institute of New Zealand. (2002) *New Zealand Wine: The Riches of a Clean Green Land*, Auckland: Wine Institute of New Zealand.

APPENDIX

This highly idiosyncratic selection of cultural artefacts has sustained, inspired and accompanied our own journeys with wine. These are offered not as an exhaustive compendium but as a tasting menu that may be of use to others in search of complementary resources for teaching or research or simply something to watch, read or listen to while enjoying a glass of wine. *The Editors*

Films – fictional

Babettes Gæstebud (Babette's Feast) (Gabriel Axel) featuring 1845 Clos de Vougeot, Veuve Clicquot etc.
Bottleshock (Randall Miller)
Ce qui nous lie (Back to Burgundy) (Cédric Klapisch)
Conte d'automne (Autumn Tale) (Eric Rohmer)
Doe San (God of Gamblers) (Wong Jing) featuring the famous line 'Uncork me a bottle of 1982 Lafite!'
★*Downton Abbey* (Julian Fellowes) (★television series with recurrent scenes of Mr. Carson, the butler, selecting, decanting and serving wines including Château Margaux, Château Chasse-Spleen)
From Russia With Love (Terence Young) in which the SMERSH bad guy blows his cover by ordering chianti with his fish!
★*Hustle* (Tony Jordan; BBC) (★television series, season 4, episode 3 ('Getting Even') features a 1797 bottle of wine sold at London auction)
Premiers crus (First Growth) (Jérôme Le Maire)
Sideways (Alexander Payne)
The Secret of Santa Vittoria (Stanley Kramer)
The Silence of the Lambs (Jonathan Demme) featuring the famous line 'I ate his liver with some fava beans and a nice Chianti'.
Tu seras mon fils (You Will Be My Son) (Gilles Legrand)

Films – documentary

Barolo Boys (Paolo Casalis and Tiziano Gaia)
Château Pékin (Boris Pétric)
Le vin se lève (Wine Calling) (Bruno Sauvard)

Mondovino (Jonathan Nossiter)
Red Obsession (David Roach and Warwick Ross)
Resistanza (Natural Resistance) (Jonathan Nossiter)
Somm; Somm: Into the Bottle; *Somm 3* (Jason Wise)
Sour Grapes (Reuben Atlas)
★*The Winemakers* (PBS) (★reality television series competition)
★*Vintage: A History of Wine* (Image Entertainment) (★television mini-series with Hugh Johnson)

Literature

A Long Finish (Michael Dibdin)
Jiǔguó (The Republic of Wine: A Novel) (Mo Yan)
Judgment of Paris (George Taber)
Kami no Shizuku (The Drops of God) (Yuko Kibayashi and Shin Kibayashi)
L'Ame du vin (The Soul of Wine) (Charles Baudelaire) (poem)
Last Call: The Rise and Fall of Prohibition (Daniel Okrent)
Ode 2.11 (Horace) ('have some good wine')
Ode to Wine (Pablo Neruda) (poem)
Passion on the Vine (Sergio Esposito)
The Accidental Connoisseur: An Irreverent Journey Through the Wine World (Lawrence Osborne)
The Bacchae (Euripides)
The Rubaiyat of Omar Khayyam (Edward Fitzgerald)
The Sun Also Rises (Ernest Hemingway)
The Vintner's Luck (Elizabeth Knox)
To Cork or Not to Cork (George Taber)
Whipbird (Robert Drewe)
Wine and War (Don Kladstrup and Petie Kladstrup)

Music

All Because of You (Françoise Hardy)
Cigarettes and Whiskey and Wild, Wild Women (Tim Spencer)
Cracklin' Rosie (Neil Diamond)
Hotel California (Eagles)
Lilac Wine (Nina Simone)
Mountain Dew (Bascom Lamar Lunsford/Scotty Wiseman)
Red, Red Wine (UB40)
Quelqu'un m'a Dit (Carla Bruni)
The Good Wine Mass (Orlande de Lassus)
Trinklied, D.183 (Drinking Song) (Franz Schubert)

Other

Grapes of Grief and Gratitude Auction Catalogue, Morrell and Co., 8 December 2001. (Fundraiser to benefit families of NYC fire and police injured and killed after the 9/11 attack, which raised approximately USD $1 million) (see Meltzer 2001 in Wine Spectator: www.winespectator.com/articles/grapes-of-grief-auction-raises-nearly-1-million-for-wtc-victims-21117)
Hundred Days – Winemaking Simulator (game: www.hundreddaysgame.com/)

INDEX

Entries in **bold** denote tables; entries in *italics* denote figures.

AAG (Association of American Geographers) 38
ABC (Department of Alcoholic Beverage Control) 102–4
Aboriginal people 178, 265–6
academic discourses, terroir in 68–9
acidity 48, 191; metaphors of 200; volatile 348
ACO (Australian Certified Organic) 437
Adelaide 110, 114
administrative work 339
adulterations, illicit 306
adverse selection 31
advertising 51; aimed at women 315; art in 55; in East Asia 420; images of champagne 218, 222, 227; whiteness in 418–19
advertising discourse 196, 198–9, 202
aesthetic goals 289, 295
aesthetic value 107, 363
aestheticization 121, 224
AFFW (Australian First Families of Wine) 304
agency 264; women's 311, 317
agricultural analysis 103
Agricultural Gazette of New South Wales 184
agriculture 4, 33, 46; anthropology of 396; biodynamic 358, 434, 437, 439; sustainable 330, 334, 357, 440
agro-food industry 74, 188, 333, 400, 402
agronomy 187–92, 342, 345–7, 369
Akerlof, G. A. 31
Albers, Josef 141
alcohol: wine as 15, 18; *see also* drinking cultures
alcohol dependence, in Ireland 152
Alessandrini, Jean 137
Algeria 248, 417
Algerian migrants 397–9
aligoté 62
Alsace 66–7, 345–6, 358, 393, 425–30, 448

Althusser, Louis 5
Amador County 103, 105, 107–8
Amarone 79
ambivalence 279, 333
America *see* United States
Americanisation, cultural 397
analysts 210–12
ancient Egypt 234
ancient Greece 250; ethnicity in 415; god of wine 234; philosophy of 5; and rural idyll 260–1; and wine islands 83–4; wine-drinking parties 313
ancient Rome: ethnicity in 415; metaphor in 250; rural idyll in 260; and viniculture 218; wine in 62; and wine islands 84–6; women and wine 313
Anglican Church *see* Church of England
Aniane 417
Anjou 426, 429–30, 448
Annales School 37–8
anthropocentrism 334
anthropology 15, 442; and the economy 119; sensory 74; on wine and culture 7, 15–18
Anthroposophy 439
antiquity 5, 39–40, 233, 313, 355
AOC Decree Law 348
AOCs (Appellation d'Origine Controlée) 44, 99, 194, 271–2; and agronomy 346; and champagne 218; cultural value of 342–3; hierarchical system of 343–5; and quality control 348; and tasting 349–50; and terroir 63–4, 118, 120, 303, 309n5, 345–7
Appadurai, Arjun 21, 119, 444
appellation systems 40, 61, 194, 293; *see also* AOCs
appellations: geography of 39; narrower 30; *see also* AOCs
Aquinas, Thomas 235
Arab Spring 241, 248

Argentina 394n1: colonisation of 239, 417–18; films of 56; missionaries in 243; wine consumption in 387; winegrape varieties in 393
aridity, increasing 427
aristocratic model 355–6, 360
Aristotle 250–2, 256
Arizona 131
Arnold, Matthew 4
art: and wine and culture 54–5; wine's potential as 29
artisanal foods 290
artisanal labour 272
artisanal winemaking 302, 305–6, 372–6, 378–80, **379**, 445
artistic logic 376, 380
Asia 233, 239; Central 406; *see also* East Asia
Asimov, Eric 52
assemblage theory 218, 228
assemblages: of connected brands *227*; rhizomatic 300, 308
assessment 31, 308, 331, 337, 349, 369
Association pour la reconnaissance des climats de Bourgogne 121–2, 262
asymmetric information 31
Ata Rangi 261–2, 265
Athens, ancient 83, 313
Atlantic islands 85–8
Aula do Comércio 7
Auslander, Leora 41
Australasian Association for the Advancement of Science 184
Australia 87–8; biodynamics in 437–9; climate change in 435–6; cultural history of 178; migrant communities and winemaking 110–15, 182, 417; rural idyll of 259, 265–6; scientific winemaking in 65–6, 180, 182–5; sustainability in 331, 338; wine tourism in 23; winegrape varieties of 394; winegrape-bearing areas 393; women in wine industry 325
Australian Women in Wine Awards 324–6
authenticity 10, 23; in champagne branding 219; ethnic 113, 115, 418; and migrant labour 400–1, 403; social construction of 271–2; of winegrapes 365
AVAs (American Viticultural Areas) 39, 86, 99–100, 108, 274, 359; in Texas 125
Avicenna 253
AWRI (Australian Wine Research Institute) 411
Azores 84–5

Bacchae 313
Bacchic Council 256
Bacchus *see* Dionysos
backyard crush *111*
baijiu 406, 408
Balmain, Pierre 172
baptism 247, 253
Barefoot brand 79, 447

Barossa Valley 10, 80
barrel aging 75
barrels, imagery of 75–6
Barthes, Roland 51, 57, 416–17; on wine as totem-drink 114, 178
Barton, Thomas 147–8
Bauhaus 140–1
Bauman, Zygmunt 402
Baumol/Bowen 28
Baxter, Richard 238
Beaujolais 348–9, 366
Beaune 53, 62–3, 117, 122; religious institutions near 235, 243
Beckert, J. 8, 31–2, 47
Beckwith, Ray 306
beer 79; in Australia 88, 111–13; consumption of 387, 444; in France 416; and gender 315; industry 445–7; in Ireland 145, 152; in Poland 155, 157–8, 161; and religion 241–2; in the US 206–9
belief 2, 4, 6–7, 46–7; and Cal-Ital 418; CET as 412; culture as system of 41–2; religious 233, 255, 312–13; and values 278
Benedictine monks 83, 218, 235
Bérard, Laurence 347
Bergerac 397
Bergonié Cancer Institute 400
Berkeley, George 146
Berkeley School 8; *see also* University of California, Berkeley
Berlan, Jean-Pierre 402
Bernard of Clairvaux 235
Berta, Pierstefano 54
best practice 270, 308, 331
Beverland, Michael 22–4, 47, 219–20, 281, 361, 380, 418
Bickerton, Leonard 166
Binet, Ana Maria 53
Biodynamic Agricultural Association of Australia 438
biodynamics 18, 67, 77, 434, 437–40; in Bordeaux 357; and rural idyll 266; use of term 334; and utopianism 304–5
BIPOC people 419
blackletters 137–9, *138*
bladders, large 75
Blake, James 180, 183
blending wines 66
BLM (Black Lives Matter) 415, 419
Bloch, Ernst 300
blood, and wine 235–6, 253, 257
BMC (Business Model Canvas) *354*, 355, 361
Boccaccio, Giovanni 314
Bogucka, Maria 159
Bohne, Louis 156
Boissenot, Jacques and Eric 305
Boisset group 361
Bond, James 173–4
Bond, Oliver 146

Bonniel, Jacques 18n1
Bordas, Jean 346
Bordeaux (region): and Burgundy 43; classification of wine estates 63; in film 56; international BMC comparison of 355–7, 361; Irish colony in 147–8, 152; migration and globalisation in 396, 398–400, 402
Bordeaux wines: and AOC system 344; blends 388; exported to Britain and Ireland 148
borders, permeable 402
Bottleshock (film) 55
Bouchard, Cedric 172
boundaries, symbolic 375
boundary work 335
Bourdieu, Pierre 42, 205, 374–5, 444
boutique wineries 86, 303–4
brand: identity 270, 274; image agents 280; images 225; meaning 22, 228; selfies 223, *224*; value 135, 143, 378–9; *see also* wine brands
Brandwatch 220–1, 225
Brereton, John 86
Britain: champagne in 165–71; and geography of wine 38; wine writing in 198
brokers 148, 192–4, 338, 349, 356
Brundtland, Gro Harlem 332
Brundtland Commission 332–4
Brunet, Raymond 189, 191
bubble trains 169
bubbles 169, 172–3, 218–19, 222–3, 226
Bucer, Martin 236–8
Buddhism 239
Bulgaria 16–17
bulk wines 75, 278, 302, 356
Bulwer-Lytton, George 165
Buoninsegna, Duccio di 165
Burckhardt, Jacob 42
Bureau of Alcohol, Tobacco and Firearms 99–101, 103, 105
Burgundian folk festivals 44
Burgundy: and AOC system 344; and Bordeaux 43; cellar doors in 94–6; in film 56; impact of climate change 436; Protestantism in 238; and terroir 63–4, 90–3, 96, 117–23, 303, 400, 447 (*see also climats*); tradition of winemaking in 269–72, 274–5; wine culture of 92
Burke, Peter 41–2, 44, 177, 443
Busby, James 88
business, and wine and culture 7–8, 20–4
business models 127, 274, 353–5, 358–61, 440
Butler, Simon 146
buyers *see* wine consumers

cabarets 188, 315
cabernet Franc 355, 367, 369, 393, 398, 426
cabernet sauvignon 80, 113, 127, 201, 304, 359, 372, 393
California: international BMC comparison of 355, 359–60; migration to 418; scientific winemaking in 65–6, 273; sustainability in 331; wineries in 213
Cal-Ital 418
Calvin, John 235–8
Calvinism 238, 246
Canada: rural idyll of 259, 264; terroir in 48
Canary Islands 85
canned wine 446
Cannes Film Festival 56, 83
Canterbury 88; *see also* North Canterbury
Cape of Good Hope 177
Cape Verde 85
capitalism: flexible 17; global 119, 436; industrial 261, 440; post-industrial 118; and wine production 16
Capus, Joseph 348
Caravaggio 54–5
Cargasacchi, Peter 306
Caring, Richard 172
Carme, Emile 188, 194
carmenère 72, 201
Carmichael, Henry 176–7, 180–2, 184–5
Carr, E. H. 41
Carreras, Nicolás 56
Carrodus, Bailey 305
Carthusians 235
Cartier, Jacques 86
Casella family 304
Castillon-La-Bataille 397–8, 401
casual manuals 137–8, *139*
category entry points (CEPs) 409, *410*
Catholicism: in Ireland 146–9, 151; and wine 236, 238, 241–4, 246–7
Cato the Elder 62
Catullus 52
Caucasus region 3, 415
celebrations 30; champagne and 174, 217, 223–4, 227, 278; harvest 386; in Ireland 151–2; religious 234, 245, 313
cellar doors 90–2, 94–7, 262–6, 284, 439
cellar hygiene 187–9
cellaring 76
cellartracker.com 212
Central Otago 88, 91–2
Central Valley of California 72, 100
certification: biodynamic 437–8; organic 78; rabbinical 247; of sustainability 304, 332, 334–9, **336–7**, 358
certification work 332, 335, 338–9
CERVIN (Centre d'Études et de Recherche sur la Vigne et le Vin) 53
CG *see* cultural goods
Chablis 189, 346, 349
Chagall, Marc 55
champagne 217–18, 309n5; bottles 170, 218, 226, 360; brand meanings 22; brands 218–21, *222*, 223–5, 227–9; in Britain 165–71; cultural history of 43–4; as cultural symbol 218–20, 278; glass

effect *174*; glasses 165–74, *173*; in Ireland 151–2; luxury image of 357; in Poland 155, 157, 160, 162, 444; posters 55; selfies 223, **225–6**, 227–8; widows 314; women drinking 315–16; women in industry 320
Champagne (region) 218; in film 56; international BMC comparison of 355, 357–9, 361
Champagne AOC 357
Champkin, Julian 174
change, understanding 9, 41–2
chaos 311
Chappaquiddick Islands 86
Chaptal, Jean-Antoine 180
chaptalisation 271, 429
Charles I of Spain 239
Charles II of England 165, 168
Château Margaux 302, 323
Château Mouton-Rothschild 55, 323
châteaux 344, 355–7, 399, 402
Chaudat, Philippe 18n1
Chauvet, Jules 349
Chauvin, Pierre-Marie 396
cheeses, artisanal 288, 290, 295
chemical analysis 76, 187–8, 192, 306
chemistry 180, 188–94
Chesterfield, Lord 145–6
Chile 72, *73*, 75; colonialism and wine in 239, 243; sustainability in 331
China 405; anthropological research on wine in 17; consumer ethnocentrism in 411–12; current state of wine market **407–9**, 413; history of wine in 405–6; tasting and talking about wine in 410–11; terroir in 48; wine and business studies in 21–2; wine industry in 420; winegrape-bearing areas 393
Chinese investors 401–2
Chinese literature 54
Chinese wine 410
Cho Lee, Jeannie 410
Christian Scientists 245
Christianity: in Poland 156; and wine 234–9, 244, 253–4, 313–14, 416
Christiansen, Ben 205–6, 209–15; tasting notes **212**
Church of England 88, 238, 241, 246, 248
Churchill, Winston 54
Cicero, M. Tullius 4
cider 151, 158, 161
Cilaos region 87
Cistercian monks 83, 235, 242, 270–2
city life 260, 398
city-country dialectics 261, 263
Clancy, Tomás 151
claret 444; cultural history of 43–4; in Ireland 146–7, 149–50, 153
class, and champagne 219, *222*
classical antiquity 35–6
classification, and hybrid wines 364–5
Clements, Henry John 149
Clements, Henry Theophilus 149

Clicquot Ponsardin, Barbe-Nicole 314, 323
climate change 18, 32, 424–5, 445; and biodynamics 434–7, 439; impact in France of 426–7; interviewees on **426**; in sixteenth century 156; and utopian winemaking 301; wine as force for good against 449–50; and winegrape varieties 386; winegrower attitudes to 427–31, 448
climats 92, 118, 120–3, 444
Clos de Tart 117, 122
Cloudy Bay 88, 304
CMS (Court of Master Sommeliers) 322, 421
CNAO (National Committee of Appellations of Origin) 344, 346, 348
CO_2 emissions 435, 448–50
coffee 15, 96, 110–11, 140, 145, 159–60, 244, 449
cognac 322, 347, 420
Colchagua Valley 72, *73*
cold discourse 188, 190, 194
Colette 54
Collins, Kourtney 126
colonial cultures 39, 82–3, 88
colonial winemaking 87, 176, 180, 182–3
colonialism 3–4, 415, 417; in Australia 176–85; and indigenous idyll 445; in Latin America 239; and migration 386, 397–8, 400; in New Zealand 94, 261; and wine consumption 43; and wine islands 82–8
Comaroff, John and Jean 402
Comité d'Agriculture de Beaune et de Viticulture de la Côte-d'Or 343
commercial logic 372, 376–80, **379**
commodifiers 210
commodity beverage 29
communion *see* Eucharist
complexity, in wine tasting 291
Coney Island 86
congestion costs 30
connected brands 227
connoisseurs 52, 150, 172, 281, 307, 359, 368, 419
connoisseurship 56, 112, 153, 159, 175, 288, 290, 294, 301, 445, 449
consciousness: altered states of 443; changing 27
consecrated wine 235–6
conspicuous production 76, 117
Constellation Brands 211
consumer behaviour 20–2, 30, 412
consumer choices 20, 79, 380, 393
consumer culture theory (CCT) 8, 22, 24, 143
consumer ethnocentrism (CET) 411–12, **413**
consumer goods: challenging 289; and identity 160
consumer images 221, 223–4, 227
consumer skills 288, 294–5
consumers, professional 213
consumption, cultural approaches to 217
contestations 2, 48, 121, 333–4, 338
conventions 9–10, 47–8, 136, 254, 288, 290, 363, 445
conviviality 46, 206, 302, 443, 447, 449–50
COO (country of origin) 411–12
coopetition 324

Coppinger, William 147
Cordier, Pierre 53
core competencies 302
Corsica 84
Cortés, Hernán 239
cosmopolitanism, in Poland 155, 160–1
cost disease 28
Côte de Nuits 117
Côte d'Or 91–3, 122, 343
Coteaux du Layon 345
Côtes de Rhone appellation 345
countrification 260
Courtown, Earl of 149
COVID-19 pandemic xxi, 206, 214, 361, 436, 446–7
creativity, in CGs 8, 28–9, 33
Crédit Agricole 397–8
Cres 111, 114
Crete 83–4
cricket 171, 262
critical discourse analysis 199
critics see wine writers
Croatia xx, 88, 111–12, 115, 444
cross-cultural encounters 44
cross-disciplinarity 442
Cullen, James 151
Cullen, Vanya 305
cult wines 273–4
cultivation 4, 417; cereal 162; of taste 33; of vines see viticulture
cultural artefacts xxi, 40, 135, 452–3
cultural assets 385–7, 393–4
cultural blindness 407
cultural capital 112, 196–7, 199, 201, 264, 291, 373–5
cultural change 24, 38; wine as marker of 43–4
cultural closure 271
cultural commodities 117, 283
cultural competition 331, 334–5, 339
cultural construction 23–4, 47–8, 425
cultural context 2; and business 20–2, 24; of Māori language 93; and semiotics 51; of terroir 68; and typography 135, 143
cultural democratisation 47, 56, 197, 288–9, 294, 350, 419, 449
cultural dimensions 2, 7, 9, 22–4, 385
cultural economics 27–9, 32–3
cultural geography, new 9, 35
cultural goods (CG): characteristics of 204; ideal consumer of 289; range of products in 215; wine as 8, 29–33, 92, 210, 212
cultural historians 9, 178
cultural history 42, 44, 155; ethics of inclusion in 178; and science 177
cultural identities 114, 266, 275
cultural imaginaries 119, 123, 311
cultural industries 27–9, 287, 418
cultural intermediaries 29, 43, 47; creating norms of taste 289–90; wine vendors as 204–5, 212–13; wine writers as 197–8

cultural intermediation, markers of 205
cultural landscapes 8, 37–9, 123, 303
cultural markets 30–2
cultural norms 119, 288, 445
cultural objects 51, 230, 280, 338
cultural product, wine as 17–18
cultural representation of wine 54, 360
cultural symbols 6, 39, 217–18, 227–8, 444
cultural system, pillars of 24n2
cultural traits 70, 353, 355, 361
cultural turn 5, 9, 42, 46
cultural value 23, 29–31; of CGs 204–5; Māori 94, 96; of wine 92, 114, 153
culture: in business disciplines 20–1; definition of 3–6, 442–3; economic analysis of 27; and geography 39; and history 41–2; intrinsic and instrumental 22, 445; production of 277, 280–1, 283, 285; sociological questions of 46–7
culture wine 10, 33
custom 4, 94, 157–8, 236
Cyprus 85

Dahl, Roald 52
Daktulosphaera vitifoliae see phylloxera
Dali, Salvador 52, 55
Dalmatians 84, 110–11, 114–15
Danebury Vineyards 262
Danler, Stephanie 52
Danowski, Déborah 436
Darpeix, Aurélie 399
Darwin. Charles 440
Daufuskie Island 86–7
Daynes, Sarah 271
de Blij, Harm 38
de Gaulle, Charles 54
de La Suze, Henriette de Coligny 54
de Leon, Miguel 419
de Villaine, Aubert 305
decolonisation 16, 396–8, 419
Delachère, François 243–4
Delaporte, Ixchel 400
Deleuze, Gilles 300–1
delimitation, of AOCs 342–3, 345–7, 349–50
demand conditions 387
demographic shifts 152, 446–7
Demolon, Albert 346
Demossier, Marion 43, 271, 400, 434
Denmark 159, 325
denomination, systems of 17
Dereoncourt, Stéphane 305
Deslandes, André Bourleau 87
destination vineyards 262
developers 210–11
Dharug people 177
dialectical materialism 5
Dickens, Charles 168
Dijon 122
Dion, Roger 37

Dionysos 55, 234, 251, 312–13; artworks of 54–5; places named after 86
disciplines 2, 5–10, 442
discourse analysis 54, 90, 363, 365
discourse democratisation 196
discursive formations 332–4
discursive practices 8, 31–2
Disraeli, Benjamin 165
distributors *see* wine distributors
diversity 2; climactic 87; for consumers 387; cultural 308; ethnic 48; gender 322, 325; in utopian wine ideals 300, 308n1; varietal 388, 390, 392–3
Diversity in Wine Leadership Forum 324
Dixon, Edmund 169
DOCG (Denominazione di Origine Controllata e Garantita) 79, 99
'doing' wine 9, 47
Dom Pérignon 219–21, 226–7
Domaine de la Romanée-Conti 305, 343, 437
domestic wines 156, 214, 410
Dominus Estate 372
Doorley, Tom 151, 239
Dougherty, Percy 38
Douglas, Mary 15
Dragon Seal Winery 406
Drennan, William 146
drinking cultures 44, 444; in Ireland 151–2; in Poland 157–9, 161
drinking vessels 55, 83, 257, 406
Drot, Christophe 398
drunkenness: and drinking culture 157–9, 161; and religion 237–8, 242; *see also* intoxication
dry wines 168, 170–1, 368
Dubaquié, Joseph 192–3
Dunstan, David 179
Dupas, Jean 55
dystopia 300, 302, 306

East Asia 387, 415, 420–1, 445
ecology 347
economic crisis of 2008 397, 420
economic development 27, 33, 113, 131, 326, 386
economic essentialism 44
economic geography of wine 39
economic singularities 122
economic value 28–32, 42, 107
economic viability 354
economics, and wine and culture 8, 27–33
economies of scale 209, 273
ecosystems, and terroir 23
efficiency 20, 302
E&J Gallo 79, 302, 359, 446–7
El Dorado AVA 103, 105
Elias, Norbert 443
elite culture *see* high culture
empiricism 181, 189, 270–1
England: rural idyll of 259, 262; sparkling wine region 304

enjoyment, as utopian 306–7
Enlightenment 4, 161, 176, 185
entanglements 300–2, 304, 308, 442–4
entrepreneurship: agricultural 305; female 320, 323–4, **327**
environmental analysis 100–3
environmental awareness 304
environmental management 329, 334
Epic of Gilgamesh 41, 443
Escudier, J. L. 323
Etherege, George 168
ethnicity 30, 415–18; and East Asian wine market 420–1; in fashion theory 278; and global middle class 264; in rural France 403; and wine consumption 21; and wine labour 418–19
ethnocentrism 405, 411–12
ethnography 7, 15, 18n1, 442; long-term 119
Eucharist 234–6, 238, 241, 243–8, 253, 416–17
Eurocentrism 363, 369, 419
European Union 388, 400
everyday devotees 211
excess 151–2, 159, 233, 245, 252
executives 210–11
experience economy 25, 96–7
experience goods 31–2
experimentation 33, 76, 83, 181–2, 184, 270, 274
expert opinion 32, 34, 211, 216
expertise: alliance of forms of 193; in Australian viticulture 179, 182–4; in wine markets 32; wine tasting as 187–92
explorers 4, 86, 211, 265
Exposition Universelle 1855 63–4, 176

Facebook 121, 357
Fair Play AVA 100–1, 105
fair-trade wine 419
Falcao da Fonseca, Luis 54
family-owned businesses 118, 213, 262, 300–1, 322–4, 328
FAO (Food and Agriculture Organization) 334
fashion: as material object 278–9; as process 277, 279–80, 283
fashion designers 279, 283
fashion diffusion models 280–1, **282**
fashion leaders 281, 283
fashion studies 277, 279–80, 283, 285
fashion systems 280
fashion theory 277, 280
fashion thinking 278, 283–5, *284*
faults and diseases of wine **189**, 190–1, 364
feasting, Polish tradition of 158–60
Federal Register 100
Federley, Maria 222
femininity 21, 138, 142, 170, 172, 311–12, 325
fermentation: malolactic 114, 293, 348; second 168; temperature controlled 302
fermentation techniques 269, 273, 293
fermented landscapes 125, 131
Ferreira, Antonia Adelaide 323

fertilisers 62, 398, 435, 437–8
fictive place 78
Fiddletown AVA 102–3, 105
figurative language 197, 199, 201
film, and wine and culture 55–7
financial crisis of 2008–9 210
finders 210
fine wines: ability to distinguish 112; in Australia 112, 183–4; as cultural good 204; normative discourse of 48; as refined good 21; tasting and chemistry 193; and wine tourism 96
Finger Lakes 30, 367–9
Fitzroy farmers 305
flagship 210
flavour: standardisation of 192; vocabulary of 189–90, 202
flute glasses *166*, 167–9, 172–4
folklore 18n1, 57, 123, 272, 345, 361
folklorisation 123
font variations 136, 141–2
fonts 135–7, *136*, 139–43: bold *142*
food: anthropology of 396; pairing 202; quality 17
formal cursives 137, *138*, 143
Foucault, Michel 42, 201, 332, 334–5
Fourcade. Marion 117
frameworks 335
France: anthropological study of wine in 16; Chinese and East Asian investment in 401–2, 421; cinema of 56; geography of 37; group identification with wine in 30; migrant labour in 396–401; national identity of 43, 416–17; Republican tradition of 400; rural idyll of 259, 262–3; sustainability in 331; wine consumption in 387; wine tourism in 23
Francis, Grant 167
Francis, Pope 247
Francis Xavier, Saint 239
Franciscan monks 127, 272, 417
Franck, Sebastian 237
Frank, Konstantin 367
fraud 187–8, 306, 348
French culture, wine in 57
French literature 53
French nationalism 400–1
French Revolution 219, 244, 400
French royal court 219
French wines: British duties on 44; in Ireland 145, 149; in Poland 155–7, 160–2; and Reunion Island 87; and terroir 303–4; and terroir 309
French-American hybrid grapes 366, 368–9
Fresno 72–4, *73*
Friedman, Jonathan 119
Friedman, Milton 5
Fripp, Robert 52
Frog's Leap Winery 67
Fukier Winery 162

Galbreath, J. 325, 327
Galen 252

gastronomy 28, 33
gatekeepers 280–1, 283
Geelong region 434
Geertz, Clifford 42, 442–3
gender, and wine preference 447
gender order 311
gender roles 33, 320–1, 326–8, 450
gender segregation 323, 326
gendered wines 326
generation Alpha 447
generation X 307
generation Y 22
Gentil, André Antoine-Pierre 270–1
geographers, as narrators of wine culture 36–9, 342
geographic designations 99
geographical indications (GIs) 261, 386, 394
geography: human 347; locational 74; people and nature in 35, *36*; and wine and culture 8–9, 35–40
geography of wine 38, 444
geology: in popular wine writing 68; and terroir 62
Georgia 83, 123
Géovino *66–7*
German migrants 178–9, 206
German wines 151, 166, 393
Germany: Nazi 300; sugar water addition 429; traditions of geography 37; wine literature 54
Gibellini, Pietro 54
Gigante, Pedro 85
GII (Gender Inequality Index) 326, **327**
Gilbert, L. A. and J. C. 320–2, 326–7
Gillet, Philippe 157
gin craze 242
Gironde department 355, 397, 402
Gladstone, William 44, 150
glass bottles 187, 446, 448–9
global North and South 338
globalisation: Burgundy's adaptation to 117–18; and demand conditions 387, 394; in France 397, 416–17; nineteenth-century 184; and rural idylls 259–60, 263, 267; and utopianism 302, 307–8; and wine in film 56
GMO (genetically modified organism) 446
Goethe, J. W. von 4
Gondwana 266
good taste 21, 24, 48; construction of canons *see* taste construction; wine professionals defining 288–9, 294
A Good Year (film) 55
Google Scholar 31, 68
Gorgona 83
gorzałka 161
Gough, J. B. 271
governance 41, 272, 320, 322, 325–6, 397
Gowlland, Geoffrey 121
grafting 364
Grands Crus 92, 117, 152, 303, 342–5, 401
grape juice 74–5, 87, 111, 243, 245–6, 248, 386

grape species, of Texas 127
grape-growing *see* viticulture
grape-growing analysis 103, **105**
grapes *see also* winegrapes
Grappe, Veronique 159–60
Graves (region), advertisement for 65
Greece: wine art of 55; wine literature of 54; wine production of 79; *see also* ancient Greece
Green, Anna 42, 44
Greening, Nigel 440
grenache 110, 114, 148
grey water 435, 449
group identity 29–30
Guattari, Félix 300–1
Guermès, Sophie 53
Guinness 153
Gutenberg, Johannes 51, 139
Guyot, Jules 180

Haass-Koffler, Carolina 55
Hage, G. 437
Hakluyt, Richard 86
Halevi, Judah 254
Halevi, Leor 41
Hall, Edward 21
Halliday, James 305
Hambledon Vineyard 262
HaNagid, Samuel 254
Hancock, Jake 68
hand selling 94, 206
Hann, Chris 17
Hardeman, Edward 149
Hartshorne, Albert 165–6
harvest: celebrating 234; and climate change 428–9, 434–6, 449; difficult 269; early-morning 440; mechanised 302; migrant workers for 399, 401; physicality of 76; praying for 243; as ritual 110
Harvey, David 119
hashtags 221, 223
Hatarask Island 86
Hautes Côtes de Beaune 62–3
health: environmental 18; of migrant workers 400; public 123; and wine 2, 41, 44, 146, 192, 406, 410, 449
health and safety regulations 78
health policy 18
Healy, Maurice 151
Heath, Dwight 157
Heath, Henry *150*
hedonic consumption 188, 264
hedonism: and cellar doors 95–6; and champagne glasses 172, 174; and gender 315; of learning 256; non-ostentatious 357; in oenological discourse 188
Heekin, Deirdre 369
heirs 156, 322, 402
Henry, Scott 434
herbicides 129–30, 358

Herder, J. G. 4
heritage: and champagne 219, *222*; cultural 111, 120, 270, 360; ethnic 112, 115, 415, 418
heritage value 92, 123
heritagisation 17, 118–20, 122, 397
Herodotus 9
Hesiod 51, 261
Hetman's cellar 162
HEV (High Environmental Value) 358
high culture 4, 46, 289, 294, 370
High Plains AVA 125, *126*, 129–31
Hilgard, Eugene 272
Hill Country AVA 125–31, *126*
Hilton Head Island 86
historical geography 8–9
history, and wine and culture 9, 41–4
hobbyists 260
Hoefler, Jonathan 137
Hofstede, Geert 21
home winemaking 110–15
homeland 91, 113–15
Homer 52, 83, 251, 257, 443
homogenisation 56, 402, 444
Hong Kong 387, 420–1
Horace 53
horizontal differentiation 357
horse breeding, thoroughbred 185
hospitality 20, 22; duty of 443; economic impact of 33
hot discourse 188, 190, 194
Houellebecq, Michel 52–4
HRVA (Hunter River Vineyard Association) 176–85
Hubinet, Adolphe 43, 170
HUE Society 419
Huetz de Lemps, Alain 36, 53
Huizinga, Johann 42
humidity 62, 77, 127, 129, 151, 364
humus colloids 439
Hungarian wines 155–7, 160–2, 444
Hunter Valley 88, 176–80, 182–5
Hus, Jan 236
hybrid grapes *see* winegrape varieties, hybrid
hybrid wines 364, 368–9
hybridisation: in business models 360–1; cultural 361, 396; in lifestyle media 196

Ibn Ezra, Moses 254
Ibn Gabirol, Solomon 254
iconic brands 280
identity assemblage 218–20, 226, 228–9
identity *see also* brand identity; group identity; national identity; wine identity
al-Idrisi, Muhammad 37
Illustrated London News 165, 167–70
image coding 221
imaginations 64, 79, 123, 193, 217–18, 229, 278
imperialism 417, 421
importers 209

INAO (National Institute of Appellations of Origin) 64, 346–9, 401
income growth 385, 387
index of similarity *390*
indigenous idylls 259, 265–6, 445; *see also* winemakers, indigenous
individualisation 199, 401
individuality, reflexive 264
industrial spirit 177
industrialisation of wine 446
inequalities 46, 48
influencers 31, 202, 227–8
information problems 31
innovations: commercial and artistic 283; women and 323, 325
INRA (National Institute for Agronomic Research) 69, 348, 428, 430
insecticides 302, 437
Instagram 217–18, 220, **221**, *222*, 225, 228–9, 357, 360
Institut Universitaire de la Vigne et du Vin 53
Institute of Masters of Wine 7
institutional logics 380
intellectual property 8, 28–9, 33, 204
interconnectedness 304
interdiscursivity 201–2
interethnic relations 401, 403, 419
intermediaries 21, 24, 29, 443–4; and international trade 43; legitimacy of 272; and wine consumers 290, 294–5; *see also* cultural intermediaries
International Wine Film Festival 56
internationalisation 325
interpretation boards 95
interpretivist approach 21–2
intersectionality 300
intersections 2–3, 6, 9, 23, 261–2, 434
intersubjectivity 8, 31
interviews, qualitative 105–7, 413
intoxicants 43
intoxication 16; in literature 52; and Polish drinking culture 160; spiritual 255–6; *see also* drunkenness
intrinsic characteristics 31
intrinsic culture 20
inventory 214
investors 118, 212–15, 244, 356, 399, 420
invisibility 121, 124, 399–400
involvement 405, 408, 411–13
IPCC (Intergovernmental Panel on Climate Change) 427, 448
Ireland 145; class system of 205; in eighteenth century 146–8; female drinking in 444; in nineteenth century 148–51; twentieth century to present 151–2; wine culture in 152–3;
Ireland, Tony 92
IRI (Information Resources, Inc.) 209
Isabella wine 87
Islam 37, 41, 239, 241, 248, 416
islandness 82

islands 39, 82–9, 299
Israel/Palestine 17, 48, 254–5, 326
Italian literature 54
Italian migrants 113, 397–8, 417–18
Italian Women Winemakers 326
italic fonts *142*
Italy: northern 32; wine consumption in 387; winegrape varieties of 394, 418; women in wine industry 323, 325

Jacob's Creek 304
Japan: wine growing in 36, 239; women and wine in 316
Japanese manga 54, 443
JCE (*Journal of Cultural Economics*) 27–8
Jenson, Nicolas 139
Jesus, and wine 234–5, 245–6, 313
Jewish wine production 247, 416
Johnson, Boris 262
Johnson, Hugh 32, 53, 205
Johnson, Randal 376
Johnston, William 147
Joly, Nicolas 305
Jones, Jason 54
Judaism 234, 246–7, 254
judgement devices 122
Judgement of Paris 55, 355, 359, 372
Jukić, Ivan 88
Jullien, André 343
Jung, Yuson 17

kaitiakitanga 265
kalimoxto 22
Kaludah Ruby 180
Kandinsky, Wassily 55
Kangaroo Island 88
Karpik, Lucien 122
Kausch, Johann Joseph 159
Keene, William 184
Kelowna 259, 264, 266
Kenna, George 55
Keynes, J. M. 5, 27
Kimmeridgian subsoils 346
King, James 176–7, 181–5
Kitá Wines 266
knowledge: formal 190, 269; scientific 177, 185, 189, 191, 425; technical 187–8, 197, 275, 332; of wine consumers 292–4; *see also* wine knowledge
kosher wine 247, 416
Kramer, Matt 52
Kulturlandschaft 37
Kurniawan, Rudy 56
kvevri 123

labelling 388
labour: ethnic division of 418–19; migrant 397–401, 403; volunteer 213, 215
Laferté, Gilles 123

Lagerfeld, Karl 172
Lagrange, Marc 53–4
Lamont, Michele 375
Landrieu-Lussigny, Marie-Helene 122
landscape 37–8, 443, 447; agricultural 125; of Burgundy 118–21; commercial 446; cultivated 95–6; distinctive 36–7; ecological 120, 272; environmental 106; of North Canterbury 94–6; transforming 95, 118, 178, 344, 417; and wine marketing 400
landscape hierarchies 347
language 6–7, 41, 52, 443; of academic cultures 69; Aristotle on 251–2; colonial 82; fashion as 278; of New Zealand wine 91–2, 94; in Rabelais 256–7; of science 194; of tasting 112; of terroir and tradition 119; of wine criticism 196–201, 379, 410–11, 419
language style 196
Languedoc 16, 417, 426
Latin America 37–8, 418–19
Latin language 252
Lawson, Wilson 443
Lawton, Abraham 148
Le Jeune, Paul 243
Le Roy, Pierre 347
leadership: and utopian winemaking 305; in wine opinion 281; women's 322–3, 325, 327
leaf plucking 303, 434–5
Lecoutre, Matthieu 159
Ledesma, Juan 306
Leeuwin Art Series 55
legitimacy, discourses of 9, 47
legitimation, processes of 9, 47
Leif Eriksson 86
Lem, Winnie 16
Lérins 83
Levitas, Ruth 300
licentiousness 312, 314
Liebig, Justus 182–3
lifestyle media 196–7, 199, 201–2, 264
Liger-Belair, Thibault 303
Lindeman, Henry 184
literature, and wine and culture 52–4
Little Ice Age 84
localism 369
locality 16–17
Loi Griffe 187
Loire Valley 37, 91, 305, 426–7, 429
Longfellow, Henry Wadsworth 366
Lorin, Philippe 53–4
low culture 4, 202
low-alcohol wine 282–3, 430, 447
lowercase 136, 141–3, *142*
Lu Ji 406
Luther, Martin 235–7
luxury brands 219
luxury products 23–4, 29
luxury wines 24, 26, 218–19, 273–4, 420

LVMH group 221, 303–4, 358
Lynch, Kermit 52
Lynch, Thomas 147

Ma, Jack 117
Macarthur, John 87
Macarthur, William 183
Macau 420–1
maceration, extended 273
Macinherney, Nicholas 147
MacLaine, Shirley 172
Macneil, Karen 373
MacQuitty, Jane 197–202
Madden, Samuel 145
Madeira 84–6, 152, 177
magic: and champagne 170, 217, 219–20, *222*, 223–4, 228; of inebriation 255; of winemaking 379–80
magpie tendency 68
Mainardi, Giusi 54
Maitland Mercury 179–81, 184
Malvasia 84–5
management 7, 20–1, 444, 448; environmental 334; and gender 322, 325; pest 336; of terroir 23; of vines 176; of wine quality 187–8; yield 308
Mandelbaum, David 43
Mandler, Peter 42
Manhattan Island 86
manner-of-motion verbs 200
Manzoni, Alessandro 54
Mao Zedong 406
Māori language 93–4
Māori winemakers 259, 265
maps, and terroir 91, 95, 121–2
Marchenay, Philippe 347
Margaret River 304–5, 437
Marie Antoinette 172
Mariposa County 100–1, 103
market clearing prices 209
market for lemons (Akerlof) 31
market orientation 373, 380
marketing, and culture 21–2
markets, cultural dynamics of 9, 48
markets from meaning 8, 31–2
Marks, Denton 1
markup 214, 408
Marlborough region 75, 88, 91
Marsala 84
Marsden, Samuel 88
Martha's Vineyard 86
Martinborough 88, 92, 259; artisanal winemaking in 305; and terroir 303; wine tourism in 261–2, 264
Marx, Karl 5, 61
Mas, Jean-Claude 306
masculinity 21, 141–2, 170, 200, 311, 375
masked cellarmen 168, *169*
material culture 2, 10, 22, 41; anthropological analysis of 119; of winemaking 76

Mathieu, Laurent 192
Matthews, Mark 272
maturation 62, 64
maturity discrepancies 429–30
McAdam Freud, Janet 172
McConnell, Tara 146
McGovern, Patrick 61, 83, 233–4, 311, 406, 415, 442–3
McInerney, Jay 52
McKay, Ian 42
McLaren Vale, South Australia 17, 266, 306
meanings, final 143
mechanisation 302, 398–9
medical metaphors 252–3
Mediterranean climate 427
Mediterranean culinary cultures 96
Mediterranean islands 83–4, 88
Mediterranean region 3, 35, 37, 51, 234, 314, 386, 448
Médoc 30, 343, 355, 397, 399, 401
Mendoza 30, 71, 76, 321
Mennell, Stephen 43, 159
menstruation 314, 321
mentoring 324–6
Mentzelopoulos, Corinne 323
merchants: in Bordeaux 356; *see also* wine vendors
merlot 127, 398; in Bordeaux 304, 355, 393; in California 359; and film 55
metaphors 4, 35, 51–2, 196–202, 250–7, 300, 443
Methodism 241–2, 246, 248
Methuen Treaty 44
métier 94, 96
metonymies 51, 174, 196, 199, 254
metro-rural idylls 263–7, 445
Michalon, Bénédicte 399
Michelangelo 55
microcelebrity 223–5, 227, *228*
micro-oxygenation 271, 273
Middle Ages: calligraphy of 136–8; gender in 314; Poland in 161–2; religion in 233, 239, 253–4
middle class 33, 155, 267, 444, 448; Chinese 405, 407; global 263–4
Middle East 303
Middleton, John 305
Middleton, Robert Hunter 141
migration 48, 112–15, 386–7, 396–9, 401–2, 417, 445
millennials 283, 307
Miller, Daniel 119
Milwaukee 205–7
Miro, Joan 55
Mission Hill Winery 77, 79, 264
Mitchum, Robert 172
Mo Yan 54
modelling 27, 431
modernisation 161, 397
Moët & Chandon 219–21, 223, 225–6
Moët, Claude 219–20

Moldova 17, 200
momentum 127, 184, 324
Mondovino (film) 56, 417
Monet, Claude 55
monks 118, 136–7, 220, 235, 271, 305
monoculture 396–7, 435
monopolistic competition 204, 213
monopoly: in labour 399; state 209–10, 419; symbolic 117; in transmitting wine knowledge 323
monopoly price 61
monopoly prices 61
monopoly rent 118–19
moral panics 311, 315–16
Moran, Warren 38, 385
More, Thomas 82–3, 299
Morel, Philippe 55
Mormons 245, 247
Mornington Peninsula 265, 303
Moroccan migrants 397–9, 401
Moss, Kate 172
Mostowski, Tadeusz 162
Mother Vineyard 86
motherhood 312, 316–17
motorisation 397
Moueix, Christian 372
Mouret, Jean-Noël 53
Mourvèdre 127, *128*, 130, 148, 201
mouthfeel 191, 349, 376
MSA (Agricultural Social Security) 397, 401
multidisciplinarity 1, *36*, 68–9
multinational corporations 387
music 306
Muspratt, Frederic 183
musto 113
Myers, Kevin 151
myths 156, 188, 332, 345, 399, 217

Naked Wines 447
Nantes 147, 152
Napa Valley: artisanal winemaking in 305; business models in 359; in film 56; and Judgement of Paris 372; scientific winemaking in 269–70, 272–5; and terroir 303; women working in 322
Napanook Vineyard 372
Napoleonic Wars 149–50
narrative analysis 366
narratives of craft and production 74–6, 79; *see also* stories of wine
National Agriculture Statistical Service 103, 105
national identity 47, 260, 300, 415–16, 444; French 43, 345, 397; Polish 160
National Women in Wine Day 326
nationalism 262, 345, 421, 449
Native American winemakers 266
natural assets 386
natural wines 2, 192–4, 304, 448
négociants 64, 260, 272, 309n4; and AOCs 343, 348; in Burgundy 94, 118, 120

neo-liberalism 16, 123, 263, 333, 417, 419
Neolithic period 233
Neoplatonism 253, 255
Nero d'Avola 83
networking 305, 317, 324–5, 419
New Australians 112–13
New South Wales 176–7, 179–80, 182–5
New World: colonisation and wine 239, 243, 386, 417–18; key countries 394n1; premium wines in 307; rural idyll of 260
New World wines: branding of 356; legitimacy of 289; and terroir 303–4
New York State 366–8
New York Times 198, 322, 363, 365–6
New Zealand 10, 38, 88; colonial history of 94; language of winemaking 92–3; rural idyll of 259–61, 265; wine regions of 75; wine tourism in 91, 94–6
New Zealand Wine (NZW) 265
Newnham-Davis, Nathaniel 170
newspapers, wine columns in 68, 196–200, 202
Nga Waka 265
Niagara wine region 290–2, 295
Nicholas II of Russia 86
Noble, Anna 199–200
noble varieties 84, 364, 394
non-replicability 270
non-script typefaces 137, 139–41
Norfolk Island 82, 87
Normand-Marconnet, Nadine 54
normative process 339, 342
norms production 338
North Africa 85, 397–8, 401, 417, 419
North Canterbury 90–6
North Yuba AVA 100–3
Norton, Mary 44
Nossiter, Jonathan 56, 417
nostalgia 114, 121, 155, 160, 162, 192
Nothomb, Amélie 53–4
Nuriootpa 80n2
Nussbaum, Katia 440

oak 72, 75–6, 79, 111, 114, 266
O'Connell, Daniel 146
oenological discourses 188–94
oenological science 179, 192
oenology 65, 188–9, 269
Oenovideo 56
off-premise sales 213–14
OIV (International Organisation of Vine and Wine) 7; and sustainability 333–4
Okanagan Syilx people 266
Okanagan Valley 77–8, 266
O'Kelly, John 179
Old World: rural idyll in 260; use of term 394n1; wine and ethnicity in 415–17
Old World wines 289, 291, 327; New World competition with 183; selling in US 208–9, 213–14

Oliver, Jamie 196
OMI (Office des Migrations Internationales) 398–9
omnivorousness, cultural 197, 289
ONI (National Immigration Office) 397–9
online selling 204, 213, 408
online shopping 210, 357
Ontario 288, 290–5
oppositions, and categorisation 364–5
Oregon 125, 321, 361
organic wines 304, 334
organoleptic characteristics 342, 347, 349
Origen 255
Orleans Island 86
Osborn, Chester 306
Osiris 234
Osterwalder, A. 353–5
Overton, John 273
Owen, Robert 149

palatability 307
Palestine *see* Israel/Palestine
Paris International Exhibition *see* Exposition Universelle 1855
Parker, Robert 273, 374, 378
Paroles Vigneronnes 121
Parrain, Charles 18n1
Parris Island 86
Pasteur, Louis 180, 187
pasteurisation 192, 246
Paton, Clive 262
patriarchy 41, 311–15, 317, 320, 327, 444
patrilinearity 327
patrimonialisation 92, 96
patrimony 111, 113–15
pattern recognition 283
Paua Cove 302
Pavillon Blanc du Château Margaux 302
PDO (Protected Designation of Origin) 355–7, 424, 426, 428–9
peasants 42; in Argentina 417; Australian migrants as 115; in France 345; grape-growing traditions of 64; in Peru 263; in Poland 156, 161
Peel, Robert 150
Penfold, Mary 179, 323
Penfolds Wines 80n2, 179, 306, 323
Pérard, Jocelyne 53
performances of winemaking 72, 79
Pernod Ricard 303, 406
Perrotti-Brown, Lisa 53
Persian poetry 37, 53
Peru 36, 239, 259, 263, 394n1, 417
Pessoa, Fernando 54
pesticides 62, 122, 129, 302, 399–400, 435
Pétain, Philippe 344
Peter Lehmann wines 304
Petric, Boris 17
Peynaud, Emile 305
Pfeiffer, Ehrenfried 438

PGRs (plant-growth regulators) 129
philanthropy 55
Philippine de Rothschild 323
Phillip, Arthur 87
Philo of Alexandria 255
Philosophical Society of Australasia 179
philosophy of winemaking 305
phylloxera 239, 364; in Australia 184; and geography 35, 38; and terroir 63–4
phylloxera crisis 44, 187–8, 365
Picasso, Pablo 379
Pierce's Disease 127, 129
Pinault, François 117, 401
pink wine 22
pinot noir xx; in film 55; in New Zealand 91; on Reunion Island 87
pisco 263
Pitiot, Sylvain 122
Pitte, Jean-Robert 36
Pizarro, Juan 239
place branding 23
place culture 42
Place de Bordeaux 355–6
place image 23
place marketing 99
place of origin 74, 90, 128, 219, 390
place specificity 10, 260, 272
Plack, Noelle 244
Planhol, Xavier de 36
Plato 5, 51
Pliny the Elder 36–7, 51–2, 62, 84
Plotinus 255
Podolinsky, Alex 438–9
Podolny, S. 48, 204, 212–13, 302, 373
poetic devices 197, 199, 201–2, 251
Poland 155–62, 235, 444
Polish identity 155–7, 161
Polish migrants 399
Polish wine 156, 161–2
Polish-Lithuanian Commonwealth 155
Polo, Marco 406
polyculture 190
polysemy of wine 52, 250, 254
Pompadour, Madame de 219
Pompeii 84
port 314–15; in Britain 43–4, 168; in Ireland 149–50; patriotic 416
Portuguese colonisation 3, 85
Portuguese migrants 398
Portuguese wines 44, 148–9
positivism 5, 20–1, 188, 192
Postgate, Raymond 172
post-socialist countries 17
Potot, Swanie 399
poverty, rural 261
poverty belt 397
power 2, 9, 46, 48, 123, 314; colonial 82, 84, 449; of consumer 444; economic 300; of ethnicity 418; global 120; inequalities of 178; male 311; of metaphor 255; of nature 436; public 187, 193; purchasing 30, 210–11, 350; soft 56; supraliminal 135; white ethnic 421
prayers 235, 243, 253
preferences 211
pregnancy 314, 316, 323
premiers crus 56, 92, 344–5
premium wines 185, 278–9, 285, 291, 307, 387
premiumisation 277
preparations, biodynamic 438–9
preservation of wine 187
price ceiling 211
price control 344
price elasticity 214
price formation 47, 49, 380
price premiums 78, 272, 292, 373, 380
price sensitivity 380
price-quality ratio 291
prices 20, 29–33; and AOC system 64, 343–4; and artisan winemakers 302; and authenticity 403; of Burgundy wines 117–18, 122–3, 272; and consumer knowledge 291–2, 294; of cult wines 273; in East Asia 421; in Ireland 148–9; official minimum 344; and sights of production 76, 79; and status 380; and terroir 304–5; in US market 209, 214
pricing policy incentive 122
product differentiation 47, 388
product involvement 412, **413**
profit gouging 260
profits 302, 308n1, 366–7; and appellation systems 61; and CGs 29–30; from hand-selling 94
Prohibition 127, 246–7, 273, 315, 364; legacy of 198, 209
prosecco 152, 202, 358
Protestantism: in Ireland 147, 149; and temperance movement 244–5; and wine 235–9, 242, 247–8
provenance, local 363
provenancing 74, 78–80, 444
pruning 62, 110, 118, 181–2, 269, 301, 398–9
psychology 8; and business 20
public goods 30
Pufendorf, Samuel von 4
Punch magazine *166–7, 171*
Puritans 237–8

quality, consistent 270
quality wines: aesthetic consumption of 263–4; commercial production of 294–5, 301–3; ranking classification 335; and technology 273
quality-price ratio 211
quantification 27, 47
Quero, Serafin 54

Rabelais, François 54, 255–7
racialisation 415, 421
racism 345, 401, 415, 419, 421, 438

radical geography 9
raisin wine 43, 246
rakija 110–11
Raleigh, Walter 86
rationalism, viticultural 275
reading, wine labels 55
reciprocity 255, 304
Red Biddy 151
Redding, Cyrus 150
regenerative agriculture 438
Regnault, Étienne 87
regulars 211
relationship management 359–60
religion 2, 39; colonial 82; and wine 233–9, 241–8, 255, 312
Renaissance 55, 250, 255, 275
Renoir, August 55
replica wines 266, 309n2
representation 2, 39, 42, 120, 155, 202, 250, 325, 426, 444–5, 448
retail: and artisanal wines 374; and commercial wines 377–8; stock-keeping units in **409**; in US market 205, 209, 211, 213–15; *see also* wine vendors
retail channels 408
retail stores 380
retail supermarkets 76, 387
retailers, big-box 265
Reunion Island 87
Revel, Gilles de 53
Revérien, Saint 243
reverse osmosis 271, 446
rhetorical devices 254
rhetorical qualities 252
rhizome 281–2, 300
Richards, Paul 86
Riedel glassware 172, *173*
riesling 290, 364, 367–9, 375, 393
Ritter, Carl 37
rituals 6; and champagne 217, 219; and drinking culture 15, 158–9; wine and 22, 24, 46, 51; of winemaking 30; women excluded from 324
Robinson, Dwight 170
Robinson, Jancis 52, 317, 373, 449
role models 324
Rolland, Michel 305
Romania 200, 324
Rome *see* ancient Rome
rosé 47
Rose, Susan 42–3
Roseworthy College, South Australia 65, 180
Roudié, Philippe 36, 397–8
Rousseau, Jean-Jacques 4, 54
Royer, Claude 18n1
Rubin, Miri 42
Ruggieri, Fulvius 158
rural communities 16, 260–1, 264
rural exodus 398
rural idylls 81, 259–62, 264, 448

rural sociality 264
rural worlds 396, 402
rurality 260–1, 443, 445
Russia 17; 'champagne' in 23

saccharometer 168, 184
sacramental wine 243, 246–7, 272
Sainte-Foy-La-Grande 397–401
Saint-Emilion 344, 349, 397–402
Saintsbury, George 198
sampling 75, 80, 221, 412
Sanchez Salas, Bernardo 56
sans serifs 137, 139–41, *140*
Sardinia 84
Sargent, Lyman Tower 300
Sarmatians 155–6, 160–1
The Saturday Times 196–7, 199, 202
saucer glass 165–6, *167*, 169–74
Sauer, Carl 37
sauternes 138, 168, 343–4
sauvignon blanc 88, 91, 282, 302, 359, 393
scale, politics of 17
Schaeffer, Phillip 87
Scheiner, Justin 130
Schiffer, Claudia 172
Schirmer, Raphaël 55–6
Schubert, Max 306
science-mindedness 177–81, 183
scientism 425
Scotland 148, 416
Scott, Walter 176, 183–5
script typefaces 137–8
A Seat at the Table (film) 56, 91
Second World War 316, 343–4, 346, 349–50, 397
secularisation 243–4, 272
selfies 220–1, 223, 225–7
self-image congruity 264
self-presentation 418
self-reflexivity 434
self-regulation 118, 120
self-sufficiency 114–15, 235
Sémichon, Lucien 192–3
semillon 182, 355, 398
serifs 137, *139*
service industries 28
Seventh-Day Adventists 245
sexual harassment 322
sexuality 312, 314, 317
Shackelford, James and Penelope 165
shame 314–15
Shapin, Steven 349
Shenandoah AVA 105, 107
sherry 25, 147, 150, 168, 315
shiraz 10, 36, 80, 113, 266
shopping 107, 206, 211; *see also* retail
Shu Okimoto 54
Sicily 83–4, 312
Sideways (film) 55–6

Sierra Foothills AVA 100–3, 105–8, 359; area of grape growing **105**; environmental analysis *102*, *103*; winery permit locations *104*
Sierra Nevada mountains, California 39, 100, 106–7
Silber and Fleming catalogue 167
Silk Road 406
Sillery region of Champagne 168
Singapore 387, 420–1
site specificity 269–70, 273–5, 447
Skinner, William 17
SKUs (stock-keeping units) **409**
Smith, Adam 5, 27
Smith, John 180, 183
Smith, Joseph 245
Smith Maguire, Jennifer 22, 24, 197, 205, 212
Sober Revolution 350
social capital 121, 324
social classes 44, 278
social identities 217
social isolation 261, 324
social media 22, 444, 446; in Bordeaux 357; in California 360; champagne on 217–18, 220–5, 229; in China 408; and wine writing 202
social networks 359, 440
social reproduction 9, 46
social systems 46–7, 192, 280, 332
socialisation, and drinking culture 157–8
societal changes 42, 44
sociological hell 436
sociological imagination 9, 46, 48
sociology 48n1, 442; and wine and culture 9–10, 46–8
soil, biodynamic approach to 438–40
sommeliers 47, 56, 187–90, 192–4, 322, 349, 411, 420
Sonoma Valley 107, 272–3, 322, 359
sophisticated wines 187, 192
South Africa: ethnicity and wine 417–20; sustainability in 331, 338; women in wine industry 326–7
South African Women's Wine and Spirits Awards 326
South Australia 17, 80, 179–80, 185, 266, 306, 411
space, social construction of 269, 274
Spain: Muslim period in 254; wine consumption in 387; winegrape-bearing areas 392
Spanish migrants 398
sparkling wines: British 262; and champagne 355, 357–8; glasses for 165, 168–9, 174
spatial mismatch 131
Spencer, Herbert 440
spending sufficiently 288–91, 293–5
Spiegel, Gabrielle 44
spirits 3; in Australia 417; consumption of 444–5; and drunkenness 161; in France 416; John Wesley on 241–2; in New Zealand 88; rice 406; in US 206–9, 214–15
spirituality 254–5, 257, 305

St. Evremond, Marquis de 43, 168
St. Romain *63*
standardisation: of flavour 192; of oenological discourse 190, 199; of practices 271; and quality wine 302
status games 373, 378–80
Stearns, Peter 41
Steiner, Rudolph 437–8, 440
stencils 137, 139–40, *141*
stories of wine 76, 85, 442–4, 448; and typography 136, 143
Strabo 36, 51, 62
stratification 9, 46, 48, 302, 308
Strutyński, Juliusz 160
students, as customers 211
stylistic devices 198–9, 201
substitutes 214, 361, 405
suburbs 110, 210–11, 213–14, 260, 305
subviving 437
Summerhill Pyramid Winery 77, *78*, 264
supermarkets 387, 408
sustainability 265, 331; concept of 332; culture of 332, 339; drivers and barriers of 334; pillars of 332–5
sustainability discourses 331–5, 338–9
sustainability knowledge 338
sustainability ranking, best 335
sustainable development 332–4, 358
Sustainable Viticulture in Champagne 358
sustainable wines 304, 331, 334, 338–9
sweet wine: and gender 315; and typography 138
Swift, Jonathan 146
Swinburn, Robert 17
SWNZ (Sustainable Winegrowing New Zealand) 265
Sydney Botanic Gardens 177
symbolic elements 178, 218, 223
symbolic meaning: and CGs 28, 33, 204; in marketing research 21
symbolic prize 335
symbolic value 8, 30
symbolism of wine 33
symmetry principle 425
symposion 313
Synge, Edward 146
syrah 148, 201, 393
systematisation 269–70

table wines 87, 112–13, 301, 343, 359, 366, 416
Tacama Vineyard 263
Tadashi Agi 54
Tanakh 234
Tannat 127, 130
tariffs 85, 148, 150
Tasmania 88
taste: contested 444; established hierarchies of 197; sociology of 48
taste construction 24, 33, 197–8

taste description 197
taste hierarchies 288–90, 294
taste individualisation 196
taste making *see* taste construction
tastemakers 283, 290, 365
tasting *see* wine tasting
Te Kairanga 265
technological innovations 269–70, 274
technology transfers 386
temperance movement 244; in Ireland 151
Tennent, Emerson 176, 183–4
terracing 62, 84
territorialisation 17
terroir xx, 2, 9–10, 90, 112, 446; anthropological study of 16–17; and champagne 218, 223, 228; in China 420; crafting of 62–7; economic analysis of 33; and French nationalism 400; and geography 74; and heritage value 118–22; hierarchy of 347; INRA/INAO definition of 69, 69–70n1; management of 23; marketisation of 447; in the mind and in print 67–9; myths about 217; narratives of 96, 269–72, 274–5; as pejorative 309n3, 343; as political and administrative space 345–7; sociology of 48; supply-side links with culture 385–6; taste of 188–90, 194, 290–2, 294, 349–50; use in New World 289; use of term 61–2; utopian 303–5; and wine tourism 90–4
terroirism 345–6
Texas 125–30, *126*
Texas A&M AgriLife Extension 130
text, and wine and culture 51–7
Thackeray, William 168
theology 5, 234–5, 252, 255
Thompson, E. P. 178
three-tier system 209, 359
Throsby, David xxi, 8, 27–9, 33, 204, 386
TNs (tasting notes) 200, **212**, 215, 378
Tokaj wine region 123
Touquette, Benoît 305
tourism 8; cultural 21–2; economics of 33
Tovey, Charles 166, 169
tractors 397–8
tradition: Burgundian 64, 91, 117, 270–1; French cinematic 56; of geographical work on wine culture 37–9; home winemaking and 113–15; and ingestion 3; family 79; Māori 93; Old World 75; terroir and 90–2, 119–20, 269, 272, 274, 275, 345; winegrowers and 270
transactions 28, 181, 209, 215
transfer, rhetorical 250–2, 256
transition 17, 120, 126, 129, 339, 368, 375
transmission 91, 205, 322–3
transnational wine companies 7, 120, 304
transubstantiation 235–6, 242
trellising 62, 85, 301–2, 434–5
Trente Glorieuses 343, 347, 350
Trubek, Amy 272, 385
truth effects 332, 335

TTB (Tax and Trade Bureau) 99–100, 108
tulip glass 169, 172, 174
tumbler glasses 167, 171, 173
Tunisia 248, 397
Tunisian migrants 397–8
tūrangawaewae 93–4
Turkey 36, 248, 416
tuscans 137, 139, *140*
TWG (Texas Wine Growers) 128
Twitter 357, 360
Tyler, Edward 4
typefaces 135–43, *136*, 444; families of 137–41
typicity 9, 61, 70, 261; of AOCs 342, 349–50; connoisseurs looking for 307–8; varietal 48, 301

unbranded wines 301, 307
understanding 1–2
UNESCO: and Burgundy wine landscape 91–2, 118–22, 262–3, 303, 394, 401; Convention on the Protection and Promotion of the Diversity of Cultural Expressions 29; and Pico Island 85; and translation of terroir 69
UNESCO Chair 'Culture and Tradition of Wine' 53
UNESCO Intangible Heritage Convention 123
Unger, Gerard 135
Union des sommeliers de Paris 188, 194
United Kingdom, gender and wine 314–15
United Nations Sustainable Development Goals 265
United States: cinema of 56; North-eastern 364–5, 367–8; wine market in 209, 372–80, **379**; wine vendors in 206–9; winegrape-bearing areas 393
University of California: Berkeley 37, 180; Davis 65, 180, 273, 349
Unwin, Tim 1, 442
uppercase 136, 138, 140–3, *141*
urban wineries 74, 266, 359
urbanisation 385, 387
Utopia (More) 83, 299
utopia, use of term 299–300
utopian goals 300, 302, 307–8
utopian goods 307–8
utopian winemaking 300–1, 305–6
utopianism 300
Utraquism 236

value 23; politics of 16
value chain 44, 280–1, 356
value creation activities 354
value proposition 354
value transmission 354
van Riebeeck, Jan 239
Vandyke-Price, Pamela 172
Variano, John 55
Vautrin, Hubert 159
Veblen, Thorstein 29, 375–6
Velasquez, Diego 55
Verga, Giovanni 54
Vermont 368–9

vernacular idylls 261–3
Verrazzano, Giovanni da 86
vertical range 357
Veuve Clicquot 219–21, 226, 314
Vichy regime 344–5, 397
Vidogna grapes 85
vignerons 271, 309n4, 432n1; and winegrape varieties 386–8, 393–4
vin de pays 367
vin de soif 448–9
Viña Montes Alpalta 72, 75, 79
vinescaping 107
vineyard management 398, 428
vineyards: Biblical imagery of 254; hierarchy of 343–5; Māori names for 265; in Poland 156, 162; religious ownership of 235, 243–4; and rural idyll 260; sale prices of 117, 122; siting of 106
vinification *see* winemaking
Vinland 86
Virgil 52
visual analysis 220–1, 225
visual reconfiguration 118, 120
viticulture 2, 8, 37, 62; biodynamic 304, 333, 437–9; in China 420; and climate change 424–31; geography of 38–9; in nineteenth century 176–7, 180; sustainable 304, 333–4, 339; and terroir 62, 64, 66–7; in Texas 127, 129–31
Vitis labrusca 86–7, 364, 366, 368
Vitis vinifera 176–8, 184, 272, 301, 363–5, 367–9, 406
Viveiros de Castro, Eduardo 436
Vizetelly, Henry 170
vodka 79, 155, 157, 161
Volnay 93, 243–4
Voltaire 54
volume discounts 214
von Humboldt brothers 4
von Mandl, Anthony 77
von Rubruk, Wilhelm 406
Vovelle, Michel 244
VQA (Vintners Quality Alliance) 290, 293
VSV (Viticultural Society of Victoria) 179

Wadmalaw Island 87
Waipara Hills 92–3
Wakefield, Edward 148
Wang Han 406
Warhol, Andy 55
WaterAid 10
WCED (World Commission on Environment and Development) 332, 334
WCTU (Woman's Christian Temperance Union) 244
websites: business communication through 357–8, 360; and rural idyll 263; terroir on 91, 93; for US vendors 207–8; wine promotion on 79; winemaker profiles on 305
Welch, Celia 305

Welch, Thomas 246
Wellington, Duke of 148
Wesley, John 241
Western Australia 177, 304, 437–8, 440
Western values 118
Whitefriars Glass 166
whiteness 418–19
wicked problems 300
Wiener, Martin 177
wilding 266
Williams, John 67
Williams, Raymond 5
Wilson, James E. 385
Wilson, Thomas 18n1, 43, 152
Windeyer, Archibald 182
Windeyer, Maria 179
wine: commodity life-cycle of 119; cultural tensions in 444–6; definition of 3; as force for good 449–50; origins of 233; and other forms of alcohol 444
The Wine Advocate 53, 373–4
wine and culture, disciplinary approaches to 6, 7–10
wine appreciation 33
wine bars 161, 211, 259, 315, 326
wine book fairs 53
wine brands: in China 408–9; creation of 372–3; hierarchy of 380; high-status 47, 375; mimicking 408; portfolios of 79–80
wine cellars, women in 314
wine classifications 16, 397
wine clusters, regional 80
wine communication 199, 278, 356, 411
wine communities, local 396
wine consumers: and artisanal logic 374–5; categories of 210–11; in China 409–12, *410*; and commercial logic 377–8; defining good 290–4; and globalisation 393; ignorance of 31; professional 213; younger 447–8
wine consumption: change over time in 279–80; as communication 278–9; demand-side influences on 386–8; female 311, 313–16; utopian 306–8
wine consumption culture 78–9
wine cooperatives 260, 357, 397–8
wine culture 2, 7–10; ancient 233–4; and anthropology 15–17; changes in 388; in China 405–6, 410–13; cultivation by vendors of 212–13, 215; cultivation of 33; economics of 33; French 342; geographical writing on 35–9; history of 42–3; in Ireland 145, 152–3; in Poland 157; regional 328, 445; and religion 238–9; and terroir 69, 91–2; in text 51–2, 57; textual fields in 52
wine distribution, inflection point in 447
wine distributors 209–10, 214, 374, 376–7, 408
wine documentary films 56
wine economies 89, 118, 401, 445
wine expertise: consumer 293; scientific 187
wine experts 8, 32, 210, 328, 372
wine fashions 277, 280–1, 285

wine festivals 8, 91
wine field 49, 331, 333, 338
wine fraud 63–4, 309
wine geese 152
wine hierarchies 343–4
wine ideals 299–300, 308
wine identity 17, 33, 347
Wine Institute of New Zealand 443
wine knowledge: of consumers 92, 291, 293–4, 307–8; and cultural capital 112; gendered transmission of 323; technical 190; and tourism 22
wine labels: images on 55; names of grape varieties on 388; typography of 135–7, 143
wine landscapes 8, 120–1, 123
wine magazine 53
wine marketing *see* advertising
wine metaphors 199, 250–3, 255; anthropomorphic 54
wine opinion leadership 281
wine potability 307
wine producers *see* winemakers
wine producing countries, new 353, 361, 428
wine production *see* winemaking
wine professionals: ethnic minority 419; evaluation of consumers 288–95; female 316–17; legitimacy of 272
wine quality: consistency in 301; global rise in 393; hierarchy of 198; new techniques for 348; perceptions of 8; and terroir 64, 67, 74; and wine tasting 187, 190; *see also* quality wines
wine regions: international cross-comparison 353–4; location and growth of 74; new 17, 387; spatial structuring of 23, 39; traditional 33, 206
wine retailing *see* wine vendors
wine segmentation 307
Wine Spectator 273, 373, 446
wine storage 180, 188–90
wine styles, diffusion of 281
wine tasting 103; bio-physical universals of 307; blind 34, 47, 306, 372; in China 410–11; as consumer education 377–8; discourse of 187–9, 191–4, 196–8; embodied sensation of 48; in Hunter Valley 182; invention of modern 349–50; as situated activity 48
wine technologies 189, 386
wine texts 51–2, 54–5
wine tourism 8; in BMC analysis 358–60; in Bordeaux 356; in Burgundy 122–3; and culture 22–3; international 387; place and terroir in 90–6; and Sierra Foothills 107; and whiteness 418; women in 323
wine trade, geography of 8, 38
wine vendors 33, 206, 214–16; categories of 210; product offerings **207**, 208
wine vocabulary 198, 419
wine widows 321
wine writing: British 198; as lifestyle writing 199–202; popular 68, 196–7; standardised 198–9;

in United States 365, 373–4, 376–9; by women 316–17
winegrape varieties: and climate change 424; hybrid 187, 191–2, 363–9, 386, 445; internationalisation of 33, 385–94, *389–92*; names of 394n2; selecting 62
winegrape-bearing areas 385, 388, *389*, 392, *393*
winegrapes, DNA manipulation of 446
winegrowing *see* viticulture
winemakers: amateur 101, 112–14; artisanal 266, 306, 373; brotherhoods of 23; in Burgundy 121; celebrity 47, 379–80; commercial 376–7; cult of 264, 305; as cultural intermediaries 47–8; female 314, 323, 326–7; in film 55–6; global 402; imagery of 74–6, 79; indigenous 259, 265–6; professionalisation of 64–6; and sociology 47–8; and viticulture 74
winemaking 2–3; amateur *see* home winemaking 113; and anthropology 16–18; colonial spread of 415; consumer understanding of 293; contribution to climate change 435–6, 449; economics of 33; and the environment 62; evolution across cultures 33; films about 56; fine 10, 47, 290; geography of 35–6, 38–9; industrialisation of 396; large-scale and craft 79; and national identity 415–16; provenance and performance of 78–80; scientific 65–6, 269, 273; sights of 72, 74–7, 79; sites of 74–5; and terroir 61–2, 64; and viticulture 64–7
winemaking cultures 37, 75–6, 275, 289, 321
winesearcher.com 207, 214
winespeak 197–9, 202
Wisconsin 30, 206–7, 209, 213
'wogs' 112, 115
women: relations with wine 311–16; in wine industry 320–8, **321**, **327**
Women Do Wine association 324
Women in Wine Leadership Symposium 324
Wood, Andrew Grant 41–2
Woodhouse, John 84
Woolf, Virginia 52
WorldClim 101–3
WWS (Waterford Wine and Spirits) 205–15, **207**; Old World wines *208*
Wyclif, John 236

xenia 443
Xu Bing 55

Yarra Valley 305
yeasts: cultured 114, 270; customised 271
Yellowtail wine 265, 292, 304, 322
Yuba County 100–1, 103

Zhang Bishi 406
Zhang Qian, famous ambassador 406
Zhou dynasty 406
Zwingli, Ulrich 235, 237